A New Star-Rating System & Other Exciting News from Frommer's!

In our continuing effort to publish the savviest, most up-to-date, and most appealing travel guides available, we've added some great new features.

Frommer's guides now include a new **star-rating system.** Every hotel, restaurant, and attraction is rated from 0 to 3 stars to help you set priorities and organize your time.

We've also added **seven brand-new features** that point you to the great deals, in-the-know advice, and unique experiences that separate travelers from tourists. Throughout the guide, look for:

Finds	Special finds—those places only insiders know about
Fun Fact	Fun facts—details that make travelers more informed and their trips more fun
Kids	Best bets for kids—advice for the whole family
Moments	Special moments—those experiences that memories are made of
Overrated	Places or experiences not worth your time or money
Tips	Insider tips—some great ways to save time and money
Value	Great values—where to get the best deals

We've also added a **"What's New"** section in every guide—a timely crash course in what's hot and what's not in every destination we cover.

Other Great Guides for Your Trip:

Frommer's Yellowstone and Grand Teton National Parks

Frommer's Rocky Mountain National Park

Frommer's National Parks of the American West

Frommer's USA

Frommer's Utah

Frommer's Colorado

Montana & Wyoming

4th Edition

by Don & Barbara Laine

Here's what the critics say about Frommer's:

"Amazingly easy to use. Very portable, very complete."

—*Booklist*

"The only mainstream guide to list specific prices. The Walter Cronkite of guidebooks—with all that implies."

—*Travel & Leisure*

"Complete, concise, and filled with useful information."

—*New York Daily News*

"Hotel information is close to encyclopedic."

—*Des Moines Sunday Register*

"Detailed, accurate, and easy-to-read information for all price ranges."

—*Glamour Magazine*

Hungry Minds™

Best-Selling Books • Digital Downloads • e-Books • Answer Networks
e-Newsletters • Branded Web Sites • e-Learning
New York, NY • Cleveland, OH • Indianapolis, IN

About the Authors

Residents of northern New Mexico for more than 30 years, **Don and Barbara Laine** have traveled extensively throughout the Rocky Mountains and the Southwest. In addition to *Frommer's Montana & Wyoming,* they are the authors of *Frommer's Colorado; Frommer's Utah; Frommer's Rocky Mountain National Park; Frommer's Zion & Bryce Canyon National Parks; Frommer's Yosemite & Sequoia/Kings Canyon National Parks;* are the lead authors of *Frommer's National Parks of the American West;* and have contributed to *Frommer's Texas* and *Frommer's USA.* The Laines have also written *Little-Known Southwest* and *New Mexico & Arizona State Parks* (both for The Mountaineers Books).

Published by:

Hungry Minds, Inc.

909 Third Ave.
New York, NY 10022

ISBN 0-7645-6575-3
ISSN 1088-2650

Editor: Christine Ryan
Production Editor: Ian Skinnari
Cartographers: Barbara Laine and Roberta Stockwell
Photo Editor: Richard Fox
Production by Hungry Minds Indianapolis Production Services

Special Sales

For general information on Hungry Minds' products and services, please contact our Customer Care department; within the U.S. at 800-762-2974, outside the U.S. at 317-572-3993, or fax 317-572-4002. For sales inquiries and reseller information, including discounts, bulk sales, customized editions, and premium sales, please contact our Customer Care department at 800-434-3422.

Manufactured in the United States of America

5 4 3 2 1

Contents

List of Maps

An Invitation to the Reader

In researching this book, we discovered many wonderful places—hotels, restaurants, shops, and more. We're sure you'll find others. Please tell us about them, so we can share the information with your fellow travelers in upcoming editions. If you were disappointed with a recommendation, we'd love to know that, too. Please write to:

Frommer's Montana & Wyoming, 4th Edition
Hungry Minds, Inc. • 909 Third Avenue • New York, NY 10022

An Additional Note

Please be advised that travel information is subject to change at any time—and this is especially true of prices. We therefore suggest that you write or call ahead for confirmation when making your travel plans. The authors, editors, and publisher cannot be held responsible for the experiences of readers while traveling. Your safety is important to us, however, so we encourage you to stay alert and be aware of your surroundings. Keep a close eye on cameras, purses, and wallets, all favorite targets of thieves and pickpockets.

New! Frommer's Star Ratings & Icons

Every hotel, restaurant, and attraction listing in this guide has been ranked for quality, value, service, amenities, and special features using a star-rating scale. In country, state, and regional guides, we also rate towns and regions to help you narrow down your choices and budget your time accordingly. Hotels and restaurants in the Very Expensive and Expensive categories are rated on a scale of one (highly recommended) to three stars (exceptional). Those in the Moderate and Inexpensive categories rate from zero (recommended) to two stars (very highly recommended). Attractions, towns, and regions are rated according to the following scale: zero stars (recommended), one star (highly recommended), two stars (very highly recommended), and three stars (must-see).

In addition to the rating system, we also use seven icons to highlight insider information, useful tips, special bargains, hidden gems, memorable experiences, kid-friendly venues, places to avoid, and other useful information:

Finds	Fun Fact	Kids	Moments	Overrated	Tips	Value

The following abbreviations are used for credit cards:

AE American Express	DISC Discover	V Visa
DC Diners Club	MC MasterCard	

FROMMERS.COM

Now that you have the guidebook to a great trip, visit our website at **www.frommers.com** for travel information on nearly 2,500 destinations. With features updated regularly, we give you instant access to the most current trip-planning information available. At Frommers.com, you'll also find the best prices on airfares, accommodations, and car rentals—and you can even book travel online through our travel booking partners. At Frommers.com, you'll also find the following:

- Online updates to our most popular guidebooks
- Vacation sweepstakes and contest giveaways
- Newsletter highlighting the hottest travel trends
- Online travel message boards with featured travel discussions

What's New in Montana & Wyoming

Montana and Wyoming are known for their rugged beauty, outdoor recreation opportunities, Wild West history, and wide open spaces. These are sparsely populated areas, where getting around means long hours in a car, and visitors get to see a section of America that is little changed from the way it was when pioneers moved through in covered wagons. Change comes slowly here—that's one of the things we like so much about these states—but gradually we are seeing more paved roads, more chain motels and restaurants, and at least a few of the more upscale facilities we expect to find in America's more modern cities.

Following are some of the recent changes in Montana and Wyoming, and we'll be watching with anticipation, and just a bit of trepidation, as these states move toward joining the modern world.

GLACIER NATIONAL PARK
Guests at the **St. Mary Lodge** resort at Glacier National Park (U.S. 89 and Going-to-the-Sun Rd.; © **800/368-3689**) now have the option of staying in one of 48 rooms at the new Great Bear Lodge. The new, upscale rooms include decks, sitting areas, and wet bars. For a full review of the St. Mary Lodge resort, see chapter 4.

MISSOULA, THE FLATHEAD & THE NORTHWEST CORNER
Missoula Ground has been broken in downtown Missoula on a new ballpark for the **Missoula Osprey**, a minor league team. The team hopes to move to the new stadium in summer 2002. Nearby, in Lolo, those seeking a resort with great cross-country skiing and other winter activities should check out the **Fort at Lolo Trail Center and Lolo Hot Springs** (38600 W. U.S. 12; © **406/273-2201**), which has added a large new building for its Lewis & Clark Exhibition Center, several hot tubs, and a convention center.

Bitterroot Valley Winter visitors can take a side trip to Lost Trail Pass to check out the new expanded ski area at **Lost Trail Powder Mountain** (90 miles south of Missoula at the Montana-Idaho border, ⅛ of a mile from U.S. 93; © **406/821-3211**). The new steeper ski area is adjacent to the original hill, and is served by two new lifts.

Kalispell A new dining choice recently emerged in Kalispell. The **Painted Horse Grille** (110 Main St.; © **406/257-7035**) has an eclectic, moderately priced menu, with culinary influences ranging from Asian to Italian.

See chapter 5 for more information.

HELENA & SOUTHWESTERN MONTANA
Helena The **Montana State Capitol** (Montana Ave. and 6th St.; © **406/444-4789**), built 100 years ago, had lost much of its historic grandeur, but the beautiful building has been revitalized with an extensive renovation project completed in early 2001. A major renovation in 2000 has done a good job of sprucing up the **WestCoast Colonial Hotel** (2301 Colonial Dr., just off I-15 at U.S. 12; © **800/422-1002**), a fairly upscale property that had become somewhat dated.

Butte & Anaconda   A new interpretive center opened at the **Anaconda Smelter Stack** (off Mont. 1 on the outskirts of Anaconda) in 2000, with a few displays detailing the 585-foot smelter stack's history and construction.

See chapter 6 for more information.

THE HI-LINE & NORTH CENTRAL MISSOURI RIVER COUNTRY Great Falls   The excellent **C.M. Russell Museum Complex** (400 13th St. N.; © **406/727-8787**), which displays the work of Western artists including its namesake, Charles M. Russell, recently completed a major expansion that doubled the area devoted to Russell's work. The **Great Falls Inn** (1400 28th St. S.; © **800/454-6010**) recently completed 10 new business-class rooms, with dataports and two telephone lines.

The Rocky Mountain Eastern Front Timescale Adventures (Bynum; © **406/469-2211**) offers a series of popular dinosaur field programs, and in 2002 is broadening its curriculum with a seminar that details American Indian lore and explores some of the sacred Indian sites in the area.

See chapter 7 for more information.

BOZEMAN, SOUTH CENTRAL MONTANA & THE MISSOURI HEADWATERS   The Gallatin Valley East-West Resorts (Big Sky; © **800/845-4428**) offers a wide range of lodging possibilities, but their new **Moonlight Lodge and Spa** in Moonlight Basin Ranch is a magnificent mountain lodge offering luxurious penthouse suites and secluded, mid-mountain cabins.

Red Lodge & the Absaroka-Beartooth Wilderness   Those longing for a good shot of coffee will welcome the new coffee bar at the **Bridge Creek Restaurant and Wine Bar** (116 S. Broadway Ave.; © **406/446-9900**), serving a wide selection of espresso, cappuccino, and latte, plus freshly baked pastries.

See chapter 8 for more information.

YELLOWSTONE NATIONAL PARK   The **Yellowstone Association Institute** (© **307/344-2294**) offers a variety of programs, lasting from 1 to 5 days, and in 2001 began a "Trails through Yellowstone" package that pairs days spent exploring little-seen park trails with nights at the comfortable Mammoth Hot Springs Hotel. See chapter 10 for more information.

JACKSON HOLE & GRAND TETON NATIONAL PARK   Jackson Hole Ski Resort (© **307/733-2292**) just keeps getting better. In 2000, it added a high-speed quad on the Après Vous run, and then in 2001 construction began on developments that will more than double the guest capacity. Also in Jackson Hole, the **Snake River Lodge & Spa** (7710 Granite Loop Rd., Teton Village; © **800/445-4655**), formerly the Renaissance, completed major renovations in early 2002, including the addition of a 17,000 square-foot spa, featuring everything from hydrotherapy to free weights.

See chapter 11 for more information.

CODY & NORTH CENTRAL WYOMING   A new addition to Cody's basic steak-and-spuds dining scene is **The Gardens** (1313½ Sheridan Ave.; © **307/587-1101**), where Paris-trained chef John McCormack serves wild game and seafood prepared with French and Italian flair. See chapter 12.

SHERIDAN & EASTERN WYOMING   The new **National Historic Trails Interpretive Center** in Casper, scheduled to open in 2002, will use state-of-the-art exhibits to give us modern travelers an idea of what life on the "road" was like for the emigrants who passed through here in the mid-1800s on the Oregon, Mormon, California, and Pony Express Trails. See chapter 13.

1

The Best of Montana & Wyoming

A mix of the rugged Wild West, the even more rugged Rocky Mountains, and a few almost modern cities—or what we might call overgrown cow towns—make the states of Montana and Wyoming a delightful vacation spot. This is especially true for those who savor outdoor adventures, but this is also an ideal region for discovering a part of the United States that many of us have only seen in the movies and on television (and that's a rather distorted view). Here you'll find some of the most breathtaking scenery in America; a vast array of wildlife that not only thinks it owns the place, but actually does; and even some first-class Western-style lodges, restaurants, and museums.

Following are what we consider some of the best experiences in Montana and Wyoming, highlights to help you begin planning your trip.

1 The Best Vacation Experiences

- **Glacier National Park** (MT): The best vacation spot in Montana is also the most obvious one. By the standard of other crowded national parks, this spectacular country is virtually undiscovered. See chapter 4.
- **Yellowstone National Park** (WY): It's the crown jewel of American parks, and it remains the prime attraction in the Rocky Mountains. This unique park offers visitors an extraordinary combination of wilderness, wildlife, and geothermal wonders. See chapter 10.
- **The Grand Tetons** (WY): The Grand Tetons are an excellent short course in Rocky Mountain parks for travelers with less time: magnificent peaks rising from the Snake River plain, alpine lakes, wildflowers, and wildlife, in a relatively small park that can be seen in a few days. See "Grand Teton National Park" in chapter 11.

2 The Best Outdoor Adventures

- **Exploring the Bob Marshall Wilderness** (MT): The 1.5-million-acre Bob Marshall Wilderness Complex in northwest Montana is one of America's most spectacular wild places. Lace up your hiking boots, tie on your bandanna, and take to the high country in Montana's northwest corner. See "The Bob Marshall Wilderness Complex" in chapter 5.
- **Enjoying the Yellowstone Backcountry** (WY): Outfitters from ranches around Yellowstone National Park will take you into the deep wilderness that surrounds the busy attractions at the park's center, and there you'll get a

Montana

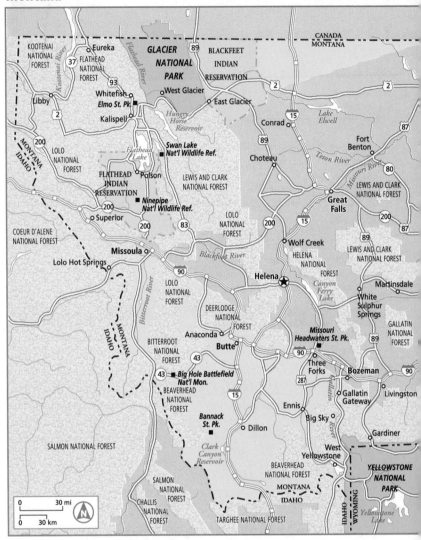

flavor of the wild as rich as the Rockies can offer. If you have the experience, you can go on your own—paddling Yellowstone Lake, backpacking into Bechtel Falls, telemark skiing the powder on Togwotee Pass. See chapter 10 for details.

3 The Best Wildlife Viewing

• **Bear-Watching in Glacier National Park** (MT): The experience of watching wildlife run wild at Glacier National Park is tough to beat. With a little energy and a lot of courage, you can see grizzlies

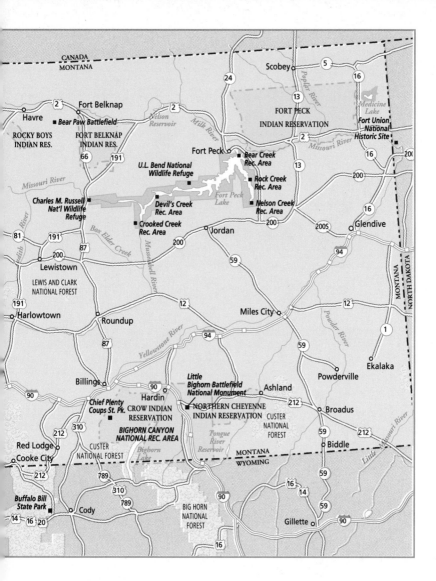

and black bears basking in their natural habitat. See chapter 4.

- **Searching for Life in the Bob Marshall Wilderness Complex** (MT): Just south of Glacier, in the Bob Marshall Wilderness Complex, roam a full complement of Rocky Mountain wildlife—although you have to wander into the backcountry to find it. See "The Bob Marshall Wilderness Complex" in chapter 5.

- **Spotting Wildlife in the Lamar Valley** (WY): You can see wildlife in many parts of Yellowstone, including the meadows across from the Old Faithful complex. But the richest trove of wildlife is

Wyoming

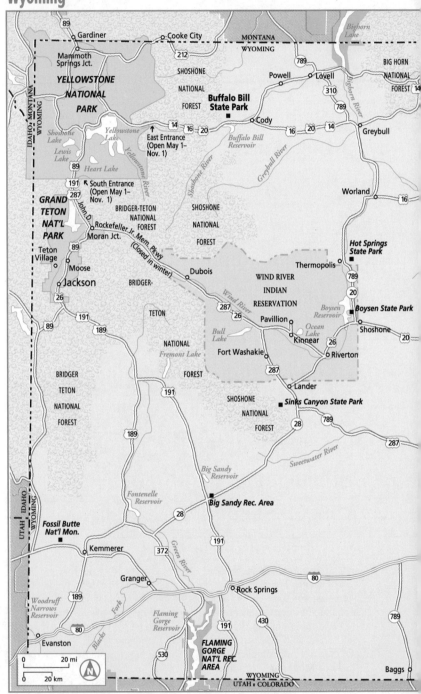

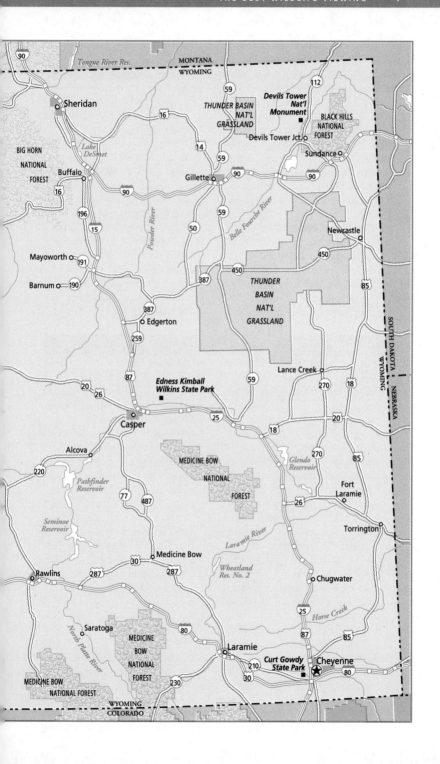

in the park's northeast corner, a less-traveled corridor that leads to the northeast entrance and Cooke City. See chapter 10.

4 The Best Winter Vacations

- **Skiing at The Big Mountain Ski and Summer Resort** (MT; ℂ **800/858-5439**): With lots of powder, lots of skiing in the trees, and plenty of runs for every level of skier, The Big Mountain is one of the best resorts in the northwestern United States. Better yet, it's still relatively undiscovered. See p. 136.

- **Wintering at Old Faithful** (WY): The chilly season in Yellowstone is increasingly popular, and it's bound be even more so now that the Old Faithful Snow Lodge has been transformed into a handsome, comfortable facility. You can take a snowcoach into the park, or cross-country ski or snowshoe to the Lone Star Geyser and other attractions. See p. 305.

- **Skiing at Jackson Hole Ski Resort** (WY; ℂ **307/733-2292**): Jackson Hole offers a vertical drop that will take your breath away, and a variety of ways to get to the bottom, from double black diamonds to intermediate slopes. Skiers who like a challenge should come here and mix the visit with some ballooning, tours of the elk refuge, and other adventures. See p. 314.

5 The Best Hotels & Resorts

- **Many Glacier Hotel** (Glacier National Park, MT; ℂ **602/207-6000**): The best thing about Many Glacier, apart from its elegant mien, its friendly service, and its cozy rooms, is the setting, along Swiftcurrent Lake and in the shadows of Mount Grinnell and Mount Wilbur. See p. 80.

- **Gallatin Gateway Inn** (Gallatin Gateway, MT; ℂ **800/676-3522**): Very old-world, the Gallatin Gateway Inn is a model of historic elegance from the days of luxury railroad travel. The Spanish-style building, with its vast interior spaces, is large enough to be a railroad station all its own. See p. 232.

- **The Pollard** (Red Lodge, MT; ℂ **800/765-5273**): You can join Buffalo Bill Cody on the guest register at The Pollard, a historic hotel that proves you don't need to sprawl all over the place to set the highest standard of comfort and elegance. See p. 242.

- **Old Faithful Inn** (Yellowstone National Park, WY; ℂ **307/344-7311**): If you ever wonder whether there is really art in architecture, look at the way the rustic simplicity and monumental structure of this inn make a perfect fit just across the way from one of nature's most astonishing creations. A lattice of logs climbs to an 85-foot ceiling, and you can find peace at one of the small writing desks in the upper balconies, or join the convivial crowds around the big stone fireplace. Corner rooms offer great views of the Old Faithful geyser. See p. 305.

- **Rusty Parrot Lodge and Spa** (Jackson, WY; ℂ **307/733-2000**): The Rusty Parrot manages to create the quiet, luxurious atmosphere of a country inn despite a location in the heart of Jackson. So you can enjoy the amenities of the lively downtown and still escape for a relaxing evening by a river-rock fireplace, or enjoy a tailor-made omelet at the expansive breakfast. See p. 321.

6 The Best Guest Ranches

- **Triple Creek Ranch** (Darby, MT; ✆ **406/821-4600**): This place is wonderful. It's pretty much the perfect guest ranch, where guests are pampered like European royalty, and the prices reflect it. It has all the traditional dude ranch activities, or you can just swim in the pool or work out in the fitness room. See p. 110.
- **Lone Mountain Ranch** (Big Sky, MT; ✆ **800/514-4644**): Lone Mountain Ranch is a winter and summer resort that has views into the Spanish Peaks Wilderness Area. In winter there are 45 miles (73km) of cross-country trails over terrain that will challenge every level of skier. In summer,

you can ride, hike, fish, or simply relax and eat in the popular restaurant. There are bird walks with naturalists and forays into Yellowstone. See p. 233.
- **Lost Creek Ranch** (Moose, WY; ✆ **307/733-3435**): Positioned next door to a national park with a beautiful view of the Tetons on one side and the Gros Ventres on the other, Lost Creek layers on the comforts and activities. You can ride, hike, swim, fish, float, play tennis, shoot skeet, play billiards, and eat gourmet food. Regulars return every year, and there are only 10 cabins, but if you can get a reservation, it's worth it. See p. 325.

7 The Best Bed & Breakfasts

- **The Garden Wall Inn** (Whitefish, MT; ✆ **888/530-1700**): This delightful B&B, built in the 1920s, is full of charm—all of the furnishings are period antiques, including claw-footed tubs and Art Deco dressers; and gourmet breakfasts include specialties like wild huckleberry crepes. See p. 139.
- **Copper King Mansion** (Butte, MT; ✆ **406/782-7580**): This is the lavishly restored home of original Butte Copper King William Clark, built in 1888 and decorated in a plush "modern Elizabethan" style. The ornamentation, from the frescoed ceilings to the pipe organ in the third-floor ballroom, reflects Clark's love of opulence. See p. 168.
- **The Sanders** (Helena, MT; ✆ **406/442-3309**): Built in 1875, this historically important B&B

has been beautifully restored. The Italianate brick-and-shingle mansion is located in Helena's historic district, and you'll settle on original 1875 furniture under the eyes of portraits hung by the original owner, U.S. Sen. Wilbur Fiske Sanders. See p. 158.
- **Spahn's Big Horn Mountain Bed and Breakfast** (Big Horn, WY; ✆ **307/674-8150**): There's lots to enjoy here: the 100-mile (161km) view from a secluded mountaintop; a rustic hideaway tucked amid the Bighorn Mountains that features a massive three-story living area and rooms decorated with country quilts and lodgepole furniture; and the chance to take a wildlife safari and search for a glimpse of moose, elk, or ever-present deer that inhabit the area. See p. 379.

8 The Best Restaurants

- **Marianne's at the Wilma** (Missoula, MT; ✆ **406/728-8549**): Chef Marianne Hoyt is a veteran of the Missoula restaurant scene, and with each incarnation her restaurants get better and better. If nothing else, the decor—call it Art Deco honky-tonk—in this restaurant makes it worth the trip. See p. 105.

- **Buck's T-4 Restaurant** (Big Sky, MT; ✆ **406/995-4111**): This is the place to experience what is often called "Montana Food"— game and beef, and lots of it. Buck's has an extensive menu of game meats, excellently prepared, and you can't beat their char-broiled steaks. See p. 234.

- **The Dining Room at Chico** (Pray, MT; ✆ **800/468-9232**): The vegetables served here are grown at the resort's own greenhouse. The game is raised here, and it's served expertly, along with beef, lamb, and other Rocky Mountain staples. Portions are generous and beautifully presented. See p. 237.

- **The Blue Lion** (Jackson, WY; ✆ **307/733-3912**): This is an old stalwart, still serving some of the best food in the region, with delicious game dishes like grilled elk loin in peppercorn sauce, and fresh seafood flown in daily. See p. 327.

- **Jenny Lake Lodge Dining Room** (Grand Teton National Park; ✆ **307/733-4647**): The five-course dinners here (from prime rib of buffalo to smoked sturgeon ravioli) are so good you might be distracted from the spectacular scenery just outside the window. You may be roughing it in the park, but you'll need to dress properly at this establishment. See p. 350.

- **Nani's Genuine Pasta House** (Jackson, WY; ✆ **307/733-3888**): Tucked away in the back of a low-rent motel, this might be the best Italian cooking in Wyoming (and Italian is the one cuisine that excels here, besides steak and beans). There is a menu of *classico* dishes, then a second menu changed monthly highlighting the dishes of a different region of Italy. See p. 327.

9 The Best Fly-Fishing

- **The Madison** (Yellowstone, MT): Brown trout are not native to this area, but no one's asking them to leave—on this popular river running from Yellowstone National Park into Montana, they're the big attraction. The Madison eventually joins up with its "holy trinity" counterparts, the Jefferson and Gallatin, at the Missouri headwaters near Three Forks, but a lot of anglers fish it around West Yellowstone, where you can find good guides. See chapter 8.

- **The Snake** (WY): It seems somehow fitting that the menacing-sounding Snake River is home to a feisty strain of cutthroat trout, making it one of the most satisfying Western rivers to fish. With picture-perfect scenery and the resort town of Jackson within casting distance, this Wyoming river is popular, but it's still an angler's paradise. See chapter 11.

10 The Best Golf Courses

- **Old Works** (Anaconda, MT): Jack Nicklaus has created a course that is as much fun to play as it is beautiful to look at. The course wonderfully integrates the rocky bluffs, the historic nature of the old copper-processing sites, and prairie grasses and sage. See p. 163.
- **Teton Pines** (Jackson, WY): You won't find a more beautiful view from any golf course in the country—except maybe the neighboring Jackson Hole club—with the granite Grand Teton looming over every shot. This Arnold Palmer design is not that long unless you're foolish enough to play from the gold tees, but water comes into play on nearly every hole. See p. 324.

11 The Best Museums

- **C.M. Russell Museum Complex** (Great Falls, MT; ✆ **406/ 727-8787**): This is a spectacular collection of the West's best-known and best-loved artist, as well as other fine artists. The museum has many of Russell's original paintings and bronzes, and includes a tour of his studio and home. See p. 192.
- **Yellowstone Art Museum** (Billings, MT; ✆ **406/256-6804**): The Yellowstone Art Museum is nationally renowned for showcasing Montana's best artists, from Charles Russell to Deborah Butterfield and Russell Chatham. See p. 249.
- **Buffalo Bill Historical Center** (Cody, WY; ✆ **307/587-4771**): An art museum, a firearm gallery, the memorabilia of the West's great showman, and exhibits about the Plains Indians comprise the finest museum in the Rocky Mountains. See p. 359.

12 The Best Performing Arts & Cultural Festivals

- **International Wildlife Film Festival** (Missoula, MT; ✆ **406/ 728-9380**): This film festival has become a required festival for international filmmakers who specialize in wildlife. It goes for a week in early April, and includes panel discussions and workshops, as well as screenings of the world's best wildlife films. See p. 96.
- **Montana Cowboy Poetry Gathering** (Lewistown, MT; ✆ **406/ 538-5436**): Held each year in mid-August, this is a rhyming good time for the bowlegged and horse-drawn set. In addition to a healthy dose of range rhyme, there are arts-and-crafts shows, and booths full of leather. See p. 201.
- **Grand Teton Music Festival** (Jackson, WY; ✆ **307/733-1128**): Under the energetic direction of Eiji Oue, the festival gathers musicians from orchestras around the country for a summer program of classical music, mixed with the occasional Duke Ellington tribute. Top international soloists appear, and there is a fine chamber-music program, too. See p.331.

2

Planning Your Trip to Montana & Wyoming

Few things can ruin a much-anticipated vacation more than poor planning: for instance, arriving at a national park in mid-January, only to discover that it's almost totally closed by snow until early May, or discovering that you missed by 2 days that dog-sled race you would have loved to see. This chapter is designed to assist you in sorting out the details that could make the difference between a trip you'll never forget and one you'd rather not remember.

1 The Regions in Brief

Planning a trip to Montana and Wyoming can be done in several ways. Those interested in a particular activity, such as hiking, might choose two or three locations and divide their time among them. Conversely, one could first select a destination, such as one of the national parks or an Old West town, and then determine the activities to be pursued there.

This book is organized geographically, and because these states are so large, many visitors will limit their vacations to one or two regions.

MONTANA
GLACIER COUNTRY & THE NORTHWEST CORNER This includes Glacier National Park, the Flathead Valley and northwest corner of the state, and Missoula, one of Montana's three largest cities. The national park draws millions of visitors each year, who come to see its soaring peaks, varied wildlife, and innumerable lakes and streams. The **Going-to-the-Sun Road,** a 50-mile (81km) scenic highway that cuts through the heart of the park from southwest to northeast, makes Glacier

surprisingly accessible. Elsewhere in the region, the increasingly popular Big Mountain draws downhill skiers, and Flathead Lake is a magnet because of its excellent water sports and quality golf courses. One of the fastest-growing areas in the state, the **Flathead Valley** shelters an interesting mix of residents: Farmers and loggers share ski lifts and trout streams with transplanted urbanites and big-bucks entrepreneurs, all looking for their slice of paradise. On the southern edge of the region is **Missoula,** a vigorous college town with good restaurants, interesting shops, and bits and pieces of Montana history.

SOUTHWESTERN MONTANA This area in the central part of the state is extremely diversified. **Helena,** a town centered around arts and politics (though not necessarily in that order), has a beautiful historic district filled with classic architecture, and access to tremendous fishing on the Missouri River. **Butte,** on the other hand, is working hard to overcome the decay caused by the exploitation, then abandonment, of its mines. A town

The Regions of Montana & Wyoming

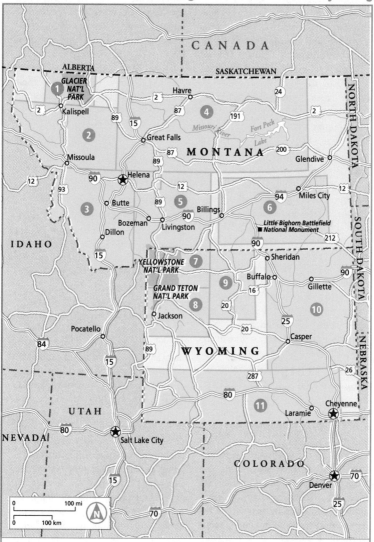

Eastern Montana **6**

Eastern Wyoming **10**

Flathead & Northwest Corner **2**

Glacier National Park **1**

Jackson Hole &
   Grand Teton National Park **8**

North Central Montana **4**

North Central Wyoming **9**

South Central Montana **5**

Southern Wyoming **11**

Southwestern Montana **3**

Yellowstone National Park **7**

that once prospered, it is searching for a new identity—perhaps as a silicon capital or movie set. Other areas in this part of the state are full of lore. Vigilantes and corrupt sheriffs dominate the stories of the "ghost towns" of Virginia City and Nevada City, both of which are kept alive today by tourists seeking a realistic glimpse into America's past.

MISSOURI RIVER COUNTRY The most distinctive trait of this region, which stretches from the mountains to the eastern border, is its prairies, which roll along interminably for hundreds of miles. One of the least populated areas in the state, its major population center is **Great Falls,** a mecca for those interested in the story of famed explorers Lewis and Clark. U.S. 2, or the **Hi-Line**—that long stretch of pavement that runs across the northern part of the state—cuts by a series of farms and ranches that perpetuate the homesteader life. New farming equipment and satellite dishes are just modern polish on an old tune.

SOUTH CENTRAL MONTANA (YELLOWSTONE COUNTRY) Though this region is almost a twin of the northwest part of the state in many ways—a nearby national park, renowned ski resorts, a university, lots of tourists—it has a unique personality. The city of **Bozeman** has its own attractions and an environment with more of a cowboy bearing, since ranching still thrives throughout the region. Anglers come from all over the world to fish these blue-ribbon trout streams, but the main attraction in this part of the state is **Yellowstone National Park.** Still, even the valleys that lead to it—the Madison, Gallatin, and Paradise—are spectacular destinations themselves.

EASTERN MONTANA The geography in this part of Montana is similar to its neighboring region to the north, but there are more people and

more things to do here. **Billings** is the supply center for eastern Montana and northern Wyoming. It's easily the largest city in Montana and has prospered without the helpful hand of tourism that the western side of the state has seen. The Bighorn Canyon and the Yellowtail Dam draw their share of visitors, especially hunters and anglers, but this region's main attraction is **Little Bighorn Battlefield,** where Gen. George Armstrong Custer led the Seventh Cavalry to defeat at the hands of the Sioux and the Northern Cheyenne.

WYOMING

YELLOWSTONE PLATEAU Yellowstone sits atop a volcanic caldera that periodically blows its top—about every 600,000 years—but in the interim provides a largely intact ecosystem of roughly 2 million acres. Protected from major development by the National Park Service, Yellowstone provides habitat no longer found elsewhere in the Lower 48, home to herds of bison, elk, grizzly bears, trumpeter swans, Yellowstone cutthroat trout, and more subtle beauties such as wildflowers and hummingbirds. The geothermal area is greater than any other in the world, with mud pots, geysers, and hot springs of all colors, size, and performance, indicative of a complex natural plumbing system that pulls water down into the earth's crust and regurgitates it at high temperatures. More than three million visitors come here annually, not just to pay homage to Old Faithful, but also to fish, hike, camp, and boat.

THE TETONS & JACKSON HOLE The Tetons are a young range, abrupt and sharp-edged as they knife up from the Snake River valley. And while the peaks get top billing, it's the valley of Jackson Hole that provides the more varied environments and experiences. **Grand Teton National Park** offers some of the most stunning scenery most of us will ever see—shimmering lakes, thickly carpeted forests, and towering peaks that are blanketed with snow throughout most of the year. It's an easy-to-see park—you can catch its breathtaking beauty on a quick drive—but there are lakes and waterfalls and even better views and adventures that you'll get to if you leave your car and take to the trails and waterways. The Tetons are especially popular with mountain climbers, who scale its peaks year-round. Elsewhere in the valley you can float the lively Snake River, visit the National Elk Refuge in the winter, or play cowboy at one of the dude and guest ranches that dot the valley. Skiers and snowboarders have a blast at the resorts here, as well as Grand Targhee on the other side of Teton Pass. And the snug town of **Jackson,** with its antler-arched town square and its busy shops, offers everything from classy art galleries to noisy two-steppin' cowboy bars.

NORTHCENTRAL WYOMING

This is the sort of basin settlers were looking for when they came this way in the 19th century—mountain ranges on all sides cradling wide, ranchable bottomlands, and some mineral wealth to pay for ranch kids' college educations. More and more, though, the oil and gas development, sheep herding and cattle driving, and beet and wheat growing are giving way to recreation and tourism. The beautiful mountains here—the Wind Rivers, the Owl Creeks, the Absarokas, the east side of the Bighorns—get less attention than the Tetons, but that only makes them more attractive. Historically, the area learned its lessons in tourism from the West's greatest showman, Buffalo Bill Cody, who helped build the fun-loving town that still bears his name. The rodeo and great museum of **Cody** are joined by other attractions, including the **Bighorn Canyon National Recreation Area,** the hot springs of **Thermopolis,** and the **Wind River Indian Reservation,** home to the Shoshone and Arapaho peoples.

EASTERN WYOMING   The plains don't begin when you pass east over the Continental Divide; there's another mountain range to cross, and then another—first the Bighorns, then the Black Hills—before you're really out there on the howling flats. The **Bighorns** are a treasure of steep canyons, snow-crowned peaks, good fishing, and good hiking, and at their feet sit two of Wyoming's nicest communities, **Sheridan** and **Buffalo.** Some of the prize ranches in this valley have become some of the best dude ranches in the country. Farther east, across the plains beyond the energy boomtown of Gillette, stands the 1,280-foot landmark of **Devils Tower,** and along Wyoming's eastern border rise the Black Hills. The region's other claim to fame lies in its history. This is the land of Butch Cassidy and his Hole-in-the-Wall Gang (also known as the Wild Bunch), of cattle rustlers, cowboys, and outlaws.

SOUTHERN WYOMING   To the millions of drivers who cross Wyoming on I-80, this is the empty quarter, mostly barren, windswept plains. But it also has its own mountainous corner—the craggy **Medicine Bow**—a lot of history and mineral wealth of many varieties, from natural gas to trona. More discerning travelers will not see a wasteland: They'll follow the routes of Oregon Trail pioneers (you can still find the wagon-wheel ruts and graves), get off the freeway to visit historic sites like Fort Laramie, and throw out a fishing line on the North Platte near Saratoga or in Flaming Gorge Reservoir south of Green River. In this country you'll find both old and new—from the re-created 1880s gold rush town of **South Pass City** to the capital city of **Cheyenne,** where the city throws the biggest rodeo party in the West during July's Cheyenne Frontier Days.

> ⌐ *Tips* **Weather Conditions**
>
> For up-to-date information on current weather, contact the **National Weather Service** at ℂ **406/449-5204;** www.wrh.noaa.gov (Montana) or **307/772-2468;** www.crh.noaa.gov (Wyoming). Statewide **road conditions** are available in Montana by calling ℂ **800/226-7623** or 406/444-6339; TDD 800/335-7592 or 406/444-7696; www.mdt.state.mt.us. In Wyoming call ℂ **888/996-7623** (within Wyoming) or 307/772-0824; http://wydotweb. state.wy.us.

2 Visitor Information

MONTANA

Travel Montana, P.O. Box 200533, 1424 9th Ave., Helena, MT 59620-0533 (ℂ **800/VISIT-MT** [800/ 847-4868] or 406/444-2654; TDD 406/444-2978; www.visitmt.com), provides information about Big Sky country and specific locales in Montana.

They put out two well-designed *Montana Vacation Guides*—one for summer, one for winter—plus the *Montana Travel Planner* that provides more detailed information, including contacts with agencies that can provide information, travel services such as airlines and rental-car agencies, and listings by town of places to stay and eat, with charts specifying price ranges and such amenities as hot tubs and access for travelers with disabilities. Travel Montana will also provide you with separate guides to some of Montana's more popular sports: snowmobiling, fishing, and skiing; as well as site-specific guides for each of six travel regions: Glacier Country in the northwest, Gold West Country in the southwest, Russell Country in north-central Montana, Yellowstone Country in south-central Montana, Missouri River Country in the northeast, and Custer Country in the southeast.

For additional information about attractions, facilities, and services in specific Montana destinations—national parks, cities, or towns—contact the **Montana Chamber of Commerce,** Box 1730, Helena, MT 59624 (ℂ **406/ 442-2405**), for the address and phone number of the nearest chamber office.

WYOMING

The **Wyoming Business Council Travel & Tourism Division,** I-25 at College Drive, Cheyenne, WY 82002 (ℂ **800/225-5996** or 307/777-7777; www.wyomingtourism.org), distributes the *Wyoming Vacation Guide,* an informative guide with information about sights and towns in the state's five travel areas: Devils Tower/Buffalo Bill Country in the north and east; Oregon Trail/Rendezvous Country in central Wyoming; Medicine Bow/Flaming Gorge along the southern border; Jackson Hole/Jim Bridger country in the west; and Grand Teton and Yellowstone; as well as special features on everything from geology to adventure travel. The nitty-gritty of agency contacts, accommodations, and eateries is in the agency's *Wyoming Vacation Directory,* which goes beyond motels to list guest ranches and B&Bs.

3 Money

Compared to much of America, Montana and Wyoming are a bargain. Especially when you get away from the national parks and major resorts, you'll find that lodging and dining is relatively inexpensive. However, you might need to budget a bit more for transportation here, mainly because distances between destinations are so great. In Montana, Canadian currency is usually accepted at the current conversion rate.

ATMS

ATMs are linked to a network that most likely includes your bank at home. **Cirrus** (✆ **800/424-7787**; www.mastercard.com) and **Plus** (✆ **800/843-7587**; www.visa.com) are the two most popular networks in the U.S.; call or check online for ATM locations at your destination. Be sure you know your four-digit PIN access number before you leave home and be sure to find out your daily withdrawal limit before you depart. You can also get cash advances on your credit card at an ATM. Keep in mind that credit card companies try to protect themselves from theft by limiting the funds someone can withdraw away from home. It's therefore best to call your credit-card company before you leave and let them know where you're going and how much you plan to spend. You'll likely get a favorable exchange rate if you withdraw money from an ATM, but keep in mind that many banks impose a fee every time a card is used at an ATM in a different city or bank. On top of this, the bank from which you withdraw cash might charge its own fee.

TRAVELER'S CHECKS

Traveler's checks are something of an anachronism from the days before the ATM (automated teller machine) made cash accessible at any time. Traveler's checks used to be the only sound alternative to traveling with dangerously large amounts of cash. They were as reliable as currency, but, unlike cash, could be replaced if lost or stolen.

These days, traveler's checks seem less necessary because most cities have 24-hour ATMs that allow you to withdraw small amounts of cash as needed. However, you're likely to be charged an ATM withdrawal fee if the bank is not your own, so if you're withdrawing money every day, you might be better off with traveler's checks—provided that you don't mind showing identification every time you want to cash one.

You can get traveler's checks at almost any bank. **American Express** offers denominations of $20, $50, $100, $500, and (for cardholders only) $1,000. You'll pay a service charge ranging from 1% to 4%. You can also get American Express traveler's checks over the phone by calling ✆ **800/221-7282**; Amex gold and platinum cardholders who use this number are exempt from the 1% fee. AAA members can obtain checks without a fee at most AAA offices.

Visa offers traveler's checks at Citibank locations nationwide, as well as at several other banks. The service charge ranges between 1.5% and 2%; checks come in denominations of $20, $50, $100, $500, and $1,000. Call ✆ **800/732-1322** for information. **MasterCard** also offers traveler's checks. Call ✆ **800/223-9920** for a location near you.

CREDIT CARDS

Credit cards are invaluable when traveling. They are a safe way to carry money and provide a convenient record of all your expenses. American Express, Discover, MasterCard, and Visa are the most commonly accepted credit cards in Montana and Wyoming, and are accepted by the great majority of businesses. However, some of the smaller, mom-and-pop establishments still refuse to go to the trouble of accepting credit cards, and a few of the more exclusive dude ranches do not accept credit cards, either.

You can also withdraw cash advances from your credit cards at any bank (though you'll start paying hefty interest on the advance the moment you receive the cash). At most banks, you don't even need to go to a teller; you can get a cash advance at the ATM if you know your PIN access number. If you've forgotten yours, or didn't even know you had one, call the number on the back of your credit card and ask the bank to send it to you. It usually takes 5 to 7 business days, though some banks will provide the number over the phone if you tell them your mother's maiden name or pass some other security clearance.

WHAT TO DO IF YOUR WALLET GETS STOLEN

Be sure to block charges against your account the minute you discover a credit card has been lost or stolen. Then be sure to file a police report.

Almost every credit card company has an emergency 800-number to call if your card is stolen. In many places, they can deliver an emergency credit card in a day or two. The issuing bank's 800-number is usually on the back of your credit card—though of course, if your card has been stolen,

that won't help you unless you recorded the number elsewhere. Citicorp Visa's U.S. emergency number is ✆ **800/336-8472.** American Express cardholders and traveler's check holders should call ✆ **800/221-7282.** MasterCard holders should call ✆ **800/307-7309.** Otherwise, call the toll-free number directory at ✆ **800/555-1212.**

Odds are that if your wallet is gone, the police won't be able to recover it for you. However, it's still worth informing the authorities, because your credit-card company or insurer might require proof of the theft.

If you choose to carry traveler's checks, be sure to keep a record of their serial numbers separate from your checks. You'll get a refund faster if you know the numbers.

In an emergency, you can have money wired to you from **Western Union** (✆ **800/325-6000;** www.westernunion.com). You must present valid ID to pick up the cash at the Western Union office.

4 When to Go

Summer, autumn, and winter are the best times to visit the Northern Rockies. The days are sunny, the nights are clear, and humidity is low. A popular song once romanticized "Springtime in the Rockies," but that season—or what most people think of as springtime—lasts about 2 days in early June. The rest of the spring season is likely to be chilly with spitting snow or rain; most of the annual moisture in these states falls during March and April.

Summer is the best season to visit for hiking, fishing, camping, and wildlife watching. It will be warm during the day and cool at night. In **Montana,** average highs in July run from 76° in **Bozeman** to 89° in **Miles City,** and lows at night from 40° to 60°. In **Wyoming,** the average high temperatures in July range from 85° to 95°—at high elevations, it almost never gets above 100°, and it's dry. The plains tend to get hotter than the mountains.

Montana's Average Monthly Temperatures (High/Low)

	Jan	Feb	Mar	Apr	May	Jun	Jul	Aug	Sep	Oct	Nov	Dec
Billings	36/12	44/17	52/24	63/33	72/42	81/50	89/55	88/53	76/43	66/34	49/23	38/14
Bozeman	33/13	38/18	44/23	55/31	64/39	74/46	82/52	81/51	70/42	59/33	43/23	34/15
Missoula	30/15	37/21	47/25	58/31	66/38	74/46	83/50	82/49	71/40	57/31	41/24	30/16
W. Yellowstone	24/0	30/4	37/10	46/20	58/29	69/37	79/41	76/39	65/31	52/23	34/12	23/1

Wyoming's Average Monthly Temperatures (High/Low)

	Jan	Feb	Mar	Apr	May	Jun	Jul	Aug	Sep	Oct	Nov	Dec
Casper	33/12	37/16	45/22	56/30	67/38	79/47	88/54	86/52	74/42	61/32	44/22	34/14
Cheyenne	38/15	41/18	45/22	55/30	65/40	74/48	82/55	80/53	71/44	60/34	47/24	39/17
Cody	34/12	40/17	47/23	56/31	66/40	76/49	84/55	82/53	71/43	61/35	45/24	36/15
Devils Tower	34/4	39/10	48/18	60/28	70/38	80/47	88/53	87/50	76/39	64/28	46/17	35/7
Jackson	26/4	32/7	41/16	51/24	62/30	72/37	82/41	80/39	70/31	58/23	39/16	27/5
Sheridan	33/9	38/15	46/22	57/30	66/39	77/47	86/53	85/52	73/41	62/32	45/20	35/10
Yellowstone	28/8	33/12	39/16	48/26	59/34	70/42	80/47	78/46	67/37	54/29	38/19	29/10

Fall brings spectacularly clear days, cool clear nights, and calm winds up until late October, when things get iffy again. Weather is changeable, however, and snow is possible—likely, even—in the high country, so don't try an extended backpacking trip unless you are experienced and well prepared. Actually, this is a requirement year-round; we've been caught in mountain snowstorms in July and August.

Winter is a glorious season here, though it can be very cold. Lows in Havre, Butte, West Yellowstone, and Jackson average single digits in January. And it can be very windy in some parts of these states, especially on the plains. But the air is crystalline, the snow is powdery, and the skiing is fantastic. If you drive around Montana and Wyoming in the winter *always* carry sleeping bags, extra food, flashlights, and other safety gear. You need to be prepared to survive if your car breaks down or you get stuck in a blizzard or snow squall. Every resident has a horror story about being caught outside unprepared. Only the north entrance at Yellowstone National Park is open to automobiles in the winter. Lodging is available in the park at Mammoth and Old Faithful only. Ski resort towns like Jackson and Kalispell stay lively all winter, but summer tourist towns like Cody are quiet.

MONTANA AND WYOMING CALENDAR OF EVENTS

January

Montana Pro Rodeo Circuit Finals. Montana's best cowboys compete in the final round of this regional competition in Great Falls. Call ✆ 406/727-8115 for information. Second or third weekend in January.

International Pedigree Stage Stop Sled Dog Race. Some of the top mushers in the world compete in this race around the Wind River Mountains. It's run in stages, with festive overnight stops in towns along the way. Call ✆ 307/733-7388. Late January to early February.

February

Wyoming State Winter Fair. They hold this one indoors in Lander, except for the chariot races. There are booths galore, music, entertainment, a livestock competition, and a big dance. Call ✆ 307/332-4011 for information. First week in February.

Race to the Sky. This weeklong event is the longest continuous dog-sled race in the Lower 48. It starts in Helena and ends in Missoula. Call ✆ 406/442-4008 for information. Second Saturday in February.

Winter Carnival. Novelty ski races and rodeo events take center stage during this Jackson, Wyoming, event that includes cowboy poetry readings, Dutch-oven cook-offs, and a barn dance. Call © **307/ 733-3316** (www.jacksonhole chamber.com) for information. Mid-February.

March

C.M. Russell Auction of Original Art. The finest Western art auction in the country, with exhibitors and attendees from around the world. Great Falls, Montana. Call © **406/ 761-6453** for information. Mid-March.

April

International Wildlife Film Festival. A unique, juried film competition in Missoula, Montana, with more than 100 entries from leading wildlife filmmakers. Call © **406/728-9380** for information. Mid-April.

Cowboy Songs and Range Ballads. With scholarly underpinning, the Buffalo Bill Historical Center in Cody, Wyoming, stages a gathering of real cowboy song and storytelling. Call © **307/587-4771** (www.bbhc.org) for the schedule. Mid-April.

May

Miles City Bucking Horse Sale. A "3-day cowboy Mardi Gras," this stock sale in Miles City, Montana, features street dances, parades, barbecues, and, of course, lots of bucking broncos. Call © **406/232-7700** for information. Third weekend in May.

Elk Antler Auction. Nearly 10,000 pounds of bull-elk antlers are auctioned off in Jackson's town square. Call © **307/733-3444** (www.jacksonholechamber.com) for information. Late May.

June

Happy Jack Mountain Music Festival. Bluegrass and fiddles prevail over this festival of mountain music in Cheyenne, Wyoming. Call © **307/777-7519** for information. Early June.

Plains Indian Powwow. Indian dancers from around the region compete in various dance categories, accompanied by traditional drum groups, on the Robbie Powwow Garden next to the Buffalo Bill Historical Center in Cody, Wyoming. Call © **307/578-4011** or visit www.codychamber.org for information. Mid-June.

Chugwater Chili Cook-Off. Thousands of hot-food pilgrims come to the Diamond Guest Ranch west of Chugwater, Wyoming, to taste the spicy contenders in this contest. Call © **307/322-2322** for information. Mid-June.

Lewis & Clark Festival. Commemoration of Lewis and Clark's journey in and around Great Falls, Montana, with historic reenactments, buffalo roasts, and float trips. Call © **406/452-5661** for information. Late June.

Shoshone Treaty Days/Eastern Shoshone Powwow and Indian Days. A celebration of American Indian tradition and culture that's followed by one of Wyoming's largest powwows and all-Indian rodeos, in Fort Washakie, Wyoming. Call © **307/332-9106** for information. Late June.

July

Cody Stampede. There are rodeo nights all summer in Cody, but this long weekend is the big one, and the rodeo ring excitement carries over to street dances, fireworks, and food. Call © **800/207-0744** (www.cody chamber.org) for details. July 1 to 4.

Grand Teton Music Festival. Fine musicians from around the world join this orchestra every summer. A varied classical repertoire includes numerous chamber concerts and some premieres in Teton Village, Wyoming. Call © 307/733-1128 for information. Mid-July to the end of August.

Legend of Rawhide Reenactment. An overeager gold miner comes to an untimely end in this production of the popular Western legend in Lusk, Wyoming. Call © 800/227-6336 (www.luskwy.com) for information. Second weekend in July.

North American Indian Days. The Blackfeet Reservation hosts a weekend of native dancing, singing, and drumming, with crafts booths and games, in Browning, Montana. Call © 406/338-7276 for information. Second week of July.

International Climbers Festival. Speakers, music, demonstrations, and climbing at the famed Wild Iris and other rock faces in Fremont County attract rock climbers from around the world to this gathering in Lander, Wyoming. Call © 307/332-6697 (landerchamber.org). Second weekend in July.

Yellowstone Jazz Festival. This music camp gathers young musicians for tutelage by some big names from the jazz world, followed by a series of performances in Powell and Cody, Wyoming. Call © 307/587-3898 for information. Mid-July.

Montana State Old Time Fiddlers Contest. A 2-day event in Polson, Montana, featuring competitions as well as impromptu and organized jam sessions. Call © 406/323-1198 for information. Third weekend in July.

Cheyenne Frontier Days. One of the country's most popular rodeos, the "Daddy of 'em All" entertains huge crowds for a full week in Cheyenne, Wyoming. Call © 800/227-6336 (www.cfdrodeo.com) for information. Last full week of July.

August

Sweet Pea Festival. A full-fledged arts festival in Bozeman, Montana, with fine art, musicians, and various entertainment for all ages. Call © 406/586-4003 for information. First full weekend in August.

Grand Targhee Bluegrass Festival. A 3-day celebration of music, arts, food, and entertainment in Jackson, Wyoming. Call © 800/827-4433 (www.jacksonholechamber.com) for information. Mid-August.

Wind River Rendezvous. A buffalo barbecue highlights this blackpowder, buckskinner event in Dubois, Wyoming. Call © 307/455-2556 for information. Mid-August.

Crow Fair. By far one of the biggest and best American Indian gatherings in the Northwest, with dancing, food, and crafts in Crow Agency, Montana. Call © 406/638-2601, ext. 104, for information. Mid-August.

Montana Cowboy Poetry Gathering. A 3-day event featuring readings and entertainment from the real McCoys in Lewistown, Montana. Call © 406/538-8278 for information. Mid-August.

River Festival and Wyoming Microbrewery Competition. Held on the banks of the North Platte River in Wyoming, festival features brews from around the state. For details call © 307/326-8855. Third weekend in August.

Big Sky Indian Powwow. A celebration of various American Indian tribes and their cultures, with traditional dancing, blanket trading, and authentic American

Indian food. In Helena, Montana. Call ℂ 406/442-4120 for information. Last weekend in August.

September

Lander Jazz Festival. Traditional jazz bands from around the country play in concerts, at street dances, and in the bars of Lander, Wyoming. For more information call ℂ 800/433-0662. Labor Day Weekend.

Nordicfest. A Scandinavian celebration in Libby, Montana, featuring a parade, a juried craft show, headliner entertainment, and an international Fjord horse show. Call ℂ 406/293-6430 for information. First weekend following Labor Day.

Western Design Conference. Western-style furniture and clothing fashions on the runway, in Cody, Wyoming. Call ℂ 888/685-0574 (www.codychamber.org) for more information. Third week in September.

Buffalo Bill Historical Center Art Show and Patrons Ball. With a big art sale to support the museum, and a black-tie dinner and ball, this is one of the Rockies' premier (and only) formal social events. Cody, Wyoming. For information call ℂ 307/578-2777 or 307/578-4032 (www.bbhc.org). Late September.

October

Art & Crafts Show. A 1-day show and sale of fine art and craft items in Helena, Montana. Call ℂ 406/449-4790 for information. Late October.

December

Christmas Strolls and Parades. Statewide, Montana and Wyoming. Check with local chambers of commerce for specific dates and locations.

5 The Active Vacation Planner

There aren't too many people coming to the Northern Rockies for amusement parks or opera festivals—the main attraction here is the outdoors. Every section of this book has suggestions for what you can do outside in the enviable setting of the Northern Rockies, but listed here are some general ideas to get you started.

OUTDOOR SAFETY

For many visitors, this is a big jump in altitude—give yourself a few days to acclimate before you embark on strenuous exercise. The weather in the Northern Rockies is capricious—it can snow in July, or give you serious sunburn in February. Be cautious around wildlife, particularly with children. Bison are not big sheepdogs, and bears are not stuffed animals; they are wild animals that can turn on you suddenly if you get too close. Never—we repeat, never—get between a mother bear and its cub.

Winter backcountry explorers should always be equipped with a shovel, a sectional probe, and an avalanche transceiver, since avalanches are common. If you're exploring during the summer, carry a can of pepper spray (bear mace), an effective deterrent to bears, available at local sporting goods stores.

If your wilderness activity takes you to a body of water, have extra clothes available in case you get wet, preferably wool and fleece fabrics, which wick away moisture. Many Western streams, rivers, and lakes are glacier-fed and run high during spring; they can be difficult to negotiate and are extremely cold.

HYPOTHERMIA Hypothermia occurs when your body gets so cold that it can no longer warm itself. It's aggravated by exhaustion, wetness, and wind, and is a leading cause of death among outdoor recreationists. It is not limited to cold weather; you can get hypothermia on a summer day that suddenly turns stormy. Always dress in layers and be prepared for bad weather, especially if you will be away from your car or lodging for an extended amount of time. When a partner gets hypothermia, you should join him or her in a sleeping bag and use your body warmth to assist.

INFORMATION ON PUBLIC LANDS

Much of the fun to be had in the Northern Rockies takes place out of doors. Throughout this book we have included contact information for national and state parks, national forests, and the like. Here are some key statewide and regional resources. The **U.S. Forest Service** has information about national forests and wilderness areas in Montana, as well as **Bridger-Teton National Forest** in Wyoming, at the Northern Region Office, Federal Building, 200 E. Broadway, Box 7669, Missoula, MT 59807 (*C* **406/329-3511;** www.fs. fed.us/r1). The rest of Wyoming's forests, as well as the **Thunder Basin National Grassland,** are covered by the Rocky Mountain Region Office, P.O. Box 25127, Lakewood, CO 80225 (*C* **303/275-5350;** www.fs. fed.us/r2).

The federal **Bureau of Land Management** also manages millions of acres of recreational lands and can be reached at its Wyoming state office, 5353 Yellowstone Rd., Cheyenne, WY 82009 (*C* **307/775-6256**), or its Montana state office, 5001 Southgate Dr., Billings, MT 59101 (*C* **406/ 896-5000**).

For information on Montana state parks, fishing, and hunting, get in touch with **Montana Fish, Wildlife, and Parks,** 1420 E. 6th Ave., Helena, MT 59620 (*C* **406/444-2535;** fwp. state.mt.us). This organization also offers a 900-number information line

(*C* **900/225-5397**) on a wide variety of recreational topics for $1.50 per minute. In Wyoming, contact **Wyoming State Parks and Historic Sites,** 122 W. 25th St., Herschler Bldg., 1-E, Cheyenne, WY 82002 (*C* **307/777-6323;** commerce.state. wy.us/sphs/index1.htm). For hunting and fishing, contact **Wyoming Game and Fish,** 5400 Bishop, Cheyenne, WY 82003 (*C* **307/777-4600;** gf. state.wy.us).

ACTIVITIES A TO Z

BACKCOUNTRY SKIING There is nothing as thrilling as skiing deep, untracked powder in completely wild terrain. To enjoy this sport you need a good set of telemark skis, good information about where to go, and expert knowledge of snow conditions and avalanche risks. Among the best places to pursue this sport is **Togwotee Pass** in Bridger-Teton National Forest in Wyoming. Otherwise, check at local ski shops and ask at the headquarters of national forests and state parks. The **Jackson Hole Ski Resort** decided in 1999 to allow skiers to ski "out of bounds" beyond the areas groomed and patrolled—as long as they sign waivers. Check with other ski resorts about forest areas around the lifts that might be accessible for backcountry adventures.

BIKING Mountain biking is a fast-growing sport. Some folks take it easy, pedaling their way to wild country on smooth, easy-grade paths; others are looking for a fast ride down on bumpy, steep trails. Bring your own bike or rent from a local bike shop; they will usually assist you in finding the best spots to ride. Bicycling on roads is also popular, but there are limitations: While automobile traffic on many roads is light, there isn't much room, because most of the roads have skimpy shoulders—Yellowstone roads are among the worst. Nor are

Value   National Parks Passes—A National Bargain

If you plan to visit a number of national parks and monuments within a year, a **National Parks Pass,** which costs $50, will save you a bundle. The passes are good at all properties under the jurisdiction of the National Park Service, but not at sites administered by the Bureau of Land Management, National Forest Service, or other federal or state agencies. The National Parks Passes provide free entrance for the pass holder and all vehicle occupants to National Park Service properties that charge vehicle entrance fees, and the pass holder, spouse, parents, and children for sites that charge per-person fees. The passes can be purchased at park entrance stations and visitor centers, or by mail order (© **888/GO-PARKS;** www.nationalparks.org).

Also available at park service properties, as well as other federal recreation sites that charge entrance fees, is the **Golden Age Passport,** for those 62 and older, which has a one-time fee of $10 and provides free admission to all national parks and monuments, plus a 50% discount on camping fees. The **Golden Access Passport,** free for blind or permanently disabled U.S. citizens, has the same benefits as the Golden Age Passport and is available at all federal recreation sites that charge entrance fees.

Available from U.S. Forest Service, Bureau of Land Management, and Fish and Wildlife areas are **Golden Eagle Passes.** At a cost of $65 for 1 year from the date of purchase, they allow the bearer, plus everyone traveling with him or her in the same vehicle, free admission to all National Park Service properties plus other federal recreation sites that charge fees. The National Parks Pass discussed above can be upgraded to Golden Eagle status for $15.

drivers in this region terribly respectful of bicyclists. So be watchful, research your routes so you can keep to the wider roads, and always wear that helmet.

BOATING & SAILING Serious sailors are not likely to put down roots at this altitude; even weekend sailors would be wise to look elsewhere for their kind of fun. But if you insist on trying, you'll find a few sails spread on the bigger lakes of these mountains. You can take a pretty big boat on pretty big **Flathead Lake,** or **Jackson Lake,** or even **Yellowstone Lake,** if you're careful about the weather. Smaller boats like Hobie Cats in some ways better suit the sudden, swirling winds typical of these mountains.

Powerboating is another matter; if you've got a motor, pack a lunch and head for any of the many lakes that dot Montana and Wyoming's landscape. **Canyon Ferry** is a popular Montana water-skiing spot, and you'll see Wyoming powerboats cruising **Boysen Reservoir** or the many impoundments on the **North Platte.** Just make sure to check around locally regarding access if you're uncertain about it. All types of boats are available locally for rent.

CROSS-COUNTRY SKIING If you don't plan to pound down the backcountry powder on telemark skis, but you want to get out in the snow, cross-country skiing can be practiced on any relatively flat, open meadow or plain where there's snow on the ground, or along old roads in the region's forests. Scores of guest ranches now groom trails for both track and "skate" skiing, and almost every ski resort in the region has a trail. If you don't want to pay to ski, **Forest Service logging roads** are typically used for cross-country trails. Many golf courses are also regularly groomed for track skiing; some are even lighted for night skiing. **Best place to cross-country ski in Montana:** West Yellowstone, training ground of U.S. Nordic and Biathlon ski teams; **in Wyoming:** Jackson Hole area and Grand Teton National Park.

DOWNHILL SKIING There are 13 downhill ski areas in Montana and 11 in Wyoming, scattered amid the towering mountain ranges found predominantly in the western parts of both states. Breathtaking summit vistas are standard fare. Usually operating from late November to mid-April, and with comparatively shorter lift lines and less expensive lift tickets than most other ski areas in the country, Montana and Wyoming ski resorts are great values for the ski enthusiast. Don't fret if you're not skiing black-diamond runs; all ski resorts have acres of beginner and intermediate trails, and seasoned instructors provide lessons at extremely affordable prices. More and more often, you'll find telemark skiers honing their skills on packed resort slopes. **Best skiing in Montana:** Big Sky Resort near Bozeman is the biggest in Montana, with runs for all abilities, and Whitefish's Big Mountain prides itself on a family atmosphere; **in Wyoming:** the Jackson Hole area wins hands down, with Jackson Hole Ski Resort, Snow King, and Grand Targhee ski hills all in close proximity.

DUDE RANCHES The dude ranch is the fabled Western experience come to life: daily rides by horseback, cowboy coffee beneath an expansive blue sky, campfire sing-alongs, and homemade food served in rustic lodges. Accommodations are usually in a comfortable cabin or lodge. You need not have any riding experience before your visit; ranch "hands" are trained to assist even the greenest of greenhorns. For additional information on dude ranches in both Montana and Wyoming, as well as other western states, contact **Dude Ranchers' Association,** Box F-417, LaPorte, CO 80535 (© **970/223-8440;** www.duderanch.org). **Best places in Montana:** the Paradise and Gallatin valleys in the southwest; **in Wyoming:** the Sheridan area and the Wapiti Valley west of Cody.

FISHING Montana and Wyoming have long been known for world-class fly-fishing, their streams and creeks teeming with native trout—rainbow, brook, brown, mackinaw, golden, and

---

⌒ Fun Fact Are You a Dude or a Guest?

A century ago, it was common courtesy in the West for ranches to feed and lodge travelers who stopped by on their treks across the great empty spaces. Gradually it became acceptable to accept a few dollars from guests, and by the 1920s a ranch visit was a full-fledged vacation.

When you make your ranch reservations, it's wise to know the difference between a "dude ranch" and a "guest ranch." A dude ranch typically requires a 1-week minimum stay, and they give you the whole package: riding, fishing, trips to the rodeo, and family-style meals. Dude ranchers look down their noses at "guest" ranches, which will take overnight guests and charge extra for activities such as riding.

Fishing Licenses

Both Montana and Wyoming require fishing licenses, which are available from most sporting goods stores, outfitters, or tackle shops. Yellowstone National Park requires an additional fishing permit (see chapter 10), and American Indian tribes located in the two states have special regulations and may require permits for fishing in their waters.

In Montana, all nonresident anglers 15 and older are required to buy fishing licenses. Those under 15 do not need a fishing license as long as they are with an adult who has a valid fishing license. A license for the period of March 1 through the following February is $45. A consecutive 2-day license is $10. In addition to fishing licenses, however, nonresident anglers of all ages must also possess conservation licenses, which cost $5 each. For information contact the Montana Department of Fish, Wildlife, and Parks, 1420 E. 6th Ave., Helena, MT 59620 (© **406/444-2535**; http://fwp.state.mt.us).

You'll also need a Wyoming state fishing license if you plan to fish that state's waters. Nonresident licenses cost $10 for 1 day or $65 for the season, plus $10 for a state conservation stamp. No license is required for kids under 14, as long as they are accompanied by an adult who has a valid fishing license. You'll also have to check creel limits, which vary from year to year and place to place. Information is available from the Wyoming Game and Fish Department, 5400 Bishop Blvd., Cheyenne, WY 82006 (© **307/777-4600**; http://gf.state.wy.us).

cutthroat—as well as kokanee salmon, yellow perch, largemouth bass, and northern pike. Warm-water species include sauger, channel catfish, and smallmouth bass. **Best places to fish in Montana:** on any one of the world-class, blue-ribbon streams in the southwest part of the state; **in Wyoming:** the blue-ribbon waters of the North Platte River near Saratoga and the Miracle Mile, or the high lakes of the Wind River Indian Reservation.

GOLF Golfers not familiar with Montana or Wyoming will be pleasantly surprised at the number of exceptional courses found in both states, particularly in Bigfork and Anaconda, Montana. Summer's long days make this a perfect place to play a round, especially when you take into consideration that average daily temperatures and humidity are much lower here than at destinations in Florida. Reserve tee times well in advance. **Best Montana courses:** the Old Works, Anaconda; Eagle Bend, Whitefish; **in Wyoming:** the Jackson Hole Golf and Tennis Club; Teton Pines, Jackson.

HIKING Hiking gives you the added bonus of moderate to strenuous cardiovascular exercise while you're seeing the sights. Remember, though, that these are the mountains, and the elevation you gain over the course of the hike is a much better indication of how difficult the hike will be than the actual distance traveled. Be sure to wear comfortable hiking shoes that have been broken in, and if you plan on hiking in prime grizzly country, be sure to carry bear mace and check with rangers for what to do in case you actually see one. **Best place to take a hike in Montana:** Glacier National Park; **in**

Wyoming: the Wind River Mountains or the Bighorn Mountains.

MOUNTAINEERING: ROCK & ICE CLIMBING The Northern Rockies provide superb opportunities for climbers to experience the year-round beauty of Montana and Wyoming's mountains, whether you seek a daylong rock climb during the height of summer in Montana's Beartooths or a technical climb up one of the faces of the Tetons. Ice climbing is becoming a hot ticket in the dead of winter, when many of the world's finest climbers congregate in Cody, Wyoming, for unforgettable winter mountaineering. Not for the faint of heart, the sport is highly technical and requires extreme fitness and stamina. **Best place to climb in Montana:** Granite Peak, the state's highest; **in Wyoming:** Grand Teton National Park or Wild Iris south of Lander.

SNOWBOARDING Forget all those stereotypes you've heard about snowboarders: This sport is a simple combination of speed, air, and style. If you've never done it, realize that you may have a very sore butt during your first few days, although seasoned shredders swear that the learning curve is much shorter than that for skiing. Experienced snowboarders will find Montana and Wyoming ski areas to be snowboard-friendly. If you're really into riding, ask around at local ski shops for winter backcountry options or summer snowboarding—**Glacier Park's Logan Pass** is a popular Fourth of July hike 'n' ride destination. **Best place in Montana and Wyoming:** The Big Mountain.

SNOWMOBILING With more than 3,000 miles (4,830km) of trails in Montana and 1,300 (2,080km) in Wyoming, snowmobilers have a vast winter playground to explore. Though rental shops are plentiful, machines are in high demand, so you're wise to make a reservation well in advance.

Though snowmobiling doesn't require an extreme level of physical fitness, you have to be able to adequately handle the snowmobile and be well versed in safety measures since avalanches are common in the areas some of these trails traverse. **Best bets for snowmobiling in Montana:** West Yellowstone and the Seeley Lake Valley; **in Wyoming:** Yellowstone National Park and the surrounding national forest lands.

WATER SPORTS: CANOEING, KAYAKING, RAFTING & SAILING Paddlers have a wealth of choices here. Montana is particularly rich in rivers worth floating: the Flathead, the Blackfoot, the Madison, the Clarks Fork near Missoula, the Dearborn, the Yellowstone, and more, even the big old Missouri. In Wyoming there is less variety, but some fine stretches of river on the Snake, the Platte, the Hoback, or Wyoming's own Clarks Fork through Sunlight Basin. If you choose white-water rafting, you leave the driving to someone else, though you may be asked to paddle. The smaller rivers have no dams to regulate flows, which means kayakers seeking fast, scary runs should come during runoff in June, while canoeists wanting to relax and bird-watch can easily handle the upper Snake or Flathead late in the summer. **Best place to paddle in Montana:** for thrills, try the Yellowstone River at Gardiner; **in Wyoming:** the Snake River.

CHOOSING AN OUTFITTER

If you're just getting started as an outdoor adventurer, it might be wise to hire an outfitter to train and guide you in the ways of the wild. Even if you're experienced, you might prefer to pay someone else to handle the logistics of food, shelter, and planning, so you can just enjoy yourself.

When considering an outfitter, think about things like group size, activity level, and guide expertise. Do you mind sleeping in a tent every night? Do you want to travel with a small group or be part of a larger one? With strangers, or friends? Is your fitness level appropriate to the type of trip you want to take? Evaluate your own limitations honestly—your health, your outdoor experience, and your travel comfort zone.

Make sure that the company is up-to-date with government permits and insurance. Find out how well the company knows the area where you're going, and ask for references from people they've taken on similar trips. Inquire about your guide's background and experience. Get a firm price, including extras like airport transfers, meals, or equipment rentals.

Throughout this book we discuss regional outfitters. You can also find an outfitter through **The Montana Outfitters and Guides Association,** P.O. Box 1248, Helena, MT 59624 (© 406/449-3578; www.moga-montana.org) and the **Wyoming Outfitters and Guide Association,** P.O. Box 2284, Cody, WY 82414 (© 307/527-7453; www.wyoga.org).

Among reputable national and international companies that offer outdoor adventure trips in this region, including multi-activity excursions, consider the following:

- **Austin-Lehman Adventures,** P.O. Box 81025, Billings, MT 59108 (© **888-338-4844** or 800/575-1540; fax 406/651-9236; www.austinlehman.com), a merger of Backcountry and Adventures Plus.
- **Backcountry Tours,** P.O. Box 4029, Bozeman, MT 59772 (© **800/575-1540** or 406/586-3556; fax 406/586-4288; www.backcountrytours.com).
- **Backroads,** 801 Cedar St., Berkeley, CA 94710-1800 (© **800/462-2848** or 510/527-1555; fax 510/527-1444; www.backroads.com).
- **GORPtravel,** P.O. Box 1486, Boulder, CO 80306 (© **877/532-4677;** fax 303/635-0658; www.gorptravel.com), formerly American Wilderness Experience.
- **Moguls Ski & Snowboard Tours,** 6707 Winchester Circle, Boulder, CO 80301 (© **800/666-4857** or 303/440-7921; fax 303/440-4160; www.skimoguls.com).
- **The World Outdoors,** 2840 Wilderness Place, Suite F, Boulder, CO 80301 (© **800/488-8483** or 303/413-0938; fax 303/413-0926; www.theworldoutdoors.org), formerly Roads Less Traveled.

6 Insurance, Health & Safety

TRAVEL INSURANCE AT A GLANCE

Check your existing insurance policies before you buy travel insurance to cover trip cancellation, lost luggage, medical expenses, or car-rental insurance. If you need additional coverage, ask your travel agent about a comprehensive package. The cost of travel insurance varies widely, depending on the cost, type, and length of your trip, and your age and overall health. More dangerous activities may be excluded from basic policies.

For information, contact one of the following popular insurers:

- **Access America** (© 800/284-8300; www.accessamerica.com).
- **Travel Guard International** (© 800/826-1300; www.travelguard.com).
- **Travel Insured International** (© 800/243-3174; www.travelinsured.com).
- **Travelex Insurance Services** (© 800/228-9792; www.travelexinsurance.com).

TRIP-CANCELLATION INSURANCE (TCI)

There are three major types of trip-cancellation insurance—one in the event that you prepay a cruise or tour that gets cancelled and you can't get your money back; a second when you or someone in your family gets sick or dies, and you can't travel; and a third when bad weather makes travel impossible. Some insurers provide coverage for events like jury duty, natural disasters close to home, and even the loss of a job. A few have added provisions for cancellations due to terrorist activities. Always check the fine print before signing on, and don't buy trip-cancellation insurance from the tour operator that may be responsible for the cancellation; buy it only from a reputable travel insurance agency.

MEDICAL INSURANCE

Most health insurance policies cover you if you get sick away from home—but check, particularly if you're insured by an HMO.

Some credit cards offer automatic flight insurance against death or dismemberment in case of an airplane crash if you charged the cost of your ticket.

If you require additional insurance, try one of the following companies:

- **MEDEX International,** 9515 Deereco Rd., Timonium, MD 21093-5375 (© **888/MEDEX-00** or 410/453-6300; fax 410/453-6301; www.medexassist.com).
- **Travel Assistance International** (© **800/821-2828;** www.travelassistance.com), 9200 Keystone Crossing, Suite 300, Indianapolis, IN 46240 (for general information on services, call the company's Worldwide Assistance Services, Inc., at © **800/777-8710**).

The cost of travel medical insurance varies widely. Check your existing policies before you buy additional coverage. Also, check to see if your medical insurance covers you for emergency medical evacuation: If you have to buy a one-way same-day ticket home and forfeit your nonrefundable roundtrip ticket, you may be out big bucks.

LOST-LUGGAGE INSURANCE

On domestic flights, checked baggage is covered up to $2,500 per ticketed passenger. If you plan to check items more valuable than the standard liability, you may purchase "excess valuation" coverage from the airline, up to $5,000. Be sure to take any valuables or irreplaceable items with you in your carry-on luggage. If you file a lost luggage claim, be prepared to answer detailed questions about the contents of your baggage, and be sure to file a claim immediately. Before you leave home, compile an inventory of all packed items and a rough estimate of the total value to ensure you're properly compensated if your luggage is lost. Once you've filed a complaint, persist in securing your reimbursement; there are no laws governing the length of time it takes for a carrier to reimburse you. If you arrive at a destination without your bags, ask the airline to forward them to your hotel or to your next destination; they will usually comply. If your bag is delayed or lost, the airline may reimburse you for reasonable expenses, such as a toothbrush or a set of clothes, but the airline is under no legal obligation to do so.

Lost luggage may also be covered by your homeowner's or renter's policy. Many platinum and gold credit cards cover you as well. If you choose to purchase additional lost-luggage insurance, be sure not to buy more than you need. Buy in advance from a trusted agent (prices will be much higher at the airport).

CAR-RENTAL INSURANCE (LOSS/DAMAGE WAIVER OR COLLISION DAMAGE WAIVER)

If you hold a private auto insurance policy, you probably are covered in the U.S., but not abroad, for loss or damage to the car, and liability in case a passenger is injured. The credit card you used to rent the car also may provide some coverage.

Car-rental insurance probably does not cover liability if you caused the accident. Check your own auto insurance policy, the rental company policy, and your credit card coverage for the extent of coverage: Is your destination covered? Are other drivers covered? How much liability is covered if a passenger is injured? (If you rely on your credit card for coverage, you may want to bring a second credit card with you, as damages may be charged to your card and you may find yourself stranded with no money.)

Car-rental insurance costs about $20 a day.

THE HEALTHY TRAVELER

The major health concerns in Montana and Wyoming are mostly associated with outdoor activities, which are discussed in "The Active Vacation Planner," earlier in this chapter. However, there are a few additional points of which all visitors to this region should be aware.

- The sun is bright and strong at the higher elevations of the Northern Rockies, so limit your exposure, use a sunscreen with a high protective factor, and remember that children need more sun protection than adults do.
- When driving in these states during the winter, even on major highways, four-wheel drive or at least front-wheel drive is wise, because it's hard to predict when a winter storm will move in. At all times of the year it's a good idea for motorists to carry a basic emergency kit that includes a flashlight and blankets or sleeping bags.

WHAT TO DO IF YOU GET SICK AWAY FROM HOME

If you suffer from a chronic illness, consult your doctor before your departure. For conditions like epilepsy, diabetes, or heart problems, wear a **Medic Alert Identification Tag** (© 800/825-3785; www.medicalert.org), which will immediately alert doctors to your condition and give them access to your records through Medic Alert's 24-hour hot line.

Pack **prescription medications** in your carry-on luggage, and carry prescription medications in their original containers. Also bring along copies of your prescriptions in case you lose your pills or run out.

If you get sick, consider asking your hotel manager to recommend a local doctor—even his or her own. You can also try the emergency room at a local hospital; many have walk-in clinics for emergency cases that are not life threatening.

7 Tips for Travelers with Special Needs

TRAVELERS WITH DISABILITIES

More and more facilities in Montana and Wyoming are becoming accessible to those with disabilities. This is especially true in national parks. The National Park Service offers a free lifetime pass to people with disabilities; see the sidebar "National Parks Passes—A National Bargain," in section 5, above). However, somewhat less has been done to accommodate those with disabilities in some of the less-developed areas of Wyoming and Montana—and particularly in historic structures.

The **Montana Independent Living Project,** Box 5415, Helena, MT 59604-5415 (© **800/735-6457** or 406/442-5755), operates an information and referral service for travelers with disabilities, providing information relating to such topics as accessibility, recreation, and transportation.

AGENCIES/OPERATORS

- **Flying Wheels Travel** (© **800/ 535-6790;** www.flyingwheels travel.com) offers escorted tours and cruises that emphasize sports and private tours in minivans with lifts.

- **Access Adventures** (© **716/889-9096**), a Rochester, New York–based agency, offers customized itineraries for a variety of travelers with disabilities.

- **Accessible Journeys** (© **800/ TINGLES** or 610/521-0339; www.disabilitytravel.com) caters specifically to slow walkers and wheelchair travelers and their families and friends.

ORGANIZATIONS

- **The Moss Rehab Hospital** (© **215/456-9603;** www.moss resourcenet.org) provides friendly, helpful phone assistance through its **Travel Information Service.**

- **The Society for Accessible Travel and Hospitality** (© **212/447-7284;** fax 212-725-8253; www. sath.org) offers a wealth of travel resources for all types of disabilities and informed recommendations on destinations, access guides, travel agents, tour operators, vehicle rentals, and companion services. Annual membership costs $45 for adults; $30 for seniors and students.

- **The American Foundation for the Blind** (© **800/232-5463;** www.afb.org) provides information on traveling with Seeing Eye dogs.

PUBLICATIONS

- **Mobility International USA** (© **541/343-1284;** www.miusa. org) publishes *A World of Options,* a 658-page book of resources, covering everything from biking trips to scuba outfitters, and a biannual newsletter, *Over the Rainbow.* Annual membership is $35.

- **Twin Peaks Press** (© **360/ 694-2462**) publishes travel-related books for travelers with special needs.

- *Open World for Disability and Mature Travel* magazine, published by the Society for Accessible Travel and Hospitality (see above), is full of good resources and information. A year's subscription is $13 ($21 outside the U.S.).

GAY & LESBIAN TRAVELERS

The murder of gay Laramie student Matthew Shepard in 1998 sent shock waves far beyond Wyoming's borders, and discouraged many gay and lesbian travelers from coming to the Northern Rockies. Nevertheless, there are gay communities in the region's larger cities—Billings, Bozeman, Helena, Missoula, Casper, Laramie, Jackson, and Cheyenne—and while these two states could generally be considered conservative, communities are generally tolerant of locals who have come out.

The **International Gay & Lesbian Travel Association** (IGLTA) (© **800/ 448-8550** or 954/776-2626; fax 954/ 776-3303; www.iglta.org) links travelers up with gay-friendly hoteliers, tour operators, and airline and cruise-line representatives. It offers monthly newsletters, marketing mailings, and a membership directory that's updated once a year. Membership is $150 yearly, plus a $100 fee for new members.

AGENCIES/OPERATORS

- **Above and Beyond Tours** (© **800/397-2681;** www.above beyondtours.com) offers gay and lesbian tours worldwide and is the exclusive gay and lesbian tour operator for United Airlines.

- **Now, Voyager** (© **800/255-6951;** www.nowvoyager.com) is a San Francisco–based gay-owned and operated travel service.

PUBLICATIONS

- *Out and About* (© **800/929-2268** or 415-644-8044; www.outandabout.com) offers guidebooks and a newsletter 10 times a year packed with solid information on the global gay and lesbian scene.
- *Gay Travel A to Z: The World of Gay & Lesbian Travel Options at Your Fingertips,* by Marianne Ferrari (Ferrari Publications; www.ferrariguides.com), is a very good gay and lesbian guidebook series.

WEBSITES

Though many gay and lesbian travel sites have no listings for Montana or Wyoming, a few do, like **Gaywired.com Travel** (www.gaywired.com).

Ferrariguides.com (www.ferrariguides.com) is a comprehensive gay travel website that grew out of one of the world's oldest gay publishing companies. Buy books, find planning and booking information on a variety of tours, and learn of upcoming gay events.

SENIOR TRAVEL

Mention the fact that you're a senior when you first make your travel reservations. All major airlines and many hotels offer discounts for seniors. Major airlines also offer coupons for domestic travel for seniors over 60. In most communities in Montana and Wyoming, people over the age of 60 (or sometimes 62) qualify for reduced admission to theaters, museums, and other attractions, as well as discounted fares on public transportation and sometimes discounts on meals.

Members of **AARP,** 601 E St. NW, Washington, DC 20049 (© **800/424-3410** or 202/434-2277; www.aarp.org), get discounts on hotels, airfares, and car rentals. AARP offers members a wide range of benefits, including a monthly magazine. Anyone over 50 can join.

The Alliance for Retired Americans, 8403 Colesville Rd., Suite 1200, Silver Spring, MD 20910 (© **301/578-8422;** www.retiredamericans.org), offers a newsletter six times a year and discounts on hotel and auto rentals; annual dues are $13 per person or couple. *Note:* Members of the former National Council of Senior Citizens receive automatic membership in the Alliance.

The **National Park Service** offers a **Golden Age Passport** (see the sidebar "National Parks Passes—A National Bargain," in section 5, above).

AGENCIES/OPERATORS

- **Grand Circle Travel** (© **800/221-2610** or 617/350-7500; www.gct.com) offers package deals for the 50-plus market, with free trips thrown in for those who organize groups of 10 or more.
- **SAGA Holidays** (© **800/343-0273;** www.sagaholidays.com) offers inclusive tours for those 50 and older. SAGA also offers a number of single-traveler tours and sponsors the "Road Scholar Tours" (© **800/621-2151**), vacations with an educational bent.
- **Elderhostel** (© **877/426-8056;** www.elderhostel.org) arranges study programs for those aged 55 and over (and a spouse or companion of any age) in the U.S. and around the world. The organization offers numerous programs throughout Montana and Wyoming. Programs generally run less than a week, and participants may find themselves meeting

American Indians, listening to a historian talk about the fur-trapping era, or learning to make beef jerky.

PUBLICATIONS

- *The Book of Deals* is a collection of more than 1,000 senior discounts on airlines, lodging, tours, and attractions around the country; it's available for $9.95 by calling © **800/460-6676.**
- *101 Tips for the Mature Traveler* is available from Grand Circle Travel (© **800/221-2610** or 617/350-7500; fax 617/346-6700).
- *The 50+ Traveler's Guidebook* (St. Martin's Press).
- *Unbelievably Good Deals and Great Adventures That You Absolutely Can't Get Unless You're Over 50* (Contemporary Publishing Co.).

FAMILY TRAVEL

The family vacation is a rite of passage for many households, one that in a split second can devolve into a *National Lampoon* farce. But as any veteran family vacationer will assure you, a family trip can be among the most rewarding times of your life.

Family groups should always ask about discounts for attractions and accommodations. If you plan to stay a week at a ski resort or dude ranch, you may find a better value by renting a condominium or lodge than multiple rooms. Ski areas often offer packages that include accommodations and lift tickets; check with the ski resort's reservation service for current prices. Before booking any type of room, event, or activity, be sure to inquire whether there are discounts for children or age restrictions.

Tip: Find out exactly what a motel means when it advertises a "continental breakfast." If it's coffee and donuts, that probably won't be enough for the kids. However, for many motels the definition of a "continental breakfast" means cereal, juice, toast, pastries, and beverages, which can save a family of four around $25 for morning meals.

AGENCIES/OPERATORS

Familyhostel (© **800/733-9753;** www.learn.unh.edu/familyhostel) takes the whole family on moderately priced learning vacations. All trip details are handled by the program staff, and lectures, field trips, and sightseeing are guided by a team of academics. The program is for kids ages 8 to 15 accompanied by their parents and/or grandparents.

PUBLICATIONS

- An especially useful resource for families traveling in the Western United States, including Montana and Wyoming, is *Frommer's Family Vacations in the National Parks.*

- *How to Take Great Trips with Your Kids* (The Harvard Common Press) is full of good general advice that can apply to travel anywhere.

WEBSITES

- **Montana Kids** (www.montanakids.com) is a website from Travel Montana that's both for kids, with games and such, and their parents, with information about places to go and things to do with families.
- **Family Travel Network** (www.familytravelnetwork.com) offers travel tips, reviews, vacation deals, and thoughtful features such as "What to Do When Your Kids Are Afraid to Travel" and "Kid-Style Camping."
- **The Busy Person's Guide to Travel with Children** (http://wz.com/travel/TravelWithChildren.html) offers a "45-second newsletter" where experts weigh in on the best websites and resources for tips for traveling with children.

Tips **Pet Safety**

Never leave your pet inside a parked car in hot climates with the windows rolled up. It's a good idea never to leave a pet inside a hot car even with the windows rolled down for any length of time.

Make sure your pet is wearing a name tag with the name and phone number of a contact person (such as your veterinarian) who can take the call if your pet gets lost while you're away from home.

TRAVELING WITH PETS

Many of us wouldn't dream of going on vacation without our pets. Under the right circumstances, it can be a memorable experience. And these days, more and more lodgings are going the pet-friendly route. Many hotel and motel chains, such as Best Western, Motel 6, Holiday Inn, and Four Seasons-Regent Hotels, welcome pets, and you'll find that many lodgings in Montana and Wyoming are pet friendly. Policies vary, however, so call ahead to find out the rules.

An excellent resource is www. petswelcome.com, which dispenses medical tips, names of animal-friendly lodgings and campgrounds, and lists of kennels and veterinarians. Also check out *The Portable Petswelcome. com: The Complete Guide to Traveling with Your Pet* (Howell Book House), which features the best selection of pet travel information anywhere. Another resource is *Pets-R-Permitted Hotel, Motel & Kennel Directory: The Travel Resource for Pet Owners Who Travel* (Annenberg Communications).

Keep in mind that dogs must be leashed at all times on all federal and state lands. They are almost always prohibited on hiking trails on federal lands administered by the National Park Service (national parks and most national monuments), but are usually permitted on trails in national forests, Bureau of Land Management areas, and state parks. However, because many of the public lands in these states have bears and other wildlife, there are sometimes site-specific regulations regarding pets.

Aside from regulations, be attentive to your pet's well-being. Just as people need extra water in this dry climate, so do pets. We particularly like those clever non-spill travel water bowls sold in pet stores. And keep in mind that trails are often rough, and jagged rocks can cut the pads on your dog's feet. Remember, too, that dogs, who usually spend most of their time sleeping, aren't used to 10-hour hikes up mountainsides.

8 Getting There

BY PLANE

Travelers flying into Montana can choose to land in one of the state's six major airports: Billings, Bozeman, Great Falls, Helena, Kalispell, or Missoula. Air service to these airports is provided by the following airlines, although only Billings can boast of service from all three: **Delta** (© 800/ 221-1212), **Northwest** (© 800/225-2525), and **United** (© 800/241-6522). Delta's commuter affiliate is **Skywest** (© 800/453-9417), and Northwest's is **Horizon** (© 800/547-9308). The busiest of the smaller connection airlines is **Big Sky** (© 800/237-7788).

In Wyoming, Jackson, Casper, Cheyenne, Cody, Gillette, Laramie, Riverton, Rock Springs, and Sheridan have airports with commercial intrastate airline service. Presently, the airlines serving the state are **Delta** (℃ 800/221-1212) and **United** (℃ 800/241-6522), with seasonal service to Jackson by **American Airlines** (℃ 800/433-7300). Commuter carriers in Wyoming include **Skywest** (the Delta Connection) (℃ 800/453-9417) and United's affiliate **United Express** (℃ 800/241-6522).

FLYING FOR LESS: TIPS FOR GETTING THE BEST AIRFARE

Passengers within the same airplane cabin are rarely paying the same fare. Business travelers who need to purchase tickets at the last minute, change their itinerary at a moment's notice, or get home for the weekend pay the premium rate. Passengers who can book their ticket long in advance, who can stay over Saturday night, or who are willing to travel on a Tuesday, Wednesday, or Thursday after 7pm, will pay a fraction of the full fare. On many flights, even the shortest hops, the full fare is close to $1,000 or more, while a 7- or 14-day advance purchase ticket may cost less than half that amount. Here are a few other easy ways to save.

- Airlines periodically lower prices on their most popular routes. Check the travel section of your Sunday newspaper for advertised discounts or call the airlines directly and ask whether any **promotional rates** or special fares are available. You'll almost never see a sale during the peak summer and holiday seasons; but in periods of low-volume travel, you should pay no more than $400 for a domestic cross-country flight. *Note:* The lowest-priced fares are often nonrefundable, require advance purchase of 1 to 3 weeks and a certain length of stay, and carry penalties for changing dates of travel.

- **Consolidators,** also known as bucket shops, are a good place to find low fares. Consolidators buy seats in bulk from the airlines and then sell them back to the public at prices usually below even the airlines' discounted rates. Their small ads usually run in Sunday newspaper travel sections. And before you pay, request a confirmation number from the consolidator and then call the airline to confirm your seat. Be aware that bucket-shop tickets are usually nonrefundable or rigged with stiff cancellation penalties, often as high as 50% to 75% of the ticket price. Protect yourself by paying with a credit card rather than cash. Keep in mind that if there's an airline sale going on, or if it's high season, you can often get the same or better rates by contacting the airlines directly, so do some comparison-shopping before you buy. And check whether you're flying on a charter or a scheduled airline; the latter is more expensive but more reliable.

  Council Travel (℃ 800/226-8624; www.counciltravel.com) and **STA Travel** (℃ 800/781-4040; www.sta.travel.com) cater especially to young travelers, but their bargain-basement prices are available to people of all ages. **The TravelHub** (℃ 888/AIR-FARE; www.travelhub.com) represents nearly 1,000 travel agencies, many of whom offer consolidator and discount fares. Other reliable consolidators include **1-800-FLY-CHEAP** (www.1800flycheap.com); **TFI Tours International** (℃ 800-745-8000 or 212/736-1140; www.lowestprice.com), which serves as a clearinghouse for unused seats; or "rebators" such as

Travel Avenue (© 800/333-3335; www.travelavenue.com) and the **Smart Traveller** (© 800/448-3338 in the U.S. or 305/448-3338), which rebate part of their commissions to you.

- Search **the Internet** for cheap fares. Great last-minute deals are available through free weekly e-mail services provided directly by the airlines. See "Planning Your Trip Online," below, for more information.

- Join a travel club such as **Moment's Notice** (© 718/234-6295; www.moments-notice.com) or **Sears Discount Travel Club** (© 800/433-9383, or 800/255-1487 to join; www.travelers advantage.com), which supply unsold tickets at discounted prices. You pay an annual membership fee to get the club's hot line number. Of course, you're limited to what's available, so you have to be flexible.

- Join **frequent-flier clubs.** It's best to accrue miles on one program, so you can rack up free flights and achieve elite status faster. But it makes sense to open as many accounts as possible, no matter how seldom you fly a particular airline. It's free, and you'll get the best choice of seats, faster response to phone inquiries, and prompter service if your luggage is stolen, your flight is canceled or delayed, or if you want to change your seat.

BY CAR

In Montana, **I-90** runs east-west from St. Regis to Wyola, near the Wyoming border southeast of Billings. **I-94** goes east from Billings to Glendive and the North Dakota border. **U.S. Highway 2,** called the "Hi-Line," is another east-west alternative, stretching across the northern reaches of Montana from Bainville to Troy. The major interstate traversing the state from north to south is **I-15,** from Sweetgrass to Monida.

Wyoming is crossed through the southern part of the state by **I-80,** a huge trucker route from Pine Bluffs in the east to Evanston in the west. **I-90** begins in the north-central part of the state near Ranchester and comes out in the northeast near Beulah. Just outside Buffalo is I-90's junction with **I-25,** a north-south route that runs through Cheyenne. The western part of the state north of Rock Springs is dominated by U.S. highways and secondary state-maintained roads.

BY TRAIN

Amtrak's *Empire Builder* (© 800/872-7245; www.amtrak.com) provides daily rail service along the northern tier of Montana, traveling west from Chicago and east from Seattle. The train stops at Wolf Point, Glasgow, Malta, Havre, Shelby, Cut Bank, Browning, East Glacier, Essex, West Glacier, Whitefish, and Libby.

BY BUS

Greyhound (© 800/231-2222) can provide you with information on specific routes to Montana's and Wyoming's most popular destinations from other cities around the country. **Rimrock Trailways** (© 800/255-7655) and **Powder River Bus Lines** (© 800/442-3682) also provide some bus services.

9 Escorted Tours and Package Deals

Before you start your search for the lowest airfare, you may want to consider booking your flight as part of a travel package such as an escorted tour or a package tour. What you lose in adventure, you'll gain in time and money saved when you book accommodations, and maybe even food and

Montana Driving Distances

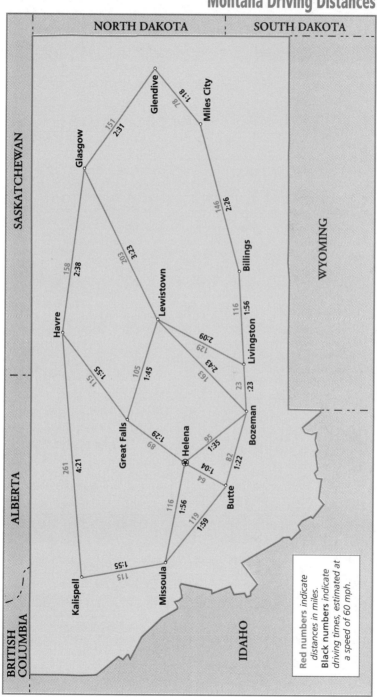

Red numbers indicate distances in miles.
Black numbers indicate driving times, estimated at a speed of 60 mph.

Wyoming Driving Distances

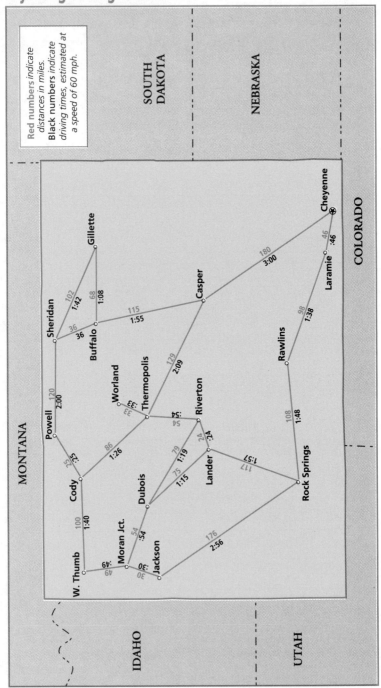

Red numbers indicate distances in miles. Black numbers indicate driving times, estimated at a speed of 60 mph.

entertainment, along with your flight. In addition to the information below, those interested in an escorted outdoor vacation should see the discussion on outfitters in section 5, "The Active Vacation Planner," earlier in this chapter.

PACKAGE TOURS FOR INDEPENDENT TRAVELERS

Package tours are not the same thing as escorted tours. With a package tour, you travel independently but pay a group rate. Packages usually include airfare, a choice of hotels, and car rentals, and packagers often offer several options at different prices. In many cases, a package that includes airfare, hotel, and transportation to and from the airport will cost you less than just the hotel alone would have, had you booked it yourself. That's because packages are sold in bulk to tour operators—who resell them to the public at a cost that drastically undercuts standard rates.

RECOMMENDED PACKAGE TOUR OPERATORS

One good source of package deals is the airlines themselves. Most major airlines offer air/land packages, including **American Airlines Vacations** (© 800/321-2121; http://aav1. aavacations.com), **Delta Vacations** (© 800/221-6666; www.delta vacations.com), **US Airways Vacations** (© 800/455-0123 or 800/ 422-3861; www.usairwaysvacations. com), **Continental Airlines Vacations** (© 800/301-3800; www.cool vacations.com), and **United Vacations** (© 888/854-3899; www.united vacations.com).

Travel packages are also listed in the travel section of your local Sunday newspaper. **Liberty Travel** (© **888/ 271-1584;** www.libertytravel.com), one of the biggest packagers in the Northeast, often runs full-page ads in Sunday papers. Or check ads in the

national travel magazines such as *Arthur Frommer's Budget Travel Magazine, Travel & Leisure, National Geographic Traveler,* and *Condé Nast Traveler.*

THE PROS & CONS OF PACKAGE TOURS

Packages can save you money because they are sold in bulk to tour operators, who sell them to the public. They offer group prices but allow for independent travel. The disadvantages are that you're usually required to make a large payment up front and you may end up on a charter flight. Packages often don't allow for complete flexibility or a wide range of choices. For instance, you may prefer a quiet inn but have to settle for a popular chain hotel instead. Your choice of travel days may be limited as well.

QUESTIONS TO ASK IF YOU BOOK A PACKAGE TOUR

- What are the **accommodations choices** available and are there price differences? Once you find out, look them up in a Frommer's guide.
- What **type of room** will you be staying in? Don't take whatever is thrown your way. Request a no-smoking room, a quiet room, a room with a view, or whatever you fancy.
- Look for **hidden expenses.** Ask whether airport departure fees and taxes are included in the total cost.

ESCORTED TOURS (TRIPS WITH GUIDES)

Escorted tours are structured group tours, with a group leader. The price usually includes everything from airfare to hotels, meals, tours, admission costs, and local transportation.

RECOMMENDED ESCORTED TOUR OPERATORS

Several regional companies provide small, personalized escorted tours of specific areas in Montana and Wyoming. These include **Aventours** (© **800/888-6639** or 406/586-8415), **Great Divide Wildlands Institute** (© **406/683-4669;** www.greatdividetours.com), **High Country Discovery** (© **406/267-3377**), **Northwest Passage** (© 406/256-9793), and **Tours by Maitland** (© **406/755-8687**). National companies that provide tours in Montana and Wyoming, often including Glacier, Yellowstone, and Grand Teton National Parks, include **Maupintour** (© **800/255-4266;** www.maupintour.com) and **Tauck Tours** (© **800/788-7885;** www.tauck.com). National bus-tour company **Gray Line** (© **800/443-6133** or 307/733-4325; www.graylinejh.com) offers tours originating in the Jackson Hole area.

Those who don't mind spending a bit of cash might want to see this country from a luxurious and nostalgic train coach with the **American Orient Express Railway Company,** 2025 First Ave., Suite 830, Seattle, WA 98121 (© **888/759-3944** or 206/441-2725; www.americanorientexpress.com). The company offers a variety of tours, including several in Montana and Wyoming, in vintage train cars outfitted in polished mahogany and brass, plus dining cars decked out with china, silver, crystal, and linen, and a cuisine to match. And speaking of trains, **Amtrak** (© **800/872-7245;** www.amtrak.com) also offers tour packages that include Montana and Wyoming.

THE PROS & CONS OF ESCORTED TOURS

If you book an escorted tour, almost everything is paid for up front, so you deal with fewer money issues. They allow you to enjoy the maximum number of sites in the shortest time, with the least amount of hassle, as all the details are arranged by others. Escorted tours give you the security of traveling in a group and are convenient for people with limited mobility.

On the downside, if you book an escorted tour you often have to pay a lot of money up front, and your lodging and dining choices are predetermined. Escorted tours can be jam-packed with activities, leaving little room for individual sightseeing, whim, or adventure. They also often focus only on the heavily touristed sites, so you miss out on the lesser-known gems. Plus, you may not always be happy rubbing suitcases with strangers.

QUESTIONS TO ASK IF YOU BOOK AN ESCORTED TOUR

- What is the **cancellation policy?** Do they require a deposit? Can they cancel the trip if they don't get enough people? Do you get a refund if they cancel? If *you* cancel? How late can you cancel if you are unable to go? When do you pay in full? *Note:* If you choose an escorted tour, think strongly about purchasing trip-cancellation insurance from an independent agency, especially if the tour operator asks you to pay up front. See the section on "Travel Insurance at a Glance," earlier in this chapter.
- How busy is the **schedule?** How much sightseeing is planned each day? Is ample time allowed for relaxing or wandering solo?
- What is the **size** of the group? Generally, the smaller the group, the more flexible the itinerary, and the less time you'll spend waiting for people to get on and off the bus. Tour operators may be evasive about this, because they may not know the exact size of the group until everyone has made reservations; but they should be able to give you a rough estimate. Some tours have a minimum

group size and may cancel the tour if they don't book enough people.

- What is included in the **price?** You may have to pay for transportation to and from the airport. A box lunch may be included in an excursion, but drinks might cost extra. Beer might be included, but wine might not. Can you opt out of certain activities, or does the bus leave once a day, with no exceptions? Are all your meals planned in advance? Can you choose your entree at dinner? Are tips included?

- What are the **names of the hotels** where you'll be staying? Once

you've gotten the names, look them up in a Frommer's guide.

- What **type of room** will you be staying in? Don't take whatever is thrown your way. Request a no-smoking room, a quiet room, a room with a view, or whatever you fancy.

- What are the **demographics** of the group with whom you'll be traveling? What is the age range? What is the gender breakdown? Is this mostly a trip for couples?

- If you plan to be traveling alone, what is the **single supplement?** Will they find you a roommate at your request?

10 Planning Your Trip Online

Researching and booking your trip online can save time and money. Then again, it may not. It is simply not true that you always get the best deal online. Most booking engines do not include schedules and prices for budget airlines, and from time to time you'll get a better last-minute price by calling the airline directly, so it's best to call the airline to see if you can do better before booking online.

On the plus side, Internet users today can tap into the same travel-planning databases that were once accessible only to travel agents—and do it at the same speed. Sites such as **Frommers.com, Travelocity.com, Expedia.com,** and **Orbitz.com** allow consumers to comparison-shop for airfares, access special bargains, book flights, and reserve hotel rooms and rental cars.

But don't fire your travel agent just yet. Although online booking sites offer tips and hard data to help you bargain-shop, they cannot endow you with the hard-earned experience that makes a seasoned, reliable travel agent an invaluable resource, even in the Internet age. And for consumers with

a complex itinerary, a trusty travel agent is still the best way to arrange the most direct flights to and from the best airports.

Still, there's no denying the Internet's emergence as a powerful tool in researching and plotting travel time. The benefits of researching your trip online can be well worth the effort.

Last-minute specials, such as weekend deals or Internet-only fares, are offered by airlines to fill empty seats. Most of these are announced on Tuesday or Wednesday and must be purchased online. Often they are only valid for travel that weekend, but some can be booked weeks or months in advance. Sign up for weekly e-mail alerts at airline websites or check megasites that compile comprehensive lists of last-minute specials, such as **Smarter Living** (www.smarterliving.com) or **WebFlyer** (www.webflyer.com).

Some sites, such as Expedia.com, will send you **e-mail notification** when a cheap fare becomes available to your favorite destination. Some will also tell you when fares to a particular destination are lowest.

Frommers.com: The Complete Travel Resource

For an excellent travel-planning resource, we highly recommend **Frommers.com** (www.frommers.com). We're a little biased, of course, but we think you'll find the travel tips, reviews, monthly vacation giveaways, and online-booking capabilities indispensable. Among the special features are our popular **Message Boards,** where Frommer's readers post queries and share advice (sometimes even our authors show up to answer questions); **Frommers.com Newsletter,** for the latest travel bargains and inside travel secrets; and Frommer's **Destinations Section,** where you'll get expert travel tips, hotel and dining recommendations, and advice on the sights to see for more than 2,500 destinations around the globe. Once your research is done, the **Online Reservation System** (www.frommers. com/booktravelnow) takes you to Frommer's favorite sites for booking your vacation at affordable prices.

TRAVEL PLANNING & BOOKING SITES

Keep in mind that because several airlines are no longer willing to pay commissions on tickets sold by online travel agencies, these agencies may either add a $10 surcharge to your bill if you book on that carrier—or neglect to offer those carriers' schedules.

The list of sites below is selective, not comprehensive. Some sites will have evolved or disappeared by the time you read this.

- **Travelocity** (www.travelocity.com or www.frommers.travelocity.com) and **Expedia** (www.expedia.com) are among the most popular sites, each offering an excellent range of options. Travelers search by destination, dates, and cost.
- **Orbitz** (www.orbitz.com) is a popular site launched by United, Delta, Northwest, American, and Continental airlines. (Stay tuned: At press time, travel-agency associations were waging an antitrust battle against this site.)
- **Qixo** (www.qixo.com) is another powerful search engine that allows you to search for flights and accommodations from some 20 airline and travel-planning sites (such as Travelocity) at once. Qixo sorts results by price.

- **Priceline** (www.priceline.com) lets you "name your price" for airline tickets, hotel rooms, and rental cars. For airline tickets, you can't say what time you want to fly—you have to accept any flight between 6am and 10pm on the dates you've selected, and you may have to make one or more stopovers. Tickets are nonrefundable, and no frequent-flyer miles are awarded.

SMART E-SHOPPING

The savvy traveler is armed with insider information. Here are a few tips to help you navigate the Internet successfully and safely.

- **Know when sales start.** Last-minute deals may vanish in minutes. If you have a favorite booking site or airline, find out when last-minute deals are released to the public. (For example, Southwest's specials are posted every Tuesday at 12:01am central time.)
- **Shop around.** If you're looking for bargains, compare prices on different sites and airlines—and against a travel agent's best fare. Try a range of times and alternative airports before you make a purchase.
- **Stay secure.** Book only through secure sites (some airline sites are not secure). Look for a key icon

(Netscape) or a padlock (Internet Explorer) at the bottom of your web browser before you enter credit card information or other personal data.

• **Avoid online auctions.** Sites that auction airline tickets and frequent-flier miles are the number-one perpetrators of Internet fraud, according to the National Consumers League.

• **Maintain a paper trail.** If you book an E-ticket, print out a confirmation or write down your confirmation number, and keep it safe and accessible—or your trip could be a virtual one!

ONLINE TRAVELER'S TOOLBOX

Veteran travelers usually carry some essential items to make their trips easier. Following is a selection of online tools to bookmark and use.

• **Visa ATM Locator** (www.visa. com), for locations of Plus ATMs, or **MasterCard ATM Locator** (www.mastercard.com), for locations of Cirrus ATMs.

• **Intellicast** (www.intellicast.com) and **Weather.com** (www.weather. com) give weather forecasts for all 50 states and for cities around the world.

• **Mapquest** (www.mapquest.com). A mapping site that lets you choose a specific address or destination, and in seconds returns a map and detailed directions.

• **Cybercafes.com** (www.cybercafes. com) or **Net Café Guide** (www.netcafeguide.com/mapindex.htm). Locate Internet cafes at hundreds of locations around the globe. Catch up on your e-mail and log onto the web for a few dollars per hour.

Tips **Easy Internet Access Away from Home**

There are a number of ways to get your e-mail on the web, using any computer.

• Your **Internet Service Provider (ISP)** may have a web-based interface that lets you access your e-mail on computers other than your own. Just find out how it works before you leave home. The major ISPs maintain local access numbers around the world so that you can go online by placing a local call. Check your ISP's website or call its toll-free number and ask how you can use your current account away from home. Also ask about the cost of the service before you leave home. If you're traveling outside the reach of your ISP, you may have to check the Yellow Pages in your destination to find a local ISP.

• You can open an account on a free, web-based **e-mail provider** before you leave home, such as Microsoft's **Hotmail** (www.hotmail.com) or **Yahoo! Mail** (mail.yahoo.com). Your home ISP may be able to forward your home e-mail to the web-based account automatically.

• Check out **www.mail2web.com**. This amazing free service allows you to type in your regular e-mail address and password and retrieve your e-mail from any web browser, anywhere, as long as your home ISP hasn't blocked it with a firewall.

• Call your hotel in advance to see whether Internet connection is possible from your room.

11 Getting Around

BY CAR

With a weak public transportation infrastructure and long distances between towns, an automobile is essential in these parts, particularly if you plan to get off the beaten path (the exception would be a ski vacation where you stay at the resort). Most paved roads are well-maintained—in fact, road-repair crews are a much bigger hazard than potholes. Be forewarned that many of the less-accessible places require driving down dirt or gravel roads, far from the nearest tow truck.

If you plan to get off the highway, rent accordingly: You'll need front-wheel drive at least, and if you're going onto the bentonite roads of the desert or foothills, you'd better get four-wheel drive. In the winter, even the interstates can turn glassy and treacherous.

Car rentals are available in every sizable city in the state and at airports. Widely represented agencies include **Alamo** (© 800/327-9633), **Avis** (© 800/831-2847), **Budget** (© 800/527-0700), **Hertz** (© 800/654-3131), and **Thrifty** (© 800/699-1025). We give detailed lists of car-rental agencies in particular areas throughout the book.

Speed limits in Montana are 75 mph on interstates and 70 mph or slower on secondary roads, depending on the road condition and contour. The interstate speed limit in Wyoming is 75 mph, while the speed limits for two-lane roads throughout the state are as posted (usually 55 or 65 mph). The limits are enforced fairly strictly, particularly in construction areas, where fines are doubled.

Take extra precautions when driving in winter, since some highways may be restricted to four-wheel-drive vehicles or those equipped with tire chains or snow tires (these highways will be clearly marked), or may be closed for hours and even days. Also, some roads (such as several in Yellowstone and Glacier National Parks) are always closed in winter. Make sure you have the following safety items: a shovel and a small bag of sand or cat litter in case you get stuck in snow or ice; a first-aid kit; jumper cables; wool blankets or sleeping bag; and an ice scraper/snow brush. Always carry drinking water, summer or winter.

Above all, winter motorists need to drive slower, not make any sudden turns or stops, and watch for wildlife: Some animals gravitate to the warmth of asphalt during cold weather.

12 Tips on Accommodations

You won't find many high-priced multistory luxury hotels here, such as those in major cities on the East and West coasts. Montana and Wyoming are mostly rural areas—some would argue that even the "cities" here are just overgrown cow towns—and the preponderance of accommodation choices will fall into one of four categories: major chains such as Best Western, Comfort Inn, and Super 8; small independent motels or clusters of cabins; historic hotels and bed-and-breakfast inns; and ranch resorts, where the

lodging is pretty much secondary to the myriad activities offered.

You usually won't have too much trouble finding a bed for the night, even without reservations, except in and near the national parks during summer, and during major events such as Cheyenne's Frontier Days. Winter can also be a problem for those looking for a room; not because they're all booked but because a lot of lodgings (and restaurants as well) simply shut down after the summer crowds have left.

TIPS FOR SAVING ON YOUR HOTEL ROOM

The **rack rate** is generally the highest rate that a hotel charges for a room, the rate you'd get if you walked in off the street and asked for a room for the night. Hardly anybody pays these prices, though, and you can usually get it reduced by 10% or more.

- **Don't be afraid to bargain.** Most rack rates include commissions of 10% to 25% for travel agents, which some hotels may be willing to let you keep if you make your own reservation and are willing to haggle a bit. Always ask whether a room less expensive than the first one quoted is available, or whether any special rates apply to you. You may qualify for corporate, student, military, senior, or other discounts. Be sure to mention membership in AAA, AARP, frequent-flier programs, or trade unions, which may entitle you to special deals as well. Find out the hotel policy on children—do kids stay free in the room or is there a special rate?

- **Watch for coupon books and advertised discounts.** State welcome centers, community visitor centers, and a variety of businesses (but not hotels) distribute free booklets that contain nothing but discount lodging coupons. These are usually for chains, and usually are for walk-ins only, so you won't be able to make a reservation. They also do not usually apply during special events. But if you can use one of these coupons (and we do quite frequently), you can often save 20% to 40% off the rack rate. These coupons are also available on the Web—try www.ustravelguide.com, www.hotelcoupons.com, and www.roomsaver.com. Also check ads in your local Sunday newspaper travel section, a good source for up-to-the-minute hotel deals, especially for lodging in resort areas.

- **Dial direct.** When booking a room in a chain hotel, compare the rates offered by the hotel's local line with that of the toll-free number. Also check with an agent and online. A hotel makes nothing on a room that stays empty, so the local hotel reservation desk may be willing to offer a special rate unavailable elsewhere.

- **Remember the law of supply and demand.** Resort hotels are most crowded and therefore most expensive on weekends, so discounts are usually available for midweek stays. Business hotels in downtown locations are busiest during the week, so you can expect big discounts over the weekend. Avoid high-season stays whenever you can: planning your vacation just a week before or after the peak season can mean big savings.

- **Look into group or long-stay discounts.** If you come as part of a large group, you should be able to negotiate a bargain rate, since the hotel can then guarantee occupancy in a number of rooms. Likewise, if you're planning a long stay (at least 5 days), you might qualify for a discount. As a general rule, expect 1 night free after a 7-night stay.

- **Avoid excess charges.** When you book a room, ask about extra charges, such as for parking. Many hotels charge a fee just for dialing out on the phone in your room. Find out whether your hotel imposes a surcharge on local and long-distance calls. A pay phone, however inconvenient, may save you money, although many calling cards charge a fee when you use them on pay phones.

- Consider the pros and cons of **all-inclusive** resorts and hotels. The term "all-inclusive" means different things at different hotels. Many all-inclusive hotels will include 3 meals daily, sports equipment, spa entry, and other amenities; others may include all or most drinks. In general, you'll save money going the "all-inclusive" way—as long as you use the facilities provided. The down side is that your choices are limited and you're stuck eating and playing in one place for the duration of your vacation.

- **Consider a suite.** If you are traveling with your family or another couple, you can pack more people into a suite (which usually comes with a sofa bed), and thereby reduce your per-person rate. Remember that most places charge for extra guests.
- **Book an efficiency.** A room with a kitchenette allows you to shop for groceries and cook your own meals. This is a big money saver, especially for families on long stays.
- Join hotel **frequent-visitor plans,** even if you don't use them much. You'll be more likely to get upgrades and other perks.

- Many hotels offer **frequent-flier points.** Don't forget to ask for yours when you check in.
- **Investigate reservations services.** These outfits usually work as consolidators, buying up or reserving rooms in bulk, and then dealing them out to customers at a profit. You can get 10% to 50% off; but remember, these discounts apply to inflated rack rates that savvy travelers rarely end up paying. You may get a decent rate, but always call the hotel as well to see if you can do better.

Among the more reputable reservations services, offering both telephone and online bookings, are: **Accommodations Express** (© 800/950-4685; www.accommodationsexpress.com); **Hotel Reservations Network** (© 800/96HOTEL; www.180096HOTEL.com); **Quikbook** (© 800/789-9887, includes fax-on-demand service; www.quikbook.com). Online, try booking your hotel through **Arthur Frommer's Budget Travel** (www.frommers.com). **Microsoft Expedia** (www.expedia.com) features a "Travel Agent" that will also direct you to affordable lodgings.

13 Suggested Itineraries

A WEEK OF FLY-FISHING IN MONTANA

Day 1 Arrive in Missoula; spend the afternoon in the local tackle shops getting the lowdown on area river conditions and what the fish are hitting.

Day 2 Find a quiet spot along the Blackfoot River outside Missoula and savor the setting of Norman Maclean's *A River Runs Through It.*

Day 3 Make your way down I-90 to Three Forks and stop in at Bud Lilly's Angler's Retreat for information on what's happening along

what many fishing enthusiasts refer to as the Southwest's holy trinity: the Madison, Jefferson, and Missouri Rivers.

Day 4 About 35 miles (56km) south of Three Forks on U.S. 287 is Ennis, a very popular spot for anglers in these parts. Stop in at any of the shops along Main Street for anything remotely connected to fishing.

Day 5 West of Ennis along Mont. 287 is Twin Bridges and the Ruby River, a blue-ribbon trout stream that's not yet quite as popular as the Madison and the Jefferson.

Day 6 As you head back to Missoula on I-90, stop off for some choice fishing in Rock Creek. It's not easy to find: take exit 126 and head south on the forest service road, which follows the creek.

Day 7 It's back to Missoula now to prepare your fables, stories, and lies before boarding your long flight home.

A WEEK IN WYOMING SEEING GRAND TETONS AND YELLOWSTONE NATIONAL PARKS

Day 1 Arrive in Jackson and head into some spectacular scenery: drive along Grand Teton National Parks' Teton Road.

Day 2 Spend the day in the park. Hiking along Jenny and Jackson Lakes ensures that, weather permitting, you'll have some good photo ops.

Day 3 Drive up to Yellowstone and spend the day around the West Thumb and Geyser Basin areas, stopping at Old Faithful. Keep an eye out for wildlife in the late afternoon.

Day 4 Follow the west side of the loop north through Madison and Norris on the way to Mammoth Hot Springs. Watch for buffalo along the way, and note the massive Obsidian Cliff on the east side of the road about halfway between Norris and the hot springs.

Day 5 Come almost full circle as you head past the Grand Canyon of the Yellowstone and Yellowstone Lake before heading out of the park on the east entrance road to Cody.

Day 6 Spend the day enjoying the Old West flavor of Cody: The Buffalo Bill Historical Center and Tecumseh's Old West Miniature Village and Museum will fill your day easily.

Day 7 Head home from Cody.

A SCENIC LOOP IN MONTANA (1 OR 2 WEEKS)

Day 1 Arrive in Billings and spend the afternoon downtown at the Western Heritage Center, shop, or wander around ZooMontana if it's sunny.

Day 2 Take a 1-hour drive east on I-90 just past Crow Agency to the site of the Battle of the Little Bighorn and Custer's Last Stand. Back to Billings for the night.

Day 3 Head east on I-94 to Miles City to see the Range Rider Museum—this is a must.

Day 4 Continue along I-94 east to Glendive, perhaps the most progressive of eastern Montana's cities. Wander around, then climb back in the car for a drive through the beautiful pastels and haunting badlands of Makoshika State Park. Another great side trip is to Fort Union Trading Post National Historic Site, just over the border in North Dakota.

Day 5 Spend the day driving west on Mont. 200—a road stretching from one end of the state to the other—stopping off in Circle and Jordan for local color and interesting museums that house more than their share of fossils and dinosaur bones. If you keep an eye out, you may just see some misplaced (or undiscovered) advertisements from Burma Shave days.

Day 6 Continue west on Mont. 200 to Lewistown for a look at a virtually untarnished Montana town with good architecture and magnificent mountains. A stroll through the historic Silk Stocking district, viewing the old homes of the town's early rich, makes for an interesting afternoon.

Day 7 If your time is up, take U.S. 87 southeast to Billings. Otherwise, head northwest on Mont. 200 to Great Falls and the C.M. Russell Museum Complex. An afternoon in nearby Fort Benton—a 45-minute drive north on U.S. 87—is a look back at Montana's beginnings in this Missouri River town that once boasted it was the "bloodiest block in the West."

Day 8 Drive north on U.S. 89 through Choteau and Browning to the St. Mary's entrance of Glacier National Park and spend the late afternoon driving through the incredible scenery of the park on Going-to-the-Sun-Road.

Day 9 From West Glacier, Whitefish and Kalispell are a little over 30 minutes away. Whitefish is a quaint ski town in winter and a recreational hub in the summer. Whitefish Lake has plenty of room on its city beach, and a gondola ride to the summit of Big Mountain provides views over the Flathead Valley and the west side of Glacier National Park.

Day 10 Bigfork, 15 minutes south of Kalispell, is a cultural oasis in summer. Electric Avenue is full of everything from a bookstore to a playhouse, including great restaurants and a marina for those who wish to spend an afternoon or evening on Flathead Lake.

Day 11 Take Mont. 35 to Polson, a shorter, though sometimes slower, route around Flathead Lake. This eastside route is full of shade and you'll see cherry trees along the roadside. From Polson head south on U.S. 93 to Missoula. Once there, spend the day on Higgins and Broadway seeing the eclectic blend of stores, then head over to the University of Montana campus. Take a hike up to the giant M on the side of Mt. Sentinel or go for a ride on the colorful horses at the brand-new carousel on the Clark Fork River's edge.

Day 12 Two hours east on I-90 takes you to Butte. Tour the Copper King Mansion, one of the most spectacular and well-maintained historic homes in the state. A visit to Butte wouldn't be complete without a walk down the tunnel to the largest and ugliest copper mine in either hemisphere, the Berkeley Pit.

Day 13 Before completing the tour, spend a day in Bozeman, the other big college town in the state. Montana State University is the biggest venue in town, and downtown has its hands full keeping up with students and newcomers. The Leaf and Bean coffeehouse on Main may have more pretensions than roasted beans, but it is a good place for gourmet coffee nonetheless, as is the less-inflated Rocky Mountain Coffee Roaster a few blocks down on Mendenhall.

Day 14 A 2½-hour drive (on I-90) from Bozeman puts you back in Billings. Fly home from here.

14 Recommended Reading

In addition to the books discussed below, those planning an extended trip to Yellowstone and/or Grand Teton National Parks will find an abundance of information in *Frommer's Yellowstone & Grand Teton National Parks.*

FICTION Start with some classics: A.B. Guthrie's *The Big Sky* (Houghton Mifflin, 1947) is now a Montana classic, as is Owen Wister's *The Virginian* (Macmillan, 1929), set in frontier Wyoming. Then move on to contemporary fiction, like the classic fly-fishing novella, *A River Runs Through It* (University of Chicago Press, 1976) by Norman Maclean. *Fool's Crow* (Viking Penguin, 1986) by James Welch (a native Montanan) and *Heart Mountain* (Viking Penguin, 1989) by Gretel Ehrlich are fictional stories that revolve around American Indian and Asian characters. Annie Proulx's *Wyoming Stories* (Harcourt Brace Jovanovich, 1999) is a recent addition by a fine writer who's spent considerable time around Sheridan. Poet James Glavin's beautifully written *The Meadow* (Henry Holt, 1992) is set in the Tie Siding area of southeast Wyoming.

Montana is fortunate to have the best of its literature compiled in one volume, *The Last Best Place* (University of Montana Press, 1988), the definitive anthology of Montana writings, from American Indian myths to contemporary short stories.

NONFICTION   Novelist Ivan Doig wrote a beautiful memoir about his youth in Montana, *This House of Sky* (Harcourt Brace Jovanovich, 1978). Gretel Ehrlich's *The Solace of Open Spaces* (Viking Penguin, 1986) is a beautifully written, evocative account of Wyoming ranch life.

If your interests lean more toward geography, check out the *Roadside Geology of Montana* (Mountain Press, 1986) by David Alt and Donald W. Hyndman, and the similar *Roadside Geology of Wyoming* (Mountain Press, 1988) by David R. Largeson and Darwin R. Spearing.

HISTORY   Perhaps the best, and easiest, read about the history and culture of Montana is found between the covers of *Montana, High, Wide and Handsome* (University of Nebraska Press, 1983), written by Joseph Howard and first published in 1944. You usually can find copies in used-book stores.

 FAST FACTS: **Montana & Wyoming**

American Express American Express travel-service representatives are located across the state. To automatically connect with the nearest agent, call ☎ **800/221-7282.**

Area Codes The statewide area code for Montana is **406.** Wyoming's area code is **307.** Intrastate long-distance calls also require these prefixes.

ATM Networks Automated teller machines are generally available for cash transactions at any time of the day; most are compatible with Cirrus, Cash Card, and PLUS system networks.

Business Hours Most businesses in these states operate at least 5 days each week and many are also open on weekends. Generally speaking, retail shops open around 10am and close at 6pm. During the two peak tourist seasons in summer and winter, many businesses extend their hours. In smaller towns, don't be surprised to find a hastily penned note on the door if the snow or sunshine conditions are perfect: Many business owners have been known to take their share of "powder days" with no advance notice.

Car Rentals See "Getting Around," earlier in this chapter.

Climate See "When to Go," earlier in this chapter.

Driving Rules See "Getting Around," earlier in this chapter.

Embassies and Consulates See chapter 3, "For International Visitors."

Emergencies Throughout most of Montana and Wyoming, call ℂ **911** for any emergency requiring the police, firefighters, or emergency medical technicians. Where 911 is not available, dial **0** and the operator will connect you to the appropriate emergency service provider.

Gambling The legal gambling age in Montana is 18, and it's a habit that's easily indulged—you'll find video gambling machines in restaurants, taverns, and filling stations. The two most popular are poker and keno (a game of chance similar to bingo). In Wyoming, gambling is illegal.

Information See "Visitor Information," earlier in this chapter.

Internet Access Access to the Internet is coming slowly to Montana and Wyoming, although there are a growing number of lodgings and even a few campgrounds that provide easy hookups for your notebook computer. There are a few cybercafes in these states; your best bet for finding one will be in fairly large cities where colleges are located.

Liquor Laws The legal age for the purchase or consumption of alcohol is 21 in both states. All liquor stores in Montana are state-controlled with minimum hours of 10am to 6pm, although individual stores may be open longer. Most are closed on Sunday. Liquor may also be bought at bars with package licenses during their operating hours. Beer and wine are available at convenience stores and supermarkets from 8:30am to 2am.

Newspapers/Magazines Checking out a community's local newspaper can provide a fascinating look into the personality of the area. Montana's major daily newspapers are The *Missoulian* (www.missoulian.com), the *Great Falls Tribune* (www.greatfallstribune.com), and the *Billings Gazette* (www.billingsgazette.com), although we have to admit a fondness for the weekly *Hungry Horse News* (www.hungryhorsenews.com). In Wyoming, the *Casper Star-Tribune* (www.trib.com) is the only statewide paper, while the *Wyoming Tribune-Eagle* (www.wyomingnews.com) is Cheyenne's daily.

Pets See "Traveling with Pets," earlier in this chapter.

Police Dial ℂ **911** or **0** (for the operator).

Safety See "Insurance, Health & Safety," earlier in this chapter.

Taxes Montana has no state sales tax, but there is a lodging tax of 4%, and certain resort communities can also charge a tax of up to 3% for goods and services. Wyoming's sales tax is 5% statewide, and local communities can add up to 2% more. The state also allows communities to impose a lodging tax of up to 4%.

Time Zone Montana and Wyoming are located in the mountain time zone and both states observe daylight savings time from spring to fall.

3

For International Visitors

The pervasiveness of American culture around the world may make you feel that you know the USA pretty well, but leaving your own country still requires an additional degree of planning. This chapter will help prepare you for the more common problems that visitors may encounter.

1 Preparing for Your Trip

ENTRY REQUIREMENTS

Immigration laws are a hot political issue in the United States these days, and the following requirements may have changed somewhat by the time you plan your trip. Check at any U.S. embassy or consulate for current information and requirements. You can also plug into the **U.S. State Department's** Internet site at **http://state.gov**.

Visas The U.S. State Department has a **Visa Waiver Program** allowing citizens of certain countries to enter the United States without a visa for stays of up to 90 days. At press time these included Andorra, Argentina, Australia, Austria, Belgium, Brunei, Denmark, Finland, France, Germany, Iceland, Ireland, Italy, Japan, Liechtenstein, Luxembourg, Monaco, the Netherlands, New Zealand, Norway, San Marino, Slovenia, Spain, Sweden, Switzerland, and the United Kingdom. Citizens of these countries need only a valid passport and a round-trip air or cruise ticket in their possession upon arrival. If they first enter the United States, they may also visit Mexico, Canada, Bermuda, and/or the Caribbean islands and return to the United States without a visa. Further information is available from any U.S. embassy or consulate. Canadian citizens may enter the United States without visas; they need only proof of residence.

Citizens of all other countries must have (1) a valid passport that expires at least 6 months later than the scheduled end of their visit to the United States, and (2) a tourist visa, which may be obtained without charge from any U.S. consulate.

Obtaining a Visa To obtain a visa, the traveler must submit a completed application form (either in person or by mail) with a 1½-inch-square photo, and must demonstrate binding ties to a residence abroad. Usually you can obtain a visa at once or within 24 hours, but it may take longer during the summer rush from June through August. If you cannot go in person, contact the nearest U.S. embassy or consulate for directions on applying by mail. Your travel agent or airline office may also be able to provide you with visa applications and instructions. The U.S. consulate or embassy that issues your visa will determine whether you will be issued a multiple- or single-entry visa and any restrictions regarding the length of your stay.

British subjects can obtain up-to-date passport and visa information by calling the **U.S. Embassy Visa Information Line** (© 0891/200-290) or the **London Passport Office** (© 0990/210-410 for recorded information).

Immigration Questions Telephone operators will answer your inquiries regarding U.S. immigration policies or laws at the **Immigration and Naturalization Service's Customer Information Center** (© **800/375-5283**). Representatives are available from 9am to 3pm, Monday through Friday. The INS also runs a 24-hour automated information service, for commonly asked questions, at © **800/755-0777.**

Medical Requirements Unless you're arriving from an area known to be suffering from an epidemic (particularly cholera or yellow fever), inoculations or vaccinations are not required for entry into the United States. If you have a disease that requires treatment with narcotics or syringe-administered medications, carry a valid signed prescription from your physician to allay any suspicions that you may be smuggling narcotics (a serious offense that carries severe penalties in the U.S.).

For HIV-positive visitors, requirements for entering the United States are somewhat vague and change frequently. According to the latest publication of *HIV and Immigrants: A Manual for AIDS Service Providers,* although INS doesn't require a medical exam for everyone trying to come into the United States, INS officials may keep out people who they suspect are HIV positive. INS may stop people because they look sick or because they are carrying AIDS/HIV medicine.

An HIV-positive noncitizen applying for a nonimmigrant visa can ask for a special waiver for visitors. This waiver is for people visiting the United States for a short time, to attend a conference, for instance, to visit close relatives, or to receive medical treatment. It can be a confusing situation, so for up-to-the-minute information concerning HIV-positive travelers, contact the Centers for Disease Control's **National Center for HIV** (© **404/332-4559;** www.hivatis.org).

Driver's Licenses Foreign driver's licenses are mostly recognized in the U.S., but you may want to get an international driver's license if your home license is not written in English.

PASSPORT INFORMATION

Safeguard your passport in an inconspicuous, inaccessible place like a money belt. If you lose it, visit the nearest consulate of your native country as soon as possible for a replacement. Passport applications are downloadable from the Internet sites listed below.

FOR RESIDENTS OF CANADA

You can pick up a passport application at one of 28 regional passport offices or most travel agencies. The passport is valid for 5 years and costs C$60. Children under 16 may be included on a parent's passport but need their own to travel unaccompanied by the parent. Applications, which must be accompanied by two identical passport-sized photographs and proof of Canadian citizenship, are available at travel agencies throughout Canada or from the central **Passport Office, Department of Foreign Affairs and International Trade,** Ottawa, Ont. K1A 0G3 (© **800/567-6868;** www.dfait-maeci.gc.ca/passport). Processing takes 5 to 10 days if you apply in person, or about 3 weeks by mail.

There are three ports of entry into Montana from Canada (and vice versa) that are open 24 hours a day: **Roosville,** the farthest west, en route from Cranbrook, B.C. (© **406/889-3865**); **Sweetgrass,** in the center near Glacier National Park, en route from Calgary (© **406/335-2434**); and **Raymond,** the farthest east en route from Regina (© **406/895-2664**). There are also 12 seasonal ports, which vary their hours and seasons of operation. For information on whether or not a specific seasonal port is open, contact one of the 24-hour ports.

FOR RESIDENTS OF THE UNITED KINGDOM

To pick up an application for a regular 10-year passport (the Visitor's Passport has been abolished), visit your nearest passport office, major post office, or travel agency. You can also contact the **London Passport Office** at ℂ **0171/ 271-3000** or search its website at www.open.gov.uk/ukpass/ukpass.htm. Passports are £21 for adults and £11 for children under 16.

FOR RESIDENTS OF IRELAND

You can apply for a 10-year passport, costing 57€, at the Passport Office, Setanta Centre, Molesworth Street, Dublin 2 (ℂ **01/671-1633;** www. gov.ie/iveagh/services/passports/pass-portintro.htm). Those under age 18 and over 65 must apply for a 12€ 3-year passport. You can also apply at 1A South Mall, Cork (ℂ **021/272-525**) or over the counter at most main post offices.

FOR RESIDENTS OF AUSTRALIA

Apply at your local post office or passport office or search the government website at www.dfat.gov.au/passports/. Passports for adults are A$126, and A$63 for those under 18.

FOR RESIDENTS OF NEW ZEALAND

You can pick up a passport application at any travel agency or Link Centre. For more info, contact the Passport Office, P.O. Box 805, Wellington (ℂ **0800/225-050**). Passports for adults are NZ$80 and NZ$40 for those under 16.

CUSTOMS
WHAT YOU CAN BRING IN

Every visitor over 21 years of age may bring in, free of duty, the following: (1) 1 liter of wine or hard liquor; (2) 200 cigarettes, 100 cigars (but not from Cuba), or 3 pounds of smoking tobacco; and (3) $100 worth of gifts.

These exemptions are offered to travelers who spend at least 72 hours in the United States and who have not claimed them within the preceding 6 months. It is altogether forbidden to bring into the country foodstuffs (particularly fruit, cooked meats, and canned goods) and plants (vegetables, seeds, tropical plants, and the like). Foreign tourists may bring in or take out up to $10,000 in U.S. or foreign currency with no formalities; larger sums must be declared to U.S. Customs on entering or leaving, which includes filing form CM 4790. For more specific information regarding U.S. Customs, call your nearest U.S. embassy or consulate, or the **U.S. Customs** office at ℂ **202/927-1770** or www.customs.ustreas.gov.

WHAT YOU CAN BRING HOME

U.K. citizens returning from a non-EU country have a customs allowance of the following: 200 cigarettes; 50 cigars; 250 grams of smoking tobacco; 2 liters of still table wine; 1 liter of spirits or strong liqueurs (over 22% volume); 2 liters of fortified wine, sparkling wine, or other liqueurs; 60cc (ml) perfume; 250cc (ml) of toilet water; and £145 worth of all other goods, including gifts and souvenirs. People under 17 cannot have the tobacco or alcohol allowance. For more information, contact HM Customs & Excise, Passenger Enquiry Point, 2nd Floor Wayfarer House, Great South West Road, Feltham, Middlesex, TW14 8NP (ℂ **0181/ 910-3744;** or 44/181-910-3744 from outside the U.K.), or consult their website at www.open.gov.uk.

For a clear summary of **Canadian** rules, write for the booklet *I Declare,* issued by **Revenue Canada,** 2265 St. Laurent Blvd., Ottawa, Ont. K1G 4KE (ℂ **613/993-0534**). Canada allows its citizens a C$500 exemption, and you're allowed to bring back duty free 200 cigarettes, 2.2 pounds of tobacco, 40 imperial ounces of liquor, and 50 cigars. In addition, you're allowed to mail C$60 worth of gifts a day to Canada from abroad, provided they're unsolicited and don't contain alcohol or tobacco (write on the package "Unsolicited gift, under $60 value"). All valuables should be declared on the Y-38 form before departure from Canada, including serial numbers of valuables you already own, such as expensive foreign cameras. *Note:* The C$500 exemption can only be used once a year and only after an absence of 7 days.

The duty-free allowance in **Australia** is A$400 or, for those under 18, A$200. Upon returning to Australia, citizens can bring in 250 cigarettes or 250 grams of loose tobacco and 1,125ml of alcohol. If you're returning with valuable goods you already own, such as foreign-made cameras, you should file form B263. A helpful brochure, available from Australian consulates or Customs offices, is *Know Before You Go.* For more information, contact **Australian Customs Services,** GPO Box 8, Sydney NSW 2001 (*℃* **02/6275-6666** in Australia; 202/797-3189 in the U.S.), or check out **www.customs.gov.au.**

The duty-free allowance for **New Zealand** is NZ$700. Citizens over 17 can bring in 200 cigarettes, or 50 cigars, or 250 grams of tobacco (or a mixture of all three if their combined weight doesn't exceed 250g); plus 4.5 liters of wine and beer, or 1.125 liters of liquor. New Zealand currency does not carry import or export restrictions. Fill out a certificate of export, listing the valuables you are taking out of the country; that way, you can bring them back without paying duty. Most questions are answered in a free pamphlet available at New Zealand consulates and Customs offices: *New Zealand Customs Guide for Travellers, Notice no. 4.* For more information, contact New Zealand Customs, 50 Anzac Ave., P.O. Box 29, Auckland (*℃* **09/359-6655**).

INSURANCE

Although it's not required of travelers, health insurance is highly recommended. Unlike many European countries, the United States does not usually offer free or low-cost medical care to its citizens or visitors. Doctors and hospitals are expensive, and in most cases will require advance payment or proof of coverage before they render their services. Policies can cover everything from the loss or theft of your baggage and trip cancellation to the guarantee of bail in case you're arrested. Good policies will also cover the costs of an accident, repatriation, or death. See "Insurance, Health & Safety" in chapter 2 for more information. Packages such as **Europ Assistance's** "Worldwide Healthcare Plan" are sold by European automobile clubs and travel agencies at attractive rates. **Worldwide Assistance Services, Inc.** (*℃* **800/821-2828**) is the agent for Europ Assistance in the United States.

Though lack of health insurance may prevent you from being admitted to a hospital in nonemergencies, don't worry about being left on a street corner to die: the American way is to fix you now and bill the living daylights out of you later.

Insurance for British Travelers Most big travel agents offer their own insurance, and will probably try to sell you their package when you book a holiday. Think before you sign. **Britain's Consumers' Association** recommends that you insist on seeing the policy and reading the fine print before buying travel insurance. **The Association of British Insurers** (*℃* **0171/600-3333**) gives advice by phone and publishes the free *Holiday Insurance,* a guide to policy provisions and prices. You might also shop around for better deals: Try **Columbus Travel Insurance Ltd.** (*℃* **0171/375-0011**) or, for students, **Campus Travel** (© 0171/730-2101).

Insurance for Canadian Travelers Canadians should check with their provincial health plan offices or call **HealthCanada** (© 613/957-2991) to find out the extent of their coverage and what documentation and receipts they must take home in case they are treated in the United States.

MONEY

Currency The U.S. monetary system is simple: The most common bills (all ugly, all green) are the $1 (colloquially, a "buck"), $5, $10, and $20 denominations. There are also $2 bills (seldom encountered), $50 bills, and $100 bills (the last two are usually not welcome as payment for small purchases). Note that newly redesigned bills of most denominations have recently been introduced. Despite rumors to the contrary, the old-style bills are still legal tender.

There are six denominations of coins: 1¢ (1 cent, or a penny); 5¢ (5 cents, or a nickel); 10¢ (10 cents, or a dime); 25¢ (25 cents, or a quarter); 50¢ (50 cents, or a half dollar); and the $1 piece.

Note: The "foreign-exchange bureaus" so common in Europe are rare even at airports in the United States, and nonexistent outside major cities. It's best not to change foreign money at a small-town bank, or even a branch in a big city; in fact, leave any currency other than U.S. dollars at home—it may prove a greater nuisance to you than it's worth. One exception is that Canadian money is welcome in many areas of northern Montana, along the Canadian border.

Traveler's Checks Though traveler's checks are widely accepted, make sure that they're denominated in U.S. dollars, because foreign-currency checks are often difficult to exchange. The three traveler's checks that are most widely recognized are **Visa, American Express,** and **Thomas Cook.** Be sure to record the numbers of the checks, and keep that information separate in case they get lost or stolen. Most businesses are pretty good about taking traveler's checks, but you're better off cashing them in at a bank (in small amounts, of course) and paying in cash. Remember: You'll need identification, such as a driver's license or passport, to change a traveler's check.

Credit Cards & ATMs Credit cards are the most widely used form of payment in the United States: **Visa** (BarclayCard in Britain), **MasterCard** (EuroCard in Europe, Access in Britain, Chargex in Canada), **American Express, Diners Club, Discover,** and **Carte Blanche.** You must have a credit card to rent a car. There are, however, a handful of stores and restaurants that do not take credit cards, so be sure to ask in advance. Most businesses display a sticker near their entrance to let you know which cards they accept. (*Note:* Often businesses require a minimum purchase price, usually around $10, to use a credit card.)

It is strongly recommended that you bring at least one major credit card. Hotels, car-rental companies, and airlines usually require a credit-card imprint as a deposit against expenses, and in an emergency a credit card can be priceless.

You'll find automated teller machines (ATMs) on just about every block—at least in almost every town—across the country. Some ATMs will allow you to draw U.S. currency against your bank and credit cards. Check with your bank before leaving home, and remember that you will need your personal identification number (PIN) to do so. Most accept Visa, MasterCard, and American Express, as well as ATM cards from other U.S. banks. Expect to be charged up to $3 per transaction, however.

> **(Tips** Travel Tip
>
> Be sure to keep a copy of all your travel papers separate from your wallet or purse, and leave a copy with someone at home should you need it faxed in an emergency.

One way around these fees is to ask for cash back at grocery stores that accept ATM cards and don't charge usage fees. Of course, you'll have to purchase something first.

SAFETY

General Safety Suggestions While tourist areas are generally safe, crime is on the increase everywhere, and U.S. urban areas tend to be less safe than those in Europe or Japan. You should always stay alert. This is particularly true of large U.S. cities. It is wise to ask your hotel front desk staff or the city's or area's tourist office if you're in doubt about which neighborhoods are safe.

Avoid deserted areas, especially at night, and don't go into public parks at night unless there's a concert or similar occasion that will attract a crowd.

Avoid carrying valuables with you on the street, and don't display expensive cameras or electronic equipment. If you are using a map, consult it inconspicuously—or better yet, try to study it before you leave your room. Hold onto your pocketbook, and place your billfold in an inside pocket. In theaters, restaurants, and other public places, keep your possessions in your sight.

Remember also that hotels are open to the public, and in a large hotel, security may not be able to screen everyone entering. Always lock your room door—don't assume that once inside your hotel you are automatically safe and no longer need to be aware of your surroundings.

Driving Safety Driving safety is important too, especially given the highly publicized car-jackings of foreign tourists in Florida. Except for a few very isolated occurrences, this sort of crime is unheard of in Montana and Wyoming. However, just to be on the safe side, keep your vehicle's door locked at all times. If you have an accident, even on the highway, stay in your car with the doors locked until you assess the situation or until the police arrive. Always try to park in well-lit and well-traveled areas if possible. If you leave your rental car unlocked and empty of your valuables, you're probably safer than locking your car with valuables in plain view. If someone attempts to rob you or steal your car, don't try to resist the thief/car-jacker—report the incident to the police department immediately by calling ✆ **911.**

2 Getting to the U.S.

There are no direct flights from any foreign countries to either Montana or Wyoming. Travelers have to go through one of the hub cities. However, several major U.S. airlines with international connections serve the states.

International travelers heading for Montana and Wyoming will likely be flying through Seattle, Denver, or Salt Lake City. One of the charms of Montana and Wyoming is that they are remote, but this remoteness means that it takes longer to reach them.

The major airports in Montana are Billings, Bozeman, Great Falls, Helena, Kalispell, and Missoula; and in Wyoming the major airports are in

Casper and Jackson. **Delta** and **Northwest** serve most of these cities, and **United** and **United Express** also provide some service.

AIRLINE DISCOUNTS Travelers can reduce the price of a plane ticket by several hundred dollars if they take the time to shop around and buy tickets well in advance. For more money-saving airline advice, see "Getting There," in chapter 2. For the best rates, compare fares and be flexible with the dates and times of travel.

IMMIGRATION AND CUSTOMS CLEARANCE Visitors arriving by air, no matter what the port of entry, should cultivate patience and resignation before setting foot on U.S. soil.

Getting through immigration control may take as long as 2 hours on some days, so be sure to have this guidebook or something else to read. Add the time it takes to clear Customs, and you'll see that you should make a 2- to 3-hour allowance for delays when you plan your connections between international and domestic flights.

In contrast, for the traveler arriving by car or rail from Canada, the border-crossing formalities have been streamlined to the vanishing point. People traveling by air from Canada, Bermuda, and some places in the Caribbean can sometimes clear Customs and Immigration at the point of departure, which is much quicker.

3 Getting Around the U.S.

BY PLANE Some large airlines (for example, Northwest and Delta) offer travelers on their transatlantic or transpacific flights special discount tickets under the name **Visit USA,** allowing mostly one-way travel from one U.S. destination to another at very low prices. These discount tickets must be purchased abroad in conjunction with your international ticket. You should obtain information well in advance from your travel agent or the office of the airline concerned, since the conditions attached to these discount tickets can be changed without advance notice.

BY TRAIN International visitors can also buy a **USA Railpass,** good for 15 or 30 days of unlimited travel on **Amtrak** (© 800/USA-RAIL). The pass is available through many foreign travel agents. Prices in 2002 for a 15-day pass are $295 off-peak, $440 peak; a 30-day pass costs $385 off-peak, $550 peak. (With a foreign passport, you can also buy passes at some Amtrak offices in the United States, including locations in San Francisco, Los Angeles, Chicago, New

York, Miami, Boston, and Washington, D.C.) Reservations are generally required and should be made for each part of your trip as early as possible.

Amtrak (© **800/872-7245**) stops along Montana's northern tier at Browning, Cut Bank, Essex, Glacier National Park, Glasgow, Havre, Libby, Malta, Shelby, West Glacier, Whitefish, and Wolf Point. Amtrak doesn't run through Wyoming.

BY BUS Although bus travel is often the most economical form of public transit between U.S. cities, it can also be slow and uncomfortable—certainly not an option for everyone (particularly when Amtrak, which is far more luxurious, offers similar rates). **Greyhound/Trailways** (© **800/231-2222**), the sole nationwide bus line, offers an **International Ameripass** that must be purchased before coming to the United States, or at the Greyhound International Office at the Port Authority Bus Terminal in New York City. The pass can be obtained from foreign travel agents and costs less than the domestic version. At press time, adult pass prices range from $135 for 4 days to $494 for

60 days. You can get more info on the pass at www.greyhound.com, or by calling ℂ **212/971-0492** (14:00–21:00 GMT) or ℂ **402/330-8552** (all other times). In addition, special rates are available for seniors and students.

BY CAR   The most cost-effective, convenient, and comfortable way to travel around the United States is by car. The Interstate highway system connects cities and towns all over the country; in addition to these high-speed, limited-access roadways, there's an extensive network of federal, state, and local highways and roads. Some of the national car-rental companies include **Alamo** (ℂ 800/327-9633), **Avis** (ℂ 800/331-1212), **Budget** (ℂ 800/527-0700), **Dollar** (ℂ 800/800-4000), **Hertz** (ℂ 800/654-3131), **National** (ℂ 800/227-7368), and **Thrifty** (ℂ 800/367-2277).

If you plan on renting a car in the United States, you probably won't need the services of an additional automobile organization. If you're planning to buy or borrow a car, automobile-association membership is recommended. See "Automobile Organizations" under "Fast Facts," below, for more information.

 FAST FACTS: For the International Traveler

Automobile Organizations   Auto clubs will supply maps, suggested routes, guidebooks, accident and bail-bond insurance, and emergency road service. The **American Automobile Association (AAA)** is the major auto club in the United States. If you belong to an auto club in your home country, inquire about AAA reciprocity before you leave. You may be able to join AAA even if you're not a member of a reciprocal club; to inquire, call AAA (ℂ **800/222-4357**). AAA has a nationwide emergency road service telephone number (ℂ 800/AAA-HELP).

Business Hours   Offices are usually open weekdays from 9am to 5pm. Banks are open weekdays from 9am to 3pm or later and sometimes Saturday mornings. Stores, especially those in shopping complexes, tend to stay open late: until about 9pm on weekdays and 6pm on weekends.

Currency & Currency Exchange   See "Entry Requirements" and "Money" under "Preparing for Your Trip," above.

Drinking Laws   The legal age for the purchase or consumption of alcohol is 21 in both Montana and Wyoming; proof of age is required and often requested at bars, nightclubs, and restaurants. Beer and wine can often be purchased in supermarkets in Montana, but not in Wyoming. Hard liquor in Montana is available in state liquor stores, usually open from 8am to 6pm Monday through Saturday. In Wyoming, liquor, beer, and wine can be purchased 7 days a week at independent liquor stores, with varying hours.

Do not carry open containers of alcohol in your car or any public area that isn't zoned for alcohol consumption. The police can, and probably will, issue you a citation. Don't even think about driving while intoxicated; the penalties for this in the U.S. are stiff.

Electricity   Like Canada, the United States uses 110 to 120 volts AC (60 cycles), compared to 220 to 240 volts AC (50 cycles) in most of Europe, Australia, and New Zealand. If your small appliances use 220 to 240 volts, you'll need a 110-volt transformer (bring one with you—they're hard to find in the United States) and a plug adapter with two flat, parallel pins.

Embassies & Consulates   All embassies are located in the nation's capital, Washington, D.C. Some consulates are located in major U.S. cities, and most nations have a mission to the United Nations in New York City. If your country isn't listed below, call for directory information in Washington, D.C. (© **202/555-1212**) for the number of your national embassy.

The embassy of **Australia** is at 1601 Massachusetts Ave. NW, Washington, DC 20036 (© **202/797-3000;** www.austemb.org). There are consulates in New York, Honolulu, Houston, Los Angeles, and San Francisco.

The embassy of **Canada** is at 501 Pennsylvania Ave. NW, Washington, DC 20001 (© **202/682-1740;** www.cdnemb-washdc.org). Other Canadian consulates are in Buffalo (NY), Detroit, Los Angeles, New York, and Seattle.

The embassy of **Ireland** is at 2234 Massachusetts Ave. NW, Washington, DC 20008 (© **202/462-3939**). Irish consulates are in Boston, Chicago, New York, and San Francisco.

The embassy of **Japan** is at 2520 Massachusetts Ave. NW, Washington, DC 20008 (© **202/238-6700;** www.embjapan.org). Japanese consulates are located in Atlanta, Kansas City, San Francisco, and Washington, D.C.

The embassy of **New Zealand** is at 37 Observatory Circle NW, Washington, D.C. 20008 (© **202/328-4800;** www.emb.com/nzemb). New Zealand consulates are in Los Angeles, Salt Lake City, San Francisco, and Seattle.

The embassy of the **United Kingdom** is at 3100 Massachusetts Ave. NW, Washington, DC 20008 (© **202/462-1340**). Other British consulates are in Atlanta, Boston, Chicago, Cleveland, Houston, Los Angeles, New York, San Francisco, and Seattle.

The only foreign consulate in Wyoming or Montana is the **Norwegian Consulate**, 490 N. 31st St., Billings, MT 59101-1256 (© **406/252-3441**). A number of countries have consulates in Denver, and some also are represented in Salt Lake City.

Emergencies   Call © **911** to report a fire, call the police, or get an ambulance. This is a toll-free call (no coins are required at public telephones). In a very few rural areas, it may be necessary to dial "0" for the operator, who can then connect you to the proper emergency service.

Gasoline (Petrol)   Petrol is known as gasoline (or simply "gas") in the United States, and petrol stations are known as both gas stations and service stations. Gasoline costs about half as much here as it does in Europe (about $1.15–$1.40 per gallon at press time), and taxes are already included in the printed price. One U.S. gallon equals 3.8 liters or .85 Imperial gallons.

Holidays   Banks, government offices, post offices, and many stores, restaurants, and museums are closed on the following legal national holidays: January 1 (New Year's Day), the third Monday in January (Martin Luther King, Jr. Day), the third Monday in February (Presidents' Day, Washington's Birthday), the last Monday in May (Memorial Day), July 4 (Independence Day), the first Monday in September (Labor Day), the second Monday in October (Columbus Day), November 11 (Veterans Day/Armistice Day), the fourth Thursday in November (Thanksgiving Day), and December 25 (Christmas). Also, the Tuesday following the first Monday in November is Election Day and is a federal government holiday in presidential-election years (held every 4 years, and next in 2004).

Legal Aid   The foreign tourist will probably never become involved with the American legal system. If you are "pulled over" for a minor infraction (speeding, for example), never attempt to pay the fine directly to a police officer; this could be construed as attempted bribery, a much more serious crime. Pay fines by mail, or directly into the hands of the clerk of the court. If accused of a more serious offense, say and do nothing before consulting a lawyer. Once arrested, a person can make one telephone call to a party of his or her choice. Call your embassy or consulate.

Mail   Mail can be sent to you, in your name, c/o General Delivery at the main post office of the city or region where you expect to be (call ☎ 800/275-8777 or see www.usps.gov for information on the nearest post office). The addressee must pick up mail in person and must produce proof of identity. Most post offices will hold your mail for up to 1 month. Post office hours vary greatly, but most are open at least Monday through Friday from 8am to 5pm.

Generally found at intersections, mailboxes are blue with a red-and-white stripe and carry the inscription U.S. MAIL. If your mail is addressed to a U.S. destination, don't forget to add the five-digit postal code (or ZIP code) after the two-letter abbreviation of the state to which the mail is addressed.

At press time, domestic postage rates were 20¢ for a postcard and 34¢ for a letter. For international mail, a first-class letter of up to one-half ounce costs 60¢ (46¢ to Canada and 40¢ to Mexico); a first-class postcard costs 50¢ (40¢ to Canada and 35¢ Mexico); and a preprinted postal aerogramme costs 50¢.

Taxes   In the United States there is no value-added tax (VAT) or other indirect tax at the national level. Every state, county, and city has the right to levy its own local tax on all purchases. Montana has no state sales tax, but there is a lodging tax of 4%, and certain resort communities can also charge a tax of up to 3% for goods and services. Wyoming's sales tax is 5% statewide, and local communities can add up to 2% more. Wyoming also allows communities to impose a lodging tax of up to 4%.

Telephone, Telegraph, Telex & Fax   The telephone system in the United States is run by private corporations, so rates, especially for long-distance service and operator-assisted calls, can vary widely. Generally, hotel surcharges on long-distance and local calls are astronomical, so you're usually better off using a **public pay telephone,** which you'll find clearly marked in most public buildings and private establishments as well as on the street. Convenience grocery stores and gas stations always have them. Many convenience groceries and packaging services sell **prepaid calling cards** in denominations up to $50; these can be the least expensive way to call home. Many public phones at airports now accept American Express, MasterCard, and Visa credit cards. **Local calls** made from public pay phones in most locales cost either 25¢ or 35¢. Pay phones do not accept pennies, and few will take anything larger than a quarter.

Most long-distance and international calls can be dialed directly from any phone. **For calls within the United States and to Canada,** dial 1 followed by the area code and the seven-digit number. **For other international calls,** dial 011 followed by the country code, city code, and the telephone number of the person you are calling.

Calls to area codes **800, 888, 877,** and **866** are toll-free. However, calls to numbers in area codes **700** and **900** (chat lines, bulletin boards, "dating" services, and so on) can be very expensive—usually a charge of 95¢ to $3 or more per minute, and they sometimes have minimum charges that can run as high as $15 or more.

For **reversed-charge or collect calls,** and for person-to-person calls, dial 0 (zero, not the letter O) followed by the area code and number you want; an operator will then come on the line, and you should specify that you are calling collect, or person-to-person, or both. If your operator-assisted call is international, ask for the overseas operator.

For **local directory assistance** ("information"), dial 411; for long-distance information, dial 1, then the appropriate area code and 555-1212.

Telegraph and telex services are provided primarily by Western Union. You can bring your telegram into the nearest Western Union office or dictate it over the phone (✆ **800/325-6000**). You can also telegraph money, or have it telegraphed to you, very quickly over the Western Union system, but this service can cost as much as 15% to 20% of the amount sent.

Most hotels have **fax machines** available for guest use (be sure to ask about the charge to use it), and many hotel rooms are even wired for guests' fax machines. A less expensive way to send and receive faxes may be at stores such as Mail Boxes Etc., a national chain of packing service shops (look in the Yellow Pages directory under "Packing Services").

There are two kinds of telephone directories in the United States. The **White Pages** list private households and business subscribers in alphabetical order. The inside front cover lists emergency numbers for police, fire, ambulance, poison-control center, and so on. The first few pages will tell you how to make long-distance and international calls. Government numbers are usually printed on blue paper within the White Pages. The **Yellow Pages** list all local services, businesses, industries, and houses of worship according to activity with an index at the front or back. The Yellow Pages also include city plans or detailed area maps, postal ZIP codes, and public-transportation routes.

Time   The continental United States is divided into **four time zones:** Eastern Standard Time (EST), Central Standard Time (CST), Mountain Standard Time (MST), and Pacific Standard Time (PST). Alaska and Hawaii have their own zones. For example, noon in New York City (EST) is 11am in Chicago (CST), 10am in Denver (MST), 9am in Los Angeles (PST), 8am in Anchorage (AST), and 7am in Honolulu (HST).

Daylight saving time is in effect from 1am on the first Sunday in April to 1am the last Sunday in October, except in Arizona, Hawaii, part of Indiana, and Puerto Rico. Daylight saving time moves the clock 1 hour ahead of standard time.

Montana and Wyoming are located in the mountain time zone and both states observe daylight saving time.

Tipping   Tipping is so ingrained in the American way of life that the annual income tax of tip-earning service personnel is based on how much they should have received in light of their employers' gross revenues. Accordingly, they may have to pay tax on a tip you didn't actually give them.

Here are some rules of thumb:

In hotels, tip **bellhops** at least $1 per bag ($2–$3 if you have a lot of luggage) and tip the **chamber staff** $1 to $2 per day (more if you've left a disaster area for him or her to clean up, or if you're traveling with kids and/or pets). Tip the **doorman** or **concierge** only if he or she has provided you with some specific service (for example, calling a cab for you or obtaining difficult-to-get theater tickets). Tip the **valet-parking attendant** $1 every time you get your car.

In restaurants, bars, and nightclubs, tip **service staff** 15% to 20% of the check, tip **bartenders** 10% to 15%, tip **checkroom attendants** $1 per garment, and tip **valet-parking attendants** $1 per vehicle. Tip the **doorman** only if he has provided you with some specific service (such as calling a cab for you). Tipping is not expected in cafeterias and fast-food restaurants.

Tip **cab drivers** 15% of the fare.

As for other service personnel, tip **skycaps** at airports at least $1 per bag ($2–$3 if you have a lot of luggage) and tip **hairdressers** and **barbers** 15% to 20%.

Tipping ushers at movies and theaters, and gas-station attendants, is not expected.

Toilets   You won't find public toilets or "rest rooms" on the streets in most U.S. cities, but they can be found in hotel lobbies, bars, restaurants, museums, department and discount stores, railway and bus stations, or service stations. Note, however, that some establishments display a notice that toilets are for the use of patrons only. Paying for a cup of coffee or a soft drink will qualify you as a patron. If possible, avoid the toilets at parks and beaches, which tend to be dirty.

4

Glacier National Park

Majestic and wild, this vast preserve overwhelms visitors, beckoning with stunning mountain peaks (many covered year-round with glaciers), verdant mountain trails that cry out for hikers, and the sheer diversity of its plant and animal life. The unofficial mascot in these parts is the grizzly, a refugee from the high plains.

Named to describe the slow-moving glaciers that carved awe-inspiring valleys throughout this expanse of nearly 1 million acres, Glacier National Park exists because of the efforts of George Bird Grinnell, a 19th-century magazine publisher and cofounder of the Audubon Society. Following a pattern established with Yellowstone and Grand Teton, Grinnell lobbied for a national park to be set aside in the St. Mary region of Montana, and in May 1910 his efforts were rewarded. Just over 20 years later, it became, with its northern neighbor Waterton Lakes National Park in Canada, Glacier-Waterton International Peace Park—a gesture of goodwill and friendship between the governments of two countries.

If your time is limited, simply motor across Going-to-the-Sun Road, viewing the dramatic mountain scenery. Visitors with more time will find diversions for both families and hard-core adventurers; while some hiking trails are suitable for tykes, many more will challenge those determined to conquer and scale the park's tallest peaks. Glacier's lakes, streams, ponds, and waterfalls are equally engaging. Travelers board cruise boats to explore the history of the area; recreational types can fish, row, and kayak.

However, to truly experience Glacier requires slightly more effort, interest, and spunk than a drive through—abandon the pavement for even the shortest and easiest hiking trail and you'll discover a window into Glacier's soul.

1 Just the Facts

GETTING THERE

The closest cities to the park with airline service are **Kalispell,** 29 miles (47km) southwest of the park, and **Great Falls,** 143 miles (230km) southeast of the park.

Glacier Park International Airport, north of Kalispell at 4170 U.S. 2 (© **406/257-5994**), is serviced by Delta, Horizon, Big Sky, and Northwest. **Great Falls International Airport** (© **406/727-3404**) is served by these same airlines.

If you're driving, you can reach the park from U.S. Highways 2 and 89. Rental cars are available in Kalispell, Great Falls, Whitefish, East Glacier, and West Glacier. **Avis, Budget, Hertz, Sears,** and **National** all have counters at Kalispell's airport. **Hertz, Avis,** and **National** have counters at Great Falls International Airport.

Amtrak's *Empire Builder* (© **800/872-7245;** www.amtrak.com), a Chicago-Seattle round-trip route, makes daily stops at West Glacier and Essex year-round and seasonally at East Glacier.

ACCESS/ENTRY POINTS

There are six entrances to Glacier National Park, but those traveling by car will most likely use **West Glacier** and **St. Mary.** These entrances are located at either end of Going-to-the-Sun Road, with West Glacier on the southwest side and St. Mary on the east. From the park's western boundary, you can enter at **Polebridge** to access Bowman and Kintla Lakes, or take the **Camas Road** to Going-to-the-Sun. The **Many Glacier** entrance provides access to the Many Glacier Hotel, Swiftcurrent Lake, and many backcountry trails. **East Glacier** takes you into Glacier Park Lodge and hiking trails at the southeastern corner of the park. The **Two Medicine** entrance is only about 4 miles (6.5km) north of East Glacier on Mont. 49, with auto access to Lower Two Medicine Lake and Two Medicine Lake, as well as hiking trails to Pumpelly Pillar and over Pitamakan Pass. **Essex** is strictly a backcountry access point to Scalplock Mountain and backcountry campgrounds along Ole Creek and Park Creek. **Cut Bank** is a dirt road, closed in winter, with only backcountry access to Triple Divide Pass and the northern route to Pitamakan Pass.

Caution: Entrance is severely restricted during winter months when the alpine section of Going-to-the-Sun Road is closed. See section 2, "Driving the Park," later in this chapter for more information.

VISITOR CENTERS

To receive information about the park before your trip, contact the Superintendent, **Glacier National Park,** West Glacier, MT 59936 (© **406/888-7800;** www.nps.gov/glac). The **Glacier Natural History Association** offers numerous publications; for a catalog, contact the association at P.O. Box 310, West Glacier, MT 59936 (© **406/888-5756;** fax 406/888-5271; www.glacierassociation.org).

For up-to-date information on park activities once you arrive, check in at visitor centers located at **Apgar, Logan Pass,** and **St. Mary.** St. Mary is open from mid-May to mid-October; Logan Pass from mid-June to mid-October; and Apgar from May through October (and weekends during the winter). Park information may also be obtained from the **Many Glacier Ranger Station** or park headquarters in **West Glacier.** General park information is available about Glacier at © **406/888-7800** and www.nps.gov/glac; or about Waterton at © **403/859-5133,** or on the Web at **parkscanada.pch.gc.ca/waterton**. The **Alberta Information Center** is located in a conspicuously modern building in West Glacier, providing information about Waterton-Glacier and other attractions in Alberta. There are also numerous exhibits about Canadian life and culture.

FEES & BACKCOUNTRY PERMITS

Rangers are on duty at most entry points to collect fees, issue backcountry permits, and answer questions.

FEES   Admission to the park for up to 7 days costs $10 per vehicle or $5 per person for those on foot, bicycles, and motorcycles. A season pass costs $20 and allows unlimited entry to Glacier National Park for 1 year. The National Park, Golden Eagle, Golden Age, and Golden Access passes are also honored (see "The Active Vacation Planner," in chapter 2). Camping fees are $12 to $17 per night at the park's drive-in campgrounds. A separate entrance fee is charged for

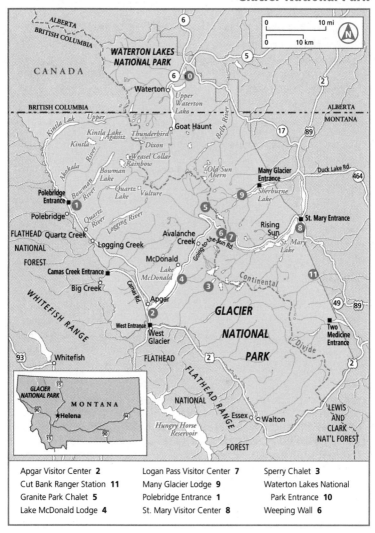

Apgar Visitor Center **2**	Logan Pass Visitor Center **7**	Sperry Chalet **3**
Cut Bank Ranger Station **11**	Many Glacier Lodge **9**	Waterton Lakes National
Granite Park Chalet **5**	Polebridge Entrance **1**	Park Entrance **10**
Lake McDonald Lodge **4**	St. Mary Visitor Center **8**	Weeping Wall **6**

visitors to Waterton Lakes National Park (see "A Side Trip to Waterton Lakes National Park," later in this chapter).

BACKCOUNTRY PERMITS These permits must be obtained in person from the Apgar Backcountry Permitting Station, St. Mary Visitor Center, or the ranger stations at Many Glacier, Polebridge, or Two Medicine. Visitors who enter Glacier's backcountry from the Canadian side (at Goat Haunt or Belly River in Waterton) can get a permit at the Waterton Visitor Reception Centre, but only with a credit card. **During summer months,** permits may be obtained no earlier than 24 hours before your trip. There is a $4 per-person per-night charge for backcountry camping. Trips are limited to 6 nights, with no more than 3 nights allowed at each campground (some exceptions apply). Campsites

---

(*Tips* **Traveling Through the Park Without a Car**

Going-to-the-Sun Tour Service (✆ **406/756-2444**) runs vans from virtually every major hotel and campground to other points in the park. Costs range from $2 for a short distance to $89 for a long-distance excursion. Reservations are recommended. A shuttle service for hikers is also offered for about $8 per person.

---

are limited. A single site has a maximum occupancy of four persons. Stoves are required in most areas (no open fires) and pets are not permitted on the trails.

To ensure a spot and avoid the hassle, order an Advance Reservation Backcountry Trip planner from Backcountry Reservations, GNP, West Glacier, MT 59936; sending them your dates with a check for $20 will reserve your spot in the wilderness.

Due to lower demand in winter, camping permits are available up to 7 days in advance. A few rules do take effect beginning each November 20, so double-check at visitor centers for details.

SPECIAL REGULATIONS & WARNINGS

Park regulations here are similar to those in other lands administered by the National Park Service, and generally prohibit damaging the natural resources. Pets must be leashed and are not allowed on trails. In addition, RVs and other vehicles longer than 21 feet or wider than 8 feet are prohibited on the 24-mile (34km) stretch of Going-to-the-Sun Road between Avalanche Campground and Sun Point on St. Mary Lake. Snowmobiling is prohibited in the park.

WHEN TO GO

Glacier is magnificent at any time of the year, but it's not always easily accessible. Most visitors come in **summer** and it seems as if they all drive along Going-to-the-Sun Road. The 52-mile (84km) two-lane road is open from late May or early June until the third Monday in October, depending upon the weather. During summer months, sunrise is around 5am, and sunset at nearly 10pm, so there's plenty of time for exploring. The shoulder seasons of **spring and fall** see budding wildflowers and seasonal colors, but these sights can be viewed only from the park's outer boundaries and a limited stretch of the scenic highway.

In **winter,** road access is limited. Going-to-the-Sun Road is plowed to Lake McDonald Lodge on the west side of the park, 12 miles (19km) from West Glacier, but the remainder of the road is closed. Snowmobiles are prohibited. All unplowed roads become trails for snowshoers and cross-country skiers, who rave about the vast wonderland. Guided trips are a great way to experience the park in winter, or you can strap on a pair of snowshoes and explore it on your own. A popular skiing expedition is to go as far up Going-to-the-Sun Road as your energy permits. Wintertime temperatures average between 15° and 30° F, but extreme lows can reach 30° below. Average winter snowfall is almost 12 feet, and it snows about half of the days from November through February.

AVOIDING THE CROWDS

If you want to avoid the crowds, travel in the off-season before mid-June, when the park begins to fill, and after Labor Day, when families traveling with youngsters have returned home (August is the busiest month). If that's not possible, consider the following: Since most people congregate in close proximity to the major hotels, find a trail head that is equidistant from two major points and head for the woods.

Going-to-the-Sun Road is nearly always jammed in the summer daylight hours. If you can, make the trip before 8:30 in the morning. In July and August, the parking lot at Logan Pass Visitor Center fills to capacity. Try to visit early in the day or late in the afternoon.

RANGER PROGRAMS

When you enter the park, you'll be given the park's publication *Nature with a Naturalist,* which lists the naturalist-led programs offered at Glacier and Waterton. There is a wide variety of hikes, boat trips, campfire programs, and family programs, and other activities. Many are accessible for those in wheelchairs. There are also campfire presentations given by members of the Salish, Kootenai, and Blackfeet tribes. Most programs are free, although those including boat trips may have a small fee associated. For schedules, check the park newspapers or call ☎ **406/888-7800.**

TIPS FOR TRAVELERS WITH PHYSICAL DISABILITIES

Information on facilities and services for those with disabilities is available at any of the visitor centers in the park, although most of the park's developed areas are fully accessible by wheelchair. The park's *Accessibility in Glacier National Park* publication describes current programs and services for visitors with disabilities.

FOR THE VISUALLY IMPAIRED   Audio tapes, park brochure recordings, and tactile nature items are available at the Apgar, Logan Pass, and St. Mary Visitor Centers. All other park facilities—restrooms, restaurants, campgrounds, gift shops—are accessible with some assistance.

FOR THE MOBILITY IMPAIRED   The Trail of the Cedars, Oberlin Bend Trail, and Running Eagle Falls Nature Trail are wheelchair accessible. A bike path at Apgar also provides magnificent views of the park's scenery. Wheelchairs are available for loan at the Apgar, Logan Pass, and St. Mary Visitor Centers and almost all of the park's facilities are fully accessible.

FOR THE HEARING IMPAIRED   Interpreters provide written synopses of most slide and campfire programs. If you plan on hiking, note that five of the park's self-guided nature trails have printed brochures available at the trail head. General park information is available by TDD at ☎ **406/888-7806.** An interpreter may be available to sign at the *Nature with a Naturalist* programs. Call ☎ **406/888-7939** a week in advance to make arrangements.

ORGANIZED TOURS & ACTIVITIES

Narrated boat tours 🚢🚢 from Lake McDonald, St. Mary, Two Medicine, and Many Glacier are offered daily from mid-June to mid-September by Glacier Park Boat Co. These "scenicruises" combine an hour-long lake cruise with a short hike or picnic. Spectacular views of Lake McDonald, the Grinnell Glacier,

---

⌐Kids   Especially for Kids

The park has a *Junior Ranger Newspaper* available at the visitor centers that lists seven activities to introduce youngsters between 6 and 12 years of age to the habitats in Glacier. Children are welcome on most interpretive activities, but should be accompanied by an adult.

Vehicle Regulations

Park regulations prohibit vehicles more than 21 feet long or 8 feet wide on the 24-mile (39km) stretch of Going-to-the-Sun Road between Avalanche Campground and Sun Point on St. Mary Lake. If you are traveling in a vehicle exceeding the 21-foot limit, park it at one of the parking areas located at Avalanche Campground and Sun Point and take the **Going-to-the-Sun Tour Service** (see "Traveling Through the Park Without a Car," above).

---

and the panoramic rugged cliffs ringing St. Mary Lake are just a few of the photo opportunities you may have. The boats typically depart every other hour, five times each day, although schedules are subject to change in late season or if the weather is inclement. For more information, contact **Glacier Park Boat Co.** at P.O. Box 5262, Kalispell, MT 59903 (✆ **406/257-2426**). Listed below are seasonal phone numbers for cruises at the following locations: **Lake McDonald** (✆ **406/888-5727**), **Many Glacier** (✆ **406/732-4480**), **Two Medicine** (✆ **406/226-4467**), and **St. Mary** (✆ **406/732-4430**).

Van tours ⚐ are given along Going-to-the-Sun Road and north to Waterton. These vans are an excellent alternative method of transportation along this scenic route. Their drivers provide the commentary, and you don't have to get vertigo peering over the roadside. They also offer hiker express and Amtrak pickup. The tours are conducted by **Glacier Park, Inc.** Call ✆ **406/756-2444**. Interpretive van tours of Going-to-the-Sun Road conducted by Blackfeet guides originate from East Glacier, Browning, and St. Mary. Contact **Suntours** (✆ **800/786-9220** or 406/226-9220). One participant told us he thought this was the best guided tour he'd ever taken, because the guides lived in the area and really knew what they were talking about.

SPECIAL ACTIVITIES

Scenic helicopter tours of Glacier are offered by **Glacier Heli Tours** (✆ **800/879-9310**), **Eagle Aviation** (✆ **406/755-2612**), and **Kruger Helicoptours** (✆ **406/387-4565**). Prices range from $60 to $90 for 1- to 2-hour tours, depending on your destination. All are located within 2 miles (3km) of West Glacier off U.S. 2.

Glacier Institute ⚐⚐ (✆ **406/755-1211**; www.digisys.net/glacinst) conducts field classes and seminars each summer to look at the geologic, wildlife, and spiritual aspects of the park. Classes run from 1 day to 1 month—most are only a day or two, and cost less than $75—and cover subjects from photography to forests. The fees include instruction, transportation, park fees, and college credit (if any). You can gather fall mushrooms, work on your journal-keeping skills, improve your writing, or search out the elusive harlequin duck.

2 Driving the Park

Because of the massive piles of rock that surround a visitor, it is impossible to drive Glacier without drawing comparisons to Grand Teton. At Teton, unless you hit the hiking trails, the mountains keep their distance. But, in Glacier, as you drive, the mountain peaks will envelop you.

GOING-TO-THE-SUN ROAD

If you plan only a day or two in Glacier, the most important thing to do is to drive **Going-to-the-Sun Road,** the 50-mile (81km) road that bisects the park between West Glacier and St. Mary. Points of interest are clearly marked along this road, and correspond to the park brochure *Points of Interest Along the Going-to-the-Sun Road*, which is available at visitor centers. Bring plenty of film.

The road gains more than 1,400 feet in 32 miles (52km), and is very narrow in places. Visitors with a fear of heights should take a van tour or shuttle. Because of the road's narrowness, oversized vehicles and trailers must use U.S. 2.

As you begin the drive from the West Glacier entrance, you'll pass the largest of the 653 lakes in Glacier—**Lake McDonald.** Numerous turnouts along the way present opportunities to photograph the panoramic views of the lake with its mountainous backdrop. You can see **Sacred Dancing Cascade** and **Johns Lake** after an easy, half-mile hike from the roadside through a red cedar/hemlock forest. The trail head for this hike is 2 miles (3km) north of the Lake McDonald Lodge along Going-to-the-Sun Road.

The **Trail of the Cedars** is a short, handicapped-accessible boardwalk trail thickly carpeted in vibrant, verdant hues. This is also the beginning of the Avalanche Lake Trail, a 2½₀-mile (3km) hike to the foot of Avalanche Lake, one of the most popular day-hikes in the park. The trail head is about 5½ miles (9km) north of Lake McDonald Lodge, just past the Avalanche Creek Campground.

Almost exactly halfway along Going-to-the-Sun is the overlook for Heaven's Peak, the massive snow-covered mountain to the south that you've just driven around. This is also the jumping-off point for **The Loop Trail,** which can take you into Granite Park Chalet. Just 2 miles (3km) farther is the **Bird Woman Falls Overlook.** Bird Woman Falls drops in a wondrous bounty of water from a hanging valley above the road. Next along the road is the oft-photographed **Weeping Wall,** which is a wall of rock with water pouring forth.

At the 32-mile mark from West Glacier is **Logan Pass,** one of the park's busiest areas and the starting point for the hike to **Hidden Lake,** one of the park's most popular. There's a visitor center here atop the Continental Divide, which has a small display about the wildlife, flora, and geology of the area, and a larger area selling books and such.

As you head downhill, you'll reach the turnout for **Jackson Glacier,** the most easily recognizable glacier in the entire park; followed by **Sunrift Gorge** and **Sun Point,** which are accessible via two short trails rife with wildlife.

WINTER ROAD CONDITIONS   Going-to-the-Sun Road is open seasonally, usually from early June to mid-October, depending on weather conditions. Call the park at ℂ **406/888-7800** to find out when tentative openings and closings are scheduled. During the winter, you may drive Going-to-the-Sun Road for 10 miles (16km) from West Glacier along Lake McDonald to the road closure; this is a popular destination for cross-country skiers.

ⓘ Tips   Picnic Paradise

The best picnicking spot on the Going-to-the-Sun Road is at the **Sun Point Lake** parking area, which is also the trail head for the 0.7-mile (1km) round-trip to Baring Falls, a trail that follows the shoreline of the lake. It's located about 9 miles (15km) east of the Logan Pass Visitor Center, or 9 miles (15km) west of the St. Mary Visitor Center. From the picnic area, the views across the lake to the mountains are unrivaled in the park. For a truly spectacular experience, get there at sunrise.

> ## Tips Glacier's Best Photo Ops
>
> Get up early to catch Glacier's best photo ops. Near bodies of water, the sunrise provides an unrivaled multitude of oranges, blues, and yellows. Then, as the earth warms, lakes are transformed to fog-covered valleys, creating a mystical photographic opportunity.
>
>   One of the most picturesque spots is the west end of St. Mary Lake; not only does it paint the lake orange and yellow, it paints the mountains red and orange. A close runner-up is the view west from an overlook across St. Mary Lake to Wild Goose Island in the foreground and the peaks and glaciers at the west end of the lake. Logan Pass, when it's carpeted with wildflowers, is not to be missed.
>
>   Late-day photos of the Garden Wall from west of Logan Pass are also very dramatic.

OTHER DRIVES

THROUGH THE LOWER HALF OF THE PARK   Circumnavigating the lower half of the park is easily accomplished in 1 long day. After a leisurely breakfast in West Glacier, you'll be in East Glacier in plenty of time for lunch at the Glacier Park Lodge (see "Where to Stay," later in this chapter) and at St. Mary or Many Glacier for dinner. To complete this counterclockwise loop from West Glacier, hop onto U.S. 2 and head along the park's southern boundary to Essex and East Glacier, then north to St. Mary.

The road between West Glacier and East Glacier—it's approximately 52 miles (84km)—is a well-paved, two-lane affair that winds circuitously around the western and southern edges of the park and follows the Middle Fork of the Flathead River. As you descend to the valley floor, you'll travel through beautiful, privately owned Montana ranch- and farmland. Shortly after entering the valley, look to the north and admire the park's massive peaks. The **Goat Lick** parking lot, on U.S. 2 just east of Essex, gets you off the beaten path and provides a view down into a canyon carved by the Flathead River; if you have time, take the short hike down to the stream.

Beyond East Glacier, as you head east on Mont. 49 and north toward Two Medicine, you'll notice that the earth appears to fall off. The contrast is inescapable—mountains tower in the west, but to the east the Hi-Line begins, sporting a horizon that extends so far and so flat as to seemingly lend credence and legitimacy to the Flat Earth Society. But round a bend on the Two Medicine Road and suddenly find yourself faced with three mountains (Appistocki Peak, Mount Henry, and Bison Mountain) bare of vegetation but as red as their Southwestern counterparts. Ten miles (16km) later, continuing the route northward on U.S. 89, you'll come across a 180° to 220° panorama of mountain peaks, valleys, ridges, and forested mountains that truly characterizes Glacier's personality. Conclude the bottom half of your long loop by wending downward from these high elevations to the village of St. Mary.

TO POLEBRIDGE   There are two ways to see the park's western boundary and to access the Polebridge area in the north; one is slow and uncomfortable; the other slightly faster and less uncomfortable. The **North Fork Road** from Columbia Falls takes about an hour to negotiate. It's a sometimes paved, mostly gravel and pothole stretch that follows the North Fork of the Flathead River. Not much is there besides water and scenery, but the area around Polebridge is a popular place to take in Montana's natural beauty without modern-day distractions like telephones and TVs.

The **Inside North Fork Road,** just inside the park's West Glacier entrance, also runs to Polebridge. However, it's totally unpaved, takes an hour longer, and is much harder on driver, passenger, and equipment. We recommend you take the faster route and spend that extra hour relaxing on a riverbank.

3 Outdoor Pursuits

BIKING   Opportunities for biking in the park are limited, since bikes may be ridden only on established roads, bike routes, or in parking areas, and are not allowed on trails. Restrictions apply to the most hazardous portions of Going-to-the-Sun Road during peak travel times from around mid-June to Labor Day; call ahead to find out when the road will be closed to bikers. During low-visibility periods caused by fog or darkness, a white front light and a back red reflector are required. A few campsites for bicyclists are held until 9pm at Apgar, Sprague Creek, Fish Creek, Many Glacier, Two Medicine, Avalanche, Rising Sun, and St. Mary Campgrounds, for $3 per person.

From June 15 to Labor Day, bikes are prohibited between Apgar and Sprague Creek campgrounds between 11am and 4pm in both directions, and from Logan Creek to Logan Pass (eastbound) between 11am and 4pm. It takes about 3 hours and 45 minutes to ride from Sprague Creek to Logan Pass.

BOATING   You can take advantage of some of those 653 lakes with a boat rental at various spots. Motor size is restricted to 10 horsepower on most lakes, and a detailed list of other regulations is available at park headquarters and staffed ranger stations. Park rangers may inspect or board any boat to determine regulation compliance. At Apgar and Lake McDonald, you will find kayaks, canoes, rowboats, and motorboats. Only human-powered or electric motorboats are available at Two Medicine. At Many Glacier you can rent kayaks, canoes, and rowboats. For details, call **Glacier Park Boat Co.** at © **406/257-2426.**

FISHING   Glacier's streams and lakes are habitat for whitefish, kokanee salmon, arctic grayling, and five kinds of trout. Try the North Fork of the Flathead to fish for cutthroat and bull trout and any of the three larger lakes in the park (Bowman Lake, St. Mary Lake, and Lake McDonald) for rainbow, brook trout, and whitefish. State of Montana fishing licenses are generally not required within the park's boundaries, although you will need one on the North Fork and Middle Fork of the Flathead River. Also, keep in mind since the eastern boundary of the park abuts the Blackfeet Indian Reservation, you may find yourself fishing in their territorial waters. To avoid a problem, purchase a $10 use permit from businesses in the gateway towns; the permit covers fishing, hiking, and biking in the reservation. Fishing outside the park in Montana waters requires a state license; check in at a local fishing shop to make certain you're within the laws.

HIKING   Glacier is a park that is best seen on foot. Its 1,600 square miles have 151 trails, totaling 753 miles (1,212km). You can hike 106 miles (171km) along the Continental Divide alone.

Trail maps are available at outdoor stores in Whitefish and Kalispell, as well as at the major visitor centers and ranger stations in the park. Before striking off into the wilderness, however, check with the nearest ranger station to determine the accessibility of your destination, trail conditions, and recent bear sightings.

Also note that the trail maps don't show elevation changes or many terrain features beyond lakes and the tallest peaks. If you plan to do any extensive hiking, it is best to purchase a U.S. Geological Survey topographic map.

The Park Service asks you to stay on trails to keep from eroding the fragile components of the park. Also, snowbanks shouldn't be traversed, especially the steeper ones. You should have proper footwear and rain gear, enough food, and, most important, enough water, before approaching any trail head. A can of pepper spray can also come in handy when you're in grizzly habitat. If you're planning to hike in Canada, be sure the bear spray is USEPA approved.

See "Exploring the Backcountry," below, for information on some of the longer hiking trails and further information on backpacking.

If you plan an extended hike, let someone know your route and when you expect to get back. Take a flashlight, in case you take longer than you think. Carry a map, rain gear, and extra clothing. Drink lots of water.

Among the park's shorter and easier trails is the **Trail of the Cedars Nature Trail** (0.25 miles [.5km] round-trip; access across from the Avalanche Campground Ranger Station), an easy, level trail that's wheelchair-accessible. It has interpretive signs along the way. The **Hidden Lake Nature Trail** ⊛ (3 miles [5km] round-trip; access from the Logan Pass Visitor Center) is an easy-to-moderate interpretative trail (with signs along the way) that climbs 460 feet to an overlook of scenic Hidden Lake. It's a popular trail, but if you hike all the way to the overlook, you'll be able to avoid some of the crowds, and you might even see a mountain goat.

The **Loop** (7 miles [11km] round-trip; access is along Going-to-the-Sun Rd., about halfway between Avalanche Campground and Logan Pass Visitor Center) offers a moderate hike that climbs to Granite Park Chalet and back. Many people use it as a continuation of the Highline Trail, but this is the section to do if you're not quite so adventurous (the Highline Trail is almost 12 miles [19km] long; see "Exploring the Backcountry," below). If you want to spend the night in the chalet, contact **Glacier Wilderness Guides** for reservations (✆ **800/521-7238**). (See the descriptions of the chalets under "Camping," below.)

The **Sun Point Nature Trail** (1⅔ miles [2km] round-trip; access is 9 miles [15km] west of St. Mary at the Sun Point parking area) is an easy walk on gentle slopes that presents commanding views of Baring Falls. Among our favorite hikes (because of its beautiful scenery) is the **Iceberg Lake Trail** ⊛⊛ (9½ miles [15km] round-trip; access at a trail head in a cabin area east of the Swiftcurrent Coffee Shop and Campstore). This is a moderate hike that traverses flower-filled meadows to a jewel of a high lake backed against a mountain wall. Even in summer, there may be snow on the ground and ice floating in the lake. Look for mountain goats or bighorn sheep on the cliffs above. And, as in many of the park's backcountry areas, keep an eye out for the grizzlies.

Swiftcurrent Lake Nature Trail ⊛ (2⅔ miles [4km] round-trip; access at a picnic area half a mile [1km] west of the hotel turnoff) is a fun and easy hike along the lakeshore, through the woods, and near a marsh, so you may see deer and birds—keep an eye out for blue grouse. If you have time, continue on the trail as it circles Lake Josephine, another easy hike, adding 2⅔ miles (4.5km) to the trip. Dramatic Mount Gould towers above the far end of Lake Josephine, and midsummer wildflowers can be spectacular. A longer, 10⅔-mile (17km) round-trip trail to Grinnell Glacier, the park's largest, is also accessed from this area.

The very easy **Running Eagle Falls Trail** (0.6 mile [1km] round-trip; access is 1 mile [2km] west of the Two Medicine entrance) winds through a heavily forested area to a large, noisy waterfall. The popular **Twin Falls Trail** (7⅜ miles [12km] round-trip; access from Two Medicine Campground) is an easy hike to scenic Twin Falls. Hikers can walk the entire distance to Twin Falls on a clearly identified trail, or boat across Two Medicine Lake to the foot of the trail head, and hike the last mile. The **St. Mary Falls Trail** ☀☀ (1⅜ miles [3km] round-trip; access from Jackson Glacier Overlook) is a fairly easy walk that takes you to rushing falls of the St. Mary River. The roar of the cascade is prodigious and satisfying.

HORSEBACK RIDING   You can bring your own horses and pack animals into the park, but restrictions apply to private stock. A free brochure detailing regulations regarding horseback riding is available from the Park Service.

Guided horseback riding at East Glacier is provided by **Two Medicine River Outfitters** (© **406/226-9220**), located a stone's throw from the front door of the lodge; the company offers hourly and half-day rides into the nearby wilderness. **Mule Shoe Outfitters** (© **406/888-5121**) offers similar rides from corrals at Lake McDonald and the Many Glacier Corral. Mule Shoe has 1- and 2-hour rides through the varied terrain of Glacier.

MOUNTAIN CLIMBING   The peaks of Glacier Park rarely exceed 10,000 feet in elevation, but don't let the surveyors' measurements fool you. Glacier has some incredibly difficult climbs, and you must inquire at the ranger station regarding climbing conditions and closures. In general, the peaks are unsuitable, except for experienced climbers or those traveling with experienced guides.

RAFTING & FLOAT TRIPS   Though the waters that are actually in the park don't lend themselves to white-water rafting, the boundary forks of the Flathead River are some of the best in the northwest corner of the state. For just taking it easy and floating on your back in the summer sun, the North Fork of the Flathead River stretching from Polebridge to Columbia Falls and into Flathead Lake is ideal. Portaging in Polebridge can be difficult, however. The same may be said for the Middle Fork of the Flathead, at the southern border of the park.

For white-water voyagers, the North Fork of the Flathead River (Class II, III) and the Middle Fork (Class III) are the best bets. Inquire at any ranger station for details and conditions, since flow rates change dramatically as snow melts or storms move through the area.

The Middle Fork is a little more severe; the names of certain stretches (such as the Narrows, Jaws, and Bonecrusher) are terror-inspiring in themselves. To assuage that terror, several outfitters offer expert and sanctioned guided trips.

The **Montana Raft Company** (© **800/521-RAFT** or 406/387-5555; fax 406/387-5656; www.glacierguides.com) is an arm of Glacier Wilderness Guides that offers rafting trips in Glacier and the surrounding area. Prices range from half-day adult for $38 (child $29), to a 3-day trip at about $430 per person. Prices cover equipment and food. Trips are scheduled throughout the season. The full-day trip puts in at Cacadilla about 15 miles (24km) up the Flathead River. You'll paddle down the relatively calm upper portion, stop for lunch, then be ready for the Class II and Class III white water below Moccasin Creek.

Great Northern Whitewater Raft & Resort (© **800/735-7897** or 406/387-5340; www.gnwhitewater.com) offers white-water rafting, kayaking, and drift-boat fishing. Full-day raft trips are $71 for adults, $46 for children (12 and under); full-day fishing trips are $295. Horseback riding and rafting combos are also available by arrangement. You can choose between trips where you paddle, or where a guide paddles for you. Other options include scenic and white-water trips, and an 8-mile (13km) barbecue dinner trip that leaves at 3pm.

Tips **Bear Warning!**

To remind you yet again: Glacier is grizzly country. Make noise when you walk, don't cook near where you sleep, and don't sleep in the same clothes you cooked in.

SNOWSHOEING & CROSS-COUNTRY SKIING   Glacier has numerous cross-country trails, the most popular of which is the **Upper Lake McDonald Trail** to the Avalanche picnic area. This 8-mile (13km) trail offers a relatively flat route up Going-to-the-Sun Road with views of McDonald Creek and the mountains looming above the McDonald Valley. For the advanced skier, the same area presents a more intense 10½-mile (17km) trip that heads northwest in a roundabout fashion to the Apgar Lookout. The most popular trail on the east side is the **Autumn Creek Trail** near Marias Pass. However, avalanche paths cross this area, so inquire about current weather conditions. Yet another popular spot is in Essex along the southern boundary of the park at the Izaak Walton Inn.

4 Exploring the Backcountry

Glacier offers every kind of backcountry experience, from 1-mile (2km) day hikes to 2-week treks. Consider your fitness level, backcountry experience, and interests, then get some advice from one of the visitor center rangers. They can provide you with area maps, but a topographical map is highly recommended if you're going for more than a short walk.

Backcountry campgrounds have maps at the entrance to show you the location of each campground, the pit toilet, food-preparation areas, and, perhaps most important, food-storage areas. If you fish while camping, it's recommended you exercise catch-and-release so as to avoid attracting wildlife in search of food. If you eat the catch, be certain to puncture the air bladder and throw the entrails into deep water at least 200 feet from the nearest campsite or trail. You will need a permit to camp; see "Backcountry Permits," earlier in this chapter.

GUIDED BACKCOUNTRY TRIPS   Glacier Wilderness Guides (© 800/521-7238 or 406/387-5555; fax 406/387-5656; www.glacierguides.com) is the exclusive hiking guide service in the park. They will put together any kind of trip for you, or offer weekly departures for 3-, 4-, and 6-day trips. Prices vary depending on the trip, but you can figure on spending $100 to $120 per person per day. They also rent equipment and provide "Sherpa service," where the guide will carry your gear. The season runs May through September.

NOTABLE BACKCOUNTRY HIKING TRAILS

DAWSON-PITAMAKAN LOOP   This difficult, 19-mile (31km) round-trip hike traverses Rising Wolf Mountain, at 9,513 feet the area's most prominent feature. There are backcountry campsites at Old Man Lake and at No Name Lake. The trail offers splendid panoramas of the park's interior and of many alpine lakes. You'll encounter lots of steep ups and downs. The trail head is at Two Medicine Campground.

KINTLA LAKE TO UPPER KINTLA LAKE TRAIL   This 24-mile (39km) round-trip hike skirts the north shore of Kintla Lake above Polebridge for about 7 miles (11km) before climbing a couple of hundred feet. This stretch of the hike is a breeze. However, once you hit Kintla Creek you may want to reconsider going any farther. With 12 miles (19km) under your belt at this point, climbing 3,000 feet may not seem like a great idea. The trail, once it breaks into the clear, offers views of several peaks, including Kinnerly Peak to the south of Upper Kintla Lake. The trail head is located 14 miles (23km) north of Polebridge after a drive along a gravel road, at the western tip of Kintla Lake.

BOWMAN LAKE TRAIL 🐾🐾   This especially scenic trail (14 miles [23km] to Brown Pass) is similar to the Kintla Lake hike in difficulty, and, like the Kintla Trail, passes the lake on the north. After a hike through the foliage, the trail climbs out of reach of anyone in bad shape, then ascends 2,000 feet in less than 3 miles (5km) to join the Kintla Trail at Brown Pass. A left turn takes you back to Kintla Lake (23 miles [37km]), a right takes you to Goat Haunt at the foot of Waterton Lake (9 miles [15km]). To reach the Bowman Lake trail head, go 0.3 miles [.5km] north of Polebridge, then turn east (right) up the Bowman Creek road. The road ends after 6 miles (10km) at the southeast end of Bowman Lake, from which the trails radiate.

QUARTZ LAKE TRAIL   Cross the bridge over Bowman Creek. The entire loop is 12 miles (19km) and runs a course up and over a ridge and down to the south end of Lower Quartz Lake. From there it's a level 3-mile (5km) hike to the west end of Quartz Lake, then it's 6 miles (10km) back over the ridge farther north (and higher up) before dropping back to Bowman Lake. An interesting aspect of this trail is evidence of the Red Bench Fire of 1988, which took a chunk out of the North Fork area.

THE HIGHLINE TRAIL   This easy-to-moderate 12-mile (19km) round-trip hike, which gains only 200 feet in elevation, begins at the Logan Pass Visitor Center and skirts the Garden Wall at elevations of more than 6,000 feet to Granite Park Chalet. Keep an eye on your watch to be certain you'll have enough time for the return hike to Logan Pass. You can continue on from the chalet to "the Loop," the aptly named section of Going-to-the-Sun Road where the trail actually terminates (an additional 4½ miles [7km]), although you'll need to plan for a shuttle back to your car.

PIEGAN PASS TO MANY GLACIER   If you're looking for a longer, tougher hike from Logan Pass, try this hike. You pick up the trail at Siyeh Bend about 3 miles (5km) on the east side of Logan Pass Visitor Center. It's a 12½-mile (20km) walk up over Piegan Pass, past Grinnell Glacier and Grinnell Lake to Josephine and Swiftcurrent Lakes before reaching Many Glacier Lodge. There are long stretches of up (and of down) walking.

5 Camping

INSIDE THE PARK

Stop at any ranger station for information on closures and availability, and consult the chart below for information on amenities and fees.

There are a variety of camping opportunities here. Campgrounds accessible by paved roads include **Apgar,** near the West Glacier entrance; **Avalanche Creek,** just up from the head of Lake McDonald; **Fish Creek,** on the west side of Lake McDonald; **Many Glacier,** in the northeast part of the park; **Rising Sun,** on the north side of St. Mary Lake; **St. Mary,** on the east side of the park; and **Two Medicine,** in the southeast part of the park near East Glacier. **Sprague Creek,** near the West Glacier entrance, offers a paved road but does not allow towed vehicles. There are also five campgrounds accessed by narrow dirt roads.

Though utility connections are not provided at these sites, fireplaces, picnic tables, washrooms (with sinks and flush toilets), and cold running water are located at each campground. Campsites are available on a first-come, first-served basis, except for Fish Creek and St. Mary campgrounds, where sites can be reserved through the **National Park Service Reservation System** (*②* **800/ 365-2267;** http://reservations.nps.gov).

A few sites for bicyclists are held until 9pm at Apgar, Sprague Creek, Avalanche, Fish Creek, Many Glacier, Two Medicine, Rising Sun, and St. Mary campgrounds, for $3 per person.

THE CAMPGROUNDS

Despite its proximity to the center of the hotel and motel activity, the **Many Glacier Campground** ⋆⋆ is a well-treed campground with more privacy than you'd expect. The campground has adequate space for small motor homes and pickup truck/camper combinations, but space for vehicles pulling trailers is limited. It is a veritable mecca for tent campers. The **Avalanche Campground** is situated in the bottom of the valley near Lake McDonald in a heavily treed area immediately adjacent to the river. The **Two Medicine Campground** ⋆⋆ lies in the shadow of the mountains near three lakes and a stream. It is a well-treed area that has beautiful sites, plenty of shade, and opportunities to wet a fishing line. Two Medicine is a little out of the way of the typical Glacier traveler, and may offer a little more solitude. The **Cut Bank Campground** road is not paved. But it's only 5 miles (8km) from the pavement to the ranger station and campground. The road and campground are best suited to recreational vehicles 21 feet or shorter.

Amenities for Each Campground in Glacier National Park

Campground	# of Sites	Fee	Max RV Length	Flush Toilets	Disposal Stations	Boat Access
Apgar	196	$14	25 sites; up to 40'	Yes	Yes	Yes
Avalanche	87	$14	50 sites; up to 26'	Yes	Yes	No
Bowman Lake*	48	$12	RVs not recommended	No	No	Yes
Cut Bank*	19	$12	RVs not recommended	No	No	No
Fish Creek	180	$17	3 sites; up to 35'	Yes	Yes	No
Kintla Lake*	13	$12	RVs not recommended	No	No	Yes
Logging Creek*	8	$12	RVs not recommended	No	No	No
Many Glacier	110	$14	13 sites; up to 35'	Yes	Yes	Yes
Quartz Creek*	7	$12	RVs not recommended	No	No	No
Rising Sun	83	$14	3 sites; up to 30'	Yes	Yes	Yes
Sprague Creek	25	$14	No towed units	Yes	No	No
St. Mary	148	$17	25 sites; up to 35'	Yes	Yes	No
Two Medicine	99	$14	13 sites; up to 32'	Yes	Yes	Yes

Campgrounds are accessible only by narrow dirt roads. RVs are not recommended.

CHALETS

Two of the park's most popular destinations, Granite Park and Sperry Chalets— National Historic Landmarks built by the Great Northern Railway between 1912 and 1914—are subjects of an extensive restoration project. The **Granite Park Chalet** is a hiker's shelter only. Guests must bring their own food, water, cooking and eating utensils, flashlights, and sleeping bags. Rooms and beds are provided, as are a kitchen with a cooking stove and dining room. No public water is available, so bring your own. The chalet has 12 rooms (all single bunk beds), and sleeps two to six per room. Cost is $60 per night per person, plus $10 per person if you want bed linens. For reservations at Granite Park Chalet, call **Glacier Wilderness Guides** (*©* **800/521-RAFT** or 406/387-5555; fax 406/387-5656; www.glacierguides.com). To get there, you'll have to walk about 3 miles (5km) from the Loop trail head off Going-to-the-Sun Road, or about 6 miles (10km) on the trail to Swiftcurrent Pass at the end of Many Glacier Road from the east side.

The **Sperry Chalet** (ca. 1913), which reopened in 1999 after closing in 1992, is an impressive stone structure in the center of the wilderness. Here you'll get a room (with linens) plus three meals daily, but no bathing facilities except cold water, and the modern composting toilets are outside. Rates are $150 for the first person in a room plus $100 for each additional person, and include all meals. For reservations contact **Belton Chalets** at (*©* **888/235-8665;** www.beltonchalet. com). To get there, walk about 4 miles (6km) from the road, up Snyder Creek, then toward Gunsight Mountain. The trail head is opposite the entrance to Lake McDonald Lodge on the lower portion of Going-to-the-Sun Road.

CAMPGROUNDS IN GATEWAY COMMUNITIES

During the busy season, it's recommended that you reserve these campsites at least 1 month in advance.

IN EAST GLACIER

Y Lazy R   Situated just off U.S. 2, this campground is conveniently located within walking distance of East Glacier and is the closest to town with laundry facilities. Plan to arrive early if you want to snag one of the few sites with trees. The Y Lazy R is a great value and an ideal place to plant the RV before heading off to explore the region.

Box 146, East Glacier, MT 59434. *©* 406/226-5573. 10 tent sites, 30 RV sites. $10 tent; $15 full hookup.

IN ST. MARY

Johnson's of St. Mary   April through September (depending on the weather), this is where you want to camp if you can get a spot. The campground is located near the southern end of Lower St. Mary Lake and provides an inexpensive overnight stop with access to the east side of the park and the tourist facilities at the St. Mary Lodge. There are also showers ($2) and a laundromat.

St. Mary, MT 59417. *©* 406/732-4207. Fax 406/732-5517. www.babbmt.com/johnsons. 50 tent sites, 65 RV sites. $14 tent; $21 RV with electricity and water only, $25 full hookup; $18 motor home, no hookup. MC, V.

IN WEST GLACIER

Glacier Campground   This campground—1 mile (2km) west of West Glacier on U.S. 2—is the closest campground outside the park. Set amid a forested area overgrown with evergreens, it's a quiet, comfortable, shady place to retreat. Most sites have water and electric hookups; the balance is perfect for tent camping. Five rather primitive cabins are also available, but furnishings are modest: sleeping beds with mattresses and electricity, but no plumbing or kitchen facilities. Recreational facilities include volleyball, horseshoes, and a basketball court; also on the premises are a laundromat and small general store.

P.O. Box 447, 12070 U.S. 2, West Glacier, MT 59936. *©* 406/387-5689. 80 tent sites, 80 RV sites, 5 cabins. $17 tent; $20 full hookup; $30–$40 cabin.

Lake Five Resort   Located 3 miles (5km) west of West Glacier and approximately 1 mile (2km) from U.S. 2 is this cabin and campground arrangement, an

Bear-Watching

If you haven't had the good (or bad) luck to run into a bear during your backcountry adventures, you can get a guaranteed sighting at the **Great Bear Adventure,** 10555 U.S. 2 E., in Coram, near West Glacier. This 10-acre compound is the home of four healthy, free-roaming black bears, including one 750-pounder, and three newly added grizzlies. The path you drive through the compound—actually, it's a private residence with a backyard full of bears—is approximately a mile (2km) long. Open daily, seasonally. Adults $5, children $4, under 3 free. Cash only.

alternative to potentially crowded park campgrounds. Situated on a 235-acre lake surrounded by private homes and summer cottages, the resort is far from the madding crowd (though still close to the park itself). Seven of the nine cabins are on the lakefront, all of them equipped with bathrooms and showers. The only distraction may be the sound of powerboats.

540 Belton Stage Rd., West Glacier, MT 59936. ✆ **406/387-5601.** www.lakefiveresort.com. 9 cabins, 6 teepee lodges, 45 sites with electricity and water (14 of which have sewer hookups). $18–$25 site; $50–$120 cabin; $40 teepee.

North American RV Park & Campground   This is a large, convenient, and conspicuous campground, close to Glacier National Park and Hungry Horse Reservoir. The RV park is associated with the **Wildlife Museum** next door. Here you'll find preserved most of the animals indigenous to this area. The museum is closed in winter. Admission is $3 for adults and $2 for children; hours are from 9am to 9pm daily, from May 1 to October 31.

P.O. Box 130449, Coram, MT 59913 (on U.S. 2 about 5½ miles [9km] west of West Glacier). ✆ **406/ 387-5800.** 18 tent sites, 91 RV sites (45 full hookups, 46 electric only). $13–$23.

West Glacier KOA   This is a neat, modern facility with a store, ice cream parlor, and playground. The campsites are wooded, and a few small cabins are available. They serve breakfast and dinner and have a new heated swimming pool and two hot tubs. The campground also sponsors occasional wildlife slide shows and lectures.

Box 215, West Glacier, MT 59936. ✆ **800/562-3313** or 406/387-5341. Fax 406/387-5209. E-mail: wgkoa@ digisys.net. $23 tent; $32 full hookup. Drive 2½ miles (4km) west on U.S. 2, then 1 mile (2km) south on a paved road.

BACKCOUNTRY CAMPING

If it's the backcountry you're bent on seeing, Glacier has 63 backcountry campgrounds. Fortunately, many are at lower elevation, so inexperienced backpackers have an opportunity to take advantage of them. For an accurate depiction of your itinerary's difficulty, and advice on what may be needed, check with rangers in the area you contemplate visiting. One of the main sources of danger is bears. Backcountry permits are available at ranger stations, and requests for sites can be made 24 hours in advance. There is no fee for a permit.

6 Where to Stay

Television reception is limited in the Glacier National Park area, so if TV is important to you, check not only that the lodging facility has in-room TVs, but also call and ask just what channels they get.

INSIDE THE PARK

With only one exception, Glacier Park, Inc. (GPI) operates the hostelries in Glacier National Park. Lake McDonald Lodge, Glacier Park Lodge, and Many Glacier Hotel are first-tier properties that have been popular destinations since early in the century. Swiftcurrent Motor Inn is typical of the casual motel-style properties at the other end of the spectrum, providing decent but undistinguished accommodations for less money. Although the lodges have a considerable charm, they don't have spas, air-conditioning, or in-room televisions.

Reserve well in advance. August dates may fill before the spring thaw. For more information on the following properties or to make a reservation, contact **Glacier Park, Inc.**, 106 Cooperative Way, Suite 104, Kalispell, MT 59901 (© **406/756-2444**; fax 406/257-0384; www.glacierparkinc.com). GPI does not accept pets at any of its facilities.

Apgar Village Lodge   The Apgar Village Lodge is located on the south end of Lake McDonald and is one of two lodgings in Apgar Village. There's a wide variety of lodging available here, but the best places—reserve early—are along Lake McDonald Creek and on the banks of the lake. There are nine river cabins, and several motel rooms overlooking the creek. The cabins are much nicer than they look on the outside. Five large cabins have been completely remodeled, with two bedrooms; most of them have kitchens with stoves and refrigerators. Some of the small ones tend to be a little dark, and the towels aren't big enough. Fans of the film *Beethoven II* might recognize the scenery—the movie was shot here.

Apgar Village, Box 398, West Glacier, MT 59936. © **406/888-5484**. Fax 406/888-5273. www.westglacier. com. 48 units. $57–$90 double motel room; $72–$210 cabin. DISC, MC, V. Closed mid-Oct to Apr. *In room:* TV, no phone.

Glacier Park Lodge ★★   Located just inside the southeast entrance at East Glacier, this is GPI's flagship inn. This imposing timbered lodge stands as a stately tribute to the Great Northern Railroad and its early attempts to lure tourists to Glacier. The hotel is stylish and impressive, but not luxurious. The rooms are fairly small, with Spartan furnishings. But you probably won't spend much time in your room anyway. The lodge's carefully manicured lawn and blooming wildflowers frame the grounds in spectacular colors. The interior features massive Douglas fir pillars, some 40 inches in diameter and 40 feet tall. A wooden deck outside the lounge provides an excellent spot for cocktails, reading, or a late-afternoon snooze. A glass-enclosed breezeway connects the main building to the annex; the oak chaise lounges provide an ideal spot to watch the sun rise.

There is always a crowd at the dining rooms of the park hotels, and the dining room of the Glacier Park Hotel is no exception. If you want to eat here, make your reservation as soon as you arrive. The room is nice, but the food is ordinary and overpriced. The menu varies, but consists mostly of beef and seafood. The service is friendly and enthusiastic but can be uneven, since the park facilities rely almost entirely on college students for staff.

The Other Gateway Communities

If the convenience of staying on Glacier's back porch is important to you, the places listed on the following pages are your best bets. See "Where to Stay" in the Whitefish, Kalispell, and Columbia Falls sections of chapter 5 for listings of places that might be more in line with your needs if the park is merely a 1- or 2-day part of your vacation.

Presentations and entertainment include Blackfeet explaining the history and culture of their tribe, naturalists' programs, and an employee-performed rock-and-roll revue. There's also an American Indian trading post offering traditional souvenirs, artwork, and clothing from tribal artisans.

Glacier National Park, MT 59936. ℭ **406/756-2444.** Fax 406/257-0384. www.glacierparkinc.com. 154 units. $135–$195 double; $299 suite. DISC, MC, V. **Amenities:** Restaurant; pool; 9-hole golf course; horseback riding arranged; a small chip-and-putt golf course occupies most of the front lawn and is very popular in the evenings.

Lake McDonald Lodge ★★
The Lake McDonald Lodge looks and feels like a lodge in the old style. It's small compared to the other GPI park lodges, and the ambience is altogether more cozy. Lodge rooms, located on the second and third floor of the lodge (no elevator), are pleasantly decorated and have a historic feel, while the motel units are simply well-maintained motel rooms. The well-preserved cottages are located in multi-unit cottage buildings in a wooded area. Situated on the shore of the park's largest lake, it provides a fine base for exploring the western part of the park. A center for boating activity, scenic cruises depart daily, or you can rent your own boat by the day. Common lounging areas are furnished with heavy couches, sofas, and chairs that surround a stone fireplace. All units are no-smoking.

Glacier National Park, MT 59936. ℭ **406/756-2444.** Fax 406/257-0384. www.glacierparkinc.com. 62 units in lodge and motel, 38 cottage rooms. $135 double lodge room; $92 double motel unit; $86–$135 cottage. DISC, MC, V. **Amenities:** Dining room, lounge, coffee shop; post office. *In room:* No phone.

Many Glacier Hotel ★★★
Many Glacier is a vast, sprawling four-story structure on Swiftcurrent Lake. It's the most popular lodging in the park, and with good reason. The setting is beautiful, and there's a wide variety of activities to embark on from here—boating, hiking, and bird-watching, to name but a few. Most of the rooms are a little larger than the ones usually associated with a Northern Pacific hotel. But this was never a "railroad hotel." Completed in 1915, it was one of a network of chalets—others were Sperry and Granite—that visitors rode to on horseback. The chalets were set 1 day's ride apart.

Rooms, decorated in keeping with the hotel's historic roots, are located in the main lodge around the balconies overlooking the lobby or in the adjoining annex. We like the lakeside rooms, for their views of Swiftcurrent Lake. Those who plan to use their room only as a place to crash at the end of the day can save money by booking one of the smaller units. You'll almost certainly see bears wandering around Many Glacier in August when the huckleberries ripen. All units are no-smoking.

Glacier National Park, MT 59936. ℭ **406/756-2444.** Fax 406/257-0384. www.glacierparkinc.com. 216 units. $106–$185 double; $209 suite. DISC, MC, V. **Amenities:** Dining room, coffee shop, lounge, nightly cabaret performances begin mid-summer.

Rising Sun Motor Inn
Located 6½ miles (11km) from St. Mary, just off Going-to-the-Sun Road, the Rising Sun consists of a complex made up of a restaurant, a motor inn, cottages, a camp store, a gift shop, and a service station. The basic motel rooms are just that—basic but uninspiring motel rooms—that are completely adequate for a good night's rest and in an excellent location for those who want to explore the eastern side of the park from Going-to-the-Sun Road. The cottages (you rent half of a duplex) are more interesting, but a bit on the rustic side. All units here are no-smoking.

Glacier National Park, MT 59936. ℭ **406/756-2444.** Fax 406/257-0384. www.glacierparkinc.com. 63 units. $82–$92 double; $86 cottage. AE, DISC, MC, V. **Amenities:** Dining room. *In room:* No phone.

Swiftcurrent Motor Inn 🅡 *Value*   The Swiftcurrent Motor Inn is located about a mile (1.5km) upstream from Many Glacier Hotel, but it attracts an entirely different crowd. The people who stay here are younger, less well-to-do, and primarily active types interested in spending lots of time exploring the back-country trails. Like Many Glacier, the inn is set against a mountain backdrop in what is considered a hiker's paradise. Motel rooms here have standard motel decor—functional but nothing special; cabins are a bit more interesting, with one or two bedrooms, and perhaps a bathroom (communal facilities are nearby). All units are no-smoking. The Swiftcurrent was built in 1936 as a motor hotel, the first in the park specifically directed at tourists arriving by car rather than train. There are three circles of cabins and two motel-style units, all set back in the trees. The inn sits in a wildlife migratory path, so you likely will see bear, elk, and moose in the parking lot. The Italian Garden Ristorante serves a mean garlic and artichoke-heart pizza. There's also a camping supplies store on the property.

Glacier National Park, MT 59936. (© 406/756-2444. Fax 406/257-0384. www.glacierparkinc.com. 88 units, most cabins without private bathroom. $82–$92 double in motor inn; $41 double in cabin. DISC, MC, V. **Amenities:** Restaurant; coin-operated laundry. *In room:* No phone.

Village Inn   Not to be confused with Apgar Village Lodge (see above), the Village Inn is the smallest of the properties operated by GPI in Glacier. Located in Apgar Village, the inn is convenient to the general store, cafes, and boat docks. Like its counterparts throughout the park, the Village Inn is comfortably outfitted with modest furnishings, making it a cozy and convenient place to set up camp. Though there's no dining room on the property, the restaurants of Lake McDonald and Apgar are all close by. Apgar Village bustles with activity during the summer and is a great choice for families.

Glacier National Park, MT 59936. © 406/756-2444. Fax 406/257-0384. www.glacierparkinc.com. 36 units (12 with kitchenette). $95–$150 double; $124 suite. DISC, MC, V. *In room:* No phone.

IN GATEWAY COMMUNITIES
IN EAST GLACIER

Backpacker's Inn   This dorm-style hostel consists of three cabins—one for men, one for women, and a private coed cabin—each sleeping up to six people (the coed cabin sleeps eight). At $10 per person, the price is right, but don't expect the rooms to include much more than a bed. The rooms are booked out of Serrano's Restaurant (see "Where to Dine," below).

P.O. Box 94, East Glacier, MT 59434. © 406/226-9392. serranos@digisys.net. 3 cabins (1 sleeps 6 women, 1 sleeps 8 men, $10 per person; 1 is private and is $20 for 1 person or $30 for 2). DISC, MC, V. Closed mid-Oct to Apr. *In room:* No phone.

Brownies Grocery and AYH Hostel   Reservations are recommended at this popular combination grocery store/hostel, which offers comfortable rooms at extremely affordable prices. Dorm and family rooms are located on the second floor of a rustic, older log building with several common rooms for guests to share, including a porch, kitchen, bathrooms, and laundry.

P.O. Box 229, East Glacier, MT 59434. © 406/226-4426 or 406/226-4456. 10 units, 2 family rooms, all with shared bathroom. AYH members $13–$26 dorm rooms, $35 family room; nonmembers $15–$29 dorm rooms, $35 family room. MC, V. Closed Oct to early May, depending on the weather. *In room:* No phone.

East Glacier Motel and Cabins *Value*   This is a small place across the street from Restaurant Thimbleberry. The average-size motel rooms are very nice, and recently remodeled. The cabins are small, with low ceilings, a small refrigerator, and a two-burner stove. The prices are very reasonable for the area, however, and the rooms were sparkling clean when we visited.

1107 Mont. 49, East Glacier, MT 59434. ☏ **406/226-5593**. 102164.356@compuserve.com. 11 cabins, 6 motel rooms. $45–$65 double. DISC, MC, V. Pets accepted. *In room:* No phone.

Jacobson's Cottages   Located in a nicely wooded area, these quaint cottages are small but comfortable. All have cable TV and one has a kitchen. Entertainment and good food are short walks away with Restaurant Thimbleberry a half block down the street, and Two Medicine an 11-mile (18km) drive. The cottages are available seasonally, and reservations are recommended.

P.O. Box 454, East Glacier, MT 59434. ☏ **406/226-4422**. 12 cottages. $50–$75 double. AE, DISC, MC, V. Closed Nov–Apr. *In room:* TV, no phone.

Mountain Pine Motel   This property is a one-story, 1950s-style motel that provides clean, well-furnished rooms equipped with cable TV. It is in a shaded, timbered area along Mont. 49. Most standard rooms have two queen-size beds, reading chairs and table, chest, and bathrooms with tub-shower combinations. The units are clustered around a small courtyard. There is also a large three-bedroom log house available with a view of the mountains. Someone will meet you at the Amtrak station if you arrive by train. All units are no-smoking.

Mont. 49, East Glacier, MT 59434. ☏ **406/226-4403**. 25 units, 1 house. $52–$68 double. AE, DC, DISC, MC, V. Small pets accepted. *In room:* TV.

IN ESSEX

Glacier River Retreat   Open only since 1998, these are two attractive but simple duplex cabins, each unit sleeping up to four. They are good-size units, with two bedrooms each, and the arched ceilings add to the feeling of openness. The cabins are located in a deeply wooded setting, a short walk to fishing in the Flathead River.

HC36 Box 11A (mile marker 173.4 on U.S. 2), Essex, MT 59916. ☏ **406/888-5002**. Fax 406/888-9002. 4 units. $120 double (2-night minimum). MC, V. **Amenities:** Sauna; recreation room. *In room:* Kitchen; no phone.

Izaak Walton Inn ★★ *Finds*   Built in 1939, this inn originally housed railway workers. It now has three floors of rooms, a restaurant, and a tavern. The rooms are not large, but they are beautifully kept, with wood-paneled walls and various Western touches. Each has a private bathroom. Some have, in addition to the double beds, futon couches that can be folded out for another bed. The halls are decorated in railroad memorabilia. The converted cabooses are similarly decorated, and what train buff can resist the temptation of spending the night in a genuine caboose? Unlike a lot of Glacier lodging establishments, the inn is booming in winter. Skiers are attracted to its 30 miles (48km) of groomed trails, and a new pavilion will house a covered ice rink. There is also an attractive Finnish sauna.

P.O. Box 653, Essex, MT 59916. ☏ **406/888-5700**. Fax 406/888-5200. www.izaakwaltoninn.com. 33 units, 4 caboose cottages. $98 double; $150 suite; $525 caboose (3-night minimum). MC, V. **Amenities:** Dining room, tavern; sauna; 30 miles (48km) of groomed cross-country ski trails; ice pavilion; self-service laundry. *In room:* No phone.

Paola Creek Bed & Breakfast ★★   This handsome log B&B sits back in the woods with a beautiful view of Mount St. Nicholas in the distance. The rooms are small but beautifully decorated in mountain lodge style, very comfortable and each with a private bathroom. Four rooms have queen-size beds; the fifth has a king bed and a whirlpool tub. The centerpiece of the inn is the great room, a large open living room dominated by a large fireplace with a three-story river-rock chimney. There is also a large deck where you can sit in awe of the Glacier Park peaks. Kelly Hostetler, who owns the B&B with her husband, Les, provides a full breakfast and evening wine and hors d'oeuvres as part of the price. She'll also cook a gourmet dinner for guests for an additional $25 per person. Paola Creek attracts a vigorous outdoor crowd who are up and out in the morning for hiking, kayaking, or fishing on the Flathead River. Although it is about 15 miles (24km) from here to the West Glacier park entrance, this is an excellent place to stay.

Box 97 (at mile 172.8 on U.S. 2), Essex, MT 59916. ℂ **888/311-5061** or 406/888-5061. Fax 406/888-5063. www.wtp.net/go/paola. 5 units. $120–$155 double. MC, V. **Amenities:** Special gourmet dinner can be arranged. *In room:* No phone.

IN POLEBRIDGE

North Fork Hostel and Square Peg Ranch   Next to the North Fork of the Flathead River, the North Fork Hostel is basic but laid-back and fun. Accommodations are rustic, with a mountain cabin feel—there's no electricity in Polebridge, so lighting is powered by kerosene and propane, and heat is from an old-fashioned wood stove. There are separate facilities for men and women, as well as couples' accommodations, washrooms with hot showers, and clean outhouses. There are also several small cabins suitable for families. Hostel guests should bring linens or sleeping bags (sheets are available for rent) and flashlights. The Square Peg Ranch offers two rustic log homes. The log homes have solar-heated showers or guests can use the hostel showers, and there are outhouses. The hostel and cabins have complete kitchen facilities, and you can take a relaxing soak in the hostel's 6-foot-long claw-foot bathtub. Serious bikers, hikers, river rats, cross-country skiers, and snowshoers stay here—use of mountain bikes, cross-country skis and boots, and snowshoes is included in the fee. There are some cabins and trailers in the back, just large enough to accommodate the beds that fill them.

P.O. Box 1, Polebridge, MT 59928. ℂ 406/888-5241. www.nfhostel.com. 12 bunks, 2 cabins, 2 log homes. $15 bunk; $30 cabin; $65 log home. AE. **Amenities:** Communal kitchen. *In room:* No phone.

Polebridge Mercantile and Cabins *Value*   There is no electricity and no running water in the lower-priced cabins, let alone bedding—it's bring your own sleeping bag or linens at the Merc. The $65 "luxury" cabin has a bathroom and running water in the kitchenette. Each cabin has a propane cooking stove and lights, and the views out over the west side of Glacier National Park make the price tag a steal, especially if you brought the kids. There's also a basic teepee that will keep the rain off your head. This may sound like an adventure in hell, but Polebridge is a happening spot in the summer when all the river rats and seasonal residents converge for good times and tall tales about the rapids they've run and their mountaineering adventures. The Mercantile sells canned goods, hot sandwiches, and souvenir T-shirts. There is a bakery with great baked goods.

P.O. Box 280042, Polebridge, MT 59928. ℂ **406/888-5105.** www.members.tripod.com/polebridge. 4 cabins, 1 teepee. $30–$65 cabin; $20 teepee. MC, V. *In room:* No phone.

IN ST. MARY

St. Mary Lodge   Owner Roscoe Black has built himself quite an empire here on the east edge of Glacier National Park. The accommodations are very nice, the restaurant is excellent, and the gift shop is huge. The cheaper units are small, but bright, with golden logs. The furniture is lodgepole. The six cottages on the hill—which will hold four adults and rent for $285 per night in season—are the best luxury accommodations anywhere in or near the park. They have a living room, full kitchen, two bedrooms, spacious decks, a good-size bathroom with a tub, and gas grills. There are only six of them, and they rent out so fast that Black says he wishes he'd built twice as many. The cottages sit high on a hill, and the view from the decks out over St. Mary Lake is spectacular. Most units are air-conditioned—a rarity in the area.

When Roscoe Black met Mike Arp, owner of the Paradise Valley's Chico Hot Springs, Arp supposedly said to him, "So, I finally get to meet the owner of the second-best restaurant in Montana." One might not give the "Montana's best" title to St. Mary Lodge's **Snowgoose Grille** (or to Chico either, for that matter), but it is certainly in the top 10. See "Where to Dine," below. The St. Mary Lodge also has the **Curly Bear Café** (serving burgers, sandwiches, and soups), and pizza, ice cream, espresso, pastry, and fudge facilities. The outdoors shop, **Trail & Creek Outfitters** (© **406/732-4431,** ext. 332) is the best around.

U.S. 89 and Going-to-the-Sun Rd., St. Mary, MT 59417. © **800/368-3689** or 406/732-4431. Fax 406/ 732-9265. www.glcpark.com. 124 total units, including 57 hotel rooms, 48 new upscale rooms and suites, and 19 cabins and cottages. $93 double hotel; $285 cottage; $140–$210 suite. AE, DISC, MC, V. Closed Oct 2 to Mother's Day. **Amenities:** Restaurant, cafe, pizza parlor, coffee/chocolate shop; coin-operated laundry; gas station. *In room:* A/C.

IN WEST GLACIER

In addition to the West Glacier properties discussed below, the **Mountain Timbers,** P.O. Box 94, West Glacier, MT 59936 (© **800/841-3835** or 406/387-5830; fax 406/387-5835; mtntmbrs@digisys.net) was a moderately priced bed-and-breakfast inn that was closed for remodeling late in 2001, with no date for reopening. Situated on 240 acres, the lodge offers easy access to the West Glacier and Camas Creek entrances to the park, and should be worth checking out when it reopens.

Belton Chalets and Lodge This old chalet and lodge immediately across from the railroad station has recently been completely restored to the elegance of a turn-of-the-century railroad hotel. The rooms are small, simple, and old-fashioned. The bathrooms are also small. But the feel of the place is comfortable and the staff is very friendly. Many of the rooms have individual balconies looking out over the rounded timber hills in the near distance, the foothills to Glacier National Park.

12575 U.S. 2, West Glacier, MT 59936. © **888/235-8665** or 406/888-5000. Fax 406/888-5005. www. beltonchalet.com. 25 units, 2 cottages. $105–$245 double high season; $95–$175 double low season. AE, MC, V. **Amenities:** Restaurant (see "Where to Dine," below), bar. *In room:* No phone.

Glacier Wilderness Resort Surrounded by Forest Service lands, the lodges at this year-round resort are as private as you can get. Each lodge is a "home," done in modern Western decor. Families will find the two-bedroom lodges to their liking, and kids can play outdoors during the day (there are 23 undeveloped acres) and there are diversions like foosball, pool, and video games in the rec center. Hiking trails abound and some even come up on some surprising waterfalls. For a summer stay, reservations should be made before March.

P.O. Box 295, West Glacier, MT 59936. © **406/888-5664.** 10 lodges. $150–$170 per lodge per night. 5-night minimum stay. MC, V. **Amenities:** Indoor heated pool; recreation center. *In room:* TV, VCR, stereo, hot tub on front porch.

Great Northern Chalets This small, family-oriented resort located near West Glacier offers log chalets that have balconies facing landscaped flower gardens and a pond, with mountain views in the distance. Two types of chalets are offered, the largest being a beautifully furnished two-story, two-bedroom unit with three queen beds, a full bathroom upstairs, and half bathroom downstairs. Smaller chalets have one large upstairs bedroom with two queen beds, and a downstairs level with a full-size sleeper sofa and a kitchen with service for six.

12127 U.S. 2 (P.O. Box 278), West Glacier, MT 59936. © 800/735-7897. www.gnwhitewater.com. 5 units. $120–$270 double. AE, DISC, MC, V. **Amenities:** 16-foot indoor hot tub spa; volleyball court that doubles as a sandbox for children; pond used for fly-fishing instruction. *In room:* No phone.

Vista Motel *Value*   Perched atop a hill at the west entrance to Glacier National Park, the Vista boasts tremendous views of the mountains. It's strictly a strip motel, old but pretty well preserved. The owner is a serious Denver Broncos fan, if that influences your choice one way or the other. Accommodations are not luxurious, but rooms are clean and comfortable, and it's a lot cheaper than the competition.

P.O. Box 98, West Glacier, MT 59936. © 406/888-5311. 27 units. $60–$140 double. AE, DISC, MC, V. Closed Nov–Feb. **Amenities:** Outdoor heated pool. *In room:* TV, no phone.

West Glacier Motel *Value*   Formerly the River Bend Motel, this property has two locations. Half of the units are in West Glacier on Going-to-the-Sun Road, about 1 mile (2km) from the park entrance, and a second set of units is 1 mile (2km) away on a forested piece of ground that presents panoramic views of the park. This 1950s-style motel has a great location, the prices can't be beat during peak season, and rates drop dramatically the week before Labor Day. The Western-style cabins are better suited to family use, since they come with two or three queen-size beds.

200 Going-to-the-Sun Rd., West Glacier, MT 59936. © 406/888-5662. 32 units. $73 double; $121–$140 cabins. DISC, MC, V. *In room:* TV, no phone, kitchens in cabins.

7 Where to Dine

INSIDE THE PARK

You'll find above-average food served at above-average prices in the dining rooms at the major properties. Glacier Park Lodge has the **Great Northern Steak & Rib House,** which has Western decor and a menu of beef, barbecued ribs, fish, and chicken, plus a full breakfast buffet; and **The Sunset Lounge,** which offers a bar menu of sandwiches and appetizers. At Lake McDonald Lodge you'll find **Russell's Fireside Dining Room** 🍴, which has a hunting-lodge atmosphere with rough-hewn beams and hunting trophies, and specializes in American standards, including beef tenderloin, roast duckling, seared mountain trout, roast turkey, Alaskan salmon, and steaks, plus has a full breakfast buffet. Also at Lake McDonald Lodge is the **Stockade Lounge,** which serves a bar menu of sandwiches and appetizers. Many Glacier Hotel has the **Ptarmigan Dining Room,** which has Swiss decor in keeping with the lodge, emphasizing spectacular mountain views, and serves continental and Swiss cuisine plus a breakfast buffet. Many Glacier also has the **Swiss and Interlacken Lounge,** with a bar menu of sandwiches and appetizers. The dining rooms open with the park and close sometime in September, depending on the facility. At each dining room, breakfast is served from 6:30 to 9:30am; lunch from 11:30am to 2pm; and dinner from 5:30 to 9:30pm. Coffee and snack shops open either at 7 or 8am and close at 9pm. All of the above restaurants are no-smoking.

The alternatives include second-tier restaurants in close proximity to the hotels, most of which are comparable to chain restaurants in both quality and price. The **Two Dog Flats Grille** at the Rising Sun Motor Inn serves "hearty American fare"; the Swiftcurrent Motor Inn restaurant is the **Italian Garden,** which serves meals from 6am to 10pm. Lunch and dinner feature combinations of salads, sandwiches, pasta dishes, and "create your own" pizzas. At Apgar you'll find the **Cedar Tree Deli,** which specializes in sandwiches, ice cream, and cold drinks, and **Eddie's Cafe,** a family dining arrangement.

IN GATEWAY COMMUNITIES
IN EAST GLACIER
In addition to the restaurants described below, the **Whistle Stop** ★★, 1020 Mont. 49 (© **406/226-9292,** call for current hours), may serve up the very best breakfasts in the area, mostly in the $5 to $10 range. Omelets and French toast are a specialty; they come in seven different styles, including a Spanish omelet with chorizo, lots of peppers, tomatoes, onions, and spinach. Definitely an eye-opener. They're also known for barbecue ribs and chicken. Try their huckleberry pie.

Glacier Village Restaurant ★ *Value* AMERICAN This family-owned, seasonal restaurant is one of the few full-service dining establishments in the area that serves three meals, starting with breakfast at 6am. Portions are healthy and prices are moderate, with standards like yummy waffles and pancakes made from homemade batter. The restaurant's impressive menu includes pork chops with huckleberry sauce, plus jams and syrups to go.

304–308 Mont. 2, East Glacier. © **406/226-4464.** Breakfast items $3–$7; main courses $5–$8 lunch, $8–$15 dinner. MC, V. Daily 6am–9:30pm. Closed Oct–Apr.

Restaurant Thimbleberry ★★ AMERICAN Locally famous for their incredible pies—the lemon meringue and raspberry are both excellent choices—the Thimbleberry also serves a great veggie omelet for breakfast, sandwiches and salads for lunch, and an excellent cornmeal-dusted St. Mary's Lake whitefish for dinner. This is a good choice for vegetarians or those looking for something other than a Montana steak or hamburger, and the calorie-conscious will find several fat-free choices. If you've never had fry bread, then this is the place to try it. The decor is charming—a rugged pine motif—and the staff is very friendly.

1112 Park Dr., East Glacier. © **406/226-5523.** Breakfast items $5–$6; main courses $5–$7 lunch, $9–$15 dinner. DISC, MC, V. Daily 7am–9:30pm. Closed Oct–Apr.

Serrano's ★★★ MEXICAN In East Glacier, if you're going to eat only one dinner, eat it at Serrano's. The farther north you go, the warier you should be of Mexican restaurants. But Serrano's only claims a kind of Mexican-California-Southwest influence, and the food succeeds very well. The seafood enchilada, with shrimp and scallops, is excellent, especially when accompanied by one of the restaurant's fabulous margaritas. Or, if you prefer, have a beer from their large selection of microbrews. Serrano's has an outstanding local reputation, so don't be surprised if you encounter masses of people during the height of summer.

29 Dawson Ave., East Glacier. © **406/226-9392.** Reservations recommended. Main courses $8–$14. DISC, MC, V. Daily 5–10pm. Closed Oct–Apr.

IN POLEBRIDGE
Northern Lights Saloon ★ *Finds* AMERICAN Polebridge is where the serious Glacier outdoorspeople hang out. And the Northern Lights Saloon is where they go to have a beer and a burger. In the dictionary, under the phrase "middle of nowhere," there's a picture of Polebridge (or at least there should be). Despite that, this small restaurant, located squarely in the middle of Polebridge, gets enough customers in summer that you actually may have to wait for a table. The fact that there are only four or five tables exacerbates the problem. The customers are usually folks who have spent the last few days in the backcountry,

on the river, or in one of the primitive lodging choices that Polebridge offers. The saloon is a classic Old West-style hangout. The food consists of burgers (including turkey and falafel burgers) plus other basic American grub.

Polebridge (next to the Polebridge Mercantile). ✆ **406/888-5669.** Main courses $9–$13. MC, V. Memorial Day to Labor Day, daily 11am–2pm and 4–9pm; off-season hr. vary, usually open weekends only, so call ahead.

IN ST. MARY

Snowgoose Grille ⟨★⟩   Located in St. Mary Lodge (see "Where to Stay," above), the Snowgoose Grille is a high-priced alternative to park food. The ambience is upscale for these parts—a glass-enclosed dining room with views of the mountains and the creek. The restaurant specializes in elegant preparation of Montana-style food like wild boar, elk medallions, buffalo, and their signature fresh St. Mary Lake whitefish. They are aided in these efforts by having their own bakery, butcher shop, and smokehouse, and they make their own buffalo sausage, hot dogs, and jerky. Lunch entrees include typical restaurant sandwiches with fancy names like the "Garden Wall," filled with such diverse items as turkey and buffalo steak. The dinner menu features Montana ground buffalo steak, lake whitefish, and prime rib.

At the St. Mary Lodge, U.S. 89 and Going-to-the-Sun Rd., St. Mary, MT 59417. ✆ **800/368-3689** or 406/732-4431. Fax 406/732-9265. www.glcpark.com. Breakfast items $4.75–$9.25; lunch $6–$9; dinner main courses $12–$28. AE, DISC, MC, V. Mid-summer daily 7–10am, 11am–3pm, and 5–10pm; shorter hr. at the beginning and end of the season. Closed Oct 2 to Mother's Day.

IN WEST GLACIER

The nightlife in West Glacier consists primarily of long walks, or having a beer at the bar portion of the **West Glacier Restaurant and Bar,** a hangout for locals that they call "Frieda's." It's very friendly, and you may find yourself drafted as a partner for a game of pool.

The Belton Tap Room and Grille AMERICAN   This restaurant, located in restored buildings that were once the Great Northern Railroad Chalet, serves up respectable food geared toward American tastes—steaks, buffalo, chicken, ribs, trout, and salmon. And although this place is deep within the heart of the meat-and-potatoes Rockies, steamed vegetables come with the meal. A large stone fireplace dominates the taproom, which serves several kinds of brewed-in-Montana beers.

12575 U.S. 2, West Glacier (across from the west entrance to the park and from the Glacier Amtrak Station). ✆ **406/888-5000.** Dinner $9–$25. AE, MC, V. Daily 5–10pm (bar open daily 3pm–midnight).

Glacier Highlander Restaurant ⟨★⟩ ⟨Value⟩ AMERICAN   This is the spot to satisfy the sweet tooth; a baker is on hand, so the pies are well worth the stop, and the cinnamon rolls are breakfast giants. The Highland Burger is, by any standard, a great hunk of beef, and the fresh trout is a dinner specialty.

U.S. 2, West Glacier (across from the west entrance to the park and from the Glacier Amtrak Station). ✆ **406/888-5427.** Breakfast items $3–$6.50; lunch $5–$7; dinner main courses $4.75–$19. DISC, MC, V. Daily 7am–10pm. Closed mid-Nov to Mar.

Heaven's Peak Dining and Spirits ⟨★★⟩ AMERICAN   This restaurant, in a massive log building, has a wonderful atmosphere, with a huge deck that overlooks a beautiful sculpted rock garden and manicured lawns. The only negative is that there's a bit too much road noise, but the beautiful views into Glacier National Park help compensate. The chef uses only fresh ingredients; gardens have been planted to provide vegetables and fruit. Dinners here are especially healthy—you won't find anything deep-fried on the menu—and include the highly recommended fresh fish, as well as pasta, chicken, buffalo (another of our favorites), beef, and roast duck.

12130 U.S. 2, West Glacier. © **406/387-4754.** thepeak@cyberport.net. Reservations not accepted. Main dinner courses $12–$22. AE, DISC, MC, V. Daily 5–10pm.

ESSENTIAL SERVICES

EAST GLACIER   The **Glacier Park Trading Company** (© **406/226-4433**), on U.S. 2, has a limited supply of fresh and canned goods. There's a shop in the back where you can purchase freshly made deli sandwiches. Also in East Glacier is a gas station, post office, several gift shops, a small market with a limited supply of fresh meats and produce as well as beer and wine, and a modest supply of fishing and camping accessories.

WEST GLACIER   A gas station, general store, laundromat, photo shop, rafting companies, post office, gift shop, bar, and restaurant are located just outside the West Glacier entrance to the park.

ST. MARY   The **St. Mary Supermart** (© **406/732-4431**) will never be confused with a metropolitan area supermarket, but it's the closest thing you will find in any of the park gateway cities except Kalispell, which is 80 miles (129km) due west. Fresh produce, canned goods, and beverages, including beer and wine, will be found here, but you can expect to pay tourist-town prices. There's also a post office.

8 A Side Trip to Browning & the Blackfeet Indian Reservation

127 miles (205km) NW of Great Falls; 68 miles (110km) E of West Glacier; 160 miles (258km) W of Havre

According to American Indian legend, the Blackfeet were named because their moccasins were blackened with soot from fires or paint. Siksika, the "Black-footed People," became their tribal name, and they eventually grew into four bands: the Blackfeet in Montana and the Kaina, Pikani, and Siksika of Alberta, Canada. Today the Blackfeet maintain a humble existence near the beautiful lands that were once their own, with about half of the tribal enrollment of 14,000 living on the reservation near the east side of Glacier National Park. **Browning,** the tribal headquarters, is a gateway town to Glacier, but many visitors pass through quickly in anticipation of the end of the prairies and the beginning of the mountains.

ESSENTIALS

GETTING THERE   To reach Browning, follow U.S. 89 south from St. Mary 32 miles (52km), or take U.S. 2, 12 miles (19km) east of East Glacier. Browning is about 69 miles (111km) east of West Glacier on U.S. 2.

SPECIAL EVENTS   Browning holds **North American Indian Days** in mid-July. This 4-day celebration draws visitors from across the region to view American Indian dance competitions, games, and sporting events at the Blackfeet Tribal Campgrounds, which are adjacent to the **Museum of the Plains Indian.**

WHAT TO SEE & DO

The **Museum of the Plains Indian** is a fairly modest effort, but it has one of the best collections of Indian dress in the West. It also features some very good art by local Blackfeet artists. June through September there is a $4 fee for adults, $1 for children ages 6 to 12. The rest of the year it's free.

A **Blackfeet Historic Site Tour** is offered daily through Blackfeet Tours and Encampment. Half- and full-day tours depart from the **Museum of the Plains Indian,** and pickups can be arranged from any of the park's hotels, lodges, or campgrounds in either the St. Mary or East Glacier area. For information on these and other programs—including arts and crafts workshops, Blackfeet Elders Storytelling Campfires, or mini-powwows—contact **Blackfeet Tours and Encampment,** Box 271, Babb, MT 59401 (*©* **800/215-2395**).

A large and eclectic art collection is on display at the intersection of U.S. Highways 2 and 89, in the **Bob Scriver Hall of Bronze** (*©* **406/338-5425**). The building does not look like an art gallery—it looks more like a warehouse on its last legs. The 20-foot-tall, 15-foot-long bucking horse and cowboy, and the equally impressive Brahma bull and bullrider that are in front of the building are both products of Bob Scriver, who has been called "the foremost sculptor in America" by H. McCracken, curator of the Whitney Gallery of Western Art. Scriver did 1,200 bronzes over a 47-year career. He died in January 1999 at the age of 84. The museum consists of two segments: a wildlife exhibit—Scriver started out as a taxidermist—and the bronze section. There are hundreds of bronzes here, arranged by subject: rodeo, animals, Indians, and so on. Admission costs $5. You can spend more if you want to, though. The bronzes are for sale, at prices ranging from $250 to $150,000.

9 A Side Trip to Waterton Lakes National Park

190 miles (306km) NW of Great Falls; 342 miles (551km) S of Edmonton, Alberta

Waterton Lakes National Park and Glacier are in many ways one park separated by an international boundary. The terrain is much the same. But Canada is a foreign country, and you'll be pleasantly reminded of that in a visit to Waterton, where you can still get British high tea and a biscuit, if you're so inclined.

Waterton is where the Canadian mountains meet the vast rolling prairies, so there's an incredible variety of flowers and animals here. As you travel along the high ridge you'll see meadows and boggy areas that are ideal habitat for moose; later, you'll find yourself surrounded by lakes, as the Canadian Rockies fill the horizon. The area is also a haven for elk, mule deer, and bighorn sheep, and both grizzly and black bears are found in the park.

Compared to its counterparts in the Lower 48, Waterton is a tiny park; the total size is only 203 square miles. However, the park has great historical significance: Based on more than 200 identified archaeological sites, historians think that Aborigines first populated the area 11,000 years ago.

The parks have been designated the Waterton/Glacier International Peace Parks to commemorate the "long history of peace and friendship" between the United States and Canada. Waterton Lakes was made a national park in 1895, with Glacier being designated 15 years later. The joint international designation came in 1932, and in 1995, the peace park became a World Heritage site.

ESSENTIALS

American and Canadian money is freely accepted in both Glacier and Waterton. Stores provide change in the local currency after adjusting for the current exchange-rate differential.

GETTING THERE   From the eastern entrance of Glacier National Park at St. Mary, drive north through Babb, until you reach the intersection of Mont. 17— it's very well marked. Head northwest to the Canadian border, where Mont. 17

becomes Alberta 6 (remember, you need proof of citizenship—and a driver's license doesn't always work). Head down into the valley until you reach the park entrance on your left.

FEES & BACKCOUNTRY PERMITS   Park entrance costs C$4 (US$2.80) per person, at a maximum of C$8 (US$5.60) per vehicle. Day hiking does not require a permit, but backcountry overnight trips do, at a cost of C$6 (US$4.20) per person per day. Permits may be obtained at the visitor center up to 24 hours in advance of your trip, or they may be reserved by calling ✆ 403/859-5133.

VISITOR INFORMATION   The Visitor Reception Centre is just inside the park, on the same road you used coming in (✆ 403/859-5133).

EXPLORING THE PARK

Unlike most "park villages," Waterton village actually is a village. It looks like it would be a nice place to live. As you cruise the perimeter of the lake headed for Waterton Village, you'll pass three large lakes, the habitat of bald eagles that are often perched atop the snags of dead trees. The park bears a striking resemblance to Grand Teton National Park in Wyoming in that its attractions spread across a narrow valley floor. But the valley is narrower and three-fourths of it surrounded by peaks, so the overall effect is cozier, but equally dramatic.

By most standards, it's also windier here—though locals say that they don't acknowledge the wind unless there are whitecaps in the restroom toilets at the Prince of Wales Hotel (see "Where to Stay," below). The Prince of Wales actually does sway noticeably in a high wind, although signs assure us that it is not a concern.

Hiking, biking, and boating on the lake are the most popular pastimes. Most of the 120 miles (193km) of trails are easily accessible from town. They range in difficulty from short strolls to steep treks for overnight backcountry enthusiasts.

BIKING   All of Waterton's roads are open for bicycling, but because they are shared with automobiles, they are narrow and potentially hazardous. Waterton allows biking on some trails. Check at the visitor center to find out which ones.

HIKING   The first thing a lot of people do at Waterton Park is hike the **Bear's Hump Trail** 𝕽𝕽. It is the park's most popular path—but not necessarily the easiest. The trail starts at the visitor center. Only about three-quarters of a mile (1km) long, it gains 700 feet in elevation from bottom to top. That is steep, squared. You'll be rewarded with a panoramic view of the park. The hike is called Bear's Hump because of the shape of the mountain, not because you're likely to run into bears—though, of course, you never know.

Right at the edge of Waterton Park, at **Cameron Falls,** Cambrian rocks are exposed from the period 600 million years ago when life exploded on earth. This is the oldest exposed formation in the Rocky Mountains. The falls are spectacular, too.

For nearly 20 years, the 10½-mile (17km) **Crypt Lake Trail** 𝕽𝕽𝕽 has been rated as one of Canada's best hikes—except for those prone to seasickness, since the trail head is reached by taking a 2-mile (3km) boat ride across Upper Waterton Lake. Contact **Waterton InterNation Shoreline Cruises** (✆ 403/859-2362) for details regarding the boat shuttle. After that, the trail leads past Hellroaring Falls, Twin Falls, and Burnt Rock Falls before reaching Crypt Falls and a passage through a 60-foot rock tunnel. The elevation gain is 2,300 feet, but veterans say the hike is doable in 3 hours, one way.

A second extended tour starts at the marina and heads south across the international boundary to **Goat Haunt,** Montana, an especially popular trip because of the sightings of bald eagles, bear, bighorn sheep, deer, and moose, as well as numerous unusual geologic formations.

The **International Peace Park Hike** is a free guided trip held on Saturdays from the end of June to the end of August. Participants meet at the Bertha trail head at 10am and spend the day on an 8½-mile (14km) trail that follows Upper Waterton Lake. At the end of the trail, hikers return via boat to the main dock. Adult fare is C$10 (US$7); children's fare is C$5 (US$3.50).

There is a wonderful nature trail in **Red Rock Canyon,** a short, easy trek through time—0.7 miles (1km), 65 million years—when the shallow sea that once lay here exposed and then oxidized mudstone rock to the color of a merlot. The rocks are banded with white slashes through the formations, portions that didn't oxidize because they were not exposed to the air from the receding and returning sea. The Red Rock Canyon Road is also an area of fairly frequent bear sightings.

WHERE TO STAY

For complete lodging information, contact **central reservations** for the Waterton area (☎ **800/215-2395;** www.watertonchamber.com/lodging).

While the **Prince of Wales Hotel** (see below) is clearly the flagship on this lake, alternative arrangements can be made at **Kilmorey Lodge** (☎ **403/ 859-2334**). This cozy country inn on Emerald Bay, at the north end of the lake, has an antique decor. Bedrooms have down comforters and a dining room and lounge are on the premises. The **Waterton Lake Lodge** (☎ **888/985-6343** or 403/859-2151) opened in July 1997. Located in the heart of Waterton Village, the lodge offers lake and mountain views, and some rooms have fireplaces, whirlpool tubs, and kitchenettes. Other facilities include a health center, spa, and indoor pool.

The Prince of Wales Hotel ✿✿✿   The stunning Prince of Wales compares to the finest park hostelries in Montana and Wyoming. Built in 1927 by the Great Northern Railway, the hotel boasts soaring roofs, gables, and balconies that convey the appearance of a giant alpine chalet. Rooms, though small, have aged well, with dark-stained, high-paneled wainscoting and heavily upholstered chairs. Standard rooms have double beds and/or twins; suites have king-size beds. Bathrooms have European-style tubs with wraparound curtains and tiny wash basins. Our choice here would be one of the pricey lakeside rooms (or one of the elegant suites, which also face the lake). Those on a budget should ask about the rooms facing the mountains, which are the lowest-priced units in the hotel. Rates from opening through about the first 2 weeks of June are considerably lower than rates the rest of the season.

The lobby, like many of the old railroad hotels, is wood, wood, and more wood—in this case accented by tufted furniture and carpeting. Two-story-tall windows overlook the lake and village, only minutes away by footpath. If you don't spend the night at the Prince of Wales, at least stop in for a traditional British afternoon tea, served daily from 2 to 5pm in the hotel lobby. All in all, the experience is very European—the gift shop even sells English bone china and Waterford crystal. The entire facility is no-smoking.

Waterton Lakes National Park, AB T0K 2M0. ☎ **403/859-2231,** or 406/756-2444 in winter. Fax 403/ 859-2630. www.glacierparkinc.com. 87 units. US$183–US$347 double; US$614–US$799 suite. MC, V. Closed late Sept to late May. **Amenities:** Restaurant (see below), tearoom, bar, gift shop.

CAMPING

At the west end of the village is **Townsite Campground** 🐾, a Parks Canada–operated facility with 235 sites that's an especially popular jumping-off spot for campers headed into the park's backcountry. Prices range from C$15 (US$10.50) to C$23 (US$16.10); half of the sites have electricity and sewage disposal; also available on the premises are kitchen shelters, washrooms, and shower facilities. The site is perched right on the lake, so views are excellent and trails await evening strollers. The campground is open from late April to early October.

There are 10 designated **wilderness campgrounds** with dry toilets and surface water, some of which have shelters, charging C$6 (US$4.20).

WHERE TO DINE

All of the village's restaurants are within a 4-block area around Waterton Avenue (which the locals call Main Street). So despite the fact that many buildings aren't numbered, you'll have no problem finding places to eat or shop.

The **Windflower Dining Room** (© 403/859-2151) at the Waterton Lake Lodge offers casual dining and spectacular views. The **Garden Court Dining Room** 🐾🐾 at the Prince of Wales Hotel (see "Where to Stay," above) serves a breakfast buffet daily from 6:30 to 9:30am, and traditional English and continental fare for lunch (daily 11:30am–2pm) and dinner (5–9:30pm).

You'll find luxurious surroundings, and slightly higher prices, at **Kootenai Brown Dining Room** 🐾🐾 (© 403/859-2211), at the Bayshore Inn, considered the luxury spot on the lake. You'll find steaks, chicken, rack of lamb, and the occasional seafood entree. **New Frank's Restaurant** (© 403/859-2240) serves conventional western fare that includes beef, chicken, and spaghetti, as well as a Chinese menu that includes an all-you-can-eat evening buffet.

5

Missoula, the Flathead & the Northwest Corner

The northwest corner of Montana is the mythological Montana, the one you probably wanted to visit when you set out for the Big Sky. This is the country of snowcapped mountains and crystal lakes. It's a land of barely explored wilderness and steel-toed lumberjacks, a land peopled with the ghosts of trappers, mountain men, and Blackfeet Indians.

It's also a booming recreational area. The central point of the region is Flathead Lake, which boasts the somewhat cumbersome distinction of being the "Largest Natural Freshwater Lake West of the Mississippi." The lake was gouged during the last glaciation about 12,000 years ago. It is very deep in places—386 feet out toward the middle—with 128 miles (206km) of shoreline, much of it taken up by vacation homes. Anglers will appreciate the fact that trophy trout, salmon, perch, and whitefish all take up residence here. And vacationers seeking a quiet getaway will be pleased by the fact that despite the busy summer season on the lake, it doesn't feel crowded, and there are plenty of places to get out of earshot of everyone.

Besides Flathead Lake, there's hiking, biking, fishing, boating, golf, parasailing, and nearly any other outdoor activity known to man in the area from Whitefish to Missoula. In winter, there are fine alpine ski areas, excellent cross-country skiing, snowshoeing, snowboarding, and innertubing accessible north to south.

Also here is the nation's largest wilderness complex, the **Bob Marshall-Great Bear-Scapegoat Wilderness,** which includes some of the most rugged, beautiful, untrammeled country in the Lower 48 states. The magnificent Chinese Wall, a vast monolith on the spine of the Continental Divide, is a symbol of wilderness in Montana, as is the grizzly bear, the king of the wild lands even when humans venture in for a visit.

1 Scenic Drives

Two major roads run through the northwest corner: U.S. 93, which runs north to south, and U.S. 2, which runs east to west. Mont. 200, one of the state's most scenic drives, bisects the lower section of the region.

U.S. 93 heads north from the Bitterroot Valley south of Missoula to the Canadian border. Much of the road slices beneath jagged peaks poking at the skyline. It's especially pretty early in the morning or early evening, when the light softens the rugged landscape. North of Missoula in the Flathead Valley near St. Ignatius and the spectacular Mission Mountains, the valley opens. At **Polson,** you've reached the southern portion of Flathead Lake, which stretches 28 miles (45km) to the north. In some places it is 8 miles (13km) wide. North

Northwest Montana

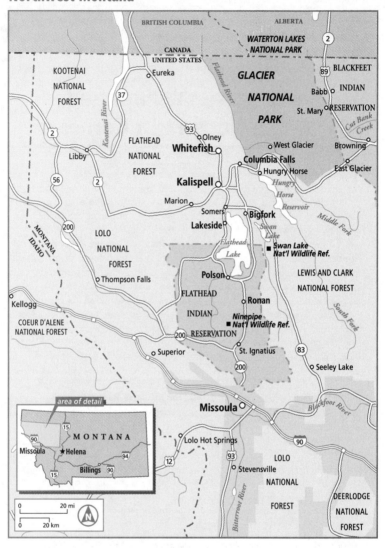

of the lake are Kalispell, Whitefish, and Columbia Falls, gateway towns to nearby Glacier National Park. The last oasis in Montana is the border village of Eureka, just minutes south of the Canadian border.

Plan on spending an afternoon making your way around Flathead Lake, which is ringed by snowcapped mountains and bright blue skies. On the east side, you can pick ripe cherries and explore the art galleries and Western boutiques of Bigfork. On the west side, you might sample a creamy huckleberry shake, poke through the antiques stores, and visit an award-winning winery.

2 Missoula ⟨★⟩

200 miles (322km) E of Spokane, Washington; 213 miles (343km) NE of Lewiston, Idaho; 339 miles (546km) W of Billings; 115 miles (185km) NW of Helena; 115 miles (185km) S of Kalispell

Missoula's current marketing slogan is "We Like It Here," and it's pretty obvious that they do. The reason is clear—Missoula is in a beautiful valley along the Clark Fork River, with a relatively mild climate that is more influenced by the Pacific Northwest than the high Rockies.

Since this is the home of the University of Montana, the crowds in Missoula's vibrant downtown are young and Birkenstocked rather than grizzled and cowboy-booted. Also in the mix are many prominent Western writers that live in or near the city; the result is an intellectual and cultural outpost.

The great outdoors—be it fly-fishing on the Bitterroot, downhill skiing, hiking in the Selway-Bitterroot, or cross-country skiing on Lolo Pass—is probably what most attracts these types to the area. The outdoors figures heavily in Missoula-area politics as well. There is a strong pro-environment sentiment among the populace.

ESSENTIALS

GETTING THERE   **Delta** (© 800/221-1212), **Horizon** (© 800/547-9308), **SkyWest** (© 800/453-9417), **United** (© 800/241-6522), and **Northwest** (© 800/225-2525) all have flights into the Missoula International Airport at **Johnson-Bell Field** (© 406/728-4381), northwest of downtown on U.S. 93.

I-90 leads into Missoula from the west (Washington State and Idaho) and the east (Billings and Bozeman). From Salt Lake City, I-15 leads up through Idaho and intersects with I-90 at Butte. For information on **road conditions** in Missoula, call © **406/728-8553.** For statewide conditions, call © **800/332-6171.** Avalanche information can be obtained by calling either the **Lolo National Forest Weekend Report** (© **406/549-4488**) or the **U.S.D.A. Forest Service** (© **800/281-1030**).

The bus terminal, 1660 W. Broadway (© **406/549-2339**), is served by **Greyhound** (© **800/231-2222**) for national travel and **Rimrock Stages** (© **800/255-7655**), which serves intrastate Montana travelers.

VISITOR INFORMATION   The **Missoula Convention and Visitors Bureau,** 825 E. Front (© **800/526-3465** or 406/543-6623; www.missoulachamber.com), has brochures, city maps, and area maps for outdoor activities, shopping, dining, and tours for most of northwestern Montana.

GETTING AROUND   Several rental-car agencies, including **Avis** (© 800/831-2847), **Budget** (© 406/543-7001), **Hertz** (© 800/654-3131), and **National** (© 800/227-7368), maintain counters at the airport; or try **Rent-a-Wreck,** 1905 W. Broadway (© 800/535-1391 or 406/721-3838). **Airport Shuttler** (© 406/543-9416) operates a transit service to and from the airport.

Missoula's city bus line is **Mountain Line Transit** (© **406/721-3333;** www.mountainline.com). It doesn't run late at night or on Sundays.

Taxi service is available 24 hours a day through **Yellow Cab, Inc.** (© **406/543-6644**).

ORIENTATION   Missoula's layout is a tad confusing, so make sure you have a good city map. Remember that downtown is bisected by the Clark Fork River, and become acquainted with the locations of the three bridges, which provide access to the university and points south. Trails alongside the river are suitable for strolling, though you'll share them with runners and bikers.

Baseball Under the Stars

Missoula is home to minor league baseball's **Missoula Osprey,** an affiliate of the Arizona Diamondbacks in the Pioneer League. As of this writing, ground had just been broken on a new downtown ballpark that the team hopes to occupy by summer 2002. The $6 million Missoula Civic Stadium will be located at the site of the former Champion lumber mill at Hickory Street and Craig Lane, just south of the Clark Fork River. For ticket information, call ☎ **406/543-3300** or visit www.missoulaosprey.com.

SPECIAL EVENTS   The International Wildlife Film Festival 🐾 founded by internationally known bear biologist Dr. Charles Jonkel in 1977, recognizes scientific accuracy, artistic appeal, and technical excellence through a juried competition. Highlights of the 1-week festival, held annually in early April, include three daily screenings, workshops and panel discussions, a wildlife photo contest, and various wildlife art displays. Contact the festival at Fort Missoula (☎ **406/728-9380;** www.wildlifefilms.org) for details.

Out to Lunch at Caras Park (☎ **406/543-4238**) is a popular summer series featuring live entertainment and numerous food vendors from 11am to 1:30pm every Wednesday June through August. Missoula's carousel is also located at this riverfront park (see below).

GETTING OUTSIDE

One of the first things you notice if you look up in Missoula is a giant "M" on Mount Sentinel. The trail to the M is a popular hike, a steep zigzag that rewards the determined hiker with panoramic views of the valley. Mount Sentinel is also a favorite spot for hang gliding. You can obtain information and maps of recreation areas before leaving town at the **Bureau of Land Management,** 3255 Fort Missoula Rd. (☎ **406/329-3914**).

ORGANIZED ADVENTURES

Venture West Vacations (☎ **406/825-6200;** P.O. Box 7543, Missoula, MT 59807) arranges a variety of Montana- and Idaho-area adventures, primarily horsepacking, fishing, hunting, rafting, backpacking, cabin rentals, and dude-ranch visits. **Adventure Connections** (☎ **406/549-5034;** www.montanatravel. com) is another recommended four-season outfitter, offering a similar variety of trips as Venture West. **10,000 Waves** (☎ **800/537-8315** or 406/549-6670; www.10000-waves.com), presents an opportunity to go hiking or rafting and absorb some Montana history in the process. The company offers two tours that focus on **Garnet Ghost Town,** one of the best-preserved old mining camps in the West. This collection of old wooden buildings offers the look and feel of a mining camp from a hundred years ago. The roads up to Garnet are dirt and treacherous. The road from the south is particularly rough; the road leading in from the north through the **Lubrecht Experimental Forest** has a number of spectacular views of the valley below.

BIKING

The best place to cycle is at the **Rattlesnake National Recreation Area.** To get there, drive northeast on Van Buren to Rattlesnake Drive. Be sure to consult one of the free trail maps available at bike shops before setting out. Bikes are prohibited in the wilderness portion of the recreation area. **Montana Snowbowl**

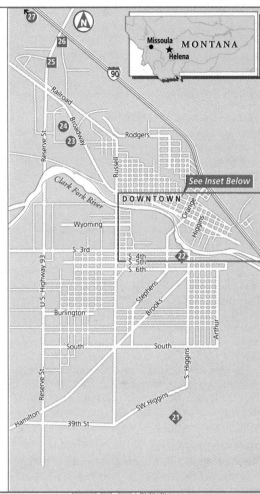

ACCOMMODATIONS ■
- Best Western Grant Creek Inn **26**
- Doubletree Hotel Missoula–Edgewater **18**
- Goldsmith's Inn **19**
- Red Lion Inn **1**
- Traveler's Inn **25**

ATTRACTIONS ●
- Aerial Fire Depot & Smoke-jumper Center **24**
- Art Museum of Missoula **4**
- Historic Ninemile Remount Depot Visitor Center **27**
- Historical Museum at Fort Missoula **10**
- Missoula Carousel **15**
- Rocky Mountain Elk Foundation **23**

DINING/NIGHTLIFE ◆
- Al and Vic's **3**
- Bernice's Bakery **22**
- The Bridge **14**
- Butterfly Herbs **17**
- The Depot **2**
- El Cazador **16**
- Hob Nob **11**
- Iron Horse Brew Pub **5**
- Kadena's **9**
- Marianne's at the Wilma **13**
- New Black Dog Cafe **8**
- Oxford Cafe **7**
- Red Bird **12**
- Sean Kelly's **6**
- Shadows Keep **21**

SERVICES ●
- The Missoula Chamber of Commerce **20**

See Inset Below

DOWNTOWN

Downtown Missoula

ski area also has trails for the serious mountain biker. For information, contact
📞 406/549-9777. To rent bikes, contact **Open Road Bicycles and Nordic
Equipment,** 517 S. Orange St. (📞 **406/549-2453**); or **Bicycle Hangar,** 1801
Brooks St. (📞 **406/728-9537**). In summer, **Snowbowl** (see "Downhill Skiing,"
below) offers mountain biking. You and your bike can ride the lift to the top, or
you can pedal on trails at the base. Five bike trails range from intermediate to
expert in difficulty, and from 1 to 8 miles (2–13km) in length.

CROSS-COUNTRY SKIING

There are hundreds of square miles of cross-country ski terrain within 30 miles
(48km) of Missoula. In nearby Garnet, the absence of gold turned a once-
prosperous mining town into a ghost town that's now become a magnet for
cross-country skiers at the **Garnet Resource Area.** With more than 50 miles
(81km) of trails and a remote location, this area offers a delightful backcountry
experience. And while out there, many like to stay in Garnet's **old-fashioned
miner's cabins** (see "Where to Stay," later in this chapter). Getting there can be
an arduous task in winter. Take I-90 east to Mont. 200, turn east for 5 miles
(8km) to Garnet Range Road, then go south along the Forest Service Road.

There are 150 miles (242km) of marked cross-country ski trails scattered
through the Lolo National Forest (📞 **406/329-3814**). Popular areas include
Pattee Canyon, Seeley Lake, and **Lolo Pass.** The Pattee Canyon Complex, 5½
miles (9km) south of town, offers several trails that range in difficulty from a
short 1.6-kilometer (1 mile) trail to a longer 5.4-kilometer trail (3¼ miles), but
don't count on them being groomed. At Lolo Pass, there's a National Forest
information center at the top of the pass with maps and permit sales. To get
there, take U.S. 12 west from Lolo for about 30 miles (48km).

The **Lubrecht Experimental Forest** is operated by the University of
Montana's Forestry Department (📞 **406/243-5521**) and has six ski trails. To
reach Lubrecht from Missoula, take I-90 east to exit 109 and follow Mont. 200
northeast to Greenough. Turn right just past the post office, and less than a half-
mile (1km) down that road is the Lubrecht camp.

DOWNHILL SKIING

Marshall Mountain Ski Area   Marshall is an unassuming ski hill as these
things go, not too steep. It's popular with families, and is an excellent place for
youngsters to learn to ski. Because of its lower, warmer elevation, its season is a
little shorter than Snowbowl's (see below). The night skiing for $12 is a bargain.

Take I-90 east to Mont. 200 and proceed northeast for 7 miles (11km). 📞 406/258-6000. www.marshall-
mountain.com. Lift tickets $19 adults, $15 students, $10 children. Open daily Nov–Apr.

Montana Snowbowl   There are 2,600 feet of vertical drop at Snowbowl,
much of it in steep runs suitable only for experts. There's not a lot of terrain for
beginners here, but the hardcore skier will have a ball. Eighty percent of the runs
are for intermediate, expert, and advanced skiers, with another 700 acres for the
extreme skier. Snowbowl has 30 reasonably priced rooms for rent during the winter, most without private bathrooms. Rentals and instruction are also available.

From I-90, exit at Reserve St.; head north on Grant Creek Rd., and turn left on Snowbowl Rd. 📞 800/
728-2695 or 406/549-9777. www.montanasnowbowl.com. Lift tickets $30 adults, $13 children; senior, student, and half-day rates available. Open Fri–Sun late Nov to early Apr.

FISHING

The **Clark Fork River,** which runs through town, has had its share of environmental problems and concerns over the years. A cleanup effort that began in the

1970s has helped, but it's never going to be an angler's first choice. The **Bitterroot River** and **Rock Creek** are better bets. Though Rock Creek has been known as a blue-ribbon trout stream, the Bitterroot is also a good spot for those who want to pull in a trout or two, and it has multiple public-access areas near the highway. Rock Creek has a full-service campground at **Ekstrom's Stage Station,** a mile (2km) off I-90 on Rock Creek Road (© **406/825-3183**), with RV hookups, showers, toilets, a store, and a swimming pool. The Missoula office for the **Montana Department of Fish, Wildlife, and Parks,** 3201 Spurgin Rd. (© **406/542-5500**), will direct you to some fine fishing spots, including Siria, a more remote site 30 miles (48km) up Rock Creek Road.

Whether guiding you along Missoula's Clark Fork River or helping you pick out the perfect fly, **Grizzly Hackle,** 215 W. Front St. (© **800/297-8996** or 406/721-8996; www.grizzlyhackle.com) can help you with your fly-fishing vacation. Seasoned guides lead you to fishing holes along the Lower Clark Fork, the Bitterroot, and the Blackfoot Rivers, as well as Rock Creek, in search of native rainbow, Westslope cutthroat, and German browns. The company also runs the Lodge on Butler Creek, not far from Missoula, where rooms rent for $160 per night for two. Grizzly Hackle advocates barbless hooks and catch-and-release fishing, donating heavily to river restoration projects and angling-oriented charities.

GOLF

Farther north, there are a number of great golf courses, but in Missoula the golf is only average. The nine-hole **Highlands Golf Club,** located at 102 Ben Hogan Dr. (© **406/728-7360**), is a short, hilly, public course with wickedly gyrating greens. A round runs $12 to $15. The clubhouse is located in **Shadows Keep** (see "Where to Dine," below). Another nine-hole course is located on the **University of Montana** campus (© **406/728-8629**) with greens fees of $16 to $18. The **Larchmont Golf Course,** 3200 Old Fort Rd. (© **406/721-4416**), the only 18-hole public course within city limits, is a long, fairly tough track that the big hitters will like. Greens fees are $20.

HIKING

An easy hike follows the **Kim Williams Trail,** along either side of the Clark Fork River through downtown. The trail is named for a deceased, much-beloved newspaper columnist. Just outside of town is the **Rattlesnake National Recreational Area and Wilderness.** To get there, drive northeast on Van Buren to Rattlesnake Drive. The Rattlesnake covers 59,000 acres, 33,000 of which are congressionally designated wilderness. Camping is prohibited within 3 miles (5km) of the road because of the heavy use the area receives. Drive northeast on Van Buren to Rattlesnake Drive. For a copy of *Trails Missoula,* a free brochure listing your options, contact the Missoula Chamber of Commerce (© **406/543-6623**).

There are two state parks in the Missoula area: **Beavertail Hill** (© **406/542-5500**) is located on the Clark Fork and is open May through September, with excellent river access and shady cottonwood trees lining the river banks. There is a day-use charge of $4; campers pay $12 per night. **Council Grove State Park** (© **406/758-5200**) is where the Hellgate Treaty establishing the Flathead Indian Reservation was signed. Open for day use only, the park has interpretive displays and picnic facilities. Take the Reserve Street exit from I-90 and drive 2 miles (3km) south, then 10 miles (16km) west on Mullan Road.

The Lolo Trail is an interesting hike. This trail was created by the constant use of the Nez Perce, Salish, and other tribes who lived in the area and moved back and forth across Lolo Pass.

You can explore a half-mile (1km) section of the original trail at Howard Creek, 18 miles (29km) west of the intersection of U.S. 93 and U.S. 12 in Lolo. Or hike a 5-mile (8km) section of the trail from Lee Creek Campground to the Idaho border. The campground is about 26 miles (43km) west of the highway intersection in Lolo.

SNOWMOBILING

The areas around Missoula have more than 500 miles (805km) of groomed snowmobile trails in a number of popular areas. In Lolo Pass, for instance, there are 150 miles (242km) of groomed trails connecting the Lolo and Clearwater national forests. There are four other nearby designated areas—Superior, Skalkaho Pass, Seeley Lake, and Lincoln—each with approximately as many miles of groomed trails. For a guide to area snowmobiling, contact the Missoula Convention and Visitors Bureau (© **800/526-3465**).

WHITE-WATER RAFTING & KAYAKING

Lewis & Clark Trail Adventures, 912 E. Broadway (© **800/366-6246** or 406/728-7609; www.trailadventures.com), offers no-nonsense white-water rafting on the Salmon River during excursions through the heart of the Frank Church No Return Wilderness. The main trip is on a 120-mile (193km) stretch of Idaho white water, where you can expect to see mountain goats, bighorn sheep, elk, deer, eagles, and otters. Other excursions take in the Lochsa River, the Alberton Gorge of the Clark Fork River, and the Missouri River (through areas in which Lewis and Clark made their famous trek). Trips run May through September. Hiking, biking, and historic tours on the Lolo Trail are also available. Five- to seven-day trips on the Salmon River run from $449 to $1,015 per person, depending on dates and length. One-day trips on the Lochsa or through Alberton Gorge range from $45 to $99 per person. Guided hikes on the Lolo Trail are between $129 (day) and $318 (overnight) per person.

The Clark Fork and the Blackfoot Rivers are the settings for white-water adventure with **10,000 Waves** ⚓ (© **800/537-8315** or 406/549-6670; www.10000-waves.com). Half-day and full-day floats feature thrilling white-water rapids along high mountain rivers and through steep, narrow canyons. Half-day trips are $48 per person; full-day floats cost $74 (includes a great lunch). The company uses self-bailing rafts, which enable the paddler to focus on the sport, not survival. If you want an even bigger thrill, consider renting an inflatable kayak for a do-it-yourself adventure. Rates are $35 for 2 hours, $62 for a half day, and $82 for a full day. 10,000 Waves also offers a rafting and kayaking trip and guided tour of Garnet Ghost town for $90.

Western Waters and Woods (© **866/703-0301** or 406/251-5212; www.westernwaters.com) in nearby Superior is another good option, offering fly-fishing and hunting trips as well as rafting expeditions. Half-day trips run $55, full-day $75, and dinner trips (with a four-course meal featuring steak or salmon) are $85.

SEEING THE SIGHTS

You can organize your own tour and check out the architectural highlights of the "Garden City" by picking up a copy of the Chamber of Commerce brochure *Historical Walking/Driving Tour.* For further information, contact the **Missoula Historic Preservation Office** (© 406/523-4650).

The **Farmers Market** ⚓ at Market Plaza (© **406/777-2636** or 406/549-0315) is the place to be during summer for organic vegetables, fresh flowers, and a diverse collection of "Made in Montana" crafts and art objects. It's open Saturday from 9am to noon, as well as Tuesday evenings from 6 to 7:30pm.

Historical Museum at Fort Missoula   Fort Missoula, one of Montana's first military posts, was established in 1877, the year Chief Joseph of the Nez Perce led his tribe toward Canada. Now the home of the National Guard and Reserve units, Fort Missoula has as its main attraction this museum, which houses rotating exhibits in its indoor galleries. A self-guided tour takes you through a Western town as it existed at the end of the 19th century, along with several old buildings subsequently moved to the site—an 1880 carriage house, a homestead cabin, an 1863 church, and other buildings.

Building 322, Fort Missoula Rd. ℂ **406/728-3476.** www.montana.com/ftmslamuseum. $3 adults, $2 seniors, $1 students, free for children under 6. Memorial Day weekend–Labor Day weekend, Tues–Sat 10am–5pm, Sun noon–5pm; after Labor Day weekend–Memorial Day, Tues–Sat noon–5pm.

Aerial Fire Depot and Smokejumper Center   This is the nation's largest training base for smokejumpers—firefighters who parachute into remote areas of national forests to combat wildfires. This facility offers a fascinating look at the life of a Western firefighter, beginning with the days when pack animals were an important part of backcountry fire fighting, through the 1939 advent of the smokejumper, up to today's heroes. The Aerial Fire Depot Visitor Center features murals, educational videos, a reconstructed lookout tower, and exhibits of firefighters that illustrate the lives and history of these rescue workers. The center also talks about the important role of fire in forest ecology.

Adjacent to Missoula International Airport, U.S. 93. ℂ **406/329-4934.** Free admission. Memorial Day–Labor Day daily 8:30am–5pm. Tours available on the hr. beginning at 10am; no tours noon–2pm; last tour begins 4pm.

Historic Ninemile Remount Depot Visitor Center   This visitor center, along with the Smokejumper Center, will educate you in the early methods of rugged fire fighting in the Northern Rockies, when pack animals were a vital part of a firefighter's "equipment." Listed on the National Register of Historic Places, the depot appears today much as it did when the Civilian Conservation Corps constructed it in the 1930s, complete with live pack mules. All tours are self-guided.

22 miles (35km) west of Missoula on I-90, then 4 miles (6km) north of exit 82. ℂ **406/626-5201.** Free admission. Memorial Day–Labor Day daily 9am–5pm.

Art Museum of Missoula   Located downtown in the historic Carnegie Library, this museum's permanent collection includes 350 works by about 100 artists, with a special emphasis on art of the Western states. Changing exhibits feature regional, national, and international art; recent displays showcased works by ceramicist Rudy Autio and painter Russell Chatham, as well as pieces originating in the Far East and Latin America. Associated programs include films, concerts, lectures, tours, and children's events.

335 N. Pattee St. ℂ **406/728-0447.** www.artmissoula.org. Suggested donation $2. Tues and Fri noon–7pm; Wed and Thurs noon–6pm; Sat 10am–3pm.

Rocky Mountain Elk Foundation   Though a relatively young conservation organization, the Rocky Mountain Elk Foundation has made a large contribution to conserving elk and elk habitat. Voicing a hunter-as-conservationist philosophy, there is a display here of trophy elk heads—some with world record racks—and a diorama of the other animals that share elk habitat: bears, coyotes, mountain sheep, rabbits, and lynxes. There are also an art gallery, theater, and gift shop.

2291 W. Broadway. ℂ **800/225-5355** or 406/523-4545. www.elkfoundation.org. Free admission. Mon–Fri 8am–5pm; Sat–Sun 10am–4pm. Closed Sun in winter.

Kids Especially for Kids

A remarkable community effort, the **Missoula Carousel** (© 406/549-8382; www.carrousel.com) was a project begun with nothing more than unrealistic optimism. During planning, funding, and assembly stages of the project, Missoula relied on the kindness of others to make it happen. The hand-carved and hand-painted horses are the result of thousands of hours of labor from volunteer workers, most of whom were novices trained in the art of carving and painting. A treat for kids, adults will also marvel at this merry-go-round by the river at downtown's **Caras Park,** which is located at the spot where Higgins Avenue crosses the Clark Fork River. The carousel is open daily year-round, with 50¢ rides for children under 18 and seniors and $1 rides for adults.

SHOPPING

Global Village World Crafts, 519 S. Higgins Ave. (© 406/543-3955), is a project of the Jeannette Rankin Peace Resource Center, selling jewelry, clothing, and musical items from communities around the world. **Butterfly Herbs,** 232 N. Higgins Ave. (© 406/728-8780), features an eclectic collection of items, including fresh herbs, jewelry, coffee mugs, teapots, and handmade paper and candles. If you begin to feel the bohemian spirit and suddenly want your own pair of Birkenstocks, just go next door to **Hide & Sole,** 236 N. Higgins Ave. (© 406/549-0666), for re-shodding.

Pipestone Mountaineering, 101 S. Higgins Ave. (© 406/721-1670), has an excellent range of outdoor gear for serious climbers, river runners, and campers. **The Trailhead,** 110. E. Pine St. (© 406/543-6966), is another good outdoors store, with gear for snowshoers, kayakers, and just about everybody in between.

Missoula is home to an impressive literary community, and the city's bookstores are among the state's best, including **Fact and Fiction,** 220 N. Higgins Ave. (© 406/721-2881). There's also a **Barnes & Noble** branch at 2640 N. Reserve St. (© 406/721-0009). The largest newsstand in Missoula is the **Garden City News,** 329 N. Higgins Ave. (© 406/543-3470), which specializes in daily newspapers from both coasts, as well as from the Rocky Mountain area. Vintage, rare, and first-edition books are available from **Bird's Nest Books** (© 406/721-1125) at 219 N. Higgins Ave.

If you're looking for clothes, the **Bon Marche,** 110 N. Higgins Ave. (© 406/542-6000), is an old standard and Missoula's only downtown department store. **Rainbow's End,** at 113 W. Main St. (© 406/829-1800), is the last refuge of hippie clothing for women.

If you haven't found that perfect Montana gift yet, try the **Moose Creek Mercantile,** 314 N. Higgins Ave. (© 406/543-6503), which offers a vast selection, much of it in wildlife themes.

Monte Dolack is one of the best-known artists in Montana. His often-humorous posters and prints are available at 139 W. Front St. in the **Monte Dolack Gallery** (© 406/549-3248). The gallery also features works of other prominent Montana artists, including Mary Beth Percival. Other worthwhile galleries include **Art Attic,** 123 South Ave. W. (© 406/728-5500), and the **Museum of Fine Arts** in the PAR/TV Building on the campus of the University of Montana (© 406/243-2019).

WHERE TO STAY

You won't find a whole lot of lodging variety within Missoula's city limits: It's dominated by chains, with a smattering of independents and Victorian-era B&Bs. For a distinctive night's sleep, try roughing it in a historic cabin. Information on rental of **old-fashioned miner's cabins** at the ghost town of Garnet is available by contacting the **Garnet Preservation Association,** Box 20029, Missoula, MT 59801-0029 (© **406/329-1031**). Rustic cabins and lookouts are available for rent through the **National Forest Service,** 200 E. Broadway (P.O. Box 779), Missoula, MT 59807 (© **406/329-3511**). Get information on camping at Missoula's **Bureau of Land Management,** 3255 Fort Missoula Rd., Missoula, MT 59804 (© **406/329-3914**).

HOTELS & MOTELS

Best Western Grant Creek Inn   Situated close to a freeway off-ramp, this Best Western is a relatively new property in Missoula. The quality of the rooms and services is what you'd normally associate with a higher-priced chain. There are a good variety of options here. Deluxe suites have a fireplace, two television sets, a dining area, a desk, a closet, and a view. Conventional rooms have two queens or one king bed. There are several restaurants and bars nearby.

5280 Grant Creek Rd. (I-90, exit 101), Missoula, MT 59802. © 888/543-0700 or 406/543-0700. Fax 406/543-0777. 126 units. $99–$159 double. Rates include continental breakfast. AE, DC, DISC, MC, V. **Amenities:** Indoor pool; exercise room; sauna. *In room:* A/C, TV, dataport, coffeemaker, hair dryer, iron.

Doubletree Hotel Missoula-Edgewater ✲   This is the premier hotel facility in Missoula. Located on the north bank of the Clark Fork, the more expensive units offer a large room with a beautiful view of the river and the University of Montana. Rooms on the second level have balconies, some overlooking the swimming pool. The property is geared toward business travelers, with meeting rooms and business services available. The lobby area is nicely finished, with a gift shop that sells Western American souvenirs, clothing, and trinkets. The Edgewater dining room, serving lunch and dinner, is just off the lobby. The wooden deck outside the lounge is a fine spot for a cocktail over the Clark Fork River.

100 Madison St., Missoula, MT 59802. © 800/222-8733 or 406/728-3100. 171 units. $109–$129 double. AE, DISC, MC, V. **Amenities:** Restaurant, lounge; outdoor pool; exercise room; outdoor Jacuzzi. *In room:* A/C, TV, dataport, coffeemaker, hair dryer, iron.

The Fort at Lolo Trail Center and Lolo Hot Springs *(Finds)*   This hot-springs resort, 25 miles (40km) west of Lolo and only 7 miles (11km) from the Montana-Idaho border, is an especially popular winter destination—the cross-country skiing on Lolo Pass is excellent, as is the snowmobiling. The Fort has recently upgraded its facilities, adding a large new building that houses the educational Lewis & Clark Exhibition Center, two hot tubs utilizing natural spring water, a dinner theater, and a convention center. Since the fabled hot springs are a separate operation, there's a fee to soak in them.

There are 18 rooms in the lodge and 16 in a motel-style unit. It's called the Fort because the design is reminiscent of television's old Fort Apache. The motel rooms are large and less expensive than those in the lodge, but they are spare in the decor department. The **Eatery** and the **Saloon** provide pretty ordinary food and drink for guests, who can also enjoy fishing, horseback riding, and hiking in nearby Lolo National Forest. There are also an outdoor hot-springs swimming pool and an indoor hot-springs soaking pool.

38600 W. U.S. 12, Lolo, MT 59847. © 406/273-2201. www.lolotrailcenter.com. 34 units. $67–$94 double. DISC, MC, V. **Amenities:** Restaurant, lounge; outdoor pool; indoor pool; 2 indoor Jacuzzis. *In room:* No phone.

Goldsmith's Bed & Breakfast ⚑   This B&B is in a beautiful 1911 brick home right on the Clark Fork River, just across the river from the University of Montana. (The home is the former residence of Clyde Duniway, the second president of the University of Montana.) Four of the seven rooms are suites with private sitting rooms, and all rooms have private bathrooms and attractive Victorian furnishings. Some also have fireplaces or reading nooks. Request the Clarkfork Suite to get a Japanese bath to soak in while looking out at the river. The Goldsmith name is famous in Missoula for making fabulous ice cream, and you can get some right next door at Goldsmith's Waterfront Pasta House.

809 E. Front St., Missoula, MT 59802. ☎ **406/728-1585.** Fax 406/543-0045. www.goldsmithsinn.com. 7 units. $95–$119 double. Rates include full breakfast. DISC, MC, V. *In room:* TV.

Red Lion Inn *Kids*   The motel-style Red Lion, which sits just west of downtown, is a good bet for families. The rooms are large and comfortable and the staff is friendly and helpful, offering popcorn and cookies upon check-in. The outdoor heated pool is open year-round and parents can take a dip in the hot tub. There is a Chinese restaurant, **Triple Dragon,** on the premises, but you're close to Missoula's downtown restaurants if you want to eat elsewhere.

700 W. Broadway, Missoula, MT 59802. ☎ **800/733-5466** or 406/728-3300. Fax 406/728-4441. 76 units. $69–$99 double. AE, DC, DISC, MC, V. Pets accepted, $5 per night. **Amenities:** Restaurant, lounge; outdoor pool; exercise room; outdoor Jacuzzi; coin-op washers and dryers. *In room:* A/C, TV, dataport, coffeemaker, hair dryer, iron.

Traveler's Inn   This one-story, white stucco building located off the interstate at exit 101 isn't the most exciting place to stay, but it is less expensive than the downtown motels and provides a clean, comfortable bed for the night. Basic rooms are furnished with queen-size beds. The closest place to grab a bite to eat is **Rowdy's Cabin,** a family diner located on the property. If the Traveler's Inn is booked, just keep searching along Reserve Street (or Motel Row, as it's known), and you're bound to find something.

4850 N. Reserve St., Missoula, MT 59802. ☎ **800/862-3363** or 406/728-8330. 29 units. $65 double. AE, DISC, MC, V. Pets accepted. **Amenities:** Restaurant (pizza/American). *In room:* A/C, TV.

A GUEST RANCH

L Diamond E Guest Ranch   A good choice for outdoors types who also want easy access to Missoula, the L Diamond E is home to an outfitting service (offering guides for hunting, fishing, horseback riding, and rafting) and a small dude-ranching operation. Located 25 miles (40km) east of Missoula near the interstate, the two western-style cabins, both with kitchenettes, are outfitted almost entirely with exposed pine with paneling on the walls, log beds and chairs, and natural pine tables. While the decor is rustic, the cabins have modern conveniences like digital satellite TV and foldout futons, plus great views in every direction. The summer pack trips include forays to a working sapphire claim and excursions in the surrounding Rock Creek Valley.

P.O. Box 885, Clinton, MT 59825. ☎ **888/725-8747** or 406/825-6295. Fax 406/825-6295. www.ldiamonde. com. 2 cabins. Guest ranch rates: $200 per person per day (includes cabin rental, horseback riding and all meals); cabin rental only: $125 double. MC, V. **Amenities:** Activities desk. *In room:* TV, kitchenettes.

WHERE TO DINE

Thanks to the university and a relatively cultured populace, Missoula is blessed with an excellent variety of restaurants, ranging from organic vegetarian to full-blown carnivorous. In addition to the options discussed below, we suggest **El Cazador,** 101 S. Higgins Ave. (☎ **406/728-3657**), for a selection of Mexican entrees, often spiced with seafood. The **New Black Dog Cafe,** 138 W. Broadway

(© 406/542-1138), is the best bet for those in search of a meatless meal, with a menu of soups, sandwiches, and eclectic dinner entrees.

EXPENSIVE

The Depot ⭐ STEAKS/SEAFOOD   A favorite of many local writers, The Depot is known for its upscale atmosphere and good food. The decor is along the contemporary cowboy and Western theme, with an inviting brick bar that looks out into an active rail yard. You might try the scallop casserole: scallops and mushrooms in white wine, Swiss cheese, and cream sauce. The beef menu features prime rib, New York strip, and filets; specialties include the garlic-roasted filet and fresh range veal chop served with fresh mushrooms and heavy cream. There is a huge wine list. Some of the finest recent vintages are some hard-to-find 1989 Bordeaux (at $95–$145 a bottle).

201 W. Railroad Ave. © 406/728-7007. Reservations recommended. Main courses $16–$23. AE, DC, DISC, MC, V. Sun–Thurs 5:30–10:30pm; Fri–Sat 5:30–11pm.

Marianne's at the Wilma ⭐⭐ CONTINENTAL/ECLECTIC   Everything about this restaurant is first class, starting with the transformation of the Wilma—a historic movie palace—into an Art-Deco dining extravaganza. The dining room's color scheme is striking, with an arched blue ceiling and golden walls and columns. There is also an attractive patio. The distinctively Northwest food, while expensive by Montana standards, is also first-rate. The dinner menu includes a savory blackened New York strip steak, a vegetarian polenta, and cornmeal-dusted salmon drizzled with a lime-chipotle sauce. Marianne's breakfast and lunch are also both excellent, consisting of inspired spins on old standards, like oatmeal pancakes stuffed with fresh berries, and a sesame-crusted ahi tuna sandwich.

131 S. Higgins Ave. © 406/728-8549. www.mariannesatthewilma.com. Reservations recommended. Breakfast $7–$10; lunch $7–$17; dinner $6–$26. Mon–Thurs 11am–3pm and 5–9pm; Fri 11am–3pm and 5–11pm; Sat 9am–3pm and 5–11pm; Sun 9am–3pm and 5pm–9pm.

Red Bird ⭐ ECLECTIC   The causally sleek Red Bird is tucked in the alley on the ground floor of the Art Deco Florence Building. Chef Christine Littig has brought fine creative cuisine to Missoula's restaurant explosion. The menu changes seasonally, but the entrees are fresh and superbly prepared year-round. One of Littig's personal favorites is halibut in saffron, lobster, zucchini, and red-pepper cream sauce. It's served on a bed of geometrically fried potatoes, for a remarkable presentation. When this dish is unavailable, there are plenty of other selections to savor, ranging from a bold oyster and spinach salad to a surf-and-turf pasta with beef tenderloin, lobster, and chives.

120 W. Front St. © 406/549-2906. Reservations recommended. Main courses $15–$24. AE, DISC, MC, V. Tues–Sat 5–9:30pm.

Shadows Keep ⭐⭐ STEAKS/SEAFOOD   After the landmark Greenough Mansion at the Highlands Golf Club burned to the ground in 1992, this castle-like restaurant, serving some of the area's best food, took its place on the very same foundation. Positioned on the bluffs of southeast Missoula, Shadows Keep oozes class, from the 30-foot ceiling in the bar to the panoramic views of the city and surrounding mountains. Shadows Keep is known for its rack of lamb and salmon entrees, but there's also an excellent pan-fried chicken (with a black-currant curry sauce) on the menu, alongside daily seafood specials and a few vegetarian dishes. The desserts are rich and decadent.

102 Ben Hogan Dr. © 406/728-5132. www.shadowskeep.com. Main courses $14–$25. AE, DISC, MC, V. Daily 5:30–10pm.

MODERATE

The Bridge ★ ITALIAN/ECLECTIC   Established in 1971, The Bridge is one of the granddaddies of Missoula's dining scene, and with good reason. Today, it's a bustling restaurant that shares space with the Crystal Theater, Missoula's artiest movie house. Order several appetizers rather than a dinner—they'll all be delicious and it's the best way to sample the restaurant's variety. The best entrees are the prawns with fettuccine, eggplant Parmesan, and salmon with a roasted red-bell-pepper cream sauce. There are also a number of thin-crusted pizzas and hints of Thai and African cuisine on the menu. The Bridge is within walking distance of the major hotels, so you can take a nice stroll across the river to get there. Alternatively, you can dine in your room: The delivery number is ✆ **406/542-0002.**

515 S. Higgins. ✆ **406/542-0638.** Main courses $13–$19. AE, DISC, MC, V. Sun–Thurs 5–10pm; Fri–Sat 5–11pm.

Hob Nob MEDITERRANEAN/VEGETARIAN   The sign outside the Hob Nob says, "Union Hall" in stark black-and-white, so it can be a little hard to find. Once located, however, the restaurant is a funky, eclectic place with humdrum photos on the walls and great live jazz 2 nights a week—Thursday and Saturday—during the summer. This is an excellent place for either vegetarians or carnivores, with a good mix of burgers, steaks, and organic dishes. The hand-rolled spinach ravioli is an especially good bet. After hours, the Hob Nob transforms into a happening club with a limited menu of fried munchies.

In the Union Club, 217 E. Main St. ✆ **406/542-3188.** Reservations required for parties of 6 or more. Lunch $5–$9; dinner $12–$14. MC, V. Mon–Fri 11am–3pm; Mon–Thurs 5:30–9:30pm; Fri–Sat 5:30–10pm. Bar open later.

INEXPENSIVE

Bernice's Bakery ★ BAKED GOODS   Bernice's is one of Missoula's most beloved culinary spots. This small, out-of-the-way place, known for its delicious baked goods, is a great place for breakfast. In addition to an outstanding soft homemade granola, Bernice's sells buttery croissants filled with flavored cream cheeses, an excellent complement to the freshly brewed organic coffee that's also a staple. Organic juices and teas are available too. This is also a great dessert spot—the cream puffs are out of this world.

190 S. 3rd St. W. ✆ **406/728-1358.** Most items $2–$5. DISC, MC, V. Sun–Thurs 6am–10pm; Fri–Sat 6am–10pm.

Kadena's GOURMET DELI   Located on the downtown riverfront, Kadena's is a fresh dining alternative with an extensive selection of unusual salads, pastas, entrees, and sandwiches. The atmosphere is akin to a typical deli, with plastic tables and plastic chairs. Regardless, there's a wonderful view of the riverfront and the Missoula Carousel. Best bets here are the Chicken Kadena (sliced chicken breast with fresh vegetables sautéed in a sherry-sesame sauce), Front Street Fried Noodles (roast pork tenderloin with fresh vegetables and linguine sautéed in teriyaki sauce), and Angel Hair Primavera. Those who like spicy food will enjoy the Cajun chicken with linguine.

231 W. Front St. ✆ **406/549-3304.** Reservations not accepted. Main courses $6–$8. AE, DISC, MC, V. Daily 11am–10pm.

The Oxford Cafe AMERICAN   You might not want to eat at the Ox, as it's known, but you really should go in and look around. Established in 1883, this dismal cafe is a Missoula institution, adorned with beer signs, a bar, a breakfast counter, a bison head, and an endless stream of eccentrics, cowboys, and bikers. Beyond stiff drinks, chicken-fried steaks are the specialty of the house; the Ox had sold more than 100,000 at last count. When a customer orders the brains and eggs—admittedly not very often—the waitress shouts to the cook, "He needs 'em!" The Oxford card room is the gathering place for the toughest, tightest poker players in western Montana. Other restaurants—all better than the Oxford—come and go, but the Ox endures, a testament to greasy food, live keno calling, and bottled American beer.

337 N. Higgins Ave. ℭ 406/549-0117. www.the-oxford.com. Breakfast $3–$6; lunch $3–$5; dinner $6–$10. Daily 24 hr.

MISSOULA AFTER DARK
WATERING HOLES FOR ANY TASTE

There are plenty of watering holes in Missoula, whether your buzz of choice is alcohol- or caffeine-induced. **Sean Kelly's,** 130 W. Pine (ℭ **406/542-1471**), serves Irish, pub-style food—bangers and mash, pot roast, Irish stew—in addition to your alcoholic beverage of choice. The weekend jazz is wonderful, and there are also pool tables in the back. **Butterfly Herbs** at 232 N. Higgins Ave. (ℭ **406/728-8780**) has a distinct 1960s feel. It's the perfect place to order up an ordinary cup of java, or an exotic beverage from an extensive specialty espresso menu. **Al and Vic's,** 119 W. Alder (ℭ **406/721-1482**), serves up ridiculously potent cocktails to a cross-section of Missoula: Blue-collar types, professionals, and college kids abound. The **Iron Horse Brew Pub** at 551 N. Higgins Ave. (ℭ **406/728-8866**) is home to Bayern, a locally produced microbrew. If you're feeling particularly cocky, ask for a beer in the boot—then see if you can drink it all.

THE PERFORMING ARTS

The **Montana Repertory Theater,** located at the University of Montana campus (ℭ **406/243-6809**), is the state's only Equity company, performing new and classical works. The **Missoula Children's Theater** is the largest touring children's theater in the United States, performing original musical productions and featuring hundreds of talented children from communities across the States, Canada, and the Pacific Rim. The theater season starts early in July and continues through the end of April. The **Missoula Community Theater** provides a year-round calendar of family entertainment. Both the Children's Theater and the Community Theater are located at 200 N. Adams St. (ℭ **406/728-1911;** www.mctinc.com).

The **Missoula Symphony Orchestra and Chorale,** 131 S. Higgins Ave. in the Wilma Building (ℭ **406/721-3194**), is composed of university students, Missoula residents, and other regional musicians, often performing with featured guests in the historic Wilma Theater. The **String Orchestra of the Rockies,** P.O. Box 8265, Missoula, MT 59807 (ℭ **406/243-5371**), a statewide professional string ensemble, is based in Missoula and performs regularly there. The **University of Montana Music Department,** Music Recital Hall at the University of Montana (ℭ **406/243-6880**), often brings in outstanding musicians performing in the university's remarkable recital hall. Regularly scheduled recitals include solo and ensemble performances by faculty and students.

3 A Detour into the Bitterroot Valley ⟨★

Extends 89 miles (143km) S of Missoula to the Idaho border

Although in part a bedroom community for Missoula, the Bitterroot Valley has become a second home and retirement paradise for folks who have fallen in love with the Missoula-area mountains, but not with the Missoula-area traffic. Though not as well known as other areas of the state, the fly-fishing in the Bitterroot River is excellent, making it a preferred destination for anglers in the know.

The Bitterroot has the reputation as Montana's banana belt, because the microclimate in the valley offers a long growing season. A lot of Missoula-area golf fanatics head to Hamilton in February because the golf course there greens up for play much earlier than the ones even a few miles farther north.

GETTING AROUND & VISITOR INFORMATION   For maps, brochures, and sage advice about the area and its happenings, consult the **Bitterroot Valley Chamber of Commerce,** which has offices at 105 E. Main St., Hamilton, MT 59840 (© **406/363-2400;** www.bvchamber.com).

DRIVING TOURS

If you'd like to take a driving tour through the area, travel south on U.S. 93 to Florence, then cross the Bitterroot River and travel south on Mont. 203/263 through a 32-mile (52km) area filled with interesting landmarks, reconnecting with U.S. 93 at Hamilton. On your trip back, take U.S. 93 south through Hamilton and Victor, Darby, and Sula. As an alternative, continue south beyond Sula to Mont. 43, the road that leads to Wisdom. Doing so will take you winding through the valley and canyons of the Bitterroot Mountains, and you'll finally emerge at the Big Hole Battlefield.

If you are feeling very brave, and you don't mind getting your car beaten up on a rough dirt road, take the Skalkaho Pass Road to the east of Hamilton. Pick up Mont. 38 just south of Hamilton—up Skalkaho Creek. The pavement runs out after a few miles, and you'll drive over a rocky, pitted, narrow road up through the Sapphire Mountains. Go slowly; the drop-offs here are as extreme as those along Going-to-the-Sun Road in Glacier National Park, but without the guardrails. But the views of forested hills are unsurpassed. It takes about 2 hours to cover the 54 miles (87km) to the **Anaconda Pintler Scenic Route,** Mont. 1, which you pick up around Georgetown Lake.

GETTING OUTSIDE

The Bitterroot Valley runs south along the Bitterroot River between the Bitterroot Range to the west and the Sapphire Mountains to the east. The Bitterroot Range is the site of the Selway-Bitterroot Wilderness, which at 1.3 million acres is one of the nation's largest wilderness areas. Numerous trail heads are located off major highways between Lolo and Darby. You can get information about hiking in the wilderness from the **Darby Historic Center/Darby Ranger Station** (© **406/821-3913**), open Monday through Saturday from 8:30am to 4:30pm and Sunday from 12:30 to 4:30pm during the summer.

The Lake Como Recreation Area is a popular day use and camping area with swimming, hiking, and boating. To get there, go 4 miles (6km) north from Darby on U.S. 93. Turn west on Lake Como Road and go about 2½ miles (4km) to the area. There are 26 camping units in two different campgrounds for $12 to $17 a night and a cabin on the lake for $50 per night. Information, and reservations for the cabin, are available at the Darby Ranger Station (see above).

If it's fly-fishing you're seeking, check out **Riverbend Fly-fishing** (© 406/363-4197), one of the longest-running acts in the Montana guiding business. Owner Chuck Stranahan is a nationally known fly-tier, with a number of his patterns chosen for the Jack Dennis fly-tying book, the bible of the business. He excels in instruction. Riverbend customizes trips for its customers, with an emphasis on the Bitterroot River, though trips also go to other rivers in western Montana. Guided trips cost $285 per day for one or two people.

SEEING THE SIGHTS

The west side of the valley has fishing access as well as places to shop, eat, and stay. The historic section of the valley is on the east side of the river, and is accessible at Florence, Stevensville, Victor, Pinesdale, and Hamilton.

Following are a lot of the attractions you'll come across if you start driving at the north end of Mont. 203/269 and head south.

Eight miles (13km) south of Florence on Mont. 203, you'll hit the **Lee Metcalf National Wildlife Refuge** (© 406/777-5552; www.fws.gov), which is free and is open daily from dawn to dusk. This wetland habitat was formed by dikes and dams that impound the water of several streams. It has helped to improve migratory waterfowl habitats and has created a nesting success, but a number of other species benefit as well, including osprey and deer. A short loop trail, open from mid-July to mid-September, leads around several ponds and blinds in the refuge's southwest corner. The picnic area is open year-round and has 2 miles (3km) of walking trails. Hunting for waterfowl is permitted on designated ponds during the fall duck-hunting season. Bow hunting for deer is permitted in season as well. Near the entrance is the well-preserved exterior of the 1885 **Whaley Homestead,** an excellent example of vernacular frontier architecture. You can drive around the refuge on the dirt road and come out in Stevensville, the next stop on the tour.

Stevensville is the oldest town in Montana, the result of the early missionary work of the indefatigable Jesuit Fr. Pierre DeSmet, who founded **St. Mary's Mission** in 1841. Capped with a bell tower, the mission is a small structure paneled with logs and white boards and an important place in the development of Montana—it was the first permanent structure in the state to be built by European-Americans. John Owen bought the mission from the Jesuits in 1850 and established a trading post, Fort Owen. Though the issue of who first found gold in Montana will doubtless never be established, in Owen's diary in 1852 he wrote: "Hunting gold. Found some."

From here, continue south on Mont. 203 to Hamilton and the Marcus Daly Mansion. Montana copper king Marcus Daly never did anything on a small scale, and his house is no exception. The **Marcus Daly Mansion** (© 406/363-6004) is a spectacular Georgian Revival mansion with classical porticoes. It occupies 24,000 square feet on three floors, with 24 bedrooms, 14 bathrooms, and 7 fireplaces. The mansion was finished in 1910, after Daly's death, and his widow Margaret lived there in the summers until her own death in 1941. It's open daily from April 15 to October 15. Admission costs $6 for adults, $5 for seniors, and $4 for students; there are tours on the hour from 11am to 4pm.

On the opposite side of the river, the village of Hamilton, several blocks long and 4 blocks wide, is worth a leisurely stroll since most of the businesses here are small, locally owned, and often interesting. For outdoor gear, head to **Bob Ward & Sons,** 1120 N. 1st St. (✆ **406/363-6204**), for a good selection of fishing, skiing, camping, and hunting equipment. Nearby is **Robbins,** 209 W. Main St. (✆ **406/363-1733**), a nice shop that sells home furnishings, crystal china, and gourmet kitchen accessories. The **BiblioJoe,** 252 W. Main St. (✆ **406/ 363-5220**), sells all manner of espresso drinks and adjoins the **Chapter One** bookstore, featuring new and used books and periodicals. At last count there were 27 antiques dealers listed in the Bitterroot antiques dealers brochure; for your copy, contact the Bitterroot Valley Chamber of Commerce (see "Getting Around & Visitor Information," above). Perhaps the most remarkable store in Hamilton is the **Main Street Rug Co.** (✆ **406/363-0338**), 126 Main St., which has a vast collection of Oriental rugs for sale, assembled by owner Miriam Kalamian.

WHERE TO STAY

Hamilton Super 8, 1325 N. 1st St., Hamilton, MT 59840 (✆ **800/800-8000** or 406/363-2940), is a clean, typically budget-minded motel with a location central to the Bitterroot Valley. The same holds true for the **Best Western Hamilton Inn,** 409 S. 1st St., Hamilton, MT 59840 (✆ **800/426-4586** or 406/363-2142), though the advantage here is the presentation of an excellent breakfast buffet, and the fact that some rooms are equipped with microwaves and refrigerators. Double rooms at both properties run around $50 to $80 per night.

Blackbird's Fly Shop and Lodge   This is a combination fly shop and lodge offering a full guiding service. In addition to supplying the necessary gear for fly-fishing, the outfit also organizes trips for guests. Fishing the Bitterroot River is the specialty here, but trips also go up to the blue-ribbon Rock Creek and other rivers early in the season. The rooms in the lodge are large and have four-poster beds and down comforters, but they are available only as a single rental to parties of four or more people. There are also two cabins adjacent to the lodge, tastefully decorated and outfitted with full kitchens. The best perk: a 1,000-square-foot deck overlooking the river.

1754 U.S. 93, Victor, MT 59875. ✆ **800/210-8648** or 406/642-6375. www.blackbirds.com. 3 units. $150–$250 double; $895–$2,395 per person for room, meals, and guided fishing for 2 to 5 days. **Amenities:** Game room; activities desk. *In room:* Kitchen, no phone.

Deer Crossing Bed & Breakfast ⭐   The 25 acres of land surrounding this pleasant, modern inn served as an apple orchard in the 1920s, and innkeeper Mary Lynch still utilizes the remaining trees to present lucky fall guests with delicious pies. The main house features three rooms and a pair of suites, ranging from the thoroughly Western Charlie Russell Suite (with a minibar, fridge, and Jacuzzi) to the small, understated Moose Meadows Room, with a plush quilt and a private entry. The property's original homesteader's cabin is still standing, recently renovated to serve as a rustic rental cabin. There's another cabin, the Bar 61, that's a bit more modern, with a television and a small kitchenette. Given a choice between a room and a cabin, go with the cabin.

396 Hayes Creek Rd., Hamilton, MT 59840. ✆ **800/763-2232** or 406/363-2232. Fax 406/375-0988. www.wtp.net/go/deercrossing. 7 units, including 2 suites and 2 cabins. $89 double; $129 suite; $149 cabin. AE, DISC, MC, V. *In room:* Kitchenettes, no phone.

Triple Creek Ranch ⭐⭐   This is one of the most elegant—and expensive—guest ranches in the West, with just about every imaginable amenity and activity. The ranch is an adults-only resort that encourages guests to relax and do things according to their own schedules. The luxury cabins have a sitting area, king bed, wet bar, and double steam shower. Tennis rackets, fly-fishing gear, and horses are available to guests. The ranch is the only Montana property to meet the Relais & Châteaux standards. The *Wall Street Journal* called a stay here "roughing it Robin Leach style."

The onsite **Triple Creek Dining Room** serves gourmet cuisine for breakfast, lunch, and dinner. It's open to the public in the evenings, but during the summer season—June, July, and August—it's filled with resort guests, and it's very difficult to get a reservation.

5551 W. Fork Stage Rd., Darby, MT 59829. © **406/821-4600.** Fax 406/821-4666. www.triplecreekranch.com. 19 cabins. $510–$995 per couple per night. Rate includes meals, drinks, and activities. AE, DISC, MC, V. **Amenities:** Restaurant; outdoor pool; putting green; tennis courts; Jacuzzi; room service; concierge; activities desk; massage; laundry service. *In room:* A/C, TV, dataport, minibar, fridge, coffeemaker.

WHERE TO DINE

Don't expect a whole lot in the way of fine dining in the Bitterroot Valley. If all your outdoor activities have you craving a juicy steak, try **Victor Steakhouse,** U.S. 93, Victor (© **406/642-3300**). The **Spice of Life Cafe,** 163 S. 2nd St. in Hamilton (© **406/363-4433**), has offerings ranging from Thai chicken to Japanese sesame noodles. **Lulu,** 315 S. 3rd St. in Hamilton (© **406/375-8330**), serves up French and Mediterranean standbys in a shimmering restored Victorian. **Maggie's Wild Oats Cafe and Coffeehouse** at 217 Main St. in Hamilton (© **406/363-4567**) is a good breakfast and lunch place in a spare cafe-style setting.

A SIDE TRIP: SKIING & HOT SPRINGS AT LOST TRAIL PASS

Lost Trail Pass is a remote and undiscovered corner of Montana about 80 miles (129km) south of Missoula on the Idaho border. This area is heavily timbered, but not heavily populated. It's also off the beaten path, because most travelers use I-15. This corner of the state is very pretty—with pine-covered peaks replacing the forbidding rock crags that dominate the skyline farther north.

With Lost Trail Powder Mountain, Lost Trail Hot Springs, and Camp Creek Inn, this pass area is an unforgettable winter vacation destination for those who loathe big crowds and the attendant ski scene.

Lost Trail Powder Mountain ski area recently expanded into a long, steeper area adjacent to the original hill, with two new lifts. Overall, this small ski area is mostly intermediate, with lots of light powder. If you like to ski the bumps but aren't a fanatic about it, the moguls develop on the intermediate runs in the afternoon, just in time to wear you out completely. The lift ticket prices are an excellent value at $20 for adults and $10 for children 12 and younger; kids 5 and younger ski free. For more information, contact Lost Trail Powder Mountain, P.O. Box 311, Conner, MT 59827. Ski reports are available during the season at © **406/821-3211** or online at **www.losttrail.com**. The ski area is 90 miles (145km) south of Missoula at the Montana-Idaho border, ⅛ mile from U.S. Highway 93.

Just down the hill to the north from the ski area is the unpretentious lodge and hot springs, **Lost Trail Hot Springs Resort,** 8221 U.S. 93 S., Sula, MT 59871 (© **800/825-3574** or 406/821-3574; www.losttrailhotsprings.com). The lodge offers summer raft trips, horseback riding, and fishing. It isn't fancy by urban standards, but the food in the restaurant, which overlooks the hot-springs pool, is good, especially if you enjoy basic American grub—burgers and pizzas. Nightly rates are $53 to $85 for lodge rooms, and $63 to $110 for cabins.

Nightly group rates start at $425 for the Clark Lodge, which sleeps 12; and $400 for the Sacajawea, which sleeps 43—23 in four furnished main rooms with lofts, and 20 more in a downstairs bunk area.

4 The Flathead Indian Reservation & the Mission Valley

42 miles (68km) N of Missoula; 75 miles (121km) S of Kalispell

The Confederated Salish and Kootenai Tribes make their home on the Flathead Indian Reservation, with tribal headquarters for the 1.2-million-acre reservation in Pablo. The tribes, however, own only slightly more than 50% of the land within reservation boundaries.

The change in culture for the tribes came quickly when fur traders, homesteaders, and the missionaries of the Catholic Church headed west. Founded in the early 1850s by Jesuit priests, the town of **St. Ignatius** (located 32 miles [52km] north of Missoula on U.S. 93) is nestled in the heart of the Mission Valley. One of the valley's larger small towns, St. Ignatius has a modest Flathead Indian Museum and trading post on the highway.

Wildlife conservation and land management have played big parts in the lives of the tribal members. The **Mission Mountain Wilderness** was the first wilderness area officially designated as such by a tribe in the United States. Hiking in the wilderness area requires the purchase of a $6 tribal permit from the Flathead Reservation Confederated Salish-Kootenai Tribes, Box 278, Pablo, MT 59855 (© **406/675-2700**). The Mission Mountain Wilderness is located in the Mission Mountain Range, east of U.S. 93. Numerous gravel roads lead up to the trail heads.

The **St. Ignatius Mission** was established in 1854 as an offshoot of the missionary work of the famous Jesuit Fr. Pierre DeSmet. A Fr. Hoecken began the mission in a small log cabin, which is still on the premises and serves as the visitor center. In 1891, the mission added this magnificent brick church in its ministry to the Indians. The ceiling is decorated with 58 murals, depicting scenes from the Old and New Testaments, by Brother Joseph Carignano, an Italian Jesuit without formal art training.

The **National Bison Range** (© **406/644-2211**), just west of St. Ignatius on reservation land, is just 7 miles (11km) southwest of Charlo on County Road 212. The 18,500 acres here contain between 350 and 500 bison, the remnants of a national bison herd that once totaled 60 million. The visitor center has a small display about the history and ecology of bison in America. The 13-mile (21km) Red Sleep Road goes through four different habitat types—grasslands, riparian, montane forest, and wetlands. In addition to the bison, you'll see deer, bighorn sheep, antelope, and maybe an occasional coyote or black bear. There's a trail here for people with physical disabilities. Gates are open from 7am to dusk daily; the visitor center is open from 8am to 7pm weekdays, 9am to 7pm weekends. Cost is $4 per car.

If you're more interested in feathers than fur, check out the **Ninepipe National Wildlife Refuge** (© **406/644-2211**), which is next to U.S. 93, 5 miles (8km) south of Ronan. Established in 1921, the refuge has 2,000 acres of water, marsh, and grassland for the double-crested cormorant and the bald eagle, among other migrating birds. There is a picnic area at Ninepipe Dam on the west side of the refuge. The refuge is open daily from dawn to dusk, although portions are closed during the fall and early winter hunting season and the bird-nesting season in spring and early summer. Admission is free. Fishing is permitted in some areas of the adjacent Pablo Reservoir, but a tribal permit is required. For information on tribal fishing regulations, call © **406/ 675-2700.**

WHERE TO STAY & DINE The **Ninepipes Lodge,** 41000 U.S. 93, Charlo, MT 59824 (© **406/644-2588;** fax 406/644-2928; www.ninepipes.com), across from the Ninepipe National Wildlife Refuge, is a pleasant motel, with 25 rooms decorated with lodgepole furniture and a wildlife/nature theme. Your choice of king, queen, double, or twin beds is offered, and all units have TVs and telephones. Rates for two are $79 to $84 in summer and $57 to $72 in winter, and American Express, Discover, MasterCard, and Visa credit cards are accepted. There is also a popular restaurant on the premises, offering a good variety of American selections for all three meals at reasonable prices. We suggest the prime rib for dinner and the charbroiled chicken salad at lunch. Also adjacent and under the same management is the **Ninepipes Museum of Early Montana** (© **406/644-3435;** www.ninepipes.com), which contains early Western art, American Indian beadwork, a life-size diorama of the area's wildlife, an Indian camp scene, and other displays on the area's history. Admission costs $4 for adults, $3 for students, $2 for children 6 to 12, and is free for children under 6 who are accompanied by an adult. Call for current hours.

A SIDE TRIP TO HOT SPRINGS

Hot Springs is a town of hand-painted signs and potholed streets, tucked into a cul-de-sac of low Montana mountains. Lots of visitors swear by the local waters' therapeutic qualities, especially as a palliative for arthritis. Situated southwest of Polson, just off Mont. 28, the tiny community is about an hour-and-a-half from Flathead Lake.

The 1928 **Symes Hotel,** 209 Wall St. (© **888/305-3106** or 406/741-2361), is a vaguely pink, Alamo-like structure that aspires to be Art Deco. You can rent rooms, or just tubs in stalls that can be filled with the famous waters. Some rooms have their own tubs, and there are two small tubs and a large hot tub outside.

Rooms run from $40 to $95 a night, in a bewildering combination of options (you get claw-foot tubs, but no TVs or phones). There's also a salon, an art gallery, and a bike rental operation on the property.

Wild Horse Hot Springs (© **406/741-3777**), 5 miles (8km) northeast of town, offers another primitive soak in blue concrete tubs. This place is located several miles down a dirt road. The private rooms are each outfitted with a "plunge" (private pool), toilet, shower, steam room, and furniture that your grandmother would have found old-fashioned. But some people swear by the place: One arthritic client has come down from Canada for 3 weeks every year since the mid-1960s. There are only two rooms to sleep in here, priced at $55 to $65 a night. A soak costs $5 an hour.

The free **Camas Bath** is located at the end of Spring Street, a small concrete pool with the same valuable waters. For more information, contact the **Hot Springs Chamber of Commerce,** P.O. Box 580, Hot Springs, MT 59845 (© **406/741-2662**).

5 The Flathead Lake Area: Somers, Polson & Bigfork ⟨★⟨★

Bigfork: 92 miles (148km) N of Missoula; 15 miles (24km) SE of Kalispell

This is one of the most beautiful areas in Montana. Glacier National Park's towering peaks rise from the valley floor on the east and the mountains of the Flathead National Forest define the edge of the valley to the west. This is a land of forests, cattle, and alfalfa—with a velvet-green valley floor, green and granite mountains, and, on a sunny day, a dramatic deep-blue ceiling.

This part of Montana seems to offer something for everyone, whether your interests lie indoors or out. There are water sports on the lake and hikes that lead to sparkling mountain streams with views. But if you want to shop or see a play, you can easily spend your day inside the shops, galleries, and theater of Bigfork.

With much of this area lying within the tribal lands of the Salish-Kootenai, there is also a long-standing American Indian heritage.

ESSENTIALS

GETTING THERE The nearest airports are **Glacier Park International** (© 406/257-5994), north of the lake between Kalispell and Columbia Falls (see chapter 4), and the Missoula International Airport at **Johnson-Bell Field** in Missoula (see section 2 of this chapter). Bigfork is just over a 30-minute drive from Glacier Park International; Polson is roughly midway between the two airports. For rental cars, **Avis** (© 800/331-1212), **Budget** (© 800/527-0700), **Hertz** (© 800/654-3131), and **National** (© 800/227-7368) maintain counters at each airport.

VISITOR INFORMATION Your best bet for information on the south end of the lake is the **Port Polson Chamber of Commerce,** P.O. Box 677, Polson, MT 59860 (© 406/883-5969; www.polsonchamber.com). For goings-on north, contact the **Bigfork Chamber of Commerce,** P.O. Box 237, Bigfork, MT 59911 (© 406/837-5888; www.bigfork.org). The **Flathead Convention and Visitor Bureau** (© 800/543-3105; www.fcvb.org), **Travel Montana** (© 800/541-1447), and **Glacier Country** (© 800/338-5072) can supplement this information.

GETTING OUTSIDE

The Flathead is one of those rare places where you see the serious golfer and the serious backpacker in the same spot, sometimes in the same body. The golfing is excellent on several courses, and the backpacking, hiking, and fishing are even better. Fishing, boating, and "yachting" are popular sports for those who can afford to practice them. If your plans take you to one of the lakes or trails on the Salish-Kootenai Reservation, don't forget to buy a tribal permit. For fishing gear, fishing licenses, and tribal permits, go to **Bear Dance Outdoor Gear** at the south end of the lake in Polson, at 13 2nd Ave. E. (© 406/883-1700). For your bicycling needs, head to **Lakeside Mountain Sports** on the west side of the lake at 306 Stoner Rd. in Lakeside (© 406/844-BIKE).

BOATING

With Flathead Lake being the largest freshwater lake west of the Mississippi River, you can bet that this is a big boating destination. Boat rentals are available at the **Bigfork Marina and Boat Center** (© 406/837-5556), **Kwa Taq Nuk Resort** (© 800/882-6363), **Bayview Resort and Marina** (© 406/ 837-4843), and **Marina Cay Resort** (© 406/837-5861).

A sailboat excursion is available from **Averill's Flathead Lake Lodge** (✆ 406/ 837-5569) on two classic racing sloops designed by L. Francis Herreshoff. Fewer than a dozen of these 50-foot "Q-Boats" remain in the world. There are four 2-hour cruises daily. Fixed-keel sailboats can be launched at the state parks around Flathead Lake. Big Arm, Yellow Bay, and Somers have fishing accesses. Because winds may blow hard during the afternoon, only ballasted boats are recommended on the main portion of the lake.

Montana Department of Fish, Wildlife and Parks has designated a **Flathead Lake Marine Trail,** showing point-to-point campsites and landing points that a human-powered craft like a canoe or kayak can reach in 1 day. You can obtain a brochure on the trail from the MFW&P (✆ 406/444-2535) or from the **Flathead Convention and Visitor Bureau** in Kalispell (✆ 800/543-3105).

CRUISES

Excursion cruises are a good way for visitors to check out Flathead Lake. The 65-foot *Far West* (✆ 406/857-3203) is one of the area's oldest, with daily dinner cruises and Sunday brunches. One of the finest charter boats on the lake, *Lucky Too,* is based at Marina Cay (✆ 406/257-5214). **Pointer Scenic Cruises** (✆ 406/837-5617) offers charter rides on high-speed powerboats that cruise to ancient petroglyphs viewable only by boat; this company also offers explorations of Wild Horse Island. The *Princess* cruise boat (✆ 406/883-2448) takes a 1½-hour tour, leaving the Kwa Taq Nuk resort marina in the early afternoon and making a loop around Wild Horse Island (no stops) before heading back. If it's a Montana sunset you're after, take the 2-hour sunset cruise, departing in the late afternoon, and look west. This evening cruise costs $17 for adults, $9 for children.

FISHING

Fishing the southern half of Flathead Lake requires a Salish-Kootenai tribal permit, which you can purchase at stores in Polson or at the tribal headquarters in Pablo. The brochure *Fishing the Flathead* is available from the **Flathead Convention and Visitor Bureau** (✆ 800/543-3105). It provides information on 14 different fishing opportunities, as well as an outline of the licensing and catch-and-release regulations. This brochure includes information on Whitefish Lake, Flathead Lake, Swan Lake, and several other lesser-known lakes where you will be able to catch some fish but avoid the crowds. To increase your odds of snagging something besides a log, contact **Glacier Fishing Charters** (✆ 406/ 892-2377). Also, "Shorty" George's **A-Able Fishing** (✆ 800/231-5214 or 406/257-5214; www.aablefishing.com) will outfit a fishing trip with qualified guides who know the area.

GOLF

There are two golf courses—one terrific, the other just pretty good—overlooking the shores of Flathead Lake. In Polson, the 18-hole **Polson Country Club** public course is the pretty good one, situated just off the lake on U.S. 93 (✆ 406/883-8230). A round of 18 holes is $28. The course is fairly short— under 6,800 yards from the tips and only 6,079 from the white tees—but it's very pretty and beautifully maintained.

The terrific course is **Eagle Bend Golf Club** (✆ 406/837-7300), a challenging Jack Nicklaus–designed track with views of Flathead Lake and the surrounding mountains, located in Bigfork just off the highway on Holt Drive. The

18-hole course is only 6,200 yards from the white tees, but it's harder than Chinese arithmetic. There are 27 excellent holes of golf here. It's $60 for 18 holes in the summer, $36 during spring and fall. *Golf Digest* has called this one of the country's top 50 courses. Be sure to call ahead for a tee time. Contact the **Flathead Valley Golf Association** (© **800/392-9795**) for a free visitor's guide and information regarding all of the area courses.

HIKING

This is bear country, and hikers should work to avoid confrontations by making noise and being watchful. Don't surprise them and they won't surprise you.

Besides strolling by the lake at one of the marinas or state parks, the best bet for trekking is in the **Jewel Basin,** a designated hiking area north of Bigfork. More than 30 miles (48km) of trails make it a great place for day-hiking as well as overnights. Before dropping into the actual basin, you'll get a great look at the Flathead Valley and Flathead Lake. For free maps of some of the more popular trails, inquire locally at one of the **Forest Service** offices in Kalispell (© **406/755-5401**) or Bigfork (© **406/837-5081**). To reach the head of the hiking area, take Mont. 83 from either Bigfork or Somers, turn north onto Echo Lake Road, and follow the signs.

A short hike, not far from Bigfork and about 45 minutes from the trail head, will take you to **Estes Lake.** Take County Road 209 out of Bigfork. Turn south at the Ferndale fire station. When the road forks, take the right fork, County Road 498. It's about a 7-mile (11km) drive from there to the parking area.

A slightly more ambitious, but still short, hike goes up to **Cold Lakes** in the **Mission Mountain** Wilderness. Take Mont. 83 south to County Road 903. Turn right (west), then follow the road to the trail head. The hike is about an hour one-way.

RAFTING

The **Flathead Raft Company** (© **800/654-4359;** www.flatheadraftco.com) runs half of its outfit from Polson at Riverside Park on U.S. 93, and half from Bigfork. Tours go down the South Fork of the Flathead River and include a swing through the Buffalo Rapids and Kerr Dam. Half-day trips are $32 to $40, and full-day trips range from $65 to $80. Meals and overnight trips are also available.

SKIING

The relatively new **Blacktail Mountain Ski Area** (© **406/844-0999;** www.blacktailmountain.com) is a big step toward making the Flathead Lake region a full-blown year-round resort area. There's an average annual snowfall of 250 inches, which ought to be enough. The area is starting out relatively small with 200 developed acres, two double chairs, a triple lift, and a beginner lift. The hill is excellent for beginner and intermediate skiers, with 1,400 vertical feet of drop. Seventy percent of the runs are rated intermediate and only 15% are black diamonds. There are two restaurants, a lounge, ski rental, and a ski school. Lift tickets cost: adults, $26 full, $19 half-day; 8 to 18 years old, $16 full, $14 half-day; ages 70 and older and 7 and younger, free. Lifts open at 9:30am and close at 4:30pm, Wednesday through Sunday and holidays. The area is located 14 miles (23km) west of Lakeside on Blacktail Mountain Road.

EXPLORING THE AREA

Miracle of America Museum   This museum contains an extensive collection of odds and ends dedicated to explaining the development of America. Like most of these efforts, it is heavily weighted toward the military and conquest sides of the story, with plenty of guns, uniforms, and battle memorabilia. But unlike a lot of the roadside museums, there is at least some effort to explain what you're looking at. There's also a collection of antique Harley-Davidsons, some dating back to 1912, and "Pioneer Village," a collection of about 30 historic structures.

58176 U.S. 93, Polson, MT 59860. ☎ 406/883-6804. www.cyberport.net/museum. $3 adults, $1 for children 3–12. Summer daily 8am–8pm; rest of year Mon–Sat 8am–5pm, Sun 1:30–5pm.

The Mission Mountain Winery   Montana's only winery is located here on Flathead Lake, producing award-winning merlot along with chardonnay and pale ruby champagne. Tours of the small facility are free and take about 15 minutes. The winery produces 7,000 cases of wine a year. Although 70% of the wines produced here are white, the winery considers the reds to be the finer vintages. The pinot noir grapes are grown in vineyards around Flathead Lake.

82420 U.S. 93, Dayton. ☎ 406/849-5524. www.missionmountainwinery.com. May–Oct tastings daily 10am–5pm.

Bigfork Summer Playhouse   Bigfork has earned a fine regional reputation for its summer stock theatrical productions, performed by rising college-age stars. Nightly performances of Broadway shows are scheduled from the end of May until the end of August. Recent productions have included *Funny Girl, The Adventures of Huckleberry Finn, Oklahoma, West Side Story, Guys and Dolls,* and *Carousel.* In the fall, the playhouse is home to a children's theater that presents adaptations of fairy tales and children's favorites.

526 Electric Ave., Bigfork. ☎ 406/837-4886 for show times and reservations. www.digisys.net/playhouse. Ticket prices vary.

SHOPPING

Bigfork is the town to find Montana chic. The main street, Electric Avenue, is littered with a variety of galleries, gift shops, boutiques, and bookstores. And it's only 4 blocks long. **Twin Birch Square,** at 459 Electric Ave., is a two-level, pine-log shopping mall where you'll find **Yellow Bay Weaving** (☎ 406/837-5454), a working studio that produces beautiful loom-woven rugs; and **Rock 'n' River** (☎ 406/837-7275), a nice shop with Montana monogrammed shirts, blankets, and a variety of gifts. At **Electric Avenue Books,** 524 Electric Ave. (☎ 406/837-6072), browsers are invited to peruse a book or a field journal, or even tinkle the ivories on a baby grand. The **Eric Thorsen Studio,** 547 Electric Ave. (☎ 406/836-4366), handles artwork from the well-known sculptor. He is best known for the sculptures he has created for Trout Unlimited, the Wild Turkey Federation, and Ducks Unlimited (at last count more than 12,000 fund-raising pieces in total). His two-level gallery is a display case for bronze and wood creations; on the second level is the artist's studio, where visitors are encouraged to observe the artist at work.

Doors away is the gallery of **Ken Bjorge** (☎ 406/837-3839), 603 Electric Ave., who also creates life-size studies of wildlife in bronze. Don't be surprised to find yourself standing next to a 6-foot-tall crane or eagle while he works his craft in your presence. Next door to Bjorge's studio is **Two River Gear** (☎ 406/837-3474), which deals in fly-fishing gear and info, and Patagonia wear. This shop is also owned by Bjorge, who is an avid fly-fisherman himself. **Artfusion,** 471 Electric Ave. (☎ 406/837-3526), is an eclectic gallery that represents more than 60 contemporary Montana artists and craftspeople. Around the corner at

Bay Books & Prints, 350 Grand Ave. (© **406/837-4646**), there are rare books and first editions. The owners carry an extensive collection of books about the explorers Lewis and Clark, some very rare and in good condition.

If you're looking for an authentic yet unusual gift item with a Western theme, visit **Electric Avenue Gifts** (© **406/837-4994**), 459 Electric Ave. At **Brookies Cookies,** 191 Mill St. (© **406/837-2447;** www.brookiescookies.com), you'll find blue-ribbon cookies and other baked goods, baked fresh daily. And for delectable jams and syrups, try **Eva Gates Homemade Preserves,** 456 Electric Ave. (© **406/837-4356**), which has been in the business since 1949.

Shopping in **Polson** at the other end of Flathead Lake is less of an upscale experience. The 3-block Main Street shopping district has few galleries. There is a good antiques store, though, the **Antique Emporium,** actually two shops at 323–325 Main St. (© **406/883-3045**). Out on U.S. 93, there is a three-store strip mall, the anchor store for which is **Three Dog Down,** 61547 U.S. 93 (© **800/DOG-DOWN**). This funky down outlet sells comforters, coats, pillows, duvets, and other cold-weather gear. Owner Robert A. Ricketts is a former opera singer who moved from Cincinnati to Polson to start a low-key dream business. Prices for high-quality down goods are lower here than in more fashionable metropolitan stores. Next door in the same strip, **Clayton's of Montana,** 61541 U.S. 93 (© **406/883-6233**), sells fine jewelry and gifts, including a wide variety of American Indian gold and silver jewelry, artwork, and hand-carved elk and wood sculptures.

WHERE TO STAY

There are five campgrounds in Flathead Lake State Park, each located at a different point around the lake: Big Arm (© **406/849-5255**) and West Shore (© **406/844-3901**) on the west side of the lake; and Finley Point (© **406/887-2715**), Yellow Bay (© **406/982-3291**), and Wayfarers (© **406/752-5501**) on the east shore. The phone numbers are operational only in summer. You can also call © **406/755-5501** for information on any of these state park campgrounds, which are open May through September.

Accommodations on and near the lake include guest ranches, water-oriented resorts with the gamut of recreational opportunities, and basic motels that offer clean but modest rooms. Less expensive options to the ranch vacation or area

---

Moments   A Visit to Wild Horse Island

Wild Horse Island, one of the largest islands in the inland United States, is run as a wildlife preserve by the Montana Department of Fish, Wildlife, and Parks (© **406/752-5501**). It contains one of the last remnants of Montana's endangered Palouse prairie plant and provides a habitat for bighorn sheep, mule deer, coyote, and a few wild horses. The island was originally created more than 17,000 years ago as a result of heavy glacial activity that formed the entire area. Sensitivity to this unusual environmental preserve by the human visitors is essential—please leave no traces of your visit. The park is open for day use only, and can be reached only by boat. Take your own or rent one from the **Big Arm Resort and Marina** (© **406/849-5622**). Several boat tours go to Wild Horse Island as well. You can take one from Bigfork with **Pointer Scenic Cruises** (© **406/837-5617**). *Note:* There are no visitor services on the island.

Jugglers, dancers and an assortment of acrobats fill the street.

She shoots you a wide-eyed look as a seven-foot cartoon character approaches.

What brought you here was wanting the kids

to see something magical while they still believed in magic.

America Online Keyword: Travel

With 700 airlines, 50,000 hotels and over 5,000 cruise and vaca-

tion getaways, you can now go places you've always dreamed of.

WORLD'S LEADING TRAVEL WEB SITE, 5 YEARS IN A ROW." WORLD TRAVEL AWARDS

Travelocity.com
A Sabre Company
Go Virtually Anywhere.

I HAVE TO CALL THE TRAVEL AGENCY AGAIN. DARN, OUT TO LUNCH. NOW I HAVE TO CALL THE AIRLINE. I HATE CALLING THE AIRLINES. I GOT PUT ON HOLD AGAIN. "INSTRUMENTAL TOP-40" ... LOVELY. I HATE GETTING PUT ON HOLD. TICKET PRICES ARE ALL OVER THE MAP. HOW DO I DIAL INTERNA-TIONALLY? OH SHOOT, FORGOT THE RENTAL CAR. I'M STILL ON HOLD. THIS MUSIC IS GIVING ME A HEADACHE. I WONDER IF SOMEONE ELSE HAS CHEAPER FLIGHTS. FORGET IT, CAN'T TAKE IT ANYMORE ... I'M HANGING UP.

YAHOO! TRAVEL
100% MUZAK-FREE

Booking your trip online at Yahoo! Travel is simple. You compare the best prices. You click. You go have fun. Tickets, hotels, rental cars, cruises & more. Sorry, no muzak.

resorts include the **Bayshore Resort Motel,** 616 Lakeside Blvd. in Lakeside (© **406/844-3131**); each unit has a kitchenette and some come with a boat slip. Summer rates are $95 for a double.

Averill's Flathead Lake Lodge ★★★ *Kids*   For an all-around vacation experience, this is the best on the lake. A beautiful log lodge surrounded by thousands of acres of forest is your home base for all activities, which include horseback riding, boating, and fishing. The Western experience is done up right at this place, complete with sing-alongs, campfires, and barn dances. The location and the atmosphere of this place (the Averills perfectly combine a ranching lifestyle with the summer vacation experience) make this one of the top picks in the state. There are 20 two- and three-bedroom cabins scattered around the property, featuring simple Western-style furnishings. Meals are served family-style in the main lodge—the food is top-notch.

P.O. Box 248, Bigfork, MT 59911. © **406/837-4391.** Fax 406/837-6977. www.averills.com. 2 lodges, 20 cabins. $2,185 per adult per week (based on 1-week minimum stay). Rate includes all meals and ranch activities. AE, MC, V. **Amenities:** 4 tennis courts; extensive water-sports equipment; activities desk; children's program; babysitting. *In room:* No phone.

Best Value Port Polson Inn   Although it's right on the highway, this is a very nice motel with an excellent view of the lake. The rooms are large and very clean, and there are two apartments and three suites that are especially good for families. The outdoor hot tub has a view of the lake, a perfect setting for unwinding after a day of fishing or hiking. Some rooms have kitchens and/or views overlooking the lake and the Mission Mountains.

502 U.S. 93 E., Polson, MT 59860. © **888/315-2378** or 406/883-5385. Fax 406/883-3998. www.bestvalueinn.com. 43 units. $79–$175. AE, MC, V. **Amenities:** Exercise room; indoor and outdoor Jacuzzis; sauna. *In room:* A/C, TV, kitchens.

The Candlewycke Inn ★ *Finds*   Tucked away on 10 acres of pine forest at the foot of the Swan Mountains, this luxurious and large B&B is a modern home that innkeeper Megan Vandegrift converted into a first-rate inn. The parlor, with 30-foot ceilings and an exposed pine staircase, draws you into a comfortable living space bedecked with an attractive selection of folk art. The large rooms have private bathrooms, and range from the somewhat frilly Botanical (with a canopied king bed, large bathroom, and private entry) to the rugged Wilderness (adorned with animal hides and a king bed with a log frame). There's a trail system on the property, an immaculate lawn, and all sorts of little touches (such as antlers converted to back scratchers). The breakfasts, anything from spinach strata to country-fried steak and eggs, are tailored to the tastes of guests.

311 Aero Lane, Bigfork, MT 59911. © **888/617-8805** or 406/837-6406. www.candlewyckeinn.com. 4 units. $110–$125 double. Rates include full breakfast. AE, MC, V. **Amenities:** Outdoor Jacuzzi; lawn games; game room. *In room:* Fridge, no phone.

Hotel Bigfork   The six rooms of this hotel are located over a popular restaurant and nightspot. Understandably, the noise from downstairs can be a problem. But to compensate, two of the rooms have large sliding glass doors opening onto a deck and a view of Flathead Lake beyond. When you aren't trying to sleep, try the restaurant for lunch or dinner—the menu includes steaks, baby-back ribs, and whitefish, and the atmosphere is pleasant with a good view of the lake. Rock-and-roll from the sound system drowns out the bar patrons' chatter about their golf games.

425 Grand Ave., Bigfork, MT 59911. ℂ 406/837-7377. 6 units. $65–$85 double. AE, MC, V. **Amenities:** Restaurant, lounge. *In room:* TV, no phone.

Kwa Taq Nuk Resort at Flathead Bay ⍟   This Best Western affiliate is a top-draw resort managed and owned by the Salish and Kootenai Indian tribes. It's the nicest property on the Polson end of the lake and offers a restaurant, marina, and art gallery. It's also the best decorated, with interesting and artful American Indian works on the walls. Lakeside rooms have commanding views, enhanced by decks furnished with chairs and cocktail tables. All the rooms are large and amply furnished.

The main lobby level is home to both a lounge and a restaurant, which provide stunning lakeside views. You can also eat or drink in the sunshine out on the deck. The retail operation is a combination gift shop–art gallery, so you'll find typical tourist souvenirs as well as authentic Western art produced by regional artists. The lower level has a large, comfortable sitting area with a large-screen cable television, swimming pool, and casino. This is the most expensive property on this end of the lake, but the amenities make it worth the extra money.

303 U.S. 93, Polson, MT 59860. ℂ 800/882-6363 or 406/883-3636. Fax 406/883-5392. www.kwataqnuk. com. 112 units. $95–$135 double. AE, DC, DISC, MC, V. **Amenities:** Restaurant, lounge; indoor and outdoor pools; Jacuzzi; activities desk; water-sports rental. *In room:* A/C, TV, dataport.

Marina Cay Resort and Conference Center   Marina Cay is a nice resort right on the water on the outskirts of Bigfork. The rooms are very large, and most open to a view on the water. The place attracts a few of the Montana glitterati, including L.A. Lakers center Shaquille O'Neal. Rooms here are sizeable, and there is a wide variety to choose from, but the walls are thin and noise carries easily from room to room.

Looking out over the marina, **Quincy's** at Marina Cay is a good restaurant, just a shade below La Provence and Showthyme (see "Where to Dine," below) in its food quality. But it's still very good, and in fact a lot of local folks rate it higher. A second restaurant, **Champs,** serves food year-round in a sports bar, casino-style atmosphere. The summer-only **Tiki** lounge serves drinks by the pool under flaring gas lamps.

180 Vista Lane, Bigfork, MT 59911. ℂ 800/433-6516 or 406/837-5861. Fax 406/837-1118. www. marinacay.com. 125 units. $65–$99 room; $199–$265 condo; $145–$275 suite. AE, DC, DISC, MC, V. **Amenities:** 2 restaurants, lounge; outdoor pool; 2 Jacuzzis; water-sports rentals. *In room:* A/C, TV.

Swan River Inn ⍟   Located in the heart of Bigfork, the Swan River Inn has a decidedly European feel, injected with a fair amount of whimsy to boot. There are only three rooms at the inn, but each is quite distinctive. The large log-cabin suite is decorated to resemble, well, a log cabin. The Victorian suite is also large, with turn-of-the-century elegance. The Art Deco suite hearkens back to the 1920s. All have beautifully restored bathrooms.

Upstairs, the **Swan River Cafe and Dinner House** serves steak, pork loin, rack of lamb, and a number of chicken and pasta dishes. In contrast to the Swiss architecture of the building's exterior, the **Grotto** is a recent makeover that converted an average lounge into a beautiful Spanish facility complete with heavy wood furniture, stucco walls, and wrought-iron fixtures.

360 Grand Ave., Bigfork, MT 59911. ℂ 406/837-2220. Fax 406/837-2327. 3 units. $90–$165. Rates include full breakfast. MC, V. **Amenities:** Restaurant, lounge. *In room:* No phone.

WHERE TO DINE

Bigfork has cornered the market on fine dining on the lake. Flathead residents from Whitefish and Kalispell routinely make their way to Bigfork to eat and take in a play at the Bigfork Summer Playhouse.

Coyote Roadhouse Grill ★★ ECLECTIC   Master chef and spice fanatic Gary Hastings labels the Coyote's cuisine "Southwestern/Tuscan/Mayan/Cajun," so it's a little hard to know what to expect. It's no big deal, because the food is uniformly superb—some locals swear the Cajun food here is better than what you get in New Orleans, where Hastings used to work. Located in the Coyote Roadhouse bed and breakfast in Ferndale, about 10 miles (16km) southeast of Bigfork, the restaurant always has a gumbo and jambalaya plate on the menu, but Hastings is forever experimenting and tinkering in the kitchen. On a given night, you might get veal saltimbocca or any number of fiery Mayan or Southwestern dishes. The seafood is flown in fresh twice weekly, and the chile peppers for the Mayan red chile sauce (usually served on a charbroiled pork tenderloin or crab cakes) are imported from Mexico. The atmosphere is rustic yet refined, and the dining room has a nice view of the Swan River.

600 Three Eagle Lane, Ferndale. ✆ 406/837-4250. Reservations required. Main courses $19–$25. No credit cards. Wed–Sun 5:30–8:30pm. Closed Oct to mid-May.

La Provence ★★ FRENCH/MEDITERRANEAN   Marc Guizol, the affable chef/owner of La Provence, made his way to Bigfork after his culinary career took him to the Ritz-Carlton in Naples and Caesar's Palace in Las Vegas. In his own eatery (occupying the space formerly filled by the Bridge Street Gallery Restaurant), Guizol's experience shines. The dinner menu is filled with lovingly prepared French standards, from escargot on a potato cake to pan-seared duck and roasted veal. He also seasonally mixes in a few game dishes and classic European desserts. The room itself is an airy, pleasant space with a simple country French flair. For lunch, the restaurant serves light fare: quiche, pastries, and sandwiches.

408 Bridge St., Bigfork. ✆ 406/837-2923. Reservations recommended. Lunch $4–$7; dinner $15–$20. AE, MC, V. Mon–Sat 11am–2pm and 5:30–10pm. Closed Mon in winter.

Showthyme ★★ ECLECTIC   When you ask locals what the best restaurant in town is, they'll more often than not tell you Showthyme—the restaurant that's located next to the summer playhouse. The atmosphere is a little bit New York, a little bit Montana. With a chef named Blu Funk and a manager named Rose Funk, you know the food has to be colorful. And it is: The Funks serve up everything from escargot and rack of lamb to baby-back ribs and chiles rellenos, all with a touch of creative flair. The grilled tuna, which is offered only as a special, is excellent, as is the Jamaican jerked pork loin with dried cranberry and hazelnut-Marsala demi-glace.

548 Electric Ave., Bigfork. ✆ 406/837-0707. Reservations recommended. Main courses $12–$22. AE, DISC, MC, V. Daily from 5pm.

Tiebuckers Pub and Eatery AMERICAN   Located in the old railroad depot in the sleepy town of Somers, Tiebuckers is a good restaurant that is prized by the locals. The fresh fish and steamed clams keep the crowds coming, but the menu also offers a good variety of beef and pasta. The chicken or ribs in Grandpa's Sauce are excellent as well. If your tastes skew toward the exotic, the restaurant also occasionally serves game: Buffalo, ostrich, or alligator might be available on a given night. There is a piano bar onsite that features live jazz on Saturdays.

75 Somers Rd., Somers. (©) **406/857-3335.** Reservations required for parties of 8 or more. Main courses $12–$18. AE, DISC, MC, V. Summer Tues–Sat 5–10pm; winter Tues–Sat 5–10pm.

The Village Well *(Value* BURGERS/PIZZA   The red neon sign outside says simply: EAT HERE. You could do worse. This loud, hip, young, ski-area kind of place (sans the ski area) is a good choice for inexpensive pizzas and burgers. If you prefer a quieter atmosphere, avoid the bar and head to the dining area to enjoy such creations as the Jimmy Buffet pizza, with chicken, mozzarella, and lime-tomato-cilantro salsa. There's a pool table, foosball, and Ping-Pong to keep the kids occupied.

260 River St., Bigfork. (©) **406/837-5251.** Lunch $5–$8; dinner $5–$15. DISC, MC, V. Daily 11am–11pm. Bar open later.

THE PERFORMING ARTS

In addition to the troupe of the Bigfork Summer Playhouse (see "Exploring the Area," above), Flathead Lake visitors can take in a play by the **Polson Players,** a talented group of thespians who take to the stage at the Mission Valley Performing Arts Center. Call the **Port Polson Chamber of Commerce** (© **406/883-5969**) for current information on plays, ticket prices, event dates, and times.

6 The Swan Valley

Extends 91 miles (147km) S of Bigfork; Southern End: 33 miles (53km) E of Missoula; 90 miles (145km) W of Helena

The 50-mile (80km) stretch of Mont. 83 from Columbia Falls to Swan, Con-don, and Seeley Lakes is far removed from Flathead Lake's tourist attractions. Though less traveled, the road boasts vistas even more lovely than those seen from U.S. 93, its cousin to the west. Opportunities for watching wildlife are quite good, and Seeley Lake, Summit Lake, and Alva Lake, all excellent recreational areas, lie close to the highway.

Swan Valley seems more authentically "Montana" than other, busier areas, perhaps because the area isn't developed for tourists. Though some think the timber industry clear-cuts are an eyesore, the remainder of this thinly populated area is crowned with snowcapped mountains and accessible lakes. Swan Valley seems remote compared to the nearby larger towns—an hour from Missoula, 2 hours from Helena—and we guess that it will remain mostly undiscovered for some time. In winter, snowmobiling, cross-country skiing, and even sled-dog mushing are the sports of choice in this out-of-the-way wonderland. Be sure to watch out for deer year-round along Mont. 83, especially at dawn and dusk—and remember, they usually travel in small groups.

Seeley Lake is one of the places where you can see the loon. Henry David Thoreau described its call as a "long-drawn, unearthly howl, probably more like that of a wolf than any other bird." The loon is a symbol of north-country wilderness, and an appropriate one for this quiet and beautiful area.

ESSENTIALS

GETTING THERE   Other than being air-dropped, the only way to get into the Swan Valley is motor vehicle via Mont. 83. Airports in **Kalispell** (© **406/257-5994**) and **Missoula** (© **406/543-8631**) are almost equidistant from the Swan. The town of Seeley Lake is 48 miles (77km) from Missoula. Take Mont. 200 east from Missoula 33 miles (53km) to Mont. 83 north. It's 42 miles (68km) from Kalispell to Swan Lake in the northern portion of the valley. Take U.S. 93 south to Mont. 82 east, then Mont. 83 south. For weather reports, call ℂ **406/449-5204.**

VISITOR INFORMATION   The Swan isn't exactly a self-promoter. Though several businesses rely on tourists, the valley-wide tendency is to remain small. The **Swan Lake Chamber of Commerce,** Stoney Creek Road, Swan Lake, MT 59911 (ℂ **406/886-2279**), can send you information on local happenings. For general information about Glacier Country, which includes the Swan Valley, call ℂ **800/338-5072** or 406/756-7128 or check out www.glacier.visitmt.com.

GETTING OUTSIDE

Densely forested and marked by a sparkling chain of lakes, the Seeley-Swan Valley offers a variety of activities for the outdoor enthusiast, with a vast network of Forest Service trails making year-round recreational opportunities for hiking, mountain biking, fishing, cross-country skiing, and snowmobiling. The **Seeley Lake Ranger District,** Seeley Lake (ℂ **406/677-2233;** www.fs.fed.us/welcome. html), will provide you with a detailed map of these trails upon request. The district office is 3 miles (5km) north of Seeley Lake near mile marker 18 of Mont. 83. One of the most popular summer activities is the **Clearwater River Canoe Trail,** a 3½-mile (6km) leisurely run down the river to the north end of Seeley Lake. The put-in is at the end of Forest Service Road 17597 and ends at the canoe landing at the ranger station.

The Forest Service publishes *Seeley Lake Area Recreation Opportunities,* which outlines a number of hikes in the national forest and wilderness areas. For a fairly short and interesting family hike, try the **Morrell Falls Trail,** a 2½-mile (4km) hike from the trail head to a series of cascades, the largest of which drops 90 feet. From Clearwater Junction, travel north on Mont. 83 for 15 miles (24km). Turn east on Cottonwood Lakes Road 477 and go 1‰ miles (2km). Turn north on West Morrell Road 4353, then go 6 miles (10km). Turn east on Pyramid Pass Road 4364 and go a quarter mile. Turn north on Morrell Falls Road 4364 and go a mile (2km) to the trail head.

OUTFITTERS & GUIDES   Swan Valley is home to several experienced guides who know parts of this vast territory like the toughened backs of their leathery hands. Guided pack trips on horseback usually run from $165 to $200 per person per day, with a normal trip into the Bob Marshall Wilderness usually lasting a week. **Buck Creek Guide Service** (ℂ **406/754-2471**) offers trips that focus on natural history and local culture. **JM Bar Outfitters** (ℂ **406/ 825-3230**) of Clinton, a tiny town south of the wilderness area, offers trips into the Bob Marshall Wilderness that may include hunting and fishing, photography, and sightseeing. Good pack trips into the Bob Marshall take at least 5 days, with 10-day trips being a little longer than normal, but certainly worthwhile. Expect to pay around $1,000 per person for a trip, with longer trips costing closer to $1,500. In Clearwater, **Monture Face Outfitters** (ℂ **406/244-5763**) offers summer backpacking trips, hunting, and fishing in the Bob Marshall Wilderness. **Montana Equestrian Tours,** P.O. Box 1280, Swan Valley, MT 59826 (ℂ **800/636-RIDE** or 406/754-2900), offers several-day horseback tours of the valley for experienced riders. Tours begin in the Seeley Lake area and go out to three or four different lodging facilities. Rides are 17 to 25 miles

(27–40km) per day at a relatively lively pace. Weather doesn't slow the riders down, so if it's raining, you'll be out there in it. Along the way you can expect to see elk, deer, and occasionally a bear. The $1,500 trips begin on Sunday and conclude on Friday.

WHERE TO STAY

The Emily A. Bed-and-Breakfast 𝕽   The Emily A. is a thoroughly modern, two-story bed-and-breakfast beautifully situated on the Clearwater River, in the middle of a stunning mountain meadow. It's located about 5 miles (8km) north of the town of Seeley Lake. The 11,000 square-foot lodge is decorated in a distinctly Western theme, emphasized by blonde pine logs. There is a large, open great room dominated by a river-rock fireplace, with an upper-tier lounge for sitting, reading, or watching television. The sun room boasts views of Swan Valley and the Mission Mountains in addition to a wide variety of wildlife that wanders right outside the B&B's door. The facility offers canoes for its guests to explore the waters that beckon just off the rear deck. The suite, with two bedrooms, a kitchen, and a private deck, is ideal for families. The entire inn is smoke-free.

Mont. 83, mile marker 20 (P.O. Box 350), Seeley Lake, MT 59868. ✆ **406/677-3474.** Fax 406/677-3474. www.theemilya.com. 6 units, 3 with private bathroom. $115 double; $150 suite. Rates include full breakfast. MC, V. **Amenities:** Water-sports equipment. *In room:* Kitchen, no phone.

The Lodges on Seeley Lake   One of only two lodges right on Seeley Lake, this 1920 lodge and cabins operation is being gradually renovated. The cabins are spacious and beautifully decorated, complete with upholstered chairs and queen beds. All the rooms have televisions and private bathrooms. Fortunately, the modern conveniences have been added without sacrificing the rustic feeling of the lodge. The best thing here though, remains the peaceful views of the lake from the beachfront, and of the wilderness beyond. The lodges have complimentary boats for guests to take out for fishing or recreation.

2156 Boy Scout Rd. (P.O. Box 568), Seeley Lake, MT 59868. ✆ **800/900-9016.** Fax 406/677-3806. www.lodgesatseeleylake.com. 11 units. $110–$137 double. MC, V. **Amenities:** Water-sports equipment. *In room:* TV, kitchens, no phone.

Swan Valley Super 8   This is the only chain hotel in the Seeley-Swan Valley. The rooms are just motel rooms, though the setting is spectacular. And the building is pretty, a two-level log structure that doesn't look like your typical Super 8. There are several restaurants nearby, and accommodations for your horse can also be arranged.

Between mile markers 46 and 47 on Mont. 83 (P.O. Box 1287), Condon, MT 59826. ✆ **800/800-8000** or 406/754-2688. Fax 406/754-2688. 22 units. $56–$59 double. Rates include continental breakfast. AE, DC, DISC, MC, V. Pets accepted. *In room:* TV.

GUEST RANCHES & RESORTS

Double Arrow Resort 𝕽   Double Arrow is 2 miles (3km) south of Seeley Lake on Mont. 83, near the Bob Marshall Wilderness Area. The resort has just about any activity that a Montana-bound vacationer could want—golf, tennis, fishing, riding, hiking, and mountain biking. There are also guided fly-fishing and float trips available on the Blackfoot River. In the winter, there's cross-country skiing, snowmobiling, and sleigh riding. You can get accommodations suited to nearly any taste, from relatively inexpensive rooms in the main lodge, to cabins, to a full-sized, four-bedroom lodge all to yourself. The cabins are large and comfortably furnished, with sitting areas featuring upholstered chairs and sofas.

Rides to trail heads in the wilderness area offer opportunities for guests to explore Clearwater Valley, Horseshoe Hills, and the Morrell Falls National Recreation Trail. Two all-weather tennis courts and an enclosed pool with a hot tub keep them busy afterwards. There's also an 18-hole golf course. The public is welcome at **The Seasons Restaurant,** which offers fine dining—mostly well-prepared beef and seafood—and a Sunday brunch on special occasions.

P.O. Box 747, Seeley Lake, MT 59868. © **800/468-0777** or 406/677-2777. Fax 406/667-2922. www.double arrowresort.com. 26 units. $75–$150 double; 2- to 4-bedroom lodges $250–$595. Call for off-season rates. AE, DISC, MC, V. **Amenities:** Restaurant, lounge; indoor pool; golf course; outdoor tennis courts; indoor Jacuzzi; water-sports equipment; activities desk. *In room:* Kitchens, no phone.

Lake Upsata Guest Ranch ★★   This family-oriented guest ranch is located along the southern border of the Bob Marshall Wilderness Area within shouting distance of Missoula and Seeley Lake. You stay in delightful but rustic cabins that have shower-only bathrooms (no tubs). Horseback riding is the number-one activity at the ranch, although fly-fishing instruction (on the nearby Black-foot River) is also arranged for guests. Hiking is another key experience, and the managers have organized several hikes that allow visitors to see wildlife and learn about the area's flora. Crafts, horseback instruction, hiking, and boating are part of a popular 5-day program for kids. Other activities here include tours to Gar-net, a nearby ghost town, and tube riding and kayaking on the lake. Meals are served family-style in the main lodge. The food is excellent; daily menus change and include baked ham, Yankee pot roast, trout, and roast turkey.

P.O. Box 6, Ovando, MT 59854. © **800/594-7687.** 8 cabins. $220 per adult per night, $190 per child per night. 3-day minimum stay. Rates include all meals and activities. No credit cards. Pets accepted. **Amenities:** Restaurant; water-sports equipment; activities desk; children's program. *In room:* Kitchens, no phone.

Tamaracks Resort   Tamaracks started out as a homestead in 1916 and became a resort in 1930. It is right on Seeley Lake with 1,700 feet of lakefront. The resort has a 1940s feel to it, with lots of room between the cabins, screened-in porches, and an attached campground (sites run $20–$25 a night). The cab-ins are clean and comfortable, though not large, but there is also a trio of full-fledged log homes for those in need of more space. Every cabin and home has a full kitchen. The resort offers boat and canoe rental, a basketball court, horseshoe pits, and volleyball in the summer, and cross-country ski, skate, and snowmobile rentals in winter.

P.O. Box 812, Seeley Lake, MT 59868. © **800/477-7216** or 406/677-2433. Fax 406/677-3503. www.tamarack resort.com. 15 cabins, including 3 log homes. $75–$205 cabin; $150–$390 log home. MC, V. **Amenities:** Water-sports equipment; activities desk. *In room:* Kitchens, no phone.

White Tail Ranch   This guest ranch is close to both Missoula and Helena, in the Blackfoot Valley, 9 miles (14km) from Mont. 200. Upon arriving, your first and biggest challenge will be to determine which of the many available activities suit your tastes. There's fly-fishing on Salmon Creek (which runs through the middle of the property), horseback riding, mountain biking, and hiking. There are also children's programs. The area is a photographer's paradise. During win-ter months it's an excellent spot for cross-country skiing, dog-sledding, and snowmobiling. Accommodations are in 10 guest cabins on the creek, with views of both the mountains and the woods. Meals are served family-style in the main lodge. All the cabins are newly redecorated and now have private bathrooms.

82 Whitetail Ranch Rd., Ovando, MT 59854. © **888/987-2624.** Fax 406/793-5043. www.whitetailranch. com. 9 cabins. $100–$200 per person per night (3-night minimum). MC, V. Well-behaved pets accepted. **Amenities:** Activities desk; children's program. *In room:* No phone.

WHERE TO DINE

In Seeley Lake, the best spot for breakfast or lunch may be the **Filling Station Restaurant and Bar** (© 406/677-2080), and the best cup of hot chocolate is undoubtedly at the **Stage Station** (© 406/677-2227). Both restaurants are in the heart of town. In Swan Lake, try the **Laughing Horse Lodge** on Mont. 83 (© 406/886-2080), which serves hearty meals and uses fresh, locally grown ingredients.

Lindey's Restaurant STEAKS   Apart from the dining room at the Double Arrow Resort (see "Where to Stay," above), this is easily the best restaurant in the area. A carbon copy of a sister restaurant in Minnesota that has achieved national acclaim, Lindey's makes ordering easy: There are only three dinner choices—chopped sirloin, prime sirloin, and special sirloin—all of which are accompanied by the restaurant's excellent greaseless hash browns plus a tossed green salad. For smaller appetites, there's a special "dinner-sharing" arrangement that allows two people to order one steak and two plates for an additional $6.25. Seating is in a comfortable glass-enclosed space with views overlooking the lake and the seaplane landing area.

Mont. 83. © 406/677-9229. Main courses $11–$22. MC, V. May–Sept daily 5–10pm; Oct–Apr 15 Tues–Sun 5–9pm. Closed Apr 16–Apr 30.

7 The Bob Marshall Wilderness Complex ★★

45 miles (72km) S of Big Fork; 78 miles (126km) NE of Missoula; 80 miles (129km) W of Great Falls

The Bob Marshall Wilderness Complex is the largest wilderness area in the Lower 48 states, covering 1.5 million acres, or about 2,400 square miles. We hate to keep picking on Rhode Island for these comparisons, but the Bob, as it is usually called, is more than twice the size of that state.

The complex includes the Bob Marshall Wilderness proper, and the Great Bear and the Scapegoat Wilderness Areas. It abuts Glacier National Park, creating a huge area of relatively untouched country extending nearly half the width of Montana from the Canadian border. Marshall himself was one of the earliest advocates of wilderness for its own sake in the U.S., and the nearly one million acres of wild lands that bear his name were among the areas designated by the federal Wilderness Act of 1964. The Great Bear and Scapegoat were set aside in the 1970s.

Just south of Glacier National Park, the complex occupies nearly the entire territory that lies between the boundaries of U.S. 2 to the north, Mont. 83 to the west, Mont. 200 to the south, and U.S. Highways 287 and 89 to the east. Access points along these roads occur infrequently and are poorly marked, so keep your eyes peeled.

The wilderness area has become very popular with hikers and horsepackers over the years, leading to a curious pattern of trail deterioration. Federal budget austerity allows the U.S. Forest Service little funding for trail maintenance, and while heavy traffic on the most popular trails has led to their corrosion, many of the secondary trails have virtually disappeared. Quite a few trails that are marked on topographical maps of the area are faint or nonexistent on the ground. You should know fundamental trail-finding and direction skills—how to read a topo map—in case a trail dies out or is covered by snowbanks.

EXPLORING THE AREA

For information, maps, and advice about traveling in the Bob Marshall Wilderness complex, contact one of the six ranger stations monitoring the wilderness.

Tips **Advice for Day-Trippers**

Day hiking is best done near **Holland Lake**. Take Mont. 83 south 61 miles (98km) from Bigfork, or north 20 miles (32km) from Seeley Lake, to reach the **Holland Lake Lodge** and the trails. Trail 42 from the north side of Holland Lake connects with Trail 110 to reach the Necklace Lakes just inside the Wilderness boundaries. To reach the Holland Lake Falls and Upper Holland Lake before crossing the Wilderness boundary at Gordon Pass, take Trail 415 a short way until it joins Trail 35. This trail, taken to its end, stretches from the western boundary into the center of the park near the South Fork of the Flathead River (not a day-hike).

In the **Lewis and Clark National Forest:** Rocky Mountain Ranger District, 1102 Main Ave. NW, Box 340, Choteau, MT 59242 (℅ **406/466-5341**). In the **Flathead National Forest:** the Spotted Bear and Hungry Horse Ranger Districts, 8975 U.S. 2 E., Hungry Horse, MT 59919 (℅ **406/758-5376**), or the Swan Lake Ranger District, P.O. Box 370, Bigfork, MT 59911 (℅ **406/837-5081**). In the **Lolo National Forest:** Seeley Lake Ranger District, HC 31 Box 3200, Seeley Lake, MT 59868 (℅ **406/677-2233**). In the **Helena National Forest:** Lincoln Ranger District, Box 219, Lincoln, MT 59639 (℅ **406/362-4265**). An excellent guidebook to the area is *The Trail Guide to the Bob Marshall Country,* by Erik Molvar (Falcon Press).

The most popular destination in the Bob is the **Chinese Wall,** a striking rock formation that stands more than 1,000 feet tall and stretches for 11 miles (18km) through the wilderness on the western boundary of the **Sun River Game Preserve.** One of the more well-traveled trails and easy accesses to the Chinese Wall is along the South Fork of the Sun River on the Holland Lake–Benchmark Trail (see below). From the east, reach the Chinese Wall by taking Trail 202 at Benchmark for 5 miles (8km) to Trail 203, then continue on this trail for roughly 11 miles (18km) before taking the Indian Creek Trail, Trail 211, to the south end of the Chinese Wall at White River Pass, elevation 7,590 feet. The Chinese Wall is unmistakable and is one of the most recognizable geologic formations in Montana. The USGS topographical maps for the trip are Slategoat Mountain, Prairie Reef, and Amphitheatre Mountain.

The high meadows at the base of the wall are very fragile, and overnight camping is prohibited along the base between Cliff and Salt Mountains. So plan your trip to allow time to reach a camping area away from this section of the wall.

Towering peaks run great lengths through the Bob and stand as some of the tallest, and certainly the most dramatic, sites in the northwest part of the state outside Glacier National Park. **Holland Peak,** just north of Holland Lake on the wilderness area's western boundary, is a spectacular 9,356-foot giant that can be seen from afar but cannot be accessed directly. A short day-hike is available from the Holland Lake Lodge (see "Advice for Day-Trippers," below, for directions to the lodge) into the wilderness to **Holland Falls.** From the trail head to the falls is only about 1½ miles (2km), an easy hike with only 240 feet of elevation gain. This trail is designated for hikers only; bikes, horses, and other pack animals are prohibited.

Once inside the wilderness area, **Big Salmon Lake** is a wonderful destination for the photographer, capturing the length and the beauty of Holland Peak's east face. To reach Big Salmon Lake, take Trail 42 from the Holland Lake Lodge on the west side of the Bob to Trail 110. It's a very long day-hike, and a reasonable 2-day hike through the Swan Range to Big Salmon Lake.

Located one-third of the way in on the **Holland Lake–Benchmark Trail** (a 60-mile [97km] trail across the midsection of the Bob that, following a series of shorter trails, takes roughly a week to traverse), Salmon Lake is simple purity without sight or sound of civilization. This trail also runs just south of the Chinese Wall.

North, in the Great Bear, is the impressive **Great Northern Mountain.** This 8,705-foot peak towers over the northeast part of the Great Bear Wilderness and can be viewed from many different points along the roadsides near the wilderness areas. You'll need a couple of vehicles if you don't have someone who can pick you up where you exit the Bob at the end of your journey. Park at Holland Lake if you plan on making it your terminus, or at Benchmark, west of Augusta, if you plan on ending there.

If you begin on the east side, the Holland Lake-Benchmark Trail follows the South Fork of the Sun River on Trails 202 and 203 before moving west along Indian Creek on Trail 211. This takes you, as mentioned above, to the south end of the Chinese Wall at White River Pass. From there, you'll take Trail 138 along the South Fork of the White River until you reach the White River and Trail 112. This trail takes you to the South Fork of the Flathead River at White River Park. Across the river, you'll find Murphy Flats and Trail 263 along the river to Trail 110. This long trail takes you along Big Salmon Lake and the Swan Range, and then to Holland Lake outside the Bob's western boundary.

To reach the summit of Great Northern, you'll have to do some off-trail hiking—8 miles (13km), if you make a round-trip. From Martin City, just northeast of Columbia Falls on U.S. 2, take the East Side Reservoir Road (38) for just over 15 miles (24km) to Highline Loop Road (1048). Take this road for just more than a half-mile across the bridge to the "trail head." Start along the left side of the creek until the landscape opens up. Trudge up to the ridge, then along it, to Great Northern's summit.

The majestic **Scapegoat Mountain** is the dominating jewel of the Scapegoat Wilderness Area. Surrounded by cliffs, this 9,204-foot summit is easily the most prominent feature in the southern part of the wilderness complex.

Wildlife abounds in the Bob, with grizzly bears being the most feared and the most difficult to spot. Moose and deer are common. Elk gather each fall for mating at the base of the Chinese Wall in the Sun River Game Preserve on the wilderness's east side. There are lots of birds, including the ptarmigan, a brown bird resembling the quail, which changes the color of its plumage each winter to snow white.

HELPFUL TIPS Some things to remember when camping: Before you set out, contact and consult a ranger at one of the district ranger stations mentioned above about distances, the wisdom of your itinerary, and restrictions. You can also pick up a topographical map. Carry plenty of water and water containers. Remember when loading up your pack that this is the weight you'll likely endure for a week or so. Restrictions are few. No vehicles are allowed in the area, including bicycles. To get around in the Bob you either walk or ride on an animal's back. It might also help to remember, too, that hunting is allowed in many areas, making backpacking in the Bob a little less inviting in the fall. Wear bright colors and make lots of noise.

8 Kalispell ⟨★⟩

115 miles (185km) N of Missoula; 249 miles (401km) E of Spokane, Washington

Located smack-dab in the center of Montana's primary vacation and tourism region, Kalispell isn't as much a destination for recreational visitors as Whitefish and Bigfork, but it is a good base for exploring the area and has a number of attractions in its own right. The city, which is also a business and industrial center, is in a beautiful setting and conveniently located for visits to Flathead Lake, skiing in Whitefish, or hiking and touring in Glacier National Park. If you come to Kalispell after visiting Glacier or the Bob Marshall Wilderness, it will seem positively urban. It has all the modern inconveniences, including a large mall and long waits at traffic lights. But it has managed to preserve a good deal of its historical character, and has a colorful arts and dining scene.

ESSENTIALS

GETTING THERE   Glacier Park International Airport (✆ 406/ 257-5994) is located north of town at 4170 U.S. 2. **Delta** (✆ 800/221-1212 or 406/257-1030), **Horizon** (✆ 800/547-9308 or 406/752-2209), and **Big Sky** (✆ 800/237-7788) have daily flights.

U.S. 2 will get you here from the east or west. From Missoula, U.S. 93 leads north into town on a scenic 120-mile (193km) route that takes you past Flathead Lake. The drive usually takes a solid 2½ hours, no matter what the season. RVs amble along the gradually curving road during summer (to the frustration of most other drivers!), and icy conditions warrant added caution and reduced speeds during the winter. Call ✆ 406/755-4949 for **road information** in the Kalispell area.

Amtrak stops at the Whitefish depot, just 15 miles (24km) north of Kalispell. The bus terminal is located at 3794 U.S. 2 E. (✆ 406/755-4011).

VISITOR INFORMATION   The **Flathead Convention and Visitor Bureau** is located at 15 Depot Park, Kalispell, MT 59901 (✆ 800/543-3105 or 406/756-9091; www.fcvb.org), and not only offers practical information concerning Kalispell, but provides information on year-round lodging, activities, and attractions, including Glacier National Park, Big Mountain Ski Resort, and Flathead Lake.

GETTING AROUND   Rental-car companies **Avis** (✆ 800/831-2847), **Budget** (✆ 800/527-0700), **Hertz** (✆ 800/654-3131), and **National** (✆ 800/ 227-7368) maintain counters at the airport.

For taxi service, call **Kalispell Taxi and Airport Shuttle** at ✆ 406/752-4022 or **Flathead-Glacier Transportation** (✆ 406/892-3390).

GETTING OUTSIDE

Kalispell itself isn't exactly a destination for the person looking for outdoor recreation, but its location near the epicenter of Glacier Park and Flathead Lake makes it a good home base for those exploring this region, during both the summer and ski seasons.

BIKING   Since motor vehicle traffic on U.S. 2 or U.S. 93 make them less than ideal for bike riding, cyclists usually head to the back roads. **Whitefish Stage Road** runs parallel to U.S. 93 (from U.S. 93, go east on Reserve Street to reach it) and offers some great views of the mountains in a bucolic environment. For area information, as well as all kinds of bicycle accessories and rentals, try **BikeRite** at 110 E. Idaho St. (✆ 406/756-0053).

FISHING There is good fishing on the main Flathead River between Columbia Falls and Kalispell for trout and whitefish. There is good shore access at Pressentine, which is 5 miles (8km) north of Kalispell on U.S. 2 (follow the fishing access signs). Or you can float from Pressentine down river to Old Steel Bridge.

GOLF Golfers should head to **Northern Pines Golf Club** ☞ (© 800/255-5641 or 406/751-1950 for tee times; www.golfmt.com), which is 2 miles (3km) north of Kalispell on U.S. 93. *Golf Digest* has already called it the second best course in Montana and the seventh best new course in the entire country—it opened in 1996. Designed by two-time U.S. Open champion Andy North and architect Roger Packard, it offers a front nine of links-style play with British Open rough. The back nine is a different style, heavily treed along the Stillwater River. The course is fairly long at 7,000 yards. Cost is $45 for 18 holes, $25 for nine. **Buffalo Hill** (© 406/756-4548; www.golfbuffalohill.com), just off U.S. 2 north of town at 1176 N. Main St., is an older course that's very hilly, with lots of trees and lots of memorable holes that can have serious golfers brushing up on their cursing. Cost is $39 for 18 holes, $25 after 3pm.

HIKING **Lone Pine State Park** (© 406/755-2706) is an attractive state park with a few hiking trails. Go west on U.S. 2. At the intersection with Meridian, you'll see signs for the park sending you left (south). Take this road for about 5 miles (8km) (in the curve to your right, the road becomes Foys Lake Rd.) to the park. Once you're there, take in the views of the valley below or hike on the trails.

SEEING THE SIGHTS
Woodland Park, on the east edge of town at Woodland Park Drive, is a little spot that offers visitors a place to sit down in the sun and relax if they want to kill a day outside without killing themselves. There's a lagoon with ducks and a swimming pool. Walking tracks skirt the park. Another worthwhile attraction is the **Central School Museum,** 124 2nd Ave. E. (© 406/756-8381), dedicated to preserving Kalispell's history.

Conrad Mansion This 23-room Victorian mansion takes up most of a city block. Built in 1895 by Missouri River freighter Charles E. Conrad, the mansion has been beautifully restored and outfitted with the original furnishings. All tours of the mansion are guided and last about an hour; tour guides are dressed in Victorian costume and explain the history of Conrad and his palatial home. Some highlights: an amazing collection of dolls and toys from three generations of the Conrad family, meticulously kept clothing from the 19th century, and the annual Victorian Christmas Bazaar in late October. The beautifully kept grounds also make for a peaceful locale for a short walk or a picnic.

330 Woodland Ave. © 406/755-2166. www.conradmansion.com. $7 adults, $1 children. Mid-May to mid-June and mid-Sept to mid-Oct daily 10am–5:30pm; mid-June to mid-Sept daily 9am–8pm. Closed mid-Oct to mid-May except for special events. Located 6 blocks east of Main St.

Hockaday Museum of Art ☞ The charming Hockaday contains art formerly located in the Carnegie Library. The museum focuses on the works of Montana artists, both contemporary and historic, including Russell Chatham, Ace Powell, and Robert Scriver. There are tours, a gift shop, and an "Arts in the Park" program each July. The Hockaday has a very fine regional reputation for the quality of its programs.

302 2nd Ave. E. © 406/755-5268. www.hockadayartmuseum.org. Suggested donation $5 adults, $4 seniors, and $1 students. Tues–Sat 10am–5pm.

SHOPPING

Although not a major shopping destination, Kalispell has enough to offer if your money is burning a hole in your pocket. The **Kalispell Center Mall** at 20 N. Main St. has more than 40 stores and restaurants. Just up the street, downtown Kalispell has a few stores of its own. **Norm's News** (see "Where to Dine," below) has the latest newspapers from around the globe as well as a comprehensive magazine rack and espresso bar. **Books West** (C 406/752-6900) is the downtown book shop on 101 Main St. The **Western Outdoor Store** (C 406/756-5818), 48 Main St., has a vast collection of Western gear for sale—4,000 pairs of cowboy boots, sterling silver Western belt buckles, and, for the wannabe dude, cowboy hats in all sizes and shapes. There's also an antiques store in the basement. The **Rocky Mountain Outfitter** (C 406/752-2446), 135 Main St., has all the gear you'll need for hiking nearby trails and scaling the peaks. You can also rent kayaks and canoes if you want to head out on the water on your own.

Mark Ogle Gallery, 101 E. Center St. (C 406/752-4217), features a selection of wildlife paintings and prints by its eponymous owner. **Columbine Glassworks** (C 406/752-7174) at 140 Main St. has stained glass and artworks in many other media.

WHERE TO STAY

Diamond Lil Inn *(Value* This boisterous hotel is across the street from the WestCoast Outlaw (see below) and offers lodging for considerably less. The rooms are fairly large; unfortunately, they all face the parking lot or the swimming pool and hot tubs. There is a casino associated with the hotel, the Rose, which also has a lounge and restaurant. The restaurant is inexpensive and offers a fairly nice atmosphere, in a riverboat gambler sort of way.

1680 U.S. 93 S., Kalispell, MT 59901. C 800/843-7301 or 406/752-3467. Fax 406/752-3489. $54–$77 double. AE, DC, DISC, MC, V. **Amenities:** Restaurant, lounge; outdoor pool; Jacuzzi; coin-op washers and dryers. *In-room:* TV.

Four Seasons Motor Inn *(Value* This is a very nicely kept older, independent motel. The rooms are in three different buildings that flank the parking area. They're bright, clean, and large, with full shower/tub combos. They are pleasantly decorated with nice artwork of Flathead Lake and Glacier National Park scenes. Some have fridges and/or modem-ready phones. None of them has a view to speak of, but this motel offers a nice, inexpensive alternative to the chains.

350 N. Main, Kalispell, MT 59901. C 800/545-6399 or 406/755-6123. Fax 406/755-1604. www.fourseasonsmotorinn.com. 101 units. Summer $62–$100 double; winter $39–$64 double. AE, DC, DISC, MC, V. Pets accepted. **Amenities:** Jacuzzi. *In room:* A/C, TV, coffeemaker.

Hampton Inn *๙* Kalispell's Hampton Inn is a very attractive three-story brick structure surrounded by lovely landscaping. The fairly large rooms have one king-size bed or two queens. The lobby has a comfortable sitting area in front of a large dome fireplace, enhanced by colorful log furniture with leather cushions. A business center provides a personal computer, fax-modem lines, calculators, copy machines, and a printer for guests.

1140 U.S. 2 W., Kalispell, MT 59901. C 406/755-7900. Fax 406/755-5056. www.northwestinns.com. 120 units. $78–$225 double. Rates include continental breakfast. AE, DISC, MC, V. **Amenities:** Indoor pool; indoor Jacuzzi; exercise room; courtesy car; coin-op washers and dryers. *In room:* A/C, TV/VCR, dataport, fridge, coffeemaker, hair dryer, iron.

The Kalispell Grand Hotel ✹   The Kalispell Grand is a historic hotel (1912) done in the Old West tradition. Located right downtown, the hotel has been beautifully refurbished, right down to the pressed-tin ceiling and elegant oak staircase. By today's standards the rooms are small, as are the bathrooms, but the historic ambience makes the lack of space worthwhile. The lobby is the center-piece of the hotel, with cherry-wood walls, a small art gallery, and a wolf-whistling cockatiel that can make a person feel downright attractive.

100 Main St., Kalispell, MT 59901-4452. ✆ 800/858-7422 or 406/755-8100. Fax 406/752-8012. www.kalispellgrand.com. 40 units. $68–$125 double. AE, DC, DISC, MC, V. Pets accepted. **Amenities:** Restaurant; spa; Jacuzzi; exercise room. *In room:* A/C, TV, dataport.

WestCoast Kalispell Center Hotel   This motel, located inside the Kalispell Center Mall, has a great location within easy walking distance to restaurants, shopping, and more shopping. Rooms, decorated in typical but attractive mod-ern hotel style, are spacious, and some overlook the patio/garden area outside. More expensive suites include kitchenettes and whirlpool baths. The Northwest Bounty Co. is the hotel's restaurant. The food is respectable, though conven-tional. But the skylights and atrium-style windows offer a nice dining experience on sunny summer days.

20 N. Main St. (attached to the Kalispell Center Mall), Kalispell, MT 59901. ✆ 800/325-4000 or 406/751-5050. Fax 406/751-5051. 132 units. $135 double; $135–$200 suite. AE, DC, DISC, MC, V. Pets accepted. **Amenities:** Restaurant, lounge; indoor pool; indoor Jacuzzi; exercise room. *In room:* A/C, TV, data-port, coffeemaker, hair dryer, iron.

WestCoast Outlaw Hotel   This is the largest property in Kalispell, located on the main highway just south of downtown. Standard rooms are accented by light-colored pine furniture and watercolors, and floral patterns on bed and win-dow coverings. All rooms come with clock radios and terry-cloth bathrobes. Business services include modem connections, fax, copiers, printers, and an air express drop-off box just outside the lobby. The dining room is more formal than in most mid-range hotels. Fitness buffs can head to the on-site handball courts, tennis court, or swimming pools (one of which is enclosed). Other serv-ices include a men's and women's styling salon and massage service, as well as a Western art gallery and gift shop.

1701 U.S. 93 S., Kalispell, MT 59901. ✆ 800/237-7445 or 406/755-6100. Fax 406/756-8994. www.best-western.com/outlawhotel. 250 units. $99 double; $134–$350 suite. AE, DC, MC, V. **Amenities:** Restaurant, lounge; indoor and outdoor swimming pools; tennis court; exercise room; salon. *In room:* A/C, TV, coffeemaker, iron.

WHERE TO DINE
MODERATE

Alley Connection ✹ CHINESE   The best place in the valley for Chinese cui-sine, the Alley Connection took several years to reach its current state of grace. What started out as a small, one-room operation has become two tastefully but simply decorated dining rooms, which serve up excellent fare. Meals of chow mein, sweet-and-sour pork, and Szechwan chicken may be ordered separately or in the more popular family-style. Lunch is a great deal for less than $6, and serv-ice is always quick and dependable.

22 1st St. ✆ 406/752-7077. Reservations recommended. Lunch $2–$5; dinner $6–$13. AE, DISC, MC, V. Tues–Thurs 11am–2:30pm and 5–9pm; Fri–Sat 11am–2:30pm and 5–9:30pm.

Cafe Max ✹✹ CONTINENTAL   Cafe Max brings a dash of New York-style culinary glitz to the Flathead Valley. Owned by chef Doug Day, the place is

small, elegant, busy, and always booked. The food is excellent, elegantly prepared and presented. While the menu changes rapidly, two standbys are the
British Columbia King Salmon with a champagne-shallot sauce and the grilled
filet mignon. (The rack of lamb, when available, also gets high marks.) The
tables aren't jammed in quite like a New York restaurant of the same size, but it's
tighter than you would expect in Montana. Nonetheless, the layout is one of
intimacy and class, and this is the town's romantic hot spot. The restaurant
serves beer and wine only, but its eclectic wine list is one of Kalispell's best.

121 Main St. ✆ 406/755-7687. Reservations strongly recommended. Main courses $19–$24. AE, MC, V.
Tues–Sun 5:30–9:30pm.

Painted Horse Grille ECLECTIC AMERICAN   A new entry in the
Kalispell dining landscape, this restaurant is located in a space that was a bar
until it was gutted in 1998. Now a sleek, long room decorated in mellow earth
tones, the Grille has quickly become a local favorite in the winter and starts
drawing in tourists when the snow melts. The approach is to bring in the best
of various culinary traditions (namely French, American, Asian, and Italian) to
its varied menu. For, lunch we recommend the delectable paella or shellfish
linguini. The dinner specialties are the roasted rack of lamb and the roast cur-
ried duck. You might even find a Cajun dish or a buffalo steak among the daily
specials.

110 Main St. ✆ 406/257-7035. Reservations recommended. Lunch $6–$7; dinner $12–$20. AE, MC, V.
Mon–Fri 11:30am–2:30pm; Mon–Sat 5:30–9:30pm.

Rocco's ✿ ITALIAN/STEAKS/SEAFOOD   You get to Rocco's after a seemingly interminable drive east of Kalispell on U.S. 2 toward the airport. It's worth
the trip, though. Rocco's has something of a reputation among locals of not
being as good as it once was, but we found the food to be terrific. The chicken
and shrimp pasta special in a homemade stone-ground Dijon mustard sauce was
excellent. We also recommend the *fettuccine pescatora*—with fish, clams, scallops, mussels, and shrimp in a garlic-cream sauce. The portions are vast. Large
windows offer some nice mountain views.

3796 U.S. 2 E. ✆ 406/756-5834. Most entrees $10–$18. AE, DISC, MC, V. Tues–Sun 5–10pm.

INEXPENSIVE

For a break while exploring Kalispell, stop at the **Avalanche Creek Coffeehouse,** 38 1st Ave. E. (✆ **406/257-0785**), which offers coffee, espresso, and
bakery items.

The Bulldog Pub and Steakhouse STEAKS/SEAFOOD   Decorated in the
style of an English pub, the Bulldog is a steak joint with a sense of humor. The
menu is fairly varied, if conventional, but the prime rib and barbecue chicken
breasts in huckleberry barbecue sauce stand out. If you're feeling adventurous,
try the full elephant roasted on a spit for $29,000. The waitress assured us that
it could be ready in 15 minutes because the elephants are parboiled ahead of
time.

208 1st Ave. E. ✆ 406/752-7522. Lunch $4–$6; dinner $8–$16. AE, DISC, MC, V. Mon–Fri 11am–2am; Sat
4pm–2am.

The Knead Café ✿ BAKED GOODS/ECLECTIC   A funky, bohemian bakery, the Knead Café is a great breakfast spot and a good destination for a casual
dinner. The brightly decorated walls are covered with the work of local artists,
and the whole place has an arty, ramshackle atmosphere. The food is tasty and

designed to please meat-eaters and vegetarians alike. The breakfast menu includes fruit-filled pancakes and omelets; lunch runs the gamut from falafel to Thai chicken curry burritos and buffalo burgers. At dinner, try a gourmet pizza or an order of Black Star fish and chips. The Knead also has a stellar Sunday brunch, featuring gumbo, huevos rancheros, and granola-crusted French toast.

25 2nd Ave. W. ℂ **406/755-7510.** Reservations accepted for large parties only. Breakfast $4–$7; lunch $6–$8; dinner $7–$12. MC, V. Tues–Sat 8am–9pm; Sun 9am–3pm; Mon 8am–3pm.

Moose's PIZZA/SANDWICHES   Very dark inside, Moose's is filled with softball players, soccer players, their kids and fans, and guys named Lefty planning their next golf outing. The food consists of pizza and sandwiches, very inexpensive, and pretty good for the price. The beer is served in frosted mugs, an important feature after a long evening on the softball field. Whatever you do, don't blow the moose horn.

173 N. Main St. ℂ **406/755-2337.** Reservations not accepted. Most items $4–$14. No credit cards. Daily 11am–2am.

Norm's News *(Kids* BURGERS   Established in 1938, Norm's is a classic old-fashioned soda fountain, with racks of magazines and daily newspapers from all around the world and an assortment of 300 kinds of candy, which should perk the kids up after a long day. It's quite a sight, from the Rock-ola jukebox to the ornate back bar carved from Mediterranean cypress. The menu is as basic as it gets: burgers, hot dogs, and fries, plus a wide variety of sundaes, ice cream sodas, and hard-packed ice cream. Try a Glacier Supreme, a concoction of 7-Up, syrup, and whipped cream, after exploring the real thing.

34 Main St. ℂ **406/755-5500.** Reservations not accepted. Most items $3–$6. No credit cards. Summer Mon–Sat 7am–10pm, Sun 8am–4pm; winter Mon–Sat 7am–6pm, Sun 8am–4pm.

9 Whitefish *(★(★(★*

12 miles (19km) N of Kalispell

Whitefish has boomed as a resort community, attracting people from all over the country and making it Montana's fastest growing area. Long-time residents have feared it will become another Jackson Hole, but that hasn't quite happened yet. In fact, as national park gateway communities go, Whitefish is fairly sedate.

Whitefish is almost two different towns—the town itself and the Big Mountain ski area. The busy season in town is the summer, and room rates are correspondingly higher there during warm weather. This may seem odd for a ski town, but Glacier National Park attracts about two million visitors a year, while the ski area brings in only about 300,000.

Up on the mountain, however, the peak season is winter, especially during Christmas vacation time. So if you don't mind the winding 5-mile (8km) drive up (or down) the Big Mountain road, you can find slightly less expensive accommodations in the appropriate season.

ESSENTIALS

GETTING THERE   Whitefish is easier to get to than virtually any other Montana vacation town. It's a quick drive up U.S. 93 from Kalispell. Statewide weather updates are available by calling ℂ **406/449-5204;** for Whitefish, call ℂ **406/755-4829.** Call ℂ **406/755-4949** for road information in the Whitefish area.

Glacier Park International Airport is 10 minutes away between Columbia Falls and Kalispell. **Delta** (ℂ **800/221-1212**), **Northwest** (ℂ **800/225-2525**),

Big Sky (☎ 800/237-7788), and **Horizon** (☎ 800/547-9308) have daily flights.

The **Amtrak** (☎ 800/USA-RAIL) station, with two trains daily—one eastbound and one westbound—is shared with **Burlington Northern** at the edge of downtown in a renovated and charmingly attractive depot. The bus terminal is located at Mike's Conoco, a gas station at 6585 U.S. 93 S., with service to and from Missoula from **Rimrock Stages** (☎ 406/755-4011).

VISITOR INFORMATION   The **Whitefish Chamber of Commerce** is located at Mountain Mall on U.S. 93 on the south edge of town. Here you'll find just about everything you need in the way of brochures, area maps, and travel information (☎ 406/862-3501; www.whitefishcamber.com).

GETTING AROUND   **Budget** (☎ 800/248-7604) and **National** (☎ 800/227-7368) maintain counters at Glacier Park International Airport. Other companies renting cars in Whitefish include **Dollar** (☎ 800/457-5335 or 406/862-1210), **Ford** (☎ 800/344-2377 or 406/862-3825), **Hertz** (☎ 800/654-3131 or 406/862-1210), and **Payless** (☎ 800/729-5377 or 406/755-4022). **Whitefish Taxi** can be reached at ☎ 406/862-0587.

SPECIAL EVENTS   Whitefish is home to the **Winter Carnival** ☀ (☎ 406/862-3501), a wild and wooly event held annually in mid-January since 1960. It includes a parade, children's events, a disco party, a snow-sculpting competition, and a battle of the bands at local bars. Of special note is the Penguin Plunge, where a group of brave locals take a dip in frigid Whitefish Lake in the name of charity.

GETTING OUTSIDE

Whitefish is truly a paradise for outdoors enthusiasts, with ski slopes, hiking trails, water-sports opportunities, and Glacier National Park just down the road. As a result, there are numerous guides and outfitters. Contact **Flathead Adventure Company** (☎ 406/249-1390; www.flatheadadventure.com). The company organizes fishing, horsepacking, skiing, snowshoeing, and river trips. Most of the trips cost $250 to $325 per day. For all kinds of outdoor equipment or apparel, check out **Sportsman & Ski Haus** at the Mountain Mall (☎ 406/862-3111) or **Ski Mountain Sports,** 200 Wisconsin St. (☎ 406/862-7541).

BIKING

Although there are some road-biking opportunities here, biking in Whitefish really means mountain biking. The same old logging roads that make the hiking only average (see below) make the mountain biking excellent. Big Mountain has added 20 miles (32km) of single-track bike trails. The trails are free, but the area offers a ride to the top on the chairlift for you and your bike for $15. The Big Mountain Ski and Summer Resort (see "Downhill Skiing," below) offers five graded mountain biking trails, the longest of which, graded as intermediate, is 8 miles (13km). There's also a short half-mile trail for beginners and two expert trails of about a mile each. The **Big Mountain Bike Academy** (☎ 406/862-2912) offers guided mountain tours ($12–$70) and private mountain-biking lessons. Trails lead across the mountain to entrances at Glacier National Park, Whitefish Lake, and Hellroaring Basin. Bicycle rentals are available as well. Another Whitefish operation shares the expertise for mountain bikers seeking adventure on seemingly undiscovered paths. **Glacier Cyclery,** 336 E. 2nd (☎ 406/862-6446), provides excellent service and maintenance as well as rentals, area maps, and up-to-date information for the serious mountain biker. This outfit has been ranked among the 100 best cycle shops in a pool of 6,800 independent dealers. For a less challenging ride, you can make the 20-mile (32km) round-trip on paved roads from downtown Whitefish to the head of Whitefish Lake.

BOATING

The boating is excellent on Whitefish Lake. You can rent water-skiing boats, fishing boats, paddleboats, and personal watercraft from the **Whitefish Lake Lodge Marina** (© **406/862-9283**) between mid-May and mid-September. Fees vary from $12 for a canoe (1-hr. minimum) to $70 per hour for a water-ski boat (2-hr. minimum). There are twilight boat cruises on Sunday and Thursday evenings.

CROSS-COUNTRY SKIING

The Big Mountain Ski and Summer Resort (see "Downhill Skiing," below) offers 12 kilometers of very challenging cross-country trails. The **Glacier Nordic Club** maintains 15 kilometers of trails on the Whitefish Lake Golf Course and another 1.6 kilometers across the street near the Grouse Mountain Lodge.

These provide an excellent outing on the hilly golf course. A small donation allows skiers to enjoy both sides of the street, and yearly passes are available. For information, contact the **Outback Ski Shack** at Grouse Mountain Lodge (© **406/862-3000**), which also rents skis and other equipment and apparel, and offers lessons. They are located in a tiny building behind the hotel and just off the track. The Flathead Convention and Visitor Bureau (see "Essentials," in section 8, above) provides a free outline of trails in or near Whitefish, as well as a list of equipment sales and rental operations.

DOG-SLEDDING

Dog-Sled Adventures (© **406/881-BARK**) lets you explore the mountains around Whitefish "at the speed of dog." The guided 12-mile (19km) rides in two-person sleds run through Stillwater State Forest, 2 miles (3km) north of Olney. Each trip takes about 1½ hours and the sleds are equipped with blankets and elk-hide furs to keep you warm. Many of the dogs pulling the sleds were rescued by the owners from unwanted homes or animal shelters and trained as sled dogs. A sled ride costs $65 per adult ($35 per child) and includes a cup of hot chocolate and homemade cookies at the end of your ride.

DOWNHILL SKIING

The Big Mountain Ski and Summer Resort ⋒⋒ (Finds) This resort offers lots of powder, lots of skiing in the trees, and plenty of runs for every level of skier. With an annual snowfall of 300 inches, night skiing for $14 (late Dec to early Mar), 11 lifts, a vertical drop of 2,500 feet, and virtually no lines, the Big Mountain is one of the best resorts in the northwestern United States. More than half the mountain is geared to the intermediate skier, but there is plenty of terrain for experts and beginners. The expert runs are pretty steep—not as steep as Jackson's Teton Village, but steep enough. There are never any crowds at Big Mountain, even in the holiday seasons, so although the prices have gone up over the years, at least you can spend your time skiing rather than waiting in lift lines.

Ski school options include half-day group lessons for kids ($18) and private lessons starting at $50 per hour. There's also a full-service ski-rental shop.

For après ski food and entertainment, the Big Mountain holds its own, with 10 restaurants in the village or on the hill. Our choice for food and beverage at the mountain is **Moguls Village Pub,** a casual, full-service restaurant and bar with a menu chock-full of Italian and American food. **Summit House** is a cafeteria that dishes up burgers and the like during the daytime; Mexican buffet dinners are served on some evenings. The **Hellroaring Saloon and Eatery** serves both lunch and dinners in a typical après ski atmosphere. The **'Stube** is the mountain's rowdiest watering hole, with a mechanical bull and a chuckwagon-style dinner.

In summer, you can take gondola rides to the top of the mountain ($9.95 adults, $7.75 children and seniors), go horseback riding with **Horsepower Adventures** (✆ 406/862-2900), or mountain bike on the trails (bike rentals are available).

P.O. Box 1400 (12 miles [19km] north of Whitefish on Big Mountain Rd.), Whitefish, MT 59937. ✆ **800/ 858-5439** or 406/862-1900. Fax 406/862-2955. www.bigmtn.com. Lift tickets $47 adults, $39 seniors, $34 children; half-day rates available. AE, DISC, MC, V. Late Nov to Apr open daily. From Whitefish, head over the viaduct to Wisconsin for 3 miles (5km) until you see the flashing yellow light. Turn right on Big Mountain Rd. and proceed 9 miles (15km) to the Big Mountain Village.

FISHING

It's not the Madison Valley, but Whitefish does have some hot spots for anglers wanting to try their hand. **Tally Lake** is a deep hole located north of Whitefish off U.S. 93. Five miles (8km) north of town, turn left onto the Tally Lake Road (signs will direct you). You can expect cutthroat, rainbow, kokanee, brook trout, and whitefish.

In town, across the viaduct toward the Big Mountain lies **Whitefish Lake.** If you can handle all the recreationists hovering about like flies, the lake offers some pretty good lake trout. Northern pike can be found here, and rainbow and cutthroat can be nabbed on dry flies in the evening. The **Lakestream Flyshop,** 15 Central (✆ **406/862-1298;** www.lakestream.com), is the best resource in town for information about fly-fishing the Flathead River and local streams. It's also a great spot for a fly-fisherman to construct a wish list, since the store sells all types of fly-fishing equipment, clothing, books, flies, dustcatchers, and memorabilia. The staff here provides full-service fly-fishing, tying, and rod-building services, in addition to good advice. Guided trips are $325 a day, $250 for a half-day.

GOLF

The **Whitefish Lake Golf Club** ⛳, U.S. 93 N. (✆ **406/862-4000;** www.golfwhitefish.com), is the only 36-hole golf course in the state. Built in the 1920s, the golf club's trees have grown up over the last 75 years or so.

While not especially long, the course offers a wide variety of shots that will require you to use all the clubs in your bag (and maybe some you forgot).

A Brewery in Whitefish

The glass-enclosed brewing "tower" at the **Great Northern Brewing Company,** on Central and Railway (✆ **406/863-1000**), gave birth to the original Black Star beer; the company has since added six new products. For a seat in the tasting room or a self-guided tour, call ahead of your planned arrival. The tasting room is open in summer Monday through Saturday, from noon to 6pm, in winter from 3 to 7pm.

Almost all the fairways are lined with trees. There are few fairway bunkers, but they have strategic placement around the greens. Both 18-hole set-ups measure a little more than 6,500 yards from the tips. There is also a driving range and putting green. This course may not be as good as the newer Meadow Lake (see the "Golf" section in "Columbia Falls," below), but it is a very fun track. Greens fees are $37 for 18, $19 for nine holes. Carts rent for $24.50. **Par 3 on 93,** U.S. 93 S. (© **406/862-7273**), is a nine-hole executive course on U.S. 93 south of town. The greens fee is $10.

HIKING

The hiking in the immediate Whitefish area is not great. For the most part, trails either stay in the woods so that you don't see anything except trees, or they go along old logging roads—which make for good mountain biking, but less inter-esting hiking. The most popular trail in town is the **Danny On Trail** to the sum-mit of the Big Mountain. Named for a Forest Service ecologist who was killed in a ski accident on the Big Mountain in 1979, it begins in the Big Mountain Village and ascends the south face of the mountain on four different paths. There's about a 4-mile (6km) trek from the top of the lift along the ridge to Flower Point and back. It takes about 2 hours. The most demanding walk is 5¾ miles (9km) from the base of the ski area to the top of the hill and then along the ridge. You can ride the lift back down. Snow can be a problem in late spring and even the early months of summer.

SNOWBOARDING

Snowboarders will find kindred spirits—as well as an extensive line of boards and apparel—at **Stumptown Snowboards** (© **406/862-0955**) at 128 Central Ave. The staff here will fill you in on the local snowboarding scene on the Big Mountain and other spots in the Flathead Valley.

SNOWMOBILING

Contact the **Flathead Snowmobilers Association** (© **406/752-2561**) for cur-rent conditions and reports, then head north on U.S. 93 for about 40 miles (64km) to **Tucker's Inn** in Trego (© **800/500-3541**) for any and all snowmo-bile adventures you may want or need; it has access to hundreds of miles of trails and rents the machines for around $175 a day.

SHOPPING

The main shopping area of Whitefish is on Central Avenue and stretches for 3 blocks. For a ski town, the shopping frenzy here is fairly subdued. The largest bookshop in town is **Bookworks,** 244 Spokane Ave. (© **406/862-4980**), which stocks the best in nature books, regional writing, and children's literature; it's also the source of current hardcover and paperback best-sellers. **Montana Art and Trading,** 216 Central Ave. (© **800/555-9049** or 406/862-9317), has some unusual and beautiful handmade paper artwork on American Indian themes. The **Artistic Touch,** 209 Central Ave. (© **406/862-4813**), sells self-described "Montana crafts of merit." The gallery is operated by a jeweler who exhibits an eclectic, diverse group of sculptures in all types of media—expect glazed wall sculptures, pottery mobiles suspended from the ceiling, wood and wire combi-nations, and even a full-size, handmade marimba. **The Tomahawk Trading Company,** 131 Central Ave. (© **406/862-9199**), has a large selection of Indian-made jewelry. The **Bear Mountain Mercantile,** 237 Central Ave. (© **406/862-8382**), is chock-full of gimcracks, knickknacks, and souvenirs, many with a bear theme.

WHERE TO STAY
IN & AROUND TOWN

Whitefish might just have the best range of accommodations in all of Montana, with everything from mom-and-pop motels to graceful inns to slopeside condos. If you're looking for an inexpensive place to stay and aren't averse to a shared bathroom, try the **Non-Hostile Hostel,** 300 E. 2nd Ave. (© **406/862-7447**), where a bunk goes for $15 a night. There's also a private room for $30. There's also a **Super 8,** 800 Spokane Ave. (© **800/800-8000**), with doubles for $60 to $80 nightly. **The Pine Lodge,** 920 Spokane Ave. (© **800/395-7463** or 406/862-7600; www.thepinelodge.com), is a good independent option, with doubles for $50 to $195.

Best Western Rocky Mountain Lodge ⚜ Located on the U.S. 93 commercial strip just south of downtown, this is a very fine Best Western. The larger rooms have their own wet bars and fireplaces. There are king and queen beds, and balconies and Jacuzzis in the higher-priced rooms. This is an especially good option for those passing through on their way to or from Glacier, but it's too far from the slopes to be the best option for skiers.

6510 U.S. 93 S., Whitefish, MT 59937. © **800/862-2569** or 406/862-2569. Fax 406/862-1154. www.rock-ymtnlodge.com. 79 units. $69–$119 double; $99–$169 suite. Rates include continental breakfast. AE, DC, DISC, MC, V. **Amenities:** Outdoor seasonal pool; Jacuzzi; exercise room; courtesy car. *In room:* A/C, TV, dataport, fridge, coffeemaker, hair dryer, iron.

Duck Inn *(Value* This is the best value in the Whitefish area. The building is right off the U.S. 93 strip, overlooking the Whitefish River. The rooms are very large, every one with a fireplace and a private bathroom with a deep soak tub. There is a lovely lobby area, and the hot tub is in a broad-windowed room overlooking the river. Even though it's right in town, the location gives the illusion of the serene, quiet countryside. The owners also own the Ford car-rental agency, and guests at the inn get unlimited mileage with their rentals.

1305 Columbia Ave., Whitefish, MT 59937. © **800/344-2377** or 406/862-3825. Fax 406/863-2533. www.duckinn.com. 10 units. Summer $79 double; winter $59 double. Rates include continental breakfast. AE, DISC, MC, V. **Amenities:** Jacuzzi. *In room:* A/C, TV.

The Garden Wall Inn ⚜⚜ *(Finds* While it's right on the main Whitefish drag, the Garden Wall Inn is a world of its own. Owner Rhonda Fitzgerald prides herself on providing the little luxurious extras. The inn is full of country charm—it was built in the 1920s, and all of the furnishings are period antiques, including claw-footed tubs and Art Deco dressers, depending on your room. Every detail is just about perfect, right down to the towels, which are large and fluffy enough to dry two adults. Since Rhonda and the innkeeper are both trained chefs, breakfast is a gourmet event (wild huckleberry crepes are just the tip of the iceberg), and afternoons end with hors d'oeuvres and beverages. Rhonda is also an avid outdoorswoman: Ask her for some tips before you head out on that excursion to Glacier or Big Mountain.

504 Spokane Ave., Whitefish, MT 59937. © **888/530-1700** or 406/862-3440. www.wtp.net/go/gardenwall. 4 units. $95–$145 double; $195 suite. Rates include full breakfast and afternoon refreshments. AE, MC, V. *In room:* No phone.

Good Medicine Lodge ⚜ The Good Medicine Lodge is an already excellent place that is continually improving itself. The two best rooms have been upgraded recently, adding gas-fired potbellied stoves and new furnishings. Several second-floor rooms have beautiful views of the mountains in Glacier National Park, and ground-floor rooms have their own patios on the green backyard. Rooms are large, modern, and clean, and decorated with various themes, like golf, Western, and Indian. The clientele tends to be the active type, but there are also older folks from warmer climes who come to Whitefish for a white Christmas—or other special occasions.

537 Wisconsin Ave., Whitefish, MT 59937. © 800/860-5488 or 406/862-5488. Fax 406/862-5489. www.goodmedicinelodge.com. 9 units. $95–$165 double. Rates include full breakfast. AE, DISC, MC, V. **Amenities:** Jacuzzi; coin-op washers and dryers. *In room:* A/C, dataport, hair dryer.

Grouse Mountain Lodge 🏔🏔   Grouse Mountain Lodge is Montana's premier vacation lodge property, and is especially popular as a meeting place for businesses. Golfers love the fact that it's immediately adjacent to the 18th hole of one of Whitefish Lake's two golf courses. The lodge combines luxury accommodations, fine service, and good food to provide a memorable experience. Standard hotel-like rooms are called the executive rooms. The executive deluxe rooms all overlook the golf course from the third floor, with vaulted ceilings and large living areas. The loft rooms—there are 12 of them, 10 with kitchens and 2 with sauna tubs—have a spiral staircase, which leads to an upper sleeping loft, where there is a king-size bed and a curtained-off area with two more beds. Our only complaint here is that the bathrooms aren't on the same level as the sleeping area. The lodge houses the popular **Logan's Bar and Grill.** The food is very good, if a little pricey. You can also eat on the deck overlooking the course.

2 Fairway Dr., Whitefish, MT 59937. © 800/321-8822 or 406/862-3000. Fax 406/862-0326. www.montanasfinest.com. 145 units. $159–$209 double. AE, DISC, MC, V. **Amenities:** Indoor pool; golf course; activities desk. *In room:* A/C, TV, dataport, coffeemaker, iron.

Hidden Moose Lodge   The centerpiece of this new property is the vaulted, high-ceilinged great room with the vast river-rock chimney fireplace. But the large, comfortable rooms are nicely done as well. Guests can savor their gourmet breakfast on their own decks if they wish. Even the bathroom mirrors are appointed with handmade ironwork. Hidden Moose has canoes and bikes available for guests at no charge. Their sign on the road is almost invisible, so it's important to know that the lodge is located about a mile-and-a-half (2km) from town on the road to Big Mountain.

1735 E. Lakeshore Dr. (on the road to Big Mountain), Whitefish, MT 59937. © 888/733-6667 or 406/862-6516. www.hiddenmooselodge.com. 8 units. $89–$140 depending on season. Rates include full breakfast. AE, DISC, MC, V. **Amenities:** Outdoor Jacuzzi; complimentary bikes; water-sports equipment. *In room:* TV.

North Forty Resort   Nestled in the pines along Mont. 40 between Whitefish and Columbia Falls, the North Forty is a great place to stay if you don't like being in town but still want to be close. Even the smaller duplex cabins all have large living areas, fireplaces, kitchens, front porches, and barbecue grills. North Forty is located in a serene and quiet area off the main highway, and there is a cross-country ski/hiking trail located at the north end of the property.

3765 Mont. 40 W. (P.O. Box 4250), Whitefish, MT 59937. © 800/775-1740 or 406/862-7740. Fax 406/862-7741. www.northforty.com. 30 units. Winter $89–$139 double; summer $115–$195 double. AE, DISC, MC, V. **Amenities:** Outdoor Jacuzzi. *In room:* TV, dataport, kitchen, coffeemaker.

Whitefish Lake Lodge Resort 🏔   The two-story condos available here may be the nicest accommodations in Whitefish. They include a very large tiled kitchen, a dining area, a deck overlooking Whitefish Lake and the marina, and a large loft bedroom, as well as a downstairs bedroom. The living rooms are tastefully appointed and mirrors on the far wall make the large rooms look even larger. The hotel-style units are much smaller—almost cramped, but they also have excellent furnishings. Managers require high maintenance standards to remain in the rental pool. Each of the one- to three-bedroom units has a spacious living area decorated in earth tones and accented with regional art and a gas fireplace; some have sofa beds. The fully equipped kitchens include double sinks, four-burner stoves and ovens, full-size refrigerators, dishwashers, generous counter space, and tableware for six. Master bedrooms have king-size beds and combination bathrooms. In summer, there is a full-service marina with boat rentals. There's even a large parking lot for storing boat trailers.

1399 Wisconsin Ave., Whitefish, MT 59937. ℂ 800/735-8869 or 406/862-2929. Fax 406/862-3550. www.wfll.com. 30 units. Hotel-style rooms $99 double; condos $240–$430. AE, MC, V. **Amenities:** Outdoor pool; indoor and outdoor Jacuzzi; water-sports rentals; coin-op washers and dryers. *In room:* TV, kitchen.

ON THE BIG MOUNTAIN

The Big Mountain is a full-service ski area, working to attract local skiers, Canadian and American vacationers, and families. It provides a wide variety of accommodations to fit almost every pocketbook. You can reach central reservations at ℂ **800/858-5439.** Be sure to ask about discounted lift and lodging packages. If you're looking for a house or condo instead of a hotel, inquire at **Glacier Village Property Management** (ℂ **800/243-7547;** www.stayatbig mountain.com) and **Big Mountain Alpine Homes** (ℂ **800/858-5439;** www.bigmtn.com). Most are available for rent on a nightly basis, although some require longer stays. You can get a low-end condo or house for as little as $280 a night, or as much as $1,250. A video-rental library is available, as is a heated indoor pool.

Alpinglow   Alpinglow is located virtually at the base of the gondola in the Big Mountain Village. The rooms are standard fare, clean and done in pastels, but those on the valley side offer spectacular views of Flathead Lake. On a clear day, you can see almost to Polson. The restaurant has broad picture windows, a deck looking out over the lift base, and respectable if unimaginative fare. The Alpinglow was the first recreational condo built in Montana, and it's showing its age a bit, but renovations have kept it quite livable.

Big Mountain Village, Whitefish, MT 59937. ℂ 406/862-6966. Fax 406/862-0076. www.alpinglow.com. 54 units. $104–$134 double. AE, DISC, MC, V. **Amenities:** Restaurant; 2 outdoor Jacuzzis; sauna; coin-op washers and dryers. *In room:* A/C, TV.

Edelweiss   The Edelweiss has some very nice large rooms, all with kitchens, full bathrooms, and fireplaces, and configurations ranging from basic studios to condo units with lofts and two bathrooms. Many of the rooms have panoramic views of the valley below, and all of them have a small balcony or patio. Convenient to the lifts, the Edelweiss has a large hot tub and a Finnish dry-heat sauna. Residents also have access to the indoor swimming pool run by Glacier Village Property Management (see above).

3898 Big Mountain Rd., Whitefish, MT 59937. ℂ 800/228-8260 or 406/862-5252. Fax 406/862-3009. www.stayatedelweiss.com. 50 units. Winter $132–$204 double. AE, MC, V. **Amenities:** Indoor Jacuzzi; sauna; coin-op washers and dryers. *In room:* TV/VCR, kitchen.

Hibernation House *(Value*   This is the least expensive place on the hill, popular with high school and college groups, ski teams, and families on budgets. And if you'll be on the slopes all day and just want a clean bed, this will do just fine. All of the rooms are exactly alike: pretty small with a double bed and a set of bunk beds. Each room has its own television—a relatively recent development—

but people still like to congregate in the lobby, where there is a large-screen TV. You can ski right to the back door on a groomed trail, and it is only a short walk to a lift in the morning. Another perk: The buffet breakfast is quite good.

3812 Big Mountain Rd., Whitefish, MT 59937. © **800/858-5439** or 406/862-1982. Fax 406/862-1956. www. bigmtn.com/html/hibhouse.html. 42 units. $65–$120 double. Rates include full breakfast. AE, DISC, MC, V. **Amenities:** Outdoor Jacuzzi; coin-op washers and dryers. *In room:* TV.

Kandahar Lodge *(★* Kandahar combines the genteel ambience of an old-fashioned lodge with the requirements of an up-tempo modern ski area. The rooms are large and elegantly appointed, featuring four-poster or sleigh beds with down comforters. About a third of the units are outfitted with kitchenettes, and the large loft bedrooms have vaulted ceilings. Overall, the lodge is one of the best (and priciest) lodging options on Big Mountain. Likewise, the Cafe Kandahar is the best restaurant on the mountain, but, ski-area food being what it is, this is not that high of a recommendation.

3824 Big Mountain Rd., Whitefish, MT 59937. © **800/862-6094** or 406/862-6098. Fax 406/862-6095. www.kandaharlodge.com. 48 units. $129–$229 double; $209–$399 suite. AE, DISC, MC, V. **Amenities:** Restaurant, lounge; Jacuzzi; sauna; coin-op washers and dryers. *In room:* TV, kitchen.

Kintla Lodge *(★* A grand native log-and-stone lodge that echoes the architecture in Glacier National Park, Kintla is the newest accommodation on the mountain, opening in 1998. It is very upscale, and the only place on the mountain with an elevator serving its four floors. (That's something people appreciate more than you might think after a day of skiing.) But it's not cheap: A three-bedroom, three-bathroom unit goes for $500 a night in peak season. All units have wood-clad French doors opening onto a patio, stone flooring in the entry and kitchens, individual ski storage, and tastefully simple pine furnishings. Best of all, Kintla is only 20 feet from the "Tenderfoot Lift." There is no restaurant on the premises, but the village's tonier shops are located on the ground level outside.

Big Mountain Village, Whitefish, MT 59937. © **800/858-4157** or 406/862-1960. Fax 406/862-2955. www.bigmtn.com/html/condos.html. 14 units. $165–$500 double, depending on season. AE, DISC, MC, V. **Amenities:** Outdoor Jacuzzi; sauna; shopping arcade. *In room:* TV.

Ptarmigan Village *(★* This is an extensive condo set-up that is spread over a lower portion of the Big Mountain. The units are pretty snazzy, featuring vaulted ceilings, fireplaces, fully equipped kitchens, and some unexpected touches: wood stoves, grills, CD players, and spiral staircases. The decks overlook a woody area where signs warn about increased black bear activity in the summer—there's a hiking trail here, too, if the bears don't scare you off. There's also a nice fishing pond where kids can spy out the turtles hiding in the reeds in summer.

3000 Big Mountain Rd., Whitefish, MT 59937. © **800/552-3952** or 406/862-3594. Fax 406/862-6664. www.ptarmiganvillage.com. 50 units. $90–$205 condo. AE, DISC, MC, V. **Amenities:** Indoor and outdoor pools; tennis courts; indoor Jacuzzi; sauna; coin-op washers and dryers. *In room:* TV, kitchens.

CAMPING

Whitefish Lake State Park is tucked on the outskirts of town in a nicely wooded area on Whitefish Lake. Call the **Department of Fish, Wildlife, and Parks** (© **406/752-5501**) for additional information. The **Whitefish KOA Kampground** (© **800/562-9734**) is about 2 miles (3km) south of town on U.S. 93 and has 76 sites ($19–$25 each) and 10 small cabins ($38–$42).

WHERE TO DINE

A good cup of organic coffee and a selection of baked goods are available at the **Montana Coffee Traders,** located at 710 Central Ave. (© **406/862-7667**), which also houses a nifty used bookstore and a nice place to sprawl out on a couch and read a book. **Wrap and Roll,** located below the Non-Hostile Hostel at 300 E. 2nd St. (© **406/862-7447**), serves inexpensive burritos, gyros, and an international array of wraps (many of them vegetarian) in a hip basement space plastered with art. There's also a pool table, Internet access, and occasional live music. **The Buffalo Cafe,** 516 3rd St. (© **406/862-2833**), is Whitefish's best breakfast spot—try their legendary bacon-and-egg-filled pies. And for good (albeit pricey) Mexican food and great margaritas, try **Serrano's,** 10 Central Ave. (© **406/862-5600**).

Mambo Italiano ⭐ ITALIAN   A swank, dimly-lit *ristorante,* Mambo Italiano has the locals raving and the tourists lined up around the block. The color scheme and the music are both loud—the walls are bright red and the stereo blasts Sinatra, Louis Prima, and Dean Martin—but it complements the rich Italian fare quite nicely. Many of the recipes have been in proprietor Billy Castronova's family since the Great Depression. For an appetizer, you can't miss with the Italian Tootsie Rolls: egg wrappers stuffed with ricotta, mozzarella, and pesto. Cooked in an open central kitchen, main courses range from crackly-crust pizza to Pappa Biagio Bolognese (ribbon noodles baked with meat sauce and mozzarella) and Pollo Con Formaggio (a breaded chicken cutlet dripping with four cheeses).

234 E. 2nd St. © 406/863-9600. Main courses $7–$15. AE, DISC, MC, V. Mon–Sat 5–10pm.

Pollo Grill AMERICAN   This farmhouse-themed restaurant, located between Whitefish and Big Mountain, has an unofficial motto: "People don't go away hungry." You can get a spit-roasted chicken or duck if you're after the house specialties, but the eatery also serves up a good seafood fettuccine and fresh salmon if your tastes tend toward the aquatic. Every rotisseried dish comes with a choice of two sides (from a long list that includes garlic mashed potatoes, Southwestern black beans, and wild rice pilaf) and a gourmet sauce—try the huckleberry merlot or the cilantro-lime glaze.

1709 Wisconsin Ave. © 406/863-9460. Main courses $10–$20. AE, DISC, MC, V. Summer daily 5–9pm; winter Wed–Sat 5–9pm.

Truby's PIZZA/BURGERS   Even if you're not crazy about pizza, you'll likely appreciate Truby's eclectic approach to the popular dish. Here you can get wood-fired, Thai-style, Athenian, veggie, or design-your-own pizza. The crusts are thin and crispy, and toppings range from Cajun andouille sausage and Jamaican jerked chicken to feta cheese and mandarin oranges. Pastas, steaks, baby-back ribs, and burgers on focaccia bread round out the menu. Truby's has a happening atmosphere with recorded blues music, lots of customers, and a cheerful staff.

115 Central Ave. © 406/862-4979. Lunch items $5–$10; dinner entrees $7–$16. AE, DISC, MC, V. Mon–Sat 11am–10pm; Sun 4–10pm.

The Tupelo Grille ⭐ CONTINENTAL/CAJUN   The Tupelo is the best restaurant in the downtown area, especially for those with a taste for New Orleans–style food. Cajun pasta (chicken, smoked sausage, and tomatoes seasoned with cilantro and chiles, sautéed and finished with cream) and a Cajun

Creole combo (a platter of shrimp Creole, crawfish *etoufée*, and chicken and sausage jambalaya) are specialties.

17 Central Ave. ✆ **406/862-6136**. Reservations recommended for large parties. Main courses $11–$19. AE, MC, V. Daily 5:30–9:30pm.

Wasabi ⚜ SUSHI   Few locals thought that a sushi joint in Whitefish would fly, but it turned out to be a serendipitous decision by proprietor/chef Scott Nagel. The contemporary space is a real eye-catcher, with lime-green walls, an orange ceiling, and a large mirror displaying the chefs hard at work above checkerboard floors. The menu includes the whole gamut of sushi, including an excellent spicy tuna roll and the Montana roll (smoked rainbow trout and whitefish caviar), as well as a nice selection of poultry and seafood entrees. There's beer, wine, and six varieties of sake, but no liquor.

419 E. 2nd St. ✆ **406/863-9283**. Sushi $3–$9 per order; main courses $10–$20. Tues–Sun 5–10pm.

Whitefish Lake Golf Club Restaurant ⚜ CONTINENTAL   There are Montanans who will enter the Whitefish Lake Restaurant as their horse in the "best restaurant in the state" sweepstakes. Located at the public golf course, it is generally conceded to be the best restaurant in the Whitefish area. It's housed in a building that was constructed in 1936 as a WPA project. The dining room has an almost church-like atmosphere: dark and quiet, with large log beams and wagon-wheel chandeliers hanging from the ceiling. There are stained-glass mountain scenes on the walls. Tables are covered with traditional Scottish tablecloths, and a large stone fireplace provides warmth on chilly evenings. The menu for the evening meal covers the culinary landscape, from vegetarian pasta to 14-ounce prime rib, lamb shank, and roast duckling; fresh seafood may include lobster, king crab, halibut, or Pacific salmon. The wine list includes an impressive collection of French and California whites and reds. As formal as a golf club ever gets, it's the only place in Whitefish that approaches dressy.

U.S. 93 N. (at the Whitefish Golf Course). ✆ **406/862-5285**. Reservations recommended. Lunch $4–$7; dinner $16–$24. AE, MC, V. Summer daily 11am–3pm and 5:30–10pm; winter Sun–Thurs 5:30–9pm, Fri–Sat 5:30–9:30pm.

WHITEFISH AFTER DARK

There's not much going on in Whitefish after hours except the bar scene, concentrated in a 2-block area on Central Avenue. A pub crawl begins at the **Palace Bar and Spirits,** a rather seedy joint that promises live rock-and-roll on weekends and holidays and $2 hamburgers. Follow that with a time-out at **Casey's,** which is equally seedy but has more character; its clientele tends to be older and more local, and the walls are covered with wildlife pictures and patriotic slogans. A third stop could be at the **Great Northern Bar and Grill,** which is upscale, at least compared to the other two joints. This place is jumping on the weekends after 7pm. Your final stop: the **Bulldog Saloon.** Not just a bar, the Bulldog turns out a pretty good burger, too.

10 Columbia Falls

11 miles (18km) N of Kalispell; 9 miles (15km) E of Whitefish

Columbia Falls gets a bad rep not only for being the home of Plum Creek, a smoke-billowing institution seen for miles even at night, but also for its not-so-subtle image as a tourist trap. And unlike Great Falls, where the falls are out of town and (gasp!) dammed, Columbia Falls goes you one better by not having any falls at all. The redeeming features and equalizers are the town's proximity to Glacier National Park, and lodging rates that are somewhat less expensive—it's a good fallback location if you have trouble finding a room in Whitefish. Residents here are real Montanans, something of an enigma in an area being inundated with out-of-staters setting up house.

ESSENTIALS

GETTING THERE   **Glacier International Airport** is 10 minutes away on U.S. 2 between Columbia Falls and Kalispell. **Delta** (✆ **800/221-1212**), **Northwest** (✆ **800/225-2525**), and **Horizon** (✆ **800/547-9308**) have daily flights. The closest **Amtrak** station is in Whitefish, 10 miles (16km) to the northwest.

Statewide **weather updates** are available by calling ✆ **406/449-5204;** for Columbia Falls, call ✆ **406/755-4829.** Call ✆ **406/755-4949** for local **road information.**

VISITOR INFORMATION   The **Columbia Falls Area Chamber of Commerce,** P.O. Box 312, Columbia Falls, MT 59912 (✆ **406/892-2072**), can provide you with pertinent area information. The chamber and the **U.S. Forest Service** jointly operate an information cabin in Maranette Park on U.S. 2 near the center of town. Columbia Falls is located in **Travel Montana's Glacier Country** (✆ **800/338-5072** or 406/756-7128; glacier.visitmt.com).

GETTING AROUND   The only car-rental agency actually located in Columbia Falls is **Dollar,** 5506 U.S. 2 W. (✆ **406/892-0009**).

GETTING OUTSIDE

Two of the best-kept secrets in this part of the state are the **North** and **South Lion Lakes.** To find them, follow the signs to the west side of the Hungry Horse Reservoir. Less than 5 miles (8km) after turning off of Mont. 40, you will come to a cutoff to the North Lion Lake and, within a hundred yards, arrive at South Lion Lake.

Both are well protected, quiet, and for the most part undiscovered by tourists—excellent for picnicking, fishing, or swimming.

There is a road around **Hungry Horse Reservoir,** a 110-mile (177km) round-trip that you can start from the town of Hungry Horse. Hungry Horse is 9 miles (15km) south of West Glacier or 6 miles (10km) east of Columbia Falls on U.S. 2. There's a small visitor center at Hungry Horse Dam (✆ **406/387-5241**). This is an excellent drive for seeing wildlife. You're almost certain to see at least an elk, and maybe a moose or bear. It's also a great place for fishing.

Another local attraction is **Wild Eyes Animal Adventures** (✆ **888/330-5391** or 406/387-5391; www.wildeyes-usa.com), a wildlife sanctuary/lodge that rehabilitates injured and abused animals and lets visitors spend a session "up close" with them for a hefty fee of $110. Lodging runs about $90 for a double.

GOLF

Columbia Falls is home to one of Montana's best golf courses, **Meadow Lake** at the Meadow Lake Resort; see "Where to Stay," below). About 6,700 yards from the back tees, the course is very challenging, especially the greens, which are "speed sensitive" and have lots of nearly invisible breaks in them. The fairways are fairly wide but lined with intimidating large trees. To reserve a tee time, call (✆ **406/892-7601.**

HIKING

Columbia Mountain, Glacier National Park, and the Jewel Basin are nearby, but the **Great Northern** is the grandpappy of 'em all in these parts. If you want a leisurely stroll with moderate difficulty, stick to the Danny On Trail on the Big Mountain in Whitefish. If you want 8 hours of hardship, then the Great Northern is for you. To get there, take U.S. 2 to Martin City, then turn onto the East Side Reservoir Road for 15 miles (24km). At that point, turn east to Highline Loop Road, and from here you should be able to see the approach route. The hike goes up the 8,705-foot high Great Northern Mountain in the Great Bear Wilderness. While there's not an official trail, enough people have beaten a path to the summit that one is clear enough to make out. This isn't a leisurely walk, nor is it the most publicized hike in the area, but it is the most rewarding for those willing to make the effort. The views of Glacier and the Hungry Horse Reservoir are remarkable.

EXPLORING THE TOWN: KITSCH & CAMP

Remember when your dad used to drive the family to the ocean or mountains for the annual family vacation? Whenever you passed the "Tent of Miracles" or the "Cave of 10,000 Rattlesnakes" or the "Fabulous Mystery House," you'd beg Dad to stop. He always ignored you and drove on as if you hadn't spoken. Columbia Falls offers you the chance to find out what attractions like these are all about.

Big Sky Waterslide & Miniature Greens, at the junction of U.S. Highways 2 and 206 (© **406/892-5025**), is the main attraction and a good place to cool off. It is the largest such park in the state of Montana. If you've always wanted to reenact the snow scenes from *The Shining* without the snow (and who hasn't?), then the **Amazing Fun Center,** at U.S. 2 E., Coram (© **406/387-5902**), is your place. Like rats hunting for an odorless cheese, tourists often enter the Fun Center's maze and emerge hours later. If mazes aren't your bag, the place also has go-karts and other games. The **House of Mystery,** 7800 U.S. 2 E., Columbia Falls (© **406/892-1210**), offers a vortex (you'll just have to go in to find out) and other bewilderments. **Just for Fun,** 1910 U.S. 2 E., Columbia Falls (© **406/892-7750**), is that place you passed coming into town from the west with the giant jackalope (a fictitious animal seen throughout the western United States that is a cross between a jackrabbit and an antelope).

WHERE TO STAY

Bad Rock Country Bed and Breakfast ℛ   This is a great choice for those who want to use Columbia Falls as a base for visiting both Glacier and Whitefish but want to avoid the hustle and bustle of being on the highway. Nestled in a green meadow at the base of the Swan Mountains, this is a very good B&B with three rooms in the main house and two duplex cabins on the grounds. The cabins are newer, built with square-cut pine logs and furnished with custom lodgepole pine trappings. In the main house, the best room is #3, with a four-poster queen bed and a private balcony perfect for watching the sunset. The Bad Rock is known for its lavish breakfasts, which begin with fresh fruit, end with a sweet dessert, and might have Montana potato pie, chicken crepes, or French toast stuffed with apricot and pineapple in between.

480 Bad Rock Dr., Columbia Falls, MT 59912. © **888/892-2829** or 406/892-2829. www.badrock.com. 7 units, including 4 cabin units. $118–$168 double. **Amenities:** Outdoor Jacuzzi.

Meadow Lake Resort ☆   Meadow Lake offers a wide variety of excellent accommodations in a modern-resort style. Development focuses on the golf course, which is one of the best in the state. Rooms are stylish in the modern sense, and many of the condo units have Jacuzzis. The resort has a recreation center with Nautilus weight machines and aerobic equipment. There are a large pool and hot tub. The inn features standard-sized hotel rooms with a king bed, double sleeper sofa, a large bathroom with double vanity sinks, and a veranda or patio. The condos come in suites (a single room with kitchen, bathroom and, usually, a Jacuzzi), or one- and two-bedroom versions.

They all have fireplaces, full kitchens, convenient washer and dryer access, private deck with barbecue, VCR, and stereo. Even if you haven't come for golf, this is still the best place to spend the night.

The Sunset Grille is a cozy place to enjoy lunch or dinner after a round or two of golf during the summer or skiing in winter. If you plan to visit during the summer, ask if the resort is hosting a Flathead Festival concert; past headline acts appearing on the course have included America, the Nitty Gritty Dirt Band, and Emmylou Harris (guests still have to buy a ticket).

100 St. Andrews Dr., Columbia Falls, MT 59912. ☎ **800/321-4653** or 406/892-8700. Fax 406/892-0330. www.meadowlake.com. 24 units in inn plus a wide variety of condos and rental homes. $89–$155 at inn; $89–$499 condo or home. AE, DC, MC, V. **Amenities:** Restaurant, lounge; Jacuzzi; golf course; exercise room; children's program; activities desk; in-room massage; dry cleaning and laundry service. *In room:* A/C, TV/VCR, coffeemaker, kitchen.

Western Inn/Glacier Mountain Shadow Resort *(Value*   This recently renovated, low-cost hostelry offers clean, comfortable accommodations with prices to match their modesty. Single rooms come with one queen-size bed, and double rooms have two queen-size beds. The accommodations are no better or worse than those found in a typical low-cost national chain. Also available for rent are a few teepees and 18 RV campsites (about $20 each).

At the intersection of U.S. Hwys. 2 and 206, Columbia Falls, MT 59912. ☎ **406/892-7686.** Fax 406/892-4575. 22 units. $75 double. Rates include continental breakfast. AE, DISC, MC, V. *In room:* TV.

WHERE TO DINE

The Back Room of the Nite Owl *(Value* AMERICAN   This greasy spoon in the back room of the Nite Owl Cafe is off the main drag in Columbia Falls. You'll be pleasantly surprised by what The Back Room has to offer—the roasted chicken, spare ribs, and country ribs (small chunks cooked in barbecue sauce) are all delicious and reasonably priced. Fry bread is the house specialty and comes with meals instead of standard bread items. The pizza and salad buffet each Sunday is a bargain for about $6.

U.S. 2 E. ☎ **406/892-3131.** Most items $6–$13. AE, DISC, MC, V. Mon–Sat 4–10pm; Sun 2–10pm.

6

Helena & Southwestern Montana

This is where Montana came of age, changing in a few short years from an isolated outback of fur traders and rugged explorers to a series of bustling, boisterous mining camps, where fortunes were made and lost overnight. Butte was once the "Richest Hill on Earth," and gold strikes were also made at Helena's Last Chance Gulch and Virginia City's Alder Gulch. Bannack, another gold-mining boomtown, was the first territorial capital.

The area has calmed down somewhat since then. The Berkeley Pit is filling with water. The Anaconda copper smelter is shut down, and the Old Works is now a golf course. Helena is the businesslike state capital, the seat of Montana's politics.

But in the Big Hole, you can still see some ranching and farming done the old-fashioned way. There are plenty of fishing and outdoor opportunities here and in the mountains that cover the area.

While signs of modern American life are now rampant, many cross-sections of this region's storied past have been meticulously preserved. The old prison at Deer Lodge can give you an eye-opening perspective on frontier justice, and the preserved mining towns of Nevada City and Virginia City provide a taste of the boomtown, mining-camp life.

1 Scenic Drives

Two high-speed highways—Interstates 90 and 15—run north to south through the region, but the best roads to take are the well-maintained back roads, the state and county highways that follow unlikely and out-of-the-way paths. Traveling from Anaconda to Dillon could be done via the interstate in good time, just over an hour. But a better, less-frequented route through the Big Hole Valley runs east of the Continental Divide and the Anaconda-Pintler Wilderness Area. A good stopping point is Wisdom, which has the dubious distinction of being one of the coldest places in the Lower 48, and the turnoff for the Big Hole Battlefield. Driving farther south on Mont. 278 takes you to Jackson, then Bannack State Park, before ending at I-15 south of Dillon. From Dillon, drive north on Mont. 41 to Twin Bridges and the junction with Mont. 287. This road runs south through the Old West towns of Sheridan, Laurin, Alder, Nevada City, and Virginia City, before ending in Ennis at U.S. 287.

DRIVING TOUR #1: THE BIG HOLE VALLEY

This short loop tour takes you through the Big Hole Valley, nicknamed "Land of 10,000 Haystacks." Begin in Dillon, the largest of the towns in this area, and keep your eye out for white-tailed and mule deer in the morning and early evening. Travel north on I-15 to Divide, then take Mont. 43 southwest to

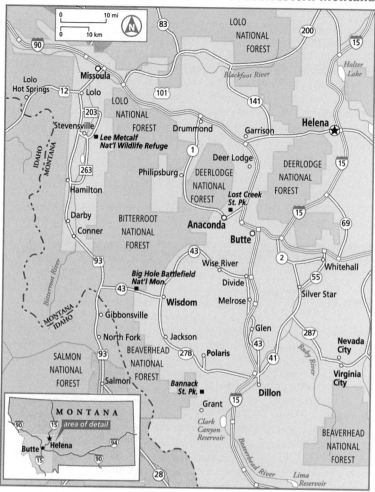

Wisdom. This is a tiny town with little other than its residents and the scenery to recommend it, but the Big Hole National Battlefield (described in detail later in this chapter) is a short drive west on Mont. 43 and is well worth the trip.

Then head back to Wisdom and take Mont. 278 towards Dillon. Along the way, stop in Jackson for a soak in the hot springs, or tour Montana's territorial capital city, Bannack, just 28 miles (45km) farther, off Mont. 278. As you stroll the boardwalks you'll discover the ease with which you can lose yourself in the state's early history—a microcosm that reflects the entire Old West. This drive is great during the summer, when haystacks fill the fields and the Bannack Days celebration re-creates early events in Montana's history. It's not so tame during winter months, though, when roads are icy and caution is required.

DRIVING TOUR #2: THE PINTLER SCENIC ROUTE

This tour is best enjoyed during summer, when area attractions open their doors to visitors and long summer days extend daylight hours.

This scenic route takes you from the mining city of Anaconda on a loop tour with ghost towns, historic buildings, and wildlife. Starting in Anaconda, where you can visit the copper-smelting display at the Copper Village Museum or admire an old Art Deco theater, **The Washoe,** which was ranked fifth in the nation by David Naylor (*American Picture Palaces*) for its architectural value—you'll head on little-traveled roads into a mountainous area that rivals any in the state.

Northwest of Anaconda on Mont. 1 lies **Georgetown Lake,** a popular tourist destination in both summer and winter, when anglers and skiers flock to the lake and nearby ski area, Discovery Basin. There are dog-sled races here on winter Sundays. Continue on Mont. 1 to Drummond, known as the "Bull Shipper's Capital of the World."

Heading southeast on I-90 will take you to **Deer Lodge,** home to the state prison, historic **Grant-Kohrs Ranch,** and the **Montana Auto Museum,** which features a slightly depleted collection of 120 antique automobiles—restored, original models from the early 1900s to the 1960s. County Road 273 takes you back to Anaconda.

2 Helena ★

64 miles (103km) N of Butte; 115 miles (185km) SE of Missoula; 89 miles (143km) S of Great Falls

Cradled in the foothills of the Montana Rockies, Helena is the focal point of the state's politics and culture. During the week, it's a bustling community of politicians, lobbyists, and bureaucrats. On the weekends, however, it seems they all turn into outdoors fanatics, heading to the lakes and mountains. Helena is also a haven for artists and other creative types, evidenced by the galleries that line the streets once dominated by mining-era saloons and houses of ill repute.

In its early days, Helena was a wild-and-wooly boomtown, built on gold mining. Last Chance Gulch was named when four miners said they had one last chance to hit it big in the West—and they did. The town boomed in the gold rush of 1865. During the height of this prosperity, only Manhattan could boast of more millionaires than the small Montana city. And along the way, the town recorded an alarming number of murders and robberies. Then, in 1935, the town was devastated by earthquakes. Beginning October 3, more than 2,000 tremors rocked the city, causing millions of dollars in damage.

After Helena took state capital rights from Virginia City in 1875, Marcus Daly, the Butte copper king with more than just a bystander's interest in the capital's location, decided to steal it away from Helena and move it to Anaconda, 25 miles (40km) from Butte. This touched off a political war that echoes throughout the state even today. As we all now know, Daly's efforts proved unsuccessful.

GETTING THERE   SkyWest (© 800/453-9417), **Delta** (© 800/ 221-1212), **Horizon** (© 800/547-9308 or 406/442-0930), and **Big Sky** (© 800/237-7788) provide commuter links to larger airports in Montana and other Western states from **Helena Regional Airport** (© 406/442-2821), northeast of the city on Skyway Drive off U.S. 15.

The **bus depot** is located at 3122 U.S. 12 E. (© 406/442-5860), with service on **Rimrock Stages,** a Trailways affiliate (© 800/255-7655).

It's easy to drive to Helena. From the east or west, take I-90; turn off and head north toward Helena. From the north or south, I-15 leads right into town.

VISITOR INFORMATION   A good starting point for local activities and area maps is the **Helena Area Chamber of Commerce** at 225 Cruse Ave., Suite A,

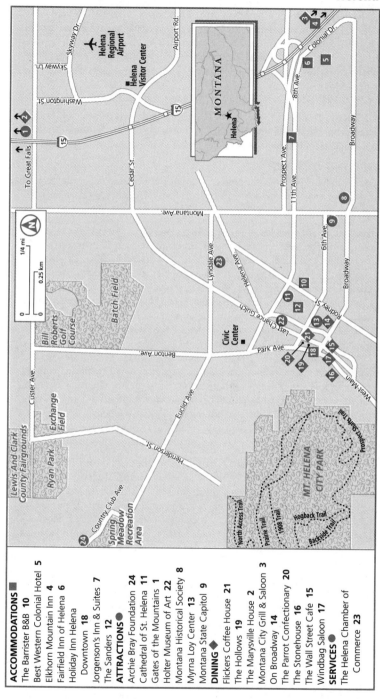

Helena

ACCOMMODATIONS ■
The Barrister B&B **10**
Best Western Colonial Hotel **5**
Elkhorn Mountain Inn **4**
Fairfield Inn of Helena **6**
Holiday Inn Helena
Downtown **18**
Jorgenson's Inn & Suites **7**
The Sanders **12**

ATTRACTIONS ●
Archie Bray Foundation **24**
Cathedral of St. Helena **11**
Gates of the Mountains **1**
Holter Museum of Art **22**
Montana Historical Society **8**
Myrna Loy Center **13**
Montana State Capitol **9**

DINING ◆
Flickers Coffee House **21**
The Hollows **19**
The Marysville House **2**
Montana City Grill & Saloon **3**
On Broadway **14**
The Parrot Confectionary **20**
The Stonehouse **16**
The Wall Street Cafe **15**
Windbag Saloon **17**

SERVICES ●
The Helena Chamber of
Commerce **23**

Helena, MT 59601 (© **800/7-HELENA** or 406/442-1530; fax 406/447-1532; www.helenamt.com). There is an information office run by the chamber out near the airport at Cedar Street off I-15. Another source is the state tourism office, **Travel Montana,** the mother lode for brochures and information about the region and the state (Helena is located in Travel Montana's Gold West Country). Contact them at 1424 N. 9th Ave., Helena, MT 59620 (© **800/VISIT-MT** or 406/444-2654; goldwest.visitmt.com).

GETTING AROUND   Car-rental agencies include **Avis** (© 406/442-4440), **Enterprise** (© 406/449-3400), **Hertz** (© 406/449-4167), **National** (© 406/442-8620), and **U-Save** (© 406/443-7283).

GETTING OUTSIDE

Just beyond the city limits, the area is chock-full of recreational opportunities, with blue-ribbon trout streams, downhill ski areas, and millions of acres of public land.

FISHING

There are several stretches of prime fishing along the upper stretch of the Missouri River. The section from **Toston Dam** downstream to **Canyon Ferry Lake** offers brown and rainbow trout in the 2- to 10-pound class. Floating with large streamers, wet flies, and lures is the most popular and productive way to catch these fish as they make their way upriver to spawn. The fishing gets progressively better from late spring to fall. The section below **Hauser Dam** to **Beaver Creek** offers a chance for really big trout. Other popular fishing areas include **Park Lake** 15 miles (24km) southwest of Helena, **Lake Helena,** and the **Smith River** to the east of the Big Belt Mountains.

Pro Outfitters, 326 N. Jackson, Helena, MT 59624 (© **800/858-3497** or 406/442-5489; www.prooutfitters.com), offers customized fly-fishing trips on the Smith River, considered in fishing circles one of the best not just in the state, but the world. Guides are helpful since river access is restricted to a limited number of permit holders by the Department of Fish and Wildlife.

HIKING

Mount Helena City Park covers 628 acres on Mount Helena, a 5,468-foot peak that looks out over the city. Nine trails cover the park, the easiest of which, the **1906 Trail,** follows the base of the limestone cliffs past Devil's Kitchen to the 5,468-foot summit. To reach the 1906 Trail, take Park Avenue to Clarke Street and turn west. Go south on Harrison to Adams Street, then west on Adams. The trail head is at the picnic area at the end of Adams Street. **Hogback Trail** is a rough and rocky hike that leads from the peak to the exposed Hogback Ridge. Contact the Helena Area Chamber of Commerce (see above) for information.

Moments Helena, au natural

Thomas McBride (© **406/443-5286**), a natural historian, river rafter, storyteller, and wildlife photographer, provides river-floating trips designed to allow you to see, understand, and connect with nature. Subjects include environmental issues, wildlife, vegetation, geologic formations, and photography instructions. McBride is a well-known and popular photographer who combines his artistic eye with a deep environmental understanding. Raft trips are $100 minimum for a day.

There are more than 700 miles (1,127km) of trails in the Helena National Forest. The **Trout Creek Canyon Trail** offers a spectacular view of Hanging Valley. Helena is also the gateway to the **Gates of the Mountains Wilderness.** For a serious hike in the wilderness area, you can go to **Mann Gulch,** the site of a forest fire in August 1949. Sixteen firefighters parachuted into Mann Gulch at about 6pm on August 5. Within 2 hours, all but three had perished. The incident is the subject of Norman Maclean's book, *Young Men and Fire.* You can get more information about hiking into Mann Gulch from the Helena Ranger district (**✆ 406/449-5490**). For a considerably less strenuous adventure, **Gates of the Mountains Boat Tours** (see below) offers boat tours of Mann Gulch along the Missouri River.

ROCKHOUNDING

Helena was founded on gold mining, and the area is still rightly famous for its gemstones, particularly Montana sapphires. Sapphires, a variety of the mineral corundum, are harder than any natural stone except a diamond. The Helena area has several commercial areas that allow visitors to dig for sapphires. Garnets, moss agates, fossils, and hematite can also be uncovered by diligent treasure seekers. See the listing for the **Spokane Bar Sapphire Mine & Gold Fever Rock Shop,** under "Seeing the Sights," below. Alternatively, contact the **Sapphire Gallery** (**✆ 800/525-0169**) or the **Eldorado Bar** (**✆ 406/442-7960**).

SKIING

Great Divide Ski Area   Great Divide is primarily a local ski hill, not a destination resort, but the resort has significantly expanded in recent years, adding a half-pipe and night lights while increasing its acreage. It is also pretty tough (15% beginner, 40% intermediate, and 45% advanced), although the Lower Mountain offers wide-open runs that cater to novice and intermediate skiers. There are a total of 140 trails on a trio of mountains served by five lifts.

There are free ski-instruction sessions for entry-level skiers, running 2 hours in length. Private lessons are also available through the ski school.

P.O. Box SKI, Marysville, MT 59640. ✆ 406/449-3746. www.greatdividemontana.com. Lift tickets $29 adults, $20 students and seniors, $10 children, free for children 5 and under with adult; rate reductions at noon and 4pm. Take exit 200 off I-15, then go west on Mont. 279 to Marysville Rd.

SNOWMOBILING

Three major trail systems are within a 30-minute drive of Helena. The Minnehaha-Rimini area grooms 120 miles (193km) of trails, and the Marysville and Magpie-Sunshine areas, with views into the Gates of the Mountains Wilderness, each groom 45 miles (72km) of trails. Guided tours can be arranged through the **Helena Snowdrifters.** For details on these tours, as well as specific trail information, contact the Snowdrifters at P.O. Box 5505, Helena, MT 59604 (**✆ 406/227-8111**).

WATER SPORTS

Canyon Ferry Lake Recreation Area, managed by the Bureau of Reclamation (**✆ 406/475-3310**), is a 25-mile-long (40km) lake within 20 minutes of Helena. In the spring, summer, and fall, the lake is primarily a rainbow trout fishery, but it does have 24 recreation and camping areas, and boat ramps. The lake is especially popular with water-skiers and water-tubers, though you'll see sailboats racing as well. This is also a prime bird-watching area—more than 1,000 eagles migrate through Canyon Ferry each year from mid-October to mid-December, and people come from all over the state and around the country to watch them feed on spawning kokanee salmon below the dam. The recreation area's **Canyon Ferry Visitor Center,** 7661 Canyon Ferry Rd., (© **406/475-3128,** is open daily from 11am to 5pm from Memorial Day to Labor Day, and from 8am to 4pm on Saturday and Sunday from the end of October until early December. To get to the visitor center, take Canyon Ferry Road east from Helena about 9 miles (14km).

Water-sports fans also head to two Helena-area state parks that are centered around man-made lakes: **Spring Meadow Lake** (day use only) and **Black Sandy** at the Hauser Reservoir. Spring Meadow is a 30-acre, spring-fed lake on Helena's western edge, noted for its clarity and depth. Open to nonmotorized boats only, the lake is popular for swimming and fishing. To reach Spring Meadow Lake, take U.S. 12 west, then head north on Joslyn to Country Club. One of the only public parks on the shores of Hauser Reservoir, Black Sandy is an extremely popular weekend boating, fishing, and water-skiing takeoff point. To get to the Hauser Reservoir, drive 7 miles (11km) north of Helena on I-15, then 4 miles (6km) east on Route 453, then follow signs 3 miles (5km) north on a county road. Information on both is available by calling © **406/449-8864,** ext. 154.

SEEING THE SIGHTS

A walking tour of the city will give you a capsule of the history of the Old West. For pointers on where to explore, contact the **Helena Area Chamber of Commerce** (© **800/7-HELENA** or 406/442-1530).

Last Chance Gulch was so named because a quartet of gold-seeking prospectors declared the spot to be their "last chance" to strike it rich. It came to be one of the richest gold-producing areas in the world and remains one of Helena's main streets. Located downtown, this historic area combines Helena's colorful past with a contemporary freshness. Architecturally significant buildings, many of which are listed on the National Register of Historic Places, house espresso shops and boutiques, while ultramodern sculptures depict historical events. Interpretive markers are scattered along the pedestrian mall, with historical information relating to period construction. **Kumamoto Prefecture** in Japan is Montana's "sister state," and the prefecture maintains a cultural center at 34 N. Last Chance Gulch (© **406/449-7904**). Visitors are welcome, and it's free. For a great place to play chess or checkers, head to the south end of Last Chance Gulch, where you'll find concrete tables with checkerboard tile inlays.

Archie Bray Foundation   Archie Bray, a Helena resident and enthusiastic supporter of the arts, established this artistic colony for potters in 1951 at the brickyard and kilns of the Western Clay Manufacturing Company. Over the years it has become a premier testing ground for ceramic artists, working together to share ideas and techniques. Various playful sculptures dot the lawns. Of special note are several larger, freestanding monuments by Robert Harrison, including "A Potter's Shrine," dedicated to Bray and incorporating some materials up to 100 years old; "Tile-X," stacked drain tiles in the shape of a pyramid; and "Aruina," a monument of brick and tile whose four arches frame the surrounding Helena landscape. Because of the intimate nature of each individual resident's art-making process, visitors are asked to respect their privacy. There is an annual summer-resident artist exhibit and sale running from mid-June to mid-August each year.

2915 Country Club Ave. © **406/443-3502.** www.archiebray.org. MC, V. Gallery open Mon–Sat 10am–5pm, Sun 1–5pm, with ceramic art for sale. Visitors may take a self-guided walking tour of the grounds during daylight hours.

Kleffner Ranch Tours ☆ (Finds) The Kleffner Ranch is a working cattle ranch with an unusual history. The ranch was founded in 1888 by William Child, a silver speculator who was ruined in the Panic of 1893. Child killed himself in the main ranch house that year, after the ranch was foreclosed by U.S. Senator-elect Wilbur Fisk Sanders. Before his downfall, Child had built a stone octagonal ranch house, the oldest of its type west of the Mississippi, and a barn that is now considered the country's largest of its vintage. After Child's death, the ranch was vacant until 1916, when a family took it over. They went broke during the Depression, and it was vacant again until 1943 when Paul Kleffner bought it. He and his wife spent the next 50 years restoring the property, and now Kleffner lives on the ranch by himself (his wife has since passed away) and is quite passionate about it. As a hobby, he gives the tours of this interesting property himself.

C. R. 518 (P.O. Box 427), East Helena. © **406/227-6645** or 406/495-9090. www.kleffnerranch.com. $5 adults, $2.50 children. June 1–Sept 30 tours at 10am and 2pm Mon–Sat, 2pm Sun. Take U.S. 12–287 through East Helena, then go south 1 mile (1.5km) on C. R. 518. You'll see the barn, then turn in at the second cattle guard.

Last Chance Tours A train engine on wheels pulls you around Helena on a tour of its historic sites, including the Atlas Block, the Montana Club, and the old governor's mansion. This is an excellent way to get oriented in Helena and learn a few things about the city at the same time.

Tours leave from the Montana Historical Society Building, 225 N. Roberts. © **888/423-1023** or 406/442-1023. www.lctours.com. $5.50 adults, $5 seniors, $4.50 children. Mid-May to late Sept; tour times vary seasonally.

Montana State Capitol Montana's beautiful state capitol building underwent extensive renovations through early 2001, revitalizing the historic grandeur that was lost during construction in the 1960s. Situated on 14.1 acres, the building was designed by architects Charles Bell and John Kent in the late 1800s. It's decorated in the French Renaissance style with frescoes, a grand stained-glass dome, and murals. The dome, faced with copper, rises 165 feet. Inside are murals by noted Montana artists Charlie Russell, Edgar Paxson, and Ralph DeCamp, including Russell's famed *Lewis and Clark Meeting Indians at Ross' Hole.* The grounds and flower gardens of the state capitol building in Helena are a designated state park, visited by thousands of people each year. In 2002, the state is celebrating the 100th anniversary of the capitol's completion.

Montana Ave. and 6th St. © **406/444-4789.** Free admission; no charge for tours. Building open Mon–Fri 8am–6pm. Montana Historical Society gives daily tours on the hour Mon–Sat 10am–4pm, Sun 11am–4pm; call ahead to make group reservations.

The Montana Historical Society The Montana Historical Society maintains a library and archives, as well as a museum. The **Montana Homeland Gallery** displays the history of Montana going back over 11,000 years. On display are petroglyphs, dinosaur bones, and implements of the earliest American Indians and first European settlers. Walls are adorned with calendars dating back to 1906, some of which have profit-and-loss calculations scribbled on them by their rancher-owners.

The **Mackay Gallery** has a permanent display of original Charlie Russell masterpieces—more than 60 artworks, including oils, watercolors, sculptures, and Russell's famous illustrated letters—that showcase one of the West's most remarkable artists. The **Haynes Gallery** displays the work of Jay Haynes, a photographer who traveled west in 1876 with the Northern Pacific Railroad to photograph farms of the Red River Valley and Black Hills of the Dakota

Territory. Haynes produced more than 10,000 views of Yellowstone's features and structures, and created a tourist-coach business along the way. A recent addition is collection of bronze sculptures by Robert Scriver that has drawn rave reviews.

Guided tours of the original **governor's mansion,** located at 304 N. Ewing, are also available through the society. This Queen Anne–style mansion with a distinctive checkerboard background was constructed in 1888 for entrepreneur William A. Chessman and his family. The state acquired the mansion in 1913 and governors resided here for half a century, during which time the mansion lost much of its original historical flavor. However, a major restoration of the building was undertaken beginning in 1969, and much of its allure has been recovered. During summer, tours operate on the hour from noon to 5pm Tuesday through Sunday. After Labor Day, call to set up an appointment to view this magnificent home.

225 N. Roberts St. ✆ 800/243-9900 or 406/444-2694. www.montanahistoricalsociety.org. Free admission and free tours. Museum: Memorial Day–Labor Day daily 8am–6pm; winter Mon–Sat 8am–6pm. Library and archives: Mon–Fri 8am–5pm, some Sat.

Cathedral of St. Helena   Completed in 1924, the Cathedral of St. Helena was modeled on a church in Vienna, Austria, and its beautiful twin 230-foot spires seem ready to soar heavenward on their own, filigreed and light. The cathedral is decorated with magnificent Bavarian stained-glass windows, hand-carved oak pews, hand-forged bronze light fixtures, and Carrara marble statues. At one time it was open to all who wandered by, but there are now times when the cathedral is left unattended and the doors are locked. So if you want to see the inside, it is best to call ahead. Masses are held here daily.

530 N. Ewing. ✆ 406/442-5825. Open to public, unless services are taking place; hours vary. Call to arrange a free group tour.

Holter Museum of Art ✸   Considered one of the premier galleries in the state, the Holter displays artwork in 7,200 square feet and features 10 to 14 different shows each year, all of which include an intriguing diversity of media and styles. Specializing in contemporary art of the Northwest region, the museum provides exhibition space for local as well as nationally prominent artists. The museum also runs a summer arts-education program for youngsters and adults.

12 E. Lawrence St. ✆ 406/442-6400. www.holtermuseum.org. Admission by donation. June–Sept Mon–Sat 10am–5pm, Sun noon–5pm; Oct–May Tues–Fri 11:30am–5pm, Sat–Sun noon–5pm.

Gates of the Mountains Boat Tours   Meriwether Lewis coined the name "Gates of the Mountains" while plying this portion of the Missouri with his party. At almost every bend in the waterway, the towering rock formations seemed to block their passage, only to magically open up as they drew closer. Visitors can have an experience similar to Lewis's through a boat tour of this scenic riverway on the *Pirogue,* the *Sacajawea II,* or the *Hilger Rose.* The 105-minute excursions take you through the mountain "gates" to a picnic area where wildlife-viewing opportunities abound. You can choose to return on a later boat and take a hike into the nearby Gates of the Mountains Wilderness Area or explore prehistoric pictographs on the limestone rocks. Mann Gulch, the setting of Norman Maclean's *Young Men and Fire,* and the site where 13 smokejumpers perished, is also within hiking distance. Markers indicate where each of the men fell.

I-15 (Gates of the Mountains exit), 18 miles (29km) north of Helena (P.O. Box 478, Helena, MT 59624). ✆ 406/458-5241. www.gatesofthemountains.com. $9 adults, $8 seniors, $6 children 4–17, free for children under 4. June–Sept; call for cruise schedule departures and returns.

Spokane Bar Sapphire Mine & Gold Fever Rock Shop If you've come to rockhound, this sapphire mine south of Hauser Lake is the place for you. A group can dig a bucket's worth for about $60, so the entire family can get into the spirit of Montana's early pioneers. The mine, 150 feet below ancient river levels, is a good source of green-blue sapphires, the most common type found. The location yields sapphires, garnets, gold nuggets, and an occasional topaz. The record sapphire taken from here was 155 carats.

5360 Castles Rd., Helena, MT 59602. *C* **406/227-8989** or 877/344-4367. www.sapphiremine.com. Call for fees. Daily 9am–5pm; winter hours vary. From I-15, take York Rd. east to mile marker 8. Turn right on Hart Lane and left on Castles Rd.

SHOPPING

Last Chance Gulch is a 4-block-long pedestrian mall. Though it is not exclusively a shopping area, the office buildings are liberally interspersed with boutiques, restaurants, pubs, and places for the kids to play. Informational kiosks are located in the center of this walking mall and at its north end. **Main News,** 9 N. Last Chance Gulch (*C* **406/442-6424**), is a tobacco shop with newspapers from various statewide and regional cities. It's located in the **Atlas Block,** one of a group of historically significant architectural structures in Last Chance Gulch. Helena's main areas were leveled several times in the last 125 years or so, once by earthquakes (in 1935) and several times by fire in the 19th century and again in 1928. In response to the fires, builders in the Atlas Block carved images of salamanders, which in mythology are impervious to fire. **Lasso the Moon,** 25 S. Last Chance Gulch (*C* **406/442-1591**), is a classic toyshop, featuring rack after rack of unique toys that aren't stocked by the mass-market retailers. Next door, at 19 S. Last Chance Gulch., is the **Ghost Art Gallery** (*C* **406/443-4536**), which features art on Western and nature themes. **Cobblestone Clothing,** 46 S. Last Chance Gulch (*C* **406/449-8684**), sells upscale women's clothing with a hint of the New West.

Reeder's Alley is a quaint shopping area that has a distinctly European feel. Its brick streets are home to a tightly packed group of old mining shanties that have been converted into offices, restaurants, and contemporary retail stores, though serious shoppers will find the pickings somewhat slim.

ESPECIALLY FOR KIDS

The Parrot Confectionery *(Kids)* Kids and adults alike will love this candy shop, established in 1922. The Parrot serves up its original cherry phosphates and caramel-cashew sundaes from the soda fountain, beneath its charming collection of ceramic elephants. Family-owned, the Parrot has provided gourmet chocolate and candy to Helena for more than 80 years, and loyal customers attest that the place and its products haven't changed a bit over time. In addition to its Helena clientele, the Parrot supplies candy to chocoholics from nearly every state in the union. It's known for its signature parrot confection, chocolate-covered caramels, and many other candies. They also have a "secret recipe" chili for lunch.

42 N. Last Chance Gulch. *C* **406/442-1470.** Mon–Sat 9am–6pm.

WHERE TO STAY

There's no shortage of good accommodations in Helena, with a bevy of historic inns and a number of business-oriented hotels and motels that cater to traveling politicos of all stripes. Aside from the options discussed below, you might try the **Fairfield Inn of Helena,** 2150 11th Ave. (*C* **800/228-2800** or 406/449-9944), with doubles for $74 to $80 and an indoor pool, or the independent **Elkhorn Mountain Inn,** 1 Jackson Creek Rd. at I-15, exit 187 (© **406/442-6625**), a top-drawer mom-and-pop with double rates of $60 to $70.

The Barrister Bed-and-Breakfast ⟨★   Located directly across the street from the Cathedral of St. Helena, the Barrister is one of many elegant homes near the original governor's mansion. Built in 1874, this Queen Anne–style gem was renovated in 1992 and opened as a B&B in 1993. The rooms are large and elegantly furnished with antiques. Each has a private bathroom—though some are across the hall. A nice touch is that each room has a black-and-white photo of what it looked like in the 19th century, courtesy of the Montana Historical Society. Most of the rooms are somewhat frilly, aside from the manly Captain's Suite, with a rich red carpet and a nautical theme. The third floor is a two-bedroom apartment that rents for $125 per night but is usually leased on longer term, by the week or month. The common areas include a sun porch, den, TV room/library, and office with high-speed DSL Internet connection.

416 N. Ewing St., Helena, MT 59601. © 800/823-1148 or 406/443-7330. Fax 406/442-7964. www.wtp.net/go/montana/sites/barrister.html. 5 units. $90–$125 double. Rates include full breakfast. AE, DC, DISC, MC, V. Pets accepted. *In room:* A/C, TV, hair dryer, no phone.

Jorgenson's Inn & Suites   Jorgenson's has been a Helena institution for more than 40 years. As you might expect in an older place, the rooms are a little smaller than those in most newer motels, but they have been religiously renovated, modernized, and refurbished throughout the years. Guests also have access to the fully equipped fitness center across the street.

1714 11th Ave., Helena, MT 59601. © 800/272-1770 or 406/442-1770. Fax 406/449-0155. 116 units. $39–$98 double. AE, DC, DISC, MC, V. **Amenities:** Restaurant; lounge; small indoor pool; courtesy car. *In room:* A/C, TV, dataport.

Holiday Inn Helena Downtown ⟨★   Formerly the Park Plaza Hotel, this seven-story hotel is on the pedestrian mall at Last Chance Gulch. In 1999 it was completely gutted and renovated to meet Holiday Inn standards. The rooms are pleasant, with modern decor, overstuffed chairs, desks, and double beds. Those at the top have exceptional city and mountain views. A few of the rooms have microwaves and fridges, so if you're in need of them, be sure to ask. Bullwhacker's Nightclub, a high-energy sports bar/dance hall that's the center of Helena's rock-and-roll scene, is just off the lobby.

22 N. Last Chance Gulch, Helena, MT 59601. © 800/332-2290 in Montana, or 406/443-2200. 71 units. $75–$79 double. AE, DC, DISC, MC, V. **Amenities:** Restaurant, 2 lounges; indoor pool; indoor Jacuzzi; exercise room. *In room:* A/C, TV, dataport, coffeemaker, hair dryer, iron.

The Sanders ⟨★★   The Sanders is a lesson in Montana history all on its own. Built and owned by Wilbur Fisk Sanders in 1875, the B&B has been beautifully restored by Bobbi Uecker (no relation to former ballplayer Bob) and Rock Ringling (a fourth-generation descendant of the famous circus family). Sanders was Montana's first U.S. senator and made his reputation by vigorously prosecuting the infamous Plummer gang in Virginia City. The Uecker-Ringlings are only the third owners of the property, and they purchased it with nearly all of its furnishings, most brought in by Sanders himself. You will sleep on beds from 1875 and look at the same pictures that Sanders did. One was painted by his wife, an important Western suffragette in her day. Bobbi Uecker's enthusiasm shows in every detail, from the fine breakfasts where she's willing to accommodate every kind of dietary restriction, to the afternoon refreshments. Our favorite accouterment is the elephant "bridle," marked with a big round disc reading "The Greatest Show on Earth." Wonder where they got that?

328 N. Ewing, Helena, MT 59601. © 406/442-3309. Fax 406/443-2361. www.sandersbb.com. 7 units. $95–$115 double. Rates include full breakfast and afternoon refreshments. AE, DC, DISC, MC, V. *In room:* A/C, TV, dataport, hair dryer.

WestCoast Colonial Hotel   This is a fairly upscale property, with a winding circular stairway inside that you might expect Scarlett O'Hara to come sweeping down at any moment. The place is somewhat dated, but a sweeping renovation in 2000 took care of most of the frayed edges. The rooms are huge for motel rooms, and the location right by the interstate is convenient for travelers. Some rooms also offer panoramic views of the valley and mountains beyond. The suites include king-size beds, refrigerators, microwaves, and some of the largest closets we've ever seen in a motel. Some suites have private Jacuzzis.

2301 Colonial Dr. (just off I-15 at U.S. 12), Helena, MT 59601. © 800/325-4000 or 406/443-2100. Fax 406/ 449-8815. 149 units. $69–$116 double. Rates include continental breakfast. AE, DC, DISC, MC, V. **Amenities:** Restaurant; lounge; indoor and outdoor swimming pools; Jacuzzi; exercise room. *In room:* A/C, TV, dataport, coffeemaker, hair dryer, iron.

CAMPING

Kim's Marina and RV Resort, 8015 Canyon Ferry Rd. (20 miles [32km] west of town), Helena, MT 59601 (© **406/475-3723**), has a complete resort facility that includes comfortable cabins situated on the lakefront. Canoes, deck boats, and paddleboats are for rent on a daily basis. You'll find 50 tent and 60 RV sites as well as tennis, volleyball, horseshoes, and boat rentals. **The Lakeside Resort,** 11 miles (18km) east of Helena on York Road near Hauser Lake (© **406/ 227-6413**), is an RV park that is open year-round with 70 full hookups and an on-site bar, restaurant, beach, and picnic area. **The Canyon Ferry RV Park,** 750 Canyon Ferry Rd., Helena (© **406/475-3811**), has full hookups and a self-serve laundry. North of town 3 miles (5km) on Montana Avenue is the **Helena Campground and RV Park,** with green grass and shade, an all-you-can-eat breakfast, and an ice-cream social in the summer. It's located at 5820 N. Montana Ave. (© **406/458-4714**).

For more primitive sites, the Bureau of Reclamation and Bureau of Land Management jointly run several campgrounds between Townsend in the south and Helena along U.S. 287 at Canyon Ferry Lake. From south to north, they are: **Indian Road Recreation Area** (1 mile [1.5km] north of Townsend on U.S. 287, mile marker 75), Silos (7 miles [11km] north of Townsend on U.S. 287, mile marker 70), and **White Earth Campground** (13 miles [21km] north of Townsend on U.S. 287 to Winston). The Indian Road Recreation Area offers a fishing pond for children and visitors with disabilities.

WHERE TO DINE

In addition to the eateries mentioned below, we like **The Hollows,** 26 N. Last Chance Gulch (© **406/443-2288**), which serves breakfast, espresso, and panini sandwiches in an attractive gallery space. **Flickers Coffee House,** 101 N. Last Chance Gulch (© **406/443-5567**), is a nice place to sit in an overstuffed chair and have a cup of coffee, baked item, or sandwich.

The Marysville House ✹ STEAKS/SEAFOOD   Every Rocky Mountain state has a barely surviving ghost town that for some reason attracts the mountain cabin crowd and a steakhouse. Marysville, an 1870 gold-mining town, once boasted a population of 4,000. And The Marysville House is the steakhouse at which they've all been eating. Located in what was once a train depot, The

Marysville House serves steaks, lobster, and crab legs in a rustic setting. The no-nonsense meals come with corn on the cob and beans. Guests have their choice of dining inside or out. And how's this for low-key Americana: Meals are served on paper plates, horseshoes can be found out back, and you can eat at a picnic table in the front yard.

In Marysville, a 45-min. drive from Helena. Take U.S. 15 North to exit 200, Mont. 279. Go north on Mont. 279 for 23 miles (37km); turn left at the sign for Marysville for 7 miles (11km) to find this living ghost town. ℭ **406/443-6677.** Meals from $10. No credit cards. Year-round Thurs–Sat; hours vary with the seasons; usually opens about 5pm.

Montana City Grill and Saloon STEAKS   This is a nice, sunny bar and grill that specializes in beef, fish, chicken, pasta, seafood, and ribs. The house specialty is the huckleberry barbecue sauce, which the cook liberally slathers on pork ribs, chicken, and pork chops. The pastel-and-wood dining room is adjoined by the bar, which has a pool table and one of the clearest big-screen televisions in the state.

Montana City, 5 miles (8km) south of Helena on I-15. ℭ **406/449-8890.** Main courses $9–$20; sandwiches and burgers $6–$8. AE, DC, DISC, MC, V. Mon–Thurs 11am–9pm; Fri 11am–10pm; Sat 8am–10pm; Sun 8am–9pm.

On Broadway ⭐⭐ ITALIAN   Located in an upscale brick building near Last Chance Gulch, On Broadway is the place to go in Helena for good Italian food. It's dressed up like any other fern-laden bar/restaurant, but the food is anything but typical, with artful combinations of meats and vegetables, fresh herbs, and pasta highlighting a menu with Italian subtitles. A local favorite is the *Petti di Pollo alla Broadway,* a chicken breast topped with fresh mushrooms and cheese, then baked in a Mornay sauce with mozzarella. The fish menu is the most imaginative, headed up by blackened tuna and oven-roasted salmon.

106 Broadway. ℭ **406/443-1929.** Reservations not accepted. Main courses $11–$25. AE, DC, DISC, MC, V. Mon–Thurs 5:30–9:30pm; Fri–Sat 5:30–10pm.

The Stonehouse STEAKS/SEAFOOD   Within a short walking distance of the shopping area on South Last Chance Gulch, The Stonehouse is a stalwart of the Helena culinary scene, although it has lost a bit of its luster in recent years. Regardless, it's a reliable bet for a romantic dinner or a huge steak. The evening specials are often the best choice; they might include veal or a surf-and-turf combo. The restaurant is also known for its prime rib dinners, offered in 10- to 20-ounce servings, and costing from $13 to $23. Fresh seafood is flown in weekly from Seattle, so the menu may include salmon, halibut, oysters, or shrimp scampi. The interior is divided into two rooms: The Victorian front is decorated in blues with a pressed-tin ceiling and Early American–style tables with high-backed chairs; the back room is surrounded by a stone wall with an ersatz waterfall under a somewhat over-the-top mountain mural.

120 Reeder's Alley. ℭ **406/449-2552.** Reservations recommended. Dinner $12–$18. AE, DISC, MC, V. Mon–Sat 5–9:30pm.

The Wall Street Café COFFEE/SANDWICHES   This small cafe is a fine way to start the day, with a pastry and some organically grown coffee or tea. Lunches consist of sandwiches and salads. All the sandwiches at lunch are $5.25 (or $3.50 for a half-sandwich), and all the salads $4.25, with daily soups and soup-salad-sandwich combos available. The restaurant is located at the end of the Last Chance Gulch pedestrian mall. The works of local artists dot the walls, with installations changing monthly.

62 S. Last Chance Gulch. ℭ **406/443-6215.** Breakfast $2–$3; lunch $3.50–$7.50. Mon–Fri 7am–4pm.

Windbag Saloon ☆ AMERICAN   Helena residents love this restaurant like you'd love an eccentric aunt: She's the most interesting relative you have and you always have a great time at her place. Who cares if she has a checkered past? So what if one of the cleanest and most respected bordellos in all of Montana once operated in the location where the restaurant now enjoys its own flourishing business? At least it's respectable, continuing the location's tradition as a focal part of Helena's nightlife. Try one of a long list of microbrews, or order something from the extensive collection of appetizers, before moving on to the Big Dorothy, one of the largest burgers you'll find anywhere, and fries so thick you'll barely be able to finish a serving.

19 S. Last Chance Gulch. © 406/443-9669. Lunch $6–$9; dinner $8–$22. AE, DISC, MC, V. Mon–Fri 11am–2pm; Mon–Sat 5:30–9:30pm.

THE PERFORMING ARTS

Make it a point to visit the **Myrna Loy Center for the Performing and Media Arts** ☆, 15 N. Ewing St. (© 406/443-0287; www.myrnaloycenter.com). Formerly the Lewis and Clark County Jail, the Myrna Loy (named after one of Helena's most famous residents, a silver-screen legend) is a multidisciplinary cultural center. Within its castle-like facade are a 55-seat cinema and a 250-seat performance hall, along with a gallery that focuses on regional art of all descriptions. The state-of-the-art facilities, where you can see independent and foreign films or attend a live production, are second to none in Montana.

3 Butte & Anaconda

Butte: 64 miles (103km) S of Helena; 120 miles (193km) SE of Missoula; 82 miles (132km) W of Bozeman; 150 miles (242km) NW of West Yellowstone

Butte may not be most people's idea of a vacation destination, but in many ways the town is the hidden soul of Montana. Butte's emergence in the 19th century as a hell-raising, wide-open mining town drew a lot of people to the state, including a variety of racial and ethnic groups. Butte has always been a strong union town in a state and region that disdain union activity. This union and socialist tradition from the rip-roaring days has made a lasting contribution to a strong progressive political tradition.

Butte used to be called "the richest hill on earth," for its production of copper, silver, and other precious metals, and during the 1880s, Butte was the world's largest copper producer. In 1955, the world's richest hill became the beginning of one of the world's largest holes, the Berkeley Pit, which provided more cost-efficient open-pit mining of copper. The pit expanded and almost swallowed the town. It is mostly closed now and filling with water, creating a gigantic pollution problem that is testing the skills of the Environmental Protection Agency.

But while Butte is proud of its rowdy past, it looks firmly to the future. It boasts Montana Tech, an arm of the University of Montana system. And full-time residents are flocking here for jobs in the city's emerging high-tech industry.

If you can look past the signs of decline that remain from the end of the mining era, Butte is full of rich history, colorful citizens, and a sort of blue-collar San Francisco–style charm. Physically, Butte is built along the sides of steep hills, which give it a cozy, provincial feel.

Anaconda was the "company town" formed when copper king Marcus Daly extended his copper empire 24 miles (39km) west. The community was spared the name "Copperopolis."

Butte

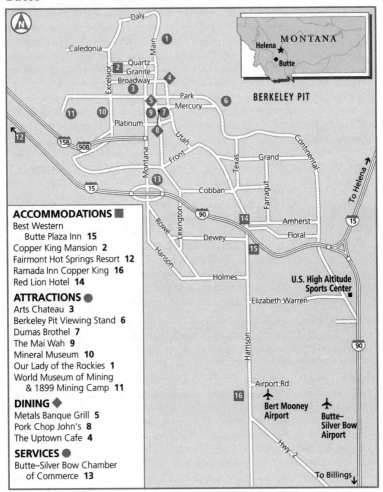

MONTANA
Helena ★
● Butte

BERKELEY PIT

ACCOMMODATIONS ■
Best Western
  Butte Plaza Inn **15**
Copper King Mansion **2**
Fairmont Hot Springs Resort **12**
Ramada Inn Copper King **16**
Red Lion Hotel **14**

ATTRACTIONS ●
Arts Chateau **3**
Berkeley Pit Viewing Stand **6**
Dumas Brothel **7**
The Mai Wah **9**
Mineral Museum **10**
Our Lady of the Rockies **1**
World Museum of Mining
  & 1899 Mining Camp **11**

DINING ◆
Metals Banque Grill **5**
Pork Chop John's **8**
The Uptown Cafe **4**

SERVICES ●
Butte–Silver Bow Chamber
  of Commerce **13**

ESSENTIALS

GETTING THERE   The Bert Mooney Airport, 101 Airport Rd. (✆ 406/
494-3771), is served by **Horizon** (✆ **800/547-9308**) and **SkyWest** (✆ **800/
453-9417**).

Butte is located at the junction of Interstates 90 and 15. For current Butte and
Anaconda **road conditions,** call ✆ **800/266-7623;** for current **weather information,** call ✆ **406/329-4840.**

The **Greyhound** station in Butte is located at 101 E. Front St. (✆ **406/
723-3287**).

VISITOR INFORMATION   The **Visitors Center and Transportation Center,** 1000 George St., Butte, MT 59701-7901 (✆ **800/735-6814;** www.butte-
info.org) is located just off exit 126 near the intersections of I-15 and I-90. The
center is a user-friendly facility just off the freeway, close to a wetlands area
where you can take a breather from driving while watching wild ducks, geese,
and muskrats go about their business.

The **Anaconda Chamber of Commerce,** 306 E. Park, Anaconda, MT 59711 (© **406/563-2400**), can give you information on Butte's sister city. For brochures devoted to area attractions and driving tours, contact **Travel Montana's Gold West Country,** 1155 Main St., Deer Lodge, MT 59722 (© **406/ 846-1943**).

GETTING AROUND   Car-rental agents in Butte include **Avis** (© 406/ 494-3131), **Budget** (© 406/494-7573), **Enterprise** (© 406/494-1900), **Hertz** (© 406/782-1054), and **Statewide Rent-a-Car** (© 406/723-4366).

The **Butte–Silver Bow Transit System** city buses run from 7am to 5:45pm Monday through Friday; for information on fares and stops, call © **406/ 723-8262. Mining City Taxi** is located at 3 S. Main St. (© **406/723-6511**) and provides local transportation 24 hours a day.

SPECIAL EVENTS   Butte has a heavy Irish heritage from its days as a mining boomtown. This legacy shines brightly (almost too brightly) on **St. Patrick's Day** ⊛, when this mining museum of a town throws a shamrock-tinted bash that is the big event of the year—even the banks shut down. The March 17 celebration is one of the biggest St. Patrick's Day parties outside of New York City, but be forewarned: It tends to be very rowdy and very drunk.

If you happen to be of Finnish extraction, or simply require a more obscure reason to party in Butte, you may want to arrive a few days earlier, when the city takes time off to honor St. Urho, the patron saint who reputedly drove grasshoppers from Finland. Contact the **Visitor Center** (© **800/735-6814**) for the dates and times of these activities.

GETTING OUTSIDE

Lost Creek State Park (© **406/542-5500**), a few miles outside of Anaconda, is a great place to camp or hike, or simply sit and admire the scenery. At the end of the road into the park, a short path will take you to pretty Lost Creek Falls, which tumble over a 50-foot drop. There are also mountain goats and bighorn sheep in residence. Several hiking trails lead off from the road. Among the most interesting things here are the rocks. Exposed on the tops of some cliffs is the 1.3-billion-year-old Newman Formation, a Precambrian rock that's among the oldest exposed rocks in the Lower 48 states. This is a primitive park, without services (and without charge). There are 25 campsites, suitable mostly for tents and car campers. To get to the park, drive 1½ miles (2km) east of Anaconda on Mont. 1, then 2 miles (3km) north on County Road 273, then 6 miles (10km) west.

GOLF

The **Old Works** ⊛⊛, 1205 Pizzini Way, Anaconda (© **406/563-5989; www.oldworks.org**), is a golf course and a work of art. This is your tax dollars at work, and you should feel good about it. The course is built on a Superfund site that has been a blight on the landscape since 1884, when the upper works began to process 500 tons of copper ore daily under Marcus Daly's voracious eye. By 1887 the lower works were necessary because of the demand. The Old Works

---

Tips **Travel Tip**

When traveling to this part of the state, many folks decide to fly into Salt Lake City, Utah. It's a 5.5-hour drive north through some spectacular country to get to this neck of the woods.

Tips **Butte Touring Tips**

The **Old No. 1 trolley tour** leaves from the Butte Visitor Center for a 1½-hour tour of the city's key attractions. Stops include the Berkeley Pit tunnel, where you'll have some time to gaze at the infamous manmade gash, and the World Museum of Mining. Driver/tour guides are chosen for their knowledge of the town's history.

---

closed in 1902, when the new Washoe Smelter—the big tower you can see from anywhere in the valley—took over all the processing. Jack Nicklaus designed the golf course, a tough but fair layout that even eight-handicappers are willing to play from the white tees. The black sand traps, the old processing works, and the vast, forbidding black tailings piles are all worked beautifully into the layout of the course. This is one of the finest courses not just in Montana, but in America. Open from mid-May to the end of October, peak season greens fees are $38 for 18 holes ($50 with cart) per person. To reach the course, take Commercial Street to North Cedar Street, turn north, then east (right) on Pizzini Way.

There's also an 18-hole course at nearby **Fairmont Hot Springs** (see "Where to Stay," later in this chapter). **Highland View Golf Course** (© 406/494-7900), at Stodden Park in Butte, has two separate nine-hole courses.

ROCK CLIMBING

Spire Rock and the Humbug Spires are the two most popular routes for rock climbers. In Butte, **Pipestone Mountaineering,** at 829 S. Montana St. (© 406/782-4994), can give you leads on the local climbing scene.

ROCKHOUNDING

From the Continental Divide east of Butte through the mountains to the south, diligent rockhounders can find smoky quartz, amethyst, epidote, and tourmaline. Ask the curator at the **Mineral Museum** (see "Seeing the Sights," below) for leads on local hot spots. The Butte Mineral and Gem Club has mining claims on **Crystal Park** 20 miles (32km) southwest of Wise River that are free and open to the public.

SKIING

In addition to **Discovery Basin** (see below), Butte visitors are within range of **Maverick Mountain** (see section 4, "Dillon & the Big Hole," later in this chapter).

Discovery Basin   This is another Montana ski resort that falls somewhere in the middle of the pack if you make a list ranking them for nearly any category. The runs on the mountain are equal parts beginner, intermediate, and expert. Five kilometers of groomed trails will satisfy the Nordic skier, or you can blaze your own trail through untracked snow.

While the scenery equals or exceeds that of other areas in the state, the real plus here is the resort's proximity to **Fairmont Hot Springs,** a four-season facility where soaking and swimming are year-round favorites (see "Where to Stay," below). Ski rentals and instruction are available (private lessons are $30 per hr.) as well as cafeteria-style food.

There are no hotels at the ski area; the nearest accommodations are at Fairmont Hot Springs or in Butte and Anaconda.

45 miles (72km) west of Butte on Mont. 1, off I-90 (P.O. Box 221, Anaconda, MT 59711). © 406/563-2184. Fax 406/563-7036. www.skidiscovery.com. Lift tickets $26 adults, $13 children 12 and younger and seniors; half-day $20 beginning at 12:30pm. Inquire about special group rates. AE, DC, DISC, MC, V.

SNOWMOBILING

The Anaconda Snowmobile Club (© **406/563-2918**) can point you to the nearest trail or take you on guided tours, most of which explore the Georgetown Lake area. The four major trail systems include Carp Ridge, which terminates at the Anaconda-Pintler Wilderness boundary; Echo Lake, at the midpoint of Georgetown Lake and Discovery Basin Ski area; Peterson Meadows, a popular spot for cookouts and picnics; and Red Lion Racetrack Lake, with ridgetop views of surrounding peaks.

SEEING THE SIGHTS

For information on the **Pintler Scenic Route,** a driving tour that begins in Butte, see section 1 of this chapter.

The Berkeley Pit is rumored to be visible from the moon. It is located just off the Continental Drive in Butte. Starting in 1955, nearly 1.5 billion tons of material were removed from the pit—including more than 290 million tons of copper ore—before mining ceased in 1982. A short walk through a dimly lit tunnel (fully accessible for those with disabilities) takes you to an observation deck where you can view the pit, which is currently filling with groundwater at a rate of about 7 million gallons per day. To keep birds from landing on the polluted water, they sometimes use flares, firecrackers, or even guys in boats waving their arms. The water flows through several thousand miles of underground pit tunnels through the mineralized zones and becomes heavily acidic. The viewing stand is at the east end of Mercury Street in the heart of downtown, and is open to the public (free admission) during daylight hours March through November.

The 585-foot **Anaconda Smelter Stack,** just off Mont. 1 on the outskirts of Anaconda, is one of the tallest standing brick structures in the world and is designated a Montana State Park, though there is no public access to the structure. Once considered the largest copper-smelting stack in the entire world, all 58 stories of the desolate shaft rise starkly to meet the Montana sky. An interpretive center opened at the site in 2000, with a few displays detailing the smelter stack's history and construction.

Our Lady of the Rockies   When you look up to the eastern heights above Butte, you'll see the large white statue of Our Lady of the Rockies in a notch at the top of a hill. The 90-foot statue was built "in the likeness of Mary, Mother of Jesus," and is dedicated to all women, and especially mothers. Private cars are not allowed up to the site, but you can get a close-up view of the statue on 2½-hour

---

⟨Fun Fact⟩ Butte's Not-So-Favorite Son

Daredevil extraordinaire Evel Knievel was born and raised in Butte before he went on to jump (or attempt to jump) his motorcycle over every imaginable obstacle. To boost the town's tourist trade, there has been talk of putting together a tourist attraction or walking tour dedicated to his childhood and later glory, but the plan has met some resistance. It seems that Knievel was something of a juvenile delinquent during adolescence, picking just about every available lock in town. Regardless, he still spends his summers in Butte and would love to see some sort of attraction come to fruition.

(Tips Anaconda Touring Tips

You can take the **Vintage Bus Tour of Historic Anaconda** from the Chamber of Commerce visitor center, 306 E. Park St. (✆ **406/563-2400**), Monday through Saturday at 10am and 2pm. The cost is $5 adults, $2 children. The tour includes a stop and inside tour of the fabulous Washoe Theater, which usually is open only at 8pm. The chamber also has a historic walking tour brochure for $2, but you won't see the inside of the Washoe unless you get lucky (see below).

---

bus tours. If you don't have time for a tour, but are interested in learning more about Our Lady of the Rockies, visit the information center and gift shop for a look at a panoramic mural of the statue. There is also a video detailing the construction: 400 tons of concrete were used just for the statue's base.

434 N. Main, Butte (gift shop and information center). ✆ **800/800-LADY** or 406/782-1221. Free admission to information center and gift shop. Summer Mon–Sat 9am–5pm, Sun 10am–5pm; winter limited hours. Tours depart daily during summer from the Butte Plaza Mall, 3100 Harrison Ave., $10 for adults, $9 children 13–17, $5 children 5–12, and free for children under 5. For tour reservations call ✆ **406/494-2656.**

Arts Chateau ⋆ Built in 1898 for Charles Clark, son of copper king William A. Clark, the Butte–Silver Bow Arts Chateau is an impressively restored mansion and art gallery. Stained-glass windows, beveled glass, ornate wrought iron, and intricately detailed woodwork contribute to the mansion's turn-of-the-century elegance. The home's magnificent staircase leads to a second-story museum, filled with period furniture, and the gallery, which houses traveling displays by Montana artists in a much more modern setting. The two galleries have exhibits that change every 6 weeks. Other highlights include the fourth-floor ballroom, which replicates a grand hunting lodge, and the first-floor gift shop, with hundreds of "Made in Montana" items for sale.

321 W. Broadway, Butte. ✆ **406/723-7600.** www.artschateau.org. $3 adults, $2 seniors, $1 children 16 and under, or $6 family. Summer Mon–Sat 10am–5pm; winter Mon–Sat noon–5pm. Tours available.

World Museum of Mining & 1899 Mining Camp ⋆ This popular museum is a re-creation of the 1899 Hellroarin' Gulch mining town. It's on the site of the Orphan Girl mine, which, though not a blockbuster by Butte standards, managed to produce 7.6 million ounces of silver, along with lead and zinc. A good way to get an overview of the museum is to ride the Orphan Girl Express, a three-car train pulled by an underground trammer engine. The ride will explain the history of mining and of Butte. The mining town is set up with typical businesses and buildings of the mining era here, with explanations of each of their functions in the community. There's also a hard-rock mining hall with tools of the trade and examples of types of framing timbers used underground.

Montana Tech Campus. ✆ **406/723-7211.** www.miningmuseum.org. $5 adults, free for children 12 and under. July–Aug daily 9am–9pm; May–June and Sept–Oct daily 9am–6pm. Closed Nov–Apr. Go uphill to the campus of Montana Tech, past the statue of Marcus Daly, where a sign in the middle of the street will direct you to the museum.

Mineral Museum   This museum displays only a percentage of the mineral specimens that belong to Montana Tech's geology department, though that still makes for a pretty impressive mineral display. The explanation of the minerals consists of their identification and place of origin. One display features a comprehensive display of fluorescent minerals, starkly illuminated by ultraviolet lights. One of the area's most exciting discoveries, a 27.5-ounce gold nugget found in the Highland Mountains south of Butte, is also on display.

Montana Tech Campus (take Park St. to the Montana Tech Campus and follow the signs to the museum). ℂ **406/496-4414.** Free admission. Summer daily 9am–6pm; after Labor Day and before Memorial Day Mon–Fri 9am–4pm; May, Sept, and Oct, Sat–Sun 1–5pm.

Dumas Brothel   Opened in 1890 as a "parlor house," the Dumas was once at the heart of Butte's red-light district. It was the city's longest-running house of prostitution, closing in 1982. Under the guidance of Norma Jean Almodovar, a former Los Angeles police officer, and later a call girl in Beverly Hills, the Dumas Brothel is being turned into a museum of prostitution. When the long-closed rooms in the basement were opened, they revealed "intact time capsules"— cigarette packs, liquor bottles, playing cards, and a rare White Cross model no. 26 metal vibrator, made in the pre–World War I era. While the project has received the unlikely support of the Butte Chamber of Commerce, it has not been universally applauded.

45 E. Mercury St., Butte. ℂ **406/723-6128.** Tours $3.50. Memorial Day–Labor Day daily 9am–5pm.

The Mai Wah   Adjacent to China Alley, the Mai Wah and Wah Chong Tai buildings stand as tributes to Butte's early Chinese population, which numbered 400 in 1890. With a first-floor mercantile and second-floor noodle parlor, the Mai Wah provided a segment of the city's ethnic community with jobs after the mines were exhausted. Today the buildings house exhibits and memorabilia honoring the rich Asian history of the area.

17 W. Mercury St., Butte. ℂ **406/782-4867** or 406/782-7329. Minimal admission fee, free for children. Summer only, Tues–Sat 11am–3pm.

Washoe Theater 🎭🎭   The Washoe shares the distinction with New York City's Radio City Music Hall of being the last two theaters done in the Art Deco style, and the Washoe is actually the more impressive. The brick exterior is unremarkable, and when you see it you'll wonder what all the fuss is about. But inside, this is a true movie palace. Considered one of the most architecturally significant theaters in the country, it's a work of art in cerulean, salmon, beige, and yellow, with a fabulous curtain. If you arrive at midday, the theater is usually closed—it's still a working movie theater and doesn't open until evening. But if owner Jerry Lussy is there, he'll turn on the lights and let you look around. Or you can take the Chamber of Commerce tour (see above).

305 Main St., Anaconda. ℂ **406/563-6161.** Movie tickets $4 adults, $3 children 11 and under. Fri–Tues, open 8pm; Wed and Thurs, 7pm.

WHERE TO STAY

Best Western Butte Plaza Inn 🎭   This property is the best motel in the area because of its facilities, services, and location next to the freeway. Rooms, with modern decor, are small but quiet and clean, all with either king- or queen-size beds, with a dataport on all the phones. The European breakfast buffet, included in the room price, includes thinly sliced meats and cheeses, fruits, muffins, hot or cold cereals, and juices and coffee. Next door, **Perkins Family Restaurant** is open 24 hours a day and serves traditional family fare. On site, **Hops** is a pub and casino decorated in the style of an English pub.

2900 Harrison Ave., Butte, MT 59701. ℂ **800/543-5814** or 406/494-3500. Fax 406/494-7611. www.best-western.com/butteplazainn. 134 units. $85–$93 double. Rates include breakfast buffet. AE, DISC, MC, V. Pets accepted, $50 deposit. **Amenities:** Indoor pool; sauna; exercise room. *In room:* A/C, TV, dataport, coffeemaker, hair dryer, iron.

Copper King Mansion ✿✿ This combination museum and bed-and-breakfast inn is an ideal choice for those who want to savor the historic ambience of one of the most lavish homes of the late 19th century. The huge home was built for mining magnate William Clark in 1888 for $260,000. There are 30 rooms on three floors. It is a lush "modern Elizabethan" style, which Clark is said to have favored. The intricate woodwork is remarkable and the owners have collected a large number of opulent furniture pieces from the period to furnish it. There are even a few original items from the period of Clark's ownership. In the third-floor ballroom, there's an 825-pipe Estey organ as well as a private collection of clothing and memorabilia dating back to the late 1800s; a small chapel is discreetly located to the side.

In addition to being a lavishly restored period mansion, the house is a bed-and-breakfast. All the rooms but one are very large (the small one, the butler's room, is seldom rented out) and beautifully furnished. There are parquet floors downstairs, and the octagon-shaped reception room, the billiard room, and the library all reflect Clark's love of luxury.

Antique lamps and chandeliers, ornate frescoed ceilings, and etched amber transoms complement the rooms' original furniture, including two matching African mahogany sleigh beds. If you stay at the B&B, you can sleep in the copper king's room, but you have to get up early. April through October, public tours ($5 per person) start at 9am and run until 5pm, when the mansion is closed to the public so that the night's guests can be admitted.

219 W. Granite St., Butte, MT 59701. ✆ 406/782-7580. www.copperkingmansion.com. 5 units, 3 with shared bathrooms. $65–$95 double. Rates include breakfast. AE, DISC, MC, V. *In room:* No phone.

Fairmont Hot Springs Resort ✿ (Kids) This oasis between Butte and Missoula is a great place for families, with a 350-foot water slide and a pair of Olympic-sized pools, a small zoo, and a playground. Parents will enjoy the wide range of activities as well, from golf and tennis to cross-country skiing in the winter. Plus, of course, the hot springs. The ski area Discovery Basin is only 30 minutes away. The standard rooms are fairly typical, hotel-style accommodations, but they all have balconies, and the suites are as large and snazzy as one could want, sleeping as many as eight guests each. The suites also have fully equipped kitchens, and, by resort standards, the cost is modest.

1500 Fairmont Rd., Fairmont, MT 59711. ✆ 800/332-3272 or 406/797-3241. www.fairmontmontana.com. 158 units. $115–$299 double. AE, DC, DISC, MC, V. **Amenities:** 2 restaurants, lounge (with casino); 2 outdoor hot-springs pools; 18-hole golf course; tennis courts; business center; massage. *In room:* A/C, TV, dataport, kitchens (suites).

Ramada Inn Copper King This very pleasant modern motel offers large rooms and good facilities. The exterior brickwork provides a nice entrance, and the interior is clean and quiet. The dome located in the back of the building is the city's only indoor tennis facility, and the indoor pool is Butte's largest. The Savoy Dining Room prepares slow-cooked beef ribs, among other items, in a subdued atmosphere.

4655 Harrison Ave. S., Butte, MT 59701. ✆ 800/332-8600 or 406/494-6666. 146 units, including 2 suites. $69–$79 double; $175 suite. AE, DC, DISC, MC, V. **Amenities:** Restaurant; indoor pool; tennis courts; indoor Jacuzzi; coin-op washers and dryers. *In room:* A/C, TV, dataport.

Red Lion Hotel The Red Lion is a good choice for families, with the largest rooms in town—decorated in typical upscale American motel style—and a very gracious staff. It has room service, which is fairly unusual in Montana motels. Its location next door to Father Sheehan City Park, with baseball diamonds, tennis courts, and a jogging track, is a plus.

2100 Cornell, Butte, MT 59701. © **800/443-1806** or 406/494-7800. Fax 406/494-2875. 134 units. $56–$89 double. AE, DC, DISC, MC, V. Pets accepted, $8 per night. **Amenities:** Restaurant; indoor pool; indoor Jacuzzi; limited room service. *In room:* A/C, TV, dataport, coffeemaker, iron.

WHERE TO DINE

Butte's ethnic tradition is most evident in its food, with pasties (pronounced "PASS-tees," or "PAH-stees" if you're British) ranking high on the list. If you've never tried one of these Cornish meat-filled pastries, you're in for a treat. Purveyed at nearly every eating establishment in the city, pasties are an essential part of the Butte experience. Another local delicacy that should not be missed is a $2.50 breaded pork chop sandwich from **Pork Chop John's,** 8 W. Mercury St. (© **406/782-0812**). This bare-bones, blue-collar diner is a Butte landmark, and the sandwiches, wrapped in wax paper and topped with pickles, mustard, and onions, are the best deal in town.

Jim and Clara's STEAKS/SEAFOOD   This is a classic Montana steak joint, with black Naugahyde booths and steaks too big to finish in one sitting. Thursday nights, you can get the large T-bone for $13. You also get the salad bar, spaghetti, and potato. One of the most popular dishes is the gourmet seafood plate, which might include a small lobster tail, crab legs, and scallops, depending on what's in season. There's also an extensive menu for seniors and kids (without such large appetites), with items that run from $8 to $10.

511 E. Park, Anaconda. © **406/563-9963** or 406/563-2311. Reservations recommended Thurs–Sat. Main courses $12–$40. AE, MC, V. Wed–Mon 5pm until the last diner leaves.

Metals Banque Grill BISTRO/MEXICAN   When restoration began on this deteriorated downtown building in 1989, workers peeled away nearly a century's worth of paint and discovered original marble, African mahogany, solid copper window frames, and an intricate 22-inch vaulted plaster ceiling. Just like that, a fine dining establishment was born. Built in 1906 to house the State Savings Bank and designed by famous turn-of-the-century architect Cass Gilbert, the Metals Banque Grill is today best known for the excellent food found inside its doors—though you'd never realize it's known locally for its Mexican food (namely the fajitas). You'll also find plenty of steaks and seafood on the extensive menu, plus an array of healthful foods and low-fat items. Our recommendation: start with an order of chicken-cilantro rolls, then move on to the N.Y. Imperial, a strip steak topped with crab meat and hollandaise sauce, for the main event.

8 W. Park St. (at Main). © **406/723-6160.** Reservations recommended, especially on weekends. Lunch $4–$15; dinner $6–$15. DISC, MC, V. Mon–Sat 11am–10pm. Shorter hours in winter.

The Uptown Café ☆ CONTINENTAL   The Uptown Café is a white-tablecloth restaurant in a no-tablecloth town. Despite the fact that the environment is casual and unpretentious, the restaurant presents five-course meals built around Montana beef and fresh seafood flown in from the Pacific Northwest. The favorite starter is Clams Maison—succulent clams prepared with white wine, chives, and butter. Other choices include soup—gazpacho if you're lucky—plus several types of salads, a pasta or vegetable dish, and the main course. We recommend the salmon or halibut, when they're available, but we wouldn't turn down a steak either. Every night at 6:30pm, the cafe also serves an early-bird special: cheese ravioli with artichokes and roasted red peppers or chicken Dijon, for example, always with a Caesar salad and French bread for only $9.50. It makes you wonder if this is really Butte.

47 E. Broadway. ☎ 406/723-4735. www.montana.com/uptown. Reservations recommended. Lunch $3–$7; dinner $9–$25. AE, DISC, MC, V. Mon–Fri 11am–2pm; Mon–Sat from 5pm; Sun from 4pm.

A SIDE TRIP TO DEER LODGE

Deer Lodge is home to Montana's state prison, which isn't ordinarily a recommendation for a tourist destination. And we won't recommend any places to stay, because you probably won't want to spend the night. But there is a collection of museums here that makes Deer Lodge worth a morning's stop— especially if you're a car buff or a fan of ranching life.

As you enter Deer Lodge from the west on County Road 275, you'll pass the **Grant-Kohrs Ranch National Historic Site** (☎ 406/846-3388; www. nps.gov/grko), another of the National Park Service's marvelous facilities. The site preserves the rich history and traditions of ranch life in the West. The ranch itself was founded in the late 1850s when Johnny Grant, a Canadian trader, moved here, eventually building up a herd of several hundred cattle. After a few years, he sold it to legendary cattleman Conrad Kohrs, and the ranch became the headquarters for a vast cattle empire scattered across the open range of Montana, Idaho, and Wyoming. Today, the site includes 88 structures, 26,000 artifacts, and a 1,500-acre cultural landscape maintained as a small-scale working ranch. Ranger-led tours of the 1890 Kohrs manor can be arranged at the visitor center. Admission is free. It's open to the public daily except Thanksgiving, Christmas, and New Year's Day.

Gold was discovered near Deer Lodge in 1862. This was an early precursor of the gold rush that reached full bloom in the discoveries at Bannack and Virginia City. One of the consequences of this gold rush is downtown—the castle-like **Old Montana Prison**, at 1106 Main St. (☎ 406/846-3111). The thievery and lawlessness that prevailed during the gold rush was initially dealt with by vigilantes, but the need for a real jail was eventually solved by the construction of this prison, which took in its first prisoner in 1871. It was used until 1979, when another facility was built about 5 miles (8km) from here. You can take a self-guided tour of the prison. Cell blocks, maximum-security areas, turreted guard towers, and the imposing arches of the "Sally Port" gate are the attractions here, as well as a tribute to officers killed in the line of duty at the **Montana Law Enforcement Museum.**

The Old Prison and the Law Enforcement Museum are only two of a collection of museums in Deer Lodge, which are all covered under one admission fee ($7.95). The prison complex also houses the **Montana Auto Museum,** the **Powell County Museum, The Frontier Montana Museum,** and **Yesterday's Playthings.** The complex is open to the public year-round, from Memorial Day to Labor Day, from 8am to 8pm, with shorter hours the rest of the year.

The **Montana Auto Museum** currently houses more than 120 exquisitely restored automobiles—mostly classic Fords and Chevys, but also vintage fire trucks, motor homes, and motorcycles. The **Frontier Montana Museum** has a collection of the tools that were used to win the West. There is a nice exhibit on Colt "peacemakers" and their effect on the keeping of the peace. There are also saddles, spurs, and Desert John's Saloon, with one of the largest bottle and whiskey-memorabilia collections in the country.

The vast weapons collection at the **Powell County Museum,** 1193 Main St., includes long guns and handguns from 1776 to 1956, as well as vintage jukeboxes and coin-operated slot machines. The museum is open from Memorial

Day to Labor Day, from noon to 5pm, and is closed in winter. **Yesterday's Playthings,** 1017 Main St., is a doll and toy museum. The collections of Harriet Free and Pat Campbell are displayed here, with dolls, toys and antiques of all descriptions: mohair Teddy bears, carriages and cradles dating back to 1835, clown dolls, and various reproductions. The collections can be viewed daily from mid-May to early October, from 9am to 5pm, but the museum is closed in winter.

For additional information on these and other activities in Deer Lodge, contact the **Powell County Chamber of Commerce,** 1171 Main St., Deer Lodge, MT 59722 (© **406/846-2094**), or **Gold West Country,** 1155 Main St., Deer Lodge, MT 59722 (© **406/846-1943;** goldwest.visitmt.com).

4 Dillon & the Big Hole

Dillon: 65 miles (105km) S of Butte; 141 miles (227km) N of Idaho Falls, Idaho

In early Western parlance, a "hole" was a valley surrounded by steep mountains. And Big Hole is, well, a big "hole," in this old sense of a valley. It is a vast expanse of hay meadows, sagebrush flats, and ranch land ringed by towering mountains in the distance. These hay meadows have also given the Big Hole its nickname of the "valley of 10,000 haystacks," which may be a rare case of Rocky Mountain understatement.

While there are plenty of haystacks, there aren't many people. This region is the least densely populated area in Western Montana. Beaverhead County, which is as large as Connecticut and Rhode Island combined, has only about 8,000 residents, and most of those live in Dillon, the county's largest town.

Dillon is primarily an agricultural center, still dependent on local farmers and ranchers rather than tourism or industry. The population jumps from 5,000 to 15,000 to 20,000 people each year around Labor Day during the event known as **"Montana's Biggest Weekend."** Among the draws are a county fair, which is wrapped around a PRCA Rodeo that draws some of Montana and Wyoming's best cowboys, as well as live musical entertainment. If you plan on attending, book a room at least 3 months in advance.

The scenic loop that takes you around this valley is one of the state's more popular driving tours, and is described in section 1 of this chapter.

ESSENTIALS

GETTING THERE The **Dillon Airport** is located at 2400 Airport Rd. and has paved runways for light planes. See Butte and Anaconda "Essentials," earlier in this chapter, for information on the closest airport to the Big Hole Valley for commercial flights, car rentals, and train and bus service. Dillon is located on I-15, about 67 miles (108km) south of Butte and 78 miles (126km) from Anaconda.

This area is also a popular destination for snowmobilers, and visitors are encouraged to call the **avalanche advisory line** (© **406/587-6981**) before setting out on a snowmobiling excursion. For **current road conditions** in the Big Hole Valley, call © **800/332-6171;** for current **weather information,** call (© **406/449-5204.**

VISITOR INFORMATION The **Dillon Visitor Information Center** (Beaverhead Chamber of Commerce) is located in the Old Union Pacific Railroad at 125 S. Montana St., Dillon, MT 59725 (© **406/683-5511**). You can also contact **Gold West Country,** 1155 Main St., Deer Lodge, MT 59722 (© **406/846-1943;** goldwest.visitmt.com), for information on the entire Big Hole Valley.

GETTING OUTSIDE

Beaverhead County has several natural hot springs, including **Jackson Hot Springs Lodge** (see "Where to Stay," below), and **Elkhorn Hot Springs,** which is located about 10 miles (16km) off Route 278 on a gravel road. Go west of Dillon on 278 about 30 miles (48km), then turn north toward Polaris at the sign. Follow the road through Polaris to Elkhorn Hot Springs, about 5 miles (8km) farther. These waters provide a therapeutic complement to various winter activities, most notably snowmobiling, downhill skiing, and cross-country skiing.

OUTFITTERS & ORGANIZED TRIPS

Montana High Country Tours, 1036 E. Reeder St., Dillon (© **406/683-4920** or 406/834-3469; www.mhct.com), is operated by sixth-generation Montanan Russ Kipp. The company offers year-round guiding services, including fly-fishing, horseback riding, big-game hunting, and snowmobiling. Whether you're a sportsman looking to bag that elusive elk or a family longing for some quality time together, Kipp has plenty of experience in arranging a unique outdoor adventure. His most popular trips center around southwest Montana's classic trout streams, picturesque limestone canyons, and stunning mountain ranges. Prices range from $625 for a 3-day/4-night snowmobiling package that includes a snowmobile (with fuel), lodging, meals, insurance, and equipment, to $2,900 for a 7-day deer- and elk-hunting trip including meals, lodging, and pack.

Great Divide Wildlands Institute (© **406/683-4669;** www.greatdivide-tours.com) offers a variety of scenic and historical tours, with a special emphasis on the route of Lewis and Clark. The packages range from day trips to where Lewis first met the Shoshone to multi-day horse-packing trips that retrace Clark's route through the Big Hole.

Another resource for trips in the Big Hole is **Maverick Travel** (© **406/ 683-2224;** www.maverricktravel.com), which maintains a list of area outfitters and guides.

FISHING

The Big Hole, Beaverhead, and Poindexter Rivers are all within easy reach of Dillon, and Jefferson is only half an hour away by car. The fishing season begins early in the year when other streams may still be clearing, and extends into October. Big Hole fishermen can find several trout species, including eastern brook, German brown, and golden. The **Clark Canyon Reservoir** provides good fishing for rainbow trout. Arctic grayling, ling, and whitefish also populate the waters of the Big Hole Valley. **The Beaverhead-Deerlodge National Forest,** 420 Barrett St., Dillon, MT 59725 (© **406/683-3900**), can provide you with a free "Lake and Fish Directory" covering all the waters in the forest. If you want to stay at a fishing lodge, check out **Craig Fellin's Big Hole River Outfitters** (see "Where to Stay," below).

For licenses, equipment, and advice on hot fishing spots, check with the locals in Dillon at **Frontier Anglers,** 680 N. Montana St. (© **406/683-5276**). You can arrange a trip on any of the local rivers with **Tom Smith's Backcountry Angler,** 426 S. Atlantic St., Dillon, MT 59725 (© **406/683-3462;** www.back-countryangler.com). Smith has been guiding in Montana since 1983, and he also has a pair of kitchenettes available for rental (call for details). In Twin Bridges (just up Mont. 41), your best bet for fishing equipment and outfitting services is the **Four Rivers Fishing Co.,** 205 S. Main St. (© **800/ BRN-TROUT**). Aficionados of the fishing world should stop at the **R.L. Winston Rod Co.,** also in Twin Bridges, at 500 S. Main St. (© **406/684-5674;**

www.winstonrods.com), for a look at some of the finest fly rods in the world. Free tours of the company museum are given each weekday at 2pm. If you're in the market, and can spare around $750, you can also buy a rod.

HIKING

Hike along the **Continental Divide National Scenic Trail** in the **Anaconda-Pintler Wilderness** for interesting geologic discoveries, fabulous scenery, and views of wildlife: Elk, moose, mule deer, antelope, and even black bears are all indigenous to the region. Covering parts of the Bitterroot and Beaverhead-Deerlodge National Forests, this 158,500-acre wilderness spans 40 miles (64km) along the Continental Divide over four counties. Highways with access to the area are U.S. 93 on the west, Mont. 38 and Mont. 1 from the north, and Mont. 43 from the east and south. The **Wise River Ranger District,** Box 100, Wise River, MT 59762 (℃ **406/832-3178**), can direct you to the area's most traveled trails. You can also obtain a *Recreation Directory for the Beaverhead-Deerlodge National Forest,* which describes many of the trails on the forest. The guide is available for free from **Beaverhead-Deerlodge National Forest,** 420 Barrett St., Dillon, MT 59725 (℃ **406/683-3900**).

HORSEBACK RIDING

Diamond Hitch Outfitters, 3405 Ten Mile Rd., Dillon, MT 59725 (℃ **800/ 368-5494;** www.mules.com), offers 2-hour rides, half-day trips, and full-day trips in the Pioneer Mountains. As an alternative, evening horseback rides include a campfire cookout. More adventurous overnight and extended backcountry rides are also available. Rates range from $25 per hour to $700 for a 5-day trip.

SKIING

In addition to **Maverick Mountain,** discussed below, Dillon is fairly close to **Lost Trail Powder Mountain** (see "A Detour into the Bitterroot Valley," in chapter 5).

Maverick Mountain Located 35 miles (56km) west of Dillon in the Beaverhead National Forest, Maverick Mountain is a small area that attracts mostly local skiers. It remains crowd-free and has yet to become a destination ski resort. It has 18 runs with 2,000 vertical feet of skiing. About half the runs are rated for the expert skier. There are some wide-open bowls, meadows, winding runs, and steep chutes. The lift tickets are very inexpensive. The area gets enough snow— 200 inches yearly—to offer some good powder days. Rentals and lessons are available for downhill skis and snowboards. There's a child-care facility, but call ahead to reserve a spot. A nursery facility is also available by reservation. There are no lodging facilities at the ski area, although there are some nice accommodations nearby. Cafeteria-style meals are available at the base lodge, or you can grab a hot toddy at the Thunder Bar.

Maverick Mountain Rd. (P.O. Box 475), Polaris, MT 59746. ℃ 406/834-3454. Lift tickets $21 adults, $14 children 6–12, free for children 5 and under. Late Nov to early Apr Thurs–Sun and holidays 9:30am–4:30pm. Take Mont. 287 west off U.S. 15 to the Polaris Rd. for 13 miles (21km).

SNOWMOBILING

The Wise River trail system features 150 miles (242km) of groomed trails in the Big Hole Valley area, including **Anderson Meadows**—which leads to backcountry lakes and a rental cabin—and **Lacy Creek,** with 10 miles (16km) of groomed and ungroomed trails to five high-mountain lakes. **The Wise River**

Jackpine Savages, Box 129, Wise River, MT 59762 (© **406/832-3258**), are the local snowmobiling authorities; call them for trail specifics.

NATURE PRESERVES & WILDERNESS AREAS

One of the Bureau of Land Management's Backcountry Byways, the **Big Sheep Creek Canyon** offers the opportunity to observe the majestic bighorn sheep in their spectacular natural habitat. The 50-mile (81km) byway begins in Dell, Montana, on I-15, 24 miles (39km) north of the Montana–Idaho border, and passes beneath the high rock cliffs of Big Sheep Canyon to the head of Medicine Lodge Creek. From here, it's just a short drive down to the Medicine Lodge Valley to Mont. 324, just west of Clark Canyon Dam.

   Clark Canyon Recreation Area, a man-made lake 20 miles (32km) south of Dillon on I-15, is a popular spot for water-skiing or trout fishing. Lewis and Clark's Camp Fortunate is located on the northwestern shore of the reservoir, where camping and boat-launching facilities are also available.

   Two Dillon-area landmarks are designated state parks because of the historical significance attached to them as a result of the Lewis and Clark expedition. **Clark's Lookout** (© **406/834-3413**) provided the explorers with a vantage point from which to view their route and is reached by taking the Mont. 41 exit from U.S. 90. Drive one-half mile (.5km) east, then another half mile north on a county road. **Beaverhead Rock,** 14 miles (23km) south of Twin Bridges on Mont. 41 (© **406/834-3413**), was a tribal landmark recognized by expedition scout Sacajawea. Both parks are day use only.

SEEING THE SIGHTS

Based in Dillon or elsewhere in the valley, you can branch out to see **Big Hole National Battlefield;** see section 5 of this chapter for details.

   The **Pioneer Mountain Scenic Byway** is a 4-mile (6km) drive that begins on Mont. 278 west of Dillon or along Mont. 43, south of the Wise River. Only the northern 28 miles (45km) of the road are currently paved, though there are plans to pave the rest eventually. Driving between the east and west Pioneer Mountain Ranges, you'll experience alpine meadows, jagged peaks, and ghost towns with numerous opportunities to camp, fish, or watch wildlife. Near Coolidge (as you drive south) you'll see the old railroad bed of the Montana Southern Railway. This was the last narrow-gauge railroad built in the U.S., to serve the Elkhorn mine.

   Visitors don't usually come to Dillon or the Big Hole Valley to shop, but there are a few stores worth mentioning. The town's **Patagonia Outlet store,** 34 N. Idaho St. (© **406/683-2580**), offers fleece pullovers and other popular outdoor gear. Right next door, at 36 N. Idaho St., is **Sagebrush Sewing Works** (© **406/683-2329**), which offers outdoor gear for everyone except the fly-fisherman. **The Bookstore,** 26 N. Idaho St. (© **406/683-6807**), makes it three in a row on the main drag. It has an excellent selection of contemporary popular Western and American Indian literature.

Beaverhead County Museum   The Beaverhead County Museum is located in the center of town next to the depot building. It's housed in an 1890s settler's cabin moved to the spot. Inside there is a little bit of everything from the pioneer era—clothes, tools, cooking utensils, furnishings, typewriters. Like a lot of small-town museums in the West, though, this one seems more interested in preserving the names of the families who donated items than in telling a coherent historic story.

15 S. Montana St., Dillon. © 406/683-5027. Free admission. Mon–Fri 9am–5pm.

Red Rock Lakes National Wildlife Refuge:
A Haven for the Trumpeter Swan

Though well off the beaten path in the Centennial Valley, 28 miles (45km) east of Monida (about an hour south of Dillon), the **Red Rock Lakes National Wildlife Refuge** is often called the most beautiful wildlife refuge in the United States. The refuge was established in 1935 to protect the rare trumpeter swan, and it is here that the endangered species has been brought back from near extinction after a century of being hunted for their meat and feathers (quill pens were a hot item in the 1800s). It was feared that these beautiful creatures, which have wingspans of 7 to 8 feet, had been completely wiped out, until biologists discovered several dozen here in 1933. (They're also found along the Pacific Coast and in Alaska.)

This is the largest population in the Lower 48 states—300 to 500 of the rare birds continue to nest and winter at the refuge. They mate for life and often return to the exact same nest each year to tend their eggs and cygnets. The best place to view the trumpeters is in the open areas near Upper Red Rock Lake, from late April to the end of September.

In addition to the swan population, the 40,000-acre refuge is home to moose, deer, elk, antelope, fox, great blue herons, sandhill cranes, ducks, and geese; more than 50,000 ducks and geese may be seen during times of migration.

The multi-use refuge is a popular spot for hiking, mountain biking, and canoeing; check with the **U.S. Fish and Wildlife Service,** Mountain Prairie Region, P.O. Box 25486 DFC, Denver, CO 80225 (✆ **303/ 236-7920,** or locally 406/276-3536), for regulations concerning these activities within refuge boundaries. The refuge lies just beyond the town of Monida, off I-15 well south of Dillon; you'll take a gravel road the remainder of the way.

Western Montana College Gallery/Museum   The most exciting exhibit at this gallery and museum is the Seidensticker Wildlife Collection of big-game trophies, featuring animals from the far-flung locales of Africa and Asia as well as North American game. The museum also houses a small permanent collection and seasonally rotating exhibits, including student artwork.

710 S. Atlantic St., Dillon. ✆ **406/683-7232.** Free admission. Open during fall and spring semesters, Tues–Fri noon–4:30pm.

WHERE TO STAY

In addition to the hotels listed below, two other chain options in Dillon are at I-15 exit 63. The **Comfort Inn,** 450 N. Interchange (✆ **800/442-4667** or 406/683-6831), has rooms for two in the $60 to $70 range; and the **Super 8 Motel,** 550 N. Montana St. (✆ **800/800-8000** or 406/683-4288), offers rooms for $58 to $65 double. If you're on a budget and not too picky, you might try the **Hotel Metlen,** 5 S. Railroad Ave. (✆ **406/683-2335**), a historic hotel that is now a bit worse for the wear. The rooms offered are only $20 to $30, but the quality is erratic (some are quite nice, some are exactly the opposite). Regardless, the place has a classic Montana saloon and card room on the first floor and a certain amount of rugged charm—but don't say we didn't warn you about the rooms.

The Best Western Paradise Inn   The Paradise Inn is a comfortable (albeit basic) two-story facility set back from one of Dillon's busier streets. The standard rooms are cozy and appointed with an eye for efficiency, not style, but the penthouse suites are well worth the indulgence, with huge bathtubs and large living areas. For families, there is one two-bedroom unit.

650 N. Montana St., Dillon, MT 59725. ✆ **800/528-1234** or 406/683-4214. Fax 406/683-4216. 65 units. $44–$70 double; $70–$80 suite. AE, DISC, MC, V. **Amenities:** Restaurant; indoor pool; indoor Jacuzzi. *In room:* A/C, TV, dataport, coffeemaker, hair dryer, iron.

Jackson Hot Springs Lodge ✿✿   A frequent comment from new arrivals at this lodge, when they enter the lobby and look up at the collection of animal heads on the wall, is "This is what you really expect a lodge to look like." The establishment effortlessly combines the trappings of a classic mountain lodge with an informal, cowboy-style atmosphere. The accommodations are in a series of attractive cabins, which are large, with pine-framed beds. The grounds are landscaped with attractive gardens. On the other hand, you would not be too surprised to see a cowboy ride his horse up to the bar and order a drink—for the horse. The large hot-springs pool—75 by 30 feet—is free to guests and available to others for a $5 fee ($3.50, 12 and under). Don't go on Wednesdays, though, because that's when it's emptied and cleaned, and it takes all day to fill up again. There is a small restaurant on the premises, with a menu that changes each night. Dinner goes for $11 to $22, depending on the meal of the day.

Main St. (P.O. box 808), Jackson, MT 59736. ✆ **406/834-3151.** Fax 406/834-3157. www.jackson hotsprings.com. 12 cabins. $65–$114 cabin. AE, MC, V. Pets accepted with additional fee. **Amenities:** Restaurant, lounge; outdoor hot-springs pool.

A FISHING LODGE

Craig Fellin's Big Hole River Outfitters ✿ *(Finds*   This is one of the finest fly-fishing lodges in the West. You can catch every species of trout—rainbow, brown, cutthroat, grayling, and brook. The Big Hole River is the only river in the Lower 48 that still has native grayling in it, and the fine guides at Fellin's will help you find them. The food is excellent and the accommodations are comfortable, though not luxurious. You will likely have moose bedding down behind your cabin, and there are often moose and deer loitering in front of the lodge in the evening. Fellin's is best for the experienced angler, but the guides are very patient and give beginners casting lessons at the lodge before hitting the streams. Craig is also an avid golfer, and he's installed a putting green on the property. You can practice your putting and casting, and then combine a half-day of fishing with a round of golf at the Old Works course in Anaconda (see above).

Box 156, Wise River Rd., Wise River, MT 59762. ✆ **406/832-3252.** Fax 406/832-3254. 4 units. $2,500 per person per week. Rates include all meals, drinks, fishing guide, and boat. No credit cards.

CAMPING

The **Dillon KOA,** 1225 C. R. 324, Dillon, MT 59725 (✆ **406/683-2749**), is only 20 miles (32km) from town and offers an RV park with fishing in the Clark Canyon Reservoir. Campers here will find 31 sites for RVs and two tent campsites. In addition to the usual bathhouse, there is a seasonal swimming pool, small grocery store, fishing supplies, propane, an RV dump station, and boat-access ramps. Rates are $21 to $26 for RV sites (which includes cable TV) and $16 to $18 for tent sites. There are also several camping cabins (which share the campground's bathhouse) at $28 to $30 double.

WHERE TO DINE

Sweetwater Coffee has freshly brewed coffee, some pastries, and light lunch fare. It's located downtown at 26 E. Bannack (✆ **406/683-4141**). Another recommended option is **Stageline Pizza,** at 531 E. Poindexter St. in the Western Montana student union building (✆ **406/683-9004**). Order takeout and head down to the riverbank to enjoy a beautiful Montana sunset.

Big Hole Crossing Restaurant AMERICAN   This is a neat little restaurant, with a black-tiled counter seating area, knotty pine furnishings, and wildlife art on the walls. The food is good yet inexpensive, although it runs toward pretty typical beef, chicken, and seafood. It's popular with the Forest Service and BLM types for breakfast and lunch, which is usually a good sign, because they tend to work up quite an appetite wrestling mountain lions, corralling grizzly bears, and arguing with ranchers about riparian habitat improvements. The pies, cinnamon rolls, and bagels are all baked in-house and are especially good. While nobody's quite sure what it is, the bumbleberry pie is excellent.

Main St., Wisdom. ✆ **406/689-3800.** Breakfast $2–$9; lunch $3.50–$8; dinner $7–$19. MC, V. May–Nov daily 7am–9pm; Dec–Apr Mon, Thurs, Sun 8am–7pm, Fri–Sat 8am–8pm.

Blacktail Station 🐾 STEAKS/SEAFOOD   Located in a basement below a local watering hole called Mac's Last Cast, Blacktail Station used to be the Mine Shaft, and some of the decorations from its past life still remain—like the trophy heads. But generally it's a more upscale, more yuppie-ish place than you'd expect in agricultural Dillon; Ansel Adams prints now adorn the walls as well as the hard-rock mining detritus. The food is very traditional and very good. The steak almost melts in your mouth. The twice-baked potato is very popular. For dessert, surprisingly, the chefs crank out a killer Key lime pie.

26 S. Montana St., Dillon. ✆ **406/683-6611.** Lunch $6–$8; dinner $8–$45. DISC, MC, V. Mon–Thurs 11am–10pm; Fri 11am–11pm; Sat–Sun 4–10pm.

Las Carmelitas MEXICAN   Located across the street from the town visitor center, Las Carmelitas focuses on traditional Mexican cuisine. Lunches are nachos, salads, enchiladas, burritos, and tacos; evening meals include rellenos, chicken mole, green chile, and other south-of-the-border standbys. The atmosphere is very basic, with square tables and metal chairs. Cold beer is available, but margaritas are not, because the establishment's liquor license allows for beer and wine only.

220 S. Montana St., Dillon. ✆ **406/683-9368.** Lunch $4–$6; dinner $6–$10. DISC, MC, V. Mon–Sat 11am–2pm and 4:30–9pm.

The Lion's Den AMERICAN   The Lion's Den is a classic Montana steakhouse, right down to the cowboy-booted guys at the bar debating what to name the new horse. Established in 1941, this is one of Dillon's oldest eating establishments, serving steak, seafood, and a little pizza if you really need it. Your best bet is the "world famous" prime rib, which probably isn't as well known as the proprietors may think, but nonetheless is slow-cooked to perfection. The bar has a casino, and the jangly notes emanating from the video poker games can be a little grating.

725 N. Montana St., Dillon. © **406/683-2051.** Lunch $5–$7; dinner $9–$19. AE, DISC, MC, V. Mon–Fri 11:30am–2pm and daily 5–10:30pm.

Papa T's *(Kids)* PIZZA   Papa T's is Dillon's version of Chuck E. Cheese's, only better. It's a converted saloon where the kids can run around without getting on anyone's nerves. There are video games lining one wall, and a little kiddies' carousel for the tykes. There's even a Ms. Pac-Man game for '80s nostalgia buffs. The food is basic American: burgers, chicken, Philly cheese steaks, and pizza. The formula has worked for more than 20 years. The family-owned restaurant is named for founder and patriarch Tom Lohman, whose kids all call him "Papa."

10 N. Montana St., Dillon. © **406/683-6432.** Reservations accepted for large parties only. Lunch $5–$9.50; dinner $5–$15. MC, V. Daily 11am–10pm.

TWIN BRIDGES

Just up Mont. 41 a piece from Dillon, a faded billboard just outside of town proclaims Twin Bridges to be the platinum capital of the Western world, an odd designation for a town that seems to be much more famous regionally for great fishing. "Floating Flotillas & Fish Fantasies" is the name given to the tiny town's annual summer festival, held in mid-July, with highlights that include the extremely popular floating parade on the Beaverhead, dances, and a barbecue. Locals are even given the chance to show their skills at fly-casting, fly-tying, and wader racing. For additional information about the Twin Bridges area and scheduled activities, contact the **Chamber of Commerce** at © **406/684-5259** or surf to **www.twinbridgeschamber.com**.

WHERE TO STAY

Also see The Old Hotel, under "Where to Dine," below.

Healing Waters Fly-Fishing Lodge *(Finds)*   Since the grand opening in 1996, Greg and Janet Lilly have built this lodge into a top-notch fly-fishing resort. It's not a surprise that they've opened a hospitality center for anglers: If you're not in the know, the Lilly name is synonymous with fishing in Montana. Nestled in a cottonwood grove on 52 acres of land, the lodge and its dining, living, and fly-tying rooms—not to mention its surprisingly elegant guest rooms, each with its own deck—are a magnet for anglers working the nearby trout waters under the tutelage of Greg and his excellent staff of guides. The package here includes rooms and meals, fly-fishing and guide service, and views from the front deck of the Ruby, Tobacco Root, and Greenhorn Mountains. Henry Winkler ("The Fonz") is a fan of this spot.

270 Tuke Lane, Twin Bridges, MT 59754. © **406/684-5960.** www.flyfishing-inn-montana.com. 6 units. $450 per person per day. Rate includes meals and guide services. DISC, MC, V. *In room:* No phone.

WHERE TO DINE

The Old Hotel CONTINENTAL   This remarkable restaurant is right on the highway in an out-of-the-way spot, serving gourmet meals out of a beautifully restored brick building decorated with a Scottish motif. Hostess and native Highlander Jane Waldie has engaged the services of a *cordon bleu* chef to prepare magnificent beef, chicken, vegetarian, and pasta dinners. While the menu changes on a regular basis, you'll always find a creative assortment of sauces accompanying the main courses; past selections have included fresh sea bass drizzled with cucumber-yogurt sauce and rack of lamb with raspberry-chipotle sauce. An excellent wine cellar features French, Italian, Australian, and

California labels. The second level has been converted to a two-suite B&B: Accommodations are tailored to the needs of the angler with rates of $125 a night.

101 E. Fifth Ave. ⓒ **406/684-5959.** www.theoldhotel.com. Reservations required. Main courses $16–$21. DISC, MC, V. Personal checks accepted. Mid-May to mid-Oct Tues–Sat 11am–2pm and 5:30–9:30pm, Sun 7:30am–2pm. Closed mid-Oct to mid-May.

5 Big Hole National Battlefield ★★

76 miles (122km) W of Dillon; 106 miles (171km) S of Missoula

The flight of the Nez Perce across Montana in 1877 is among the most heroic and epic stories of the Indian Wars period. About 800 non-treaty Nez Perce left the Wallowa area of Idaho in June of 1877. In an attempt to join Sitting Bull in the relative safety and freedom of Canada, the Nez Perce eluded the pursuing forces of the United States until early October, when they surrendered—not so much from military defeat but from exhaustion and starvation. On October 5, 1877, only 431 remained.

The **Big Hole National Battlefield** commemorates the flight of the Nez Perce over 1,200 miles (1,932km) of some of the roughest land in the Lower 48 states, through Yellowstone National Park, across Montana's high plains, all the while outwitting and outfighting the U.S. cavalry. There were several battles along the way, but by far the largest skirmish took place here. Between 60 and 90 members of the band were killed. Only 12 of the dead were warriors—the rest were women, children, and the elderly. The U.S. military suffered 29 casualties and 40 soldiers were wounded.

The Nez Perce had traditionally lived in eastern Washington, Idaho, and Oregon. They had always maintained good relations with the white explorers, assisting Lewis and Clark in 1805 by caring for the expedition's members when they arrived in their country sick, tired, and low on provisions. They gave them food, two dugout canoes, and guides. The Nez Perce were also the subjects of the first major Protestant mission effort among the Indians, when the stern and domineering Eliza Spaulding—an associate of the later martyred Marcus Whitman—urged them to give up their traditional ways in return for eternal salvation.

The Nez Perce's problems multiplied in 1860, when gold was discovered. Most were sent to reservations, but Joseph—known as "Young Joseph"—led a non-treaty band to live on his traditional homeland in the Wallowa Valley. Pressure from settlers eventually led to an order forcing Joseph's band onto a reservation.

In the summer of 1877, several Nez Perce braves ignored advice from the tribal elders and attacked and killed four white settlers in Oregon to exact revenge for the earlier murder of the father of one of the braves. This attack raised the ire of settlers, and the cavalry was called in to hunt down the Nez Perce. On June 1, 1877, Joseph's band joined four other Nez Perce groups and crossed the swollen Snake River, fleeing to Canada.

Battles erupted in Idaho before the Nez Perce entered Montana, fleeing from U.S. Army troops under the leadership of Gen. Oliver O. Howard. When the Nez Perce reached the Big Hole Valley, they decided to make camp, thinking all the while that they left their troubles behind them in Idaho.

However, in addition to Howard's troops behind them, a second group of soldiers, under the command of Col. John Gibbon, was advancing up the Bitterroot Valley toward the unsuspecting tribe. On the morning of August 9, 1877, Gibbon's soldiers, along with a contingent of local volunteers, attacked the sleeping tribe in what is today known as the Battle of the Big Hole. Less than 48 hours after they'd set up camp, the remaining Nez Perce once again found themselves fleeing for their lives and their freedom. They headed toward Canada, but the U.S. Army troops caught up to them at Bear Paw, only 40 miles (64km) from the Canadian border. The capture of Joseph's tattered band was the last major military effort of the Indian Wars period.

The Battle of the Big Hole is somewhat unusual among Indian fights in that a number of descriptions of the battle exist, many from the Indian point of view. André Garcia, a scout and adventurer, married a Nez Perce woman, In-who-lise, who was wounded in the battle. In his marvelous book *Tough Trip Through Paradise,* he says that he visited the battlefield 2 years later and human bones and skulls were still scattered everywhere.

Begun as a military reserve in 1883, the area became a national monument in 1910 and was designated a national battlefield in 1963. Today, the National Park Service maintains an interpretive center, where rangers help visitors understand the significance of the battle that occurred at Big Hole. Guided tours, a museum, exhibits, a bookstore, movies, and three self-guided walking trails are available.

Trails begin at the lower parking lot and lead to several points of interest. **The Nez Perce Camp,** where soldiers surprised the sleeping tribe, is considered sacred ground. The **Siege Area** marks the place where soldiers were besieged for nearly 24 hours as the Nez Perce fought to save their families from certain death. A fairly steep walk will lead you to the **Howitzer Capture Site,** where soldiers suffered a heavy blow as Nez Perce warriors captured and dismantled the military weapon. This spot affords a spectacular view of the battlefield and surrounding area.

The Big Hole Battlefield represents only a small fraction of the Nez Perce's tragic flight across the West. The 1,200-mile (1,932km) Nez Perce (Nee Me Poo) National Historic Trail follows the entire route of the Nez Perce War, from Wallowa Lake in northwestern Oregon to Bear Paw Battlefield in north-central Montana (see chapter 7). Crossing four states, the trail features several Nez Perce war sites with interpretive markers telling the story of the tribe's fight for freedom. The trail is administered by the U.S. Forest Service, and the Beaverhead-Deerlodge National Forest (see "Visitor Information," below) can provide you with an excellent map of the four-state area.

GETTING THERE   From Missoula, you can reach the Big Hole Battlefield by going south on U.S. 93 through the Bitterroot, 80 miles (129km) to Lost Trail Pass. Then turn east 16 miles (26km) to the site. From Butte, go south on I-15 20 miles (32km) to Mont. 43, west for 51 miles (82km) to Wisdom, then continue west on Mont. 43 to the site for about 10 miles (16km). From Dillon, take Mont. 278 west to Wisdom, then go west on Mont. 43 for 10 miles (16km).

VISITOR INFORMATION   You can obtain a pamphlet with an auto tour of the flight of the Nez Perce through the Big Hole, Horse Prairie, and Lemhi valleys from the **National Park Service, Big Hole National Battlefield,** Box 237, Wisdom, MT 59761 (© **406/689-3155**); or from the **Beaverhead-Deerlodge National Forest,** 420 Barrett St., Dillon, MT 59725 (© **406/683-3900**).

The **Big Hole Battlefield Visitor Center,** P.O. Box 237, Wisdom, MT 59761 (© **406/689-3155;** www.nps.gov/biho), is open daily (except on Thanksgiving, Christmas, and New Year's Day) with summer hours from 9am to 5:30pm and winter hours from 8am to 4:30pm. Admission costs $5 per car, $3 per bike. Picnic tables are located at the lower parking lot, though there are no camping or overnight facilities on the premises. Fishing is allowed within the battlefield's boundaries and adjacent national forest, but there are restrictions on the private land adjoining the battle site.

The nearest facilities—restaurants, gas stations, grocery stores, and lodgings—are located in Wisdom, 10 miles (16km) to the east.

6 The Old Mining Towns: Virginia City, Nevada City & Bannack ⭐⭐

Virginia City: 72 miles (116km) SE of Butte; 67 miles (108km) S of Bozeman; 84 miles (135km) NW of West Yellowstone

Virginia City and nearby Nevada City have both a boisterous and colorful past and present. They are old towns, but Virginia City never turned into a ghost town; in fact, it's one of the oldest continuously occupied towns in the West.

In 1863, a group of miners led by Bill Fairweather took $180 in their first day of gold panning from a creek, which they later named Alder Gulch after the trees growing on the bank. A gold rush soon followed and a mining town grew. The nation was in the midst of the Civil War, and the Southern sympathizers in the crowd wanted to name the new city Varina after Jefferson Davis's wife. But G.G. Bissell, a northerner and a miners' judge, said, "I'll see you damned first." He wrote "Virginia" on the founding document instead, a sort of a compromise, but since Virginia housed the capital of the Confederacy, no one complained.

Just as the cities have very interesting and significant pasts, so do they have a present that reflects Montana's pride in the part these towns played in the state's culture.

The restoration of Virginia City began in 1946 when Charles and Sue Bovey began the painstaking task of preserving and restoring many of the structures you see in town today. Most of the buildings were erected during Virginia City's heyday as the state's second territorial capital.

In 1991, following the deaths of Sue and Charles, son Fred Bovey determined that he was unable to continue to operate the properties and attractions. He decided to sell the whole kit and caboodle, including millions of dollars of antiques (Sotheby's estimate: $60 million). The State of Montana and Montana Historical Society attempted to have the area designated a national park, but to no avail. Even the National Trust for Historic Preservation got into the act, declaring Virginia City an endangered historic site.

Finally, partly because of a public outcry and due to the efforts of Governor Marc Racicot, the 1997 Montana legislature took dramatic fiscal measures and agreed to fund the $6.5-million purchase (such a bargain), and added $3 million for operational expenses. Today, the cities operate under the supervision of the Montana Historical Society and its foundation.

The dusty main drag of Bannack also pays tribute to the mining era. The town grew up quickly after the state's first big gold strike occurred here in 1862, but the vein was a shallow one, and Bannack quickly turned into a ghost town. Despite its short life, Bannack has a colorful history. One writer said, "It is probable that there never was a mining town of the same size that contained more desperadoes and lawless characters than did Bannack during the winter of 1862 to '63."

GETTING THERE Virginia City and Nevada City are 13 miles (21km) west of Ennis on Mont. 287. From Bozeman, take Mont. 84 west to Norris, then go south on U.S. 287 to Ennis, then west on Mont. 287 to the sites. From Butte, take I-90 east to the Whitehall exit (Mont. 55), then go south 27 miles (43km) to Twin Bridges. From Twin Bridges, take Mont. 287 east 30 miles (48km) to the sites. They are only about a mile apart, with Nevada City being the farther west.

Bannack is located about 15 miles (24km) west of Dillon on Mont. 278, then south on a gravel road at the sign for Bannack State Park.

VISITOR INFORMATION   There are remains of many other Montana ghost towns in this part of the state; it's just that information about them is often hard to find and the towns themselves even harder. Your best bet: Contact the **Virginia City Chamber of Commerce,** P.O. Box 218, Virginia City, MT 59755 (© **800/ 829-2969;** www.virginiacitychamber.com), and **Gold West Country,** 1155 Main St., Deer Lodge, MT 59722 (© **406/846-1943;** goldwest.visitmt.com). These two agencies can provide you with free information about the historic ghost towns of Montana. While you're at it, request copies of two brochures that will enhance your visit to the area: *Walking Tour,* a historical, block-by-block guide to Virginia City; and *A Walking Tour of Nevada City, Montana.*

Most attractions in Virginia City (and all of them in Nevada City) are run by the **Montana Heritage Commission,** P.O. Box 38, Virginia City, MT 59755 (© **406/843-5247; www.edheritage.org/heritagecommission**), and they're open only during the peak summer season, from Memorial Day to Labor Day. Before driving in this area during winter, check on weather conditions and road reports statewide (© **800/332-6171**).

VIRGINIA CITY

As Virginia City boomed after Bill Fairweather discovered gold, it became the site of a dramatic ordeal of Western lawlessness and revenge that has fueled a thousand cowboy movie plots. Much of Virginia City's history was driven by the vigilante movement, and the town launched the career of Wilbur Fisk Sanders, who eventually went to Washington as Montana's first U.S. senator.

By 1864, when the Montana Territory was created by President Abraham Lincoln, nearly 30,000 people were living along the gulch's 8 miles (13km). Virginia City was named territorial capital in 1865—taking that title from Bannack, virtually a ghost town by then—and held the position until 1875. For many years after its founding, the only currency acceptable to Virginia City merchants was gold dust.

As the town boomed, the incidence of robberies and murders increased. Many of the robberies depended on inside information by people usually called "road agents." The miners' sheriff, Henry Plummer, who had "persuaded" the sheriffs in Bannack, Nevada City, and Virginia to turn over their duties to him, turned out to be the leader of the road agents. As sheriff, he knew the timing of the gold movements.

No legal relief was possible, because the nearest officials to administer an oath were 400 miles (644km) away. In 1863, when a popular miner, Dutchman Nicholas Thiebalt, was murdered for $200, the other miners were outraged. The killer, George Ives, was captured and tried by a miners' court, then hanged. The site of his hanging is preserved in Nevada City. The local residents formed "vigilance committees" to capture and bring the road agents to justice. They hanged at least 21 more of the road agents—including Plummer—and some order was restored to the area.

Virginia City is the largest of the two towns; Nevada City is entirely a ghost town, a collection of original and transplanted buildings from the period. A pair of beautifully restored trains make seven round-trips daily between the two.

SEEING THE SIGHTS

Virginia City has a number of operating commercial enterprises interspersed with the historical stuff. Along the main thoroughfare you'll find the village centerpieces: the **Fairweather Inn,** the **Wells Fargo Overland Company build-ing,** and the **Virginia City Historical Museum.** One of the oldest structures, the **Montana Post Building,** once housed the state's first newspaper; the paper's original press is still used locally for menus, playbills, and placards.

You should start your visit to Virginia City at the **Visitor Center and Museum Store,** at the end of Main Street. The center has photos and a brief explanation of the history of the town, and a friendly staff of volunteers. The government shut down gold mining for good in 1942, and a few years later the Boveys began buying up the property.

The **Virginia City Players** completed its 50th season in 1999, operating out of the Smith and Boyd Livery Stable, built in 1900. The players are Montana's oldest professional acting company. For information on show times, prices, and days for the Virginia City Players, call ☎ **800/829-2969** or 406/843-5377 or visit **www.vcplayers.com**.

A little farther up the hill is the **Hangman's Building.** On January 4, 1864, the building was still being constructed, and a stout beam was exposed in the unfinished structure. The vigilantes took advantage of this situation to hang four road agents. The **Virginia City–Madison County Historical Museum** (☎ **406/843-5500**), also on the main street, has some photos of the vigilantes on exhibit and a nice collection of period clothing. Museum visits cost $2 per person or $5 per family.

Up above the town, looking down over the main street, is **Boot Hill,** the last resting place of several road agents, who required hasty burial after they died with their boots on.

If you *really* want to see the Old West come to life, check out a **Brewery Follies** production. Famous statewide for its cabaret-style revues and entertain-ing period melodramas, the company performs most nights during the summer. The Brewery Follies have a loyal following. For information on show times, prices, and days for the Brewery Follies, call ☎ **406/843-5218.**

WHERE TO STAY

Bennett House Country Inn   The Bennett House is an eclectically furnished B&B run by some very friendly folks. All the rooms have shared bathrooms, though the proprietors hope to add private bathrooms to two rooms by the 2003 season. The nicest room is the honeymoon suite, with a large bay window on the second floor. There's also one cabin.

115 E. Idaho, Virginia City, MT 59755. ☎ **877/843-5220** or 406/843-5220. www.bennetthouseinn.com. 7 units, 1 cabin. $75–$95 double. Rates include full breakfast. MC, V. *In room:* No phone.

Fairweather Inn   This small hotel, located right in the middle of downtown Virginia City, has a great upstairs porch that's a fun place to sit and people-watch. Though most of the rooms are tastefully decorated in an Old West theme, a few of them are distinguished by odd combinations of bright paint and mismatched quilts. Only five of the hotel's 15 rooms have private bathrooms; the rest are rooming house–style.

315 W. Wallace St. (Box 57), Virginia City, MT 59755. ☎ **800/829-2969** or 406/843-5377. Fax 406/843-5402. 15 units. $55–$70 double. MC, V. *In room:* No phone.

Stonehouse Inn   Built in 1884 by a local blacksmith/rancher/miner, this Gothic Revival–style B&B is a cozy place to hang your hat while in town for a night. Clad in locally quarried stone, the gray exterior is softened by a few brightly painted accents and a sweeping porch with a rocking chair. Your options range from a masculine room embellished with antique snowshoes and a "No

Spitting" sign to a romantic upstairs room with stained glass, a private balcony, and rather frilly decor. All of the rooms have brass beds that are predominately full-sized. While the bathrooms are shared, they are exceptionally spacious and feature antique commodes, showers, and tubs.

306 E. Idaho St., Virginia City, MT 59755. ℭ 406/843-5504. www.stonehouseinnbb.com. 5 units, none with private bathroom. $65–$100 double. Rates include full breakfast. MC, V. *In room:* No phone.

CAMPING
The **Virginia City Campground and RV Park,** P.O. Box 188, Virginia City, MT 59755 (ℭ **888/833-5493** or 406/843-5493), has 17 RV sites and 27 tent sites, and is open from mid-May to the end of September. The campground has a dump station, propane sales, horseshoe pits, and a recreation field, and is in a great location just east of downtown. Tent sites are $16 and the RV sites are $18 to $21.

WHERE TO DINE
The Roadmaster Grille 🅖 *Kids* AMERICAN   When this nostalgic eatery opened in 1998, some locals complained that it wasn't nostalgic enough—its decor harks to the 1950s, not the 1890s. They've since warmed up to it, however, probably because of the consistently good food. The distinctive features here are four cars: a 1950 Buick Roadmaster sits in the center of the dining room, flanked by a salad bar made out of a 1948 Chevy truck. Then there's a 1949 Cadillac and a 1957 Chevy that were dismantled and converted into four booths, with the trunks and hoods hanging overhead as lampshades. Lunch here is basic, with plump sandwiches and burgers, while dinner features a selection of steaks, chicken, and seafood. The specialties are rotisseried chicken and pork dinners, served with mashed potatoes and gravy. Adjoining the diner is the Copper Palace Pub, a painstakingly recreated 1890s-era saloon with a pressed-copper ceiling and plush couches.

126 W. Wallace Ave. ℭ 406/843-5234. www.roadmastergrille.com. Lunch $5–$8; dinner $11–$17. Reservations recommended for car booths. AE, MC, V. Summer daily 11–8pm; winter daily 11:30–7:30pm.

NEVADA CITY
The distance between Nevada City and Virginia City is only a mile or so, but back in the days before the vigilance committees formed, it was a dangerous mile. Miners dared not go between the two cities after dark. One miner known as Dutch Fred was waylaid by a robber. When the highwayman found that Fred had only $5 with him—and paper money, not gold dust, at that—the bandit cursed and told him, "If ever you come this way with only $5, I'll shoot you." The robber shot Dutch Fred anyhow, wounding him in the arm.

Nevada City is the site of the resurgence of law and order in these Montana mining camps. Two thousand people reportedly came to town to watch the trial of George Ives for the murder of Nicholas Thiebalt. Emotions were running high on both sides, and it was in the face of these feelings that Wilbur Fisk Sanders began his place in Montana history by courageously prosecuting Ives before the crowd. The spot where Ives was hung is marked in town.

Today Nevada City is a tourist attraction—a collection of historic wooden buildings, including an open-air museum depicting the gold-mining and settlement period of the area's turbulent history. Nevada City also exists as the result of Charles Bovey's diligence and dedication to the preservation of history. In the mid-1950s, Bovey began to re-create an authentic Western town with buildings he'd accumulated around the West. The buildings are authentic, though their setting may not be. It looks like a perfect cowboy movie set, though, and has in fact been used for a couple of oaters, including *Missouri Breaks, Little Big Man,* and *Return to Lonesome Dove.*

Admission to the Nevada City site costs $5 for adults, $4 for seniors, and $3 for kids; the site is open daily from 7am to 7pm from mid-May to mid-September. For information, call ℂ **800/829-2969** or 406/843-5247.

SEEING THE SIGHTS

With your walking-tour booklet in hand, begin your excursion behind the **Nevada City Hotel,** where you can view the state's only double-decker outhouse, and stroll along the streets to see what a Western mining town might have looked like. Boardwalks pass barber shops, homes, a schoolhouse, and even an Asian section. Some of the buildings are closed, but many include period furnishings and wares.

When you hear a cacophony of horns and whistles, follow the noise to the **Nevada City Music Hall,** located next door to the hotel. There you can see the "famous and obnoxious horn machine from the Bale of Hay Saloon!" A sign on the machine begs visitors not to miss hearing "the machine that has driven 28 change-makers, 72 bartenders, and near a million tourists to the brink of insanity!" The music hall is a fascinating place to spend an hour listening to the many music machines and reading about their history. It's one of the largest collections of its kind on display in the United States today. The building was originally the Canyon Lodge Recreation Hall in Yellowstone.

Across the street is the railroad museum, where you can board the steam-powered **Locomotive No. 12** for the short train ride to Virginia City (the railroad depot there is at the west end of town). The museum has an observation car once used by Calvin Coolidge and the last "Catholic chapel car" in the world. The train runs every hour, and costs $10 for a round-trip, $6 one-way.

WHERE TO STAY & EAT

You can believe the **Star Bakery's** claim that it has the best biscuits and gravy in town, because it's also the *only* restaurant in town. Best known for its breakfasts, the small restaurant begins serving home-style food at 7 in the morning and closes after lunch. It's small, but full of cozy country charm. The kids will love the old-fashioned soda fountain.

Just an Experience Bed-and-Breakfast   If you want something more modern than the Nevada City Hotel and Cabins (see below), this B&B is your only other choice in Nevada City proper (dare we say, "downtown Nevada City?"). Two of the rooms in the house share a bathroom, and one has a private bathroom. The rooms are large, with iron-post beds, but the cabins are larger, with enough room for six people, and include loft bedrooms for the kids and full kitchens. The original log house here was built in 1864, but it has been remodeled and incorporated into a modern cedar-sided home. Pets are permitted outdoors only, not indoors. There's a restaurant nearby.

1570 Mont. 287, Virginia City, MT 59755. ℂ **866/664-0424** or 406/843-5402. www.justanexperience.com. 5 units, including 2 cabins. $50–$90 double. AE, DISC, MC, V. *In room:* Kitchens, no phone.

Nevada City Hotel and Cabins   Entering this hotel is like taking a step back in time. Constructed in the 1860s, it was originally a stage stop near Twin Bridges, and still has the cool, musty smell of a mining-camp hotel. Most of the rooms are small and spare, but the upstairs Victorian suites are huge, furnished in rough but exquisite Victorian style, complete with polished burl wood furniture and private bathrooms. There's a restaurant nearby. If you rent a cabin, be certain to lock your door—many tourists mistake the cabins for museum exhibits and may come exploring.

Box 57, Nevada City, MT 59755. $\copyright$ **800/648-7588** or 406/843-5377. Fax 406/843-5402. 30 units. $60–$90. AE, DISC, MC, V. Closed Oct to mid-May. *In room:* No phone.

BANNACK

Bannack was the site of the state's first big gold strike in 1862. With more than 60 of the town's original buildings preserved, the tumbledown town is a stark reminder of the heyday of the frontier: vigilantes stalking road agents stalking prospectors, in a favored place where the rivers yielded gold dust.

Born out of the discovery of placer gold in 1862, Bannack quickly grew to a town of 3,000 people, largely composed of those hoping to strike it rich. Blacksmiths, bakeries, stables, restaurants, hotels, dance halls, and grocery stores rapidly sprang up to complement an expanding mining industry.

Bannack became the first territorial capital and the site of the first territorial legislative session in 1864. But the placer veins in Grasshopper Creek were thin. Only a few years later, it was a ghost town, and the boosters of the capital movement had turned their attention to Virginia City and the richer mines at Alder Creek.

Notorious Henry Plummer killed his first local man in Bannack in Goodrich's saloon. The victim was Jack Cleveland, who had threatened another man about a debt, which the other man had already paid. Cleveland bragged that he wasn't afraid of him. Plummer, apparently a bystander, got to his feet, cursed Cleveland, roared, "I'm tired of this," and commenced to shooting. Cleveland got the worst of it, dying 3 hours later.

Plummer was an enigmatic outlaw. He was considered a "gentleman" by the standards of the era. He married a schoolteacher, though she left him after only 10 weeks of wedded bliss. Only a few weeks before he was hanged (see the section on Virginia City, above), Plummer held an elaborate dinner for territorial officials, including the governor and some of the vigilantes, for which he had ordered a $60 turkey from Salt Lake City. His guests apparently saw nothing unusual about enjoying the hospitality of a man they had already decided to hang.

VISITOR INFORMATION Designated a state park in 1954, Bannack is open year-round. Summer hours are from 8am to 9pm; winter hours 8am to 5pm. There are a visitor center, camping and picnic grounds, a group-use area, and hiking trails. Other lodging facilities are available in nearby Dillon (see section 4 of this chapter). Day-use fees are $4 per vehicle, $1 per person, and $8 for a campsite ($7 in the off-season).

Bannack is located 4 miles (6km) south of Mont. 278, 25 miles (40km) west of Dillon. To get there, turn west off I-15, 3 miles (5km) south of Dillon. Head west 17 miles (27km) on Mont. 278, then south 4 miles (6km) when you see the sign. For additional information, call $\copyright$ **406/834-3413.**

A SPECIAL EVENT **Bannack Days,** staged annually during the third weekend in July, is a 2-day event commemorating the history and heritage of Montana's early pioneers, with activities centering around frontier crafts, music, pioneer food, and dramas. A black-powder muzzleloader shoot, Sunday church services, and horse-and-buggy rides bring the "toughest town in the West" to life and are fun for the entire family.

7

The Hi-Line & North Central Missouri River Country

This portion of Montana is classic cattle and wheat country, the true home of the American cowboy. This vast section of Montana was once a wilderness of tall grass, rolling in the wind like the sea, home to a million antelope and 60 million buffalo.

Lewis and Clark reported vast herds of buffalo on the plains, but that wasn't all they saw here. When the adventurers entered Montana in 1805 just past the confluence of the Yellowstone and Missouri Rivers, they saw their first grizzly bear, and Lewis made the first extensive description of the animal for science.

As you travel through this region, you'll likely be closely following the trail of Lewis and Clark to the portage of the Great Falls. In the city of Great Falls, take time to visit the Lewis and Clark National Historic Trail Interpretive Center and experience vicariously one of the great American adventures. This portion of the state is also the landscape that Charles M. Russell memorialized in his famous Western paintings and bronzes.

But the region isn't all history and vanished mythology. There's plenty of outdoor activity, including fishing and boating on Fort Peck Lake, birdwatching at the C.M. Russell National Wildlife Refuge, rafting on the wild and scenic Missouri River, and both downhill and cross-country skiing.

1 Scenic Drives

DRIVING TOUR #1: KINGS HILL SCENIC BYWAY

The Kings Hill Scenic Byway is a 71-mile (114km) drive through the Little Belt Mountains and the Lewis and Clark National Forest. You pick it up about 22 miles (35km) southeast of Great Falls, where U.S. 87 and U.S. 89 divide. Take U.S. 89 south toward the towns of Monarch and Neihart. From the south, take U.S. 89 north from just east of Livingston on I-90. For a leisurely tour, you can watch the wildlife and the scenery, then visit the ghost towns at Castle Town and Hughesville, and the historic mining site at Glory Hole. For a more active trip, go to **Sluice Boxes State Park** just north of Monarch to hike along the abandoned rail line there, or fish in Belt Creek. In winter, there is cross-country skiing at the Silver Crest Trail System (just north of Showdown Ski Area; see below), and snowmobiling at Kings Hill. Memorial Falls has a nature trail that is accessible to visitors with disabilities. There are camping sites and national forest access points at numerous spots along the highway.

DRIVING TOUR #2: THE CHARLES M. RUSSELL TRAIL

The Judith Basin inspired the work of one of the West's seminal artists, Charles M. Russell. This drive on U.S. 87/Mont. 200 between Great Falls and Lewistown provides an intimate glimpse at the unsettled West through Russell's eyes. The drive is lovely in a pastoral way, but it helps to have a copy of the

North Central Montana

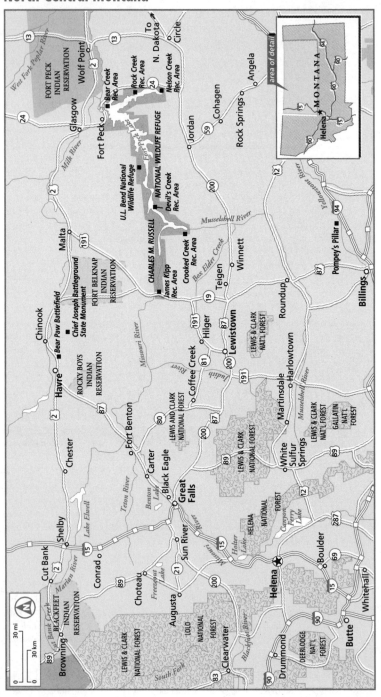

interpretive guide of the trail from Travel Montana's **Russell Country** (© **800/ 527-5348** or 406/761-5036; www.russell.visitmt.com) if you want to get the full experience. The guide uses Russell's art to illuminate the history of the basin.

These highways were designated the Russell Trail by the Montana legislature. The scruffy cowhands and toughened Indians that Russell painted have been replaced by carefully tended fields of grain, but with the help of Russell's art and a little imagination, you can put yourself back in the saddle in 1880s Montana.

From Great Falls, you go southeast through the towns of Raynesford, Geyser, and Moccasin, taking in the history of the Blackfeet, the wolves of the basin in Stanford, and the role of the railroads in Hobson. Spring and fall are the best times to match Russell's color palette with that of the scenery. If you're traveling between May and September, be sure to stop at The Charles M. Bair Family Museum (© **406/572-3314;** www.bairmuseum.org) in Martinsdale (see below).

There are roadside turnouts along the highway for many of the 25 interpretive sites, including the settings for two of Russell's best-known paintings, *Buffalo in Winter* and *Paying the Fiddler.* Yogo Creek Road and Memorial Way are single-lane gravel roads included in the guide, but they are not recommended for RVs.

2 Great Falls

89 miles (143km) N of Helena; 219 miles (353km) NW of Billings

Great Falls, named for a series of waterfalls on the Missouri River, is a big city. An important cog in the U.S. military strategy, it is the control point for a number of U.S. Intercontinental Ballistic Missiles. Malmstrom Air Force Base is also the launching point for the new X-33, the space shuttle of the future.

But the country around Great Falls looks much as Charlie Russell found it and painted it at the end of the 19th century. Russell made his home Great Falls, and did much of his painting in his studio there.

Lewis and Clark came through with the Corps of Discovery, making an 18-mile (29km) portage around the falls. It is a sign of Great Falls' progress that it is now known as the electric city, because the falls that Lewis and Clark marveled at have been tamed by a series of dams to provide electric power.

ESSENTIALS

GETTING THERE Great Falls serves as the hub for north central Montana east of the Rockies. The **Great Falls International Airport** (© **406/727-3404**) has daily service from **Delta** (© **800/221-1212**), **Northwest** (© **800/ 225-2525**), **Horizon** (© **800/547-9308**), and **Big Sky** (© **800/237-7788**). Shelby, 88 miles (142km) northwest, provides the closest **Amtrak** service (© **800/872-7245**).

Great Falls is located on I-15, which runs north-south from Butte on I-90 to Helena, then through Great Falls, and then north to Canada. From Missoula, you can take Mont. 200 east, or you can take I-90 a little southeast, pick up U.S. 12, and go east to Helena, then north to Great Falls. Mont. 200 is more scenic. From Billings, you can take Mont. 87 north to Lewistown and then west to Great Falls. Or you can go west on I-90 to Livingston, then take Mont. 89 and the Kings Hill Scenic Byway (see the driving tour earlier in this chapter) northwest to Great Falls. From Bozeman, take U.S. 287 at Three Forks, then I-15 to Great Falls.

VISITOR INFORMATION Request tour information from **Russell Country, Inc.,** at P.O. Box 3166, Great Falls, MT 59403 (© **800/527-5348** or 406/761-5036; www.russell.visitmt.com). The Great Falls Chamber of

Great Falls

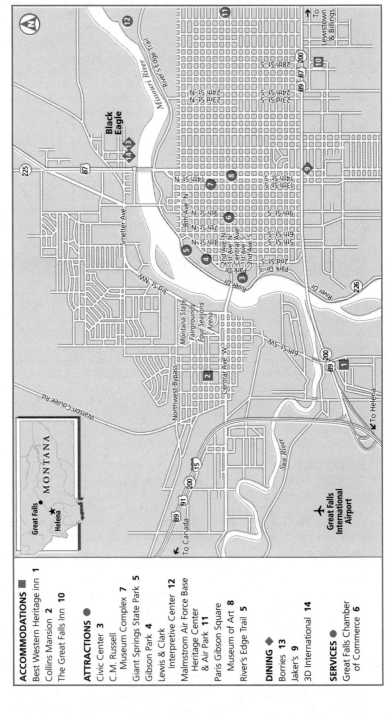

ACCOMMODATIONS ■
Best Western Heritage inn **1**
Collins Mansion **2**
The Great Falls Inn **10**

ATTRACTIONS ●
Civic Center **3**
C.M. Russell
  Museum Complex **7**
Giant Springs State Park **5**
Gibson Park **4**
Lewis & Clark
  Interpretive Center **12**
Malmstrom Air Force Base
  Heritage Center
  & Air Park **11**
Paris Gibson Square
  Museum of Art **8**
River's Edge Trail **5**

DINING ◆
Borries **13**
Jaker's **9**
3D International **14**

SERVICES ●
Great Falls Chamber
  of Commerce **6**

Commerce is at 710 1st Ave. N. There is also a visitor center at the Broadwater Overlook at 10th Avenue South and Second Street South, by the tall flagpole (© **800/735-8535**). For a Great Falls road report, call © **406/453-1605.**

GETTING AROUND   The best way to explore Great Falls and environs is by car. Rental franchises in town include **Avis** (© 800/331-1212), **Enterprise** (© 800/736-2227), **National** (© 800/227-7368), **Rent-A-Wreck** (© 800/ 962-5344), and **Hertz** (© 800/654-3131).

You can also use public transportation. Great Falls Transit System operates eight lines from early morning to early evening Monday through Saturday (no service Sun and holidays). Call © **406/727-0382** for information.

ORGANIZED TOURS   To see the town, take the 2-hour **Great Falls Historic Trolley** tour, $20 for adults, $5 children 2 to 12, with one stop at the Rainbow Falls. You pick up the tour at the visitor information center at the Broadwater Overlook. Call © **888/707-1100** or 406/771-1100 for information or browse **www.greatfallshistorictrolley.com** online. The company also does a cultural tour, a parks tour, and out-of-town day trips.

A SPECIAL EVENT   Great Falls hosts the **Lewis and Clark Festival** each year in late June. Events include history workshops, tours, food booths, and children's activities. For information and tickets call © **406/452-5661.**

GETTING OUTSIDE
FISHING & BOATING
Great Falls is the unofficial dividing line for cold- and warm-water fish. You can fish for trout from Giant Springs, or take one of the many tours available on the Missouri. For 2- to 7-day fishing and whitewater trips on the Missouri, try **Montana River Outfitters,** 923 10th Ave. N., Great Falls (© **800/800-8218** or 406/761-1677; www.mt-river-outfitters.com). You can also paddle the Upper Missouri in 34-foot voyageur-style canoes with **River Odysseys West** (© **800/ 451-6034;** www.rowinc.com), which offers tours in the style of the fur trappers (but with first-class tenting accommodations). Price for a 5-day trip on the Missouri is $1,200 for an adult, $1,050 for youths age 10 to 16, and $795 for kids age 5 to 9. The company also guides day trips and riverside hiking tours.

GOLF
The city offers two public golf courses: **Anaconda Hills** on Smelter Hill northeast of town (© **406/761-8459**), and the **Eagle Falls Golf Club** at 29th Street and River Drive North (© **406/761-1078**).

HIKING & BIKING
The 8-mile (13km), paved River's Edge Trail along the Missouri River starts downtown at the Oddfellows Park and runs out past Rainbow Dam to Crooked Falls. There is also an unpaved trail going another 8 miles (13km) or so out to the Cochrane Dam. The trail is ideal for hiking, biking, running, walking, and skating. The Great Falls Chamber of Commerce (see "Visitor Information," above) can provide you with information and trail maps.

WINTER SPORTS
Showdown Ski Area   Although relatively undiscovered, this is a full-service ski area, with 34 trails, two chair lifts, two land lifts, and 1,400 vertical feet of drop. The area is perfect for beginning and intermediate skiers (30% beginner, 40% intermediate, 30% expert), with long, uninterrupted runs and lots of dry, light powder. There are ski rentals and a restaurant and bar. Family-oriented

perks include a day-care center and a children's program. Just north of Showdown is the Silver Crest Trail System for cross-country skiing, and there is snowmobiling at Kings Hill. Call 🕓 **406/236-5358** for snowmobile rentals.

65 miles (105km) southeast of Great Falls on U.S. 89, near Neihart. 🕓 **800/433-0022** or 406/236-5522. For snow conditions, call 406/771-1300. www.showdownmontana.com. Lift tickets $28 adults, $16 juniors and seniors, free for children under 6. Winter Wed–Sun and all holidays except Christmas and Thanksgiving; plus daily mid-Dec to late Dec. Lifts open 10:30am (9am mid-Dec to late Dec).

SEEING THE SIGHTS

Gibson Park, located 1 block north of the Civic Center along Park Drive, is a serene, local favorite, with a large pond, playgrounds, flower gardens, and picnic areas. This is a good place to pick up the trail system along the Missouri River. Meriwether Lewis was chased into the Missouri River near here by a grizzly bear in 1805, at Sacajawea Island. Every Wednesday evening there is a free concert at the band shell. No word on whether the grizzly will be in attendance.

Benton Lake National Wildlife Refuge Established in 1929 by President Herbert Hoover, the refuge is physically unimpressive, a small lake in a broad, open, treeless plain. But the 12,283 acres are important nesting grounds for waterfowl, especially mallards, pintail, teal, and canvasback. Bird-watching for waterfowl and prairie species is best early in the morning or in the evening. There's a 9-mile (14km) auto-tour route that takes about an hour, marked with signs to provide information about what you're seeing, but Mother Nature is constantly changing the refuge attractions.

922 Bootlegger Trail, Great Falls, MT 59404. 🕓 **406/727-7400.** Fax 406/727-7432. Free admission. Open daily during daylight hr. Go 1 mile (1.5km) north of Great Falls on Mont. 87, take a left on Bootlegger Trail, then proceed about 9 miles (14km) north to well-marked entrance.

Paris Gibson Square Museum of Art Located in a national historic landmark building that served as Great Falls' first high school, Paris Gibson Square is now the cultural and art center of the city. The changing art shows display the works of artists from around the Northwest, as well as pieces from the permanent collection. The selection includes both contemporary and historical exhibits in a comfortable, beautifully restored space. The museum cafe serves gourmet lunches by reservation only (Tues–Fri with seatings at noon and 12:30pm). Call 🕓 **406/727-8255** for the current menu and reservations.

1400 1st Ave. N. 🕓 **406/727-8255.** Fax 406/727-8256. Free admission, donations suggested. Tues 10am–5pm and 7–9pm; Wed–Fri 10am–5pm; Sat–Sun noon–5pm. Also open Mon 10am–5pm in summer.

C.M. Russell Museum Complex 🕓🕓 You can divide the world into two kinds of people—those who like cowboy art, and those who don't. It is a measure of Charlie Russell's greatness that, although he was a cowboy artist, almost everybody likes his work. This facility, which includes tours of Russell's studio and home, is one of the high points of any trip to Montana, and it's worth going out of your way to see.

Russell and the dime novelists practically invented the West. But the power of his work is that the personality of everyone and everything portrayed—American Indians, cowboys, even the landscape—shines through. Much modern "Western art" concentrates on the scenery and fierce animals without making much of a statement. Conversely, Russell had something to say about a celebrated but passing way of life, and he said it powerfully.

The museum houses the largest collection of Russell's work around, and tour guides are quite knowledgeable. You can spend a few minutes or all day here. There are also a number of his bronzes, which are much admired, but in our opinion less interesting than his paintings. The artist's studio, also on the tour, contains some of Russell's personal belongings, including many of the Indian artifacts he collected to help maintain his art's authenticity.

A number of other excellent artists working on Western themes are shown to good advantage here as well; their exhibits change several times a year. The museum recently completed a major expansion, debuting a new entrance and doubling the square footage devoted to Russell's work.

400 13th St. N. ℂ 406/727-8787. www.cmrussell.org. $6 adults, $4 seniors, $3 students, free for kids 5 and under. May–Sept Mon–Sat 9am–6pm, Sun 1–5pm; Oct–Apr Tues–Sat 10am–5pm, Sun noon–5pm. Closed major holidays.

Lewis and Clark National Historic Trail Interpretive Center ★★

Located on a bluff overlooking the Missouri River, this facility is hands down the best Lewis and Clark exhibit between St. Louis and the Pacific Ocean. The facility is cleverly arranged to follow the adventurers' path to each major point along the way. You start in Washington with Thomas Jefferson's instructions to the Corps of Discovery. Then you go from one high point to the next along the journey. You visit a Mandan earth lodge, see the grizzlies, and feel the voyagers sweat as they pull their 3,000-pound boat along the portage of the Great Falls. Of this portage Clark wrote, "To state the fatigues of this party would take up more of this journal than other notes which I find scarcely time to set down." An excellent facility, it will take a few hours to see properly. The docents are wonderfully informed and entertaining. Interpretive programs are held year-round, outdoors at a "River Camp" setting during the summer months.

4201 Giant Springs Rd. ℂ 406/727-8733. www.fs.fed.us/r1/lewisclark/lcic.htm. Fax 406/453-6157. $5 adults, $4 seniors and students, $2 children 6–17, free for children under 6. Memorial Day–Sept 30 daily 9am–6pm; Oct 1–Memorial Day Tues–Sat 9am–5pm, Sun noon–5pm. Closed major holidays.

Giant Springs State Park

Lewis and Clark also discovered and described the Giant Springs, purportedly the largest freshwater spring in the world. The spring now also feeds a fish-breeding facility nearby. It burbles out of the 250-million-year-old Madison Formation, a large water-bearing formation that provides a lot of groundwater throughout the northern West. The springs send out 234,000 gallons a minute into the 201-foot-long Roe River, credited in the *Guinness Book of World Records* as the shortest in the world. The entire park covers 218 acres.

The Great Falls that gave Lewis and Clark so much trouble have been dammed, but you can see a few remnants of their former glory from overlooks. In the spring, especially, you can see the power of the river flowing through the spillways at Rainbow Dam, spewing mist hundreds of feet into the air, creating the rainbows in the sunshine that so entranced the explorers. Lewis called Rainbow Falls "one of the most beautiful objects of nature." The Montana Department of Fish, Wildlife, and Parks also operates a fish hatchery and visitor center nearby, where visitors can purchase hunting and fishing licenses.

4600 Giant Springs Rd. ℂ 406/454-5840. $1 per person or $4 per vehicle. Open daily during daylight hours. Take River Dr. east along the Missouri River to Giant Springs Rd. Turn left and drive about a quarter of a mile, just past the Lewis and Clark Interpretive Center.

Malmstrom Air Force Base Heritage Center and Air Park

The air park has a number of aircraft from various eras, primarily from the 1950s and 1960s, but the real attractions here are the implements of nuclear weaponry: a Minuteman III ICBM and its transporter erector. Inside, amidst scads of military equipment and uniforms and a reconstruction of a World War II–era barracks, is the control panel used to fire the base's nuclear missiles and the only air-to-air nuclear missile ever deployed. Interpretation of the exhibits is minimal, unfortunately. This is mostly a volunteer effort, and funds are short.

Malmstrom Air Force Base, east end of 2nd St. N. past 57th St. ☎ **406/731-2705.** Free admission; civilian passes are available at the gate's visitor center. Air park: Open daily during daylight hr. Museum: Memorial Day–Labor Day daily 10am–4pm; Labor Day–Memorial Day Mon–Fri 10am–4pm.

SHOPPING

There are at least 19 antiques stores in Great Falls, and the chamber can give you a map of their locations. The **Stagecoach Gallery** (☎ **406/761-8845**), 508 1st Ave. N., combines an antiques store with fine art and things Western. **Hoglund's,** 306 1st Ave. S. (☎ **406/452-6911**), has an awe-inspiring selection of cowboy boots and hats. You can find Montana-made souvenirs or gifts at **Best of Montana,** 2912 10th St. S. (☎ **406/761-1233**).

WHERE TO STAY

Best Western Heritage Inn   The hotel has a sedate New Orleans motif, and is the preferred business stop-off in Great Falls, located a little closer to the interstate than downtown. The rooms are comfortable, a notch above your typical chain, and many of them adjoin the central gardened atrium where the pool is located. It has the largest convention center in Great Falls, and a latte bar to boot.

1700 Fox Farm Rd., Great Falls, MT 59404. ☎ **800/548-8256** or 406/761-1900. Fax 406/761-0136. www.bestwestern.com/heritageinngreatfalls. 240 units. $89 double; $89–$129 suite. AE, DC, DISC, MC, V. **Amenities:** Restaurant, lounge/casino; indoor pool; exercise room; indoor Jacuzzi; sauna; coin-op washers and dryers. *In room:* A/C, TV, dataport, coffeemaker, hair dryer, iron.

Collins Mansion ★★   Built in 1891 and listed on the National Register of Historic Places, this grand Queen Anne–style mansion was carefully converted into a stylish bed-and-breakfast in 1998. At 8,000 square feet, this gleaming white structure stands out (it sits in an otherwise typical neighborhood overlooking the west side of Great Falls) with a wraparound veranda and ornate details. All of the rooms contain period antiques and a private bathroom. The pinnacle is the Master Suite, decorated in black and gold, featuring a half-canopied queen-size bed with an antique iron frame and a city view from the bay window. The more feminine Cherub room is done in burgundy and mauve with an angelic headboard above its iron-framed queen bed.

1003 2nd Ave. NW. Great Falls, MT 59404. ☎ **877/452-6798** or 406/452-6798. www.collinsmansion.com. 5 units. $80–$100 double. Rates include full breakfast. AE, MC, V. *In room:* A/C.

The Great Falls Inn _Value_   This is a reliable independent hotel away from the bustle, located near the hospital and medical center. The rooms are quiet and very well kept, with contemporary furnishings. All have queen-size beds, reclining lounge chairs, refrigerators, and microwaves. The inn has 10 new business-class rooms with dataports and two telephone lines. While there is a complimentary continental breakfast, there are few other amenities. The property does offer transportation from the airport, if needed.

1400 28th St. S., Great Falls, MT 59405. ☎ **800/454-6010** or 406/453-6000. Fax 406/453-6078. 61 units. $55 double. Rate includes continental breakfast. AE, DC, DISC, MC, V. **Amenities:** Coin-op washers and dryers. *In room:* Fridge.

WHERE TO DINE

There are a couple of landmark restaurants in Black Eagle, a ramshackle neighborhood just across the Missouri River from downtown Great Falls. Try **Borries,** 1800 Smelter Ave. (☎ **406/761-0300**), a family-owned eatery that has been serving Italian standards and steaks for dinner since 1938; or the eclectic **3D**

International, 1825 Smelter Ave. (© **406/453-6561**), an Art Deco facility serving a bewildering variety of Italian, American, Chinese, Thai, and Mongolian dishes for lunch and dinner.

Jaker's STEAKS/RIBS/FISH   Jaker's is a regional chain, with six locations in Montana and Idaho, but the atmosphere is more refined than one might expect. Decorated in dark woods with wide windows, the Great Falls Jaker's offers a very extensive menu in the not-cheap-but-not-expensive-either range. And the casino is kept in its own room, instead of ka-chinging in the diners' ears. Carnivores are well provided for with steaks, including a 20-ounce T-bone and a 24-ounce porterhouse, or else the ribs and seafood dinners. Those looking for lighter fare won't be disappointed with Jaker's long and varied list of salads, either, especially the terrific stuffed avocado and crab-meat salad.

1500 10th Ave. S. © 406/727-1033. www.jakers.com. Lunch $5–$14; dinner $10–$30. AE, DC, DISC, MC, V. Mon–Thurs 11:30am–10pm; Fri 11:30am–11pm; Sat 5–11pm; Sun 5–9pm.

A SIDE TRIP TO FORT BENTON

Thirty-six miles (58km) north of Great Falls on Mont. 87, you can drop down to the historic town of Fort Benton. The town faces the Missouri River, which formed its destiny. There is a pleasant waterfront park with an interesting series of murals detailing the town's history.

The Lewis and Clark expedition made a critical decision a short distance downstream from Fort Benton, where the Marias River enters the Missouri. The expedition was divided on which was the main branch of the Missouri. The vote was 30-to-2 for the Marias being the main branch. The two who went for the other branch were Lewis and Clark. Had they chosen the Marias branch, there is a good chance that the expedition would have failed, because they would not have been able to get over the Rockies before winter. A statue of the explorers at this decisive point dominates one end of Front Street in Fort Benton. A small visitor center at the Bureau of Land Management (BLM) office on Front Street offers some information about this event.

Next to the Lewis and Clark statue is the **Keelboat Mandan,** a full-scale replica 62 feet long and 12.5 feet wide built for the movie *The Big Sky.* In the heyday of keelboating, broad-shouldered men could push a boat upstream at a pace of about 2 miles (3km) a day. There is also a monument on the riverfront to Shep, a collie sort of dog whose master died and was sent East by train for burial. After that, Shep met every train in Fort Benton from 1936 until 1942, waiting for his return.

The first steamboat reached Fort Benton in 1850, and 600 of them stopped here from 1859 to 1870. Furs, goods, and gold were all shipped through the town. **The Museum of the Northern Great Plains,** in the Old Fort Park (20th and Washington; © **406/622-5316**), tells the story of settlement. Admission is $4, which includes admission to the Museum of the Upper Missouri at Old Fort Park and Front Street. There is a vast collection of farming equipment here, testifying to the fortitude and ingenuity of the settlers on the Great Plains. **The Museum of the Upper Missouri** (© **406/622-5316**) has an excellent historical collection, including the rifle that the Nez Perce Chief Joseph surrendered at the Bear Paw battle, and the history and personality of Fort Benton as expressed by the artist Charlie Russell, the preacher Brother Van, and the infamous "Madame Mustache," the woman who reputedly introduced Calamity Jane to prostitution. Both museums are open daily from 10am to 5pm from Mother's Day to late September.

The BLM manages 149 miles (240km) of the Missouri here as a federally designated Wild and Scenic River, and canoeing and keelboating are both good ways to take in the landscape. Contact the **Fort Benton Chamber of Commerce** (© **406/622-3864;** www.fortbenton.com) for a list of river outfitters.

For lodging, try the **Grand Union Hotel,** 1 Grand Union Square (P.O. Box 119), Fort Benton, MT 59442 (© **888/838-1882** or 406/622-1882; www.grandunionhotel.com), right on the river. Built in 1882 at a cost of $50,000, it was completely restored to its original splendor in 1999. Said to be Montana's oldest hotel, the Grand Union has 27 small but luxurious guest rooms (with modern conveniences: phones with dataports and TVs), a riverside restaurant, and a brewpub. The three suites are larger. Rates start at $79 for a double and up to $159 for the suites, a price that includes a deluxe European breakfast.

3 The Rocky Mountain Eastern Front

53 miles (85km) W of Great Falls

The eastern front of the Rockies is an isolated, sparsely populated section of Montana, but it is no less beautiful than the peaks and valleys to the west. A great paleontological mystery was solved here. Scientists had discovered many dinosaur fossils in the far-eastern part of the state, but no nests or eggs. When fossilized dinosaur eggs turned up along the Rocky Mountain Eastern Front— the shoreline of a shallow sea 65 million years ago—paleontologists learned that the beasts had migrated to this area to lay their eggs. You can explore the site of the first discovery on Egg Mountain near Choteau via a guided tour.

There are two towns with distinctive personalities on the front: Choteau and Augusta. Choteau bills itself the gateway to the Rockies. Named for the president of the American Fur Co., who brought the first steamboat up the Missouri, it is one of the oldest towns in Montana.

Tiny Augusta is a cheerful, friendly community. Unlike a lot of small Western towns, it is not hustling to turn itself into something else. It's only about 2 blocks long, with weathered wood exteriors on the buildings. Folks are out and about, the guy at the gas station gives you full service at the self-service pump, and everybody's on a first-name basis with just about everybody else. The pace picks up a bit the last weekend in June when the rodeo hits town.

ESSENTIALS

GETTING THERE The closest airport is in Great Falls, about 52 miles (84km) from Choteau (see the "Great Falls" section earlier in this chapter for airport information). From the airport, take I-15 north to the U.S. 89 exit (about 12 miles [19km]), then go west on U.S. 89 for 40 miles (64km) to Choteau.

To reach the area by car from the northwest, drive on U.S. 2 along the southern border of Glacier National Park. At Browning, go south on Mont. 89. Augusta's position (and that of the front in general) along Mont. 287 is roughly parallel with that of Great Falls on I-15, which lies to the west about 40 miles (64km). From points south and east of Great Falls, refer to the Great Falls "Essentials" section earlier in this chapter for appropriate driving directions to this area.

VISITOR INFORMATION For an information packet, contact the regional tourism office for **Travel Montana's Russell Country,** P.O. Box 3166, Great Falls, MT 59403 (© **800/527-5348** or 406/761-5036; www.russell. visitmt.com) In Choteau, write to the **Choteau Chamber of Commerce** at P.O. Box 897, Choteau, MT 59422 (© **800/823-3866** or 406/466-5316; www. choteaumontana.com). For hunting and fishing info, contact the **Montana**

Tips Rental-Car Tip

A reliable four-wheel-drive vehicle is strongly recommended for touring the back roads of the Rocky Mountain Eastern Front. Many are unpaved, gravel roads that turn into a slippery mush locally known as "gumbo." Car-rental companies keep such vehicles in stock, but requests for four-wheel-drives should be made weeks in advance. See the "Great Falls" section earlier in this chapter for information on renting a car.

Department of Fish, Wildlife and Parks, 4600 Giant Springs Rd., Great Falls, MT 59406 (© **406/454-5840**).

GETTING AROUND   The only way to travel this country is to drive. See the "Great Falls" section earlier in this chapter for information on renting a car.

OUTFITTERS & ORGANIZED TRIPS

Pine Butte Guest Ranch Summer Trips and Workshops ⭐   The Nature Conservancy's Pine Butte Guest Ranch offers eight learning vacations over the summer covering grizzly bears, mammal tracking, geology, wildflowers, and dinosaurs, among other topics. Some are built around day hikes, while others have overnight trips. A number of guests have noted that their time at the ranch and the nature workshops made up the best week of their lives.

HC 58, Box 34C, Choteau, MT 59422. © **406/466-2158**. Reservations required. $1,400 per person per week. Rate includes shuttle from airport, meals, rooms, and the nature program.

Timescale Adventures *Kids*   Timescale Adventures runs some popular dinosaur field programs, designed for all ages and levels of interest. The 3-hour seminar is a walk along the Rocky Mountain Eastern Front covering identification of dinosaur bones and eggs, and what to do when you find one. The 2-day seminar includes a dig and instruction in fossil-preservation techniques. In the summer of 2001, Timescale was excavating three large meat-eating dinosaurs and five duckbill dinosaurs from one of its sites. For 2002, Timescale is broadening its curriculum, offering a seminar (in conjunction with the Old Trail Museum in Choteau) that will detail American Indian lore and take authorized trips to some of the sacred Indian sites in the area. All of the programs originate from a new building in the town of Bynum, 14 miles (23km) north of Choteau on U.S. 89.

P.O. Box 786, Bynum, MT 59419. © **800/238-6873** or 406/469-2211. www.timescale.org. 3-hr. day tour, $25 adults, $15 children 12 and under. 1-day program, $85 per person per day. Longer programs, $75 per person per day. Advance registration is required; space is limited.

A SCENIC DRIVE & A SCENIC MOUNTAIN

The beautiful **Sun Canyon Drive** on Sun Canyon Road starts out along the plains west of Augusta, and then weaves up the canyon past a 1913 Bureau of Reclamation dam. During the time of Lewis and Clark, the Blackfeet called the river that carved the canyon the Medicine River, but it is now known as the Sun River. The canyon, a gray-granite jumble with snowcapped peaks in the distance, is a weekend getaway spot for residents all along the front. There are opportunities for fishing, boating, hiking, and four-wheeling in the area. The road up here is an easily navigable gravel track for the most part, but it can be very rugged in portions, especially if they've been trying to fix it. After you get to the national forest, however, the road is paved. Go figure.

Kids **Especially for Kids**

The Pine Butte Guest Ranch (see "Where to Stay," below) offers a number of educational programs for kids ages 7 to 14, from late June to mid-August, on topics such as fly-fishing, dinosaurs, field journals, and story-telling. The classes are held at the Old Nelleview School 17 miles (27km) west of Choteau. The cost is $15 a day. Call ℂ **406/466-5430** or e-mail belanger@3rivers.net for more information.

Egg Mountain (ℂ **406/466-5332**) is where Jack Horner of the Museum of the Rockies and Bob Makela discovered dinosaur eggs in the late 1970s. It is now on a portion of land owned by The Nature Conservancy, and the tours are conducted in cooperation with the Pine Butte Swamp Preserve (see above) and the Old Trail Museum in Choteau. The only way to see the area is on a guided tour; reservations are required and tours leave from the museum.

SHOPPING

Latigo and Lace on Main Street in Augusta (ℂ **406/562-3665**) is an eclectic shop run by Texas native Sara Walsh, who sells the work of Montana artists, plus books, games, cappuccino, and knickknacks. There is a spectacular collection of "made in Montana" souvenirs, collectibles, and art. Latigo and Lace can also put your brand on a coffee mug, if you have a hankering. Walsh is a great source for information and advice on things to see and do around Augusta.

WHERE TO STAY

The Bunkhouse Inn   This is the cowboy way. Housed in a building that dates back to 1912 and that is constantly under renovation, the Bunkhouse is sort of a bed-and-breakfast without the breakfast. Proprietor Terry Taillon sends his guests to Mel's Diner across the street. Taillon says that Mel doesn't rent rooms, so he won't serve food. That's the sort of town this is. The rooms are small and basic; there are no phones or televisions, but instead of staring at the idiot box, you can sit out on the second-floor porch watching the slow-paced bustle on Main Street. On Memorial Day weekend, you'll have a front-row seat to Montana's smallest parade as the gray-haired American Legionnaires march to the strains of Sousa marches played on a boom box carried by two of the ladies' auxiliary.

122 Main St. (P.O. Box 294), Augusta, MT 59410. ℂ **800/553-4016** or 406/562-3387. 9 units. $26–$57 double. MC, V. *In room:* No phone.

JJJ Wilderness Ranch   The Triple J is a guest ranch located in the extraordinary Sun Canyon near Gibson Reservoir. It offers everything the outdoorsy type could want—horseback riding, hiking, fishing, pack trips into the Bob Marshall Wilderness Area (at an extra charge), and pure and simple relaxation. Nestled in a forest of aspen and spruce, the rustic cabins accommodate a total of 20 guests, so you're never crowded. Though there are few amenities, it's not due to an oversight. Those who come here don't want phones and televisions.

Box 310, Augusta, MT 59410. ℂ **406/562-3653.** Fax 406/562-3836. www.triplejranch.com. 7 cabins. $1,239 per week, double occupancy with a 1-week minimum stay. Rate includes all meals and ranch activities (except pack trips), and transportation from and to the Great Falls Airport. No credit cards. **Amenities:** Outdoor pool; children's programs; activities desk. *In room:* No phone.

Pine Butte Guest Ranch ⋆ *Finds*   Located deep in the Sawtooth Range along the Rocky Mountain Eastern Front, Pine Butte Guest Ranch is the property of

The Nature Conservancy, a national land-preservation organization. Since seven or eight endangered grizzly bears have made this 15,500-acre Pine Butte Swamp Preserve their home, the Conservancy saw fit to buy it to protect the delicate ecosystem. The preserve is the only place left in the Lower 48 states where grizzlies use both the mountain and prairie ranges as they did before settlement of the West drove them to the remnant habitat in the mountains.

Pine Butte Guest Ranch focuses on education, running numerous workshops on appreciating and understanding the natural world. You can also do the usual dude-ranch activities—riding, hiking, swimming, and the like. Pine Butte was first homesteaded in the 1930s, but it has always been a guest ranch, not a cattle ranch, which accounts in part for the largely undisturbed habitat. Average winter winds of 80 mph have helped keep development to a minimum.

Each of the ranch's log cabins has a river-rock fireplace and is comfortably equipped with handmade furniture. However, the little time you'll be indoors will likely be spent in the lodge, with a handsome pine interior with Western decor and a few photos of Kenneth and Alice Gleason, who owned and ran the place before the Conservancy bought it. There's also a bookstore and nature center.

The Conservancy's preserve is not open to those not staying at the ranch, but to get a taste of the country, you can hike some trails in the Bureau of Land Management's Ear Mountain Outstanding Natural Area nearby. This is grizzly country, so be very cautious.

HC 58, Box 34C, Choteau, MT 59422. ✆ 406/466-2158. 10 cabins. Summer $1,200 per person per week; May 13–June 23 and Sept 17–Oct 6 $825 per person per week; natural-history workshops $1,400 per person per week. Rates include room, board, riding ranch facilities, and transportation to and from Great Falls International Airport. AE, MC, V. **Amenities:** Activities desk. *In room:* No phone.

Viewforth Bed & Breakfast ☆   The best place to stay in Augusta is, strictly speaking, not in Augusta, but a short drive north. After a sojourn in Oregon, long-time Montanans Terese and Keith Blanding returned to their home state and opened the Viewforth, an elegant Craftsman-style bungalow with softly washed walls the color of clouds.

Each of the Viewforth's two rooms has a mellow quality, with queen beds and private bathrooms, plus excellent views of Sawtooth Mountain and Castle Reef in the Rockies. The highlight of a stay here will likely be the time spent enjoying the silence, watching sheep graze in the meadows below as an ominous storm peers over the horizon. Breakfast here is a treat, featuring fresh-baked goods, fruit, and a hot entree such as eggs Blanding (the owners' version of eggs Benedict).

4600 U.S. 287, Fairfield, MT 59436. ✆ 406/467-3884. www.viewforth.com. 2 units. $80 double first night, $75 thereafter. Rates include full breakfast. 7 miles (11km) north of Augusta on Route 287. *In room:* No phone.

CAMPING

Wagons West   This is a no-frills campground located on the edge of Augusta, but it is a place to put your RV or your tent, and it has a pretty view of the mountains. There is also a small associated motel (double rooms run $45–$50 a night), a restaurant, and a bar.

Augusta, MT 59410. ✆ 406/562-3295. 50 tent sites, 40 RV sites. $10 tent site; $20 RV site. DISC, MC, V.

WHERE TO DINE

Buckhorn Bar STEAKS/AMERICAN   Gordon Dellwo has run this bar in the same location for more than 40 years. His son and daughter-in-law help him out these days, serving a selection of steaks, chicken, and burgers. Your best bet is a charbroiled 12-ounce rib steak with a salad and choice of potato for $12. The food is decent and moderately priced, the atmosphere classic woody Western, complete with animal-head trophies, cowboy-hatted patrons, and pool tables.

Main St., Augusta. © 406/562-3344. All dishes $3–$12. No credit cards. Daily 8am–2am.

Mel's Diner AMERICAN   Everyone in town will send you to Mel's for breakfast. It's a tiny place with four booths and one large table. You'll get good food at good prices: bacon and eggs, hotcakes, and biscuits and gravy for breakfast; fish and chips, burgers, and sandwiches for lunch and dinner. You can also take your pick of ice-cream treats, shakes, and malts. The hours depend on how business is doing.

Main St., Augusta. © 406/562-3408. All dishes $1–$6. No credit cards. Daily 6am–6pm (or later).

Outpost Deli SANDWICHES   This is a very friendly sandwich shop with good sandwiches and excellent milkshakes. Locals keep their regular coffee cups on a shelf, and they sit together at a large table by the window. But they'll visit with the out-of-towners too, and even bring them coffee.

819 N. Main St., Choteau. © 406/466-5330. Breakfast $2–$6; lunch $3–$8. MC, V. Daily 6am–3pm.

Western Bar AMERICAN   The main job of the Western is serving beer, but the food isn't bad, and the place is very clean for a small-town bar. You can sit at the bar or some inconspicuous tables in the back, near the woodstove, or else head to the seasonal outdoor beer garden. Favorites are the burgers and thick, juicy steaks. The bar also has live music twice a month, and sponsors winter and summer fishing derbies. The ice-fishing derby in February is Montana's largest.

142 Main St., Augusta. © 406/562-3262. All dishes $5–$17. No credit cards. Daily 10am–midnight. Bar open later.

4 Lewistown

105 miles (169km) E of Great Falls; 128 miles (206km) N of Billings

Lewistown is not right on the way to any particular tourist destination, so if you find yourself here, you probably meant to come. It is the hub of a large agricultural region in Charlie Russell country, known as the Judith Basin. The town is blessed with mountains, great downtown architecture, stately homes, and solid and modest citizens. And there are some notable recreational activities here—especially hunting and fishing. The city is also home to two of the best B&Bs in Montana.

Lewistown is located in a broad valley surrounded by three mountain ranges— the Big and Little Snowies, the Moccasin, and the Judith. This is the center of the Judith Basin. While Charlie Russell lived in Great Falls later, the Judith Basin is where he worked as a cowboy, and where he fell in love with Montana.

ESSENTIALS

GETTING THERE   **Big Sky Airlines** (© 800/237-7788) provides commuter airline service to and from Billings daily. The **Rimrock Stages bus depot** (© 406/538-9227) is located at 513 1st Ave. N. and provides service from and to Billings and Great Falls.

Lewistown is connected to other Montana cities by two-lane U.S. highways that radiate from the town. From Billings, go north 92 miles (148km), then west 31 miles (50km) on U.S. 87. From Great Falls, Lewistown is 105 miles (169km) east on U.S. 87.

VISITOR INFORMATION   The **Lewistown Chamber of Commerce** has its offices adjacent to the Museum of the Central Montana Historical Association at Symmes Park at 408 NE Main (© 406/538-5436; www.lewistown-chamber.com). Maps from the Bureau of Land Management, the U.S. Forest Service, and the C.M. Russell Wildlife Refuge, and local maps are all available. **Travel Montana's Russell Country** includes Lewistown (© **800/527-5348** or 406/761-5036; www.russell.visitmt.com). Local road reports are available at © **406/538-1358.**

GETTING AROUND Rental-car agencies in Lewistown include **Budget** (© **406/538-7701**) and **Dean Newton Olds, Cadillac, and GMC** (© **406/ 538-3455**).

SPECIAL EVENTS The **Chokecherry Festival,** held on the Saturday following Labor Day, honors that smarter-than-the-average-berry, the chokecherry, one of the few indigenous fruits of the prairie. Generally overlooked by poets and songwriters—no one has ever been the chokecherry of someone's eye, nor has life ever been a bowl of chokecherries—Lewistown attempts to place the chokecherry on its proper pedestal in the berry pantheon with parades, bake sales, and pie cook-offs. It may be that the pit-spitting contest (for distance and accuracy) is not the best PR tool to accomplish this, but the cook-off could launch the chokecherry into the fruit pie hall of fame.

Lewistown lassoed the **Montana Cowboy Poetry Gathering** ✪ when the event got too big for the venue in Big Timber, about a hundred miles (161km) south. Each year in mid-August at the Yogo Inn and a local high school, cowboys, ranchers, large animal vets, and other swaybacked and bowlegged Montana literati gather to swap lies and poems. Those who may have considered the term "cowboy poetry" an oxymoron are usually pleasantly surprised to find a relentless rhyming vitality to the poetry, along with a lot of humor, and an honest and healthy appreciation of fellow poets. There are also a juried arts-and-crafts show, booths full of leatherwork, and other activities. For details on these events, call the **Lewistown Chamber of Commerce** at © **406/538-5436.**

GETTING OUTSIDE

For information on activities in the national forest lands in this area, contact the **Lewis and Clark National Forest,** P.O. Box 869, Great Falls, MT 59403 (© **406/791-7700**).

CROSS-COUNTRY SKIING

You have to make your own fun in Lewistown. If you're here in the winter, there is good cross-country skiing in any of the three mountain ranges that ring the valley—the Big and Little Snowies, the Moccasin, and the Judith ranges. There are a number of trails accessible by car in the Judith Mountains north of town, on old logging and mining roads unused except by skiers and snowmobilers when the autumn snows begin to fall. Head north on U.S. 191 to the Maiden Canyon sign, then take a left and follow the road for 5 miles (8km) to the trails.

FISHING

High in the Big Snowy Mountains is **Crystal Lake,** about 35 miles (56km) southwest of Lewistown. This is a popular and somewhat remote recreational area that offers good fishing, hiking, and camping. You have to travel about 25 miles (40km) on gravel road to get there. Take U.S. 87 west of town for 8 miles (13km), then turn south at the sign for Crystal Lake. After about 16 miles (26km) it runs into Forest Service Road 275, which you should follow for another 9 miles (14km) to the lake. Motorized boats are prohibited, but overnight RV and tent camping is available. For good trout fishing closer to

Must-See in Martinsdale: The Charles M. Bair Family Museum

The **Charles M. Bair Family Museum** (© 406/572-3314; www.bair museum.org) opened in 1995, the legacy of an unusual—and unusually successful—sheep rancher. Charles Bair came west in 1883 as a conductor on the Northern Pacific Railroad, and then developed the largest sheep ranch in the country. His flock at one time numbered 300,000, spread across 50,000 acres. In 1 year, he filled 47 railway cars with 1.5 million pounds of lamb.

But sheep was not all Bair accumulated. With his wife Mary and daughters Alberta and Marguerite, the family compiled a treasure trove of European antiques, silver, and American Western paintings by contemporaries C.M. Russell and J.H. Sharp. They also collected American Indian artifacts and other Western memorabilia.

Guided tours of Bair's former residence, which begin every hour on the hour (until 4pm), offer a look into the lifestyle of one of the wealthiest families in Montana. The museum is located 81 miles (130km) southwest of Lewistown (or 74 miles [119km] north of Livingston) in Martinsdale. From Lewistown, go west on U.S. 87 to the intersection of U.S. 191, then south 39 miles (63km) to Harlowton. Go west 23 miles (37km) on U.S. 12 to County Road 294, then 2 miles (3km) south. From Livingston, go 49 miles (79km) north on U.S. 89, then east on County Road 294 to Martinsdale, about 27 miles (43km).

The museum is open from early May to the end of September. In May and September, hours are Wednesday through Sunday, from 10am to 5pm, with the last tour offered at 4pm. In June, July, and August, the hours are the same, but the museum is open 7 days a week.

town, try **Big Spring Creek,** which begins south of Lewistown and flows north through town to join the Judith River. You can easily access Brewery Flats on Big Spring Creek about 2 miles (3km) outside of town on Mont. 238. Flatwillow Creek in the Forest Grove area of the Little Snowies provides some rainbow and cutthroat fishing. For **flat-water fishing,** try Upper and Lower Carter's Pond, man-made ponds 6½ miles (10km) north of Lewistown on U.S. 191. There are picnic facilities and overnight camping as well. The **James Kipp Recreation Area** (© 406/538-8706), 78 miles (126km) north of town on the western tip of Fort Peck Lake in the Charles M. Russell National Wildlife Refuge, also has fishing, camping, hiking, and a boat ramp. Take Mont. 191 northeast until it intersects with Mont. 19, then go north about 35 miles (56km). For advice, licenses, and gear, head to **The Bait Shop,** 638 NE Main St. (© 406/ 538-6085).

GOLF
The 18-hole **Judith Shadows Golf Course** (© 406/538-6062) is an alternative-spikes-only facility located at the end of Marcella Avenue in the northeast corner of Lewistown. Greens fees are $12 for 9 holes, $20 for 18, with an additional $1-per-hole fee for the use of a cart.

HIKING

At **Crystal Lake** (see "Fishing," above), there are numerous trails into the Lewis and Clark National Forest, including the Crystal Lake Loop National Recreation Trail. There is also good hiking along the Wild and Scenic Missouri River from the James Kipp Recreation Area. The **Judith Resource Area of the Bureau of Land Management,** Lewistown District Office, Box 1160, Airport Road, Lewistown, MT 59457 (℃ **406/538-7461**), can give you information on additional hiking trails in the nearby mountains.

SEEING THE SIGHTS

A little too cutely named, the **Charlie Russell Chew-Choo Dinner Train** (℃ **406/538-5436** for information, or 406/538-2527 for reservations) runs from Lewistown to Denton and back every Saturday from Memorial Day through the end of September, with special trains on Christmas, New Year's Eve, and Valentine's Day. On the 56-mile (90km) round-trip ride, the train crosses three large trestles and navigates a 2,000-foot tunnel during its 3½-hour run through the Charlie Russell country of the Judith Basin. The schedule varies, so call ahead. A regular summer run on the train with dinner is $85 per adult, $50 for children 12 and under; the New Year's Eve trip is $125 per person.

Big Spring, located 7 miles (11km) south of Lewistown on County Road 466, is the third-largest freshwater spring in the world. The spring is the water source for the town, and is considered one of the purest in the nation. It is bottled by the Big Spring Water Company and sold at stores in the west-central part of the U.S. The spring also feeds the Montana State Fish Hatchery nearby.

Lewistown became a regional commercial center after a ranching and mining boom in the early part of the 20th century. The industry barons built large homes in a range of styles, primarily Gothic and Victorian. The first to build was a gold miner and organizer of the Empire Bank & Trust, J.T. Wunderlin. Others soon followed, creating a neighborhood of elegant homes. They lived in the **Silk Stocking District,** which is just northeast of downtown on Boulevard. (Not the section of Boulevard near Symmes Park; if you're there, you're lost.) The Lewistown Chamber of Commerce (℃ **406/538-5436**) can provide information on self-guided tours. The homes, however, are private residences and not open to the public. At 220 W. Blvd., there is a plaque outside the Symmes-Wicks House (see below) describing the area. At the top of the hill overlooking the Silk Stocking District, check out the **Fergus County Courthouse** (7th Ave. and Main St.), a gold-domed mission-style courthouse built in 1906.

WHERE TO STAY

Circle Bar Guest Ranch   The Circle Bar is a full-service, year-round guest ranch that offers everything from riding to volleyball. If you've always wanted to work a cattle drive, this is your chance—the ranch holds them in June and October. There are also hiking and fishing on the Judith River in summer, bird and big game hunting in the fall, and horse-drawn wagon rides in the winter. (The regular guest season runs from June 1–Sept 15, but the ranch also has winter activities available by special arrangement.) The cabins here are roomy log affairs, recently redecorated, with porches, woodstoves, and private bathrooms. The best cabins are located right at the river's edge.

P.O. Box 61, Utica, MT 59452. ℃ **888/570-0227** or 406/423-5454. Fax 406/423-5686. www.circle barranch.com. 9 units. $1,500 per adult per week, $1,300 per child 12 and under per week, free for children under 3. Rates include meals and ranch activities. MC, V. 35 miles (56km) west of Lewistown;

take U.S. 87 west to Windham, then turn south on C. R. 541 to Utica. Then go 12 miles (19km) southwest along the Judith River on a gravel rd. **Amenities:** Outdoor pool; outdoor Jacuzzi; activities desk. *In room:* No phone.

Pheasant Tales Bed-and-Bistro ✿

While the Symmes-Wicks House (see below) offers a turn-of-the-century experience, the Pheasant Tales is a thoroughly modern, beautifully constructed and furnished guest house with some unique touches. Proprietors Chris and Rick Taylor are both avid pheasant hunters. After Chris began preparing gourmet meals with the birds brought down by friends, hunters told the couple that if they opened a bed-and-breakfast, they would stay there on hunting trips. Since Chris prefers fixing dinners, she instead opened a bed-and-bistro specializing in eclectically prepared game birds, with very impressive results. The building is done in reddish pine, and the rooms are large and comfortably furnished. With reservations, Chris can often prepare a gourmet dinner in the evening (for an additional $25). Chris will also consider requests for dinner from visitors not staying at the Pheasant Tales if they call ahead. The Taylors also breed English setters, so there is almost always a brace of puppies providing entertainment. There's an extensive deck, land to walk on, and good fishing nearby as well. A full breakfast is available on request for $9 per person.

RR1, Box 1615, Lewistown, MT 59457. ✆ **406/538-7880.** www.tein.net/pheasant. 6 units. $78 double; $156 4-person kitchen suite. Located 5 miles (8km) south of Lewistown. **Amenities:** Guest laundry. *In room:* No phone.

The Symmes-Wicks House Bed & Breakfast ✿

Charles and Carole Wicks have beautifully restored this 1909 shingle-style, Arts-and-Crafts home, which sits right in the heart of the Silk Stocking District. Though you can easily see the stately exteriors of all of the surrounding homes, a stay here provides the unique opportunity to view the inside of one, replete with Tiffany glass and period antiques. Upstairs, the guest rooms are tastefully decorated in two opposing themes. The room facing east, in masculine hunter-green tones, has a sleigh bed and a reproduction Degas figure. The bathroom is a wooden work of art. The room facing south has a more feminine touch. The bathroom isn't so much a room as it is a tasteful area partitioned off from the main room, with a green-marble shower as its centerpiece. In the early 20th century, there was an influx of Croatian stonecutters to Lewistown. Some of their work can be seen on this house, as well as on other buildings in the area.

220 W. Boulevard, Lewistown, MT 59457. ✆ **406/538-9068.** Fax 406/538-5331. 3 units, 2 with private bathroom. $45–$75 double. Rates include breakfast. MC, V. *In room:* No phone.

Yogo Inn

Ignore the outside of the Yogo—it looks better on the inside, with clean, functional, and quiet rooms that are otherwise unremarkable. There is a well-kept, interior courtyard that catches the sun and contains the motel's swimming pool. The Yogo is popular with business travelers, and everything is functional but not fancy. It's the locus of the annual Montana Cowboy Poetry Gathering every August, and it books up pretty quickly for the event.

211 E. Main St., Lewistown, MT 59457. ✆ **800/860-9646** or 406/538-8271. www.yogoinn.com. 121 units. $69 double. AE, DISC, MC, V. Pets accepted. **Amenities:** 2 restaurants, lounge; outdoor pool; indoor Jacuzzi. *In room:* A/C, TV, dataport.

WHERE TO DINE

The Whole Famdamily AMERICAN

This is an inviting, cafe-style restaurant with some character. The sandwiches are your best bet; they are big and reasonably priced. Each night, the dinner menu offers up two new specials. The sandwiches are named after locals—like the Hungry Hubert, a mountain of a sandwich piled high with turkey, ham, and roast beef. During the week, you can get a hearty home-style dinner special. The offerings change nightly, with beef ribs and Mexican plates recurring regularly.

206 W. Main St. ℂ 406/538-5161. Menu items $4–$7. AE, DISC, MC, V. Mon–Fri 11am–8pm; Sat 11am–4:30pm.

5 The Hi-Line: U.S. 2

Havre: 115 miles (185km) NE of Great Falls; Fort Belknap: 46 miles (74km) E of Havre; Glasgow: 279 miles (449km) N of Billings

If you're not from Montana and find yourself on the Hi-Line, you're probably on the way somewhere else. There isn't a great deal of anything up here, except for wheat, birds, lots of ground squirrels, and the occasional pronghorn.

There are a number of National Wildlife Refuges along this drive: the gigantic **Charles M. Russell NWR,** and the smaller **Black Coulee, Bowdoin,** and **Medicine Lake**—the latter on the far-eastern border of the state. Like most of the refuges nationwide, they are managed primarily for the benefit of birds, especially migratory waterfowl. So this is a good place to bring your field guide: Even if you don't leave your car, you'll be able to identify many species, possibly including the Franklin's gull with its telltale black wingtips, the melodious western meadowlark, or the marsh hawk (or harrier, not a true hawk). The latter flies low to the ground, flapping its wings more often than the gliding hawks, and is gray when mature, brown when young, with a white bar across its rump.

The roadsides here are dotted with white crosses—memorials to people who have died in auto accidents. Maintained by friends and family, many are decorated with flowers, flags, and ribbons, and there are a lot of them. Don't be fooled by the long, straight stretches of road. Drive carefully.

FROM HAVRE TO FORT BELKNAP

Havre probably isn't anyone's idea of a vacation spot, but it has its moments. There are some interesting historic sites, including the nearby **Bear Paw Battleground,** the site of the last major battle between the army and the Indians in the Indian War period. Nearly every tour in Havre itself is a guided tour and requires advance reservations. The best place to start is the **H. Earl Clack Museum,** located in the Heritage Center downtown, 306 3rd Ave. (ℂ 406/265-4000) The museum is open year-round from noon to 5pm Tuesday through Saturday. Admission is $3 for adults, $1 for students. You can reserve a spot on most of the guided tours at the museum.

Start your exploration of this region just south of Havre on Mont. 87, coming up from Great Falls. Drive north to Havre until you reach the junction with U.S. 2. Take U.S. 2 east until it converges with Montana's version of Route 66, a state highway running south through the Fort Belknap Indian Reservation. Take 66 through the reservation to the intersection of U.S. 191. Turn left (northeast) and drive until the road joins U.S. 2 again, about 57 miles (92km).

SEEING THE SIGHTS

Rocky Boys Indian Reservation and the Rocky Boy Powwow   Southwest of Havre lies the home of 2,000 Chippewa and Cree Indians on this rather small plot of land at the Western Front of the Bear Paw Mountains. For years the U.S. government tried to keep the Cree from settling in the United States, and the tribe was homeless. In 1911, when Fort Assinniboine was abandoned, the Chippewa and Cree had part of the land set aside as a reservation. Then, as now, employment was difficult to come by. Each July the Rocky Boy Powwow is held near Box Elder.

From Mont. 87 turn east at Box Elder onto Duck Creek Rd. Drive 14 miles (23km) to the Tribal Headquarters. Call the Havre Area Chamber of Commerce (© 406/265-4383; www.havremt.com) for precise dates and further information about the powwow.

Fort Assinniboine   This well-preserved fort was established in 1879, after it was already obsolete. It was intended to protect settlers from Indian attacks, but all the tribes had already been defeated. After the defeat of Chief Joseph in the nearby Bear Paw Battle, the Fort Assinniboine troops didn't have much to worry about. After the fort closed, much of the land around it was turned into the Rocky Boys Reservation. Only guided tours are permitted because the fort is now run by Montana State University as an agricultural research station.

3 miles (5km) south of Havre on Mont. 87. Guided tours only, originating from the H. Earl Clack Museum in Havre daily at 4pm. © 406/265-4000 or 406/265-6233. $4 adults, $1.50 students, free for children under 6. Open June–Aug.

Havre Beneath the Streets 🎯   This tour of Havre's boisterous history as a railroad and cowboy town provides an interesting look at the past, when racism was rampant. When a devastating fire in 1904 destroyed Havre's business district, the labyrinth of tunnels and basements under the town served as a subterranean "shopping mall." Many local "businesses" of the last century were located here. Their products included honky-tonk, gambling, opium, and prostitution. There is also a railroad museum attached to the underground, focusing on the area's rail history.

120 3rd Ave., Havre. © 406/265-8888. $6 adults, $5 seniors, $4 children 6–12. Reservations recommended. Summer daily 9am–5pm, tours 9:30am–3:30pm; winter Mon–Sat 10am–5pm, tours at 4pm.

Wahkpa Chu'gn Bison Kill   From a steep cliff above the Milk River called Wahkpa Chu'gn, the Assinniboine drove bison to their deaths to provide food for the tribe. Indians used the jump from between 2,000 and 600 years ago. The hour-long guided tours are very informative, in part because this is one of the largest and most studied buffalo jumps in existence. Visitors are also given the opportunity to try their skill with an "atl-atl," or throwing stick.

Behind the Holiday Village Shopping Mall on U.S. 2 W. © 406/265-6417 or 406/265-4000. www.buffalo-jump.org. Tour info available at H. Earl Clack Museum. $5 adults, $4 seniors, $2.50 students, free for children under 6. Tours, June to Labor Day weekend, daily 10am–5pm, 1 evening tour at 7pm. Winter tours available by reservation, weather permitting.

WHERE TO STAY

The **El Toro Inn,** 521 1st St. (© 800/422-5414), is a reliable and inexpensive roadside hotel charging $51 for two. Rooms are well kept but basic, although they do have refrigerators and microwaves. On Route 2, in the eastern part of town, there is a pleasant RV campground (right next to the Best Western) called the **Havre RV Park** (© 800/278-8861). There are showers, a saloon, a casino, laundry, and a store. Cost is $27 for an RV, $19 for a tent.

Best Western Great Northern Inn 🎯   This is a relatively new entry in the Havre lodging scene and a relatively upscale one. The rooms have a tad more square footage than your typical Best Western, and there are more extensive facilities than anyplace else in Havre. There is no restaurant, but across the street at the Vineyard or Mediterranean Room (see "Where to Dine," below), you can charge your meal to your room. There are a bridal suite and a corporate suite. The 24-hour business center has fax, copying, and computer capabilities.

1345 1st St., Havre, MT 59501. ℂ **888/530-4100** or 406/265-4200. Fax 406/265-3656. www.best western.com/greatnortherninn. 64 units. $80–$100 double; suites from $129. Rates include continental breakfast. AE, DC, DISC, MC, V. **Amenities:** Lounge/casino; indoor pool; exercise room; indoor Jacuzzi; sauna; game room. *In room:* A/C, TV, dataport, coffeemaker, hair dryer.

WHERE TO DINE

PJ's AMERICAN   You're out on the Hi-Line, driving through Havre, so you might as well eat in a typical Western place. PJ's is across the street from the railway station; there's a poker game in the corner with the clickety-clack of chips, and the boop-boop-boop of the electronic games of chance. The food isn't bad at all, especially the trademark burgers and beef, and the folks are friendly.

15 3rd Ave. ℂ **406/265-3211.** Breakfast $3–$7; lunch $5–$9; dinner $9–$20. MC, V. Sun–Thurs 6am–10pm; Fri–Sat 6am–11pm.

The Vineyard/Mediterranean Room STEAKS/SEAFOOD   The faux Italian decor at these adjoining restaurants might be a tad overdone, but the food is actually pretty good. The menus at both places are essentially the same, but the Mediterranean Room's portions are a bit bigger and the prices a tad higher. Both restaurants share the same salad bar, which is quite extensive, and you can get all of the usual surf-and-turf entrees, from porterhouse steaks to fresh lobster. If you're here in the midst of Havre's short summer, grab a seat on the outdoor patio.

1300 1st Ave., Havre. ℂ **406/265-6111.** Dinner $8–$20. AE, DISC, MC, V. Mon–Thurs 5–10pm; Fri–Sat 5–10:30pm; Sun 4–9:30pm.

FORT BELKNAP RESERVATION

Established in 1888, the Fort Belknap Reservation is home to the Gros Ventre and Assinniboine tribes. It was named for William W. Belknap, who was secretary of war under President Ulysses S. Grant. The Gros Ventre call themselves the A'a'nin, or White Clay People. They had lived in North Dakota's Red River Valley from A.D. 1100 to 1400, gradually being pushed west by competition from other tribes. After coming to the Missouri River country in about 1730, they split into two tribes, and the southern branch became known as the Arapaho.

The Assinniboine split from the Yanktonai Sioux in the early 1600s, supposedly over a squabble. Two of the first ladies of the tribe fought about a local delicacy, a buffalo heart. They call themselves the Nakota, The Generous Ones. There is also a branch of the tribe at the Fort Peck Reservation to the east.

There is a small **museum** and visitor center at the intersection of Mont. 66 and U.S. 2 (ℂ **406/353-2205**). From here you can arrange a tour of the tribe's herd of 300 buffalo and learn a little bit about the tribe's culture.

Nearby Snake Butte was often used as a site of vision quests, where individuals sought supernatural powers or medicine. These powers came with a price. It was said few who had them lived long lives. The Army Corps of Engineers quarried Snake Butte for stone to build the dam at Fort Peck in the 1930s.

If you head south from here to Hays, then turn to the east, you'll come to **St. Paul's Mission,** a solid stone structure established by Jesuit missionaries in 1886. Next to it is a tiny chapel built in 1931 that is dedicated to Our Lady of the Little Rockies. A local devotee has carved a statue practically identical to the supposedly miraculous one at Einsiedeld in Switzerland. To get here, take Mont. 66 south from U.S. 2 at Fort Belknap for about 40 miles (64km) to the sign for

Bear Paw Battlefield: The Nez Perce Surrender

One of the most remarkable events of the Indian Wars culminated at the Bear Paw Battlefield in Nez Perce National Historic Park, located 26 miles (42km) south of Chinook on County Road 240.

In 1877, in what is now northeast Oregon, the Army tried to force a band of Nez Perce Indians under the leadership of Chief Joseph onto a reservation far from their native lands. The Nez Perce decided to escape, trying to reach Canada where they hoped to join Sitting Bull's Lakota, who had already found homes there.

Joseph led 800 of his tribal members on a 1,700-mile (2,737km) flight through Yellowstone National Park and eventually north to this site, a mere 45 miles (73km) south of the Canadian border and freedom.

The U.S. Army under Gen. Oliver O. Howard pursued the tribe as it fled. A Civil War hero known as "the praying general," Howard, a deeply religious Christian, developed considerable hostility toward some of the Nez Perce leaders because he considered them heathens. Through a series of brilliant maneuvers, Joseph and his band of warriors, women, children, horses, and cattle escaped or defeated the army at every turn. Even Howard was forced to admit in his memoirs about the chase, "The leadership of Chief Joseph was indeed remarkable. No general could have chosen a safer position or one that would be more likely to puzzle and obstruct a pursuing foe."

They fought several battles along the way, but Col. Nelson A. Miles finally caught Joseph and his band in a snowstorm at Bear Paw, a rolling, grassy landscape achingly close to the freedom promised by the Canadian border. After a 6-day fight, Joseph surrendered on October 5, 1877. The chief's rifle is now in the Museum of the Upper Missouri in Fort Benton.

Chief Joseph is believed to have delivered this famous speech, translated by an interpreter:

Hays. Turn left (east). Once you get to Hays, follow the road south after it turns to gravel. The mission is on the left (east) side of the street about a quarter mile after the road turns south.

Up the road is Mission Canyon, a steep, narrow, cool gash in the otherwise open landscape. Just after entering the canyon, you'll see a natural stone arch. The very brave can climb nearly to the top, and there are several ledges where you can pose for the photographer.

Gros Ventre and Assinniboine Tribes Buffalo Tours These tribes have been rebuilding their bison herd since 1974, starting with 27 animals. There are now about 300 grazing on 10,000 acres of the tribal buffalo reserve. You're likely to see other wildlife on the tour, including golden eagles and America's fastest land animal, the pronghorn. In 1998, federal and state agencies relocated 52 extremely rare black-footed ferrets to the reservation, so there's a chance you could spot one of these notoriously elusive critters, too. The tour includes insights into the tribes' history, culture, and relationship to the plains and its animals.

"Tell General Howard I know his heart. What he told me before I have in my heart. I am tired of fighting. Our chiefs are killed. Looking Glass is dead. Toohoolhootze is dead. The old men are all killed. It is the young men who say yes or no. He who led the young men is dead. It is cold and we have no blankets. The little children are freezing to death. My people, some of them, have run away to the hills, and have no blankets, no food; no one knows where they are—perhaps freezing to death. I want time to look for my children and see how many of them I can find. Maybe I shall find them among the dead. Hear me, my chiefs. I am tired; my heart is sick and sad. From where the sun stands now, I will fight no more forever."

That night, White Bird and 200 of his followers slipped away to Canada. Of the 431 remaining, 21 died by the end of spring. The survivors moved to a reservation in Oklahoma, where another 47 of Joseph's people died and many more became ill. Finally, in 1885, 118 Nez Perce who agreed to convert to Christianity were allowed to relocate to the Lapwai Agency near Lewistown, Idaho. The rest, including Joseph, were settled on the Colville Reservation in Nespelem in northeast Washington State.

Joseph never gave up hope of a return to his homeland in the Wallowa Valley. He met with President William McKinley in 1897, and tried unsuccessfully to purchase the land in 1900. He died at Colville in 1904 at age 64. Even in death, he wasn't returned to the Wallowa Valley, but was buried at Nespelem.

For more insight into the flight of Chief Joseph and the Nez Perce, stop at the **Blaine County Museum**, 501 Indiana St. in Chinook (© **406/357-2590**), and take a look at the interpretive displays and the 40-minute film, *Forty Miles from Freedom.*

RR1, Box 66, Fort Belknap Agency, Harlem, MT 59526. © **406/353-2205**. Reservations required. Tours are run from the visitor center, located at the intersection of U.S. 2 and Mont. 66 at Fort Belknap. $15–$20 per person (charge based on group size). Open May–Sept.

FROM GLASGOW TO THE FORT PECK INDIAN RESERVATION & THE C.M. RUSSELL WILDLIFE REFUGE

People moving through the northeast extremes of Montana can find themselves a little disoriented by the sheer vastness of the horizons that stretch unbroken all the way to the Dakotas. Although this is mostly wheat country, it's not totally flat. In fact, it is sharply rolling and canyon-scored country, but it's open to the eye in all directions.

In 1879, Robert Louis Stevenson rode an immigrant train through here and later wrote: "What livelihood can repay a human creature for a life spent in this huge sameness? He is cut off from books, from news, from company, from all that can relieve existence but the prosecution of his affairs. A sky full of stars is the most varied spectacle he can hope. He may walk five miles and see nothing; ten, and it is as though he had not moved; twenty, and he is still in the midst of the same great level, and has approached no nearer to the object within view, the flat horizon which keeps pace with his advance."

There is a story, usually attributed to an area just over the border in western North Dakota, but in the same sort of landscape, of a lone Indian who watched patiently as a recently arrived farmer plowed into the virgin earth, turning the soil with its deep and tangled roots to begin the civilization of the already vanishing native prairie. After some time, the Indian came over to the farmer, pointed to the plowed earth and said, "Wrong side up."

The story is probably another of the long chain of myths on which the West is built in the American imagination. But there are two contrasting sentiments made flesh here in the northeast corner that illustrate the conflicting impulses of America: progress and preservation.

The first and easiest to spot is the Fort Peck Dam and Lake. Construction of the dam began in 1933, at the height of the Great Depression, as a way to put men to work and to provide inexpensive water to the growing agricultural area.

The dam is the largest hydraulically earth-filled dam in the world, nearly 5 miles (8km) across, backing up a lake that is 134 miles (216km) long with 1,600 (2,576km) miles of shoreline—more shoreline, it is said, than the entire coast of California. The dam is one of the many Corps of Engineers projects that have turned the cantankerous Missouri River that Lewis and Clark navigated into a tame and regulated lake from the Mississippi River to the Rockies.

Seven thousand men and women went to work on the dam in 1933, and at the peak of employment nearly 11,000 were employed here. Locally, the attitude toward the dam was ambivalent, as the residents were losing their homes to the slowly rising water. On the other hand, they could appreciate the need for jobs, for irrigation water, for electric power, even for a large recreational lake. The story of the dam is told at the **Fort Peck Dam Interpretive Center and Museum** (© **406/526-3421** or 406/526-3411). The powerhouse looms over the landscape like a chunky Art Deco skyscraper that somehow got lost on its way to Des Moines. The museum (it's free and open 9am–5:30pm daily) offers tours of the power plant on the hour from Memorial Day to Labor Day weekend (the last one leaves at 4:45pm). The museum also houses a fine collection of dinosaur fossils. It's located on Mont. 24 at Fort Peck Dam.

SPECIAL EVENTS   Fort Peck Lake, backed up by the dam, is the best spot in Montana for walleye fishing. An annual competition, **the Governor's Cup,** takes place there each spring. Contact the Corps of Engineers at © **406/526-3411** or the Glasgow Area Chamber of Commerce (© **406/228-2222**) for the schedule and details.

OUTFITTERS & SEEING THE SIGHTS

The tiny town of Fort Peck is Montana's only planned community, the result of its heyday as the housing base for the workers at the dam in the 1930s. It started out as a trading post in 1867, then grew with the dam, then faded when construction was finished. It is testimony to the remoteness of this region that in 1934, months after the U.S. Army Corps of Engineers had begun construction of this $100 million project (big money during the Depression), a New York supplier asked the New York army headquarters how to address some equipment it was sending out to Montana. The army solemnly replied that there was no such place as Fort Peck—it had been abandoned in the 1880s.

The Fort Peck Theatre is a large former cinema built in the 1930s for the workers. The surprisingly beautiful theater seats 900 people for summer stock. Its season runs approximately from the last week of June to the last week of August. Call ℂ **406/526-9943** for information and tickets ($24 adults, $15 students).

Surrounding the many miles of shoreline at Fort Peck Lake is the **Charles M. Russell Wildlife Refuge,** named for the famous Western wildlife cowboy artist Charlie Russell. Born in 1864 in St. Louis, Russell was a working Montana cowboy at the age of 16 and drew much of his artistic inspiration from those years. He greatly admired the region's American Indians, and deplored the plowing of the grasslands. Russell knew that destroying the native grass would destroy the habitat for the animals, the bison would be lost, the Indian conquered. Russell didn't like seeing the West civilized, and he had little use for "settlers."

Turnoffs and campsites are located all along the perimeter of the refuge, as are boat ramps for anglers. Flat Creek, Rock Creek, and Nelson Creek boat ramps are easy to reach, located just off Mont. 24, which skirts the eastern side of the lake. There are 15 campgrounds scattered along the lake margin. The camping varies from rugged to semi-civilized. Only two campgrounds—the West End Campground and Downstream Campground—have flush toilets and showers; both are located near the dam. Contact the Corps of Engineers (ℂ **406/526-3411**) for information.

The **Fort Peck Indian Reservation** is home to the Assinniboine and the Sioux. The Sioux, who had been on the reservation by themselves, were joined by the Assinniboine nation after smallpox killed more than half of the tribe farther west along the Missouri River and again threatened the tribe after it resettled near Fort Belknap. The escape from the deadly disease brought them to Fort Peck. Now the reservation is home to many non-Indians, with American Indians now possessing less than half of the actual reservation.

This has been an extremely important area for the study of dinosaurs. The world's first Tyrannosaurus rex remains were discovered in 1902 just south of where the lake is in Garfield County. The **Garfield County Museum** (ℂ **406/557-2517** or 406/557-2519) in Jordan has replicas of the T. rex skull there, along with a duckbill dinosaur and triceratops. It is open June through August, from 1 to 5pm. Jordan is located at the intersection of Mont. 59 and Mont. 200 in the plains south of Fort Peck Lake. From Miles City, drive north on Mont. 59 for 83 miles (134km). From Glendive, take Mont. 200 west 111 miles (179km). From Fort Peck Dam, take Mont. 24 south 59 miles (95km) to Mont. 200, then take Mont. 200 west 36 miles (58km).

WHERE TO STAY

The Cottonwood Inn   This motel and convention center is far and away the nicest place in Glasgow: modern and clean, if a little small in the lobby. The rooms are conventional motel rooms, with queen or king beds and, for the most part, refrigerators. The restaurant, the Prairie Rose, is the most popular one in town. It specializes in homemade soups, bread, and pies, all made from scratch. The motel has valet and room service, unusual out here in Hi-Line Country.

U.S. 2 E., Glasgow, MT 59230. ℂ **800/321-8213** or 406/228-8213. Fax 406/228-8248. 92 units. $56–$65 double. AE, DC, DISC, MC, V. Pets accepted. **Amenities:** Restaurant; indoor pool; sauna; Jacuzzi; coin-op washers and dryers. *In room:* A/C, TV, dataport.

Fort Peck Hotel   A stone's throw from U.S. 2, this registered historic site is an intimate, old-fashioned hotel. Built in 1934 during the heyday of the WPA, it hearkens back to the slower way of life in Montana. There are no televisions or telephones in the rooms, a situation that tends to usher people out into the bar in the lobby for (gasp!) conversation. There is a good restaurant that serves three meals a day and has summertime dinner buffets that cater to the theater crowds (see the information about the Fort Peck Theatre in "Outfitters & Seeing the Sights," above). The rooms are small but serviceable, with high ceilings and spare furnishings reminiscent of the 1930s and 1940s.

Missouri Ave. (P.O. Box 108), Fort Peck, MT 59223. (C) **800/560-4931** or 406/526-3266. Fax 406/526-3472. 35 units. $36 double with shared bathroom, $48 double with private bathroom; $78 for 2 adjoining rooms. AE, DISC, MC, V. Closed Dec–Apr. **Amenities:** Restaurant, lounge. *In room:* No phone.

8

Bozeman, South Central Montana & the Missouri Headwaters

Relatively unspoiled, south central Montana is a world-class playground for the outdoor recreation enthusiast. Its biggest draws are the mountains that are a haven for hikers and campers, and the fly-fishing waters of the four major rivers that flow through its valleys—the Madison, Jefferson, Gallatin, and Yellowstone—which are also prime locations for rafting, kayaking, and canoeing.

During the winter, downhill skiing takes over at Big Sky, which claims to have the largest vertical drop of any hill in the United States (4,180 ft.). The region is also excellent for cross-country skiing—Lone Mountain Ranch and Bohart Ranch are two of the best Nordic skiing facilities in the state.

Bozeman, home of Montana State University, provides the hip, intellectual charm and culture of a college town—good bookstores and restaurants, charming shops, even a brewpub—as well as cultural events that appeal to both the cosmopolitan and cowboy cultures. The Sweet Pea Festival, a celebration of music and the performing arts, is complemented by the Livingston rodeo, one of the best in the region.

A few years ago the area around Bozeman bounded by the Bridger, Gallatin, Madison, and Tobacco Ranges seemed like an undiscovered bargain for real estate opportunists. Those times have changed; the communities of Bozeman, Livingston, and Belgrade experienced a boom as newcomers moved in, attracted to the easygoing Montana lifestyle and the wide range of outdoor activities. It's also been discovered by some rebellious Hollywood types who have purchased ranches in the area, such as writer Tom McGuane and actor Peter Fonda. Livingston has attracted a number of writers, including Peter Bowen, author of a series of Western detective novels.

1 A Scenic Drive

The Bozeman-Livingston-Three Forks area is one large intersection. **Interstate 90** runs east to west through this region, and from it, three valley highways extend south. The westernmost of these highways, **U.S. 287,** runs south from Three Forks, and extends 120 miles (193km) south through the Madison Valley to the town of Ennis (a fishing mecca) and West Yellowstone, the western gateway to Yellowstone National Park. From Bozeman, **U.S. 191** parallels U.S. 287 down the Gallatin Valley, past the resort community of Big Sky, to West Yellowstone.

The third highway, **U.S. 89,** runs 57 miles (92km) south from Livingston through the Paradise Valley to Gardiner and the north entrance of Yellowstone.

South Central Montana

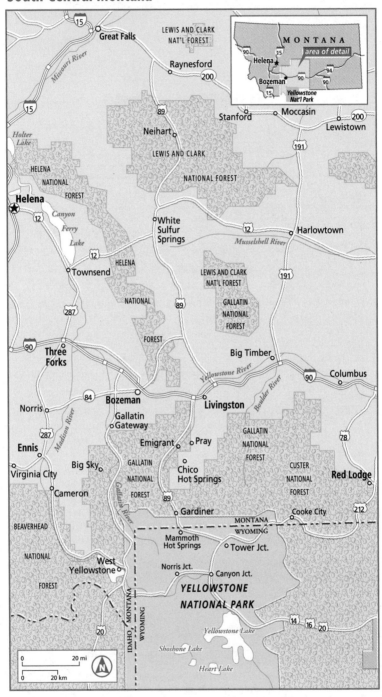

Though the area is populated primarily by ranchers and there are few developed attractions, it's a beautiful drive, especially through Yankee Jim Canyon.

Red Lodge can be reached a few different ways, but the most scenic is by taking I-90 to exit 408 at Columbus and heading south on Mont. 78 through Absarokee and Roscoe for 48 miles (77km). It's a much prettier and less traveled road than the freeway.

THE BEARTOOTH SCENIC BYWAY

This loop drive takes you to altitudes of almost 11,000 feet, taking in the sights that led Charles Kurault to call this the most scenic road in America.

Begin in Livingston. Drive south, following the Yellowstone River through Paradise Valley, 53 miles (85km) to Gardiner, and then into Yellowstone National Park. Once inside the park, you can stop off at Mammoth Hot Springs, a geothermal wonderland just inside the park's northern boundary. Then, take the road from Mammoth Hot Springs east to Tower Junction, continuing east to the park's northeast entrance at Silver Gate to pick up U.S. 212 (this is the Beartooth Byway). From here, the road begins to wind upward along the Montana and Wyoming border for nearly 40 ear-popping miles (64km) until it reaches the Beartooth Pass (elevation 10,947 ft.). From that spectacular altitude, you'll see miles and miles of mountains across both Wyoming and Montana. The road then drops for 24 miles (39km) as the byway continues on to Red Lodge. From Red Lodge, drive north on Mont. 78 down into the high plains before heading back to the mountains of Bozeman, west on I-90. The entire trip takes between 6 and 8 hours, depending on the time of day you choose to drive it and the condition of the roads.

2 Bozeman

82 miles (132km) E of Butte; 142 miles (229km) W of Billings; 91 (147km) miles N of West Yellowstone

Bozeman is a college and tourist town whose cowboy edge has been mostly chipped away to reveal a sophisticated Western chic. The vibrant downtown area is filled with independent shops and restaurants. The area bustles all year long—whatever the season, the locals always seem to be out and about.

Bozeman has experienced its greatest growth during the last 10 years, and it shows little sign of slacking off. Longtime residents worry that the town may be getting a little too chic. The city probably has more nice restaurants per capita than any other town in Montana. The university, Montana State, is a good one, and the students gravitate here for the excellent downhill skiing at nearby Bridger Bowl. The fact that Bozeman is only 2 hours from Yellowstone National Park certainly hasn't hurt its popularity either.

The city has become the unofficial capital of Montana environmental politics, with several nationally important groups based here. The combination of university and outdoor interests provides a good habitat for them.

But Bozeman hasn't always been a hotbed of activity. In the 1930s, for instance, local ordinances prohibited dancing anywhere in town after midnight, and in beer halls at any time. It was illegal to drink beer standing up, so all the bars had plenty of stools.

ESSENTIALS

GETTING THERE   Bozeman's **Gallatin Field** (© **406/388-8321**) serves a wide region in this part of the state. Daily service is available from **Delta**

(© 800/221-1212), **Northwest** (© 800/225-2525), **Horizon Air** (© 800/ 547-9308), and **United Express** (© 800/241-6522).

Bus service is available through **Greyhound,** with a terminal at 625 N. 7th Ave. (© 406/587-3110). **Rimrock Stages** (© 800/255-7655) operates intrastate service to Helena and thence to Missoula or Great Falls, a well as from Bozeman to Billings.

By car, Interstate 90 handles most of the traffic. It is 140 miles (225km) along I-90 from Billings to the east and 120 miles (193km) from Missoula to the west. For **local road reports,** call © 406/586-1313.

VISITOR INFORMATION   The **Bozeman Area Chamber of Commerce** is located at 200 Commerce Way (© 800/228-4224 or 406/586-5421; www.bozemanchamber.com). From Memorial Day to Labor Day, there's an information kiosk at 1001 N. 7th Ave., and there's a **Downtown Bozeman Visitor Center** (© 406/586-4008) at 224 E. Main. The chamber publishes an extensive Visitors Guide. Travel Montana calls this region **Yellowstone Country.** For info from them, call © 406/556-8680.

GETTING AROUND   There are a number of car-rental agencies in Bozeman, including **Avis** (© 406/388-6414), **Budget** (© 406/388-4091), **Enterprise** (© 800/736-2227), **Hertz** (© 406/388-6939), **National** (© 406/ 388-6694), and **Practical** (© 800/722-4618). For taxi service, call **All Valley Cab** (© 406/388-9999).

A SPECIAL EVENT   Stalking the wild sweet pea may not have been something you'd had in mind while traveling. Reconsider. The **Sweet Pea Festival,** at Lindley Park and throughout Bozeman (© 406/586-4003), is a wonderful diversion in Bozeman. Held the first full weekend each August, it was founded in the early 1900s as a community festival. Today, it is a music, arts, and sports festival, with bands from rock to reggae, dance, art, and even a little Shakespeare from the MSU Shakespeare troupe. A Saturday-morning run, including one for children, is followed by the Sweet Pea Parade.

GETTING OUTSIDE

Many of the outdoor activities discussed in this section take place in the **Gallatin National Forest.** For additional information, including current road and trail conditions, contact the Bozeman Ranger District, 3710 Fallon St., Suite C, Bozeman, MT 59718 (© 406/522-2520; www.fs.fed.us/r1/gallatin). The office is open Monday through Friday from 8am to 5pm.

ORGANIZED ADVENTURES

Yellowstone Safari Company ✇ (© 406/586-1155; www.beyondyellowstone. com) specializes in wildlife biologist-guided trips in Montana, Yellowstone, and Grand Teton National Parks, and along the Lewis and Clark Trail. Founded by biologist Ken Sinay—once called "Vesuvian in his enthusiasm"—the company offers guide services for both individuals and groups. Using specially adapted vehicles and boats, their activities include single and multi-day safari-style expeditions to observe wildlife and explore the natural and cultural history of the area. They offer seasonal hiking and backpacking trips, horse-riding and pack trips, river trips, snowshoe and cross-country ski trips in winter, plus bird-watching, wildlife photography, and bear and wolf viewing. They can tailor the tour's activities to the abilities and desires of your group, so choose your group-mates well. Full-day trips include guides, transportation, binoculars, spotting scopes, food, and beverages. Although they can't guarantee what wildlife you'll

Bozeman

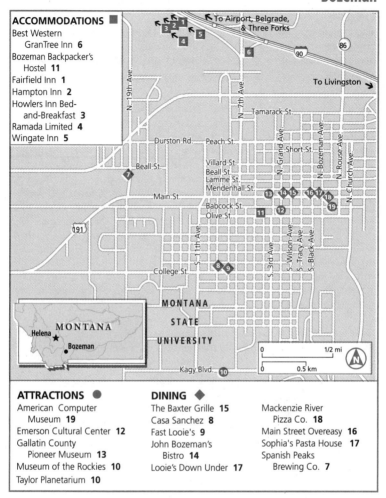

see, they do guarantee "diverse wildlife and learning opportunities." Rates depend on group size and the kind of tour, with full-day rates varying from $420 for one person to about $130 per person for seven people. A half-day Gallatin Valley wildlife or Lewis and Clark tour is $80 per person. Advance reservations are required, and the earlier the better as they are always fully booked.

Founded in 1982 and the first of its kind, **AdventureWomen** (15033 Kelly Canyon Rd., Bozeman; ✆ **800/804-8686;** 406/587-3883 outside the U.S.; www.adventurewomen.com) offers customized trips to just about anywhere in the world for "women born to be wild," age 30 and older. Around Bozeman, the company organizes hiking trips in Yellowstone National Park ($1,895, moderate to high-energy); a "Cowgirl Sampler" offering a variety of activities ($1,895, easy to moderate); horseback riding on a working Montana cattle ranch ($1,895, moderate); and canoeing the Lewis and Clark Trail on the Missouri River ($1,995, moderate).

BIKING

There are plenty of biking opportunities here, mostly off-pavement. Some of the best mountain biking is in the Gallatin National Forest—check with the Bozeman Ranger District office (see the intro to this section, above) for tips on where to go.

CROSS-COUNTRY SKIING

If you want to explore on your own, many drainages provide excellent skiing around Bozeman. Some local favorites are the 10-mile (16km), moderately difficult **Bozeman Creek to Mystic Lake Trail** that gains 1,300 feet of elevation over its course (go south of S. 3rd St. for 4 miles [6km] to Nash Rd., then east on Nash Rd. for a mile to Bozeman Creek Rd., then 1 mile [1.5km] south to the parking area), and the **Hyalite Reservoir Ski Loop,** a 4-mile (6km), relatively flat track around the Hyalite Reservoir, also rated moderately difficult (see the "Hiking" section, below, for directions). The road may not be plowed or maintained in winter. Two ski mountaineering routes for the adventurous are the 14-mile (23km) **Hyalite Ski Loop** and the 5½-mile (9km) **New World Gulch to Mystic Lake Trail.** Check with the Bozeman Ranger District office (see above) for directions.

Bohart Ranch, 16621 Bridger Canyon Rd., Bozeman, MT 59715 (© **406/ 586-9070**), next to the Bridger Bowl downhill area, offers 25km of groomed and tracked trails for all levels of skiers. There are a biathlon range, a ski school, and ski rentals. In summer, the ranch offers a Frisbee golf course (also known as folf), and trails for hiking, mountain biking, and horseback riding. Located in Bridger Canyon 16½ miles (27km) northeast of Bozeman on U.S. 86, it's open in winter daily from 9am to 4pm, and summer daily from dawn to dusk. Cost is $10 for adults, $5 for children 7 to 12.

DOWNHILL SKIING

Bridger Bowl is just 16 miles (26km) north of town, on Mont. 86 (15795 Bridger Canyon Rd., Bozeman, MT 59715; © **800/223-9609** or 406/587-2111; www.bridgerbowl.com). Although not as steep as Teton Village in Jackson Hole, Bridger Bowl is plenty steep for most of us, and a great hill for good skiers, with a lot of expert terrain. The ski area has quite a bit of beginner terrain as well, but the intermediate skier gets squeezed between the two. Lift tickets cost $34 adults, $28 seniors, $13 children 6 to 12, free for those 5 and under or 72 and over; half day $28 from 12:30 to 4pm. The fixed-grip quad, two triple, and four double chairs can haul people up the hill at the rate of 7,300 an hour. With 20 feet of snowfall annually, Bridger sees a lot of powder days. Usually open from the second Friday in December to mid-April, daily from 9am to 4pm. Oh, and there are seldom any lift lines.

FISHING

At **The River's Edge,** 2012 N. 7th Ave. (© **406/586-5373;** www.theriversedge. com), Dave and Lynn Corcoran operate a highly professional fly-fishing specialty shop "in the heart of Montana's blue-ribbon trout streams." They offer guided fishing trips year-round—including float fishing and walking or wading trips, plus equipment rental and shuttle service. Wading trips are excellent learning experiences, because guides can focus on your fly-fishing skills. They also offer a special program for women only. A guided trip for two costs $330 per day and includes lunch.

A full-line Orvis shop, **Montana Troutfitters,** 1716 W. Main St. (© **800/ 646-7847** or 406/587-4707; www.troutfitters.com), has been operating guide services since 1978. Owner Josh Stanish and outfitter Dave Kumlien offer guided float, walk and wade, and tube trips to rivers, lakes, and streams; plus 2- and 4-day fly-fishing schools. Kumlien is especially good at teaching youngsters the basics of the sport. Guided trips cost $300 per day for two people, including lunch.

The Bozeman Angler, 23 E. Main St. (© **800/886-9111** or 406/587-9111; www.BozemanAngler.com), provides guided trips in the Madison, Gallatin, Yellowstone, Jefferson, and Missouri Rivers plus numerous creeks, reservoirs, and lakes. Anglers can choose float trips in hard-sided drift boats, walk and wade, or backcountry fishing trips. Full-day trips include transportation, food, beverages, and instruction from a licensed professional guide. These trips start at $315; a half-day walk/wade excursion is $235 and doesn't include lunch.

GOLF

Bridger Creek Golf Course at 2710 McIlhattan Rd. (© **406/586-2333;** www.bridgercreek.com) is a scenic and challenging 18-hole layout, 6,400 yards from the back tees; this has been rated one of the 10 best courses in Montana by *Golf Digest.* It costs $28 for 18 holes on the weekend, $26 during the week.

HIKING

There's a beautiful and popular hiking area near Bozeman, known as the **Hyalite drainage,** on the Gallatin National Forest (see above for contact information). The area includes Hyalite Canyon and reservoir, Palisades Falls Trail, and many trail heads for access to the national forest. A lot of the trails here are steep and difficult, though. An excellent introductory hike to get the lay of the land is the half-mile **Palisades Falls National Recreational Trail.** From Bozeman, take 19th Avenue south for 7½ miles (11km) to the Hyalite Canyon Road, and follow the road to the reservoir. Continue east around the reservoir for 2 miles (3km) to the East Fork Road, and proceed to the Palisades Falls parking area.

The trail gains 540 feet in a little more than half a mile, which makes it very steep and gives it a rating of "most difficult" for a recreational trail. **Hyalite Reservoir** itself contains cutthroat and grayling, and there are two campsites here. **The Grotto Falls Trail** is a "difficult" 1¼-mile (2km) graveled trail to Grotto Falls located 13 miles (21km) up the West Fork Road in Hyalite Canyon. For a longer hike, go the 7¼ miles (12km) up the **Hyalite Peak Trail** to the peak. There is a 3,300-foot elevation gain on this hike.

If you're interested in combining a little bird-watching with your hiking, you can get a brochure on the **Birding Hotspots of the Gallatin Valley** (for $1 from Sacajawea Audubon Society, Box 1711, Bozeman, MT 59771). Try Kirk Hill in the foothills transition zone, where you might spot a colorful western tanager or a great gray owl. Take South 19th Street south for 5 miles (8km) until the road curves west. The entrance to the preserve is on the left.

LLAMA TREKKING

Yellowstone Llamas (© **406/586-6872;** fax 406/586-9612; www.yellowstone-llamas.com) offers a unique backcountry adventure that combines a rugged trek into Yellowstone and the surrounding area with fine dining and no-impact camping. Days begin with a hearty breakfast followed by 5- to 6-mile (8–10km) hikes in the company of llamas transporting provisions for the gourmet meals—accompanied by wines—that are served at campsites. Afternoons are unstructured, allowing time for the leisurely exploration of alpine surroundings and fishing. No experience with llamas is necessary. The cost is $195 per day, per person over 12; $145 for children 12 and under. Average length of a trip is 3 to 5 days. No credit cards are accepted. The 10 trips between July 1 and Labor Day are usually fully booked by April.

WHITE-WATER RAFTING

Montana Whitewater (© **800/799-4465** or 406/763-4465; www.montana whitewater.com) can get you sprayed in the face by the waters of both the Yellowstone and Gallatin Rivers. You paddle the raft as you fly through the nearly continuous rapids of the Gardiner section of the upper Yellowstone or through the dauntingly named rapids of Snake Bite and Mother Eater on the Gallatin. In addition to the white-water trips, the company offers more sedate scenic trips and "saddle and paddle" outings in which the morning is spent riding and the afternoon rafting. Half-day trips on the Gallatin cost $40 adults, $29 ages 12 and under; on the Yellowstone it's $30 and $20 respectively. Full-day Gallatin trips cost $68 adults and $54 ages 12 and under; and on the Yellowstone $58 and $46 respectively. Saddle and paddle jaunts range from $76 to $92.

If you want to try a rafting adventure on your own, the staffs at the rental shops (see "Where to Find Equipment & Supplies," below) will help guide you to the right spot for your abilities and thrill-seeking level.

WHERE TO FIND EQUIPMENT & SUPPLIES

It's easy to find whatever outdoor recreation equipment you need for your particular adventure. Mountain-bike rentals are usually in the range of $20 to $25 per day, and rafts and canoes are usually in the $40 to $60 per day range, with discounts for weekly rentals. Among rental outlets we recommend are **Panda Rentals,** 621 Bridger Dr. (© **406/587-6280**), which rents bikes, rafts, canoes, skis, and snowboards; **Chalet Sports,** on Main and Willson (© **406/ 587-4595**), a full-line sporting goods store that sells skis as well as rents bikes, in-line skates, skis, and snowboards; **The Round House Ski and Sports Center,** 1422 W. Main St. (© **406/587-1258**), which specializes in sales and rentals of bikes, rafts, and skis; and **Northern Lights Trading Co.,** 1716 W. Babcock St. (© **406/586-2225**), a high-end store selling gear for everything from kayaking to telemark skiing, and renting canoes, rafts, and kayaks.

SEEING THE SIGHTS

American Computer Museum ⚐   This unique museum traces the history of computing technologies from the abacus to the Apple. More than 4,000 years of computing circuits are fully explained, from those found in watches and microwaves to automated bank tellers. Though you won't find any T. rexes here, you can view computing's dinosaurs: slide rules and room-size computers with a mere fraction of the power of today's super-powered miniatures.

234 E. Babcock St. © 406/587-7545. www.compuseum.org. $3 adults, $2 children 6–12, free for children under 6. June–Aug daily 9am–5pm; Sept–May Tues, Wed, Fri, and Sat noon–4pm. Closed major holidays.

Emerson Cultural Center   Once a home for schoolchildren, this historic building (ca. 1918) was converted in 1993 into an arts and cultural center. The non-profit organization hosts a variety of professional and contemporary art exhibits, offers a fine arts education program, and provides retail and studio space for over 80 artists in converted schoolrooms. The Emerson also hosts free community events such as Lunch on the Lawn in summer, with live music and food vendors every Wednesday afternoon; plus special holiday activities in December. There's also a restaurant serving lunch and dinner, and a theater and ballroom for a variety of programs.

111 S. Grand Ave. © 406/587-9797. Free admission. Gallery and shops Tues–Sat 10am–5pm.

Gallatin County Pioneer Museum *Kids*   Located in the old city jail, which was in use until 1982, this museum features county history, focusing in part on law enforcement (as you might expect), the area's military history, and local daily life of the past. There's a display and memorabilia from actor Gary Cooper, known as Frank in the days he grew up in Bozeman and Helena. The museum also contains a cell from its days as the jail. There's also a collection of 11,000 historic photos and a research library devoted to Lewis and Clark.

317 W. Main St. ℂ 406/522-8122. www.pioneermuseum.org. Free admission. Oct–May Tues–Fri 11am–4pm, Sat 1–4pm; June–Sept Mon–Fri 10am–4:30pm, Sat 1–4pm.

Museum of the Rockies ★★   This first-class museum explains the history, geology, wildlife, and people of the Rocky Mountains all the way back to the Big Bang. The centerpiece of the museum is the fabulous dinosaur exhibit, which includes a life-size cast of a Tyrannosaurus rex skull, and the even larger Gigantosaurus carolinii, a recently discovered theropod dinosaur from Argentina. You can watch the fossil preparers as they clean recently discovered bones. Also at the museum, and almost as popular as the dinosaurs, is **Taylor Planetarium,** a state-of-the-art, 40-foot domed multimedia theater whose computer graphics simulator provides the illusion of flying through space in three dimensions. Programs take you from the evening sky to the farthest galaxies and are enhanced by superb visual effects and sound. The **Living History Farm** is a turn-of-the-century homestead with costumed interpreters who demonstrate tasks like baking bread in a wood-burning stove, forging iron, working in the garden, and other farm chores.

600 W. Kagy Blvd. (on the Montana State University campus). ℂ 406/994-2251. www.museumoftherockies. org. Museum $7 adults, $4 children 5–18, free for children under 5. Planetarium: $3 ages 3 and up. June 15–Labor Day museum and planetarium daily 8am–8pm; Martin Discovery Room 9am–4pm. After Labor Day–June 14 museum and planetarium Mon–Sat 9am–5pm, Sun 12:30–5pm; Martin Discovery Room Mon–Sat 9am–4pm, Sun 12:30–4pm. Living History Farm May 26–Sept 15 daily 9:30am–5pm (opens at 12:30pm some Sundays—call for details). Closed Thanksgiving, Christmas, and New Year's Day.

SHOPPING

Main Street offers an Old West feel and New West selection, starting at about 7th Avenue and running out to I-90. The chief part of the shopping district is easily accessible on foot. Among our favorite stops here are **Vargo's Jazz City and Books,** 6 W. Main (ℂ 406/587-5383), which sells an eclectic mass of new, used, and out-of-print books, CDs, and LPs (or the elusive, vanishing vinyl); **The Montana Gift Corral,** 237 E. Main (ℂ 800/242-5055 or 406/585-8625), which offers a wide selection of made-in-Montana gifts, in case you need a moose clock to take home; **Thomas Nygard Gallery,** 127 E. Main (ℂ 406/586-3636), which sells high-end art from noteworthy artists on American themes, not just Montana; and **Poor Richard's News,** 33 W. Main (ℂ 406/586-9041), the best newsstand and tobacco shop in town. The **Gallatin Valley Mall,** 2825 W. Main (ℂ 406/586-4565), has department and specialty stores, art galleries, and a food court.

Big Sky Carvers Outlet Gallery ★, 324 Main St., Manhattan (ℂ 800/746-8245 or 406/284-6067; www.bigskycarvers.com), is a local manufacturer in tiny Manhattan, about 15 miles (24km) west of Bozeman on I-90. They create a wide variety of carvings—mostly wildlife, including decoys, fish, birds, and lots of bears—plus furniture including tables, cabinets, armoires, and bed frames. The company has garnered an international reputation for its products, which also include bronzes and castings.

WHERE TO STAY

Bozeman has a full complement of chain motels, most just off I-90. In addition to the places listed below, you can stay at the **Best Western GranTree Inn,** 1325 N. 7th Ave., Bozeman, MT 59715 (© **800/624-5865** or 406/587-5261); the **Fairfield Inn,** 828 Wheat Dr., Bozeman, MT 59715 (© **406/587-2222**); the **Hampton Inn,** 75 Baxter Lane, Bozeman, MT 59715 (© **406/522-8000**); or the **Ramada Limited,** 2020 Wheat Dr., Bozeman, MT 59715 (© **406/ 585-2626**). The above are all at I-90 exit 306, and have rates for two in the $60 to $100 range, with the highest rates in the summer.

Bozeman Backpackers Hostel *(Value*   These bunkhouse accommodations are located in a quiet residential neighborhood near the MSU campus. The bunk rooms are coed, allowing couples to stay together. There's also a private room available. Full kitchen and bathroom facilities are available to guests.

405 W. Olive St., Bozeman, MT 59715. © **406/586-4659.** 15 bunks, 1 private room. $14 per person; $30 private room. No credit cards. **Amenities:** Coin-operated laundry. *In room:* No phone.

Howlers Inn Bed-and-Breakfast *(Finds*   Located on 84 acres in Bridger Canyon, the Howlers Inn is not only a beautiful B&B, but is also home to eight resident wolves who live in a 3-acre penned area adjacent to the main house. Owner Dan Astrom worked with wolves and big cats as a volunteer at a refuge in California, and when he came to Bozeman, he continued his interest by keeping wolves. Although guests can't interact directly with the animals, you can observe them from the house. The rooms here are large and well appointed, and the views of Absaroka and Bridger Mountains are marvelous. There's also a two-story chalet that can be rented as either a three- or two-bedroom unit. The chalet comes with a deck and a satellite television.

3185 Jackson Creek Rd., Bozeman, MT 59715. © **888/469-5377** or 406/586-0304. www.howlersinn.com. 5 units. $85–$105 double; $120 chalet. MC, V. Take I-90 east from Bozeman to exit 319, then go north for 3 miles (5km) to the inn. **Amenities:** Rec room with pool table; hot tub; sauna; well-equipped weight room.

Wingate Inn   The Bozeman Wingate Inn opened in April of 1999 and is the westernmost member of this East Coast chain. There is a large and elegantly appointed lobby and breakfast room, where an expanded continental breakfast is served. The rooms are average size, very clean, and well kept.

2305 Catron St. (I-90, exit 305), Bozeman, MT 59718. © **800/228-1000** or 406/582-4995. Fax 406/ 582-7488. www.wingateinns.com. 86 units. $73–$135 double. Rates include expanded continental breakfast. AE, DC, DISC, MC, V. **Amenities:** Indoor pool; exercise room; whirlpool; steam room; business center with free use of computer, fax, printer, and copier; guest laundry. *In room:* TV, dataport, coffeemaker, hair dryer, iron, safe.

CAMPING

The **Bozeman KOA** (© **406/587-3030**) is the city's largest campground, with sites for 100 RVs and 50 tents. It has a natural hot-springs pool, laundry, store, and a variety of other amenities. It is located 8 miles (13km) south of Belgrade on Mont. 85, with sites from $18 to $45. There are also numerous places to camp in the **Gallatin National Forest;** contact the Bozeman Ranger District, 3710 Fallon St., Suite C, Bozeman, MT 59718 (© **406/522-2520;** www.fs.fed. us/r1/gallatin) for details.

WHERE TO DINE

The Baxter Grille *★★* STEAK/SEAFOOD   This upscale restaurant serves some of the finest steaks and seafood in the state, and is a great choice for a romantic evening. In summer you can dine al fresco on the Main Street sidewalk, or on the back deck. Popular house specialties include a fresh seafood bouillabaisse and a creamy seafood pot with fresh dumplings, and the Tuesday-night all-you-can-eat snow-crab legs for $19.95. Our favorites are the roasted salmon filet and the prime rib. There's also an extensive wine list. Also on premises is the Bacchus Café, with a more casual atmosphere, and serving down-home meals between 8am and 9pm. For breakfast you might try the huevos rancheros or eggs benedict, and for lunch and dinner choose from among salads, burgers, sandwiches, and ribs, or opt for their year-round Thanks-giving dinner. You can enjoy live music several nights of the week in the lounge, where the full Bacchus Café menu is also available.

105 W. Main St. ✆ 406/586-1314. Main courses $12.95–$22.95. AE, DISC, MC, V. Summer daily 4:30pm–close; call for winter hrs.

Casa Sanchez MEXICAN   This 100-year-old house is home to the best Mexican food in Bozeman—and it's all homemade. If you consider yourself a nacho connoisseur, Ron's Nachos has what you're looking for: a plate full of chips, shredded chicken, salsa, and jalapeños, topped with mounds of gua-camole and sour cream. Burritos, enchiladas, chimichangas, and tacos are the basic food groups on the Casa Sanchez menu, with the occasional tostada thrown in for good measure. There's a large deck open in summer, and beer and wine to complement your meal choice. Takeout is available.

719 S. 9th Ave. (at College St.). ✆ 406/586-4516. Most dishes $6–$9. DISC, MC, V. Mon–Thurs 11am–9:30pm; Fri 11am–10pm; Sat 5–10pm.

Fast Looie's ECLECTIC   If you like to sample from several cuisines, or everybody in your group wants something different, this is the perfect choice. Looie's offers Thai, Japanese, Indian, Italian, Sushi, and American salads and wraps—all made to order speedily—not to mention the added incentive of fresh-baked breads and desserts.

815 W. College St. ✆ 406/522-0800. Most items $3.95–$9.95. MC, V. Daily from 11am.

John Bozeman's Bistro CONTEMPORARY AMERICAN   One of the most popular and upscale restaurants in town, this restaurant offers an eclectic and often innovative menu that may include buffalo, Jamaican jerk chicken, beef tenderloin, or an interesting vegetarian entree. The menu varies, but past favorites have included the Healthy Happy Bowl—stir-fried vegetables and soba noodles topped with marinated tofu. The atmosphere is a cut above casual.

125 W. Main St. ✆ 406/587-4100. Lunch items $9–$12; dinner entrees $12–$26. AE, DC, DISC, MC, V. Tues–Sat 11:30am–2:30pm and 5–10pm.

Looie's Down Under CONTINENTAL/PACIFIC RIM   Looie's is a great place, with a wide variety of well-prepared items. The menu features lots of seafood—we suggest the scallops in a citrus sauce or the seafood pasta, which includes tuna, sea bass, and artichoke hearts—and you can also get lamb, pasta, and veal. This is all served up in an informal San Francisco–cafe atmosphere. A sushi bar in the lounge offers sushi hand rolled to order.

101 E. Main St. ✆ 406/522-8814. Reservations recommended. Brunch $7.95; dinner $13–$24. AE, MC, V. Daily 5:30–10pm; Sun brunch 9am–2pm.

Mackenzie River Pizza Co. ☆☆ PIZZA   These folks do pizza a decidedly new way, one which matches the decor—funky, in a slightly overdone Western style with a log structure in the middle of the dining room. The tomato-based pizzas are delicious, and there are plenty of old standbys with traditional toppings. Innovations include the pesto-based pizzas from the "Back Forty" side of the menu. Names match the ingredients: The Athenian features feta, the Mexican, salsa, and the Angler—what else?—smoked trout.

232 E. Main St. ✆ 406/587-0055. Reservations not accepted. Sandwiches $5–$6; entrees $13–$16. AE, MC, V. Mon–Sat 11:30am–9pm; Sun noon–9pm. Second location at 145 Rawhide Ridge (✆ 406/582-0099) offering delivery and takeout, with limited dine-in availability.

Main Street Overeasy BREAKFAST/SANDWICHES   Chef Erik Carr opened this restaurant in 1998, and it rapidly became a local favorite, especially for breakfast. Breakfast dishes include old-fashioned oatmeal, a Belgian waffle, eggs Benedict, or cinnamon bread pudding with vanilla-bean sauce. Lunches consist of large gourmet sandwiches and salads.

9 E. Main St. ✆ 406/587-3205. Breakfast $3–$7; lunch $5–$7. AE, MC, V. Tues–Sun 7am–2:30pm.

Sophia's Pasta House ITALIAN   Sophia's Pasta House boasts 41 delicious ways to enjoy pasta. Home of the $4.95 lunch, it has replaced O'Brien's as the lunch spot of choice for some of the Bozeman business crowd. Every dish is carefully prepared and the portions are huge.

101 E. Main St. ✆ 406/582-0393. Fax 406/582-0398. Lunch $5–$7; dinner $7–$15. AE, DISC, MC, V. Mon–Sat 11:30am–2:30pm; daily 5:30–10pm.

Spanish Peaks Brewing Co. AMERICAN   Spanish Peaks Brewing Co. is one of the West's most successful microbreweries. Choose your tipple from among fine handcrafted ales, lagers, ciders, cigars, wines, and spirits. And the food is a cut above the usual brewpub fare: Chefs Dave and John "make everything right here, all from fresh ingredients." There are brick-oven pizzas, homemade pastas, steak, fish, and chicken dishes. The sage-grilled New York strip and bourbon-seared filet mignon were particularly good, as was the Peak's Cobb salad with roast chicken, avocado, cucumber, bacon, and Gorgonzola piled atop baby greens and drizzled with a delightful ancho-citrus vinaigrette. Spanish Peaks is popular with the MSU crowd and is noisy during happy hour.

14 N. Church Ave. at the corner of Main St. ✆ 406/585-2296. www.spanishpeaks.com. Main courses $6–$23. DISC, MC, V. Mon–Sat 11:30am–10:30pm; Sun noon–10:30pm.

BOZEMAN AFTER DARK

Bozeman is a college town, so there are lots of places to get a casual drink accompanied by loud music. We like **Spanish Peaks Brewing Co.** (see "Where to Dine," above), which does an excellent job on its microbrews, and also offers mixed drinks and wine and a good selection of cigars. Other popular watering holes include **Boodle's,** 215 E. Main St. (✆ 406/587-2901), which has live jazz on the weekends; the lively **Crystal Bar,** 123 E. Main St. (✆ 406/587-2888); and **Ruppert's Tap House,** just off West Main at 2711 W. College St. (✆ 406/522-8960), which has a stock of microbrews on tap.

   Montana Shakespeare in the Parks, Montana State University, Bozeman, MT 59717-0400 (✆ 406/994-3901), is a professional touring company that was formed in 1972. Based in Bozeman, the troupe of 10 to 12 actors produces 66 performances during the summer at communities throughout Montana, Wyoming, and Idaho—often in a different town each day. Some summer weekends find them at their Bozeman stage—located on the MSU campus on 11th Avenue near the corner of Grant Street—for "Shakespeare Under the Stars." Parking is available just north of the MSU field house. Call for schedule. Performances are free.

3 The Madison River Valley: Three Forks & Ennis

Ennis: 54 miles (87km) SW of Bozeman; 71 miles (114km) N of West Yellowstone

The Madison Valley is an almost mythical place surrounded by spectacular mountain scenery where anglers from all over gather to fish. The main attraction is the Madison River, which flows through the valley at the base of the Madison Range, a stretch of peaks that runs toward Yellowstone Park.

Besides the phenomenal fishing, the historical significance of the Madison Valley makes it a worthy tourist destination. **The Missouri Headwaters State Park** is at the confluence of the Jefferson, Madison, and Gallatin Rivers, where Lewis and Clark paused to take shelter; **Lewis and Clark Caverns State Park,** with its spectacular underground peaks, is just up the road; and **Madison Buffalo Jump State Park** is nearby.

ESSENTIALS

GETTING THERE   The Bozeman airport, **Gallatin Field** (discussed earlier in this chapter), is the closest airport to the valley.

Greyhound stops at the Sinclair station in Three Forks at 2 Main St.

Three Forks is located on I-90, 30 miles (48km) from Bozeman, 170 miles (274km) from Billings, and 173 miles (279km) from Missoula. Three Forks is 66 miles (106km) from the capital in Helena. Ennis is 45 miles (72km) south of Three Forks on U.S. 287.

VISITOR INFORMATION   Contact the **Three Forks Chamber of Commerce,** P.O. Box 1103, Three Forks, MT 59752 (© **406/285-4753,** www.threeforksmontana.com); or the **Ennis Chamber of Commerce,** P.O. Box 291, Ennis, MT 59729 (© **406/682-4388**). For information on **Yellowstone Country,** the Montana region that includes the Madison Valley, call © **800/736-5276** or 406/556-8680 (www.yellowstone.visitmt.com).

GETTING AROUND   If you're flying into Bozeman, pick up a car at the airport (see the section on Bozeman for more information). For local **road reports,** call © **406/586-1313.**

GETTING OUTSIDE

There is plenty of fishing water along the road from Three Forks to Quake and Hebgen Lakes along U.S. 287. The first fishing access is **Cobblestone,** just a few miles south of Three Forks on the right side of U.S. 287. If you plan to base yourself in Ennis, the **Valley Garden, Ennis Bridge, Burnt Tree,** and **Varney Bridge** fishing accesses are within minutes of town along 287. Between Ennis and Quake Lake, the accesses begin popping up frequently. **McAtee Bridge, Wolf Creek, West Fork,** and **Reynolds Pass** are all accessible from the roadside. Hebgen Lake, just south of the dam, and Quake Lake are also great fishing spots.

On Ennis's Main Street, it seems that every second door houses a fly-fishing outfitter. The **Madison River Fishing Company,** 109 Main St. (P.O. Box 627), Ennis, MT 59729 (© **800/227-7127** or 406/682-4293; www.mrfc.com), has a good stock of fishing supplies and a guide service. Guided trips, for one or two people, cost $195 for a half day and $295 for a full day; fall day trips include lunch. They also offer a free brochure that contains a map of the Madison from Ennis to Quake Lake, listing fishing spots and camping and toilet facilities along the way. Other guide services, with similar rates, include **Eaton Outfitters,** Box 351, Ennis, MT 59729 (© **800/755-3474** or 406/682-4514); **Clark's Guide**

Service, Box 572, Ennis, MT 59729 (✆ **406/682-4679**); **Howard Outfitters,** Box 247, Ennis, MT 59729 (✆ **406/682-4834**); and **The Tackle Shop Outfitters,** 127 Main St. (Box 625), Ennis, MT 59729 (✆ **800/808-2832** or 406/682-4263).

SEEING THE SIGHTS

National Fish Hatchery   The Ennis National Fish Hatchery, constructed in 1931, is probably the only place in America where you can observe two genetic mutants of ordinary rainbow trout: albino and blue. (These fish are not released into the wild trout population.) Some of the trout in the hatchery ponds weigh more than 20 pounds and are more than 5 years old. The hatchery cultivates seven different strains of rainbow trout. You can learn about the operation in the small exhibit area and tour the facility. When some of those huge adults are past their use as brood stock, they too are released into lakes and streams to test fishermen.

180 Fish Hatchery Rd., Ennis. ✆ **406/682-4847**. www.r6.fws.gov/hatchery/ennis/Ennis.htm. Free admission. Daily 8am–4:30pm. The 10-mile (16km) access road is pretty rough.

Lewis & Clark Caverns ✮   These lovely limestone caverns are named for the famous explorers, but there is no evidence that their party ever saw or visited them. Originally called Morrison Cave for surveyor Daniel Morrison, who discovered them in 1902, these caverns are a succession of vaulted chambers and passageways, thickly decorated with stalactites and stalagmites, as well as other underground formations such as massive, gleaming organ pipes; silky, delicate soda straws; intricate filigrees; and weirdly hung draperies. Plan at least 2 hours for the 2-mile (3km) guided tour through the caverns; and above ground there are hiking trails, several picnic areas, and a large campground (see "Camping," below). A Christmas candlelight tour is held on 2 weekends in December. Reservations should be made in November for one of the 200 or so spots available. There are three cabins on the premises with electric heat; $39 in summer and $25 in winter.

Located 19 miles (31km) west of Three Forks (midway between Butte and Bozeman) on Mont. 2. ✆ **406/287-3541**. www.fwp.fwp.state.mt.us. Entrance fee $4 per vehicle or $1 per person, whichever is less. Cave tours $8 adults, $5 children 6–11. Park open daily year-round. Guided cave tours May–Sept daily 9am–4:30pm; mid-June to Labor Day 9am–6:30pm. Tours leave as required by demand; call for group reservation.

Madison Buffalo Jump State Monument   This is one of a few buffalo jumps, or *pishkun,* that have been excavated. Prior to the advent of the horse, the Northern Shoshone and the Bannock drove the bison off this steep cliff to their death on the rocks below. Long rows of rocks funneled the animals to the cliff. There is a well-worn trail up to the base of the cliff, making for a short but steep hike.

23 miles (37km) west of Bozeman, off I-90 exit 283. ✆ **406/994-4042**. www.fwp.state.mt.us/parks. Entrance fee $4 per vehicle or $1 per person, whichever is less. Open daily 24 hr. From the Logan exit off I-90, 7 miles (11km) south on Buffalo Jump Rd.

Missouri Headwaters State Park ✮✮   You can easily spend an hour just exploring the interpretive signage at this historic state park. Begin by following the Missouri River out from Three Forks. The headwaters themselves are no great shakes—just another river—but the sunsets from the bank of the river are breathtaking. From the headwaters, drive back toward Three Forks where, on the opposite side of the road, you'll see a parking area with interpretive markers. Allow plenty of time to read about Lewis and Clark and Sacajawea, the young

Shoshone guide, as well as early American Indians, trappers, traders, and settlers. Camping and RV units are available as well as access to hiking, boating, and fishing.

4 miles (6km) northeast of Three Forks (east on C. R. 205, then north on C. R. 286; follow signs). ℂ **406/ 994-4042.** www.fwp.state.mt.us/parks. $4 per car or $1 per person, whichever is less. Open daily 24 hr.

Quake Lake Just before midnight on August 17, 1959, a massive earthquake measuring 7.5 on the Richter scale jolted Yellowstone and the Madison River canyon, sending large chunks of mountain into the river. A campsite just below the mountain was covered with rubble and 19 people were buried alive. The rubble that collapsed into the river created a dam and the aptly named Quake Lake. The ghostly fingers of trees that died when they were swamped still poke skyward from the lake. The visitor center off to the left of the highway offers exhibits, a video every half-hour, and an observation area from which you can see the massive slides. The area around Yellowstone and Quake Lake is still very seismically active: Between June 13 and 22, 1999, more than 630 small earthquakes occurred in the area just east of Hebgen Lake. The visitor center has a great deal of information about the area's seismic activity and hypotheses of how it got this way.

Off U.S. 287, 27 miles (43km) west of West Yellowstone and 43 miles (69km) south of Ennis. ℂ **406/ 682-7620** or 406/823-6961. $3 per car. Visitor center Memorial Day–Labor Day daily 8:30am–6pm.

WHERE TO STAY
IN THREE FORKS

Bud Lilly's Anglers Retreat Having Bud Lilly mastermind your fishing itinerary is reason enough to stay here, but it's by no means the only reason. Formerly a railroad hotel belonging to Bud's mother, the Anglers Retreat has been refurbished and is now a cozy lodge. The three upstairs bedrooms share a bathroom with a claw-foot bathtub and shower, and each of the suites has a full bathroom with shower as well as a fully equipped kitchen. There's also a shady verandah and upper balcony overlooking a well-kept back yard; a collection of fly-fishing memorabilia, art, and antiques; and a comfortable TV room with an extensive library of fishing and Montana videos. The private cottage has its own kitchen and living area, and sleeps four.

But the big draw here is the fishing. Every reservation at the Anglers Retreat includes a personalized, detailed itinerary of where to fish locally, based on your preferences and length of stay.

16 W. Birch St., Box 983, Three Forks, MT 59752. ℂ **406/285-6690.** Fax 406/586-8713. 5 units, 3 with shared bathroom. $65 double; $135–$176 suite; $135 cottage. MC, V. **Amenities:** Laundry facilities; videos. *In room:* A/C, TV.

IN ENNIS

In addition to the properties discussed below, the **Rainbow Valley Motel,** 1 mile (1.5km) south of Ennis on U.S. 287 (Box 26), Ennis, MT 59729 (ℂ **800/ 452-8254** or 406/682-4264; www.rainbowvalley.com), offers large, well-maintained cabin-style rooms at rates for two of $70 to $90 in summer and $50 to $60 in winter.

El Western Resort It's a little hard to categorize this place, which has some inexpensive log duplex-style cabins as well as large, expensive two- and three-bedroom lodges. The original portion was built in 1948 and is done with knotty-pine interiors and built-in wooden cabinets. The newest lodge is the Eagle's Loft, a three-bedroom, three-bathroom, two-story cabin with vaulted ceiling and rock fireplace, plus a whirlpool tub and washer and dryer. Every unit enjoys spectacular views of the Madison Range, including Fan Mountain and the Spanish Peaks. You can't go wrong here, and the overnight cabins are as affordable as anything in the valley. There's no restaurant or lounge associated with the property, but a new conference center building with a large, inviting deck and picture windows serves both business and family groups.

P.O. Box 487, Ennis, MT 59729 (1 mile [1.5km] south of Ennis on U.S. 287). © **800/831-2773** or 406/682-4217. Fax 406/682-5207. www.elwestern.com. 29 units. $68–$78 double; $90–$100 kitchen cabin, $140–$185 deluxe kitchen cabin; $190–$325 lodge unit. AE, DISC, MC, V. *In room:* TV.

Wade Lake Resort This secluded resort, which consists of five cabins, is located in a picture-perfect forested canyon on Wade Lake. The cabins are fairly primitive, with only a refrigerator, running water, heat, a gas stove, and a gas barbecue grill. The shared, heated bathhouse is out back. Although there are overhead electric lights, there aren't any stand-alone reading lamps by the bed. There aren't even any electric outlets to plug in your computer (which we consider a major plus). Bring food to cook because the nearest restaurant is 11 miles (18km) back up the road. The area is very beautiful, though—Wade has been designated a Montana Wildlife Viewing Site. The area is rich in wildlife, with eagles and osprey nesting on the lake, and moose, elk, bear, and other locals dropping in occasionally. It also helps you remember what real quiet and real darkness are like.

P.O. Box 107, Cameron, MT 59720. © **406/682-7560.** 5 cabins. $50–$75 double. No credit cards. Drive 40 miles (64km) south of Ennis to the Wade Lake turnoff, marked by a sign. Turn west on the bumpy, gravel Wade Lake Rd. and follow the signs about 6 miles (10km) to Wade Lake. **Amenities:** Wildlife viewing; cross-country skiing; snowshoeing. *In room:* No phone.

A GUEST RANCH

Diamond J. Ranch *Kids* Twelve miles (19km) east of town you'll find this 200-acre dude ranch, among the first established in Montana in the 1930s. Tucked into a narrow canyon in the Madison Range and surrounded by the Beaverhead National Forest, this family-oriented vacation spot lacks the stylishness of some of its competitors but provides adults and children alike with a good variety of outdoor activities. Overstuffed leather chairs and sofas fill an appealing lounge area in the lodge, and meals are served at long tables in the same building. Children usually dine in a separate room, while their parents socialize at the Branding Iron. The cabins are comfortable but rustic, made of lodgepole pine and with rock fireplaces, hickory furniture, and hardwood floors. Riding is the primary focus here, and rides are organized to suit the abilities and preferences of guests. Other activities include fly-fishing on Ginny Lake, a stocked pond; tennis on the court inside the barn; swimming in the small pool; trap and skeet shooting; and volleyball, table tennis, and horseshoes.

P.O. Box 557, Ennis, MT 59729. © **406/682-4867.** Fax 406/682-4106. www.diamondjranch.com. 8 units. $1,330 per adult per week, lower for children under 13. Rate includes all meals and activities. AE, MC, V. **Amenities:** Dining room; small outdoor pool; indoor tennis court; horseback riding; fishing. *In room:* No phone.

CAMPING

Lewis & Clark Caverns (see "Seeing the Sights," above; © **406/287-3541**) has 40 campsites ($12), showers, a dump station, and a river, plus hiking trails and interpretive programs. **Missouri Headwaters State Park** (see "Seeing the Sights," above; © **406/994-4042**) has a year-round campground ($12) with 20 sites scattered along the river, plus numerous hiking trails and plenty of fishing access. Maximum trailer length is 25 feet; there's a boat ramp and dump station. Those wanting RV hookups and the usual commercial campground amenities should head to **Three Forks KOA,** on U.S. 287, 1 mile (1.5km) south of I-90 exit 274 (© **800/562-9752** [reservations] or 406/285-3611), which has a clean bathhouse, swimming pool, rec room, playground, and sauna. It's open May through September, with sites for both tents and RVs at rates of $18 to $25.

WHERE TO DINE
NEAR THREE FORKS
Wheat Montana Bakery and DeliAMERICAN   This is a very popular place where Montana-grown wheat is turned into bread, and the smell of bread baking alone makes it worth the stop. For breakfast, munch on a fresh cinnamon roll or muffin with a cup of gourmet coffee, or enjoy homemade biscuits and gravy or the popular egg croissant. Later in the day, come back for our favorite: the wheat-chile soup served in a bread bowl, or build your own sandwich from the wide array of meats and cheeses, or choose one of the daily specials. There are cookies and brownies to satisfy your sweet tooth, and you can always take home a couple of loaves of bread or just get the flour to bake your own.

I-90 and U.S. 287, Three Forks. © **800/535-2798** or 406/285-3614. www.wheatmontana.com. Sandwiches $2.50–$4.50. AE, MC, V. Daily 6am–8pm.

Willow Creek Café and Saloon ★★ Finds AMERICAN   This place is a find, if you can find it—it's located 7 miles (11km) southwest of Three Forks on the Old Yellowstone Trail. It's worth the search, though, because Willow Creek gets our vote for the best restaurant in the area (don't let the bullet holes in the ceiling scare you off). It began as the Babcock Saloon around 1916, and continues as a remarkable reflection of what's best in Montana: hearty meals and friendly people. The ever-popular baby-back pork ribs draw repeat customers from around the country, but the local cowboys know that the beef is tops here, so the hand-pounded chicken-fried sirloin steak is their recommendation. The pasta dishes are very good and the homemade soups really taste homemade.

21 Main St., Willow Creek. © **406/285-3698.** Dinner reservations recommended in summer. Lunch $4–$8; dinner $8–$18. DISC, MC, V. Tues–Sat 11am–9pm; Sun 8am–noon.

IN ENNIS
Scotty's Longbranch Supper Club and SaloonAMERICAN   Scotty's has a sign that reads: "No burgers. No fries." So don't ask. And there is classical music on the CD player. But the atmosphere otherwise is pure Western steak-house, as is most of the food. Our choice is the steak béarnaise, though veal Parmesan, crab cakes, and shrimp scampi are also on the menu. Scotty's serves twice-baked and regular baked potatoes, but like the sign says—no fries. The restaurant is located in the rear of the Longbranch Saloon.

125 Main St. © **406/682-5300.** Main courses $10.95–$21.50. MC, V. Mon–Sat 5:30–10pm; hr. vary somewhat in winter.

4 The Gallatin Valley

Big Sky: 53 miles (85km) S of Bozeman; 48 miles (77km) N of West Yellowstone

According to legend, the Sioux and Nez Perce once engaged in a bloody battle in the lower Gallatin Valley. On the third day of the fighting, the sun was blotted out and a booming voice told the warriors to forget old wrongs and stop fighting, because they were in the Valley of Peace and Flowers.

Since those days, the sun still mostly shines around here, but the only booming voices heard are those calling you for your tee time or your dinner reservation. The transition of Big Sky from peace and flowers to year-round resort was not entirely without dissension, however. When legendary NBC newsman Chet Huntley—a Montana native—proposed the Big Sky resort, there was an outcry from the budding environmental movement. But Huntley's dream was realized in 1973, and the resort has blossomed into a world-class facility.

The valley is a narrow, shining slice of Montana edged by the Absarokas and Gallatin Ranges to the east and the Madison Range on the west. The Big Sky Ski Area covers two of the western peaks—Lone Mountain, elevation 11,186 feet, and Andesite Mountain, 8,800 feet.

There are three distinct "villages" in Big Sky. The **canyon area** along U.S. 191 has a haphazard collection of motels, taverns, restaurants, gas stations, and whatnot. The **Meadow Village,** 2 miles (3km) west of the highway, includes a community of condos, a few overnight lodging places, and the golf course. The main **base area** for the ski resort is at the Mountain Village, 8 miles (13km) west of the highway, with condos, restaurants, and hotels.

The main season in Big Sky is winter, but the Lone Mountain Guest Ranch, which was once the only destination spot in this valley, offers fine, year-round accommodations and activities—dude-ranch style in summer, and cross-country skiing in winter. The summer months bring excellent fly-fishing, horseback riding, and white-water rafting. And this beautiful scenery may seem familiar—the Gallatin River was the setting for the film *A River Runs Through It.*

ESSENTIALS

GETTING THERE   Big Sky is about 40 miles (64km) south of Bozeman on U.S. 191. Fly into Bozeman's **Gallatin Field** for easiest access to Big Sky.

From the airport, you can ride to the ski area with **4×4 Stage** (© 800/517-8243 or 406/388-6404), a company that has a transportation fleet of sturdy four-wheel-drive vehicles. The ride is $43 round-trip per person in winter; summer transportation can be arranged by calling ahead. Or you can take a taxi provided by **Mountain Taxi** (© **406/995-4895**) for $65 for one and $70 for two people.

GETTING AROUND   A car gives you the greatest flexibility in getting around this area. For service between condominiums, hotels, restaurants, and activities within the ski area, take the **Snowexpress,** Big Sky's free local shuttle-bus system, which operates daily during the ski season.

GETTING OUTSIDE
BIKING

Big Sky Resort rents mountain bikes (around $55 for 8 hr.) and offers bike rental/lift ticket combos. Call © **406/995-5840** for details.

CROSS-COUNTRY SKIING

Big Sky Resort (see below) offers some groomed trails for cross-country skiing. But for the real deal, go to **Lone Mountain Ranch** ★★ (P.O. Box 160069, Big Sky, MT 59716; © **800/514-4644** or 406/995-4644, or 406/995-4734 for the outdoor shop; www.lmranch.com), which has about 45 miles (72km) of cross-country trails over terrain that will challenge every level of skier. Near the ranch headquarters, in the meadows, lies some flat terrain that beginners might appreciate. There's also a steeper portion to practice your telemark technique. Intermediate trails with more hills make up about 60% of the area, and expert trails provide plenty of challenging downhill runs. Ski and snowshoe rentals are also available. Full-day trail passes cost $18, and half days cost $15. The entrance to Lone Mountain Ranch is off Lone Mountain Trail (the main road to the Big Sky Resort), about 4 miles (6km) west of its intersection with U.S. 191 and 2 miles (3km) east of the Mountain Village.

DOWNHILL SKIING

Big Sky Resort   Tennis, golf, and rock climbing are all very nice, but the real reason to come to Big Sky is to ski. It's a huge hill, with more than 3,600 acres of terrain and 85 miles (137km) of trails. You can ski for nearly a vertical mile from the top of the tram at 11,150 feet elevation to the bottom of the Thunderwolf lift, at 6,970 feet. There is terrain here for everybody, with 43% for advanced skiers, 47% for intermediate, and 10% for beginner.

Big Sky gets 400 inches of snowfall, offering plenty of powder days. The season begins on Thanksgiving and goes through April. There's an ambitious children's program, offering lessons for kids as young as three, and day care for kids who don't want to ski. Full ski-rental packages are available.

P.O. Box 160001, Big Sky, MT 59716. (✆) **800/548-4486** or 406/995-5900 for reservations; 406/995-5900 for snow conditions; 406/995-5743 for ski school. Fax 406/995-5001. www.bigskyresort.com. Lift ticket $56 adults, $28 seniors (70 and over), $44 children 11–17 and college students with ID, free for children 10 and under. Half-day (afternoon only) ticket $42. Hours vary; call for information.

FISHING

According to an Indian legend, folks who drink the water of the Gallatin River will return to the valley before they die, but of course you should no longer drink untreated water out of even high mountain streams, because of the possibility of giardia, an intestinal microbe that you don't want traveling back home with you. We're not sure if eating the fish that live in the water counts toward the legend, but it's worth a try. Several guides offer half-day and full-day trips for prices ranging from $165 (half day for two, walking) to $310 (full day for two, floating). For details contact **Lone Mountain Ranch** (✆ **406/995-4644**), **Gallatin River Guides** (✆ **406/995-2290**), or **East Slope Anglers** (✆ **406/995-4369**).

GOLF

Big Sky Golf Course, Meadow Village (✆ **406/995-5780**), is a striking Arnold Palmer design that is fairly short, fairly open, and harder than it looks on the card. A few of the holes wander next to the West Fork of the Gallatin River, which runs through the property. Cost, which includes the cart fee, is $40 to $47 for 18 holes, $29 to $40 for nine; ask about twilight rates. Tee times can be reserved up to a week in advance.

HIKING

As you might expect in an area surrounded by three mountain ranges and two national forests, there is an abundance of hiking opportunity not far from Big Sky. An easy, 4-mile (6km) hike to **Porcupine Creek** is accessible nearby. Go south 2¾ miles (4km) on U.S. 191 from the intersection with the mountain village road. Turn left at the sign that announces Porcupine Creek, and go about a half mile to the trail head. The first mile of the hike wanders along Porcupine Creek, then offers a choice of either a north or south fork. The left (north) fork goes up into the foothills, offering a view of the creek below.

If you want more of a workout, try the **Lava Lake** trail, which begins about 13 miles (21km) north of the intersection of the mountain village road and U.S. 191 on the highway. Take the Lava Lake turn. The trail climbs steeply and without much relief for 3 miles (5km) to an alpine lake in the shelter of three mountains.

Yellowstone National Park is only about 40 miles (64km) south of Big Sky, and you can hike there, too. See chapter 10 for specifics.

WHERE TO STAY

Big Sky Resort (P.O. Box 160001, Big Sky, MT 59716; ⓒ **800/548-4486** or 406/995-5000; fax 406/995-5002; www.bigskyresort.com) handles a wide variety of lodgings—from economy to full-fledged luxury scattered among some 15 properties. The three-story **Huntley Lodge,** with 205 units, was the beginning of late NBC newsman Chet Huntley's original vision for Big Sky. It offers rooms that can sleep up to four, and several loft rooms that can accommodate six. The 97-unit **Shoshone Condominium Hotel** combines the living quarters of a condo with the amenities and services of a hotel, with sleeping for four to six. Weight-training centers, saunas, an outdoor pool, gift shops, and ski storage are included at both places. **The Summit at Big Sky,** with 213 luxury condominiums, offers European sophistication in a Western style. All three properties are slope-side and offer ski-in/ski-out convenience. Rates in prime season (Jan 30 to mid-Mar) are $186 to $196 double, $229 to $443 suite or loft; Christmas season (Dec 25–Jan 2) runs $220 to $230 and $262 to $554 respectively; and off-season, $160 to $170 and $200 to $377.

East-West Resorts (P.O. Box 160058, Big Sky, MT 89716; ⓒ **800/845-4428** or 406/995-2665; fax 406/995-3299; www.eastwestresorts.com) offers properties ranging from condos to private residences to luxurious penthouses. Their new **Moonlight Lodge and Spa** in Moonlight Basin Ranch is a magnificent mountain lodge offering luxurious penthouse suites (sleeping eight to ten people and starting at around $1,300) and secluded, mid-mountain cabins; plus a sophisticated yet down-home restaurant, a relaxed-atmosphere bar, and a deli. There's also a full-service spa with treatment rooms, complete fitness center, steam rooms, heated pool, and a cascading waterfall hot tub; a concierge ready and able to organize everything from fly-fishing trips, to backcountry skiing, to dog-sled adventures; and even an ice-skating rink just outside in winter.

In the Big Sky area, rates vary with the season and within the ski season. The highest rates are over Christmas vacation, the lowest in the spring and fall "shoulder" seasons.

Best Western Buck's T-4 Lodge   Buck's offers a woody, Western ambience on the highway a little away from the ski resort lodgings. The lodge offers large, comfortable rooms in bewildering variety. Begun in 1946 as a hunting camp, Buck's T-4 got to the valley before electricity did. It has grown somewhat randomly since then. The current lodge is thoroughly modern, including two hot tubs large enough for the kids to swim in, a game room, and all of the other amenities you want in ski-and-Yellowstone–area accommodations. The best thing about the place, though, is the restaurant (see "Where to Dine," below). Regular motel rooms, suites, and suites with kitchenettes are available. Ask about ski packages and vacations when making reservations.

P.O. Box 160279, U.S. 191 (about a half mile south of its intersection with Lone Mountain Trail), Big Sky, MT 59716. ⓒ 800/822-4484 or 406/995-4111. Fax 406/995-2191. www.buckst4.com. 74 units. $79–$109 double; $94–$219 suite. AE, DC, DISC, MC, V. Pets accepted with additional fee. **Amenities:** Restaurant, lounge; 2 hot tubs; game room. *In room:* TV w/pay movies, dataport, hair dryer.

Gallatin Gateway Inn ⚘   Located about 28 miles (45km) north of Big Sky on U.S. 191, the Gallatin Gateway Inn is a model of historical elegance from the days of luxury railroad travel. The hotel opened in the summer of 1927, as visitors were beginning to come to Yellowstone in large numbers. The Spanish-style building recalls pre–World War II elegance, and you almost expect to see Winston Churchill relaxing on the porch with a cigar. With lavish appointments that include Polynesian mahogany woodwork, decoratively carved beams, and high arched windows, the Gallatin Gateway has maintained its proud history of lavish style and refinement. The spacious guest rooms provide a tastefully understated balance to the regal lobby and dining room. They maintain the refined historic feel, but have been updated with light colors, providing a more open and airy feeling than you usually find in hotels of this vintage. The restaurant's seasonally changing menu includes regional specialties showcasing ingredients from local growers, and prepares hearty dishes with an eye toward imaginative combinations and generous portions. The wine list is carefully selected to complement the food.

76405 Gallatin Rd. (U.S. 191), P.O. Box 376, Gallatin Gateway, MT 59730. ℂ **800/676-3522** or 406/763-4672. www.gallatingatewayinn.com. 34 units. $85–$175 double. Rates include continental breakfast. AE, DISC, MC, V. **Amenities:** Restaurant, lounge; outdoor pool and whirlpool; angler's casting pond. *In room:* A/C, TV.

Lone Mountain Ranch ★★★ *Kids*

Back before there was even a community of Big Sky there was Lone Mountain Ranch. Started in 1926 as a working cattle ranch, Lone Mountain Ranch rapidly blossomed into a year-round destination as a guest ranch and cross-country ski area.

In the summer, the ranch blends traditional guest-ranch activities—riding, hiking, fishing, and eating—with naturalist programs that will improve your understanding of the Yellowstone ecosystem. They'll not only guide you into the Spanish Peaks, but also into an understanding of wildflowers, bird habits and habitat, and geology. They offer guided fly-fishing trips, and the shop on the premises is an Orvis outlet. Lone Mountain prides itself on a family atmosphere and has separate activities for children, including animal tracking and wildflower pressing. In the winter the ranch is a cross-country ski destination, with 45 miles (72km) of trails (see "Cross-Country Skiing," under "Getting Outside," above).

The accommodations here are varied, from small cabins to the large new Ridgetop Lodge, which can host an entire family reunion. Some of the cabins are quite old, from the original ranch, while the new lodge was built in the 1990s. All are spacious with private bathrooms and attractive pine interiors. They are spread out, assuring quiet and privacy for the guests.

Lone Mountain's restaurant is good, and in the winter, there is a sleigh ride and dinner at the ranch's North Fork cabin. There is a buffet breakfast and lunch each day. Call ℂ **406/995-2782** after 3pm for dinner reservations.

P.O. Box 160069, Big Sky, MT 59716. ℂ **800/514-4644.** Fax 406/995-4670. www.lmranch.com. 24 cabins, 1 lodge, 1 house. Winter: cabin, $1,938–$2,703 first person, $1,173 each additional person; Ridgetop Lodge, $2,856 first person, $1,173 each additional person; Douglas Fir House, $3,417 first person, $1,173 each additional person. Rates include 7 nights' lodging, 3 meals daily, an 8-day trail pass with unlimited access to the ranch's trail system, evening entertainment, a sleigh-ride dinner, a trail buffet lunch, and airport transfers. Summer rates are slightly higher. DISC, MC, V. From Bozeman, head south on U.S. 191 about 40 miles (64km). **Amenities:** Restaurant; massage; cross-country ski and snowshoe trails and lessons; rafting, fishing, hiking, and climbing trips arranged. *In room:* No phone.

River Rock Lodge ★

The River Rock Lodge is a substantial, beautiful rock-and-log structure that delivers Montana style with European service. The rooms are large and beautifully appointed, with all the little extras like evening turndown service, the fax version of the *New York Times,* and cider upon check-in. The place is fairly new, presenting a lodge atmosphere with small-hotel service. There is no restaurant or lounge, but the hotel provides in-room bars and a European-style continental breakfast. The hotel has been a favorite stopover for television personalities such as Jay Leno and Conan O'Brien.

3080 Pine Dr., Big Sky, MT 59716. ℭ 800/995-9966 or 406/995-2295. Fax 406/995-2727. www.river rocklodge.com. 29 units. $100–$275 double. Rates include breakfast. AE, DISC, MC, V. **Amenities:** Outdoor whirlpool tub. *In room:* TV, minibar.

WHERE TO DINE

There are almost two dozen eateries at Big Sky, so you know you won't go hungry. Be aware that the closer you are to the slopes, the more expensive the food is. Restaurants range from simple snack bars dispensing hot dogs and sandwiches to family-style restaurants and the upscale **Huntley Lodge Dining Room** (ℭ 406/995-5783), which has a good breakfast buffet in the morning and fine dining in the evening. Big Sky also has more than a dozen nightspots.

In the **Meadow Village** area, there are about a dozen restaurants, including the **Huckleberry Cafe** (ℭ 406/995-3130), which has the best breakfast in Big Sky (lunches and dinners aren't bad, either); and we also like the **Blue Moon Bakery** (ℭ 406/995-2305), which is also open for all three meals and has good sandwiches and fresh-baked pastries, along with salads, soups, and pizza, and free delivery after 5pm. In the **Gallatin Canyon** area, we suggest the **320 Ranch** (ℭ 406/995-4283), which does a great job with steaks and wild game. It's located at mile marker 36 on U.S. 191, about 11 miles (18km) south of its intersection with Lone Mountain Trail.

Buck's T-4 Restaurant ★★★ CONTEMPORARY AMERICAN Buck's offers an adventurous menu of "Montana cuisine," with about a half dozen wild game dishes, including pan-seared elk chops (a bone-in elk rib chop, pan-roasted and served medium rare), and the New Zealand red deer (a chargrilled filet served with a sauce of Port wine, thyme, and shallots). Our choice here, though, are any of the charbroiled steaks, served with roasted-garlic mashed potatoes. Check the Buck's T-4 website for the complete current menu and some of the restaurant's most requested recipes. For our money, Buck's is in the running for the best-restaurant-in-Montana sweepstakes. Chef Chuck Schommer was the first Montana chef invited to cook at the prestigious James Beard Foundation, and the restaurant has been named one of the top 10 ski-area restaurants (by *Snow Country* magazine) and one of the best restaurants in the Rockies (by the *Chicago Tribune*).

U.S. 191 (about a half mile south of its intersection with Lone Mountain Trail), Big Sky. ℭ 406/995-4111. www.buckst4.com. Reservations recommended. Entrees $15.95–$34.50. AE, DC, DISC, MC, V. Daily 6–9:30pm.

5 Livingston & the Paradise Valley

Livingston: 26 miles (42km) E of Bozeman; 110 miles (177km) W of Billings; 58 miles (93km) N of Mammoth Hot Springs in Yellowstone National Park

Livingston is caught between very cowboy and very hip. As the largest community in the Paradise Valley, it has been discovered by the Hollywood set who want to get away from it all, but unfortunately still bring some of it with them. Peter Fonda has a ranch here. You might see Dennis Quaid or Tom McGuane. Robert Redford is also a fan of the area.

The Paradise Valley is carved out by the Yellowstone River. Along with the two valleys paralleling it to the west—the Gallatin and Madison—this portion of Montana is a fly-fishing paradise. There are lots of fishing guides and tackle shops, and millions of acres to wander in and wonder at.

ESSENTIALS

GETTING THERE   The nearest airport is Bozeman's **Gallatin Field,** 26 miles (42km) west along I-90. It's also possible to fly into Billings' **Logan Airport,** 116 miles (187km) east along I-90.

The Gardiner entrance to Yellowstone National Park is 53 miles (85km) south on U.S. 89. For local road reports, call *C* **406/586-1313.** Bus service is provided by **Greyhound.** The bus depot is at 105 W. Park St. (*C* **406/222-2231**).

VISITOR INFORMATION   The Livingston Chamber of Commerce is located at 303 E. Park St. (*C* **406/222-0850;** www.yellowstone-chamber.com). The **Gardiner Chamber of Commerce** is at 222 W. Park St. (*C* **406/848-7971;** www.gardinerchamber.com). For information on **Yellowstone Country,** Travel Montana's region including Livingston and the Paradise Valley, call *C* **800/736-5276** or 406/556-8680 (www.yellowstone.visitmt.com).

GETTING AROUND   Car-rental agents in Livingston include **Avis** (*C* 406/388-6414), **Hertz** (*C* 406/388-6939), **National** (*C* 406/388-6694), and **Rent-A-Wreck** (*C* 406/587-4551). All have desks at Gallatin Field. Or call a cab at **VIP Taxi** (*C* 406/222-0200).

GETTING OUTSIDE

Much of the outdoor recreation in this area takes place in the **Gallatin National Forest.** Check with the Livingston Ranger District, 5242 U.S. 89 S., Livingston, MT 59047 (*C* **406/222-1892;** www.fs.fed.us/r1/gallatin). Another good source of information on hiking, mountain biking, cross-country skiing, and snowshoeing, as well as equipment rentals and sales, is **Timber Trails Outdoors Co.,** 309 W. Park St. (*C* **406/222-9550**).

CROSS-COUNTRY SKIING & SNOWSHOEING

The most popular spots are in the national forest. For specific locations and current conditions, check with the Livingston Ranger District (see above), or in Livingston at **Timber Trails Outdoors Co.,** 309 W. Park St. (*C* **406/222-9550**), which rents skis and snowshoes and will provide information on trails.

FISHING

Montana has the best trout fishing in the country, and the area around here is the best trout fishing in Montana. Livingston is the gateway to classic Montana fly-fishing in the blue-ribbon Madison River, the Paradise Valley, and the Yellowstone River. **Dan Bailey's Fly Shop,** 209 W. Park St. (*C* **800/356-4052**), in business since 1938, offers all manner of fishing tackle for sale or rent. Bailey's can give you some tips on where to fish on your own, or provide a guide for about $315 a day, depending on where you want to go and how many are in the group. **Hatch Finders Fly Shop,** 113 W. Park St., no. 3 (*C* **406/222-0989**), can tie your custom flies and also provide outfitters almost anywhere in the state. A full-day guided trip in the Yellowstone River area is about $300 for two anglers (plus Montana fishing licenses).

About a quarter-mile (.4km) south of town on U.S. 89, **George Anderson's Yellowstone Angler** (*C* **406/222-7130**) is another fully equipped equipment store and guide service. Anderson also offers a fly-fishing school. About 20 miles (32km) south of Livingston in the town of Pray is **Knoll's Yellowstone Tackle and Fly Shop,** 104 Chicory Rd. (*C* **406/333-4848**). Calling itself an "honest and angler-friendly" shop, here you can learn firsthand how feathers mysteriously become fishing flies, and purchase unique Montana gifts, jams, and jellies.

Take U.S. 89 south to Emigrant then east and northeast on County Road 540 to Pray.

Early-season fishing before runoff starts—in late April and early May—offers excellent dry fly-fishing. In late May and June, the water on most of the rivers is running high and muddy, but the Firehole River in Yellowstone National Park has a heavy early hatch, and the fishing is good. All fishing in the park is catch and release. The rivers drop in July and August, and there are hatches daily for good fishing.

HIKING & BIKING

This area is nearly surrounded by the **Gallatin National Forest,** which has several thousand miles of trails, including more than 800 miles (1,288km) in two designated wilderness areas—the Lee Metcalf and Absaroka-Beartooth. Popular trails that are relatively easily accessible include **Pine Creek Falls** south of town off the East River Road. The falls themselves are a short walk from the campground at the end of the access road, and Pine Creek Lake is about 4 miles (6km) farther along. **Livingston Peak** (or Mount Baldy Trail) is east of town off Swingley Road, and the **Big Timber Canyon Trail** is north of the town of Big Timber. The **Livingston Ranger District of the U.S. Forest Service** and **Timber Trails Outdoors Co.** (see above) can provide information about trails and access routes to them. Timber Trails also rents mountain bikes, starting at about $25 per day.

HORSEBACK RIDING

Wineglass Mountain Trailrides, 5237 U.S. 89 (© **406/222-5599**), features half-day, breakfast, and evening steak rides. **Chico Hot Springs** (© **406/ 333-4933**), about 22 miles (35km) south of Livingston off U.S. 89 to the east, also offers horseback riding.

R.K. Miller's Wilderness Pack Trips, 409 Cokedale Rd. (© **406/222-1717**), offers 7- to 10-day horse-packing trips into Yellowstone National Park. Call for their current schedules and rates.

RAFTING

Both scenic and white-water rafting and kayaking are available on the Yellowstone River throughout the Paradise Valley. **Rubber Ducky River Rentals,** 4 Mount Baldy Dr. (© **406/222-3746**), provides guided trips June through September, or will rent boats and equipment and provide river shuttles. Chico Hot Springs (see "Where to Stay," below) (© **406/333-4933**) also offers raft trips. Call for current schedules and rates.

SEEING THE SIGHTS

The main attractions in downtown Livingston are its three museums (www. livingstonmuseums.org), all of which contain gift shops.

Livingston Depot Center ⭐   This is a beautifully restored 1902 Northern Pacific railway depot, built in handsome Italianate style, that is one of the most stunning railroad stations we've ever seen (it was designed by the same architects that designed Grand Central Station in New York City). The depot houses a museum with exhibits that concentrate on the history of the railroad and how it contributed to the development of the area. There are videos and interactive displays in this thoroughly modern look at the olden days, and the museum also hosts changing exhibits on some aspect of local history, such as explorers Lewis and Clark (the depot is a designated stop on the Lewis and Clark Trail).

200 W. Park St. ⓒ **406/222-2300.** $3 adults, $2 seniors and students, free for children under 6. Usually open late May to Sept only, Mon–Sat 9am–5pm, Sun 1–5pm.

Yellowstone Gateway Museum of Park County   This museum offers exhibits about the early history of Livingston—including an 1889 train caboose, a Yellowstone National Park stagecoach, and exhibits stepping back to the prehistoric people who lived in this area some 10,000 years ago.

118 W. Chinook St. ⓒ **406/222-4184.** $3 adults, $2 seniors and children 6–12, free for kids under 6. Memorial Day–Labor Day, daily 10am–5pm; open by appointment in winter.

International Fly Fishing Center   You'll find some 10,000 flies on display here, plus exhibits on the history of fly-fishing, displays showing the evolution of the fishing rod, fishing-related art, and two aquarium rooms—one containing warm-water species, the other with cold-water fish. The center also offers fly-casting lessons (call for times).

215 E. Lewis St. ⓒ **406/222-9369.** $3 adults, $2 seniors and children 7 to 14, free for children 6 and under. Summer daily 10am–6pm; 10am–4pm the rest of the yr.

SHOPPING

Livingston is a center of Western art and artists, and there are about a dozen galleries in town. For Western wildlife and fly-fishing art, try the **Visions West Gallery** at 108 S. Main St. (ⓒ **406/222-0337**), with wood carvings, bronzes, and original oils. You'll find the work of Russell Chatham, a Livingston artist known for his oils and lithographs of Western landscapes, at the **Chatham Fine Art Gallery,** 120 N. Main St. (ⓒ **406/222-1566**). The **Danforth Gallery,** 106 N. Main St. (ⓒ **406/222-6510**), is a nonprofit gallery of contemporary Western art that changes its exhibits every few weeks in the summer.

WHERE TO STAY

Livingston has several chain motels, including **Comfort Inn,** 114 Loves Lane, Livingston, MT 59047 (ⓒ **800/228-5150** or 406/222-4400), with rates from $55 to $95 double; and **Super 8,** 105 Centennial Dr., Livingston, MT 59047 (ⓒ **800/800-8000** or 406/222-7711), with rates from $50 to $65 double. Rates here are highest in summer.

Chico Hot Springs Resort ⟨⟨   Rambling over 150 magnificent acres in the Paradise Valley, just 30 miles (48km) north of Yellowstone National Park, the Chico offers a taste of gentility, cowboy style. The hot springs were discovered in 1876. The lodge opened in June 1900 and has been going strong ever since. There's a bewildering variety of lodgings from small rooms that share a bathroom to their newest—built in 1999—deluxe rooms, plus rustic log cabins and a five-bedroom, two-bathroom private house. The three-story original Main Lodge is furnished mostly with antiques, and houses the casually elegant restaurant. Two open-air mineral hot-springs pools are just outside and are open daily from 6am to midnight year-round. In the film *Rancho Deluxe*—screenplay by local resident Tom McGuane—Sam Waterston and Jeff Bridges soak in a Chico hot pool in their cowboy hats.

Vegetables are grown in the resort's own hot-spring–heated greenhouses, which are also open for scheduled visits by guests. The **Dining Room at Chico** (dinner reservations recommended) offers large steaks and fresh seafood, a fine wine cellar, and a Sunday brunch. The antelope served here is as tender and tasty as that available anywhere. The **Poolside Grille** offers burgers, soup, salads, and

"E.R.'s famous and fabulous ribs." **E.R.'s Saloon** features barbecued chicken, slow-cooked beef, and more of the famous ribs.

1 Chico Rd., Pray, MT 59065. © **800/468-9232** or 406/333-4933. www.chicohotsprings.com. 104 units. Lodge: $85–$109 double, $45–$60 double with shared bathroom, $119–$189 suite; $75–$85 cabin; $149–$315 private house. DISC, MC, V. Pets accepted, $5 fee. **Amenities:** 2 restaurants, saloon; 2 hot-springs pools; children's programs; horseback riding; rafting; hiking; fishing; evening entertainment in summer; cross-country skiing; dog-sledding. *In room:* No phone.

CAMPING

There are plenty of camping opportunities in the Gallatin National Forest, including **Pine Creek** and **Miller Creek** campgrounds to the south of town toward Yellowstone National Park. For information, contact the Livingston Ranger District, 5242 U.S. 89 S., Livingston, MT 59047 (© **406/222-1892;** www.fs.fed.us/r1/gallatin).

Nine miles south of Livingston on Pine Creek Road is the **Livingston/ Paradise Valley KOA,** 163 Pine Creek Rd., Livingston, MT 59047 (© **800/ 562-2805** or 406/222-0992). Open from May to mid-October, the facility boasts an indoor heated pool, a snack bar, LP gas sales, and a bathhouse. The campground is situated along the Yellowstone River, with shady sites that cost about $18 for tents and $24 to $28 for RVs. **Yellowstone's Edge,** 3502 U.S. 89 S., Livingston, MT 59047 (© **800/865-7322** or 406/333-4036; www.mtrv. com), is located on a bluff overlooking the Yellowstone River. Open from May to mid-October, it has 60-foot pull-through sites that can accommodate large RVs, back-in sites along the river, plus grassy tent sites and a log lodge housing a convenience store, game room, laundry facilities, and the usual bathhouse. There's also a dump station and LP gas available. Tent sites cost $16.50 and RV sites cost $28.50.

WHERE TO DINE

Chatham's Livingston Bar and Grille 🟊🟊 CONTINENTAL   If you're going to eat only one meal in Livingston, this is the place to go. All the locals will direct you here. The walls are decorated with the original paintings of the owner, local artist Russell Chatham, who opened the place in 1996. Some favorites here include the veal-spinach ravioli and the capellini with shrimp.

130 N. Main St., Livingston, MT. © **406/222-7909.** Reservations recommended. Main courses $14–$25. AE, DISC, MC, V. Summer Mon–Sat 5:30–10pm, Sun 5–9:30pm; winter Mon–Sat 5–9:30pm, Sun 4:30–9pm.

Grand Hotel LAMB/SEAFOOD   This beautiful restaurant is located in downtown Big Timber, about 30 miles (48km) east of Livingston, in an 1890 hotel that has been beautifully restored. The main attraction on the extensive menu is Big Timber lamb. The restaurant has also won the *Wine Spectator* Award of excellence 5 years in a row for its all-American wine list of 90 wines. There's also a large selection of Scotch, with 30 different single malts.

139 McLeod, Big Timber. © **406/932-4459.** www.thegrand-hotel.com. Lunch $4–$8; dinner $14–$22. DISC, MC, V. Daily 11am–2pm (Sun brunch) and 5–9pm.

The Sport Restaurant AMERICAN   This early-1900s bar looks and feels much the same as it did back then, with plank floors and animal heads on the walls. It's evolved into a family-friendly place, and our choice for the best spot in town for a burger—they're build-your-own, so you have lots of choices. We also like the charbroiled steaks—all Montana beef—and The Sport also serves seafood and a variety of hot sandwiches. For dessert, try Grandma's Swedish apple pie, topped with locally made vanilla ice cream. Adjoining the restaurant is **The Sport Next Door** (open daily 4pm–2am), a sports bar/night club that serves the same menu as The Sport Restaurant, and also has lots of TVs, keno/poker machines, some video games, two pool tables, and a busy dance floor.

114/116 S. Main St., Livingston. ℂ **406/222-3533.** Lunch $4–$10; dinner $8–$20. MC, V. Mon–Thurs 11am–9pm; Fri–Sat 11am–10pm.

6 Red Lodge & the Absaroka-Beartooth Wilderness

60 miles (97km) SW of Billings; 62 miles (100km) NW of Cody, Wyoming

Nestled in a steep valley at the edge of the Absaroka-Beartooth Wilderness and surrounded by the spectacular Beartooth Mountains, the community of Red Lodge is not quite a tourist town, not quite a destination ski resort, but still not the sleepy little town it once was, either. It has elements of all three, giving it a homey and still busy feel. While it is slowly losing its small-town identity in favor of a resort persona, this hasn't happened completely.

Founded as a coal-mining community in the late 1880s, it did fairly well until the mines closed in the 1930s. Today it's the beautiful scenery and outdoor activities around Red Lodge that attract us. It doesn't hurt that the town sits at the northern end of the Beartooth National Scenic Byway, which the late Charles Kurault called the most beautiful road in America.

ESSENTIALS

GETTING THERE   To reach Red Lodge, you'll have to fly into **Logan International Airport in Billings** (see the section on Billings "Essentials," in chapter 9). From Billings, take I-94 to Laurel, about 16 miles (26km), then go south on U.S. 212–310. The route diverges after about 12 miles (19km) at the small town of Rockvale. Follow U.S. 212 southwest 44 miles (71km) to Red Lodge. Rental cars are rare in town, but **Red Lodge Chevrolet** (ℂ **406/446-2720**) at 210 N. Broadway offers limited rentals. For **road conditions** concerning the Red Lodge area and closures of the Beartooth National Scenic Byway, call ℂ **406/657-0209** or 307/237-8411.

VISITOR INFORMATION   Contact the **Red Lodge Area Chamber of Commerce,** P.O. Box 998, Red Lodge, MT 59068 (ℂ **406/446-1718;** www.redlodge.com).

SPECIAL EVENTS   Each June the **Red Lodge Music Festival** brings professional classical musicians to town and gives local high school students the opportunity to study with them. In August the **Festival of Nations** is a get-together of townsfolk from different cultural backgrounds. The weeklong extravaganza is devoted to residents of Scottish, Scandinavian, Finnish, Italian, Slavic, English, Irish, and German extraction, whose ancestors were brought here during the mining boom days.

Call the Chamber of Commerce (ℂ **406/446-1718**) for specific dates and information about these events.

GETTING OUTSIDE

Many of the outdoor activities in these parts take place in the Custer National Forest. For information, contact the **Beartooth Ranger District Office** of the Custer National Forest, at the south end of town along U.S. 212 (HC49, Box 3420, Red Lodge, MT 59068; ℂ **406/446-2103;** www.fs.fed.us/r1/custer). The office is open from 8am to 5pm daily in summer, and 8am to 4:30pm Monday through Friday in winter.

And They're Off . . . to the Pig Races

Bored with the rodeo? Horse racing make you ho-hum? Just head down to the **Bear Creek Saloon & Steakhouse;** behind the bar is Bearcreek Downs, site of the famed local pig races.

Pig races? After the famous fires in Yellowstone in 1988 created a slow tourist season, the Bear Creek Saloon & Steakhouse owners decided that a **pig race** might generate some visitor interest. There was some question over whether the races were legal, but the Montana legislature stepped in and said pig races were okay by them, provided the proceeds went to charity. So Bearcreek Downs porkers are sending Carbon County students to college—almost $50,000 has gone for scholarships so far. Pig races are held Friday through Sunday at 7pm, from late May to the end of September.

Even if you don't come for the piggy track meet, the **Bear Creek Saloon & Steakhouse** (© 406/446-3481; www.redlodge.com/bearcreek) is a great place to eat. It looks and smells like an authentic Western tavern, and the grub is mostly beef. We especially recommend the charbroiled steaks, such as the 18-ounce T-bone or 8-ounce filet. You can also get a buffalo rib eye, Cajun shrimp, a one-third-pound burger, or chicken. Prices range from $5 to $19.50, and food is served Friday through Sunday from 5 to 10pm. The saloon is 7 miles (11km) east of Red Lodge on County Road 308 in Bear Creek.

GOLF
The **Red Lodge Mountain Golf Course** (© 406/446-3344) is notorious for swallowing golf balls. Water comes into play on 13 of the 18 holes. The signature hole is the 238-yard, par three Number 6, where you hit to an island green from an elevated tee about 80 feet above the hole. The cost is about $28 for 18 holes.

HIKING
There are some popular and challenging day hikes not far from Red Lodge. Drive south on Route 212 about 10 miles (16km) to County Road 2346, then 2 miles (3km) down that road to the **Lake Fork of Rock Creek.** From here you can do a full loop of 19 miles (31km) to the West Fork of Rock Creek trail head (or do it as an overnight backpacking trip), or just walk up a few miles to some great fishing in the streams and lakes along the way and return.

Other popular hikes leave from the trail head at the **West Fork of Rock Creek.** Head west on the road to Red Lodge Mountain Ski Area, known locally as Ski Run Road. When the road forks, stay left and continue for several miles past a number of campgrounds. The road turns to gravel and ends at the Wet Fork trail head. The hike from here to Timberline Lakes is a moderate 9 miles (14km) round-trip. If you're not feeling that energetic, you can hike for about a mile to a picturesque waterfall. The fishing in Lake Mary near the trail is very good.

The **Absaroka-Beartooth Wilderness area** is a 950,000-acre wilderness that extends from the boundary of Yellowstone through two national forests. It's some of the most spectacular country in the Lower 48 states. Because of its proximity to the park, it is heavily used. There are lots of great hikes, incredible vistas, and pristine lakes with excellent trout fishing. **Granite Peak,** at 12,799 feet, is the tallest mountain in Montana, but it's only one of the 28 mountains topping 12,000 feet in the Absaroka-Beartooth.

For information about the above trails, contact the **Beartooth Ranger District Office** (see above).

SKIING

Red Lodge Mountain (Box 750, Red Lodge, MT 59068; *©* **800/444-8977** or 406/446-2610; www.redlodgemountain.com) is a relatively small, family-oriented ski area. But it's growing: The skiable terrain recently increased to 1,600 acres of mountain, and plans are in the works for an additional 400 acres. Vertical drop is 2,400 feet, and more than half the mountain (55%) is rated for intermediate skiers, 15% for beginners, and 30% for advanced. Of the seven lifts, two are new high-speed quads, and plans include eventual replacement of all the old lifts. An average of 250 inches of snow falls each year, plus Red Lodge has one of the largest snowmaking operations in the Rockies, so it frequently has the earliest opening dates in Montana, with top-to-bottom skiing often available by Thanksgiving. Lift tickets cost $36 for adults, $33 for juniors, and $14 for children; a half-day ticket (morning or afternoon) costs $30. The season usually runs from November to the end of April. From Red Lodge, go south on Broadway and turn right at the sign for the ski area. Known locally as Ski Run Road, it has no official name and no street sign. The ski area is 6 miles (10km) up the road.

SEEING THE SIGHTS

As you've read elsewhere in this guide, the **Beartooth National Scenic Byway,** a 64-mile (103km) stretch of U.S. 212 from Red Lodge to Cooke City, is an incredible road that takes you to almost 11,000 feet elevation. Make sure a camera is handy when Pilot Peak comes into view, just outside Cooke City.

Beartooth Nature Center   The Beartooth Nature Center is the only nature center in Montana that provides a home exclusively for animals that have been injured, orphaned, or too accustomed to humans to be returned to the wild. Residents, more than 45 at a recent count, include mountain lions, wolves, coyotes, black bears, sandhill cranes, and other Montana residents or migrants, along with some non-natives (like the Arctic fox) and some domesticated animals. There is also a petting zoo for the kids.

2nd Ave. N., Red Lodge, MT 59068. *©* **406/446-1133.** $6 adults; $3 seniors and children 2–12. Memorial Day–Labor Day 10am–5:30pm; rest of yr. visitors are welcome during morning feeding hr. starting at 10am.

Carbon County Peaks to Plains Museum   Highlights of this well-run and interesting museum include a simulated coal mine that recalls Red Lodge's underground past, and the Greenough Collection of cowboy and rodeo gear. There's also a Crow Indian teepee and camp setup, and pioneer displays. This is the place to find out more about "Liver Eatin'" Johnston, who got his name because . . . no, it's too repulsive. You'll have to find out for yourself.

224 N. Broadway and 8th Ave., Red Lodge, MT 59068. *©* **406/446-1920.** $3 adults, $2 children, free for children 5 and under. Mon–Fri 10am–5pm; Sat–Sun and holidays 1–5pm.

WHERE TO STAY

In addition to the properties discussed below, we recommend the **Comfort Inn of Red Lodge,** 612 N. Broadway, Red Lodge, MT 59068 (*©* **888/733-4661** or 406/446-4469; www.wtp.net/comfortinn), which charges $50 to $110 double.

Chateau Rouge   The Chateau Rouge offers excellent accommodations at a very reasonable price, especially for families. Though run like a motel, the

Chateau Rouge is actually a collection of privately owned condominiums. Most are two-story, two-bedroom affairs with a living room and kitchen on the first floor and the sleeping rooms upstairs. The two-story condos have large, fully appointed kitchens, while the studios have small but complete kitchens. All are attractively decorated and maintained. The only drawback—a minor one in our opinion—is that they are not air-conditioned, which can be uncomfortable on those rare summer days when the mountain temperatures reach the 90s.

1505 S. Broadway, Red Lodge, MT 59608. ℭ **800/926-1601** or 406/446-1601. Fax 406/446-1602. www. chateaurouge.com. 24 units. Winter, $76 studio, $89 2-bedroom condo, $15 for each extra person; summer, $65 studio, $89 2-bedroom condo, $10 for each extra person. AE, DC, DISC, MC, V. **Amenities:** Indoor pool. *In room:* TV.

The Pollard 👍👍   Built in 1893 by the Rocky Fork Coal Company at an initial cost of $20,000, The Pollard has recently undergone a magnificent restoration, integrating modern conveniences with historic character and elegance. It has been a stopover for a number of Old West celebrities, including Buffalo Bill Cody, Calamity Jane, and Jeremiah "Liver Eatin'" Johnston. The Pollard has a three-story gallery with a wood-burning fireplace. Six of the rooms have balconies overlooking the lobby. All the rooms are very large, done with manly oak furniture and ladylike flower-print comforters, and the entire operation is first-class. Many of the rooms have Jacuzzi tubs.

For fine dining in Red Lodge, **Arthur's Grill at the Pollard Hotel** is the best choice. The food is excellent—we suggest the steaks, grilled over a wood fire. Reservations are recommended. Arthur's is open daily from 7:30am to 2pm and 5:30 to 9pm.

2 N. Broadway, Red Lodge, MT 59068. ℭ **800/765-5273** or 406/446-0001. Fax 406/446-0002. www. pollardhotel.com. 38 units. $75–$235 double. AE, DISC, MC, V. **Amenities:** Large health club; sauna; hot tub; 2 racquetball courts. *In room:* A/C, TV/VCR.

Rock Creek Resort 👍👍   This property was built in 1963 as a dormitory for members of an international ski-racing camp founded by owner Pepi Granshammer. Rock Creek retains much of the ski atmosphere that produced it, although the ski hill is a good 6 miles (10km) away. The cedar-sided Beartooth Lodge, the main building, boasts a huge fireplace made of river rock and windows that offer mountain views. There is a wide variety of accommodations, from mountain lodge-style units, with lots of wood, to luxurious condominiums and three-bedroom town houses, decorated in a Western theme. Many units have wood-burning stoves or fireplaces, and patios or balconies. It would be a challenge to find a room here without a wonderful view.

In addition to the Old Piney Dell (see "Where to Dine," below), Rock Creek recently opened the Kiva Restaurant in Beartooth Lodge. It serves breakfast and lunch either on the deck overlooking Rock Creek or in a room walled with windows.

HC 49, Box 3500, Red Lodge, MT 59068. ℭ **800/446-1119** or 406/446-1111. Fax 406/446-3688. www. rockcreekresort.com. 88 units. $88–$295 double. AE, DC, DISC, MC, V. **Amenities:** 2 restaurants; indoor pool; 4 tennis courts; sauna; hot tub; weight room; stocked trout pond; barbecue area; volleyball and horseshoe area; soccer field. *In room:* TV, dataport, some kitchenettes, whirlpools.

CAMPING

There are 16 Forest Service campgrounds available in the Red Lodge area, with sites for over 700 campers. Seven of the larger campgrounds accept reservations through the **National Recreation Reservation Service** (ℭ **877/444-6777;** www.reserveusa.com), and the rest are first-come, first-served. For information, contact the **Beartooth Ranger District Office** of the Custer National Forest, at the south end of town along U.S. 212 (HC 49, Box 3420, Red Lodge, MT 59068; © **406/446-2103**).

Those seeking commercial campgrounds, with all the usual RV hookups and other amenities, can head to the **Red Lodge KOA** (HC 50, Box 5340, Red Lodge, MT 59068; © **406/446-2364**), 4 miles (6km) north of Red Lodge on U.S. 212. It has grassy and shady sites, a heated outdoor pool, and a convenience store, and charges about $20 for tents and $20 to $26 for RVs. It's open from mid-May to early September.

WHERE TO DINE

In addition to the restaurants discussed below, see the sidebar "And They're Off . . . to the Pig Races," above, for information on the **Bear Creek Saloon & Steakhouse;** and the "Where to Stay" section for information on the excellent restaurant at **The Pollard.**

Bogart's MEXICAN/PIZZA   Bogart's menu consists of great sandwiches, Mexican entrees, and pizza. As you might have guessed, the place is named after Humphrey himself. Other than the humble homage of naming sandwiches after some of his movies, don't expect more of a tribute. The chimichangas are toasted to a golden turn, and the chiles rellenos are excellent.

11 S. Broadway. © 406/446-1784. Reservations not accepted. Most dishes $6–$15. MC, V. Daily 11am–9pm.

Bridge Creek Restaurant and Wine Bar ECLECTIC   Bridge Creek is a local favorite, with a widely varied, moderately priced menu. Lunches include wraps, salads, sandwiches on fresh-baked breads, and homemade soups. At dinner you'll find fish, chicken, steaks, chops, and pasta. The wine bar is a small, bright room with an extensive wine list that for several years has received the *Wine Spectator* award of excellence. The atmosphere is casual; sort of California cafe with a Western flavor. New in 2001 is a coffee bar, serving a wide selection of espresso, cappuccino, latte, mocha, and iced drinks plus freshly baked pastries from 7am Monday through Saturday.

116 S. Broadway Ave. © 406/446-9900. Lunch $4–$9; dinner $10–$20. MC, V. Mon–Thurs 11am–9pm; Fri–Sat 11am–9:30pm.

Old Piney Dell ★★★ *Finds* INTERNATIONAL/WESTERN   Located in a quaint, low-ceilinged cabin on the banks of Rock Creek, this is where locals come for a special evening. Both the service and food are excellent, and there's jazz playing in the background. If you like Wiener schnitzel, this place is for you—the veal is lightly breaded and delicately pan-fried to perfection. And the steaks: the bleu cheese–crusted tenderloin practically melts in your mouth and the grilled New York strip in peppercorn butter satisfies the heartier appetite. There's also chicken, pork, and fish on the menu. Ask about the daily mixed grill and pasta specials, created from the best find of the day. Their homemade desserts add the right finish to any meal.

In Rock Creek Resort, 6 miles (10km) south of Red Lodge. © 406/446-1111. www.rockcreekresort.com. Reservations recommended. Dinner $15.75–$22.50. Mon–Thurs 5:30–9pm; Fri–Sat 5:30–10pm.

9

Billings & Eastern Montana

The plains of eastern Montana offer a more subtle beauty than the rugged mountains to the west. A land of rolling hills, dusty bluffs, and an occasional rock-walled canyon, this is classic cattle and wheat country, with grass thick and green in spring, brown and dry by fall, and blanketed by snow in winter. Temperatures can be extreme; hot in the summer under a blazing sun, and bitter cold in the winter, dipping below zero for long stretches.

Eastern Montana's history is rich: Lewis and Clark trekked along the Missouri River, and one of the most famous battles of the American West, the Battle of the Little Bighorn, was fought here.

In the old days, travel in eastern Montana was defined by the railroads. Virtually every town with 300 people and a tavern could be reached by either the main line or a spur. But the romantic days of rail travel have been replaced by the automobile, and interstates rival the rails. I-94 sweeps across the state west to east, I-15 cuts through the Rockies from Idaho to the Canadian border, and I-90 dips south from near Billings to the Crow Reservation in Sheridan, Wyoming.

1 Billings

104 miles (167km) W of Cody, Wyoming; 123 miles (198km) N of Sheridan, Wyoming; 142 miles (229km) E of Bozeman; 339 miles (546km) E of Missoula

The most populous city in Montana, Billings rivals Missoula for the honor of being the "most citified" place in the state. You'll find real shopping malls here, along with the tallest freestanding hotel west of the Mississippi, and the occasional five o'clock traffic jam. Since its 1880s development by Frederick Billings as a railroad town, the city has evolved into the economic hub for much of the eastern portion of the state and parts of northern Wyoming.

Once a booming oil town, as well as a crossroads for the railroads, Billings has now positioned itself as the progressive regional medical center for all of eastern Montana, the Dakotas, and Wyoming. The economy is still based on cattle and grain, but downtown Billings boasts new banks and contemporary business centers, plus beautiful historic buildings in various stages of restoration. Billings also has its share of scenic splendor: From the heights of the city you can see three mountain ranges—the Pryor Mountains, the Bighorns, and the majestic Beartooths to the west.

ESSENTIALS
GETTING THERE Billings' **Logan International Airport** is the state's busiest, located about 2 miles (3km) north of downtown. Service is provided by **Big Sky Airlines** (✆ 800/237-7788 or 406/245-2300), **Delta** (✆ 800/221-1212), **Horizon** (✆ 800/547-9308), **Northwest** (✆ 800/225-2525), and **United** (✆ 800/241-6522).

Eastern Montana

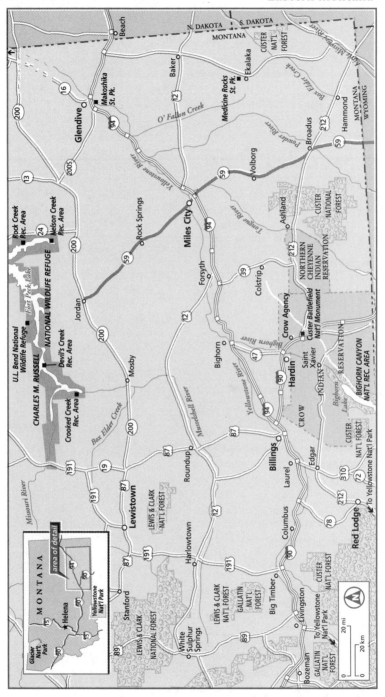

245

If you're traveling by car, I-90 connects Billings to Bozeman, Butte, and Missoula in the west before crossing into Idaho; I-90 east heads southeast into Wyoming. I-94 branches off I-90 10 miles (16km) east of town and runs northeast through Miles City and Glendive before reaching North Dakota. U.S. 87 heads north out of Billings to Roundup, and U.S. 310 goes south to Lovell, Wyoming.

VISITOR INFORMATION   The **Billings Area Chamber of Commerce & Visitor Center,** 815 S. 27th St. (P.O. Box 31177), Billings, MT 59107 (✆ **800/ 735-2635** or 406/245-4016; www.billingscvb.visitmt.com), has brochures, maps, and area information. The area is also part of Travel Montana's **Custer Country** (✆ **800/346-1876** or 406/628-1432; www.custer.visitmt.com).

GETTING AROUND   Billings' downtown street system might be a bit confusing at first, but can be mastered if you remember that Montana Avenue is the dividing line between north and south. Numbered avenues run parallel to Montana, starting with 1st North and South 1 block each side of it and increasing from there. The numbered streets run perpendicular to Montana, changing from north to south as they cross it, and increase numerically from east to west. The heart of downtown lies north of Montana and is relatively compact. Its boundaries are North 27th and North 29th Streets and 1st and 6th Avenues North.

To access downtown from I-90, which skims the southern edge of the city, take exit 450 and go north on 27th Avenue; the Business Loop follows Montana Avenue between exits 446 and 452. Coming from the north, from Roundup, U.S. 87 turns into a four-lane road before heading west into the Heights, the northeastern part of the city. Follow this road into downtown, or turn right on Airport Road to reach Logan International Airport.

The best way to see Billings is to drive. Car-rental companies at the airport include **Avis** (✆ **800/831-2847** or 406/252-8007), **Budget** (✆ **800/527-0800** or 406/259-4168), **Hertz** (✆ **800/654-3131** or 406/248-9151), and **National** (✆ **800/227-7368** or 406/252-7626).

The city bus service is **Billings Met Transit** (✆ **406/657-8218**). Taxi service is available from **City Cab** (✆ **406/252-8700**), **Yellow Cab** (✆ **406/ 245-3033**), and **Silver Eagle Shuttle** (✆ **406/252-8700**).

GETTING OUTSIDE
FISHING
Though the Yellowstone River runs through the city, it is wide, busy, and often muddy. The best nearby fishing is in the **Bighorn Canyon National Recreation Area** (see section 3, later in this chapter). Fishing guides come and go pretty often in the Billings area, so to find a local one the best bet is to check with **The Base Camp,** 1730 Grand Ave. (✆ **406/248-4555**).

GOLF
Lake Hills Golf Club (✆ **406/252-9244**) and the **Peter Yegen, Jr. Golf Club** (✆ **406/656-8099**) are the two 18-hole public golf courses in Billings. **Circle Inn Golf Links** (✆ **406/248-4201**) and **Par 3 Exchange City Golf Course** (✆ **406/652-2553**) are public par-three courses. The private 27-hole **Pryor Creek Golf Course** (✆ **406/256-0626**) and, one of the best courses in the state, the 18-hole **Briarwood Country Club** (✆ **406/248-2702**), offer limited public play. Call ahead for availability.

NEARBY PARKS & NATURE PRESERVES
An unusual side trip is to **Pictograph Caves State Park,** where you can see cave paintings made by prehistoric people over 4,500 years ago. There are over 100

Billings

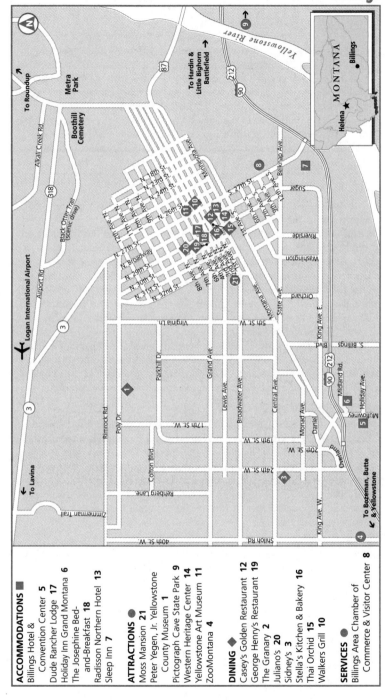

ACCOMMODATIONS

Billings Hotel &
  Convention Center **5**
Dude Rancher Lodge **17**
Holiday Inn Grand Montana **6**
The Josephine Bed-
  and-Breakfast **18**
Radisson Northern Hotel **13**
Sleep Inn **7**

ATTRACTIONS

Moss Mansion **21**
Peter Yegen, Jr. Yellowstone
  County Museum **1**
Pictograph Cave State Park **9**
Western Heritage Center **14**
Yellowstone Art Museum **11**
ZooMontana **4**

DINING

Casey's Golden Restaurant **12**
George Henry's Restaurant **19**
The Granary **2**
Juliano's **20**
Sidney's **3**
Stella's Kitchen & Bakery **16**
Thai Orchid **15**
Walkers Grill **10**

SERVICES

Billings Area Chamber of
  Commerce & Visitor Center **8**

Black Otter Trail Scenic Drive

The Black Otter Trail Scenic Drive, following about 3 miles (5km) along the edge of the sheer rimrock overlooking Billings, affords a spectacular view of the city and the three mountain ranges in the distance. To get there, take Montana Ave. east to U.S. 87 and turn left (north). After you pass Metro Park on your right, turn left onto Airport Road, and shortly thereafter, left again onto Black Otter Trail. Boot Hill Cemetery is at this end of the road, and contains 40 of the unlucky residents of the town of Coulson, most of whom "died with their boots on." It's also the final resting place of the famous scout, Yellowstone Kelly, who asked to be buried here above the land he scouted.

pictographs, in red and black pigments made from ashes, clay, and animal fat. The meaning of the designs is continually debated—were they ceremonial, or perhaps celebrations of a successful hunt or battle (there are many images of shield-bearing warriors)? A short, but fairly steep, interpretive trail leads up to the caves, which are more like large stone alcoves than caves in the usual sense. They lie in a classic, sheer, broad sandstone canyon inhabited by rabbits and an occasional rattlesnake—so stay on the trail. From Billings, take I-90 to exit 452 and follow the signs for 6 miles (10km). The park is open from 8am to 8pm from April 15 to October 1, and has an entrance fee of $4 per vehicle. In season, call ✆ 406/252-4654 for information.

Locals go to nearby **Lake Elmo State Park,** 10 miles (16km) north of Billings on U.S. 87 (✆ 406/247-2955), for picnicking, swimming, windsurfing, fishing, and volleyball. Boat rentals and windsurfing lessons are available in the summer; gas-powered boats are prohibited. Entrance fee is $1 per person over age 6.

SEEING THE SIGHTS

To view some modern artists' contributions to decorating the West, drive the **Avenue of the Sculptures** along 27th Street (from I-90 exit 450 to the airport) for an outdoor art show. The first work, *The Cattle Drive Monument,* is right outside the Chamber of Commerce's visitor center. *The Trough,* a contemporary piece that looks like a fragment of collapsed concrete, is in front of the Norwest Bank Building at 175 N. 27th. *The Sheriff Webb Memorial Marker* is on the courthouse lawn, and finally, in front of the airport is the *Range Rider of the Yellowstone,* posed for by silent-screen cowboy actor William Hart.

The Moss Mansion   This massive red-sandstone, three-story mansion, built in 1901 for Billings banker Preston B. Moss, was designed by prominent New York architect Henry Janeway Hardenbaugh. It has many European influences, including a Moorish entry, a Shakespearean library, and a French Louis XVI parlor. Oak and mahogany millwork gives an elegant feel to the upstairs bedrooms. The mansion, listed on the National Register of Historic Places, has been used in various TV miniseries and Hollywood films, and was featured on A&E's *America's Castles* in 1997. Visitors view a short video about Moss and early Billings before taking the 1-hour guided tour of the home. The Moss Mansion also hosts various events during the spring and summer months, and is elaborately decorated for Christmas.

914 Division St. ✆ 406/256-5100. www.mossmansion.com. $6 adult, $5 senior, $3 children 6–12. MC, V. Summer, guided tour every hour on the hour, Mon–Sat 9am–4pm, plus 1 evening tour Wed 7pm, Sun 1–3pm; winter, daily 1–3pm. Closed Thanksgiving, Christmas, and New Year's Day.

Western Heritage Center A lot of Western museums are just vast collections of dusty reminders of bygone eras. But this facility has done an excellent job of interpreting and editing its extensive collection, making the panoramic history of Western settlement accessible to casual visitors. In addition to the usual exhibits of the area's settlement by white people, the Heritage Center includes sensitive displays on the Crow tribe and on Japanese and other minority settlers. Interactive presentations include videos and recorded memories of three Yellowstone County homesteaders. The museum also has an outreach program, revolving shows, and a gift shop.

2822 Montana Ave. © **406/256-6809**. www.ywhc.org. Free admission. Tues–Sat 10am–5pm; Sun 1–5pm.

Peter Yegen, Jr. Yellowstone County Museum The museum, located next to the airport, has a large collection housed in a 104-year-old cabin, which has had such eminent visitors as Teddy Roosevelt and Buffalo Bill Cody. Rotating exhibits describe the history and diverse cultures of Montana and the Yellowstone River Basin, from prehistory through the 1950s. At any one time, these might include the Northern Plains Indians, American expansion into the West, mining, the herding and transportation industries, the military from 1870 to the 1950s, plus household and personal goods. The recently opened Lewis and Clark Fur Trading Post exhibit is fascinating, with its displays of trade goods and fur-trader accoutrements. There are changing exhibits of contemporary local and national artists in the Landmarks Gallery. Also on the grounds, for the mechanically minded, is a vintage steam engine; and the view of Billings and the surrounding countryside from the museum's deck is terrific.

1950 Terminal Circle, adjacent to Logan International Airport. © **406/256-6811**. www.pyjrycm.org. Free admission. Mon–Fri 10:30am–5pm; Sat 10:30am–3pm. Closed legal holidays.

Yellowstone Art Museum 🏛🏛 Montana art aficionados are justifiably proud of the Yellowstone Art Museum, a leader in the contemporary Western art movement. The museum showcases the best the new West has to offer, from Deborah Butterfield's ranch sculptures to Russell Chatham's gauzy landscapes to Rudy Autio's colorful, erotic ceramics. Additionally, the museum's permanent collection—some 2,000 pieces—includes the largest public gathering of the drawings, paintings, books, and memorabilia of cowboy illustrator Will James, plus paintings and drawings by other historic regional artists such as J.H. Sharp and Charles M. Russell. Changing exhibitions have included the William I. Koch Collection, which featured works by Degas, Monet, Picasso, Dalí, and Chagall, plus a number of Greek and Roman antiquities; a display of works depicting the Hudson River School—Albert Bierstadt, John Kensett, and Thomas Cole; and a wonderful exhibit representing American art from 1719 to 1989, which included works by Rembrandt Peale, Winslow Homer, and Andy Warhol. Thursday at noon there's a docent-led museum tour. The Museum Store is outstanding and offers pottery and other regional crafts; a children's area, stationery and postcards; lovely jewelry, textiles, and clothing; plus posters, books, and educational items.

401 N. 27th St. © **406/256-6804**. http://yellowstone.artmuseum.org. $3 adults. Tues–Wed 10am–5pm; Thurs 10am–8pm; Fri–Sat 10am–5pm; Sun noon–5pm.

SHOPPING

In the downtown area, the shopping district covers about 4 blocks on North 29th Street, Broadway, and 1st and 2nd Avenues North. The area is heavy in the antiques line, but it also has a few boutiques and independent bookshops. The **Yesteryear Antique and Craft Mall,** 114–118 N. 29th St. (© **406/259-3314**), is the first stop for collectors. You can find old bones, fine Western writing desks,

(Kids   **Especially for Kids: Animals, Animals**

ZooMontana   The only wildlife and botanical park within 500 miles (800km) of Billings, this ambitious zoo covers 70 acres and is continually changing and growing. There are nature trails meandering among the natural habitats of Siberian tigers, red pandas, eastern gray wolves, Manchurian sika deer, bald eagles, great horned owls, black-footed ferrets, and the North American river otter; there's a petting zoo in a farm and ranch setting, a Discovery Center, and Nature Store.

Current exhibits include bald eagles, river otters, and two of the 300 Siberian tigers remaining in the world. The zoo also has two black-footed ferrets (North America's rarest mammal), and is planning an extensive high plains habitat exhibit. The zoo is also concentrating on northern plains wildlife, some of which you may see on your trip through the state.

Take exit 443 north off I-90, head northwest on King Avenue to Shiloh Road, then south (*©* **406/652-8100**; www.zoomontana.org). Admission is $5 adults, $2 children 3 to 15, $3 seniors over 65. Open daily in summer, from 10am to 8pm; winter, daily from 10am to 4pm. Closed Thanksgiving, Christmas, and New Year's Day.

and American Indian artifacts and jewelry. There are numerous antiques shops in Billings, and the Chamber of Commerce has the *Antiquers Trail Guide of Greater Billings,* showing the location of more than two dozen stores.

For contemporary art, try the **Toucan Gallery,** 2505 Montana Ave. (*©* **406/ 252-0122**), in the city's historic district, offering prints, oils, handmade furniture, and ceramics.

The fashion conscious can find clothing from around the world at the **Cactus Rose,** 202 N. 29th St. (*©* **406/252-9126**). The classic Western department store, where lots of real cowboys get their gear, is **Lou Taubert Ranch Outfitters** (*©* **406/245-2248**), at 123 Broadway. For outdoor clothing and equipment, check out **The Base Camp** (*©* **406/248-4555**), at 1730 Grand Ave.

WHERE TO STAY

In addition to the properties discussed below, you might consider the **Holiday Inn Grand Montana,** 5500 Midland Rd. (I-90 exit 446), Billings, MT 59101 (*©* **877/554-7263** or 406/248-7701) with rates for two of $79 to $129; or the **Sleep Inn,** 4904 Southgate Dr. (I-90 exit 447), Billings, MT 59101 (*©* **800/ 753-3746** or 406/254-0013) with rates for two of $55 to $75.

Billings Hotel and Convention Center   This is just what you might expect from an upscale convention center in a Western city: The large lobby is graced by a grand piano and a freestanding fireplace; and rooms are very comfortable— large with modern country decor.

1223 Mullowney Lane, off I-90 at exit 446, Billings, MT 59101. *©* **406/248-7151.** 241 units. $79–$100 double; $99–$200 suite. AE, DC, DISC, MC, V. Small pets accepted with $50 deposit. **Amenities:** Restaurant, lounge; heated indoor pool; whirlpool; exercise room; game room; volleyball. *In room:* A/C, TV w/pay movies, dataport, coffeemaker, radio; some units microwave, fridge.

Dude Rancher Lodge   The Dude Rancher has been offering real Western hospitality since it opened in 1949. The rooms, which surround an inner courtyard, are comfortable and quiet, with ranch oak furniture and king- and queen-size beds. Its downtown location puts you within walking distance of numerous restaurants, shopping, banks, the library, and the Alberta Bair Theatre.

415 N. 29th St., Billings, MT 59101. © 800/221-3302 or 406/259-5561. www.duderancherlodge.com. 57 units. $48–$63 double. AE, DISC, MC, V. **Amenities:** Restaurant. *In room:* A/C, cable TV.

The Josephine Bed-and-Breakfast   For a trip back to the elegance of 100 years ago, book a room at The Josephine. Named for a steamboat that once plied the waters of the Yellowstone between here and St. Louis, this B&B is located within walking distance of downtown, offering a quiet retreat amid Billings' urban bustle. Owners Doug and Becky Taylor have put a modern whirlpool tub in one room, but most rooms feature the classic, high-sided, claw-foot tubs familiar to Western movie buffs. The Captain's Room offers a masculine feel, from the pipes on the night table (but don't light one up; the entire inn is no-smoking) to the four-poster bed. The other rooms have more feminine touches. There are a library, parlor, and dining room for breakfast, and a wraparound porch where you can sit and read. Breakfasts are memorable: Doug's signature dish is a fantastic cheese strata—but don't turn up your nose if you happen to be there on the day he makes champagne waffles.

514 N. 29th St., Billings, MT 59101. © 800/552-5898 or 406/248-5898. www.thejosephine.com. 5 units. $75–$160 double. AE, DISC, MC, V. *In room:* A/C, cable TV, dataport.

Radisson Northern Hotel   The Northern Hotel has long been Billings' land-mark hotel, going back to the days of the railroaders. It was the finest place to stay from its construction in 1902 until it was destroyed by fire in 1940—although it was rebuilt almost immediately. Early dignitaries who stayed here include painter C.M. Russell, Teddy Roosevelt, and Prince Olaf of Sweden. A recent renovation retained and polished its elegance and style. It has a contemporary Western flair, but isn't pushy about it. For business travelers who have to use their computers, it is excellent, with comfortable desks, accessible power outlets, and dataports on the phones in the suites. The parlor suites come with 6-foot conference tables. The Golden Belle is an elegant restaurant, and there's live music in the saloon, which is patronized by lots of long and lean cowboy types.

Broadway and 1st Ave. N., Billings, MT 59101. © 800/542-5121 or 406/245-5121. 160 units. $99 double; $109 junior suite; $129 parlor suite. AE, DC, DISC, MC, V. **Amenities:** Restaurant, saloon; exercise room. *In room:* A/C, TV.

WHERE TO DINE
EXPENSIVE

The Granary 🐾🐾 STEAKS/SEAFOOD   This dimly lit establishment is the place for those who take their beef very seriously. Among the most popular, most recommended, and most expensive restaurants in Billings, since 1980 The Granary has been serving wet-aged, hand-cut beef. We especially recommend the New York steak—we like it grilled, but you can also get it blackened—and the slow-cooked prime rib—seasoned just enough for our taste. Those who pre-fer seafood should like the halibut, available steamed, blackened, grilled, or sautéed, and everyone seems to love the shrimp. Alaskan king crab is a popular special (usually offered Wed). The outside deck is a favorite of many locals just wanting to quaff late-afternoon beers and cocktails.

1500 Poly Dr. © 406/259-3488. Reservations recommended on weekends and Wed. Main courses $15–$35. AE, DISC, MC, V. Mon–Sat 5:30–10pm; Sun 5:30–9pm.

Juliano's ★★★ PACIFIC RIM/CONTEMPORARY AMERICAN   Quite possibly the best restaurant in Montana, Juliano's serves excellent, original food in a casually elegant atmosphere. It's a little hard to categorize the food here. Chef Carl Kurokawa is a native of Hilo, Hawaii, and his menu describes the cuisine as "Fun American with European and Asian influences." Privately, Kurokawa says to call it "Carl food." The menu changes monthly, but you can depend on it having the fresh Hawaiian fish that Kurokawa insists on flying in. For dinner you might get Montana ostrich or Rocky Mountain elk, or maybe steak topped with crab cakes. At lunch there are salads—if you're feeling adventurous, try the grilled salmon and spicy watermelon salad—plus sandwiches and pasta dishes. The building was originally the stable of the sandstone "castle" next door, built in 1902. A pressed-tin ceiling with Bacchus hoisting a glass covers one of the dining rooms, and there is an outdoor patio for nice days. There is an extensive wine list, and about six times a year special wine dinners are presented (call for dates).

2912 7th Ave. N. ✆ **406/248-6400.** Lunch items $6.95–$7.95; dinner entrees $13.95–$23.95. AE, DC, DISC, MC, V. Mon–Fri 11:30am–2pm; Wed–Sat 5:30–9pm.

MODERATE

George Henry's Restaurant AMERICAN   Housed in an 1882 home, the ambience of George Henry's recalls a 1920s tearoom with a lot of stained glass and Old World charm. The food is mainly innovative and well-prepared variations on American standards, with a fairly extensive menu. The Steak Oscar—an 8-ounce filet mignon topped with crab, asparagus, and Béarnaise sauce—is a popular dinner choice, but we especially recommend the broiled Grecian-style lamb chops. You also might like the orange roughy (broiled with a Parmesan crust) or the pan-fried walleye pike, topped with slivered almonds and a lemon-dill sauce. Desserts, such as the strawberry shortcake torte, are all homemade. The lunch menu includes lots of salads, plus sandwiches, burgers, and our choice—the quiche of the day.

404 N. 30th. ✆ **406/245-4570.** Main courses lunch $5–$7.50; dinner $10–$20. AE, DISC, MC, V. Mon–Fri 11am–2pm and 5:30–9pm; Sat 5:30–9pm.

Sidney's *Kids* PASTA/PIZZA   With the freshest possible ingredients, including their own handmade pasta, Sidney's has created a menu of matchless taste, in every sense of the word. The coconut chicken from their pasta selection is a feast for the palate and eyes, with vegetables and angel-hair pasta highlighted by subtle flavors of coconut, lime, and red curry. Popular pizza choices include the Mediterranean and the fajita chicken. But don't be put off if you've got kids in tow—Sidney's is family friendly, with children's portions and even a peanut-butter-and-jelly pizza (I guess you gotta be a kid to appreciate that), plus a friendly, cheerful staff. The decor is Southwestern fresh, with stucco walls painted in an adobe-colored wash and teal umbrellas covering the patio tables outside. The location at the mall makes this place even more popular, so if you don't want to wait, be sure to come early.

300 S. 24th St. W., Rimrock Mall. ✆ **406/652-6000.** Lunch $5–$10; dinner $8–$12. AE, DC, DISC, MC, V. Mon–Thurs 10am–10pm; Fri–Sat 10am–11pm; Sun 10am–8pm.

Stella's Kitchen and Bakery AMERICAN   Serving breakfast and lunch, this combination bakery and restaurant (take it out or eat it there) has been making delicious homemade baked goods since the mid-1980s. They make melt-in-your-mouth cinnamon rolls that are a meal (or two) in themselves, plus yummy cookies, and plate-sized pancakes. They even stone grind wheat for their whole-wheat breads—homemade wholesome is their motto.

110 N. 29th St. ✆ **406/248-3060.** Breakfast $3–$8; lunch $5–$9. MC, V. Mon–Sat 6am–4pm; bakery 6am–6pm.

Thai Orchid THAI   This long-established Billings restaurant has moved downtown, and the dark burgundy walls are a soothing backdrop for the hot and spicy Thai meals. The chef serves his own regional specialties such as yellow curry (mildest), red curry (medium), and green curry (hottest), plus several ethnic curries like Panang, massaman, and purple curry with pineapple. If you're feeling adventuresome, try their special Thai Hot Wings—you'll never go back to those tame old buffalo wings. There is a daily all-you-can-eat luncheon buffet that's very popular with the downtown office crowd, so get there early to avoid the crush. Beer and wine are served, including specialty Asian ones.

2926 2nd Ave N. © **406/256-2206.** Lunch and dinner $6–$10; buffet $6. MC, V. Mon–Fri 11am–2pm and 5–10pm.

Walkers Grill AMERICAN BISTRO   Walkers offers a San Francisco–coastal feel here on the plains. The restaurant is done in an understated light wood, with a hint of a Japanese motif, and diners can see into the kitchen from the dining room. The original chef has moved on, but his two assistants, whom he trained, have taken over and the food remains very good. From spring into early summer, people come especially for the morel mushrooms served in a port-cream reduction. We enjoyed the apricot and chipotle–glazed pork medallions with peach-apricot chutney, and the chicken breast stuffed with thinly sliced ham, mozzarella, and Swiss in a light lemon and pepper sauce. If Montana lamb is a special the day you're there, be sure to order it—it's a real treat. The wine list is very extensive, including many French wines—often difficult or impossible to find on the plains. Definitely a place that attracts locals—all the diners seem to know each other.

301 N. 27th St. © **406/245-9291.** Reservations recommended. Main courses $9.25–$22.50. AE, DISC, MC, V. Mon–Sat 5–10pm.

BILLINGS AFTER DARK

Casey's Golden Restaurant, 222 N. Broadway (© **406/256-5200**), has been around since 1935. It features a blend of blues, jazz, reggae, and rock music, leavened with Cajun food, including the "famous gumbo" (food is served 11:30am–11pm). On Monday nights, there is an open mike, and the locals come in to jam, as do some of the famous touring musicians. The stage has been visited by B.B. King, Chuck Mangione, Vince Gill, and Wynton Marsalis. The 3,000-square-foot ceiling Mural of Musicians pays tribute to legendary musicians—Buddy Holly, Billie Holiday, Bob Marley, and many more. One night a mysterious stranger in a dark trench coat sat down at the piano and proceeded to blow the room away with runaway blues. Then he got up and walked out. Never said a word. Never seen again. There are also pool tables, poker and keno video games, shuffleboard, and a gift shop—something for everybody. Casey's is open Monday through Saturday nights.

A SIDE TRIP TO POMPEY'S PILLAR

A 150-foot-high sandstone butte 29 miles (47km) east of Billings holds the only concrete evidence left along the way of the famous journey of Lewis and Clark through the Louisiana Purchase. On July 25, 1806, Capt. William Clark carved his name and the date on the side of the rock. He noted in his famous journals for that day, "The nativs have ingraved on the face of this rock figures of animals &c near which I marked my name and the day of the month and year." Clark then walked to the top and described the panoramic view of the river and plains that can be captured from the top. Clark had to scramble up through the yucca and sagebrush, but visitors now are aided by stairways and enthusiastic and

informative volunteer guides who will point out the historic sites and wildlife—
from ant lions to eagles' nests.

Clark's name is now locked under a protective glass cabinet, but many others
have added their names. The pillar was originally called Pompy's Tower by
Clark, using the nickname he'd given the youngest member of their expedition,
little Baptiste Charbonneau, the son of Sacajawea and Touissaint Charbonneau,
the expedition guides. The boy traveled in Clark's dugout, and the captain called
him "my boy Pomp."

The park, operated by the Bureau of Land Management, is open from Memorial Day to Labor Day, from 8am to 8pm; then into early October from 9am to
5pm; after that you have to park a half-mile away and walk in. The fee is $3 per
carload during the season; free at other times. For more information call the visitor center (© 406/875-2233). To get there, go 29 miles (47km) east of Billings
to I-94 exit 23.

2 The Crow Reservation

54 miles (87km) E of Billings

The beautiful Crow Reservation—the Crow People call themselves the
Apsaalooke, "Children of the Large-Beaked Bird"—encompasses 3,565 square
miles in southeastern Montana. It consists of seven main communities, of which
Crow Agency, on I-90, is the hub of tribal management and government.

One of the main Indian Nation events of the summer-long powwow trail is
Crow Fair, in August. Powwows are social gatherings featuring traditional food,
dress, and dances. Visitors are welcome at powwows, but flash photography is
not allowed during contests, and you should always ask dancers for permission
before taking their photographs. For more information contact the **Tribal
Headquarters,** P.O. Box 159, Crow Agency, MT 59022 (© 406/638-2601).

The most famous and historic site here is the **Little Bighorn Battlefield** (see
"Little Bighorn Battlefield National Monument," below), a somewhat ironic
inclusion on this reservation. The Crow scouted for Custer, and the Little Bighorn
is the site of the cavalry's most infamous defeat at the hands of the Indians.

A good place to learn about the Crow culture is at **Chief Plenty Coups State
Park** (© 406/252-1289). The tribe's last traditional chief, Chief Plenty Coups
deeded his home and lands as a memorial to the Crow Nation, and the museum
houses many of the Crow leader's personal items plus interpretive displays about
the Crow people. The park is in the town of Pryor, and the easiest access is from
Billings. Drive about 25 miles (40km) south on Mont. Highways 416 and 418
to Pryor, then go a mile west, following signs. There are picnic facilities but no
overnight camping. It's open May through September daily from 8am to 8pm;
visitor center 8am to 5pm. Entrance fee is $1 per person.

3 Bighorn Canyon National Recreation Area

Fort Smith: 83 miles (134km) SE of Billings

Over eons, the Bighorn River carved a steep, sheer canyon out of the rolling
plains of present-day southeastern Montana and into northwestern Wyoming.
The construction of the Yellowtail Dam—named for Crow chairman Robert
Yellowtail—near Fort Smith on the Crow Reservation, not only provides power
and irrigation, but also marvelous recreational opportunities on and around 71-
mile-long (114km) Bighorn Lake. Established on October 15, 1966, the

Bighorn Canyon National Recreation Area encompasses over 70,000 acres and straddles the Montana–Wyoming border.

The lake and recreation area are remote and not easy to get to, requiring long drives on winding roads through small towns. The Wyoming and Montana portions of the recreation area are not connected by a road, although a boater can cruise easily up and down the reservoir. But it's worth the effort to get here: Steep walls soar above the deep waters, and there's superb water fun, some hiking, and tremendous photo opportunities.

ESSENTIALS

ACCESS POINTS   There are two portions of the recreation area and two different access points. On the **Montana** side, from Billings, exit I-90 at Hardin and follow Route 313 south to Fort Smith and Yellowtail Dam.

The **Wyoming** section is accessed about 3 miles (5km) east of Lovell. From I-90 north of Sheridan, head west on U.S. 14 and turn north on Wyo. 37. The route is well marked.

FEES   The daily entrance fee is $5.

VISITOR INFORMATION   Contact **Bighorn Canyon National Recreation Area,** P.O. Box 7458, Fort Smith, MT 59035 (© **406/666-2412;** www.nps. gov/bica).

Bighorn Canyon has visitor centers with exhibits and a descriptive film in each of its sections. The **Yellowtail Visitor Center** (© **406/666-3234**) at the Yellowtail Dam in **Montana** is open from 8am to 5pm daily from Memorial Day to Labor Day; weekends only through mid-September and in May. You can take a guided tour into the dam, view the 1,480-foot-long dam, and, for those who don't suffer from vertigo, look down the 525 feet to the river below.

Near Lovell, Wyoming, the **Bighorn Canyon Visitors Center** (© **307/ 548-2251**) is open daily year-round from 8:15am to 5pm. The facility has a large relief map of the area and a gift shop.

REGULATIONS & WARNINGS   The park has a number of black bears, which are not generally as dangerous to people as grizzlies, but can cause problems when they learn that humans carry food. Therefore, NEVER feed the bears, not only for your safety but for theirs as well.

GETTING OUTSIDE

Bighorn Canyon is primarily a flat-water recreation area with excellent boating and fishing, plus swimming, water-skiing, and scuba diving. There are limited hiking trails and scenic drives.

Tips Travel Tip

You can't drive through the **Bighorn Canyon National Recreation Area** from the Montana side to the Wyoming side. To get from one to the other, you must make a very long, circuitous drive either east from Fort Smith to I-90 at Lodge Grass, south to Sheridan, Wyoming, then west to the recreation area. Or you can go north from Fort Smith to I-90 at Hardin, back to Billings and then south on Mont. 72 to U.S. 310, which winds eventually into Wyoming and Lovell. It's best to choose either north or south, and stick to it.

Anglers, take note: **Fishing regulations** are tricky in these parts since the Crow Reservation encompasses nearly all of the Montana portion of the canyon. A state fishing license from whichever state you'll be fishing in is needed, and unless you are certain which it will be, it's best to get both. The visitor center has information on limits, regulations, and fishing conditions.

ON THE MONTANA SIDE

The **Ok-A-Beh Boat Landing** (© 406/665-2216) outside Fort Smith has a marina and campsites, rents boats, and sells gas and fishing supplies.

A park ranger can help you find the **Om-Ne-A Trail,** which stretches for 3 steep miles (5km) along the canyon rim. The **Beaver Pond Trail** is a short trip from the visitor center along Lime Kiln Creek.

ON THE WYOMING SIDE

The south side of the park offers some of the more sensational canyon views and is a prime viewing spot of some of the last wild horses to run free in North America. The **Horseshoe Bend** area, on Wyo. 37, has a full-service marina (© 307/548-7230), open from Memorial Day to Labor Day, and sometimes a little longer.

Leaving Horseshoe Bend, you'll pass burgundy-colored hills and enter the **Pryor Mountain National Wild Horse Range,** which has been home to wild mustangs—the virtual emblem of the West, along with the buffalo—for more than a century. Sometimes, you can catch a glimpse of a few from the road. Just across the Montana border is the **Devil Canyon Overlook,** offering a view of the river as it winds through a steep, winding canyon of gray limestone and orange shale.

At the end of the highway is **Barry's Landing,** with a boat ramp and fishing access, and the focus for most of the recreational opportunities in the southern part of the park.

The self-guided **Canyon Creek Nature Trail** (½ mile; 1km), which starts at Loop C of the campground at Horseshoe Bend; and the trail from **Barry's Landing** to the campground at Medicine Creek (2 miles; 3km), are the only hikes on this side of the park.

WHERE TO STAY

Accommodations on the south side of the park are at Lovell, 3 miles (5km) west of the intersection of Wyo. 37 and U.S. 14A.

The camping and motels in this area are generally undistinguished, but you'll likely be spending most of your time outside doing things anyway. Three miles (5km) north of Fort Smith is **Cottonwood Camp** (© 406/666-2391), with a few cabins, 15 full-hook-up RV sites, and 24 tent sites. It also has a laundry, showers, and convenience store.

There's a park-service campground at each end of the recreation area: **Afterbay,** 1 mile (1.5km) northeast of Yellowtail Dam in Montana, has 48 sites, water, toilets, fishing, and a boat ramp; and **Barry's Landing** in Wyoming has nine sites, toilets, a boat ramp, hiking trails, and fishing.

Forrester's Bighorn River Resort (P.O. Box 7595, Fort Smith, MT 59035; © 800/665-3799 or 406/666-9199; fax 406/666-9179; www.forrester-travel. com) is an outfitting company owned and run by former wildlife biologist Nick Forrester and his wife, Francine, a Manhattan-trained chef. There are seven rustic but very comfortable private cabins and a lodge with a massive river-rock fireplace in the living room, cigar loft, pro shop, and dining room where Francine serves meals to soothe weary fishermen. Located about a half-mile

(1km) north of Fort Smith, the cabins sit on a bluff overlooking the Bighorn River. The Forresters offer packages that include all meals and lodging (3-night minimum, double occupancy), plus Orvis-endorsed fishing guides, starting at $990 per person. Credit cards are not accepted.

4 Little Bighorn Battlefield National Monument

56 miles (90km) E of Billings

Perhaps there is no phrase in the English language that serves as a better metaphor for an untimely demise than "Custer's Last Stand." It was on this battlefield, on the dry sloping prairies of southeastern Montana, that George Armstrong Custer met his end. Though the details of the actual battle that took place on June 25, 1876, are sketchy at best, much remains for the visitor to explore and ponder in this mysterious place. The **Little Bighorn Battlefield National Monument** chronicles the history of this world-famous engagement, offering a coherent look at how the battle developed, where the members of Custer's contingent died, and how it might have looked to the swarming warriors.

ESSENTIALS

GETTING THERE   The monument is located 54 miles (87km) southeast of Billings. Take I-94 east to I-90 south; just past Crow Agency take exit 510 for U.S. 212. The battlefield is located a few hundred yards east.

ADMISSION & HOURS   The park is open daily from 8am to 9pm from Memorial Day to Labor Day; spring and fall hours are 8am to 6pm; winter hours are 8am to 4:30pm. The visitor center is open from 8am to 7:30pm, but closed on Christmas, New Year's Day, and Thanksgiving. There is a $10 admission fee per vehicle; $5 for those on foot.

VISITOR INFORMATION   At the **Visitor Center** just inside the park entrance, you'll see actual uniforms worn by Custer, read about his life, and view an eerie reenactment of the battles on a small-scale replica of the battlefield. For advance information, contact the Superintendent, Little Bighorn Battlefield National Monument, P.O. Box 39, Crow Agency, MT 59022-0039 (© **406/ 638-2621;** www.nps.gov/libi).

TOURING THE MONUMENT   It's possible to view the site in less than a half-hour, but you'll shortchange yourself with that approach. Instead, plan to spend enough time to explore the visitor center, listen to interpretive historical talks presented by rangers there, and then tour the site. You'll leave with a greater appreciation for the monument and an understanding of the history that led up to the battle.

After stopping at the **visitor center,** drive 4½ miles (7km) to the **Reno- Benteen Monument Entrenchment Trail,** at the end of the monument road, and double back. Interpretive signs at the top of this bluff show the route followed by the companies under Custer, Benteen, and Reno as they approached the area from the south, and the positions from which they defended themselves from their Indian attackers.

As you proceed north along the ridge, you'll pass **Custer's Lookout,** the spot from which the general first viewed the Indian village. This was the spot at which Custer sent for reinforcements, though he continued marching north.

Capt. Thomas Weir led his troops to **Weir Point** in hopes of assisting Custer, but was immediately discovered by the Indian warriors and forced to retreat to the spot held by Reno.

The **Medicine Trail Ford,** on the ridge, overlooks a spot well below the bluffs in the Medicine Trail Coulee on the Little Bighorn River, where hundreds of warriors who had been sent from the Reno battle pushed across the river in pursuit of Custer and his army.

Further north, the Cheyenne warrior Lame White Man led an attack up **Calhoun Ridge** against a company of the Seventh Cavalry that had charged downhill into the coulee. When Indian resistance overwhelmed the army, troops retreated back up the hill, where they were killed.

As you proceed to the north, you will find detailed descriptions of the events that occurred on the northernmost edges of the ridge, as well as white markers that indicate the places where army troops fell in battle. The bodies of Custer, his brothers Tom and Boston, and nephew Autie Reed, were found on Custer Hill.

Indian casualties during the rout are estimated at 60 to 100 warriors. Following the battle, which some say began early in the morning and ended within 2 hours, the Indians broke camp in haste and scattered to the north and south. Within a few short years they were all confined to reservations.

The survivors of the Reno-Benteen armies buried the bodies of Custer and his slain army where they fell. In 1881, the graves that could be located were reopened, and the bones re-interred at the base of a memorial shaft found overlooking the battlefield. Custer's remains were eventually reburied at the U.S. Military Academy at West Point in 1877.

The adjacent **National Cemetery,** established in 1879, incorporates a self-guided tour to some of the more significant figures buried there. There are three **walking trails** within the monument for visitors wishing to explore the battle in greater depth.

A SPECIAL EVENT   The **Hardin Area Chamber of Commerce** (I-90 exits 497 and 503) sponsors **Little Big Horn Days,** around June 25th each year, but not at the monument. The events include a reenactment, parade, symposiums, and of course food. For information, call ☎ **406/665-1672.**

5 Miles City ⟨★⟩

145 miles (233km) E of Billings; 70 miles (113km) SW of Glendive

Miles City gets its name from Col. Nelson A. Miles—the commander of the Fifth Cavalry who was ordered to return bands of Indians to reservations in the summer of 1876. As the world moves on around it, Miles City has retained its Western flair for over a century. In the early days, as portrayed in Larry McMurtry's novel *Lonesome Dove,* Miles City was a cowboy town on the verge of becoming a leading cattle market; the market came with the arrival of the Northern Pacific Railroad in 1881.

Today, Miles City maintains its cowboy traditions with its annual Bucking Horse Sale—which attracts rodeo stock contractors from all over the country—and the Range Riders Museum, a thorough collection of photographs and firearms from the old days. It's where remote ranchers come when they need barbed wire or tractor axles, and it's the closest business and agricultural center to Billings.

Miles City still boasts a traditional Main Street with a saloon and lunch counter, and local merchants make conscious efforts to keep up this city's Old West appeal. Its citizens take an active pride in the town's lack of parking meters—a vestige of its civility and small population.

ESSENTIALS

GETTING THERE   It's an easy 145-mile (233km) drive on I-94 from Billings. Miles City's **Frank Wiley Field** is serviced by **Big Sky Airlines** (✆ **800/237-7788** or 406/232-5058), a regional airline that offers connecting flights to Billings.

VISITOR INFORMATION   The **Miles City Chamber of Commerce,** at 315 Main St., Miles City, MT 59301 (✆ **877/632-2890** or 406/232-2890; www.mcchamber.com), provides maps and guides to the town. Or get an area vacation guide from **Custer Country,** P.O. Box 160, Laurel, MT 59044 (✆ **800/346-1876** or 406/628-1432; www.custer.visitmt.com).

GETTING OUTSIDE

There's an attractive municipal swimming facility at the west end of Main Street, and a pond, surrounded by cottonwood trees, with piers for jumping from.

FISHING & BOATING

Miles City isn't classic Montana fishing country, but there is plenty of access to the Yellowstone and Tongue Rivers for walleye, sauger, catfish, crappie, and, occasionally, the unusual paddlefish (see "Paddlefishing," in section 6, below). Fishing throughout the area is best in late spring and early fall. **Twelve-Mile Dam,** 11 miles (18km) south of Miles City on Mont. 59, then 1 mile (1.5km) south on Tongue River Road, has camping facilities and a boat launch, and a handicapped-accessible fishing platform.

   Pirogue Island State Park is just north of Miles City. Go 1 mile (1.5km) north on Mont. 22, then 2 miles (3km) north on Kinsey Highway, then 2 miles (3km) east on a gravel road. Stop by **Red Rock Sporting Goods,** 2900 Valley Dr. E. (✆ **406/232-2716**), for gear and information.

GOLF

Miles City has the nine-hole **Town and Country Club golf course** running along the banks of the Tongue River southeast of town. It's relatively short—3,280 yards. For fees and tee times, call the pro shop at ✆ **406/232-1500.**

 The World-Famous Miles City Bucking Horse Sale

Ever since 1914, rodeo contractors—the men who supply the animals for the West's rodeos—have been meeting in Miles City and lining up their stock. This gathering, which began as an informal event, has now become the "World-Famous Miles City Bucking Horse Sale," held every May on the third weekend of the month. More than 200 horses are sold at auction, from untried stock to spoiled saddle horses. There are pari-mutuel horse races, a parade, trade show, and rodeos, as well as wild-horse racing. The downtown area is virtually closed down at night, bands play on the streets, and beer is swilled and spilled while the city's open-container ordinances are suspended inside the "people corral." There's also a "quick-draw art and auction," music, and a barbecue in the city park. Tickets cost $8 for the Friday night sale session, and $10 for Saturday and Sunday. Children under 12 are $5. Call the Miles City Area Chamber of Commerce (✆ **406/232-2890;** www.buckinghorsesale.com) for the current schedule.

SEEING THE SIGHTS

Range Rider Museum   The amazing thing about this collection is its size—the Western memorabilia collection fills 11 buildings and includes a frontier town, an art gallery that includes the work of Charles Russell, and a gun collection of more than 400 firearms, including an elephant gun. Items on display also include American Indian artifacts and French sabers. There are 500 photos of local celebrities in the Wilson Photo Gallery, and a replica of Old Milestown—as the town was originally called—of 1877. Of particular interest are the excellent photos of Cheyenne tribal members taken in the 1890s.

U.S. 12 (on Main St., just west of town at I-94 exit 135). © **406/232-6146** or 406/232-4483. $5 adults, $4 seniors, $1 high school and college students, 50¢ children, free for children under 6. Apr 1–Oct 31, daily 8am–6pm. Closed Nov–Mar.

Custer County Art Center ⭐ (Kids)   The old city water plant (ca. 1910) has been reincarnated as an art museum, with changing exhibits of traditional and contemporary art from the museum's notable permanent collection of some 400 works, plus national and regional touring exhibits. There are some especially interesting photographs of the Wyoming frontier from the late 1800s. Listed on the National Register of Historic Places, the museum building is actually an attraction itself. In 1979, it was awarded the governor's trophy for best adaptation of a historic structure. The art center hosts the Western Art Roundup, an annual show (late May–early July) of Western art, and an art auction each year in late September. The "Kids Create" program each summer offers workshops for school-age children, with half- and full-day sessions (call for the current schedule).

Waterplant Rd. off W. Main St. (just over the Tongue River Bridge west of town). © **406/232-0635**. Free admission. Tues–Sun 1–5pm.

WHERE TO STAY & DINE

There are several properties at I-94 exit 138 in Miles City. The impressive **Holiday Inn Express,** 1720 S. Haynes (P.O. Box 1348), Miles City, MT 59301 (© **888/ 700-0402** or 406/232-1000; www.hiexpress.com), is a relatively new and well-maintained facility with 52 units. There's a pool and whirlpool; rooms have dataports, irons and boards, hair dryers, and coffeemakers. Rates are $79 double, and include an expanded continental breakfast. The **Best Western War Bonnet Inn,** 1015 S. Haynes Ave. (P.O. Box 1055), Miles City, MT 59301 (© **406/232-4560** or 800/528-1234), has 54 units, including three suites with microwave and refrigerator. Rates are $69 to $95 double, including continental breakfast; plus there's an indoor pool, hot tub, and sauna. The **Miles City Comfort Inn,** 1615 S. Haynes Ave., Miles City, MT 56301 (© **800/228-5150** or 406/232-3141), has 54 units, an indoor pool, and a hot tub, and rates of $60 to $85 double including a deluxe continental breakfast. A new property, with an exercise room and swimming pool, is the **Guesthouse Inn & Suites,** 3111 Steel St., Miles City, MT 59301 (© **406/ 232-3661;** www.guesthouseintl.com). It has 61 spacious rooms with microwaves, refrigerators, VCRs, coffeemakers, hair dryers, and irons and boards, and rates for two of $76 to $79 including a hot breakfast.

The **Miles City KOA Campground,** 1 Palmer St., Miles City, MT 56301 (© **406/232-3991**), is shaded by more than 70 cottonwoods and has full RV hookups, tent sites, a pool, and a store, and rates from $18 to $27. It also has several camping cabins (you share the bathhouse) for about $32 per night.

For a small Montana town, Miles City offers several pretty good restaurants. The **Stagecoach Station,** 3020 Stower St., by Wal-Mart (© **406/232-2288**), offers steak, seafood, really good barbecue, and pasta (dinner items mostly in the

$6–$15 range) with Old West hospitality and atmosphere to match—from the boot upholstery to "old Gabby" greeting you at the door. It's open daily from 6:30am to 11pm. Getting a bit more modern is the **Airport Inn** (north of town on Mont. 59 overlooking the Yellowstone River; *C* **406/232-9977**), where you're greeted by a vintage airplane—a 1934 Aerocoupe—and have models dangling overhead while you eat. Try the "finger steaks" or munch on some pizza. A variety of sandwiches, burgers, and homemade soups are also served. Prices range from $2.95 to $8.25. In summer it's open daily from 11am to 11pm, and it closes at 10pm the rest of the year. For fine dining, visit **Club 519,** 519 Main St., on the second floor of the Professional Building (*C* **406/232-5133**), a softly lit, quiet, comfortable restaurant serving very good steaks and seafood, with dinner prices in the $11 to $22 range. It's open daily from 5 to 10pm.

MILES CITY AFTER DARK

The cowboys in their dress hats come out after dark in Miles City, mostly in the bars. The historic **Montana Bar** *⚘*, 612 Main St. (*C* **406/232-5809**), has a Montana map for a sign, with Miles City marked by a check. Built in 1893, this is where stockmen gathered. It was enlarged and received a new facade in 1914, but has changed little since, and is known as one of the most authentic Western bars in the state. It has a multicolored tile floor, antique back bar, pressed-tin ceiling, and a bullet hole in one leaded-glass panel. Patrons used to have to stand up to the bar and "drink like a man," but bar stools have been added for the modern tippler. Within a few steps of the Montana is **Range Riders,** 605 Main St. (*C* **406/232-4584**), and down the street is **The Texas Club,** 716 Main St. (*C* **406/232-0100**). All three offer a friendly atmosphere for cold beer and hot country music.

6 Glendive

222 miles (357km) E of Billings; 196 miles (316km) W of Bismarck, North Dakota

A cattle town in the 1880s, Glendive has gradually become a farming community, producing mostly sugar beets and wheat. The city's most curious attraction is paddlefishing (see below). Lodging here includes the **Best Western Jordan Inn,** 223 N. Merrill Ave., Glendive, MT 59330 (*C* **888/453-6348** or 406/377-5555), with rates of $58 to $88 double; and **Days Inn,** 2000 N. Merrill Ave., Glendive, MT 59330 (*C* **800/329-7666** or 406/365-6011), which charges $40 to $70 double.

GETTING THERE It's a long but easy 222-mile (357km) drive on I-94 from Billings. **Big Sky Airlines** (*C* **800/237-7788** or 406/687-3360) flies to the **Dawson County Airport** from Billings.

VISITOR INFORMATION The **Glendive Area Chamber of Commerce and Agriculture,** 313 S. Merrill Ave., Glendive, MT 59330 (*C* **406/365-5601;** www.midrivers.com/~chamber), provides brochures and maps.

PADDLEFISHING

Thousands of anglers come every year to try to snag one of these prehistoric hundred-pounders from the bottom of the Yellowstone River. The season is from May 15 to June 30, and the best fishing spot is at the intake diversion dam on the Yellowstone, 15 miles (24km) northeast of town on Mont. 16. These large non-skeletal monsters are "snagged"—caught on treble hooks dragged along the bottom of the river—and the limit is one fish per fisherman. You'll need both a Montana fishing license and a special tag, which several places in town sell. Ask at the Chamber of Commerce. Other sport fish include sauger, walleye, catfish, ling, and sturgeon.

MAKOSHIKA STATE PARK

Montana's largest state park, at 11,500 acres, **Makoshika State Park** (© **406/365-6256**) is a few blocks from town via the railroad underpass. The name is Sioux, meaning "bad earth" or "bad land." Erosion has done wonders with the park's upper and most malleable layer, forming magnificent spires in some places and coulees that cut deep into the multicolored valleys in others. Stunted ponderosa pine trees are scattered over much of the park. The amazing thing about this state park is not necessarily the uncanny resemblance to Badlands National Park in South Dakota, but the abundance of dinosaur bones that have been removed from under the loess. The actual skull—not a replica or cast—from a young triceratops uncovered in the park is on view inside the visitor center.

A partially paved road—steep and narrow even by Montana mountain standards—winds about 2 miles (3km) to an overlook that provides a wonderful view of the badlands. Don't take your RV—the road is too narrow and there is nowhere to turn around. The visitor center (open daily 10am–6pm, Memorial Day–Labor Day; the rest of the year, Mon–Sat 9am–5pm and Sun 1–5pm) has a fine display of the history, prehistory, and geology of the park. The day-use fee is $4.

A SIDE TRIP TO FORT UNION

Strictly speaking, the **Fort Union Trading Post National Historic Site** is in North Dakota. The Montana–North Dakota border bisects the parking lot, and the fort itself is a few paces east. But Fort Union is so important to the development of Montana that it should be included in any trip through the eastern part of the state.

For 30 years after 1828, Fort Union was the edge of the frontier—the most important trading post in John Jacob Astor's beaver pelt and buffalo robe empire in the Northern Plains. This National Park Service site has been spectacularly reconstructed from pictures and descriptions. The main gate of the glistening, whitewashed wooden stockade overlooks the wide Missouri, and two tall stone bastions stand sentinel over the river at the fort's corners.

Lewis and Clark camped near here on their trip to the Pacific, on April 25 and 26, 1805. Lewis commented in his journals on the "wide and fertile vallies" and how ideal the site would be for a fort. The Bourgeois House has been converted into a modern visitor center, and contains excellent exhibits detailing the life and times of the fur traders. Artist George Catlin visited in 1832, as did Karl Bodmer in 1833, and John James Audubon in 1843. In 1867, the fort was acquired by the U.S. Army and its lumber was used to expand nearby Fort Buford and to fuel steamboats.

Fort Union has been a Park Service site since 1966. Reconstruction started in 1987, and was completed to its current level in 1991.

GETTING THERE & VISITOR INFORMATION   From I-94 exit 213 at Glendive, take Mont. 16 northeast to the North Dakota border, then North Dakota 58 north to the fort (it's about 75 miles [121km]). Contact **Fort Union Trading Post National Historic Site,** 15550 N. Dak. 1804, Williston, ND 58801-8680 (© **701/572-9083;** www.nps.gov/foun). Admission is free and the park is open from 8am to 8pm during the summer and 9am to 5:30pm in winter.

10

Yellowstone National Park

For all the epic wonder of the geysers and the antlered elk and the towering waterfalls, visitors to our nation's first national park often bring home memories more subtle and personal: the fine grades of pastel colors in a small hot spring, or the flight of an osprey above the river, or a spider web sagging with steam droplets in the early morning light. Yellowstone isn't just about beauty. At every turn it raises questions about the mysteries of nature, awakening a curiosity you might have thought died during that long-ago biology exam.

After the initial reaction of wordless awe to a bubbling mud pot or a meadow of brightly colored wildflowers, it's human nature to want to know how it all works. And only in Yellowstone can you observe firsthand how wolves wander amidst an elk herd seeking prey; or smell the sulfurous vapors venting from the volcanic caldera beneath the plateau; or touch the fireweed and pine seedlings sprouting within the forests burned by the 1988 fires.

It was a prescient move in 1872 when the U.S. Congress set aside 2.2 million acres of the West as a geothermal and wildlife preserve and "pleasuring ground for the benefit and enjoyment of the people." Since then, Yellowstone has been the model for the creation of parks around the world. For Americans, it's become a kind of national touchstone to our wilderness past, visited by more than three million pilgrims a year.

Despite all we get out of Yellowstone, not much has been put back. There is a backlog of work to be done, from road repair to sewer improvements, and there are also issues of ecological health. Imported Mackinaw trout are crowding out the native cutthroat in Yellowstone Lake, and increasing traffic congestion interferes with the wildlife.

But there are success stories, too, such as the reintroduction of wolves to the Yellowstone ecosystem, and the devoted work of park scientists and managers. People who know the park well remain optimistic that our mistakes will not dislodge nature's plan. For 600,000 years, since the last time the Yellowstone caldera blew its top, the forces of nature have been reshaping Yellowstone and populating it with flora and fauna. These things take time. Likewise, as much time as you and your family can invest here will be richly rewarded.

1 The Gateway Towns: West Yellowstone, Gardiner & Cooke City

West Yellowstone: 91 miles (147km) SW of Bozeman; 30 miles (48km) W of Old Faithful; 320 miles (515km) NE of Salt Lake City. Gardiner: 79 miles (127km) SE of Bozeman; 163 miles (262km) SW of Billings. Cooke City: 127 miles (204km) SW of Billings.

WEST YELLOWSTONE

By making itself the headquarters for snowmobilers who want to travel the park's roads in winter, **West Yellowstone**—just outside the park's west gate—has

Yellowstone National Park

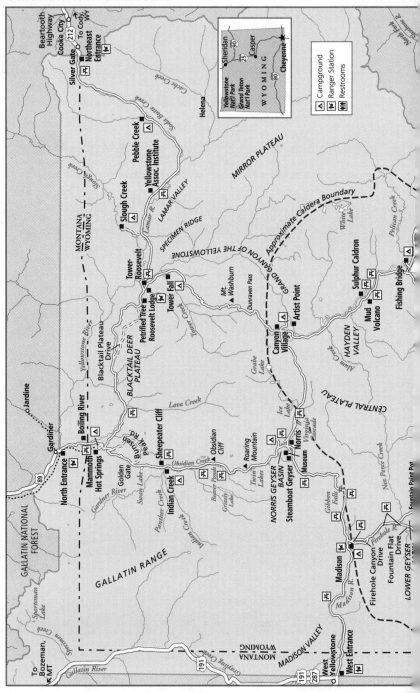

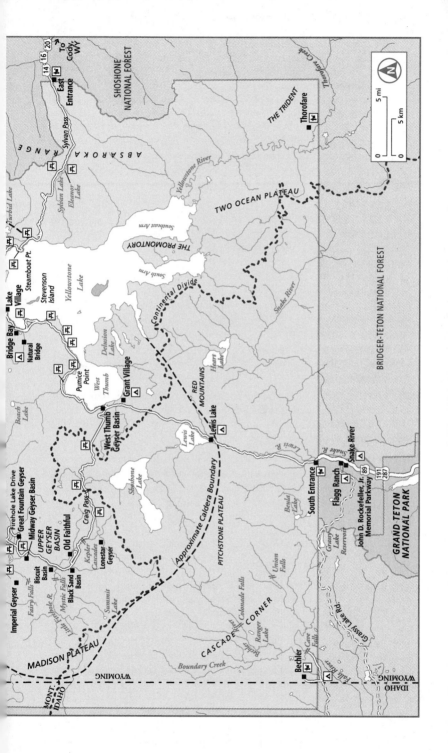

created a year-round tourist economy and attracted an ever-growing number of big hotel chains. The quiet fly-fishing town that once was is no more; the shops are chock-full of curios and the streets are clogged with tour buses, and, in the winter, rumbling snow machines.

One could argue that West Yellowstone made its Faustian bargain with tourism long ago, when the Oregon Short Line's Yellowstone Special train first arrived in 1909. Originally called Riverside, then Yellowstone, the name was grudgingly changed to West Yellowstone in 1920 when Gardiner residents complained that tourists would mistakenly believe the town was the park. This place is about shopping, not nature, and its biggest attraction is a zoo-like look at wildlife in the Grizzly Discovery Center.

ESSENTIALS

GETTING THERE   The **West Yellowstone Airport,** U.S. 191, 1 mile (1.5km) north of West Yellowstone (© 406/646-7631), provides commercial air service seasonally, June through September only, on Delta's commuter service, **Skywest** (© 800/453-9417). If you're driving to West Yellowstone from Bozeman (91 miles; 147km), take U.S. 191 south (a pretty drive along the Gallatin River) to its junction with U.S. 287 and head straight into town. From Idaho Falls, take Interstate 15 north to U.S. 20, which takes you directly into West Yellowstone, a 53-mile (85km) drive.

VISITOR INFORMATION   Visitor information is available by contacting the **West Yellowstone Chamber of Commerce,** 30 Yellowstone Ave. (P.O. Box 458), West Yellowstone, MT 59758 (© 406/646-7701; www.westyellow stonechamber.com).

GETTING AROUND   In West Yellowstone, **Avis** (© 800/831-2847 or 406/ 646-7635) operates May through September. **Budget** (© 800/527-0700 or 406/646-7882) is available year-round. **Yellowstone Taxi** (© 406/646-1111) provides local service.

GETTING OUTSIDE

Most people arrive here on their way to the park, but there is no fence along the park's boundary, so some of the best wild country is actually to the west. Particularly if you like fishing, the rivers—the Gallatin and the Madison, particularly—are among the best in the country. The following tackle shops offer the full gamut of guided fishing trips and instruction: **Arrick's Fly Shop,** 37 Canyon St. (© 406/646-7290); **Bud Lilly's Trout Shop,** 39 Madison Ave. (© 800/854-9559 or 406/646-7801); **Eagle's Tackle Shop,** 9 Canyon St. (© 406/646-7529); **Jacklin's,** 105 Yellowstone Ave. (© 406/646-7336); and **Madison River Outfitters,** 117 Canyon St. (© 406/646-9644).

Come winter, **cross-country skiers** hit the trails (see "Winter Sports & Activities," below). Ski rentals are available in West Yellowstone at **FreeHeel and Wheel,** 40 Yellowstone Ave. (© 406/646-7744), or **Bud Lilly's,** 39 Madison Ave. (© 406/646-7801).

Snowmobiling is a huge draw for West Yellowstone, where sleds are more common than cars on snow-packed winter streets. In addition to driving machines on the snow-packed roads of Yellowstone—where speed limits are strictly enforced—there are trails in surrounding national forests with fewer restrictions. There are tricks to riding on backcountry snow, so if you're inexperienced, rent a guide as well as a machine. All the major hotels and motels in West Yellowstone arrange snowmobile rentals that include gear, and there are

Moments Frommer's Favorite Yellowstone Experiences

Witness the World's Most Famous Geologic Alarm Clock. ★★★ Old Faithful is known for its reliability, but it's slowing down a little with age. Still, about once every 75 minutes you can watch her blow, as she has for at least 120 years. This is the busiest place in the park. While you're there, get a good look at the beautiful and historic Old Faithful Inn. See section 4, "Seeing the Highlights."

Escape to the Backcountry. If the packed benches at Old Faithful give you the impression that Yellowstone is overrun, venture into the backcountry for a dose of true wilderness. It will restore your spirits and perhaps your belief in national parks. Get advice from a ranger on how to travel safely in bear country, and then have it mostly to yourself—most of the three million annual park visitors rarely leave the roadways. See section 8, "Hiking."

Get Hooked on Yellowstone Trout. There is some fine fly-fishing water in and near the park. Try the Madison, the Gibbon, and the Firehole rivers, or troll the lakes for cutthroat, brown, rainbow, and brook trout. When a big trout slaps the twilight surface of the Yellowstone River, Izaak Walton smiles in fly-fishing heaven. See section 6, "Summer Sports & Activities."

Have a Howling Good Time at Lamar. Since wolves were reintroduced in Yellowstone in 1994, they have surprised biologists by making frequent morning and late-afternoon appearances along Slough Creek and in other parts of Lamar Valley. This less-traveled area in the northeast corner of Yellowstone is loaded with wildlife: bison, elk, coyotes, and grizzly bears. See section 8, "Hiking."

Make Like Teddy and Be a Rough Rider. At Roosevelt Lodge, visitors relive the Old West by taking organized rides on horseback, stagecoach, or wagon. A more adventurous alternative is the Old West cookout; you will arrive by either horseback or wagon for hearty, meat-and-potatoes grub. See section 11, "Where to Dine in the Park."

Learn Something at the Yellowstone Institute. You can take classes on everything from bears to butterflies at the Yellowstone Association Institute, which inhabits the old Lamar Buffalo Ranch in the park's northeast corner. It's a friendly, communal way to get a more intimate knowledge of the ecosystem. See section 3, "A Park Primer."

Sleep on a Historic Pillow in the Park. Old Faithful Inn, dating back to 1904, is a log cathedral within view of the geyser. Relax with a drink on the second-floor terrace, or climb the timber lattice that holds up the great roof. Original rooms may not all have private bathrooms, but it's still the nicest place to stay in the park. Ask for Suite 3014 or Room 229 to watch the geyser erupt from your room. See section 10, "Where to Stay in the Park."

numerous independent operations offering rentals and guides, including **Yellowstone Arctic/Yamaha,** 208 Electric St. (© **406/646-9636**), and **Backcountry Adventure Snowmobile Rental,** 224 Electric St. (© **800/924-7669**).

Expect to pay $100 to $150 per day per snowmobile, and unless you have a helmet and winter gear to protect you from sub-zero wind chill, plan on spending another $25 for clothing. Also popular are **snowcoach tours,** offered in vans equipped with tank-like treads to travel on snow. Check with **Yellowstone Alpen Guides Co.,** 535 Yellowstone Ave. (© **800/858-3502**), or with snowmobile outfitters, who often offer snowcoach rides as well.

SEEING THE SIGHTS

Grizzly Discovery Center   For those who aren't able or willing to search for and observe from a distance the free-ranging wildlife of Yellowstone National Park, there is this not-for-profit educational center. You can see plenty of grizzlies here, and the interpretive center gives a well-mounted and detailed explanation of the grizzlies' and wolves' history in this country, and the difficult and controversial efforts to revive them in the wild. This is a closer look at these animals than you'll get in the wild, but some find it a bit depressing since even in a roomy, landscaped enclosure, you will often see bears and wolves pacing the edge of the fence line—instinctively, these animals want to roam.

201 Canyon St. in Grizzly Park. © **800/257-2570** or 406/646-7001. www.grizzlydiscoveryctr.org. $8.50 adults, $4 children 5–12, free for children under 5. Year-round daily 8am–dusk.

Museum of the Yellowstone 🙇   Located in the 1909 Union Pacific depot, this is the only museum that focuses on the park's cultural history and provides an look at the park's first tourists, with scads of memorabilia, postcards, and concessionaire ephemera. There are also displays on the Yellowstone ecosystem, covering epochal events such as the 1959 earthquake that created Quake Lake and the 1988 fires, along with a mounted grizzly bear known in his animate days as "Old Snaggletooth." There are videos and films on the region's history, as well as occasional historic walking tours and evening programs.

Canyon St. and Yellowstone Ave. © **406/646-1100.** www.yellowstonehistoriccenter.org. $20 family, $7 adults, $5 seniors and children, free for children under 5. Mid-May to mid-Oct daily 9am–9pm.

Yellowstone IMAX Theater 🙇 *Kids*   This theater is next door to the Grizzly Discovery Center and, together, they form the centerpieces of a real estate development on the edge of the park, which includes several new hotels. Despite keeping such company, the IMAX concept works pretty well here—there are things an airborne camera can show you on a six-story-tall screen that you'll never see on your own two feet. Six channels of stereo Surround Sound add to the sense of "being there." A film called *Yellowstone* plays fairly often, with swooping views of the canyon and falls and other sights, but there are other big-screen extravaganzas as well.

101 Canyon St. © **888/854-5862** or 406/646-4100. www.imax.com/theatres/yellowstone.html. $8 adults, $6 children 3–12, free for children under 3. Call for show times.

WHERE TO STAY

Make your reservations early if you want to visit in July or August, or if you're going to spend Christmas to New Year's here. If you can, come in the fall, when there are plenty of empty rooms and better rates, and spend your days fishing the Henry's Fork or one of the other great streams in the vicinity. Rates for rooms often reflect the seasonal traffic, and prices fluctuate. Unless noted, all these establishments are open year-round.

West Yellowstone Central Reservations handles booking for many of the hotels (© **888/646-7077**). You'll find chains like the **Marriott Fairfield Inn** (© **800/565-6803**) at 105 S. Electric St., with summertime doubles for $129;

and the **Days Inn** (✆ **800/548-9551**) at 301 Madison Ave., around $85 a night
for a double. There are a bunch of Best Western affiliates, including the **Best
Western Desert Inn,** 133 Canyon St. (✆ **800/528-1234** or 406/646-7376);
the **Executive Inn,** 236 Dunraven St. (✆ **800/528-1234** or 406/646-7681),
the largest with 82 rooms; and the **Best Western Weston Inn,** 103 Gibbon St.
(✆ **800/528-1234** or 406/646-7373). The Best Western doubles range from
$80 to $120 a night during the summer. The **Stage Coach Inn,** at 209 Madison
Ave. (✆ **800/842-2882** or 406/646-7381), is another good choice, with
doubles for $69 to $139, with three different levels of rooms.

Less-expensive options (doubles run $67–$99) include the **Brandin' Iron Inn,**
201 Canyon St. (✆ **800/217-4613** or 406/646-9411), with 84 rooms; and the
City Center Motel, 214 Madison Ave. (✆ **800/742-0665** or 406/646-7337).
There's also a good hostel/motel with some history, the 1912 **Madison Hotel,**
139 Yellowstone Ave. (✆ **800/838-7745** or 406/646-7745), where historic
rooms go for $36 to $42 for two, and newer motel rooms are $45 to $60.

Firehole Ranch ✭✭   Visitors can take a boat ride to this lodge's location on
a mile of private shore along Hebgen Lake, only 16 miles (26km) from Yellowstone National Park. The resort is surrounded by thousands of acres of national
forest in which guests ride horses, hike, canoe, and make use of the ranch's
supply of mountain bikes. The focus is squarely set on angling, however, with
guided fishing trips (for a fee) on Hebgen Lake and in six different streams near
the park, and there's a full-service fly shop on the premises. Lodging is in 10
cabins, most suitable for two guests. The nicest units have separate living quarters, complete with wood-burning stoves, bedrooms furnished with king-size
beds, and private bathrooms with tub-shower combinations. There are no
television sets on the property, and telephone service is limited. You can enjoy a
cocktail, served in a cozy nook, before dining on exquisite meals prepared by a
French chef. Breakfast is made to order, and there are box lunches at midday.

11500 Hebgen Lake Rd., West Yellowstone, MT 59758. ✆ 406/646-7294. Fax 406/646-4728. www.
fireholeranch.com. 10 cabins, each sleeps up to 4. $270–$300 per person per night double. Rate includes all
meals. 4-day minimum stay required. No credit cards. Kids under 12 allowed only with prior approval.
Amenities: Restaurant; airport shuttle; bike rental; self-serve laundry. *In room:* No phone.

The Hibernation Station   These luxury cabins, each named after a local river
or stream, are furnished Western-style with hand-hewn log beds draped in down
comforters, wall tapestries, fireplaces, and enormous bathrooms with jetted tubs.
They can fit from two to eight people, and some have kitchenettes. Every year a
few more cabins go up, and the owners say a big lodge will eventually be added.
The outdoor sculptures on some of the roofs are eye-catching if not gallery quality, and you can rent a snowmobile and all the requisite gear with your cabin.

212 Gray Wolf Ave., West Yellowstone, MT 59758. ✆ 800/580-3557 or 406/646-4200. www.hibernation
station.com. 40 cabins. $99–$269 per cabin. AE, DISC, MC, V. **Amenities:** Jacuzzi. *In room:* Cable TV, kitchenette.

Three Bear Lodge ✭✭ *Kids*   The cozy, pine-furnished rooms of this inn are
located less than 3 blocks from the park entrance. The motel-style rooms are of
above-average quality, reliable and clean, and there are some in-room hot tubs
and a few large rooms for families. Like every other lodging in West Yellowstone,
the Three Bear offers park tour and snowmobile packages with or without
licensed guides—but unlike elsewhere, they also offer some inexpensive cycling-
tour packages. Three Bear Lodge's restaurant and lounge are great spots for
refueling and relaxing after a long day of playing in the snow.

217 Yellowstone Ave., West Yellowstone, MT 59758. ℂ 800/646-7353 or 406/646-7353. www.three-bear-lodge.com. 74 units. $73–$108 double. DISC, MC, V. **Amenities:** Restaurant, lounge; outdoor heated pool (seasonal); 4 indoor Jacuzzis; children's activities; self-serve laundry. *In room:* Cable TV.

West Yellowstone Conference Hotel–Holiday Inn SunSpree Resort ★★★

This hotel is West Yellowstone's standout offering. From its rooms to its restaurant to its conference facilities, this big new resort is first-rate. At the activities desk you can arrange fishing and rafting trips, bike and ATV rentals, and chuck-wagon cookouts. Snowmobilers who have been rattling around all day relax in the Jacuzzis in the King Spa suites. The Iron Horse Saloon serves regional microbrews, and the Oregon Short Line Restaurant serves Western cuisine including buffalo and elk as well as seafood dishes. At the center of the restaurant sits the restored railroad club car that brought Victorian gents to Yellowstone a century ago.

315 Yellowstone Ave., West Yellowstone, MT 59758. ℂ 800/HOLIDAY or 406/646-7365. www.yellowstone-conf-hotel.com. 123 units. $79–$144 double; $90–$200 suite. AE, DISC, MC, V. **Amenities:** Restaurant, lounge; large indoor pool; exercise room; Jacuzzi; sauna; bike rental; activities desk; children's program; self-serve laundry. *In room:* A/C, cable TV, microwave, fridge, coffeemaker, hair dryer, iron.

WHERE TO DINE

Just as the chain motels have arrived, so have garden-variety fast-food joints, so West Yellowstone is a good place to stop for a quick bite on your way into the park. Apart from the choices listed below, **Jocee's Baking Company,** 29 Canyon St. (ℂ **406/646-9737**), is a small but excellent alternative to steak-'n'-eggs breakfast joints. The bakery combines fresh morning pastries with coffee and espresso, and offers deli sandwiches and pizza in the afternoon. Next door at the same address is the **Arrow Leaf Ice Cream Parlor** (ℂ **406/646-9776**), which brags about its 2,001 different ice-cream flavors. For the best variety of coffee drinks and baked goods, visit **the espresso bar** at the excellent Book Peddler in Canyon Square (ℂ **406/646-9358**). At **Pete's Rocky Mountain Pizza Company,** 104 Canyon St. (ℂ **406/646-7820**), you can design your own pizza. The **Texas Rose,** 335 Firehole Ave. (ℂ **406/646-0095**), is one of the few 24-hour joints in town, serving respectable Tex-Mex all summer long.

Bullwinkle's Saloon, Gambling and Eatery ★ AMERICAN

Boisterous and noisy crowds, families and fishermen, gamblers and goof-offs fill this restaurant frequently, and they don't leave hungry. Both luncheon and dinner menus are packed with traditional entrees: burgers and salads for lunch; ribs, steaks, pastas, and seafood at dinner. Try the inexpensive and plentiful Bullwinkle's salad (served with shrimp) or the house specialty—the hazelnut-crusted scallops—and check the updated fishing conditions charted on the wall. You can gamble on video poker machines, featured in many Montana bars.

19 Madison Ave. ℂ 406/646-7974. Lunch $5–$8; dinner $9–$24. MC, V. Summer daily 11am–2am.

The Canyon Street Grill ★★ (Value) AMERICAN

It's hard not to like a restaurant whose slogan is, "We are not a fast food restaurant. We are a cafe reminiscent of a bygone era when the quality of the food meant more than how fast it could be served." This delightful, 1950s-style spot serves hearty food for breakfast, lunch, and dinner. Hamburgers and chicken sandwiches are popular, accompanied by milkshakes made with hard ice cream. A combo of steak, mashed potatoes, and veggies goes for around $12.

22 Canyon St. ℂ 406/646-7548. Most dishes $6–$13. MC, V. Mon–Sat 7am–10pm.

Eino's Tavern ★ (Finds) AMERICAN

Locals snowmobile out from West Yellowstone to Eino's (there's a trail that follows U.S. 191) to become their own chefs at the grill here. It's a novel concept, and one that keeps people coming back for more to a restaurant with a fine view of Hebgen Lake. If you want to blend in with the locals, go up to the counter and place your order for a steak, teriyaki chicken, hamburger, or hot dog, and keep a straight face when you're handed an uncooked piece of meat. Go to the grill, slap it on, and stand around, drink in hand, shooting the breeze with other patrons until your food is exactly the way you like it. Steaks and chicken come with your choice of a salad (or twice-baked potatoes in the wintertime), and hamburgers come with chips. Snowmobilers can purchase gas and oil here, too.

8955 Gallatin Rd. (6 miles N of West Yellowstone on U.S. 191). © 406/646-9344. Main courses $5–$16. No credit cards. Daily winter 9am–9pm; rest of year daily noon–9pm. Closed Thanksgiving to mid-Dec.

The Outpost Restaurant (★) (*Value*) AMERICAN   This restaurant is tucked away in a downtown mall. The food is presented in a family-oriented, home-cooking style—exemplified by the beef stew. There's also salmon, steaks, trout, liver, and an excellent salad bar. For breakfast, if you're really hungry, you can't beat the Campfire Omelette, smothered in homemade chili, cheese, and onions. The menu isn't all that adventurous, and you won't find any of the vices you'll find in the local taverns (video poker, beer, wine, liquor, or smoking), just solid fare in a quiet, family-friendly atmosphere.

115 Yellowstone Ave. (in the Montana Outpost Mall). © 406/646-7303. Main courses $6–$18. AE, DISC, MC, V. Daily 6am–11pm. Closed Oct 15–Apr 15.

GARDINER

Of all the towns that stand sentry on the roads into Yellowstone, none seems more like a gateway town than Gardiner. This is partly due to the historic stone Roosevelt Arch that marks the entrance through which the earliest visitors passed into the park. This is the only park entrance that's open to auto traffic year-round, in order to keep a connection open to Cooke City, which in winter can be reached only through the north entrance.

Gardiner sits at the junction of the Gardner and Yellowstone Rivers (the town's eight-letter name has been attributed to a 19th century spelling error), still looking like the gritty little mining town it once was. Nobody puts on airs in the coffee shops and bars, and nobody raises an eyebrow when a bison or deer wanders through town. If you need additional information, contact the **Gardiner Chamber of Commerce,** 222 Park St., P.O. Box 81, Gardiner, MT 59030 (© **406/848-7971;** www.gardinerchamber.com).

GETTING THERE   From Bozeman (the nearest jet service airport), take I-90 26 miles (42km) east to Livingston, then take U.S. 89 south 53 miles (85km) to Gardiner.

WHERE TO STAY

As with all the gateway towns, make your reservations early if you're coming during the peak season. The steep fall-off in the off-season leads to great discounts—inquire when making reservations.

Chain motels are moving in and filling up during the summer months: The new **Motel 6** (109 Hellroaring Dr.; © **877/266-8356** or 406/848-7520) and the virtually new **Super 8** (on U.S. 89 South; © **800/800-8000** or 406/848-7401) are open year-round with rates during the high season between $80 and $100 for a double. The **Best Western by Mammoth Hot Springs,** on U.S. 89 (© **800/828-9080** or 406/848-7311) is another solid option, with doubles for $89 to $109 in the summer.

Absaroka Lodge ★★ Every room in this lodge has its own furnished balcony, many with jaw-dropping views of the Yellowstone River and the mountain scenery beyond it. The lodge's riverbank location is just a few blocks from the village center, and the rooms are well-appointed with queen-size beds. Suites with kitchenettes cost a little more. Like most other properties in town, the lodge has staff ready and able to assist in arrangements with outfitters for fly-fishing, rafting, and, in the fall, hunting.

U.S. 89 at the Yellowstone River Bridge. ✆ **800/755-7414** or 406/848-7414. www.yellowstonemotel.com. 41 units. $40–$100 double. AE, DC, DISC, MC, V. *In room:* A/C, cable TV, kitchenette.

Comfort Inn This log cabin–style hotel looks like it belongs here, unlike a lot of other chain operations. The centerpiece is a 3,000-square-foot rustic lobby, decorated with wild-game trophies, and a large second-floor balcony that offers views of Yellowstone scenery and passing wildlife. The standard modern motel rooms are what you would expect from a member of this well-established chain. Family suites that sleep six and luxurious Jacuzzi suites are also available, along with a self-service laundromat.

107 Hellroaring Dr., Gardiner, MT 59030. ✆ **800/228-5150** or 406/848-7536. Fax 406/848-7062. www. yellowstonecomfortinn.com. 80 units. Summer $65–$150 double; winter $50–$80 double. Rates include complimentary continental breakfast. AE, DC, DISC, MC, V. **Amenities:** 3 indoor Jacuzzis; self-serve laundry. *In room:* A/C, cable TV.

Yellowstone Suites Bed and Breakfast ★ This quiet B&B on the north bank of the Gardner River is a good alternative to the motels that line U.S. 89. Originally built in 1904, legend has it that the second story's quarried-stone exterior is actually a leftover from the Roosevelt Arch. The rooms are frilly and cozy, with a teddy bear motif in the Roosevelt Room and a Victorian theme in the Jackson Room, and the Yellowstone Suite has a television and a kitchenette. The real perks here are the impeccably gardened backyard and the breakfasts, which might feature French toast stuffed with cream cheese, or ham and cheese quiche.

506 4th St., P.O. Box 277, Gardiner, MT 59030. ✆ **800/948-7937** or 406/848-7937. www.wolftracker.com. 4 units. Summer $80–$110 double; winter $47–$69 double. Rates include complimentary full breakfast. AE, MC, V. **Amenities:** Outdoor Jacuzzi. *In room:* Kitchenette, no phone.

WHERE TO DINE

The Chico Inn ★★ *(Finds* CONTINENTAL It's 30 miles (48km) north of Gardiner, but if you're in the area, stop here for some of the best food in the Rockies, and a quick soak in the resort's hot springs. The carnivorous traveler will enjoy the selection of top-drawer beef, and the pine nut–crusted Alaskan halibut is a seafood aficionado's dream. Many of the incredibly fresh veggies originate in the resort's garden and greenhouse, and the menu always includes a vegetarian selection. You'll want to linger over the food, so consider a night's stay in either the old lodge or the newer additions.

Old Chico Rd., Pray, MT. ✆ **800/HOT-WADA.** Reservations recommended. Main courses $20–$30. AE, DISC, MC, V. Summer daily 5:30–10pm; winter Sun–Thurs 6–9pm, Fri–Sat 5:30–10pm.

K-Bar ★★ PIZZA This Gardiner mainstay might not be much to look at—beer signs and video poker machines are the standout decor—but it serves the best pizza and calzones in town, as well as a good selection of subs. Touting its thick-crusted pies as "the best pizza in the West," the K-Bar makes its dough from scratch, and the resident Yellowstone concessionaire workers swear by the stuff. The full-service bar attracts throngs of locals and tourists, and there's a pool table for entertainment.

Main St. and U.S. 89. ✆ **406/848-9995.** Reservations not accepted. Main courses $4–$8; pizzas $8–$15. DISC, MC, V. Daily 11am–11pm. Bar open later.

Park Street Grill and Cafe ★★ ITALIAN/STEAKS   Adding a dash of zest to Gardiner's staid meat-and-potatoes dining scene, this excellent eatery opened in 1999 to rave reviews. Served in a simply decorated room with an exposed pine interior, the menu here is a refreshing mix of gourmet Italian entrees, fresh seafood, and good old American chicken, pork, and beef dishes. The Crazy Mountain Alfredo is a good choice from the pasta menu: Reputedly served in Italy's insane asylums, the delectable sauce is spiced with sweet and hot peppers, julienne chicken breast, and Italian sausage. Hearty appetites won't mind the huge racks of barbecue pork ribs (served with a fresh-fruit salsa) or the slow-roasted prime rib, and there's a decent selection of lighter fare as well.

204 Park St. ℂ 406/848-7989. Main courses $14–$21. MC, V. Daily 5:30–10pm. Closed mid-Oct to May.

Sawtooth Deli ★ ECLECTIC   This restaurant can fit the needs of almost any appetite, with a casual deli atmosphere during lunch hours and a decidedly more upscale dinner atmosphere. On warm summer nights, the breezy garden patio is the best place in town to take in a meal. The deli menu includes sandwiches both traditional (BLT, pastrami and Swiss) and unexpected (vegetarian, chicken Parmesan), but the real treats are the dinners, especially the mesquite-smoked chicken and the seafood specials, and the indulgent homemade desserts. Pasta, steaks, salads, and a respectable wine list round out the offerings.

270 W. Park St. ℂ 406/848-7600. Reservations not accepted. Lunch $4–$6.50; dinner $9–$15. Credit cards not accepted. Mon–Sat 9am–10pm. Closed Nov–Apr.

COOKE CITY

If little ol' Gardiner seems just a little too connected to the civilized world, you ought to spend a winter in tiny Cooke City or even tinier Silver Gate, just outside Yellowstone National Park's northeast entrance. In the winter, when the cloud-scraping Beartooth Pass closes to the north, supplies for these towns have to come through the park. Better to visit in the summer and take the breathtaking drive north over the pass (U.S. 212 toward Red Lodge), or south along the scenic Chief Joseph Highway (Wyo. 296). For a hundred years, the lifeblood of this town was mining gold, platinum, and other precious metals, but now there is only park tourism, which seems a little anemic by comparison. Less than 100 residents live year-round in the town today, and Silver Gate, right next to the park entrance, is barely in double figures. Contact the **Colter Pass/Cooke City/Silver Gate Chamber of Commerce** at Box 1071, Cooke City, MT 59020-1071 (ℂ 406/838-2495; www.cookecity.com), for information and a map of hiking and snowmobiling trails in the area.

GETTING THERE   From Billings, Montana, drive west on I-90 to Laurel, then south on U.S. 212 to Red Lodge, a total distance of 60 miles (97km); then continue another 67 miles (108km) south over spectacular Beartooth Pass, dipping into Wyoming and back up into Montana at Cooke City.

WHERE TO STAY & EAT   Lodging here will be less expensive than in other gateway towns, ranging from $35 to $80 a night. The 32-room **Soda Butte Lodge** (ℂ 406/838-2251) is the community's largest motel. It includes the good **Prospector Restaurant**—with great mountain views from the bar—and a small casino. We also like the **Alpine Motel,** also on Main Street (ℂ 406/838-2262), a well-kept and very reasonably priced mom-and-pop motel. For a bite to eat and a great selection of beers, try the funky **Beartooth Cafe** (ℂ 406/838-2475). If you find yourself in Silver Gate one evening, stop by the historic **Range Rider Lodge** (ℂ 406/838-2359), a cavernous log building with a huge dance floor.

2 Just the Facts

BEFORE YOU GO

To obtain maps and information about the park prior to arrival, contact **Yellowstone National Park,** P.O. Box 168, WY 82190 (② **307/344-7381;** www.nps.gov/yell). Information regarding lodging, some campgrounds, tours, boating, and horseback riding in Yellowstone is available from **Yellowstone Park Lodges,** Yellowstone National Park, WY 82190 (② **307/344-7311;** www.travelyellowstone.com). For information regarding educational programs in Yellowstone, contact **Yellowstone Association,** P.O. Box 117, Yellowstone National Park, WY 82190 (② **307/344-2293;** www.yellowstoneassociation.org), which operates bookstores in park visitor centers, museums, and information stations, and oversees the **Yellowstone Association Institute** and the courses taught at the old Lamar Buffalo Ranch in the park's northeast corner. They also have a catalog of publications you can order by mail.

GETTING THERE

If interstate highways and international airports are the measure of accessibility, then Yellowstone is as remote as Alaska's Denali National Park or the Serengeti Plains of Africa. But three million people make it here every year, on tour buses, in family vans, on bicycles, and astride snowmobiles.

The closest airport to Yellowstone is in **West Yellowstone,** Montana, which sits just outside the park's west entrance. For information on flying into West Yellowstone, see "Essentials" in section 1 of this chapter.

Visitors can reach the park from the south by flying into **Jackson,** Wyoming (only 14 miles [23km] from the southern entrance to Grand Teton), then driving 56 miles (90km) through Grand Teton to the southern entrance of Yellowstone. **American Airlines** (② 800/433-7300); **Delta** (② 800/221-1212); **Skywest,** the Delta Connection (② 800/453-9417 or 307/733-7920); and **United Express** (② 800/241-6522) all have flights to and from **Jackson Airport.**

To the north, **Bozeman,** Montana, is 87 miles (140km) from the West Yellowstone entrance on U.S. 191. Or you can drive east from Bozeman to Livingston, a 20-mile (32km) journey on Interstate 90, and then south 53 miles (85km) on U.S. 89 to the northern entrance at Gardiner. Bozeman's airport, **Gallatin Field,** provides daily service via **Delta** (② 800/221-1212), **Northwest** (② 800/225-2525), and **United** (② 800/241-6522), as well as **Horizon** (② 800/547-9308) and **Skywest** (② 800/453-9417) commuter flights. If you're driving to West Yellowstone from Bozeman (91 miles; 147km), take U.S. 191 south to its junction with U.S. 287 and head straight into town.

Also to the north, **Billings, Montana,** is 129 miles (208km) from the Cooke City entrance. Billings is home to Montana's busiest airport, **Logan International,** 2 miles (3km) north of downtown. Daily intrastate service is provided by **Big Sky Airlines** (② 800/237-7788 or 406/245-2300); and regional daily service is provided by **Delta** (② 800/221-1212), **Horizon** (② 800/547-9308), **Northwest** (② 800/225-2525), and **United** (② 800/241-6522). From Billings, it's a 65-mile (105km) drive south on U.S. 212 to Red Lodge, then 30 miles (48km) on the Beartooth Highway to the northeast entrance to the park. Keep in mind that the Beartooth Highway (U.S. 212), which takes you on a high, twisting journey over a spectacular pass, is open only from Memorial Day weekend until late October.

From **Cody, Wyoming,** it's a gorgeous 53-mile (85km) drive west along U.S. 14/16/20 to the east entrance of the park. **Cody's Yellowstone Regional**

> ⌒*Tips* **Flying for Less**
>
> Flying into the closest airports to Yellowstone can be an expensive proposition. You can save significant airfare dollars by flying to **Salt Lake City,** or the more distant **Denver.** Salt Lake City is 390 driving miles (628km) from Jackson, a route that takes you through rolling Idaho countryside and alongside the dramatic western slope of the Rockies, then high above it all over Teton Pass.

Airport (© 307/587-5096) serves the Bighorn Basin as well as the east and northeast entrances of Yellowstone National Park with year-round commercial flights via **Skywest** (© 800/453-9417) and **United Express** (© 800/241-6522).

Most of the major auto-rental agencies have operations in the gateway cities. **Avis** (© 800/831-2847), **Budget Auto Rental** (© 800/527-0700), **Thrifty Auto** (© 800/367-2277), and **Hertz** (© 800/654-3131) all have operations in Bozeman, Billings, and Jackson. **National Car Rental** (© 800/227-7368) has locations in Bozeman and Billings. Thrifty, Avis, Hertz, and Budget serve Cody. **Alamo Auto Rental** (© 800/327-9633) serves Jackson.

ACCESS/ENTRY POINTS

Yellowstone has five entrances. The **north entrance,** near Mammoth Hot Springs, is located just south of Gardiner, Montana, and U.S. 89. In the winter, this is the only access to Yellowstone by car.

The **west entrance,** just outside the town of West Yellowstone on U.S. 20, is the closest entry to Old Faithful. Inside the park, turn south to see Old Faithful or north to the Norris Geyser Basin. This entrance is open to wheeled vehicles April through November and during the winter to snowmobiles and snowcoaches.

The **south entrance,** on U.S. 89/191/287, brings visitors into the park from neighboring Grand Teton National Park and the Jackson area. As you drive north from Jackson, you'll get a panoramic view of the Grand Tetons. Once in the park, the road winds along the Lewis River to the south end of Yellowstone Lake, at West Thumb and Grant Village. It is open to cars May through November and to snowmobiles and snowcoaches December through March.

The **east entrance,** on U.S. 14/16/20, is 52 miles (84km) west of Cody, Wyoming, and is open to cars May through September and to snowmobiles and snowcoaches December through March. The drive up the Wapiti Valley and over Sylvan Pass is especially beautiful, if not marred by road-repair delays.

The **northeast entrance,** at Cooke City, Montana, is closest to the Tower-Roosevelt area, 29 miles (47km) to the west. This entrance is open to cars year-round, but beginning on October 15, when the Beartooth Highway closes, until around Memorial Day, the only route to Cooke City is through Mammoth Hot Springs. When it's open, the drive from Red Lodge to the park is a grand climb among the clouds.

Regardless of which entrance you choose, when you enter the park you'll be given a good map and up-to-date information on facilities, services, programs, fishing, camping, and more.

Check **road conditions** before entering the park by calling the visitor center at © 307/344-7381. There always seems to be major road construction in one part of the park or another, so be forewarned.

VISITOR CENTERS & INFORMATION

There are five major visitor and information centers in the park, and each has something different to offer. Unless otherwise indicated, summer hours are from 8am to 7pm.

The **Albright Visitor Center** (℃ 307/344-2263), at Mammoth Hot Springs, is the largest. It provides visitor information and publications about the park, has exhibits depicting park history from prehistory through the creation of the National Park Service, and houses a wildlife display on the second floor.

The **Old Faithful Visitor Center** (℃ 307/545-2750) is another large facility. An excellent short film describing the hot springs' microscopic life, *Yellowstone Revealed*, is shown throughout the day in an air-conditioned auditorium. Rangers dispense various park publications and post projected geyser-eruption times here. An informative seismographic exhibit is an added attraction. By 2003, the Park Service hopes to open a state-of-the-art $15 million visitor education center in place of the current (and architecturally maligned) building.

The **Canyon Visitor Center** (℃ 307/242-2550), in Canyon Village, between Tower Junction and Lake Yellowstone, is the place to go for books and an informative display about bison in the park. It's staffed with friendly rangers used to dealing with crowds.

The **Fishing Bridge Visitor Center** (℃ 307/242-2450), located near Fishing Bridge on the north shore of Yellowstone Lake, has an excellent wildlife display. You can get information and publications here as well.

The **Grant Village Visitor Center** (℃ 307/242-2650), in Grant Village just south of West Thumb on the west side of Yellowstone Lake, has information, publications, and a fascinating exhibit that examines the effects of fire in Yellowstone.

Other sources of park information can be found at the Madison Information Station; the Museum of the National Park Ranger and the Norris Geyser Basin Museum, both at Norris; and the West Thumb Information Station.

FEES & PERMITS

Entrance for up to 7 days costs $20 per vehicle and covers both Yellowstone and Grand Teton National Parks. A snowmobile or motorcycle pays $15 for 7 days, and someone who comes in on bicycle, skis, or foot pays $10. You can buy an **annual permit** for $40, but the various national park passes, which are also honored, are a better deal (see "The Active Vacation Planner," in chapter 2).

BACKCOUNTRY PERMITS   Backcountry permits are free, but you have to have one for any overnight trip, on foot, on horseback, or by boat. Camping is allowed only in designated campsites, many of which are equipped with food-storage poles to keep wildlife away. These sites are primitive and well situated, and you won't feel at all like you're in a campground. If designated campsites in a particular area have already been reserved, you're out of luck. So while you can pick up a permit for hiking or boating the day before beginning a trip, you would be wise during peak season to make a reservation in advance (you can contact the park for reservations for the upcoming year beginning Apr 1), although it costs $20. The **Yellowstone Backcountry Office** (P.O. Box 168, Yellowstone National Park, WY 82190) will send you a useful "Backcountry Trip Planner" with a detailed map showing where the campsites are. Call the office for more information at ℃ **307/344-2160.**

Pick up your permit in the park within 48 hours of your departure, at one of the following visitor ranger stations any day of the week during the summer:

Bechler, Canyon, Mammoth, Old Faithful, Tower, West Entrance, Grant Village, Lake, South Entrance, and Bridge Bay. Boating permits for motorized craft can be obtained at only the last four ranger stations.

BOATING PERMITS   Any vessels used on park waters must have a permit. For motorized craft, the cost is $20 for annual permits and $10 for a 7-day pass. Fees for non-motorized boats are $10 for annual permits and $5 for 7-day permits. Rivers and streams are closed to boats of any kind, except for the stretch of the Lewis River between Lewis and Shoshone Lakes, which is restricted to hand-propelled craft. Coast Guard–approved personal flotation devices are required for each person boating.

FISHING PERMITS   Permits are required for anglers; the permit costs $10 for 10 days and $20 for the season. Children 12 to 15 years of age must have a permit, but there is no charge, and children under 12 may fish without a permit under adult supervision. Permits are available at all ranger stations, visitor centers, and Hamilton stores. The season usually begins on the Saturday of Memorial Day weekend and continues through the first Sunday in November, with some exceptions: Yellowstone Lake opens June 15, and its tributary streams open July 15 (after the bears are done fishing). Sections of the Yellowstone River also have briefer seasons. In the search for ecological equilibrium, the regulations have two key wrinkles: any non-native lake trout caught within the park must not be released alive and cutthroat trout are catch-and-release only.

REGULATIONS

You can get more detailed information about these rules from the park rangers or at visitor centers throughout the parks or at the park's website.

DEFACING PARK FEATURES   Picking wildflowers, or collecting natural or archaeological objects, is illegal. Only dead-and-down wood can be collected for backcountry campfires.

BICYCLES   Bicycles are not allowed on the park's trails or boardwalks, but the park is a popular destination for pavement cyclists. Because of the narrowness of park roads and the presence of large recreational vehicles with poor visibility, it's recommended that you wear helmets and bright clothing. There are some designated off-pavement bicycling areas—contact the park for more information.

CAMPING   In any given year, a person may camp for no more than 30 days in the park, and only 14 days during the summer season. Food, garbage, and utensils must be stored in a vehicle or container made of solid material and suspended at least 10 feet above the ground when not in use.

CLIMBING   Because of the loose, crumbly rock in Yellowstone, climbing is discouraged throughout the park and prohibited in the Grand Canyon of the Yellowstone.

FIREARMS   Loaded guns are not allowed in the park. However, unloaded firearms may be transported in a vehicle when cased, broken down, or rendered inoperable, and on certain trails for access to areas outside the park, with a special permit. Ammunition must be carried in a separate compartment of the vehicle.

LITTERING   Littering in the national parks is strictly prohibited—remember, if you pack it in, you have to pack it out. Throwing coins or other objects into thermal features is illegal.

MOTORCYCLES   Motorcycles, motor scooters, and motorbikes are allowed only on park roads. No off-road or trail riding are allowed. Operator licenses and license plates are required.

PETS   Pets must be leashed and are prohibited in the backcountry, on trails, on boardwalks, and in thermal areas. If you tie up a pet and leave it, you're breaking the law.

SMOKING   No smoking in thermal areas, visitor centers, ranger stations, or any other posted public areas.

SNOWMOBILING   Pending litigation, snowmobiling in Yellowstone may be banned by 2003. Regardless, snowmobilers must have valid driver's licenses, stay on the designated unplowed roadways, and obey posted speed limits.

SWIMMING   Swimming or wading is prohibited in thermal features or in streams whose waters flow from thermal features in Yellowstone. (An exception is the "Boiling River" near Mammoth, where visitors can take a warm soak between daybreak and dusk except during spring runoff.) Swimming in Yellowstone Lake is discouraged because of the low water temperature and unpredictable weather. Bathing suits are required.

WILDLIFE   It is unlawful to approach within 100 yards of a bear or within 25 yards of other wildlife. Feeding any wildlife is illegal. Wildlife calls such as elk bugles or other artificial attractants are forbidden.

WHEN TO GO

During the quiet "shoulder" seasons of spring and fall, there are more bison and elk around than autos and RVs. Before the second week in June, you'll be rewarded by the explosion of wildflowers as they begin to bloom, filling the meadows and hillsides with vast arrays of colors and shapes. After that, roads become progressively busier. Traveling before peak season has economic advantages, as well, since gateway-city motel rates are lower, as are the costs of meals. After Labor Day weekend, crowds begin to thin again and the roads become less traveled. In addition to wildlife and improved fishing conditions in some areas, the fall foliage transforms the area to a calendar-quality image.

In the winter, Yellowstone has a storybook beauty, as snow and ice soften the edges of the landscape and shroud the lumbering bison. Geyser basins appear even more dramatic, the frigid air temperature in stark contrast to the steaming, gurgling waters. Nearby trees are transformed into eerie "snow ghosts" by frozen thermal vapors. Wildlife cluster at the thermal areas to take advantage of the softer ground and more accessible vegetation. Lake Yellowstone's surface freezes to an average thickness of 3 feet, creating a vast ice sheet that sings and moans as the huge plates of ice shift.

The only dissonance to this winter wilderness tableau is the roar of snowmobiles, which inhabit the park's snowpacked roads in ever-growing numbers. In response to growing concerns about pollution and wildlife safety, the Park Service moved toward a snowmobile ban for 2003, with strict quotas for the winters of 2001 and 2002; but, as of press time, the concept was mired in a lawsuit brought on by the snowmobile manufacturers.

You can also enter the park in tracked vehicles that deliver visitors to the beautifully rebuilt Old Faithful Snow Lodge and tour the park. From the lodge or Mammoth—which also stays open to cars during the winter—you can ski, snowmobile, or visit the thermal areas. The only road within the park open for automobile traffic is the Mammoth Hot Springs–Cooke City Road.

SEASONS

Natives of the region describe weather in the Yellowstone ecosystem as predictably unpredictable. Because of the high elevations of the parks, and changing weather systems, the region is characterized by long, cold winters and short, though usually warm, summers.

The first sticking snows typically fall by November 1, and cold and snow may linger into April and May, though temperatures generally warm up by then. The average daytime readings during that time are 40° to 50° F, gradually increasing to 60° to 70° F by early June. Yellowstone is never balmy, but temperatures during the middle of the summer are typically 70° to 80° F in the lower elevations, and are especially comfortable because of the lack of humidity. Even during the summer months, nights will be cool, with temperatures dropping into the low 40s. No matter how warm you expect it to be, it's a good idea to bring a warm jacket, rain gear, and water-resistant walking shoes. And, because this is high altitude, bring plenty of sunscreen and a wide-brimmed hat to protect yourself in the thin atmosphere. As summer thunderstorms are common, a tarp and an umbrella are also recommended.

During winter months temperatures hover in single digits, and sub-zero overnight temperatures are common. You should bring fleece underwear, heavy shirts (not cotton!), vests and coats, warm gloves, and warm, wicking socks. The lowest temperature recorded at Yellowstone was –66° F, in 1933.

AVOIDING THE CROWDS

One of the things you'll discover when you venture down a trail is that the majority of Yellowstone's three million annual visitors aren't going to follow you. (Less than 10% of visitors wander beyond the trail heads.) Some are afraid of grizzly bears; some are in a hurry; some just don't want the exertion. Regardless, Yellowstone rewards those who expend a bit of shoe leather: A mere half-mile from the traffic jams, you'll find few people and much better opportunities to smell the wildflowers.

If you really want a Yellowstone experience that's all your own, head for the backcountry. This is some of the deepest, most exquisite wilderness in the country, and you definitely won't be fighting a mob. While visitation at Yellowstone increases yearly, backcountry permits do not—they've been level since 1980. Our favorite areas are the Thorofare region, in the park's southeast corner at the headwaters of the Yellowstone River, and the shores of Shoshone Lake, the largest backcountry body of water in the Lower 48, but there's so much wilderness here that you will surely find views of your own.

EDUCATIONAL PROGRAMS

Yellowstone offers free **ranger-led educational programs** ★★ that will significantly enhance a visitor's understanding of the area's history, geology, and wildlife. Most programs run through late September. Detailed information on location and times is listed in the park newsletter, which is distributed at the entrance gates. On a more informal basis, you'll run into ranger-naturalists roaming the geyser basins and along the rim of the Grand Canyon in Yellowstone, and in areas where wildlife gather in both parks, leading informative walks and answering the questions of inquisitive visitors.

Evening campfire programs are presented nightly in the summer at Mammoth, Norris, Madison, Old Faithful, Bridge Bay, Grant, and Canyon. Many of these activities are accessible to those with disabilities. It's a good idea to bring a flashlight, warm clothing, and rain gear. Rangers also conduct walking, talking, and hiking programs throughout the park.

As one would expect, there are more tours and evening programs in the **Old Faithful** area than anywhere else in the park. The topics of the guided walks, which can run as long as 1½ hours, usually focus on the geysers, their fragile plumbing, and their role in the Yellowstone ecosystem.

Beginning in June, daily hikes in the **Canyon** area head out to the Hayden Valley and the rim of the Grand Canyon; a ranger talk on the art inspired by the falls is held several times a day at the lower platform of Artist Point. An explanation of the origins of the hot pools and mud pots is conducted daily beginning in June at the **Grant** area as part of a walk of the Lakeshore area of the West Thumb Geyser Basin. The **Lake/Fishing Bridge** agenda includes walking tours of the Mud Volcano area, and along the shores of Yellowstone Lake and Indian Pond. There is an afternoon talk at the Fishing Bridge Visitor Center about managing wildlife like grizzlies and wolves, and a discussion of fisheries management that is held on the west end of the Fishing Bridge. For a full schedule, consult the park newsletter that is distributed at the entrance gates.

Mammoth Hot Springs is host to several interesting ranger-led programs, namely a pair of "Daily Special" talks on the park's natural wonders and a historical tour of the original site of Fort Yellowstone, established more than 125 years ago. There is also a guided tour of the hot-springs terraces. The hottest, most dynamic, and oldest geyser basin in the park is at **Norris,** where a popular 1½-hour tour begins at the Norris museum three times daily.

There are also special exhibitions at the various visitor centers around the park. *Yellowstone Revealed,* a new film on the teeming microbial life in the park's hot pools, plays regularly at the Old Faithful Visitor Center, and an excellent exhibit on bison, mounted by the park and Cody's Buffalo Bill Historical Center, is quartered at the Canyon Visitor Center.

The ranger/naturalist programs are one of several activities that make up the **Junior Ranger** program. For $3, kids can pick up an activity paper at one of the visitor centers, then follow its guidelines for hiking and learning about the park. When they complete the program, their enrollment as Junior Rangers is announced to the public with great fanfare.

Photographers can get some lessons and free advice through **Kodak's photo walks and demonstrations,** which are held at various locations around the park during the summer. Check the *Yellowstone Today* newspaper for locations and times. Astronomers from the **Museum of the Rockies** in Bozeman, Montana, bring their telescopes and stories to a series of stargazing sessions throughout the park—contact the museum at ℭ **406/994-2251** for a schedule.

The **Yellowstone Association Institute** ℛℛ (P.O. Box 117, Yellowstone National Park, WY 82190; ℭ **307/344-2294;** www.yellowstoneassociation.org) operates at the Lamar Buffalo Ranch, on the road through the Lamar Valley to the park's northeast entrance, and offers more than 100 courses, winter and summer, covering everything from wildlife tracking in the snow to wilderness medicine to the history of fur trappers on the plateau. The courses run from 1 to 5 days, with forays into the field, and lectures and demonstrations at the Institute's cozy quarters. Participants share meals and stories in the common kitchen. Prices are reasonable (around $60 a day for tuition), and some classes are specifically oriented to families and youngsters. To make the most of a class, you'll want to stay at the ranch itself, where there are simple, comfortable cabins available for $20 a night per student.

New in 2001, the Institute teamed with Yellowstone National Park Lodges to offer "Trails through Yellowstone," a 4-night package offering the best of two worlds: days spent exploring little-seen trails with knowledgeable and witty guides and nights at the comfortable Mammoth Hot Springs Hotel. Rates (around $500 per person) include box lunches, breakfast, and in-park transportation. Contact the Yellowstone Association Institute (see above) or Yellowstone National Park Lodges (© **307/344-7311;** www.travelyellowstone. com) for reservations.

SERVICES & SUPPLIES

Hamilton Stores, Inc. is the oldest private concessionaire in the park. The **stores** are located throughout the park, including Old Faithful, Mammoth Hot Springs, Lake, Fishing Bridge, and Grant Village, and feature gift shops, grocery supplies, and soda fountains. Depending upon the location, you may find a limited supply of fresh veggies and canned goods (as at the Canyon store), plus fishing supplies, souvenirs and, of course, ice cream. **Service stations** are located at major visitor areas: Old Faithful, Canyon, Mammoth Hot Springs, and Grant Village. Exact locations of all services and stores are listed in the park newspaper you receive at the entrance gates.

If you have medical problems while visiting the park, Yellowstone Park Medical Services provides help at the **Lake Hospital** (© **307/242-7241**), an acute-care facility; the **Old Faithful Clinic** (© **307/545-7325**); and the **Mammoth Clinic** (© **307/344-7965**).

ORGANIZED TOURS & ACTIVITIES

A number of tour companies offer bus tours of the park originating in gateway communities: **Powder River Coach USA** (© **800/442-3682** ext. 114; www. coachusa.com) out of Cody offers daylong trips; **Gray Line of Yellowstone** (© **800/523-3102;** www.graylineyellowstone.com) takes travelers around the park from West Yellowstone, as does **Buffalo Bus Lines** (© **800/426-7669**). If you are looking for specialized guided trips—such as photo safaris or snowcoach tours—contact the chamber of the gateway community where you want to begin (see section 1, "The Gateway Towns: West Yellowstone, Gardiner & Cooke City").

Within the park, the hotel concessionaire, **Yellowstone Park Lodges** (© **307/344-7311;** www.travelyellowstone.com), has a variety of general and specialized tours.

Three different **motor-coach tours** are available from all of Yellowstone's villages. For $29, you can explore either the **Washburn Expedition** (Norris Geyser Basin, the Grand Canyon of the Yellowstone, and Mammoth Hot Springs) or the **Circle of Fire** (Old Faithful, Yellowstone Lake, and the Hayden Valley); or, for $33, you can do the whole thing, the **Yellowstone in a Day.** These are full-day tours, with stops at all the sights and informative talks by the guides. Specialty trips include photo safaris, wildlife trips up the Lamar Valley, and Yellowstone Lake sunset tours in historic buses from the 1930s.

From June to the end of September, 1-hour **scenicruse** tours around the northern end of Yellowstone Lake depart throughout the day from Bridge Bay Marina. You view the Lake Hotel from the water and visit Stevenson Island, while a guide fills you in on the history, geology, and biology. Fares are $9 for adults, $5 for children 2 to 11. Guided fishing trips on 22-foot and 34-foot cabin cruisers are also available from Yellowstone Park Lodges at Bridge Bay

($55 and $72 per hr., respectively), and you can rent smaller outboards and row-boats.

Buses are replaced in the winter by **snowcoach tours.** These are closer in size to a van than a bus, mounted on tank treads with skis in front for steering. The snowcoach can pick you up at the south or west entrances, or at Mammoth, and take you all over the park. You can spend a night at Old Faithful and then snow-coach up to Mammoth the next night, or do round-trip tours from the gates or wherever you're staying in the park. One-way trips range from $46 to $51, while round-trips cost $92 to $99.

Guides tell tales of the areas as you cruise the park trails, and pull over for photo ops. Snowcoaches aren't the most comfortable mode of transportation, and they're a bit noisy, but they allow larger groups the option of traveling together in the same vehicle. They are also available for rent at most snowmobile locations if you want to do the coaching yourself.

FOR TRAVELERS WITH DISABILITIES

Wheelchair-accessible accommodations are located in the Cascade Lodge at Canyon Village, in Grant Village, in the Old Faithful Inn, and in the Lake Yellowstone Hotel. For a free *Visitors Guide to Accessible Features in Yellowstone National Park,* write to the Park Accessibility Coordinator, P.O. Box 168, Yellowstone National Park, WY 82190, or pick up the guide at the gates or visitor centers. There are **accessible campsites** at Madison, Canyon, and Grant campgrounds, which may be reserved by calling © **307/344-7311.**

Accessible restrooms with sinks and flush toilets are located at all developed areas except West Thumb and Norris. Accessible vault toilets are found at West Thumb and Norris, as well as in most scenic areas and picnic areas.

Many of Yellowstone's roadside attractions, including the Grand Canyon of the Yellowstone's south rim, West Thumb Geyser Basin, much of the Norris and Upper Geyser Basins, and parts of the Mud Volcano and Fountain Paint Pot areas, are negotiable by wheelchair.

Visitor centers at Old Faithful, Grant Village, and Canyon are wheelchair accessible, as are the Norris Museum and the Fishing Bridge Visitor Center.

Handicapped parking is available at Old Faithful, Fishing Bridge, Canyon, Norris, and Grant Village, though you'll have to look for it; at some locations it is near a Hamilton store.

3 A Park Primer

A BRIEF HISTORY

A trip to Yellowstone has changed considerably since the days of George Cowan: When he visited the park in 1877, he set a new standard for "roughing it." Cowan was kidnapped from his horse-packing camp and shot by the Nez Perce Indians, then subsisted on roots and coffee grounds as he dragged his paralyzed body for days through the wilderness.

Let's just say the United States government had a bit to learn about how to run the world's first national park. It still does, but it's getting better all the time. For more than 125 years, the National Park Service has been directing traffic at this complex intersection of wilderness and tourism, juggling the protection of powerful natural wonders while allowing for civilized comforts. And if anyone complains that the roads are potholed or the coffee is cold . . . well, George Cowan would not be sympathetic.

Yellowstone was never known as a hospitable place. Nomadic Indian bands crossed the plateau but never settled there, except for a small group of Shoshone known as "Sheepeaters." The first non-Indian to lay eyes on Yellowstone's geothermal wonders was probably John Colter, an explorer who broke away from the Lewis and Clark expedition in 1806 and spent 3 years wandering a surreal landscape of mud pots and geysers. When he described his discovery on his return to St. Louis, no one believed him, and he settled down to life as a farmer. Later, miners and fur trappers followed in his footsteps, occasionally making curious reports of a sulfurous world still sometimes called "Colter's Hell."

The first significant exploration of what would become the park took place in 1869, when a band of Montanans led by David Folsom completed a 36-day expedition. Folsom and his group traveled up the Missouri River, then into the heart of the park, where they discovered the falls of the Yellowstone, mud pots, Yellowstone Lake, and the Fountain Geyser. But it was an 1871 expedition led by the director of the U.S. Geological Survey, Ferdinand Hayden, that brought back astonishing photographs of Yellowstone's wonders by William H. Jackson and drawings by artist Thomas Moran.

Crude health spas and thin-walled "hotels" went up near the hot springs. A debate soon followed over the potential for commercial development and exploitation of the region. Many people take credit for the idea of creating the national park—members of the Folsom party later told a story about thinking it up around a campfire in the Upper Geyser Basin. In any case, the idea caught on as Yellowstone explorers hit the lecture circuit back East. In March 1872, President Ulysses S. Grant signed legislation declaring Yellowstone a national park.

No one had any experience in managing a wilderness park, and many mistakes were made: Superintendents granted favorable leases to friends with commercial interests in the tourism industry; poachers ran amuck, decimating the wildlife population; a laundry business near Mammoth cleaned linens in the hot pool.

By 1886, things were so bad that the Army took control of the park; their firm-fisted management practices resulted in new order and protected the park from those intent upon exploiting it, although the military participated in the eradication of the plateau's wolf population. By 1916, efforts to make the park more visitor-friendly began to bear fruit: Construction of the first roads had been completed and guest housing was available in the area. Stewardship of the park was then transferred to the newly created National Park Service.

THE PARK TODAY

The job of the National Park Service will never be easy in Yellowstone, where rangers must preserve a natural environment for a wide range of species—including one very demanding creature, the human being. Tourists come from around the world to visit Yellowstone, some with high expectations of creature comforts in the wilderness.

It's challenge enough to provide an unimpaired view of the wildlife, scenery, and thermal features of the park to three million visitors a year. It's even harder to amend the environmental impact of those visitors on the forests, meadows, thermal areas, and wildlife habitat. The powers that be debate a number of issues today: the reintroduction of wolves, their protection, and their impact on livestock around the park; the invasion of Yellowstone Lake by man-introduced species such as Mackinaw trout; the crush of automobile and snowmobile

Wildlife & Where to Spot It

Biologists consider Yellowstone one of the most important wildlife habitats in the world. You'll find all sorts of creatures here, from the dramatic bald eagle and grizzly bear to the less-publicized reptiles and insects of the thermal areas. What particularly distinguishes this collection of wildlife is that the giant herds of elk, the thousands of bison, and all their brethren are free-roaming. Grizzly bears and wolves in the wild are currently extremely rare in the Lower 48.

Some claim the **bison** (buffalo) that once blanketed the Great Plains were only driven to the Yellowstone Plateau when they were hunted off the plains. Regardless, this herd is right at home here, wandering along the main thoroughfares without much regard for their human spectators. They are easy to view in the summer months, often seen munching grass, wallowing in dust pits, and even wrestling sumo-style for mates in the **Lamar, Hayden,** and **Pelican Valleys;** the **Bechler River area;** and in the geyser areas **near the Firehole River.** A caution: Keep your distance from these behemoths. They have poor eyesight and cranky dispositions, and, like moose, they can move with sudden speed (up to 35 mph) to batter anyone who enters their personal space.

Biologists have trouble agreeing on how many **bears** there are in Yellowstone, but most will acknowledge that their numbers are on the rise. Their food supplies seem to have stabilized a bit with the wolf reintroduction (more carcasses) and pro-cutthroat fishing regulations. In the Yellowstone Ecosystem there are probably about 1,000 black bears and 600 grizzlies.

Decades ago, bears foraged in open-pit garbage dumps near the lodges, or guests hand-fed bears who begged along the park roads. When the dumps were closed in the 1970s and bear-feeding was prohibited, the population of bears plummeted. Diminishing habitat around the park also had an impact. However, bears are creative omnivores, and they've found new food sources in the wild. Come spring, they tend to gravitate toward elk and bison (either the very young or very old) and wolf kills, but their diet has been assessed as being about three-quarters vegetarian.

Black bears are most commonly sighted in the spring, sometimes with cubs, in the Canyon-Tower and Madison–Old Faithful areas, where they feed on green grass and herbs, berries, ants, and carrion. The more aggressive grizzly's unpredictable behavior makes them the likely suspect in the rare instances of bear attacks on humans, but blacks have demonstrated that they also are capable in this regard. Rangers closely monitor their movements during late spring in areas near trout-spawning streams and carrion sites to minimize the possibility of an encounter.

Odds of seeing a grizzly are best during May and June, in the Lamar Valley, Hayden Valley, and the Geyser area, before they retreat into the backwoods for the summer. Backcountry travelers often see bears in the remote Thorofare Country on the park's southeast border, where bears (and avid anglers) journey to the Yellowstone River headwaters for the spawning cutthroat trout in the spring.

It is estimated that 63,000 **elk** (wapiti) populate the ecosystem. You should have no problem telling elk from deer or antelope by their size (typically 900 lb.), the males' large antler racks, and their chestnut-brown heads and necks, with a distinctive tan patch on their rumps. One herd can usually be located around **Mammoth Hot Springs;** others are often seen in the meadows between Old Faithful and Madison Junction.

During winter months, the northern Yellowstone herd heads to a winter grazing area near Gardiner. Listen in the fall for the distinctive bugling of the males, a throaty gargle that slips into a piercing, high whistle.

Moose are more solitary than elk; they're grumpy loners, and not very patient with the tourists that flock around whenever they appear. Those appearances are usually in alder thickets and marshes around streams, particularly around Canyon and near Shoshone Lake in the backcountry (not to mention Grand Teton National Park). They are recognizable by their dark coats, massive antlers, and the fleshy dewlap that hangs beneath their necks like a bell. A moose is capable of traveling at 30 mph; cows will charge any perceived threat to a calf, and bulls become particularly ornery in the fall. Give them a wide berth.

The **pronghorn,** usually labeled antelope (although they are unrelated to true antelope), is often sighted grazing near the northern entrance to Yellowstone. These fleet and flighty animals have excellent vision, and they'll take off at 45 mph when photographers try to get near. You might have better luck in the fall, when lonely males wander stoically by themselves. The pronghorn is identified by its short, black horns, tan-and-white body, and black accent stripes.

Not to be outnumbered by their larger cousins, thousands of **mule deer** live within park boundaries. Most often spotted near forest boundaries or in areas covered with grass and sagebrush, their most distinguishing characteristics are their huge ears and white rumps with black-tipped tails.

For a long time, the **coyote** has been the predator most often spotted by park visitors, but the arrival of wolves has taken its toll on the smaller canine. Coyotes may be seen alone or in small packs—they're particularly visible in winter—with brown to gray coats that grow silvery after the snow falls. They prey on small animals like squirrel and rabbit, or larger ungulates like elk and deer that have grown old or ill. They'll also scavenge the leftovers of other predators. Biologists estimate there are around 500 coyotes in the park. You'll see them out in the open meadows of the **Hayden Valley,** and you might get lucky and see the interaction between wolves and coyotes in places like **Slough Creek.**

Gray wolves from Canada were reintroduced to the park in 1995, and while many have been killed or relocated, it appears they're here to stay, feasting on the smorgasbord of elk in the northern end of the park. There are about 165 wolves in the ecosystem today. The **Lamar Valley** is where they were first released, and patient observers at dawn and dusk can sometimes see the Druid Peak Pack along the river or the Rose Creek Pack on the slopes above Slough Creek. Look for ranger Rick McIntyre—he's there most of the summer—and ask for his advice, or check at the east gate or Mammoth Visitor Center for the best sighting opportunities. A laminated one-page guide, *Wolves of Yellowstone* (available at park bookstores), is a must for the serious lupine tracker.

traffic; the privatization of park operations; and the diminishing store of undeveloped land around the park, which traditionally provides a cushion for Yellowstone's wildlife populations.

The National Park Service is determined that the laws of nature should remain unaffected by human intrusion; that's why firefighters let the 1988 fire burn until fears arose about the loss of park buildings and human lives. A similar situation may develop with the wildlife population, which is protected within the park but not outside of it, and therefore has stretched certain food supplies to their limits. Herds of elk, deer, and bison have ballooned in size, raising questions about the ecosystem's ability to support them; some say the reintroduction of wolves and the rebounding bear population may solve the problem naturally.

When Canadian gray wolves were transplanted to the park's northeast corner in 1995, the reintroduction proved astonishingly successful: The wolves reproduced rapidly and immediately began enlarging their range, breaking into new packs and roaming beyond the park boundaries. When a few developed a taste for calves and lambs, ranchers were incensed, lawsuits began to fly, and a federal judge in Wyoming ruled in 1998 that all reintroduced wolves should be removed. This decision was overturned in 2000, and the wolves are finally entrenched in Yellowstone for the long haul.

Then there are the snowmobilers. They come from the flatlands, singing praises for the fine trail system in and around the park. The noisy, pollution-heavy engines are not exactly ecologically friendly, but the gateway towns are staunch snowmobile proponents, because the activity boosts their economies in the moribund winter. The park adopted a controversial plan in 2000 that would ban all snowmobiles by 2003. So far, litigation has prevented the park from finalizing the plan, but snowmobilers might have to settle for the trails in surrounding federal lands instead of those in Yellowstone in coming years.

There are summer traffic problems, too, particularly involving house-sized motor homes and trailers navigating the narrow, twisting park roads. They create traffic jams and force bicyclists off the road. Along with cars, they interrupt the passage of wildlife like bison and elk. Traffic studies suggest the problem will worsen, and the government has shown little inclination to spend the money necessary to fix Yellowstone's beaten-up roads.

At press time, the primary road-construction projects include bridge work at Dunraven Pass, which will be closed during the 2002 season, short-circuiting plans to complete the Grand Loop for the summer; and upgrades between Madison and Norris during both the 2002 and 2003 seasons.

"Privatization" has been a watchword since the Reagan era, and increasingly the parks are allowing concessionaires to take over management duties, such as campground management, in order to put private dollars to work where federal funds once did the job. Critics fear that this leads to profit-driven decisions: Certainly the expansion of winter activities makes more economic than environmental sense. On the other hand, the beautiful new Old Faithful Snow Lodge is a vast improvement over the lodge it replaced, thanks to Yellowstone Park Lodges. Park management has taken matters into its own hands by steadily increasing entrance and user fees. A good portion of these fees will be used for building maintenance, salaries, roads, and other park infrastructure needs.

PLANT LIFE OF THE PARK

The large mammals may be the stars of Yellowstone National Park, but flower-lovers will find plenty to enjoy here, too. Flowers and shrubs broadcast bright shades of blues, purples, yellows, and oranges throughout the park, providing a colorful accent to the forests and meadows.

The plateau's volcanoes, fires, and glaciers have created a series of tumultuous changes that have had an enormous impact on plant life. At one site in the Lamar Valley, the inspection of petrified tree stumps exhumed by erosion resulted in the identification of 27 distinct layers of forests, one atop the other.

The plants have evolved with the ever-changing Yellowstone environment. Forests once populated with hardwood, like maple, magnolia, and sycamore, are now filled with conifers, the most common of which are pine, spruce, and fir. A smattering of cottonwood and aspen thrive in the cool park temperatures.

Vegetation zones tend to reflect altitude: Lower-elevation valleys tend to be dry and grassy, with sagebrush and few trees; forests of fir dominate between about 6,000 and 7,500 feet, followed by lodgepole pine stands and then spruce and more fir up to the timberline, with open meadows where wildflowers explode in the spring. At high elevations, shrubs and carpet-like vegetation take over, and you have to lean over to examine the tiny blossoms.

Attempts by park officials to manage the ecosystem have had an impact, too. Climax forests—a plant succession leading to conifers that create a shady canopy and block the growth of seedlings—had a prolonged reign in Yellowstone because of fire suppression, which contributed to the ferocity of fires in the dry summer of 1988. However, once the fires were allowed to burn, it became clear that fire was crucial in the life cycle of lodgepole pine. Since its cones release seeds only after a burn, many of the areas that were "ravaged" in 1988 now have an astounding 1 million saplings per acre.

4 Seeing the Highlights

This is a wonderland you can return to again and again, sampling a different pleasure each time. All the sites mentioned here are easily accessible along the loop tours detailed in section 5, "Driving the Park." The farther you get from the pavement, and the farther from July and August you schedule your visit, the more private your experience will be.

We've organized this list geographically, following the roadways that form a figure-8 at the heart of the park. We'll begin in the north, then move south, first

Moments Hot Spring Hot Spot ★★

Once upon a time, travelers in Yellowstone bathed, cooked, and laundered their clothes in the hot springs, but such activities are illegal nowadays. There is one spot on the east side of the road to the North Entrance, however, where the public is allowed to take a dip. Called Boiling River, the hot springs here run into the Gardner River and create a series of temperature-graded (around 100° F) pools. This was once a late-night skinny-dipping secret, but we can't do that anymore: There's a parking lot, gate, and posted hours (daybreak–dusk, closed during the high springtime runoff). Regardless, this is just about the best possible way to cap off a day of touring and hiking: sitting in Mother Nature's hot tub, surrounded by beautiful scenery.

along the east side, then the west. Get out the oversized map you receive at the gate or by mail and follow along:

MAMMOTH HOT SPRINGS

At the park's north entrance, 5 miles (8km) south of Gardiner, Mammoth Hot Springs is home to spectacular limestone terraces, historic park buildings, and the Mammoth Hot Springs Hotel. It's one of the older park settlements, with stone buildings dating back to the late 19th century, when the army was stationed here at Fort Yellowstone.

There are no geysers at **Mammoth Hot Springs Terraces,** but this cascading staircase of hillside hot pools, among the oldest in the park, offers a boardwalk tour of gorgeous pastels in shades of white, yellow, orange, and green, the unintentionally artistic work of microscopic bacteria in the sediments. The mineral-rich springs constantly bubble to the surface, depositing travertine as the water cools in contact with the air. It's a vivid illustration of the park's unusual geological situation: a rare geologic hot spot of seismic activity in the middle of the continent, where molten rock nearly makes it to the earth's surface.

Whether or not you spend the night at the **Mammoth Hot Springs Hotel**—not the most distinguished lodging in the park, but it has historic character—you should drop by the **Albright Visitor Center.** This building once housed Fort Yellowstone's bachelor officers, but you won't find a pool table here today; rather, you'll find displays on park history, wildlife and photography exhibits, smiling rangers dispensing advice, and numerous park publications and maps. Films on the park's origin and the art it inspired are shown throughout the day. A special treat for international visitors is the opportunity to get their visas stamped with the official Yellowstone National Park document stamp. For more information, call © **307/344-2263.**

TOWER–ROOSEVELT AREA

East of Mammoth Hot Springs you enter a delicious mix of high plains, deep forest, and twisting rivers. Toward the northeast corner lies one of the most beautifully serene valleys in the Rockies, the **Lamar.** This glacier-carved swath of grassy bottom and forested flanks sits apart from the vehicular chaos at the center of the park, a good thing because the traffic here is not automobiles, but the bison, bears, wolves, and elk whose presence has earned the valley the nickname, "The Serengeti of the United States." If you continue east and leave Yellowstone via the park's northeast entrance, you'll be heading up to the spectacular views of the **Beartooth Highway.**

The area around the Tower–Roosevelt Junction was once a favorite spot of U.S. president Teddy Roosevelt. At **Roosevelt Lodge,** visitors can enjoy the kind of simple accommodations that fit the tastes of the Bull Moose himself: those with the rustic flavor of the Old West. This is the most relaxed of the park's villages, and a great place to take a break from the more crowded attractions. Get into the cowboy spirit by taking a **guided trail ride,** a **stagecoach ride,** or a **wagon ride.** You can skip the dining room and ride out for an **Old West cookout,** served from a chuck wagon to patrons who arrive by either horseback or wagon. The nearby 132-foot **Tower Falls** is named for the looming volcanic pinnacles at its brink and provides an excellent photo opportunity. While in the area, take time to view the petrified forests on **Specimen Ridge,** where a wide variety of fossilized plants and trees date back millions of years. All things considered, Roosevelt is a great place to escape the hordes.

Finds **Petrified Wood**

With so many hot pots, mountain peaks, geysers, and bison to gawk at, it's not surprising that many visitors to Yellowstone miss some of the finest examples of petrified forest found anywhere. The trees were preserved, scientists believe, when their organic matter was replaced by volcanic material during one of the many eruptions on the plateau. Some of the tree trunks still stand, particularly in the Specimen Ridge area in the northeast area of the park, and they are a monument to the region's warmer, swampier past: sycamore, magnolias, and dog-woods are all preserved in stone. Check at the Tower Ranger Station for maps showing you where to find petrified wood. This is not a renewable resource: Don't touch or take.

Further south, **Pelican and Hayden Valleys** are the two most prominent remnants of large, ancient lakebeds in the park. They are now vast, sub-alpine meadows, thriving with plant life that provides feed for sizeable bison and elk populations. You might see a bear here, too.

THE GRAND CANYON OF YELLOWSTONE

Hayden Valley flanks the featured attraction of the park's center: the **Grand Canyon of the Yellowstone River** ★★★, a colorful, 1,000-foot-deep, 24-mile-long (39km) gorge that some can't resist comparing to its larger counterpart in Arizona. Okay, then: This canyon is greener, the water clearer, the air cooler, and it has two dramatic waterfalls, the big one taller than Niagara. As it drops through this gorge, the Yellowstone River in some places moves at 64,000 cubic feet of water per second.

Volcanic explosions and glaciers surging and receding shaped the canyon. The geological story is told in the canyon itself, where hard lava flows formed the lip of the falls next to softer quartz-rich rock that gave way, allowing the river to cut deeply through the layers of red, orange, tan, and brown hue. Plumes of steam pinpoint vents along the canyon's rock spires, where viewing opportunities are extensive and varied. There are many hikes along and down into the canyon, which is 24 miles (39km) long and up to 1,200 feet deep, and you'll be surprised at how few people you encounter away from the parking areas. Many do trek down to a view of the Lower Falls on **Uncle Tom's Trail** ★★ from the South Rim, and a short path from a parking area for Upper Falls View also offers breathtaking views. Two other favorite trails are **Inspiration Point** and **Artist Point;** both are handicapped-accessible.

Canyon Village has a sprawling 1950s look, which puts off some visitors. It's also crowded, but you can find many useful services there, and some of the newer lodging is an improvement.

NORRIS GEYSER BASIN

If you travel south from Mammoth on the west side of the park, you pass some interesting rock formations, **Obsidian Cliff** and **Roaring Mountain,** before coming to **Norris Geyser Basin** ★. Norris is not nearly as famous as the Mammoth terraces or the crowd of geysers around Old Faithful, but there's a lot going on here, from the steaming pools of the **Porcelain Basin** to the eruptions of **Echinus Geyser.** If you're the patient type, you can sit by the blowhole of **Steamboat Geyser** and hope that this, the largest of park geysers with a maximum height of 400 feet, will erupt. But be prepared to wait: It has erupted only twice in the last 15 years, once in 2000 and once in 1991. This is one of the hottest, most active thermal areas on the plateau, at the intersection of three faults in the earth's crust; when they shift, new geysers pop up and old ones disappear. The **Norris Geyser Basin Museum** explains geothermal features, and the nearby **Museum of the National Park Ranger** tracks the history of the park's stewards.

OLD FAITHFUL

About a quarter of the world's geysers are crowded into hills, valleys, and riverbanks around Old Faithful, where the hot pools and spouts are divided into three areas: **Lower, Midway,** and **Upper Geyser Basins.** Here you'll find burbling mud pots, radiant pools like **Chromatic Spring,** and geysers with a variety of tricks, from the angled shots of **Daisy Geyser** to the witches' cauldron of **Crested Pool.**

But the grand old dame of geysers, the star of the show, is **Old Faithful.** Over the last 100 years, its eruptions have been remarkably consistent, blowing 21 to 23 times daily with a column averaging about 134 feet and a duration of about 40 seconds. Recent seismic activity has elongated the intervals between eruptions a tad, but it's still the most predictable geyser in the world. Estimates posted at the visitor centers are give-or-take 10 minutes; if the last eruption was a long one, you might have to wait 2 hours for the next burst. (No big deal—there's plenty else to see here.)

Since the geyser is one of the key park attractions, the **Old Faithful Visitor Center** (© 307/545-2750) is larger than most of its counterparts. An excellent film describing the geysers and their microscopic inhabitants is shown throughout the day in an air-conditioned auditorium—quite a relief on hot July afternoons. The Park Service hopes to close the existing visitor center by 2003 and cut the ribbon on a new state-of-the-art building, which will feature interactive exhibits and a environmentally-integrated architectural style.

A National Historic Landmark, the shingled, steep-roofed **Old Faithful Inn** was built of local stone and hand-hewn timber, including a pair of interior balconies above the lobby floor. See "Where to Stay in the Park," later in this chapter, for a full description and review.

YELLOWSTONE LAKE

West of Old Faithful, over Craig Pass, or south of Canyon, through the wildlife-rich **Hayden Valley,** is gigantic **Yellowstone Lake,** another natural wonder unique to Yellowstone. At 20 miles (32km) long, 14 miles (23km) wide, and more than 300 feet deep in places, it's the largest lake in the world above 7,000 feet in elevation. If you took a dip in the frigid water (not recommended), you could hardly guess that the caldera underneath the lake is filling with hot liquid magma, actually tilting the lake northward at a measurable pace. The caldera is the sunken remainder of a huge volcanic blast 600,000 years ago, and another 600,000 years before that. Experts believe it's due to blow again sometime in the next 100,000 years. Volcanic underpinnings aside, grizzlies work the tributary streams in the spring when fish spawn (some campgrounds are closed), and lots of other wildlife congregate here, including moose and osprey.

The lake has long been a favorite fishing spot, but recent regulations have made cutthroat trout a catch-and-release species parkwide. This is part of a desperate attempt by park biologists to help the cutthroat come back against the planted Mackinaw or lake trout, which dine on small cutthroat and therefore are not to be released alive. You'll see some big sailboats braving the quirky winds of the lake, and experienced paddlers may want to **kayak** or **canoe** into the south and southeast arms of the lake, which are closed to motorboats. These deep bays are true wilderness, and great areas to fish and view wildlife. When you pick up a boating permit, you'll also get a stern warning from rangers to watch out for the changeable weather if you get out on the lake's open water. They're right to urge caution; even the best paddlers risk their lives in a sudden afternoon storm.

Lake Village, on the north shore of the lake, offers a large range of amenities, including fine restaurants at either the rustic **Lake Lodge** or the majestic 100-year-old **Lake Yellowstone Hotel.** This hotel has Greek columns and a spacious solarium overlooking the lake, the best place for a cocktail within park boundaries. It's very different from the Old Faithful Inn, but a rival for its beauty and history. Just south of Lake Village is **Bridge Bay Marina,** the park's water-activity center. Here you can obtain guided fishing trips, small-boat rentals, and dock rentals; there's also a store and tackle shop.

WEST THUMB & GRANT VILLAGE
On the south end of the lake, at **West Thumb,** the boiling thermal features extend out into the lake. You can see steaming cones and churning water created by the action of the underwater hot springs. **Fishing Cone** is rumored to be the place where fishermen once used the "hook and cook" method, immediately tossing their catch into a hot pot for instant meal preparation. Don't try it—it's illegal to drop anything into a thermal feature, and the geyser water has traces of mercury and arsenic. You can walk among the lakeshore pools at the **Central Basin** and look at the colorful, thick fudge of the **Thumb Paint Pots.**

Grant Village, named for President Ulysses S. Grant, was completed in 1984 and is the newest of Yellowstone's villages. It has some of the most modern facilities in the park, but it's also the least inspired. On the plus side, this area is a great vantage point for watching sunrises and afternoon squalls move across the lake, and you may see **river otters** and **cutthroat trout** in the old marina's waters. (Come wintertime, the otters like to use holes melted by the underwater thermal features as base camps for ice-fishing escapades.) The **Grant Visitor Center** plays a video that explores the role of fire in the Yellowstone ecosystem.

5 Driving the Park
Yellowstone has approximately 370 miles (596km) of paved roads, and in recent years the park has struggled to catch up with a backlog of maintenance—filling potholes, widening shoulders, and redoing some roads completely. The wear and tear of heavy RVs and trailers undoes the work as quickly as it's done, and since road construction is limited to the warm months of summer, drivers often

 Tips Roadwork Hot Spots for 2002 and 2003

Dunraven Pass will be closed during the summer of 2002, creating a break in the popular Upper Loop between Canyon Village and Tower-Roosevelt. And while it will not be closed, an ongoing project between Madison and Norris is expected to continue through the 2003 season.

> **Tips** **Winter Road Conditions**
>
> Be cautious if you're planning a winter road trip to Yellowstone. Icy roads and blinding snowstorms take their toll every year. The park itself is largely closed to automobiles in the winter—only the northern entrance is open to wheeled vehicles. The road through Lamar Valley to the northeast gate is kept open to get essential supplies to Cooke City, but from there you can go no farther north into Montana, because the Beartooth Highway is impassable in winter. The rest of the park's primary roads are open during the snowy months to snowcoaches and snowmobiles . . . and bison, which find the packed roads convenient and think nothing of lolling along with a line of frustrated snowmobilers waiting for a chance to pass. For up-to-the-minute information on weather and road conditions, call the **visitor information center** at ⓒ 307/344-7381.

encounter delays along the park's roads. If you travel in July or August, you'll share these frustrations with a lot of other drivers. But you can see a surprising number of interesting sights along the figure-8 roadways at the heart of the park. You can take in both north and south loops—together known as the **Grand Loop**—in 1 day if a quick blink at each stop is enough for you. Better, though, to take your time, or explore different areas on different trips.

THE UPPER LOOP
At 70 miles (113km), the Upper Loop, which begins at the north entrance, is the shorter of the two loop drives. If you start by going east from **Mammoth Hot Springs** and the park headquarters, orient yourself at the **Albright Visitor Center,** then take in the **Blacktail Plateau** or rustic **Roosevelt Lodge** (a good place for lunch). If you'd prefer, take a side trip up the pretty **Lamar Valley** ⚑ for wildlife viewing at least as far as Slough Creek—checking out the views of **Tower Falls** and **Mount Washburn** (the highest point in the park)—and up **Dunraven Pass** to look out over the Mirror Plateau. Then, if road construction permits, head west from Canyon Junction to Norris Junction and north to the **Norris Geyser Basin** ⚑⚑, with pastel pools and a few burbles and spouts, and its fine museum. You'll continue north past **Roaring Mountain** (a travertine cascade by the road; get out only if you have some extra time) and **Obsidian Cliff** (same advice), and then have dinner in the dining room at the historic **Mammoth Hot Springs Hotel.**

If you're doing only the Upper Loop on this trip, you should include the **Grand Canyon of the Yellowstone** on your tour—it's a short ways south of Canyon Village, where the loop runs west to Norris.

THE LOWER LOOP
The longer **Lower Loop** covers some of the more famous park landmarks in its 96-mile (155km) circuit. Beginning at the south entrance, you would join the loop at the **West Thumb** of Yellowstone Lake, where there are hot springs and mud pots. If you go east, the loop skirts the west shore of **Yellowstone Lake** to the handsome **Lake Hotel** at the north end, where the Yellowstone River outlet is spanned by **Fishing Bridge.** The route then encompasses the **Grand Canyon of the Yellowstone, Madison Junction** and the **Firehole Canyon Drive,** the **Lower Geyser Basin** and the **Fountain Paintpots,** the **Midway Geyser Basin,**

and the **Upper Geyser Basin** and stalwart **Old Faithful,** where you can top off the day with a meal at historic **Old Faithful Inn.** Then head east over **Craig Pass** to the lake again.

Put the two loops together and you've done the Grand Loop of approximately 166 miles (267km). At its conclusion, you will have seen most of the major attractions in the park.

OUT OF THE LOOPS: ENTRANCES & OTHER DETOURS

Rapturous descriptions of the **Lamar Valley** ✸ elsewhere in this guide should encourage you to take a run out of the park's northeast entrance. The valley is wide and beautiful, with elk and bison grazing by the river, and coyotes, wolves, and grizzly bears making guest appearances. Beyond the park gate you'll find Cooke City, a friendly little town, and then a switchback climb north on the Beartooth Highway, with its spectacular views.

Roads to the other entrances also have allure. If you head east along the north shore of Yellowstone Lake, you'll begin climbing into **Sylvan Pass,** the 8,530-foot exit route that will take you through the east gate into the beautiful Wapiti Valley and eventually to the town of Cody (see chapter 12, "Cody & North Central Wyoming"). The north and east shores of the lake have beaches where you can sun, swim, or begin a paddling journey to the remote southern corners of the lake. The **south entrance road** skirts **Lewis Lake** and follows the **Gardner River,** where you'll often see the graceful parabolas of fly-fishing lines at work. You'll also see some of the stark handiwork of the 1988 fires. Similarly, areas along the **west entrance road** are still marked by the burnt husks of trees; there are also peaceful views of the **Madison River** along this road.

There are also some trips off the main roads that are worth taking. Try the short **Firehole Canyon Drive** (just south of Madison Junction, head west on the one-way loop) for a look at Firehole Falls and a dip in the idyllic spring-warmed swimming hole a bit farther down the road. For a chance at sighting wolves, drive into **Slough Creek** in the Lamar Valley in the early morning or late afternoon. Drive across the Yellowstone River just south of Canyon Village and hike from majestic overlook to majestic overlook along the **South Rim.** Drive to the **Mount Washburn** picnic area off Dunraven Pass, and if you're feeling energetic, hike to the top of the 10,243-foot peak.

6 Summer Sports & Activities

BICYCLING

Considering the vast expanse of real estate the parks cover, the challenging terrain, and the miles of paved roads and trails, a cyclist could conclude that the park is a prime area for biking, on or off the roads.

It looks good on paper, but the reality borders on harrowing. The narrow and twisty roads have no bike lanes, so bikers continually fight for elbow room with wide-bodied RVs and trailers. Off-road opportunities are limited because bikes are allowed on only a small number of trails.

Nevertheless, plenty of bicyclists take the challenge. The following trails are available to bikers, but know that you will share the roads with hikers. The **Mount Washburn Trail,** leaving from the Old Chittenden Road, is a strenuous trail that climbs 1,400 feet. The **Lone Star Geyser Trail,** accessed at Kepler Cascade near Old Faithful, is an easy 1-hour ride on a user-friendly road. Near Mammoth Hot Springs, **Bunsen Peak Road** and **Osprey Falls Trails** present a combination ride/hike: The first 6 miles (10km) travel around Bunsen Peak;

getting to the top requires a fairly short (but fairly steep) hike. A round-trip hike to Osprey Falls adds another 4 miles (6km) to the journey.

Bike rentals are available in West Yellowstone at **Yellowstone Bicycles** (© 406/646-7815) and in Jackson at **Hoback Sports** (© 307/733-5335).

BOATING

The best place to enjoy boating in Yellowstone is on **Yellowstone Lake,** which has easy access and panoramic views. The lake is one of the few areas where powerboats are allowed; you can rent rowboats and outboard motorboats at **Bridge Bay Marina** (© 307/242-3876). Motorboats, canoes, and kayaks can be used on Lewis Lake (about 15 miles [24km] north of the south entrance) also.

FISHING

There are two primary types of anglers in Yellowstone. First are the fly casters, purists more interested in the artistry and seduction of fly-fishing than in keeping what they catch. There are stretches of the Yellowstone and Madison Rivers where the anglers are packed tippet to tippet and the trout must be punch drunk from catch-and-release.

Then there are the powerboat fishermen who troll the deep waters of **Yellowstone Lake.** Seven varieties of game fish live in the parks: five trout species (cutthroat, rainbow, brown, brook, and lake), grayling, and mountain whitefish. Of the trout, only the cutthroat are native, and they are being pressured in the big lake by the larger lake trout. As a result, you can't keep any pink-meat cutthroat caught in Yellowstone Lake, and you must keep any lake trout. These limits seem to have diminished the number of fishing boats on Yellowstone Lake in recent years, but they're necessary.

The Yellowstone fishing season typically opens on the Saturday of Memorial Day weekend and ends on the first Sunday in November, except for Yellowstone Lake, which has a slightly shorter season, and the lake's tributaries, which are closed until July 15 to avoid conflicts between humans and grizzly bears, both of which are attracted to spawning trout.

The **required Yellowstone fishing permit** is available at any ranger station, visitor center, or Hamilton Store in the park. Anyone older than 15 needs a fishing permit, which costs $10 for 10 days or $20 for the season. Fishers aged 12 to 15 also need a permit, but it's free. Casters under 12 can fish without a permit when supervised by an adult. Season permits can be obtained by mail, from **Visitors Services,** P.O. Box 168, Yellowstone National Park, WY 82190.

In June, one of the best fishing spots is on the **Yellowstone River** downstream from Yellowstone Lake, where the cutthroat trout spawn; anglers head to **Madison River** near the west entrance in July and then again in late fall for rainbow and some brown trout; in late summer, the **Lamar River** and **Soda Butte Creek** in the park's beautiful northeast corner are popular spots to hook cutthroats in September. You'll find more isolation at **Trout Lake,** a small backcountry lake about 10 miles (16km) west of the northeast entrance.

You can fish the **Yellowstone River** below the Grand Canyon by hiking down into **Seven Mile Hole,** a great place to cast (thanks to the dearth of vegetation to snag on) for cutthroat trout from July to September, with the best luck around Sulphur Creek.

Other good fishing stretches include the **Gibbon and Firehole Rivers,** which merge to form the Madison River on the park's west side, and the 3-mile (5km) **Lewis River Channel** between Shoshone and Lewis Lakes during the fall spawning run of brown trout.

There is an access for anglers with disabilities at the **Madison River,** 3½ miles (6km) west of Madison Junction at the Haynes Overlook. Here you'll find a fishing platform overhanging the river's edge for 70 feet.

HORSEBACK RIDING & LLAMA TREKKING

People who want to pack their gear on a horse, llama, or mule must get permits to enter the Yellowstone backcountry, or hire an outfitter with a permit (see below). If you're looking for just a short ride, Yellowstone Park Lodges offers 1- and 2-hour guided trail rides daily aboard well-broken, tame animals. Stables are located at Canyon Village, Roosevelt Lodge, and Mammoth Hot Springs. Roosevelt Lodge also offers **evening rides** from June into September.

If you're looking for a longer, overnight horse-packing experience, contact the park and request a list of approved concessionaires that lead backcountry expeditions. Most offer customized, guided trips, with meals, horses, and camping and riding gear provided. Costs will run from $200 to $400 per day per person, depending on the length of the trip and number of people. In Gardiner, at the north entrance to the park, **Wilderness Connection** (© **406/848-7287**) offers horseback trips in the park for groups of 4 to 10; coming from the south side of the park, try **Press Stephens, Outfitter** (© **307/455-2250**) in Dubois.

While not a horseback excursion per se, you might also try **Yellowstone Llamas** (© **406/586-6872;** www.yellowstone-llamas.com). Beasts of burden carry the heavy gear, leaving you free to wander the trails. They typically cover 5 to 8 miles (13km) per day, and serve gourmet meals with stream-chilled bottles of wine. Cost is $195 a day per person, $145 for children 12 and under.

7 Winter Sports & Activities

Yellowstone's average snowfall of 4 feet every year provides the perfect backdrop for a multitude of winter activities. The north entrance remains open, so you can drive in from Gardiner for a day, and drive back out. You can travel throughout the park by snowmobile or snowcoach, and spend the night either at Mammoth or at the handsomely rebuilt Old Faithful Snow Lodge. For additional information on all of the following winter activities and accommodations, as well as snowcoach transportation and equipment rentals, contact **Yellowstone Park Lodges** (© **307/344-7311**). There are also many activities, outfitters, and rental shops in the park's gateway towns.

CROSS-COUNTRY SKIING

The best cross-country trails in Yellowstone are the **Lonestar Geyser Trail,** a fairly level 5-mile (8km) round trip through a remote setting, starting at the Old Faithful Snow Lodge, and the **Fern Cascades Trail,** which begins in the Old Faithful housing area on the south side of the road and winds for 3 miles (5km) through a rolling wooded landscape. Energetic skiers can tackle the 12-mile (19km) **Mallard Lake Trail,** though it may take them all day—it departs north of the Old Faithful Lodge area along the north side of the Upper Geyser Basin, then loops north and east to Mallard Lake and back to Old Faithful.

Equipment rentals, ski instruction, ski shuttles to various locations, and guided ski tours are all available at the **Old Faithful Snow Lodge** and the **Mammoth Hot Springs Hotel,** the park's two winter lodging options. Discounts are available for multi-day rentals of skis or snowshoes. Ski instruction costs around $20 per person for a 2-hour group lesson. A half-day guided excursion is around $34 per person; a full day is $60 to $100 per person.

Snowmobiling: To Ban or Not to Ban?

Before President Clinton left office in 2001, he ended an ongoing controversy by establishing a ban on snowmobiles in Yellowstone, effective beginning the winter of 2003–04, with a gradual decrease in the number of snowmobiles permitted to enter each winter until then.

However, gateway communities and snowmobile manufacturers filed lawsuits in 2001, throwing the situation into limbo until another environmental study is completed in 2002. This new study, not yet released at press time, will likely shape the future winter landscape in Yellowstone, whether it is punctuated by the wail of snowmobiles or not.

The **Yellowstone Association Institute** ★★ (© **307/344-2294**) offers winter courses based out of its headquarters in Lamar Valley. Past offerings have included 3-day classes devoted to "Snowshoeing in Yellowstone," "Family Winter Adventure," and "Snow Tracking Ecology." The institute's faculty and staff are a knowledgeable and friendly bunch, and a class is one of the best ways to acquaint yourself with the park in any season.

ICE SKATING

The **Mammoth Hot Springs ice rink** is located behind the old Mammoth Hot Springs Recreation Center. On a winter's night you can rent a pair of skates ($1 an hr.; $4 per day) and glide across the ice of this outdoor rink, while seasonal melodies are broadcast over the PA system. It's cold out there, but there's a warming fire at the rink's edge.

SNOWMOBILING

Roads that are jammed with cars during the summer fill up with bison and snowmobiles during the winter. In deference to the shaggier road warriors, moderate speed limits are strictly enforced, but this is still an excellent way to sightsee at your own pace (a driver's license is required for rental and children under 12 ride free). The cost is $165 for a single rider, $175 per day for two at **Mammoth Hot Springs Hotel** or **Old Faithful Snow Lodge.** A quick lesson will put even a first-timer at ease. A helmet is included with the snowmobile, and you can rent a clothing package for protection against the bitter cold for about $20. **Warming huts** are located at Mammoth, Indian Creek, Canyon, Madison, West Thumb, and Fishing Bridge. They offer snacks, a hot cup of coffee or chocolate, and an excellent opportunity to recover from a chill. *Caution:* Keep an eye on snow conditions. While it's true that snowmobile trails are groomed for travel, when snow cover is scanty, a normally smooth trip can become something akin to riding on a jackhammer. Also, if engine noise is what you came to Yellowstone to escape, this is probably not for you.

Snowmobile rentals are also available in the **gateway communities** of Gardiner and West Yellowstone, Montana, and at Flagg Ranch (see section 1 of this chapter for detailed information). Most rental shops accept reservations weeks in advance, so reserving at least 2 weeks ahead of time is a good idea. Plan on making reservations for the week between Christmas and New Year's at least 6 months in advance.

8 Hiking

Getting your car snarled in one "wildlife jam" after another in pursuit of a glimpse of one of the park's four-legged denizens is one way to enjoy the outdoors. Another is taking a hike, even a short one, because you'll see a whole new side of the park. There are gentle hikes where you never lose sight of the road; there are moderate hikes where you might spend an afternoon penetrating the forest to visit a spot of secluded beauty; and there are overnight trips where you can hike and camp for days without seeing anyone but the people who embarked on the journey with you.

Part of the reason so few people hike and camp in the Yellowstone wilderness is fear of bears. Bear attacks are extremely rare, and usually involve a sow protecting her cubs, but you should carry pepper spray, just in case; when you camp, secure your food and cooking gear in a tree well away from tents. Park rangers can advise you on current bear activity and safe practices. This is true wilderness, but if you equip yourself properly and learn proper techniques, you'll be safer than you are on a city street. If you go into the backcountry, you need a permit (see "Where to Go & How to Reserve a Spot," below), which also ensures that someone knows where you are.

For those who would rather sleep in a bed, there are still excellent day hikes that allow you to escape the crowd and view wildlife in their own habitat, take in the scenery, or climb a peak. Rangers at visitor centers can advise you on a hike to match your interests and abilities, and provide maps of the extensive trail system in the park. Besides a good map, always bring a good supply of water (and, if you can, a purifier or iodine pills) and rain gear.

Here is a small selection of good hikes, long and short. In addition to these individual hikes, the **Continental Divide Trail** (CDT) links many of them together as part of a continuous trail from Mexico to Canada, roughly following the spine of the continent. The Yellowstone Backcountry Office maintains a guide to CDT trails. The Howard Eaton Trail system once went all through the park, but was supplanted by the Grand Loop Road. Sections of the old trail are still maintained and will be found in trail guides, though some of them closely parallel park roads. For a more extensive list of trails and details than what follows here, pick up longtime ranger Mark C. Marschall's excellent *Yellowstone Trails* (Yellowstone Association, $9.95), or the maps provided by the park.

HIKES AROUND MAMMOTH

The **Beaver Ponds Loop Trail** starts in Mammoth at Clematis Gulch (between Liberty Cap and an old stone Park Service residence) and makes a 5-mile (8km) loop to a series of beaver ponds, where your best chances of seeing the big-tailed beasts are early morning or afternoon. There are some good views coming and going, including Mount Everts. More ambitious hikers can link up with the **Sepulcher Mountain Trail,** which features hot springs, gardens of oddly shaped limestone boulders, and scenic views from the ridges of the Mammoth area. Be in shape for this one and bring a good map of the crisscrossing trail system, because you'll cover at least 12 miles (19km), depending on your route.

Nearby is the **Mount Bunsen Trail** ☆, a short but steep trip to the summit of this volcanic remnant, with a 1,300-foot gain in elevation. Make the hike early and you can watch the morning sun strike Electric Mountain, which glows with a golden hue. The 2-mile (3km) trail passes through mosaic burns from the 1988 fires, and when you get to the top you'll have a view from 3,000 feet above the Yellowstone Valley. After topping the peak, you can take an alternative route down Bunsen's east side and come back along the Old Bunsen Peak Road Trail for a 6-mile (10km) round trip. If you're looking for more, hike the **Osprey Falls Trail** 𝄢 and add 4 miles (6km) and a great view of a 150-foot waterfall to the trek.

HIKES IN THE TOWER-CANYON AREA

The **Tower Falls** overlook is easy to get to; it's only 100 yards from the Tower Falls parking area. Walk a half-mile more along some steep switchbacks and you'll be at the less crowded base of the falls for a stunning view. You can also hike 3½ miles (6km) to the falls from Roosevelt Lodge, a good car-free choice if you happen to be staying there. Begin on the **Lost Lake Trail** and take a left when the trail forks a half-mile from the lodge.

Just south of Canyon Village, the **Chittenden Bridge** crosses from the Loop Road to the South Rim Road near the top of the Grand Canyon of the Yellowstone. You can park and hike either the **South Rim** or **North Rim Trails,** with spurs that drop steeply (but briefly) down to viewing platforms at the Upper and Lower Falls. If you want a more complete and less crowded view of this deep gorge, take the **7-Mile Hole Trail** (which is actually 5½ miles [9km] long) along the north canyon rim. You'll see the Silver Cord Cascade from the rim, and then drop down to the river after a couple of miles in an area where the canyon widens enough for trees. There are some active hot springs along this hike. This is quite a drop (1,400 ft.), and hikers should be prepared for a fairly demanding climb out.

Across the road from Uncle Tom's Trail parking area (the first parking area to the left after crossing the bridge to the South Rim) is the trail head for the **Clear Lake/Ribbon Lake Loop Trail** 𝄢. The hike to Clear Lake is 1½ miles (2km), a gradual climb across a high plateau, and Ribbon Lake lies less than 2 miles (3km) beyond. Bears are often active in this area early in the year, so check with rangers for current conditions before heading out. Views of the plateau improve with each footstep, until you find yourself surrounded by a panoramic view of the mountains surrounding the canyon area. During early and late spring it's a bit more difficult because snow runoff and rain can make trails wet and muddy, but that shouldn't be an impediment to anyone interested in the spectacular views. Clear Lake itself is intimately small, and gives you the opportunity to see subsurface activity of the thermal areas below the lake. On a circumnavigation of the lake along a trail, you will see—and smell—venting activity making its way to the surface; in some spots the lake looks like a small, boiling pot. This trail also connects to the **Howard Eaton Trail,** an arduous, 14-mile (23km) trail to Fishing Bridge and Yellowstone Lake.

The **Mount Washburn Trail** 𝄢𝄢 falls into the "if you can only do one hike, do this one" category. It's a short hike to panoramic views, with wildflowers decorating the way and nonchalant bighorn sheep often browsing nearby. Trail heads are located at the summit at Dunraven Pass (elevation 8,895 ft.), and on Old Chittenden Road, where there's more parking available. Either hike is 6 miles (10km) round-trip, with an increase in elevation of 1,400 feet; however, the climbs are fairly gradual and interspersed with long, level stretches. From the summit, the park will lie before you like a map on a table: You'll see the Absaroka Mountains to the east, Yellowstone Lake to the south, and the Gallatin Mountains to the west and north. In addition to the sheep, you may see marmots and red fox; bears have also made use of the area in recent years. You'll be climbing a summit more than 10,000 feet, so pace yourself, and bring warm clothing to

---

> ⌒ **Finds   An Old Faithful Secret**
>
> For a spectacular view of Old Faithful from above, take the **Observa-
> tion Point Look Trail** ☆, a 2-mile (3km) jaunt (beginning at the Old
> Faithful Visitor Center) that will take you by numerous thermal fea-
> tures on the other side of the Firehole River. Follow the Geyser Hill Trail
> across the river and then climb the switchbacks to the observation
> point to watch Old Faithful burst in relative solitude.

---

fend off the storms that often buffet the top. The hike to the summit is an easy
90-minute walk at a steady pace, which can stretch to 2 hours if you take time
for breaks. There's a day-use shelter in the base of the ranger lookout, with viewing telescopes and restrooms.

HIKES NEAR OLD FAITHFUL

The popular trail to **Lonestar Geyser** covers a little more than 2 miles (3km) of
mostly level terrain to the geyser, which rewards visitors with eruptions up to 50
feet tall every 3 hours. The trail follows the Firehole River, with a forest canopy
to keep it cool in the summer, widening now and then into broad riverbank
meadows. The geyser erupts from a brown cone about 12 feet high, and is surrounded by a meadow pocked by steam vents and thermal features. The path
begins from a parking lot on the Old Faithful–West Thumb road just south of
the Kepler Cascades. It's partially paved to the geyser and open to bicyclists. If
you want to try a less busy (and less scenic) route, take the **Howard Eaton Trail**
just east of the Old Faithful overpass, 3 miles (5km) to the geyser. From the
geyser, you can continue on—bicycles can't—over Grants Pass to join the
Bechler River Trail to Shoshone Lake.

From the Biscuit Basin parking lot, you can take a fine 3-mile (5km) round-
trip hike to **Mystic Falls,** which fall 100 feet to the Firehole River. Continue up
switchbacks to the top of the falls and beyond, and you'll link up with the **Little
Firehole Meadows Trail** to return to Biscuit Basin, with more views on the way.
You can make this trip in less than 2 hours, with only a 460-foot elevation gain.

Fairy Falls plummets a more impressive 200 feet, and can be reached by
hiking 2½ miles (4km) on the Fairy Falls Trail, which begins from the Old
Faithful–Madison road just south of the Midway Geyser Basin parking area.
Hikers who don't mind a slightly longer haul (about 8 miles [13km] round-trip)
will be rewarded with better wildlife-viewing opportunities by starting from the
Imperial Meadows trail head a mile south of the Firehole River bridge on Fountain Flat Drive. The hike winds through an area populated by elk along Fairy
Creek, then past the Imperial Geyser, where it joins the Fairy Creek Trail and
travels east to the base of the falls. The total gain in elevation is only 100 feet. If
you turn west instead, you'll find an unmarked trail north to the Imperial
Geyser.

HIKES NEAR YELLOWSTONE LAKE

At the north end of the lake, the **Pelican Valley Trail** takes a loop north of the
lake around an area loaded with elk, bison, sandhill cranes, trout, eagles, grizzlies, and the new kids on the block, wolves. You can take hikes of different
length, up to a 16-mile (26km) loop, but a lot of folks, having had their fill of
wildflowers and beasts, go no farther than Pelican Creek Bridge, a 7-mile

(12km) round trip. If you continue on, you'll pass through forest and "bear meadows." This is a daytime-only hiking area (9am–7pm), and it's closed in the early summer until July 4 because of bear activity.

The **Elephant Back Loop Trail** is an opportunity to get a bird's-eye view of the island-dotted expanse of Yellowstone Lake, the Absaroka Mountains, and the Pelican Valley—and maybe a moose. It's a great photo opportunity and a fairly easy 4-mile (6km) loop, beginning a mile south of Fishing Bridge Junction off the road to Lake Village.

You can walk along the north shore of Yellowstone Lake on the **Storm Point Trail** ✿ (be aware that it's occasionally closed due to grizzly bear activity). This easy, level 2-miler (3km) terminates at a point jutting into the lake where you'll find lovely panoramic views. It begins in the Indian Pond area, 3½ miles (5.6km) east of Fishing Bridge directly across from the Pelican Valley trail head.

HIKES TO REMOTE AREAS AND OVERNIGHT BACKCOUNTRY TRIPS

The **Bechler Meadows Trail** enters the southwest corner of the park, an area rich in waterfalls, cascades, and thermal features rarely seen by human eyes. The access is by Idaho 47 from Ashton, Idaho, which will take you to the Bechler Ranger Station in the southwest corner of the park. About 5 miles (8km) into the hike, the trail makes several fords of the river as it enters Bechler Canyon, passing Collonade Falls and Iris Falls. There are places on this trail where you can view the Grand Tetons in the distance, and some thermal features bubble and churn on the Bechler River's banks. This is a camping trip—you can cover nearly 30 miles (48km) if you hike all the way into the Old Faithful area—best made late in the summer to avoid high water during creek crossings. You'll need a backcountry permit for overnight stays (see "Camping," later in this chapter).

The **Slough Creek Trail,** which begins in the Lamar Valley of the park's northeast corner, takes hikers through some of the best wildlife habitat in the park. You can see elk, bison, trumpeter swans, the occasional grizzly bear, and the wolves that have quite happily taken up residence among abundant prey. The presence of wolves has made this area more popular, and the trail is also used by horse-packers. The trail starts from the road to Slough Creek campground, following the creek's valley north, then crossing a ridge to a second valley. You can hike a few miles, or take your camping gear and head for the park boundary, 11 miles (18km) to the north.

The **Thorofare Trail** follows the eastern shore of Yellowstone Lake and then skirts the Yellowstone River up into some of the most remote and beautiful backcountry in the Rockies. It's a long, steep trail, but you'll be rewarded with views of the Upper Yellowstone Valley, Two Oceans Plateau, and abundant wildlife. Eventually you'll reach a gorgeous alpine valley just outside the park's boundary, with a ranger station known as Hawk's Rest. Fishermen love this area, as do grizzly bears, especially during the cutthroat trout–spawning season. This is the most remote roadless area in the Lower 48, a good 30 miles (48km) from the trail head at the lake, and even the most capable hikers should consider riding with an outfitter. You can cut 9 miles (14km) off the trip by getting a boat shuttle (about $60 an hr.) to the mouth of the lake's southwest arm (call the marina at ✆ **307/242-3876**), or you can come in through the Bridger–Teton National Forest to the south (check with the forest's Blackrock Ranger Station in Moran, WY, ✆ **307/543-2386**).

9 Camping

WHERE TO GO & HOW TO RESERVE A SPOT

The National Park Service has shifted management of five major campgrounds to Yellowstone Park Lodges, the park concessionaire, which means, predictably, higher fees, but also allows you to make reservations ahead of arrival. The other seven campgrounds still managed by the park are available only on a first-come, first-served basis. These lower-cost campgrounds ($10–$12 per night) are located at Indian Creek, Lewis Lake, Mammoth, Norris, Pebble Creek, Slough Creek, and Tower Fall. We happen to prefer Lewis Lake and Indian Creek, which tend to be available when others are full. Check with rangers about campsite availability when you enter the park; some campgrounds fill up as early as 8am.

Yellowstone Park Lodges operates the large campgrounds at Bridge Bay, Canyon, Grant Village, Madison, and Fishing Bridge, where the fees are $15 per night. The **Fishing Bridge RV Park** is the only campground equipped with water, sewer, and electrical hookups for RVs and trailers, though it accepts hard-sided vehicles only (no tents or tent trailers), and the fees are $28 per night. The **Madison campground** is the first to open on May 1, while **Grant Village** is closed until June 21 to avoid bear conflicts during trout-spawning season. These campgrounds are usually busier, and some, like Bridge Bay, are rather barren of trees unless you get a site on the fringes. Most campgrounds close in September, but Madison is open until mid-October. If you plan to travel in July or August, make your reservations 6 months ahead of time by calling © **307/344-7311;** by writing **Yellowstone Park Lodges,** P.O. Box 165, Yellowstone National Park, WY 82190; or by visiting **www.travelyellowstone.com**.

Camping is allowed only in designated areas and visitors are limited to 14 days between June 15 and Labor Day, and to 30 days the rest of the year, except at Fishing Bridge, where there is no limit. Checkout time for all campgrounds is 10am. Quiet hours are strictly enforced between the hours of 8pm and 8am.

There are plenty of opportunities for backcountry camping as well. Some areas in the Yellowstone backcountry include delicate habitat—the southeast arm of Yellowstone Lake is an example—and visitors must camp in designated areas for a limited time only. Check with the **Yellowstone Backcountry office** (© **307/344-2160**) for rules, reservations, and advice.

WHAT TO EXPECT

Remember, these are campgrounds, not motels, so the amenities are spare. But some have showers and bathrooms and potable water. Check the chart below to determine the level of comfort at each campground. Showers and laundry facilities are available at Canyon, Fishing Bridge, Grant Village, and Madison campgrounds. In addition, campers may use the shower and laundry facilities at Lake Lodge and Old Faithful Lodge.

In the northeast area of the park, the **Tower Fall campground** is near a convenience store, restaurant, and gas station at Tower Lodge, 19 miles (31km) north of Canyon Village and 18 miles (29km) east of Mammoth. **Slough Creek campground** is located in a remote section of the Lamar Valley near the northeast entrance; the good news is there are fewer people, good fishing, and the possibility of wolf sightings; the bad news is that rest room facilities are pit toilets. **Canyon campground** is the busiest in the park. Sites are in a heavily wooded area; the store, restaurants, visitor center, and laundry at Canyon Center are nearby. Because it's in an area of spring bear activity, attempts have been made over the years to close the

RV park at **Fishing Bridge.** It's still open, but only hard-sided camping vehicles are allowed here. **Bridge Bay** is located near the shores of Yellowstone Lake, so you get tremendous views, especially at sunrise and sunset. Unfortunately, though surrounded by the forest, much of the area has been clear-cut, so there's not a whole lot of privacy. It's close to boat-launching facilities and the boat-rental operation. **Madison** and **Norris campgrounds** are attractive, wooded locations in the heart of the park, close to wildlife activity, hiking trails, and rivers. These camp areas seem less like outdoor motels than the big campgrounds on the park's east side.

Amenities for Each Campground, Yellowstone National Park (where flush toilets are not available, vault toilets are provided)

Campground	# Sites	Fee	Showers/ Laundry	Flush Toilets	Disposal Stations	Generators Permitted
Bridge Bay*	430	$15	No	Yes	Yes	Yes
Canyon*	272	$15	Yes	Yes	Yes	Yes
Fishing Bridge*	344	$28	Yes	Yes	Yes	Yes
Grant Village*	425	$15	Yes	Yes	Yes	Yes
Indian Creek	75	$10	No	No	No	No
Lewis Lake	85	$10	No	No	No	No
Madison*	280	$15	No	No	Yes	Yes
Mammoth	85	$12	No	No	Yes	No
Norris	116	$12	No	No	Yes	No
Pebble Creek	36	$10	No	No	No	No
Slough Creek	29	$10	No	No	No	No
Tower Fall	32	$10	No	No	No	No

Reserve through Yellowstone Park Lodges, ℂ **307/344-7311;** TDD 307/344-5395; **www.travelyellowstone.com**.

10 Where to Stay in the Park

For accommodation listings just outside the park, see the section on gateway towns in section 1 at the beginning of this chapter.

The first thing you should know: no televisions. Private bathrooms have arrived and phones are in place, but there are no televisions in the rooms.

Railroad companies built most of the park's hotels and lodges around the turn of the century, and they would offer their primped Victorian guests a package tour that delivered them by train and stagecoach to luxurious resorts with rocking chairs on the verandas and gourmet food. A good deal of that old-style ambience has been thankfully retained at Yellowstone. Many of the newer facilities erected by the park concessionaire (in particular, the Old Faithful Snow Lodge and the new lodges at Canyon) are suitably matched to older buildings, at least on the exterior. However, the push for more features may come in the near future, and, during recent upgrades at the Lake Hotel, the wiring was installed for televisions—just in case. Many of the hotels provide beautiful examples of architecture and craftsmanship, but they're not perfect: The plaster walls transmit some sound and the bathrooms tend to be smallish. However, even the most budget-conscious traveler will find a room in the park that fits the pocketbook. Look over the descriptions below carefully, though, because some of the cheaper lodgings are primitive indeed.

> ⌒*Tips* **Making Reservations**
>
> Yellowstone accommodations are normally open from May to mid-October. The winter season begins in mid-December and runs through March, with accommodations and meals available at either Mammoth Hot Springs or Old Faithful Snow Lodge and Cabins. Vacancy increases before June 15 and after September 15. Rooms are typically fully booked during the peak season in July and August, so reservations should be made up to 6 months in advance. For information or reservations at any of the following locations, contact **Yellowstone Park Lodges** at P.O. Box 165, Yellowstone National Park, WY 82190 (✆ **307/344-7311;** www.travelyellowstone.com).

Canyon Lodge and Cabins   This complex is one of the newer facilities in the park (the Cascade and Dunraven Lodges here both were completed in the '90s), but it can't escape the Disneyland-style atmosphere of the sprawling Canyon Village. However, the lodges are located a mere half-mile from the Grand Canyon of the Yellowstone and Inspiration Point, one of the most photographed spots in the park. Cascade offers simple rooms appointed with tasteful log furnishings in the three-story building; the newer Dunraven is similar, although it is more modern (with an elevator) and located adjacent to a woodland setting. There are also clusters of cabins scattered throughout the village: clean, motel-style configurations. The cabins are single-story duplex and four-plex structures with private bathrooms that are among the largest in the park. They're much nicer than their more rustic counterparts in other centers, but given the sheer number of units involved, this wouldn't be the place to "get away from it all."

In Canyon Village (P.O. Box 165), Yellowstone National Park, WY 82190. ✆ 307/344-7311. www.travel yellowstone.com. 595 units. $127 double; $51–$101 cabin. AE, DC, DISC, MC, V. Closed Oct to late May. **Amenities:** Restaurant, lounge; activities desk; self-serve laundry. *In room:* No phone.

Grant Village   The southernmost of the major overnight accommodations in the park, Grant Village was completed in 1984 and is one of the more contemporary choices in Yellowstone. It's not as architecturally distinctive as the Old Faithful options, consisting of six motel-style chalets set back from the water's edge, but it's also less touristy and more isolated. Rooms are tastefully furnished, most outfitted with light-wood furniture, track lighting, electric heat, and laminate counters. Nicer and more expensive rooms affording lake views have mullioned windows, one queen or one or two double beds, and full bathrooms.

On the West Thumb of Yellowstone Lake (P.O. Box 165), Yellowstone National Park, WY 82190. ✆ 307/ 344-7311. www.travelyellowstone.com. 300 units. $93–$108 double. AE, DC, DISC, MC, V. Closed late Sept to late May. **Amenities:** Restaurant, lounge; activities desk.

Lake Lodge Cabins   These cabins, which surround Lake Lodge, face the lake just around the corner north of the Lake Yellowstone Hotel and Cabins. The old Western lodge's most attractive feature is a large porch with rockers that invite visitors to sit and gaze out across the waters. Two small rock fireplaces contribute a bit of ambience to the main lodge room, but it's not nearly as lavish as the larger lodges in the park. The accommodations are in well-preserved, clean, free-standing cabins near a trout stream that threads through a wooded area. There are nature walks around the lodge, but this is a trout-spawning area, so access is usually restricted early in the summer when grizzlies emerge from hibernation. These cabins come in two grades: Western cabins provide electric heat, paneled walls, two double beds, and shower/tub combination bathrooms, while Frontier cabins are smaller, with only one double bed each and small shower-only bathrooms. You'll need to head outdoors to enjoy the lake views; the only things you can see from your cabin are other cabins. Because the dining options here are a tad short on atmosphere, you might want to make the short trek to the Lake Yellowstone Hotel for a more sumptuous meal in a more appetizing setting.

On Lake Yellowstone (P.O. Box 165), Yellowstone National Park, WY 82190. 🕐 **307/344-7311.** www.travel yellowstone.com. 186 cabins. $53 Frontier cabin; $116 Western cabin. AE, DC, DISC, MC, V. Closed mid-Sept to early June. **Amenities:** Restaurant, lounge; activities desk; self-serve laundry.

Lake Yellowstone Hotel and Cabins 🌟🌟   The ionic columns, dormer windows, and deep porticos on this classic yellow building faithfully recall the year it was built: 1891. It's an entirely different world from the rustic Western style of other park lodgings, but when you find yourself sipping a cocktail in a wicker chair in the huge sun room overlooking the lake while a classical pianist tinkles the keys, you'll appreciate those Victorians' refined tastes. The facility was restored in the early 1990s, and its better rooms are the most comfortable and roomy in the park, with soul-stirring views of the massive lake.

The three- and four-story wings house the hotel rooms, and there are also an annex and an assortment of cabins. The upper-end rooms here are especially lavish for Yellowstone, with stenciled walls and traditional spreads on one queen or two double beds. Annex rooms bring to mind a typical motel chain—we prefer the freestanding cabins, decorated with knotty-pine paneling and furnished with double beds and a writing table, as a low-priced alternative. *Note:* If you take a cabin, request a single rather than a duplex, since walls are paper thin.

On the north side of the lake (P.O. Box 165), Yellowstone National Park, WY 82190. 🕐 **307/344-7311.** www. travelyellowstone.com. 296 units, including 1 suite. $127–$167 double; $68 cabin; $411 suite. AE, DC, DISC, MC, V. Closed Oct 4–May 13. **Amenities:** 2 restaurants, lounge; activities desk; self-serve laundry. *In room:* No phone (cabins).

Mammoth Hot Springs Hotel and Cabins   On the site of historic Fort Yellowstone, near the steaming terraces of Mammoth Hot Springs and 5 miles (8km) from the north entrance, is the only park hotel open during both summer and winter seasons. It began life as a hostelry in 1911 and was replaced by a lodge, built in 1937, that has been incorporated into the current Mammoth Hot Springs Hotel. The quiet pace here, where elk often graze the strips of lawn around the hotel, is somewhat quickened by the flow of tourists stopping by the park headquarters and stores. The hotel itself is less distinguished than the Lake Hotel or the Old Faithful Inn, but its dormer windows and wood floors are attractive, and the high-ceilinged lobby is comfortable and relatively quiet, particularly if you drift into the adjacent Map Room (named for the massive inlaid map of the U.S. on one of the broad-paneled walls), with overstuffed sofas, desks, and huge windows for admiring the scenery.

The only high-end accommodations are the suites. Standard rooms and cabins are arranged around three grassy areas, where the resident elk often graze. Rooms offer minimal but apt appointments and various bed arrangements. If you require a tub, be sure to request one when you make your reservation— some rooms have showers only, and some share a bathroom down the hall. Personally, we prefer the cabins: cozy cottage-style buildings, some with private hot tubs and sun decks. In wintertime, the employee housing adjacent to the hotel is converted into the Aspen Lodge, another mid-range option for guests.

(*Tips* **Rooms with a View**

When staying at the **Old Faithful Inn,** if you want to watch the geyser erupt from your room, ask for Suite 3014 or Room 229. The suite is the "best in the house," with a spacious bathroom, bedroom, and sitting room, and goes for $351 a night. Room 229 is a high corner room with views of Old Faithful and the geyser basin, and because it's one of the older rooms, it costs only $71 a night. The problem with 229 is that you have to plan far ahead: People vie for this room, and you probably won't get it if you don't reserve it 18 months before your visit.

At Mammoth Hot Springs (P.O. Box 165), Yellowstone National Park, WY 82190. ℂ **307/344-7311.** Fax 307/ 344-7456. www.travelyellowstone.com. 224 units, including 2 suites. $66–$93 double; $274 suite; $55–$88 cabin; $127 hot-tub cabin. AE, DC, DISC, MC, V. **Amenities:** 2 restaurants, lounge; activities desk. *In room:* No phone (cabins).

Old Faithful Inn ★★   There are three hotels within viewing distance of the geyser, including a very nice new one, but this is undoubtedly the crown jewel of Yellowstone's man-made wonders. Seven stories tall with dormers peaking from a shingled, steeply sloping roof, it's an architectural wonder that was designed by Robert Reamer to blend into the natural environment—and it works. Inside, you can climb the stairs to its internal balconies, but seismic activity eventually closed the crow's nest, where, in the inn's early years, a chamber orchestra would perform for the Victorian guests below.

Guest rooms are in the main building and in wings that flank the main lodge. Original rooms are well appointed with conservative fabrics and park-theme art, but may not have private bathrooms; the wing rooms offer better facilities and more privacy. Make reservations far ahead if you're traveling during the summer.

At Old Faithful (P.O. Box 165), Yellowstone National Park, WY 82190. ℂ **307/344-7311.** Fax 307/344-7456. www.travelyellowstone.com. 327 units, including 9 suites. $117–$167 double with private bathroom; $71–$126 double without bathroom; $263–$351 suite. AE, DC, DISC, MC, V. Closed mid-Oct to mid-May. **Amenities:** 2 restaurants, lounge; activities desk.

Old Faithful Lodge Cabins *Value*   These are the leftovers from the days when crude cabins littered the landscape around the world's most famous geyser. The ones closest to the geyser were hauled away years ago, but you still get a sense of what tourism was like in the park's early days, especially if you rent one of the **budget cabins,** which are just slightly less flimsy than tents, and have basic beds and sinks, no more. Showers and restrooms are a short walk away. Next up the scale are the **economy cabins,** which have beds, sinks, and toilets. **Frontier cabins** are the best units, adding a private bathroom to other amenities. The lodge is perhaps the busiest spot in the geyser area, featuring several snack shops and a huge cafeteria dishing up varied fast food.

At Old Faithful (P.O. Box 165), Yellowstone National Park, WY 82190. ℂ **307/344-7311.** www.travel yellowstone.com. 97 cabins (some without private bathroom). $44–$68 double. AE, DC, DISC, MC, V. Closed mid-Sept to mid-May. **Amenities:** 2 restaurants; activities desk. *In room:* No phone.

Old Faithful Snow Lodge and Cabins ★★   If your last visit to Yellowstone included a stay at the Old Faithful Snow Lodge, put the memory out of mind. The old dormitory-style lodge was torn down in 1998, and this new, award-winning place could aptly be called the New Faithful Snow Lodge. Its contemporary big-beam construction and high ceiling in the lobby echo the Old Faithful Inn, and a copper-lined balcony curves above the common area, where guests can relax in wicker furniture. The structure's wooden components were recycled from the actual mill that provided the lumber for the Old Faithful Inn in 1904, and wrought-iron bears abound on everything from lamps to fireplace grates. The modern rooms are spacious and comfortable, second only to the upper-end accommodations at the Lake Hotel, and there's also the usual selection of surrounding cabins with motel-style furnishings.

At Old Faithful (P.O. Box 165), Yellowstone National Park, WY 82190. ℂ 307/344-7311. Fax 307/344-7456. www.travelyellowstone.com. 134 units. $137 double; $118 cabin. AE, DC, DISC, MC, V. **Amenities:** Restaurant, lounge; activities desk. *In room:* No phone (cabins).

Roosevelt Lodge Cabins *(Kids)* This is considered the park's hideaway treat, a family-oriented, low-key operation with primitive cabins, horseback rides, and a lodge restaurant that's more like a big ranch house. It's named after Teddy Roosevelt, who loved this area (the northeast part of the park) and slept in a tent near here. You'll share a communal bathroom if you choose one of the bare-bones **Roughrider** cabins, furnished with two simple beds, clean linens, a writing table, and a woodstove that may or may not suffice for the chilliest nights. **Frontier** cabins are a step up, with their own private bathroom; and **Economy** cabins have toilets and sinks but no showers or bathtubs.

The lodge is a ruggedly charming stone edifice with a long, deep porch outfitted with rockers so guests can converse with each other, nature, or the squirrels that scurry about. Stagecoach rides, horseback trips, and Western trail cookouts give this place a cowboy flavor that many enjoy, and it's a calmer scene than the other park villages. Since the cabins are just north of the Grand Canyon of the Yellowstone and Tower Falls, and isolated from crowds at larger hotels and campgrounds, the appeal here is clearly to budget-conscious, outdoor types interested in exploring the northeast part of Yellowstone without having to pay through the nose.

P.O. Box 165, Yellowstone National Park, WY 82190. ℂ 307/344-7311 for reservations. 80 cabins. $40–$77 cabin. AE, DC, DISC, MC, V. Closed early Sept to June. **Amenities:** Restaurant; activities desk. *In room:* No phone.

11 Where to Dine in the Park

While they're not world-class establishments, Yellowstone's restaurants are well suited to their location and the appetites of their patrons: The portions definitely won't leave anyone going hungry. Most of the menus include a selection of unadventurous, all-American meat-and-potatoes grub alongside several more creative entrees with a splash of zest. The college-age wait staff is generally enthusiastic and talkative, brandishing name tags that identify hometowns from Memphis to Moscow.

If you're not up for restaurant dining, but you don't want to cook over your camp stove the whole time, there is counter-style fast-food service at the **Hamilton General Stores** as well as snack shops and cafeterias at Canyon, Mammoth, Grant Village, Lake Lodge, and Old Faithful. Try the new **Geyser Grill** at the Old Faithful Snow Lodge, or the old lunch-counter scene at the **Fishing Bridge Hamilton Store.** The **Canyon Lodge Cafeteria** is a fast-food alternative located across the parking lot in the Canyon Lodge area, open from June to early September.

Canyon Lodge Dining Room STEAKS/SEAFOOD This is a spacious dining area, with the 1950s feel that infects most of Canyon Village, and when it fills up, it's noisy. The salad bar is long and loaded, but otherwise the dinner fare is largely geared toward the carnivore, with a wide selection of steaks alongside some seafood and pasta selections. The breakfast buffet is a good way to start your day, with all the standard American fixings. The crowds can be large at Canyon Village, but there is a relaxed and unhurried feel to the place that you don't find at some of the park's other busy points, and it's kid friendly.

At Canyon Lodge. Ⓒ **307/344-7901.** Reservations required. Breakfast $3–$8; lunch $5–$10; dinner $12–$20. June to mid-Sept daily 6:30–10:30am, 11:30am–2pm, and 5:30–10pm.

Grant Village AMERICAN   Breakfast and lunch at the Grant Village restaurant are much like those at the other restaurants in the park, but the chef often surprises diners with unusual dinner items. Lunch may include pan-fried trout covered with toasted pecans and lemon butter, huge burgers, and a top-notch taco salad. The dinner menu ranges from huckleberry chicken to swordfish with lemon-dill beurre to blackened prime rib, but the specialty is trout, prepared in a variety of creative ways. Quality and ambience here are comparable to those of the better dining rooms at the major park hotels. **The Lake House,** a second restaurant footsteps away, specializes in less-expensive entrees, including a pasta bar, pizza, fresh fish, and beer. Meals are served here from 5:30 to 9pm.

At Grant Village. Ⓒ **307/344-7901.** Dinner reservations required. Breakfast $4–$8; lunch $6–$10; dinner $10–$23. AE, DISC, MC, V. June–Sept daily 6:30–10am, 11:30am–2:30pm, and 5:30–10pm.

Lake Yellowstone Hotel ✦✦ CONTINENTAL   This represents the finest dining Yellowstone has to offer, with a view of the lake stretching south from a vast dining room that doesn't feel crowded even when it's full. One of the best ways to start your day is a generous breakfast buffet, but the huevos rancheros and pan-fried trout and eggs are also quite good. There's also a wide selection of fresh fruit, juices, pastries, and cereals. The dinner menu is even more inviting. Appetizers include duck quesadillas and *spanakopitas* (a tasty Greek pastry stuffed with spinach and cheese), while entrees include lovingly prepared sea scallops, pan-seared yellowfin tuna, and, of course, several beef dishes. The food here is of the quality one expects at a grand hotel.

The deli just off the hotel lobby by the dining room entrance serves lighter fare, including sandwiches, from an area slightly larger than a broom closet. Just down the road, the Hamilton store offers three meals in a section of the store that is shared with tourist items; the best bets here are breakfast or a burger. Inexpensive meals are also served cafeteria-style at the Lake Lodge.

On the north side of the lake. Ⓒ **307/344-7901.** Dinner reservations required. Breakfast $4–$8; lunch $5–$13; dinner $10–$25. AE, DC, DISC, MC, V. Mid-May to early Oct daily 6:30–10am, 11:30am–2:30pm, and 5:30–10pm.

Mammoth Hot Springs Dining Room STEAKS/SEAFOOD   At Mammoth, there's a good balance between casual and formal, reminiscent of a above-average neighborhood restaurant: comfortable and pleasant without too much of the hotel's Victorian past. The view of the Old Fort Yellowstone buildings and surrounding slopes is also quite enjoyable. The breakfast buffet is the same as other locations, featuring scrambled eggs, French toast, and the like. The lunch menu focuses on an array of sandwiches, including teriyaki chicken breast, a grilled vegetarian sandwich, and grilled German bratwurst. Dinner is a bit more substantial, and the house-smoked entrees are quite good. At the opposite end of the building, typical fast-food fare is served in a less distinctive room.

At Mammoth Hot Springs. Ⓒ **307/344-7901.** Dinner reservations required. Breakfast $4–$8; lunch $6–$11; dinner $9–$23. AE, DC, DISC, MC, V. Summer daily 6:30–10am, 11:30am–2pm, and 5:30–10pm.

Obsidian Dining Room STEAKS/SEAFOOD In the snazzy new snow lodge, a spacious restaurant provides a comparatively contemporary alternative to the dining room at the Old Faithful Inn. It's a little quieter, a little less expensive, and a little less formal, which is reflected in a menu heavy on burgers and salads. It still has some flash on the menu—teriyaki salmon and huge porterhouse pork chops—and there is a breakfast gem in the Southwestern eggs. If you come in the winter, it's a huge improvement over the cramped restaurant of the old Snow Lodge.

At the Old Faithful Snow Lodge (C) **307/344-7901**. Breakfast $4–$8; lunch $5–$12; dinner $9–$18. AE, DC, DISC, MC, V. Late May to mid-Oct and mid-Dec to mid-May daily 6:30–10am, 11:30am–2:30pm, and 5–10pm.

Old Faithful Inn STEAKS/SEAFOOD There's nothing wrong with the food here, but the real highlight is the gnarled-log architecture of this distinguished historic inn. Breakfast is buffet or a la carte, and there's a lot to choose from. There's another buffet at lunchtime (headlined by barbecue beef and chicken), as well as a generous assortment of salads and sandwiches. The dinner menu is extensive, with four cuts of prime rib, several fish dishes, meatloaf, and pastas. The fare has gotten more distinguished in recent years, with such creative options as roasted pork loin with jalapeño-cream sauce and shrimp scampi making regular appearances on the menu. We recommend that you have at least one dinner here while you're visiting the park to at least take in the ambience of the inn—and top it off with a decadent Yellowstone Sundae.

At the Old Faithful Inn. (C) **307/545-4999**. Dinner reservations required. Breakfast $7–$9; lunch $5–$11; dinner $9–$24. AE, DC, DISC, MC, V. May to mid-Oct daily 6:30–10am, 11:30am–2:30pm, and 5–10pm.

Roosevelt Lodge STEAKS/SEAFOOD This is supposed to be the cowboy alternative to the fancier cuisine served at the bigger Yellowstone hotels, but the unadventurous menu will win over only the most naive city slickers. Like the aging cabins that take you back to the early days of auto camping, Roosevelt's dining area is simple and spare, a collection of tables that take up one side of the lodge's big lobby. For breakfast, it's eggs and flapjacks; lunch is burgers and sandwiches. Come suppertime, the Roosevelt beans are the standout (an indication of the establishment's creativity), and the short menu is dominated by middle-of-the-road American specialties like ribs and steaks. A better idea: Join Roosevelt's Old West Dinner Cookout, and ride by horse or wagon thorough the Pleasant Valley to a chuck-wagon dinner that includes cornbread, steak, watermelon, those famous beans, and apple crisp. It's a daily summer event (reservations required) that costs $42 to $52 for an adult, depending on the route of your horseback ride, or $32 if you go by wagon. Children pay $10 less.

At Tower Junction. (C) **307/344-7901**. Breakfast $4–$8; lunch $6–$13; dinner $9–$22. AE, DC, DISC, MC, V. Summer daily 7–10am, 11:30am–3pm, and 5–9pm.

11

Jackson Hole & Grand Teton National Park

Grand Teton compares to Yellowstone somewhat the way a Generation X snowboarder compares to an old ski patrol graybeard: It's younger, flashier, and closer to the bars. The Tetons are a young mountain range in geologic time, and Grand Teton is a young national park, on the rolls in its present form since 1950; Yellowstone, by comparison, dates back to 1872. And whereas the geysers of Yellowstone are a pretty long drive from anywhere, you can come off a climb at Grand Teton and be in a posh Jackson eatery 20 minutes after you hit the valley floor.

That's not a knock on Grand Teton National Park. Jackson, after all, is a spiffy resort town with a little cowboy still in it. And within the park's borders are beautiful lakes and rivers, wildlife galore, and lots of recreational opportunities. In the summer, you can climb, hike, boat, balloon, backpack, raft, bird-watch, and fish. In winter, the park and nearby resorts become a magnet for skiers of every style and skill level. Jackson Hole Ski Resort is upgrading furiously to keep its status as a premier national skier's destination, and its neighbor on the west side of the mountain, Grand Targhee, has some of the best powder in the Rockies.

1 Jackson Hole

57 miles (92km) S of Yellowstone National Park; 432 miles (696km) NW of Cheyenne; 275 miles (443km) NE of Salt Lake City; 177 miles (285km) SW of Cody

Of the few communities in the Rockies that have successfully toed the line between promoting themselves as resort towns and retaining some semblance of indigenous character, Jackson is a standout. The million-dollar homes are sprouting all over the valley, but there is still open space, a memory of the cowboy past, and some resistance to letting in too much commercial glitz.

The remaining open spaces allow visitors to imagine what it was like early in the 19th century, when fur trappers first camped here. They were followed by ranchers, who soon became *dude* ranchers. Today, the community holds an interesting mixture of ski bums, blue bloods, nouveau riche, avid outdoor types, and even a few old-time cowboys. The cosmopolitans of this motley crew came not just with a hunger for scenery, but also with a taste for music, art, and good restaurants, too, and the selection here is unrivaled in Wyoming. The big ski hill lures a younger crowd, with the final ingredient for resort status—celebrities—supplied by transplants like Harrison Ford.

ESSENTIALS

GETTING THERE The **Jackson Airport** is located north of town at the southern end of Grand Teton National Park. **American Airlines** (© **800/ 433-7300**) flies in seasonally from Chicago, and regular service is provided from

Jackson or Jackson Hole—What's the Difference?

You'll likely see every kind of merchandise imaginable fashioned with an image of the Tetons and the words "Jackson Hole, Wyoming" scrawled over it. You may notice that on the map, the town just south of Grand Teton National Park is called Jackson. But your plane ticket says Jackson Hole. But wait a minute—the postmark just says Jackson. What gives?

The mystery of the town's name is actually pretty simple. Three mountain men ran a fur-trapping company in these parts in the 1800s: one named David Jackson, another named Jedediah Smith, and a third named William Sublette. Mountain men in those days referred to a valley as a hole. As the story goes, Sublette called the valley Jackson's Hole, because Jackson spent a great deal of time in it. That name was shortened, and when the town materialized, it was also named for David Jackson. So the city itself is Jackson, Wyoming, and it lies in the great valley that runs the length of the Tetons on the east side, Jackson Hole.

Denver and Salt Lake City by **Delta** and **Delta Connection** (✆ **800/ 221-1212**), and by **United** and **United Express** (✆ **800/241-6522**).

If you're getting here on your own wheels, come north from I-80 at Rock Springs on U.S. 189/191, or come east from I-15 at Idaho Falls on U.S. 26 and either come through Snake River Canyon on that highway or veer north over Teton Pass on Wyo. 32. If you are coming south from Yellowstone National Park, you can stay on U.S. 89, which runs north-south through both parks and into town. For up-to-date weather information and local road conditions, contact the Chamber of Commerce (see below).

VISITOR INFORMATION   The **Jackson Hole Chamber of Commerce** is a source of information concerning just about everything in and around Jackson. Along with the U.S. Forest Service and National Park Service, representatives of the chamber can be found at the informative **Visitors Center,** 532 N. Cache, about 3 blocks north of Town Square with a view of the National Elk Refuge. For information on lodging, events, and activities, contact the chamber at P.O. Box 550, Jackson, WY 83001 (✆ **307/733-3316;** www.jacksonhole chamber.com).

GETTING AROUND   Once you're on the ground, major car-rental operations serving the airport include **Alamo** (✆ 800/327-9633 or 307/733-0671), **Avis** (✆ 800/331-1212 or 307/733-3422), **Budget** (✆ 800/527-0700 or 307/733-2206), **Hertz** (✆ 800/654-3131 or 307/733-2272), and **Thrifty** (✆ 800/699-1025 or 307/739-9300). Also providing rentals in the area are **Aspen** (✆ 877/22ASPEN or 307/733-9224) and **Rent-a-Wreck** (✆ 800/ 637-7147 or 307/733-5014). Downtown at 375 N. Cache is **Eagle Rent-a-Car** (✆ 800/582-2128 or 307/739-9999), where you can rent everything from minivans to RVs to snowmobiles. Eagle also provides free pickup and delivery.

Taxi service is available from **Buckboard Cab** (✆ 307/733-1112). **Alltrans, Inc.** (✆ 800/443-6133 or 307/733-4325) offers shuttle service from the airport and national park tours. Many of the hotels and car-rental agencies in the Jackson area offer free shuttle service to and from the airport.

Jackson

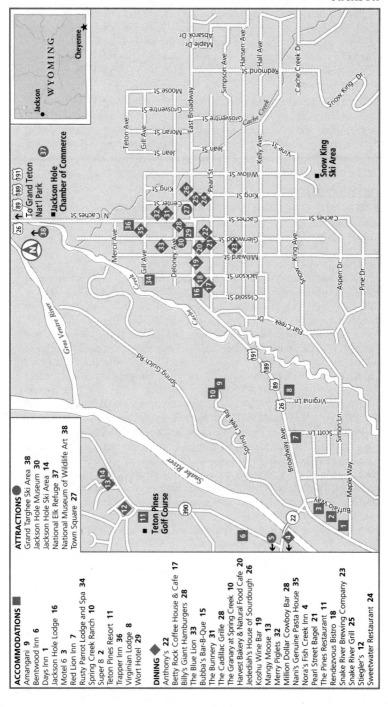

ACCOMMODATIONS ■

Amangani **9**
Bentwood Inn **6**
Days Inn **1**
Jackson Hole Lodge **16**
Motel 6 **3**
Red Lion Inn **7**
Rusty Parrot Lodge and Spa **34**
Spring Creek Ranch **10**
Super 8 **2**
Teton Pines Resort **11**
Trapper Inn **36**
Virginian Lodge **8**
Wort Hotel **29**

DINING ◆

Anthony's **22**
Betty Rock Coffee House & Cafe **17**
Billy's Giant Hamburgers **28**
The Blue Lion **33**
Bubba's Bar-B-Que **15**
The Bunnery **31**
The Cadillac Grille **28**
The Granary at Spring Creek **10**
Harvest Bakery & Natural Food Cafe **20**
Jedediah's House of Sourdough **26**
Koshu Wine Bar **19**
Mangy Moose **13**
Merry Piglets **32**
Million Dollar Cowboy Bar **28**
Nani's Genuine Pasta House **35**
Nora's Fish Creek Inn **4**
Pearl Street Bagel **21**
The Pines Restaurant **11**
Rendezvous Bistro **18**
Snake River Brewing Company **23**
Snake River Grill **25**
Stiegler's **12**
Sweetwater Restaurant **24**

ATTRACTIONS ●

Grand Targhee Ski Area **38**
Jackson Hole Museum **30**
Jackson Hole Ski Area **14**
National Elk Refuge **37**
National Museum of Wildlife Art **38**
Town Square **27**

The **Southern Teton Area Rapid Transit (START)** offers bus transport from Teton Village to Jackson daily for $2 (students up to high school age ride free). Service includes 60 trips a day between downtown and Teton Village in the winter, 10 in the summer, and shuts down around 11pm year-round. For specific schedule information, contact START at ✆ **307/733-4521** or browse **www.startbus.com**.

SPECIAL EVENTS   Held annually in late May, **Old West Days** is a 4-day event dedicated to Jackson's frontier past, with a shootout, cowboy poetry readings, a parade, and a rodeo. The other big annual event is the **Jackson Hole Fall Arts Festival**, a weeklong extravaganza in September with special events every day. Contact the Jackson Hole Chamber of Commerce (see above) for further information on either.

GETTING OUTSIDE
SPORTING GOODS & EQUIPMENT RENTALS
Jackson adventurers may like to flirt with danger, but generally they like to do so fully equipped and handsomely attired. Serious climbers with serious wallets will appreciate the gear at **Teton Mountaineering** ✦ at 170 N. Cache St. (✆ **800/850-3595** or 307/733-3595), a block from the square, where you can get karabiners, killer Nordic skis, and high-grade fleece jackets. Fishermen are lured to **High Country Flies** ✦ at 185 N. Center St. (✆ **877/732-7210** or 307/733-7210; www.highcountryflies.com), and the **Jack Dennis Outdoor Shop** on the square at 50 E. Broadway (✆ **800/570-3270** or 307/733-3270; www.jackdennis.com). **Adventure Sports**, at Dornan's in the town of Moose (✆ **307/733-3307**), has a small selection of mountain-bike, kayak, and canoe rentals, and advice on where to go with the gear. When snowboards are put away for the summer, the **Boardroom** switches to BMX bikes and skateboards, at 225 W. Broadway (✆ **307/733-8327**). The competition, in Teton Village, is **Jackson Hole Sports** (✆ **307/739-2687**), open in winter only. **Hoback Sports**, 40 S. Millward St. (✆ **307/733-5335**), has a large selection of skis, boards, and summer mountain bikes for rent and sale, and a second location at the Snow King (✆ **307/733-5200**). Equally hip, with a smaller but high-quality selection of bikes and skis, is **Edge Sports**, 490 W. Broadway (✆ **307/734-3916**). **Skinny Skis**, at 65 W. Deloney Ave. off Town Square (✆ **307/733-6094**), is a year-round specialty sports shop and has an excellent selection of equipment and clothing. For a supply of inexpensive, serviceable factory seconds at severely discounted prices, head north to the little town of Moose near the entrance to Grand Teton National Park and shop **Moosely Seconds** ✦ (✆ **307/733-1801**). The friendly folks at **Leisure Sports**, 1075 S. U.S. 89 (✆ **307/733-3040**), offer fishing boats, camping equipment, and rafting items in summer. In winter, look for snowmobiles, cross-country skis, and ice-fishing equipment.

BIKING
You can rent a bike and pick up maps at several of the shops listed above, or take a guided trip in Yellowstone, Grand Teton, or the national forest with **Teton Mountain Bike Tours** (✆ **800/733-0788**; www.tetonmtbike.com) or Hoback Sports' **Fat Tire Tours**, 40 S. Millward St. (✆ **307/733-5335**), which places bikes in the Snow King chairlift for an easy ride up the mountain.

CLIMBING
The sight of the 13,770-foot Grand Teton towering above the valley has been setting hearts pumping for generations. A century ago no one had reached the top;

now, thousands have, often carefully roped and cared for by professional guides. Experienced guides and established routes assure a modicum of safety, but climbing accidents and deaths still occur. There are two reliable, long-standing guide services: **Exum Mountain Guides,** P.O. Box 56, Moose, WY 83012 (© 307/ 733-2297; www.exumguides.com), has been around since 1931 and offers climbs on several mountains guided by well-known names in the climbing world. A trip to the top of Teton costs $400 to $700, depending on the route and the size of the group. Group preparation classes cost from $95 to $155 per person. **Jackson Hole Mountain Guides,** 165 N. Glenwood St., Jackson, WY 83001 (© 800/239-7642; www.jhmg.com), offers intermediate climbing courses for $100 and a 2-day Grand Teton summit climb for $600. On rainy days, the **Teton Rock Gym,** 1116 Maple Way (© 307/733-0707), is an inexpensive alternative, setting you loose on its walls and climbing ropes for $11 a day.

CROSS-COUNTRY SKIING

With five Nordic centers and a couple of national parks at your feet, plus the 3.5-million-acre Bridger-Teton National Forest, cross-country skiers have plenty of choices. If you're new to cross-country skiing, you might choose to start on the groomed, level trails at one of the Nordic centers. If, however, you have experience in the steep, deep powder of untracked wilderness, visit or call the National Park Service in **Grand Teton National Park** (© 307/739-3300) or the **Bridger-Teton National Forest** in downtown Jackson at 532 N. Cache (© 307/739-5500) and check in before you go.

The local ski shops are an excellent source of unofficial advice about the area's backcountry. Keep in mind that many of the trails used by cross-country skiers are also used by snowmobiles. The **Jackson Hole Nordic Center,** 7658 Teewinot, Teton Village (© 307/733-2629), located on the flats just east of Teton Village, is a small part of the giant facility that includes some of the best downhill skiing around (see "Downhill Skiing," below). The price of a downhill pass includes the price of skiing on the cross-country trails.

Teton Pines Cross Country Skiing Center (© 307/733-1005) offers 8 miles (13km) of groomed trails. Rates are about $10 (see also "Where to Stay," below). **Spring Creek Ranch Touring Center,** 1800 N. Spirit Dance Rd., Jackson (© 800/443-6139), located below the ridge resort (see "Where to Stay," below) maintains 8½ miles (14km) of groomed trails, and you don't have to be a guest to enjoy them. The fee for skiers (guests or non) is $10 per day.

At **Grand Targhee** (© 307/353-2304), you can rent or buy anything you need in the way of cross-country ski equipment and take off on the resort's 8 miles (13km) of groomed trails.

For those seeking instruction, lessons are available at the Nordic centers, or you can check the schedule of **Teton Parks and Recreation** (© 307/ 733-5056), which offers inexpensive courses for those who want to ski all day and have brought their own equipment.

For cross-country information in **Grand Teton National Park,** call © 307/ 739-3300, or 307/739-3611 for recorded weather information. Also, see section 2, "Grand Teton National Park," below.

DOG-SLEDDING

If your idea of mushing is not oatmeal but a pack of yipping dogs, you might want to try your hand at dog-sledding. **Jackson Hole Iditarod,** P.O. Box 1940, Jackson, WY 83001 (© 800/554-7388 or 307/733-7388; www.jhsleddog.com), associated with Iditarod racer Frank Teasley, offers both half- and full-day trips in five-person sleds (the fifth companion is your guide) and you can take a turn in the driver's stand. The half-day ride costs $135 per person, gives the dogs an 11-mile (18km) workout, and includes a lunch of hot soup and cocoa before you head back to the kennels. For $225 a head, you can take the full-day excursion out to Granite Hot Springs, a 22-mile (35km) trip total. You get the hot lunch, plus your choice of freshly barbecued trout or steak for dinner. Another Iditarod veteran, Bill Snodgrass, leads trips in the national forests around Togwotee Pass with his **Washakie Outfitting** (© 800/249-0662; www.dogsledwashakie.com). These trips fill up quickly, so call at least 3 to 4 days in advance to reserve a spot.

DOWNHILL SKIING

Low temperatures, black-diamond runs, remote location, and an intimidating vertical drop haven't scared skiers away from Jackson Hole—this is what *attracts* them. The two largest ski resorts in the area have been expanding, putting in faster chairs, and eliminating long waits in lift lines. The quality of snow on the mountain can vary, but skiers who seek challenges will not be disappointed.

Jackson Hole Ski Resort 🐾🐾 Every year, there's something new at this resort—in 2000, it was a high-speed quad on the Après Vous run; in 2001, construction began on new developments that will more than double the guest capacity. There is special grandeur to this ski resort, from its spectacular mountaintop views to its daring black-diamond runs. Take the tram to the top of **Rendezvous Mountain** and plunge down Tensleep Bowl if you want to get a taste of skiing on the edge. You'll find an inexhaustible supply of steep runs that require skiing expertise. There are lesser runs to the north, including gentler journeys down the sides of **Apres Vous Mountain** that will better suit an intermediate skier. At the bottom, two small chairs serve beginning skiers.

Crowded days have been few in recent years—lucky for skiers, if not the owners. With 2,500 acres of skiable terrain, there's plenty of room. Nine lifts, a gondola, an aerial tram, and 76 runs are available from December 1 to the beginning of April. For an orientation, join the Mountain Hosts, who gather groups at the top of the Rendezvous lift to escort newcomers on a 2-hour tour.

The competition among ski resorts compels growth—not just on the slopes, but also in the resort villages below. A variety of restaurants, lodging, a medical clinic, shops, and entertainment—from sleigh-ride dinners to a skating rink—make it unnecessary to leave the complex during a ski vacation.

If you've never skied in powder up to your kneecaps, make an early-morning trip to the **Hobacks Zone,** just under Cheyenne Bowl. The ski patrol closes it off as soon as the snow gets tracked out.

7658 Teewinot, Teton Village, WY 83025. © **307/733-2292** or 307/733-4005; 307/733-2291 for snow conditions; 800/443-6931 for central reservations. www.jacksonhole.com. 3-day lift tickets $165 adults, $124 young adults (15–21), $83 seniors and children 14 and under. AE, DISC, MC, V. Open Dec to early Apr 9am–4pm. From Jackson, take Wyo. 22 west to Wyo. 390 and go north to Teton Village, about 5 miles (8km).

Grand Targhee Resort 🐾 The Grand Targhee resort has struggled at times, changing ownership, wheeling and dealing with federal land managers, and sparring with local conservationists over expansion plans and real-estate development. None of that affects the snow, however, which is terrific. Or the deep, forgiving powder from November through spring (more than 500 in. annually), and a more peaceful, less-crowded village that provides a worthy alternative to Teton Village. Many skiers break up a Jackson ski trip by driving over Teton Pass for a day or two on these slopes.

This may also be a better place for less-aggressive skiers. There is a beginner's powder area and hundreds of acres of wide-open powder slopes for intermediates and other cruisers. You can take a new high-speed quad to the adjacent Peaked Mountain and ski in thigh-deep, untracked snow. A problem you might encounter is, oddly enough, fog. Now and then the mountain gets socked in with gray moisture, forcing skiers to ski below the thick blanket. The **Lost Groomer Chute,** a run that takes full advantage of the weather moving west to east, will provide the most insatiable powder hound with enough dust.

Here are a few of the other treats at Targhee: You can ride a sleigh on a starlit evening to a roundtable dinner in a snow-buried yurt; your kids can enroll in the Powder Scouts program, which gives kids ages 6 to 14 a full day of instruction, food, and skiing for $68; and a spa offers everything from massage to a mineral mud wrap, along with hot tubs, sauna, exercise room, and heated outdoor pool.

Ski Hill Rd., Box SKI, Alta, WY 83422. © **800/TARGHEE** or 307/353-2300. www.grandtarghee.com. Lift tickets $47 adults, $29 seniors (62 and older) and children 6–14. From Jackson, take Wyo. 22 over Teton Pass into Idaho, then Id. 33 north to Driggs, then follow the signs west (back into Wyo.) to Targhee Resort, about 38 miles (61km).

Snow King Resort   If you enter Jackson from the north on a winter night, the lit slopes of Snow King are an appealing sight. Snow King offers a variety of recreation, from tubing hill to ice rink to snowboard park. Plus, it's conveniently located near the heart of town. It's the oldest ski hill in Wyoming, operating since 1939, and the hotel has attractive, moderately priced rooms. The only problem is the skiing itself: There's a limited number of fairly steep runs that don't offer much variety. The beginner's slope is small and amounts to only 15 percent of the terrain, and there's not enough intermediate snow to satisfy all levels of ability. The two other area resorts are much bigger, with more and longer runs and a greater variety of challenges. "Town Hill," as it's known, has 500 acres of skiable terrain, a triple chair, two double chairs, and a Poma lift.

400 E. Snow King, Jackson, WY 83001. © **800/522-5464** or 307/733-5200; or **307/734-2020** for snow conditions. www.snowking.com. Lift tickets $32 adults, $22 seniors and children under 16. Take Cache St. south to Snow King Ave. Turn left and follow the signs to the resort.

FISHING

Yellowstone and Grand Teton National Parks are home to some fabled fishing spots (see the park sections for details), but some of the best angling in the region is found outside the park boundaries.

The **Snake River** emerges from Jackson Lake Dam as a broad, strong river, with decent fishing from its banks in certain spots—like right below the dam— and better fishing if you float the river. Fly-fishermen should ask advice at local stores on recent insect hatches and good stretches of river, or hire a guide to keep them company. **High Country Flies** 🎣, 185 N. Center St. (© **307/733-7210;** www.highcountryflies.com), has a vast selection of high-quality fishing gear, flies, and fly-tying supplies, along with lessons, guided trips, and free advice if you just want to gab about where to cast. The **Jack Dennis Outdoor Shop** on Town Square, at 50 E. Broadway (© **307/733-3270;** www.jackdennis.com), is a much bigger store with room to display some big boats, and it also offers lessons and guides. There's a smaller edition of the Dennis store in Teton Village (© **307/733-6838**). **Westbank Anglers,** 3670 N. Moose-Wilson Rd. (© **307/ 733-6483;** www.westbank.com), is another full-service fly shop that sells gear and organizes trips around Jackson Hole.

GOLF

More than one American president has played a round of golf in Jackson, which despite its short putting season has some world-class links. The **Jackson Hole Golf and Tennis Club** (© 800/628-9988 or 307/733-3111), north of Jackson off U.S. 89, has an 18-hole course that's recently been rated one of the nation's top 10 resort courses by *Golf Digest,* as well as six tennis courts. Greens fees are $135 for 18 holes, but you can save by taking advantage of lower evening rates. The **Teton Pines Resort and Country Club,** 3450 N. Clubhouse Dr. (© 800/238-2223 or 307/733-1005), designed by Arnold Palmer and Ed Seay, is a challenging course and prime real estate; Vice President Dick Cheney owns a house on it. Greens fees are $60 to $80 for 18 holes. Both are open to the public.

HIKING

One benefit of having so many mountain ranges converging around Jackson is that you have *choices*—especially when it comes to hiking. The most popular place to go for a stroll in the vicinity of Jackson is **Grand Teton National Park,** which shows off some glorious aspen colors in the fall. Less traveled are the forests that abut the park, particularly **Bridger-Teton National Forest** just east of Jackson. Bridger-Teton and its east-side counterpart, **Shoshone National Forest,** encompass a huge piece of mountain real estate, including glaciers, 13,000-foot peaks, and some of the best alpine fishing lakes in the world. Among the mountain ranges included in these forests are the **Absarokas,** the **Gros Ventre,** the **Wyoming,** and the **Wind River Range,** or "Winds," as they're called by locals, which stretch about 120 miles (193km) from just southeast of Jackson near Pinedale to the South Pass area and the Red Desert. A **visitor center,** located in a sod-roofed A-frame at 532 N. Cache in downtown Jackson (© 307/739-5500), provides all of the hiking and access information you'll need for the national forest as well as for the Gros Ventre and Teton Wilderness Areas. If you want guided hikes, ask for information at the visitor center.

HORSEBACK RIDING

Some hotels, including those in Grand Teton National Park, have stables and operate trail rides for their guests. For details, contact **Jackson Hole Trail Rides** (© 307/733-6992), **Snow King Stables** (© 307/733-5781), **Spring Creek Ranch Riding Stables** (© 800/443-6139), or the **Mill Iron Ranch** (© 307/733-6390). Rates usually run about $25 an hour, and many trips include breakfast or lunch.

KAYAKING, CANOEING & SAILING

With the Snake and Hoback Rivers and the lakes of Grand Teton National Park, it's no surprise to see all kinds of watercraft towed or tied to the roofs of SUVs in Jackson. Canoeists and kayakers enjoy the upper Snake River, from Jackson Lake Dam down to Moose, and expert kayakers are attracted to the ride through Snake River Canyon and Hoback white water. Beginners should be wary of the upper Snake—snags and spring currents have claimed lives, so a guide is advisable. Canoeists paddle Jenny Lake and, with a small portage or two, String and Leigh Lakes. The big lake, **Jackson,** attracts sailboats and sea kayaks, but beware of the sudden afternoon eruptions of gusty wind and thunderstorms.

Several operators in Jackson run schools and guide services for beginners, intermediates, and advanced paddlers. The two major outfits are the **Snake River Kayak and Canoe School,** 365 N. Cache St. (© 800/KAYAK-01; www.snakeriverkayak.com); and **Rendezvous River Sports,** 235 N. Cache St. (© 307/733-2471; www.jhkayakschool.com).

(Tips Boating Regulations

If you're going to set out in your own boat, you should know that before launching in the park you'll need a boat permit. Ask at the visitor center at Moose, or call the **National Park Service** at © **307/739-3300** for information. Once you get outside the park, you're in the jurisdiction of the **Bridger-Teton National Forest,** with offices in Jackson at 340 N. Cache (© **307/739-5500**).

RAFTING

There are two parts to the Snake River—the smooth water, north of Jackson, and the white water of the canyon, to the south and west. A rafting trip down the upper Snake, usually from Jackson Lake Dam or Pacific Creek to Moose, is not about wild water but about wildlife: Moose, bald eagles, osprey, and other creatures come to the water just like we do. Several operators provide scenic float trips, charging around $40 for a half day, $70 for a full day. Ask at **Barker-Ewing** (© **800/365-1800** or 307/733-1800; www.barker-ewing.com); **Flagg Ranch,** in the north part of Grand Teton National Park (© **800/443-2311** or 307/543-2861); **Grand Teton Lodge Company** (© **800/628-9988**); and **Lewis and Clark Expeditions** (© **800/824-5375** or 307/733-4022; www.lewisand clarkexpeds.com).

SNOWMOBILING

Though West Yellowstone is the most popular base for snowmobiling in the Yellowstone area (for now—there's a proposed ban for 2003 that's tied up in court), Jackson has a growing contingent of snowmobile aficionados and outfitters. You don't really need a guide to tour Yellowstone, where you're required to stay on groomed roads, and you can also handle Togwotee Pass and the Granite Hot Springs area if you stick to groomed trails. Snowmobilers also head for the rugged Gros Ventre Mountains and the Greys River area, 45 miles (72km) west of Jackson. The operators who rent snowmobiles (including the necessary clothing and helmets) also offer guides to take you on 1-day and multi-day tours of Jackson Hole and the surrounding area. **High Country Snowmobile Tours,** at 3510 S. U.S. 89 in Jackson (© **800/524-0130**), offers touring service for Jackson Hole, Yellowstone, and the Gros Ventre Mountains. **Jackson Hole Snowmobile Tours,** 1000 S. U.S. 89 (© **800/633-1733** or 307/732-0784), offers 1-day trips in Yellowstone and multi-day trips along the Continental Divide. In addition to renting snowmobiles, **Wyoming Adventures,** 1050 S. U.S. 89 (© **800/637-7147**), also takes trips along the Continental Divide, as well as Grey's River. Typical 1-day outings range from $150 to $200, including pickup and drop-off service, equipment, fuel, continental breakfast, and lunch. Multiday trips range from $300 to $450 per day per person (including all equipment, guide, meals, lodging, and fuel), depending on the destination.

   Flagg Ranch Snowmobiles, at the south entrance to Yellowstone (© **800/443-2311**), provides rentals and guided tours from the resort near that park's south gate. Also in Jackson, snowmobiles can be rented at **Leisure Sports,** 1075 S. U.S. 89 (© **307/733-3040**).

WHITEWATER RAFTING

The Snake River Canyon's fame has not diminished its Class IV allure to expert paddlers—but they avoid the midday crowds and take their white-water jollies more toward twilight. If you want to join them jolting over Lunch Counter Rapids, but you'd rather be in a raft steered by somebody who knows what they're doing (you'll be asked to paddle, and you may feel like your life depends on it), contact **Barker-Ewing** (© **800/448-4202**), **Charlie Sands Wildwater** (© **800/358-8184** or 307/733-4410), **Dave Hansen Whitewater** (© 800/ 732-6295), **Jackson Hole Whitewater** (© **800/648-2602**), **Lewis and Clark Expeditions** (© **800/824-5375**), or **Mad River Boat Trips** (© **800/458-7238** or 307/733-6203).

OFFBEAT BUT MEMORABLE WAYS TO SEE THE TETONS
AERIAL TOURING

For a much quicker climb to the tops of the mountains, call **Jackson Hole Aviation** (© **307/733-4767**; www.jhaviation.com), at the Jackson Hole Airport, or **Teton Aviation,** Driggs Airport, Driggs, ID 83422 (© **208/354-8131** or 800/472-3100). You'll get a new perspective on the immensity of the Grand Teton (though you won't get too close—the park has some air-space restrictions). Jackson Hole Aviation offers airplane trips ($75 an hr.), and Teton offers the Super Teton Ride ($160), in a glider that takes you to 11,800 feet on the west side of the Grand. Flights in the two-seater glider (you and the pilot) cost $140 for an hour; Jackson Hole Aviation charges $225 per hour for its Cessna, which can carry four passengers comfortably.

BALLOONING

It used to be that only anglers were up at the crack of dawn in Jackson, but now you can add balloonists. The folks at the **Wyoming Balloon Company,** P.O. Box 2578, Jackson, WY 83001 (© **307/739-0900**; www.wyomingballoon. com), like to fire up early, in the still air that cloaks the Teton Valley around 6am. Their "float trips" stay aloft for a little more than an hour, cruising over a 3,000-acre ranch with a full frontal view of the Tetons. The journey concludes with a champagne breakfast at the landing site. Flights in a balloon cost $195 per adult and $125 per child.

EXPLORING THE AREA

Jackson Hole Aerial Tram Rides   Here you can see the Tetons from an elevation above 10,000 feet, but don't expect a private tour. During busy summer days the tram carries 45 passengers, packed in like the skiers that take the lift in the winter. The top of Rendezvous Mountain offers an incredible view, but it can get pretty chilly, even in the middle of summer, so bring a light coat.

At Jackson Hole Ski Resort, 7658 Teewinot, Teton Village. © **307/739-2753**. Tickets $15 adults, $13 seniors, $5 children, free for children 5 and under. Late May to Sept daily 9am–5pm; mid-June to Aug daily 9am–7pm. Tram runs approximately every half hr.

National Museum of Wildlife Art ⭐   If you don't spot this museum on your way into Jackson from the north, consider that a triumph of design: Its jagged, red-sandstone facade is meant to blend into the steep hillside facing the elk refuge. Within this 50,000-square-foot castle is some of the best wildlife art in the country, as well as exhibits on the elk refuge wildlife and a 200-seat auditorium where there are regular slide shows and lectures on a wide range of subjects. There are 14 exhibit galleries that display traveling shows and collections dating from the 19th century to the present, including John James Audubon and local great Carl Rungius. The museum houses a repository of internationally acclaimed wildlife films, and in the winter it's the take-off point for sled tours of the elk refuge (you can also view the wildlife through spotting scopes on the balcony). There's a good little cafe, too.

2820 Rungius Rd. (3 miles [5km] north of town on U.S. 89, across from the National Elk Refuge). © 307/733-5771. www.wildlifeart.org. Admission $6 adults, $5 students and seniors, free for children under 6. Summer daily 8am–5pm; winter daily 9am–5pm.

Jackson Hole Museum Dedicated volunteers maintain this repository of early photographs, artifacts, and other items of historical significance, and they'll guide you through the collections. You can browse the exhibits or go down the street to the Historical Society at Glenwood and Mercil to do some research. At the museum, you'll find collections of trade beads, antique pole furniture, pistols, and Indian artifacts, spread out in 3,000 square feet of floor space.

105 N. Glenwood (at the corner of Deloney). © 307/733-2414. www.jacksonholehistory.org. Admission $6 families, $3 adults, $2 seniors, $1 students and children. Mon–Sat 9:30am–6pm; Sun 10am–5pm. Closed Oct–May.

WILDLIFE-WATCHING

National Elk Refuge The U.S. Fish and Wildlife Service makes sure that the elk in this area eat well during the winter by feeding them alfalfa pellets. It keeps them out of the haystacks of area ranchers, and creates a beautiful tableau on the peaceful flats along the Gros Ventre River: thousands of elk dotting the snow for miles. Drivers along U.S. 89 may also see trumpeter swans, coyotes, moose, bighorn sheep, and wolves. As autumn begins to chill the air in September, you'll hear the shrill whistles of the bull elk in the mountains; as snow begins to stick on the ground, they make their way down to the refuge. Though the cultivated meadows and pellets help the elk survive the winter, some biologists say this approach results in overpopulation and the spread of diseases like brucellosis.

Regardless, this is a great opportunity to see these magnificent creatures up close. Each winter from mid-December until March the Fish and Wildlife Service offers **horse-drawn sleigh rides** that weave among the refuge elk. Rides early in the winter will find young, energetic bulls playing and banging heads, while late-winter visitors wander through a more placid scene. Rides embark from the National Museum of Wildlife Art between 10am and 4pm on a first-come, first-served basis. Tickets for the 45-minute rides cost $12 for adults and $6 for children 6 to 12, and can be purchased at the museum. Ask about a combination pass ($15) for the sleigh ride and the museum.

Located 3 miles north of Jackson on U.S. 26/89 (P.O. Box 510), Jackson, WY 83001. © 307/733-9212. www.nationalelkrefuge.fs.gov. Free admission. Visitor center: summer daily 8am–7pm; winter daily 8am–5pm.

SHOPPING

In recent years stores like the **Gap** (on Town Square; © 307/733-7927) and **Eddie Bauer** (55 S. Cache St.; © 307/733-7336) have opened factory-outlet stores in Jackson, and among the ever-changing array of shops (rents are high; so is turnover) you can find everything from American Indian crafts to cowboy boots to Oriental rugs. But these are what you'll find in most resort towns. The areas where Jackson excels are its art galleries and outdoor-wear shops.

Standouts in the outdoor clothing category include **Teton Mountaineering** (170 N. Cache St.; © 307/733-3595), also a great spot for climbing, camping, and winter gear; and **Moosely Seconds** (150 E. Broadway; © 307/733-7176), where you'll find surprisingly deep discounts on quality outdoor wear.

Some collectors, tired of countless images of bighorn sheep and weather-beaten cowboys, dismiss Western art. But while Jackson has plenty of that genre

---

⟨Kids⟩ Especially for Kids

Snow King may not have the best skiing in the valley, but it caters to kids and families. In the summer, kids can frolic on the **Snow King's Alpine Miniature Golf Course and Alpine Slide** (✆ 307/733-5200). A round of 18 holes is $4.75 for children, $5.75 for adults.

The **Alpine Slide** is the golf course's untamed neighbor. It's a wild ride down the 2,500-foot ophidian highway running from the top of the blue-and-yellow chairlift to the bottom of Snow King Mountain; it's like a water slide without the water.

In the winter, there are ski schools for kids with day-care options at all the ski resorts. Once again, Snow King has something extra: an ice-skating rink, which opens in October and features skating and hockey until spring. For prices and hours, call ✆ **307/733-5200.**

---

in stock, some of its abundant galleries have become more adventurous and sophisticated. The **Martin-Harris Gallery,** at 60 E. Broadway (✆ **307/ 733-0350**), looks down its nose (well, it's located upstairs) at the less sophisticated Western art in neighboring galleries, but it backs up its snobbery with beautifully displayed art, original and contemporary, while still sticking largely to Western themes. Prices are second-story as well. The beauty of Tom Mangelsen's wildlife photography has been somewhat diluted by its display in airports and malls, but Jackson is where he started, and at the **Images of Nature Gallery,** 170 N. Cache St. (✆ **307/733-9752**), you'll find some of his work signed and numbered. The **Center Street Gallery,** 110 Center St. (✆ **307/ 733-1115**), has the lock on abstract Western art in Jackson. A mile north of town, at 1975 U.S. 89 (toward the park), is the **Wilcox Gallery** (✆ **307/ 733-6450**), which showcases more than 20 painters and sculptors from across the nation.

WHERE TO STAY
IN JACKSON

There's a wide variety of lodging options in Jackson Hole, but be prepared to shell out some cash. Prices have steadily increased, to the point where it's difficult to find a room for less than $100 in the summer. Many of the least-expensive chain properties are clustered together near the junction west of town where Wyo. 22 leaves U.S. 26/89 and heads north toward Teton Village: **Motel 6** (600 S. Wyo. 22; ✆ 307/733-1620) and the not-just-numerically superior **Super 8** (750 S. Wyo. 22; ✆ **800/800-8000** or 307/733-6833). In the vicinity are the more upscale and expensive **Days Inn,** at 350 S. Wyo. 22 (✆ **800/329-7466** or 307/733-0033), with private hot tubs and fireplaces, and the 73-room **Red Lion Inn,** at 930 W. Broadway (✆ **800/844-0035** or 307/734-0035). High-season rates for these properties run about $90 to $170, with double rooms at the Red Lion starting at $229 a night. Sales tax adds about 6% to the listed rates.

Jackson Hole Lodge   Though it sits near one of the busiest intersections in Jackson, and it's packed into a small space, this lodge is quiet and well designed, so that its location in the heart of town becomes a plus. The pool is not just for splashing—you can lap its 40-foot length, sit in one of the whirlpools, take a sauna, or sit out on your own sun deck. The rooms are more comfortable and complete than what you'll find at a chain property, blending Western ambience with scads of in-room options. Best of all are the condo lodgings, with two upstairs bedrooms, a full kitchen, and a living room with foldout couch. This gives families a little space, and it's also affordable.

420 W. Broadway, Jackson, WY 83001. (C) 800/604-9404 or 307/733-2992. www.jacksonholelodge.com. 59 units. $109–$134 double; $184–$304 condo. AE, DC, DISC, MC, V. **Amenities:** Outdoor pool; 2 Jacuzzis; sauna; game room. In room: A/C, TV, some kitchens.

Rusty Parrot Lodge and Spa 🏕🏕   The name sounds like an out-of-tune jungle bird, but since 1990 the Rusty Parrot has shown excellent pitch, cultivating a country lodge and spa right in the heart of busy Jackson. Located across from Miller Park, the Parrot is decorated in the nouveau-Western style of peeled log, with an interior appointed with elegant furnishings and river-rock fireplaces. One very attractive lure is The Body Sage, where you can get yourself massaged, painted with Austrian moor mud, and treated to all sorts of scrubs, wraps, and facials, for prices ranging from $45 for a hot herbal wrap to $170 for a "Himalayan Experience" that includes aromatherapy, hot-oil massage, and a hot linen pack. Breakfast includes omelets, fresh pastries, fruits, cereals, and freshly ground coffee; food also appears later in the day, but the lodge likes to make that a surprise (sorry). Rooms are gigantic and several have private balconies.

175 N. Jackson, Jackson, WY 83001. (C) 800/458-2004 or 307/733-2000. www.rustyparrot.com. 31 units. $108–$275 double; $500 suite. Rates include full breakfast. AE, DC, DISC, MC, V. **Amenities:** Restaurant, lounge; spa. In room: TV.

Trapper Inn   The employees here are some of the most helpful you'll find in Jackson. Just 2 short blocks from Town Square, the Trapper is hard to miss if you're walking north on Cache from Town Square. On the west side of Cache you'll notice the crazy Trapper guy on the sign. You can walk anywhere downtown within minutes. The rooms are spacious, featuring cozy quilts and stately lodgepole-pine furnishings. There are two structures here: Fittingly, the newest building, erected in 1991, features rooms with a more modern feel.

235 N. Cache, Jackson, WY 83001. (C) 800/341-8000 or 307/733-2648 for reservations. www. trapperinn.com. 54 units, including 4 suites. $98–$178 double; $170–224 suite. AE, DC, DISC, MC, V. **Amenities:** Jacuzzi; self-serve laundry. In room: A/C, TV, microwave, fridge, coffeemaker.

Virginian Lodge 🏕   It's not brand-new; it's not a resort; it doesn't have a golf course; and the highway is right outside the door, but since its overhaul in 1995, the Virginian is attempting to earn its spurs as one of the better motels in Jackson. Given its location on the busy Broadway strip, that's not likely to happen, but the prices remain reasonable, and it's a busy, cheerful place to stay. You can get a room with a private Jacuzzi or a kitchenette, and many have "dry" bars and sofa sleepers. Kids can romp in the arcade, everyone can eat in the Howling Coyote restaurant, and parents can relax in the Virginian Saloon.

750 W. Broadway, Jackson, WY 83001. (C) 800/262-4999 or 307/733-2792. Fax 307/733-4063. www. virginianlodge.com. 181 units. $95–$109 double; $125–$185 suite. AE, DC, DISC, MC, V. **Amenities:** Restaurant, lounge; outdoor pool; Jacuzzi; game room; self-serve laundry. In room: A/C, TV, kitchenette.

Wort Hotel 🏕🏕   Located on Broadway just off Town Square, the Wort stands like an old tree, though its Tudor-style two-story building was largely rebuilt after a 1980 fire. Opened in the early 1940s by the sons of Charles Wort, an early-20th-century homesteader, it has an old-fashioned style to it, both in the noisy and relaxed **Silver Dollar Bar** and the quiet, formal dining room (there's also a Starbucks Coffee outlet on-site). The lobby is graced by a warm, romantic fireplace; another fireplace and a hand-carved mural accent a mezzanine sitting area. The rooms aren't Tudor at all—the Wort labels them "New West" and has totally renovated each of them since 2000. The comfortable rooms have modern decor. The Governor's Suite boasts a traditional parlor.

The famous Silver Dollar Bar is a casual watering hole; the bar itself is inlaid with 2,032 silver dollars, the most precious piece of furniture rescued during the fire. Country-and-Western music emanates from the jukebox, and live entertainers appear nightly during the summer. Totally made over in 2001, the Silver Dollar Grill serves three meals a day and focuses on steaks and ribs come suppertime.

50 N. Glenwood, Jackson, WY 83001. (✆ 307/733-2190. www.worthotel.com. 60 units. $140–$245 double; $275–$485 suite. AE, DISC, MC, V. **Amenities:** Restaurant, lounge; exercise room; Jacuzzi. *In room:* A/C, TV.

NEAR JACKSON

Amangani 🏵🏵 Cut into the side of East Gros Ventre Butte, Amangani's rough rock exterior blends incredibly well, so that at night the lights from its windows appear to glow from within the mountain. The decor is understated and rustic, but every detail is done with expensive style. Owner Adrian Zecha has resorts like this around the world, from Bali to Bora Bora, and while the designs are tailored to the landscape, the approach is the same: personal service, luxury, and lots of little touches. To name a few of the latter, there are CDs in every bedroom, cashmere throws on the daybeds, and stunning slate and red-wood interiors. You can get massages and facials at the health center, or dine at the Grill at Amangani. Some Jackson competitors are jealous: One suggested that Amanresorts operate on the theory that if you set your prices sky-high, a certain clientele feels it has to stay there.

1535 NE Butte Rd., Jackson, WY 83002 (on top of East Gros Ventre Butte). (✆ 877/734-7333 or 307/734-7333. www.amangani.com. 40 units. $625–$900 double. AE, DC, DISC, MC, V. **Amenities:** Restaurant, lounge; outdoor pool; spa; Jacuzzi. *In room:* A/C, TV, VCR, minibars.

Bentwood Inn 🏵 *Finds* This B&B is an architectural marvel. Built from 200-year-old timber cleared from Yellowstone to make room for a rest area, the inn is a 6,000-square-foot log mansion with an amazing 43 corners. The parlor, featuring 30-foot ceilings and a three-story river-rock fireplace, is an ideal place to while away a thunderstorm reading a book or playing a game of backgammon. But the real beauty here is outside; the inn is situated just east of the Snake River on three acres of cottonwood and pine forest with a breezy deck and back lawn. The rooms themselves, all with remote-controlled gas fireplaces, private balconies, and Jacuzzi tubs, are extensions of the innovative design, with touches equally urban and rural, from ornate tilework to longhorn skulls above the bed. Innkeepers Bill and Nell Fay (the former designed the inn himself) pay a great deal of attention to detail and it shows: One room is pet-friendly, the breakfasts are simultaneously hearty and gourmet, and the fridge is always stocked with a wide range of soft drinks and libations.

4 miles west of Jackson on Teton Village Rd. (P.O. Box 561), WY 83001. (✆ 307/739-1411. Fax 307/739-2453. www.bentwoodinn.com. 5 units, including 1 suite. $165–$325 double. Rates include full breakfast and evening cocktails. AE, DISC, MC, V. **Amenities:** Game room. *In room:* TV.

Spring Creek Ranch 🏵 Perched atop East Gros Ventre Butte, 1,000 feet above the Snake River and minutes from both the airport and downtown Jackson, this resort commands a panoramic view of the Grand Tetons and 1,500 acres of land populated by deer, moose, and the horses at its riding facility in the valley below. It seems a little less exclusive now that Amangani has opened next door. But Spring Creek still has much going for it: The rooms, divided among nine buildings with cabin-like exteriors, all have fireplaces, Native American floor and wall coverings, and balconies with views of the Tetons. Most rooms have a king-size or two queen-size beds, and the studio units boast kitchenettes. In addition to its own rooms, the resort arranges accommodations in the privately owned condominiums that dot the butte—large, lavishly furnished, and featuring completely equipped kitchens and sleeping accommodations. Winter skiing at Teton Village is only 15 miles (24km) away.

1800 Spirit Dance Rd. (on top of the East Gros Ventre Butte; P.O. Box 4780), Jackson, WY 83001. © **800/ 443-6139** or 307/733-8833. 125 units. $210 double; $375–$1,200 condo. AE, MC, V. **Amenities:** Restaurant (see "Where to Dine," below); outdoor pool; tennis; spa; Jacuzzi; room service. *In room:* A/C, cable TV, VCR, fridge, coffeemaker, kitchenette.

IN TETON VILLAGE

Teton Village is gradually becoming the self-contained resort town now typical of better ski resorts—it has everything you need, from food to powder to a massage, a short limp from the chairlifts. The village is located on the west side of the Snake River, surrounded by ranchlands that have been protected from development. While lodging in the town of Jackson tends to be a little cheaper in the winter than the summer, the ratio is reversed at Teton Village—rooms by the ski hill get more expensive after the snow falls.

Very Expensive

Alpenhof Lodge * * No other spot in the village has quite the Swiss chalet flavor of this longstanding hostelry, which has a prize location only 50 yards from the ski resort tram. Four stories tall, with a pitched roof and flower boxes on the balconies, it offers a little Old-World atmosphere, as well as excellent comforts and service. The management continues to upgrade, most recently redoing the dining room and deluxe accommodations with brightly colored alpine fabrics, newly constructed handcrafted Bavarian furnishings, and tiled baths. Among the accommodations, you can choose from two junior suites with wet bars and five rooms with fireplaces; and many rooms have balconies or decks.

Your choices for dinner include award-winning and expensive continental fare that is served in The Alpenhof dining room; or pork, game, and pasta, which are staples in the Alpenhof Bistro, a casual and cozy second-level dining area overloaded with Bavarian furniture. After dinner, you may relax over cocktails by a stone fireplace, or on the outside deck.

3255 W. McCollister Dr., Teton Village, WY 83025. © **800/732-3244** or 307/733-3242. Fax 307/739-1516. www.alpenhoflodge.com. 42 units. Dec–Apr $119–$258 double, $183–$538 suite; May–Oct $88–$168 double, $118–$408 suite. AE, DC, DISC, MC, V. Closed Nov. **Amenities:** 2 restaurants; lounge. *In room:* A/C, cable TV, kitchenette.

Jackson Hole Resort Lodging * * The wide variety of prices below indicates the wide variety of properties now under the wing of this management group. Most of them are in the Teton Village area, and they range from the relatively inexpensive and simple Village Center Inn to some deluxe private homes. Also on the roster here are the condos at the Jackson Hole Racquet Club, 4 miles (6km) south of the ski resort at Teton Village on 550 acres along the Moose-Wilson Road. The condos come with fireplaces, washer-dryers, and fully equipped kitchens. You can comfortably fit a family in many of these loft-style condos with balconies, and the resort has extras (some require a fee) including tennis courts, a health club, and an outdoor pool. Don't expect coddling from the staff, which checks you in and lets you be.

3200 McCollister Dr. (P.O. Box 51087), Teton Village, WY 83025. © **800/443-8613** or 307/733-3990. Fax 307/734-1077. info@jhresortlodging.com. 300 units. Spring $52–$64 double, $126 2-bedroom loft, $190–$606 3–5 bedroom home; winter $90–$100 double, $340 2-bedroom loft, $635–$1,440 3–5 bedroom home. AE, DISC, MC, V. **Amenities:** Varies, depending on location. *In room:* TV, kitchen.

Snake River Lodge & Spa ⭐   Major renovations on what was once the Renaissance were completed in 2002, and this perpetually changing establishment looks to have gained some stability under the ownership of Vail Resorts. Wooden walls, stone floors and fireplaces, and a stuffed bison accent the main reception area. The main lodge provides accommodations where classy overshadows rustic, with exposed wooden-beam ceilings, down comforters, and luxurious furnishings. There are three levels of suites, from oversized versions of the standard rooms to three-bedroom versions with top-of-the-line kitchens, good sound systems, and Jacuzzi tubs. **Gamefish** restaurant serves regional game and seafood, and the bar offers a place to unwind with just about any beer you can think of, including microbrews plus pool tables, and sports on television. The 17,000-square-foot **Natura Spa** is a new addition, featuring everything from hydrotherapy to free weights. Winter visitors can ski directly to a locker room with whirlpool and sauna, and drop their skis off for an overnight tune-up.

7710 Granite Loop Rd. (Box 348), Teton Village, WY 83025. ✆ **800/445-4655** or 307/732-6000. Fax 307/732-6009. www.snakeriverlodge.com. 135 units. May to early June and Sept to mid-Dec $169–$299 double, $300–$900 suite; June to mid-Sept $229–$329, $400–$1000 suite; mid-Dec to Apr $340–$380, $450–$1,050 suite. AE, MC, V. **Amenities:** Restaurant, lounge; indoor/outdoor pool; health club and spa; Jacuzzi; children's programs; concierge; room service; dry cleaning. *In room:* Cable TV, kitchenette, hair dryer, safe, coffeemaker.

Teton Pines Resort ⭐   Arnold Palmer and Ed Seay designed the challenging 18-hole golf course attached to this luxury resort. Don't expect to improve your handicap on this course, but you can soothe your frustrations on the green in the comfortable rooms, which feature, among other things, his-and-her bathrooms, one with tub, one with shower. There is also a pair of condo units, complete with kitchens and washer/dryer combinations. This upscale resort offers a range of recreation (though some activities cost extra): tennis, heli-skiing, fly-fishing, and more. Five minutes away is the Jackson Hole Ski Resort. The dining room, **The Pines Restaurant,** is in the Teton Pines Clubhouse, and it's one of the better places to eat in Jackson Hole, though it's pricey.

3450 N. Clubhouse Dr., Jackson, WY 83001. ✆ **800/238-2223** or 307/733-1005. 18 units. Summer $395–$750 suite; rest of year $100–$675 suite. AE, MC, V. **Amenities:** Restaurant; outdoor pool; golf course; tennis courts; access to nearby health club; Jacuzzi; activities desk; room service; dry cleaning. *In room:* Cable TV, kitchen.

Moderate

Hostelx ⭐ (Value)   If you came to Wyoming to ski, not to lie in the lap of luxury, get yourself a room at Hostelx and hit the slopes. Called "the soul of Jackson Hole," it's a great bargain for skiers who don't need the trimmings, and it's not a dormitory, either—comfortable private rooms (above the caliber of a roadside motel) with king-size beds hold up to four people, and there's a good place to prep your skis, a library, and a common room with a fireplace, where ski movies run during the winter. You can walk to the Mangy Moose and other fun spots, and nobody will be able to tell you apart from the skiers staying at the Ritz.

Box 546, Teton Village, WY 83025. ✆ **307/733-3415.** Fax 307/739-1142. www.hostelx.com. Summer $48–$54 double; winter $47–$60 double. MC, V. **Amenities:** Game room; self-serve laundry. *In room:* No phone.

NEARBY GUEST RANCHES

Though there have been ranches in the valley for more than a century, Jackson Hole's white residents have always made part of their living hosting visitors from Europe and the eastern U.S. who came to hunt, see the sights, and enjoy the outdoors. Somewhere around 1900, the term "dude ranching" came into discourse, and Jackson joined Sheridan and Cody as popular Wyoming destinations for folks who wanted a cowboy experience. You can come out to work hard on horseback, move cattle, eat wranglers' grub, and pay dearly for it; but many of the dude ranches offer a more relaxed vacation, with riding, river floating, fine food, and plenty of boots-up porch time.

Flying A Ranch 𝄢   Nestled at 8,300 feet between the Gros Ventre and Wind River Ranges of Wyoming, the Flying A stuns its visitors with panoramic views. Quaking aspen, stream-fed ponds, and curious antelope are hardly disturbed by this exclusive operation, which hosts only 14 guests at a time. Built in the 1930s, the ranch cabins have been carefully restored, with evocative touches that include wood-burning stoves, handmade pine furniture, and regional artwork. Typical of a dude ranch, everything is included: unlimited horseback riding, fly-fishing (with lessons, if you wish), mountain biking, guided hikes, gourmet meals, and unlimited hot-tub time. The cabins are rustic on the outside, but have complete bathrooms and fireplaces, porches, and views. The quiet intimacy of this small operation is underlined by an adults-only policy. It's a 50-mile (80km) drive from the ranch to Jackson for shopping and sightseeing excursions.

771 Flying A Ranch Rd., Pinedale, WY 82941 (50 miles [80km] southeast of Jackson on U.S. 191). ✆ **307/ 367-2385**, or 800/678-6543 in winter. www.flyingaranch.com. 7 cabins. $1,100–$1,675 per person per week. Rates include all meals and ranch activities. No credit cards. **Amenities:** Jacuzzi; activities desk. *In room:* Kitchenette, no phone.

Heart 6 Ranch *Kids*   Slightly more than an hour's drive north of Jackson, just east of the Moran Junction, is the Heart 6, a fistful of fun for families. The Heart 6 isn't the fanciest of the guest ranches in and around Jackson Hole, but it's certainly not short on entertainment. Fishing, horseback riding, hiking, or just sitting and talking lead the long list of outdoor activities. A naturalist from the Park Service is also on hand to educate guests on the local wildflowers. The ranch offers an airport-shuttle system, Saturday trips to the rodeo in Jackson, and extensive children's programs. Babysitting service is also available for infants and for children up to age 4. In fact, Heart 6 is the only ranch in the valley that takes care of infants. On rainy days, kids and adults alike can enjoy the recreation center, with bumper pool, Foosball, and Ping-Pong.

16985 Buffalo Valley Rd., 5 miles (8km) outside Grand Teton National Park (35 miles [56km] north of Jackson on U.S. 26/287), Moran, WY 83013. ✆ **888/543-2477** or 307/543-2477. www.heartsix.com. 15 cabins. $1,072–$1,265 per person per week. Rates include all meals. DISC, MC, V. **Amenities:** Jacuzzi; game room; activities desk. *In room:* No phone.

Lost Creek Ranch 𝄢𝄢   The Lost Creek is so popular that one guest has stipulated in his will that his family will inherit annual trips after his demise. Reservations are at a premium with a short season and a maximum capacity of about 50 guests. If you manage to wrangle a reservation, however, this ultra-plush ranch offers a wide range of outdoor activities, crowned by sumptuous gourmet meals. All the usual dude-ranch activities are available, and then some: hiking, riding, touring the parks, and gourmet meals are part of the package.

After all that activity, you can pamper yourself in the spa (not included in the room rates): get a massage, a sea-salt body scrub, or a facial, or else take a yoga class or work out with weights. If you want to get away from the children, there's a lounge with billiards and cards or a skeet-shooting range.

Duplex cabins, representing the height of rustic elegance, can be rented or subdivided; each section is outfitted with queen-size and twin beds and a private combination bath. There's also a large two-bedroom cabin that has a living area with fireplace and sleeping quarters for seven.

P.O. Box 95 (off U.S. 89, 20 miles [32km] north of Jackson), Moose, WY 83012. ℂ **307/733-3435.** Fax 307/733-1954. www.lostcreek.com. 10 cabins. $5,585–$12,860 per cabin per week. Rates include all meals, float trips, and rodeo. Call for discounted group and off-season rates. AE. Closed mid-Sept to May. **Amenities:** Outdoor swimming pool; tennis courts; health club and spa; Jacuzzi; children's program; activities desk; babysitting; laundry service. *In room:* Fridge, coffeemaker, no phone.

Red Rock Ranch *Kids* This working cattle ranch makes room for families who want a fun experience amidst the peaceful wilderness of the Gros Ventre Mountains east of Grand Teton National Park. With excellent catch-and-release fly-fishing on a private stretch of Crystal Creek, horseback riding in the mountains, and activities that include overnighters for the kids, cookouts with live music, trips to the rodeo in Jackson, and weekly country dances, this guest ranch northeast of Jackson is a great spot to bring the whole bunch. All nine cabins (one or two bedrooms) are comfortable log structures built in the 1950s, each busily decorated with Western trappings and a charming woodstove.

The kids will have a blast here. The **Children's Riding Program** (for those 6 and older) is a great learning experience and takes kids all over the ranch by horseback, but the overnight camp-out is the real Western treat. After a horseback ride, the kids (with the help of a couple of wranglers) set up camp and cook supper over an open fire. The night is spent playing games, telling stories, and looking up at a million stars.

P.O. Box 38 (30 miles [48km] northeast of Jackson on U.S. 26/287), Kelly, WY 83011. ℂ **307/733-6288.** www.theredrockranch.com. 9 cabins. $1,350 per cabin per week. Rate includes all meals and horseback riding. Minimum 6-day stay (Sun–Sat). No credit cards. Closed Sept–May. **Amenities:** Lounge; outdoor pool; Jacuzzi; game room; activities desk. *In room:* Fridge, no phone.

CAMPING

There are several places to park the RV around Jackson Hole. Most are going to charge around $25 and up, though prices seem to change at the drop of a hat, rising just like local motel prices.

There aren't a lot of campsites for trailers close-in to this resort town anymore, because property values attract more upscale investments. The biggest is the **Virginian RV Campground,** 750 W. Broadway (ℂ **800/321-6982**), behind the Virginian Motel. You'll pay between $35 and $40 for a site. Also in town, the **Wagon Wheel Campground** (ℂ **307/733-4588**) is about 5 blocks north of Town Square at the Wagon Wheel Motel and has sites for $30. There's also the **Snake River Park KOA Campground,** on U.S. 89, 10 miles (16km) south of town (ℂ **307/733-7078**) and the **Teton Village KOA** (ℂ **307/733-5254**), 12 miles (19km) northwest of Jackson in Teton Village, both with sites for about $30. If you're looking to set up a tent when the parks are full, **Curtis Canyon Campground** (ℂ **307/739-5500**) is a great campground up behind the elk refuge in Bridger-Teton National Forest, and it will cost only $10 a night.

See also section 2, "Grand Teton National Park," for details on camping in Grand Teton National Park.

WHERE TO DINE

In addition to the choices reviewed below, you can get smaller, quicker bites to eat at **The Merry Piglets,** 160 N. Cache St. (ℂ **307/733-2966**), a snug Mexican restaurant that also serves Thai chicken wraps. **Harvest Bakery and Natural Food Cafe,** 130 W. Broadway (ℂ **307/733-5418**), serves smoothies, vegetarian meals, and other breakfast and lunch entrees made from organic ingredients. At the other end of the spectrum is **Bubba's Bar-B-Que,** 515 W. Broadway (ℂ **307/733-2288**), a late-night institution dishing out ribs and other meats. If you need a good shot of espresso with your morning paper, stop at **Pearl Street Bagel,** 145 W. Pearl St. (📞 **307/739-1218**), or the **Betty Rock Coffee House & Cafe,** 325 W. Pearl St. (📞 **307/733-0747**), where you can sit outside on the deck and nosh on a designer sandwich and salad.

EXPENSIVE

The Blue Lion 🎇 ECLECTIC In the fast-moving, high-rent world of Jackson dining, the Blue Lion stays in the forefront by staying the same. On the outside, it's a two-story blue clapboard building across from the town park that looks like a comfy family home. On the inside, in intimate rooms accented with soft lighting, diners enjoy slow-paced and elegant meals. The menu features rack of lamb and the usual (in Jackson) wild game specialties, like grilled elk loin in a peppercorn sauce. Fresh fish is flown in daily for dishes like the wine-basted rainbow trout stuffed with snow crab. Summer diners can eat outside on the patio.

160 N. Millward. 📞 307/733-3912. Reservations recommended. Main courses $15–$28. AE, DC, MC, V. Wed–Mon 5:30–10pm.

The Cadillac Grille CALIFORNIA ECLECTIC The 1950s neon and hip American cuisine give this restaurant a trendy air that attracts see-and-be-seen visitors more than locals. The chefs work hard on presentation, but they also know how to cook, despite the wide-ranging variety of dishes, from fire-roasted elk tenderloins to garlic-painted Chilean sea bass. A *Wine Spectator* favorite, the wine list is long and varied. The menu changes regularly, but the place itself has become one of Jackson's longer-lived establishments.

55 N. Cache. 📞 307/733-3279. Reservations recommended. Lunch $5–$18; dinner $15–$25. AE, MC, V. Daily 11:30am–3:30pm and 5:30–10pm.

The Granary at Spring Creek AMERICAN Perched atop Gros Ventre Butte, 15 minutes from downtown Jackson, this restaurant at Spring Creek Ranch has one of the best views of the Teton Range, especially enjoyable over a plate of fresh snapper wrapped in prosciutto and potato. Breakfast (our favorite: rainbow trout and eggs) and lunch are particularly pleasant when weather allows dining outside on a wood deck. The menu changes seasonally, but you may find elk-flank fajitas and gourmet sandwiches at lunch or grilled elk tenderloin with blackberry-barbecue sauce at dinner.

On top of the East Gros Ventre Butte (P.O. Box 3154), Jackson, WY 83001. 📞 800/443-6139 or 307/733-8833. Reservations recommended. Breakfast $9–$13; lunch $8–$15; dinner $15–$28. AE, DC, MC, V. Daily 7:30–10am, noon–2pm, and 6–9pm.

Nani's Genuine Pasta House 🎇 *(Finds* ITALIAN The setting is simple but the food is extraordinary at Nani's, where you are handed two menus: a *carta classico* featuring pasta favorites like *amitriciana* (tomato, onion, pancetta, and freshly ground black pepper) and a bowl of mussels in wine broth; or a list of specialties from a different featured region of Italy, which might include veal seared in a Marsala sauce or swordfish stuffed with bread crumbs, Parmigiano Reggiano cheese, capers, and garlic. Your only problem with this restaurant might be finding it—it's tucked away behind a rather run-down motel.

240 N. Glenwood. 📞 307/733-3888. www.nanis.com. Reservations recommended. Main courses $10–$17. MC, V. Tues–Sat 5–10pm.

The Pines Restaurant CONTEMPORARY AMERICAN The Teton Pines golf resort is home to what locals consider one of the finest restaurants in the valley. The posh eatery overlooks a placid trout pond and Teton Pines golf course. An impressive menu includes a succulent array of well-prepared steak and veal

Old West Cookouts

If you don't have time or money (or desire) for the full dude-ranch experience, one stomach-filling alternative is to make a beeline for the nearest guest ranch around mealtime to enjoy Western cuisine served up to the strains of yodelin' cowpokes.

Before you take your appetite to the ranches, check to see if reservations are necessary. The **Bar-J Ranch** (✆ 307/733-3370), Teton Village Road, 1 mile (1.5km) north of Wyo. 22, is a big operation, with room for more than 700 people beneath its awnings. They serve a big meal of barbecue beef, beans, biscuits, and more, and there is cowboy humor and music ($15–$22 for adults; $6 for children under 9; children in laps free). Reservations are recommended. The **Bar-T-5,** 790 E. Cache Creek Dr., Jackson (✆ 800/772-5386 or 307/733-5386), offers a covered-wagon ride through Cache Creek Canyon to the "dining room" for an evening of Western victuals and after-dinner songs from the Bar-T-5's singing cowboys. The covered-wagon dinner runs around $30 for adults, $23 for youngsters 6 to 12; children 5 and under enjoy the night free.

dishes, as well as the obligatory pastas. The seafood arrives daily—for an appetizer, try the tempura nori roll, with tuna, Dungeness crab, and Arctic char; for dinner, there's lamb chops with pear-and-mint salsa and pistachio couscous.

3450 N. Clubhouse Dr. off Teton Village Rd., Jackson, WY 83001. ✆ 800/238-2223 or 307/733-1005. Reservations recommended. Main courses $15–$28. AE, MC, V. Mon–Sat 11:30am–2:30pm and 6–9pm; Sun 9am–1pm.

Snake River Grill ★★ CONTEMPORARY AMERICAN   This is a popular drop-in spot for locals, including some of the glitterati who sojourn in the area—like Harrison Ford and Uma Thurman to name but a couple. The front-room dining area overlooks the busy Town Square, but there's a more private, romantic room in the back. It's an award-winning restaurant for both its wine list and its menu, which features regular fresh-fish dishes (ahi tuna is a favorite), crispy pork shank, and some game meat entrees like venison chops and Idaho trout. The pizzas—cooked in a wood-burning oven—are topped with exotic ingredients like duck sausage or eggplant with portobello mushrooms.

Town Square, Jackson. ✆ 307/733-0557. www.snakerivergrill.com. Reservations recommended. Main courses $20–$40. AE, DC, MC, V. Daily 5:30–9:30pm. Closed Nov and Apr.

Stiegler's AUSTRIAN/CONTINENTAL   Since 1983, Stiegler's has been confusing, astonishing, and delighting customers with such favorites as venison St. Hubertus (game dishes are de rigeur at finer Jackson dining establishments), bratwurst, and schnitzel, as well as less recognizable (but equally tasty and heavy) delicacies. You'll be familiar with the desserts, at least: apple strudel and chocolate bread pudding. Peter Stiegler, the Austrian chef, invites you to "find a little *Gemütlichkeit*"—the feeling you get when you're surrounded by good friends, good food, and, of course, good beer.

Teton Village Rd., at the Aspens. ✆ 307/733-1071. Reservations recommended. Main courses $18–$30. AE, MC, V. Tues–Sun 4–9:30pm. Closed Mon.

Sweetwater Restaurant AMERICAN   Though this little log restaurant serves American fare, it does so in a decidedly offbeat way. The eclectic menu includes, for example, a Greek salad, a Baja chicken salad, and a cowboy grilled roast beef sandwich. During the summer, there's outside dining. The dinner menu is just as quirky, and livened by nightly specials; try the unique smoked buffalo carpaccio before diving into a giant grilled salmon filet. Vegetarians will want to sample the spinach-and-feta casserole, topped with a cheese soufflé.

85 King St. ℂ **307/733-3553.** Reservations recommended. Lunch $5–$8; dinner $13–$22. AE, DISC, MC, V. Daily 11am–3pm and 5:30–10pm; shorter hr. in winter.

MODERATE

Anthony's ITALIAN   There was a time when Anthony's was THE Italian restaurant in Jackson, and you would stand in line for a table in an atmosphere of friendly frenzy. The menu has changed a bit since those days, and Anthony's is no longer the pinnacle of fine dining in Jackson. It's still a very respectable eatery, but the competition has gotten so stiff over the years that Anthony's has suffered a bit by comparison. The menu offers selections of pasta, veal, poultry, and seafood, alongside the requisite antipasti selections and a kids' menu. A personal favorite: the rich lasagna verde, an arresting concoction with layers of grilled eggplant, Italian cheeses, and roasted red peppers.

62 S. Glenwood St. ℂ **307/733-3717.** Main courses $10–$17. AE, MC, V. Daily 5:30–9:30pm.

Koshu Wine Bar ⚛ ECLECTIC   A relatively new entry in Jackson's frenetic dining scene, the Koshu Wine Bar has quickly emerged as one of the hippest restaurants in town. Both locals (including the area's resident celebrities) and tourists crowd the small, sleek dining room for chef Joel Holland's ingenious, addictive creations. His ever-changing menu reads "Asian inspired food," but the Far East is just a starting point for Holland, who melds dozens of other influences into dishes like tamarind pork with coconut milk, green onions, and rice; sweet miso–marinated black cod with spinach and mushrooms; and an out-of-this-world ahi sashimi. Thanks to its location in the Jackson Hole Wine Company, patrons can choose from 800 varieties of wine at retail price (plus a nominal corking fee). The brunch has quickly become a favored hangover cure for locals—the wok-fried catfish is sure to roust the cobwebs on one's brain.

200 W. Broadway in the back of the Jackson Hole Wine Company. ℂ **307/733-5283.** Reservations not accepted. Main courses $12–$18; brunch dishes $6–$11. AE, MC, V. Tues–Sat 6pm–midnight; Sun 11am–2pm and 6–10pm. Bar open later.

Mangy Moose AMERICAN   Coming off the slopes at the end of a hard day of skiing or snowboarding, you can slide right to the porch of this Teton Village institution. Good luck getting a seat inside, but if you like a lot of noise and laughter, a beer or glass of wine, and a tasty dish like buffalo meatloaf, be patient—it beats getting into your car and driving into town. The decor matches the pandemonium: It looks like an upscale junk shop, with bicycles, old signs and, naturally, a moose head or two hanging from the walls and rafters. The food is customary Wyoming fare (steak, seafood, and pasta), with a good salad bar and a smattering of Mexican dishes. Try the hot spinach and artichoke-heart dip as an appetizer and move on to the elk fajitas or buffalo prime rib. There is often music on weekends in the bar, sometimes a well-known name like James McMurtry.

1 McCollister Dr., Teton Village. ℂ **307/733-4913.** Reservations recommended for larger parties. Main courses $15–$35. AE, MC, V. Daily 5:30–10pm.

Nora's Fish Creek Inn ⚛ *Finds* AMERICAN   If you like to eat among locals, Nora's is the place to hang out in Wilson, 6 miles (10km) northwest of Jackson—just look for the 15-foot trout on the roof. Rough but pleasant to look at, it's an institution, and if you come here often you'll start to recognize the regulars, who grumble over their coffee and gossip about doings in the valley. Breakfast is especially good, when there are pancakes and huevos rancheros that barely fit on the huge plates. Prices are inexpensive compared to those at any of the other restaurants in town. Dinner is fish, fish, and more fish, like fresh Idaho trout.

5600 W. Wyo. 22, Wilson. ℂ **307/733-8288.** Breakfast $5–$8; lunch $4–$9; dinner $12–$21. AE, DISC, MC, V. Daily 6am–1:30pm and 5–9:30pm.

Rendezvous Bistro AMERICAN/SEAFOOD   The Rendezvous opened in 2001 and quickly garnered a local following. It's easy to see why: The place is contemporary yet casual; the food is affordable but very good; and the service is well above average. Climb into one of the intimate booths and order a dozen oysters on the half shell and slurp away, but save some room for a main course, ranging from grilled New York strip *frites* to whole Maine lobster. It might sound formal, but it's really not—the beauty is that the food is top notch, while the atmosphere is laid-back and friendly.

380 W. Broadway. ℂ **307/739-1100.** Reservations recommended. Main courses $9–$20. AE, MC, V. Daily 5:30–10:30pm. Closed Nov.

Snake River Brewing Company PIZZA/PASTA   Microbreweries are sprouting (and spouting) all over the country, but this one is a cut above the others, judging from the prizes it's won for its pale ale and Zonker Stout. In this roomy, high-ceilinged new building, the brewery also serves excellent pizza cooked in a wood-fired oven—try the prosciutto and roasted red pepper or the barbecue chicken. There are also pastas, calzones, a spicy brat, and various sandwiches. The 15 brewing vats are all around and above, sometimes humming a bit too loudly, and you can play foosball and pool on the mezzanine. Beer lovers will appreciate the happy hour from 4 to 6pm, and there is sometimes live music—jazz or traditional Celtic.

265 S. Millward St. ℂ **307/739-2337.** Main courses $8–$12. Daily 11:30am–11pm.

INEXPENSIVE

Billy's Giant Hamburgers *Value* BURGERS   If you take a wrong turn while entering the posh Cadillac Grille (right instead of left), you find yourself in this cramped '50s-style lunch booth and counter shop . . . and you might just stay. Big, juicy burgers are what you'll get, cooked right in front of you. You can actually sit in here and order from the fancy Cadillac—perhaps Atlantic salmon and a fine sauvignon blanc—but won't you feel silly when the guy in the next booth has a giant cheeseburger in his hand? Go easy on the pocketbook, relax, order a big one and a brewski, with a pile of fries on the side.

West side of Town Square. ℂ **307/733-3279.** Most dishes $4–$6. AE, MC, V. Daily 11:30am–11pm. Closed Nov.

The Bunnery BREAKFAST/SANDWICHES/SOUPS   A Jackson mainstay, this bakery and restaurant is a great place for breakfast—perhaps a spinach omelet with sour cream and Swiss, or a Bunnery Benedict, served on a healthful oat, sunflower, and millet bun. It's popular and small, though, so you'll often find yourself waiting in a line that stretches down the boardwalk of the Hole-In-The-Wall Mall just off the square—that's not bad in the summer, but tough on a cold winter morning. Sandwiches like the Roadrunner (tarragon chicken salad) are reasonably priced and the portions are large. If you're in a hurry, there's also the Bunnery Express: muffins, baked goods, and drinks with a rapidly moving line.

130 N. Cache St. ℂ **307/733-5474.** Main courses $6–$8. MC, V. Summer daily 7am–3pm and 5–9pm; winter 7am–2pm.

Jedediah's House of Sourdough AMERICAN   You feel like you've walked into the kitchen of some sodbuster's log cabin home when you enter Jedediah's—the structure was built in 1910, and now resides on the National Register of Historic Places. (The sourdough starter is even older, 100 years old and going strong.) Bring a big appetite for breakfast, and a little patience—you may have to wait for a table, then you may have to wait for food, while you stare at the interesting old photos on the wall and listen to the families packed closely around you. But it's worth it, especially for the rich flavor of the sourjacks, a stack of sourdough pancakes, served with blueberries if you like. The "Diah's" omelet is a big three-egg concoction stuffed with bacon, onions, and cheddar cheese and served with a side of potatoes. During summer months, Jedediah's also serves dinners: steaks, barbecue chicken, rainbow trout, and the like.

135 E. Broadway. © 307/733-5671. Reservations not accepted. Breakfast $4–$8; lunch $5–$9; dinner $8–$18. AE, DC, DISC, MC, V. Year-round daily 7am–2pm; summer 5:30–9pm.

JACKSON AFTER DARK

Talented musicians from well-known orchestras around the country do a little slumming in the mountains every summer, participating in the **Grand Teton Music Festival** ⚡ (© 307/733-1128; www.gtmf.org) held at Teton Village in the amphitheater next to the tram lift. Under new Music Director Eiji Oue, the classical and contemporary programs have a new exuberance, highlighted by top-notch guest artists from around the world. Tickets are usually available on short notice, especially for the terrific weeknight chamber-music performances.

The summer-only **Jackson Hole Playhouse,** 145 W. Deloney (© **307/ 733-6994;** www.jacksonholetheatre.com), and the year-round **Pink Garter Mainstage Theatre,** 50 W. Broadway (© 307/733-3670), produce musicals, melodramas, and other light fare. Get tickets in advance for these shows.

If your idea of theater is a bunch of folks wearing cowboy hats in a bar, visit the famous **Million Dollar Cowboy Bar,** on the west side of the square at 25 N. Cache St. (© 307/733-2207), where you can dance the two-step to live bands. You can hear yourself talk more easily at the Wort Hotel's **Silver Dollar Bar** at 50 N. Glenwood (© 307/733-2190), where real or imagined cowpokes belly up to the bar. And, yes, those 1921 silver dollars under your glass are authentic, commemorating the original owner's wedding day. But if you want some high-octane dancing fun led by some talented local hoofers, head out to Wilson (west of Jackson 5 miles [8km] on Wyo. 22) and the **Stagecoach Bar** (© 307/733-4407) on a Sunday night. It's the only night they have live music in this scruffy bar and hamburger joint, and the place is jammed wall to wall. You'll see some folks who really know how to dance, fueled by a lively band, often with drop-in guitar aces and occasional celebrities (but don't count on Bob Dylan showing up *again*).

2 Grand Teton National Park

12 miles (19km) N of Jackson

Since people often think of Grand Teton in conjunction with either Yellowstone National Park or Jackson Hole, they imagine it's been around since the days of exploration, trappers, and ranch homesteads. But it's a fairly new park, about 50 years old, just as the dramatic Tetons are a fairly young mountain range—a mere 10 million years old, give or take a millennium.

It's also a small park, at least by Yellowstone standards, comprising the eastern slope of this brief mountain range and a portion of the Snake River plain below.

Jackson Hole & Grand Teton National Park

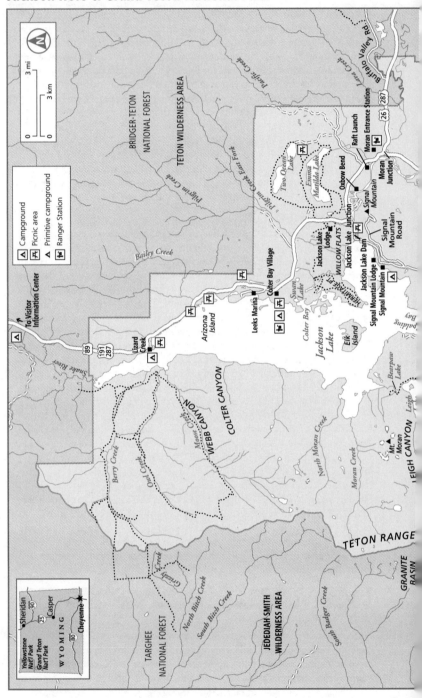

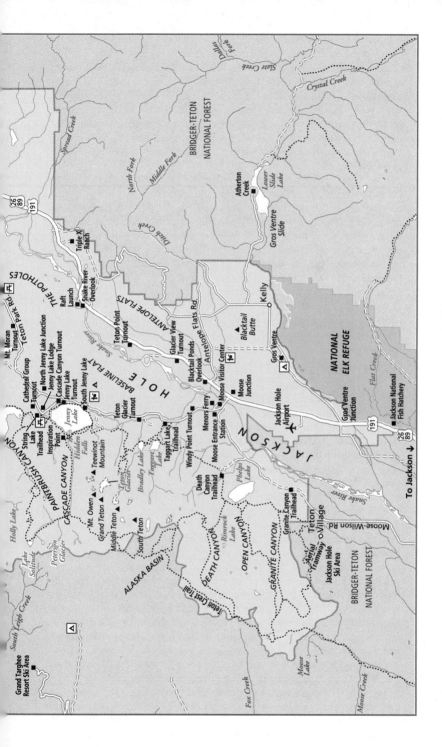

It lacks the unique geothermal features of its northern neighbor, but few mountains stand in such dramatic relief as the towering Cathedral Group, "Les Trois Tetons" (or "the three breasts," as some lonesome French trappers named them): **Mount Owen, Teewinot,** and **Grand Teton.** The Grand, as the locals call it, rises highest, to 13,770 feet, and it has lured climbers since the Depression era, when young Paul Petzoldt and a friend scrambled their way to the top in tennis shoes, to the astonishment of locals. Now commercial guides take hundreds of people to the summit every year, while adventurers find new and more difficult climbs in the range, or new ways of challenging themselves, like snowboarding or paragliding off the summits.

But Grand Teton is not merely an amusement park for risk-takers. There are beautiful lakes where you can sail or fish, and hikes that take you to waterfalls and panoramic views of the valley and mountains. There are historic sites like Menors Ferry, built a century ago to get folks across the Snake River, and some beautiful old lodges where you can experience holidays the way our grandparents did. Alpine wildflowers explode during the late spring, and hikers will often see elk, moose, trumpeter swans, bald eagles, and the occasional bear. There are peaceful nights under the stars when you might hear a chorus of coyotes yapping, or, more recently, the husky howls of wolves.

More than Yellowstone, Grand Teton is a modern park, beset by complex issues that sometimes pit wilderness values against modern conveniences like the commercial airport that operates here, or other uses, like the irrigation water behind Jackson Lake Dam or the cattle that graze the park's meadows.

A BRIEF HISTORY

Your first look at the Tetons, rising like spears from the Snake River plain, will take your breath away. Geologists say these mountains are still growing along a crack in the earth's crust that thrusts the range upward from the west as the valley sinks to the east. The lakebed sediments of the valley floor are actually "younger" than the pre-Cambrian rock of the peaks. Recent earthquakes in the area indicate the fault is still active. Like much of the Rocky Mountains, this range has been sculpted by glaciers, which gouged out the deep U-shaped valleys between the peaks. When the ice sheet that covered Jackson Hole melted for the last time, 15,000 years ago, it left a depression and a big mound of debris—called a terminal moraine—that formed a natural dam at the end of Jackson Lake.

The receding layers of ice created beautiful glacial lakes like Phelps, Taggart, Bradley, Jenny, String, and Leigh; polished the sides of Cascade canyon; and honed the peaks to their present jagged state. The glaciers live on, the most prominent being the five that have survived on Mount Moran.

The first human inhabitants of the region appeared about 12,000 years ago. Among the tribes who hunted here were the Blackfeet, Crow, Gros Ventre, and Shoshone. Summers were spent here hunting and raising crops; winters meant migration to warmer climes. The trappers and explorers who followed the tribes into the valley were equally distressed by the harsh winters and short growing season, which made Jackson Hole marginal ranchland at best. These early homesteaders quickly realized that their best hope was to market the beauty of the area, which they began doing in earnest as early as a century ago.

The danger of haphazard development soon became apparent. There was a dance hall at Jenny Lake, hot-dog stands and piles of debris along the roads, and vacation homes going up on prime wildlife habitat. In the 1920s, Yellowstone park officials and conservationists met to discuss how the Grand Teton area might

Tips **Travel Tip**

If you're considering a visit to the area's parks before mid-June, you should begin your exploration in Grand Teton before working north to Yellowstone. Elevations are slightly lower and snow melts earlier, so trails are more navigable and temperatures a bit more moderate.

be protected, and eventually they enlisted philanthropist John D. Rockefeller, Jr., to acquire lands for a future park. In 1929 a park was established to protect the mountains, while Rockefeller continued buying up ranches at the base of the Tetons, using a dummy corporation to hide his involvement. Wyoming's congressional delegation fought hard against park designation in the valley as Jackson Hole public opinion swayed like a pendulum, so President Franklin D. Roosevelt created the Jackson Hole National Monument in the 1940s. In 1950 the park was expanded to its present form.

JUST THE FACTS
ACCESS/ENTRY POINTS

Like the range of mountains it protects, Grand Teton National Park is a strip of real estate centered on a north-south axis. Teton Park Road, the primary thoroughfare, skirts along the lakes that pool at the mountains' base. From the **north,** you can enter the park from Yellowstone National Park, which is linked to Grand Teton by the **John D. Rockefeller Jr. Memorial Parkway** (U.S. 89/191/287), an 8-mile (13km) stretch of highway, where you may see wildlife through the trees, some of which are bare and blackened from the 1988 fires. When you come this way, you will already have paid your entrance to both parks, so there is no entrance station, but you can stop at **Flagg Ranch,** approximately 5 miles (8km) north of the park boundary, and get park information. December through March, Yellowstone's south entrance is open only to snowmobiles (though a potential ban is pending for 2003) and snowcoaches.

You can also approach the park from the **east,** via U.S. 26/287. This route comes from Dubois, 55 miles (89km) east on the other side of the Absaroka and Wind River Mountains, and crosses **Togwotee Pass,** where you'll get your first—and one of the best—views of the Tetons towering above the valley. Travelers who come this way can continue south on U.S. 26/89/191 to Jackson without paying an entrance fee, though they are within the park boundaries.

Finally, you can enter Grand Teton from Jackson in the **south,** driving about 12 miles (19km) north on U.S. 26/89/191 to the Moose turnoff and the park's south entrance. Here you'll find the park headquarters, a visitor center, and a small community that includes dining and shops.

For details on how to fly into the region, see "Getting There," in section 1, "Jackson Hole," above.

VISITOR INFORMATION

There are three visitor centers in Grand Teton National Park. The **Moose Visitor Center** (© 307/739-3399) is a half-mile west of Moose Junction at the southern end of the park; it's open from 8am to 7pm daily from June to Labor Day, and 8am to 5pm the rest of the year. The **Colter Bay Visitor Center** (© 307/739-3594), the northernmost of the park's visitor centers, is open 8am to 8pm from early June to Labor Day, and from 8am to 5pm after Labor Day to early October. There is also **Jenny Lake Visitor Center,** open from 8am to 7pm daily from early June to Labor Day and from 8am to 5pm after Labor Day to early October. Maps and ranger assistance are available at all three, and there are bookstores and exhibits at Moose and Colter Bay.

To receive park maps and information prior to your arrival, contact **Grand Teton National Park,** P.O. Drawer 170, Moose, WY 83012 (© **307/ 739-3600**). Other key park numbers include emergency park dispatch (© **307/ 739-3300**), and recorded information on climbing (© **307/739-3604**) and campgrounds (© **307/739-3603**). The park's website is **www.nps.gov/grte**.

Other sources of useful information include **Travel Montana,** P.O. Box 200533, Helena, MT 59620 (© **800/847-4868;** www.visitmt.com); **Wyoming Division of Tourism,** I-25 at College Drive, Cheyenne, WY 82002 (© **800/ 225-5996;** www.wyomingtourism.org); **Yellowstone Country,** P.O. Box 1107, Red Lodge, MT 59068 (© **800/736-5276**); **Jackson Chamber of Commerce,** P.O. Box 550, Jackson, WY 83001 (© **307/733-3316;** www.jacksonholechamber. com); and **Park County Travel Council,** P.O. Box 2454, Cody, WY 82414 (© **307/587-2297;** www.pctc.org).

FEES & BACKCOUNTRY PERMITS

There are no park gates on U.S. 26/89/191, so you get a free ride through the park on that route. But if you want to get off the highway and explore, you'll pay $20 per automobile for a 7-day pass for entry into both Grand Teton and Yellowstone National Parks. If you expect to visit the parks more than once within a year, you can buy a $40 annual permit, but we consider the various national park passes, which are also honored here, to be a better deal (see "The Active Vacation Planner," in chapter 2). For information on camping fees at Grand Teton National Park, see "Camping," below.

Backcountry permits are required from the Park Service for overnight use of backcountry campsites. The permits are free, but they can be reserved only from January 1 to May 15 (and the reservation itself costs $15); thereafter, all backcountry permits are issued on a first-come, first-served basis up to 24 hours before your first night out. Permits are issued at the Moose and Colter Bay visitor centers and the Jenny Lake ranger station. Reservations may be made by writing the **Permits Office,** Grand Teton National Park, P.O. Drawer 170, Moose, WY 83012, or by sending a fax to **307/739-3438.** Phone reservations are not accepted.

Boating permits are required if you bring your own boat (for motorized craft, $20 for an annual permit and $10 for a 7-day permit; for human-powered vessels, $10 for an annual permit and $5 for a 7-day permit). You can get permits at Moose or Colter Bay; the cost is included in the price of a boat rental. Motorized boats are permitted on Jenny, Jackson, and Phelps Lakes; sailboats, windsurfers, and jet skis are allowed on Jackson. Boats paddled by humans are permitted on most park lakes and the Snake River.

State of Wyoming **fishing licenses** are required for fishers over 14 years of age. An adult nonresident license costs $10 per day, $65 for the season. Youth fees (ages 14–18) are $3 per day, $15 for the season. (A Wyoming resident pays $15 for a season permit.) You can buy them at sporting-goods stores or park visitor centers. The entirety of the Snake River is open for fishing from April 1 to October 31; Jackson Lake is closed October 1 to 31. Because the Snake River flows into, and exits, Jackson Lake, different regulations apply to various sections of the river, and several are closed; the prudent angler will become knowledgeable of these laws to avoid a hefty fine.

REGULATIONS

The rules here are similar to those in most national parks. It is illegal to damage or collect natural, archaeological, or historic objects, and even picking wild-flowers is prohibited. Pets must be leashed and are not allowed more than 50 feet from roadways; on trails, boats, or boardwalks; or in the backcountry. They are allowed in campgrounds, but must be restrained at all times.

Loaded guns are not permitted in the park. However, unloaded firearms may be transported in a vehicle when cased, broken down, or rendered inoperable. Ammunition must be carried in a separate compartment of the vehicle.

SEASONS

Spring is an excellent time to visit the park—but remember that spring starts later in Wyoming than in most other parts of the country. In **May** and **June,** mild days and cool nights intersperse with occasional rain and snow. The snow level usually remains above valley elevation until mid-June. Wildflowers are in bloom, and, on a clear day, the snow-covered Tetons stand out boldly against a crisp blue sky. Better yet, trails are virtually devoid of hikers, though at higher elevations snow might still block the paths; check in at one of the ranger stations for trail conditions.

Summer is the most intense season at Grand Teton, with flowers blooming, fish and wildlife feeding, and all sorts of activity crammed into a few months of warm weather, from July to early September.

In **September,** sunny days and cooler nights alternate with rain and occa-sional snowstorms, and by the middle of the month, fall colors begin to make their way across the landscape.

The first big snow usually arrives by the beginning of **November** (though it's not unheard of in July!). In winter months, temperatures stick in the single digits, with sub-zero overnight temperatures common.

AVOIDING THE CROWDS

Summer is the busy time here, but crowds thin in the park after Labor Day, and you can enjoy sunny days and brilliant aspen yellows well into October. When there are crowds, you can avoid them by staying away from the centers of activity, which are Colter Bay, Jenny Lake, and Moose. Check out the overlooks, photograph the sites, and take in a few educational exhibits, then abandon the paved areas for unpaved trails.

TIPS FOR TRAVELERS WITH DISABILITIES

Visitor centers at Moose, Colter Bay, Jenny Lake, and Flagg Ranch provide interpretive programs, displays, and visitor information in several formats, including visual, audible, and tactile. Large-print scripts, Braille brochures, and narrative audiotapes are available at Moose and Colter Bay.

Accessible parking spaces are located close to all visitor center entrances; curb cuts are provided, as are accessible restroom facilities.

Campsites at Colter Bay, Jenny Lake, and Gros Ventre campgrounds are on relatively level terrain; Lizard Creek and Signal Mountain are hilly and less accessible. Picnic areas at String Lake and Cottonwood Creek are both acces-sible, though the toilet at Cottonwood is not.

Accessible dining facilities are located at Flagg Ranch, Leek's Marina, Jack-son Lake Lodge, and Jenny Lake Lodge.

More information is available by contacting **Grand Teton National Park,** P.O. Drawer 170, Moose, WY 83012 (© **307/739-3600;** www.nps.gov/grte).

Tips **Seeing the Park for Free**

Those who are only passing by, and never plan to get far from their cars, can see the full spectacle of these mountains without paying a park entry fee. If you come from the east, you will pass no tollbooths on your way south on U.S. 26/89/191, but there are frequent pullouts on the west side of the road that give you a panoramic overview of the Snake River and the Tetons. For that matter, you get a more distant, but equally grand, view of the mountains coming over **Togwotee Pass** on U.S. 26/287.

VIEWING THE PEAKS

Grand Teton National Park is famous for its mountains, and rightly so. The Cathedral Group is composed of **Grand Teton** (elevation 13,770 ft.), **Teewinot** (elevation 12,325 ft.), and **Mount Owen** (elevation 12,928 ft.). Nearby, almost as impressive, are **South Teton** (elevation 12,514 ft.) and **Middle Teton** (elevation 12,804 ft.).

If you come from the north and Yellowstone National Park, you will have paid a park-entry fee and be entitled to explore along **Teton Park Road,** west of the Snake. You'll be looking at mountains as you drive the east shore of Jackson Lake, and you'll find plenty of opportunities to pull over and snap your shutter. Four miles (6km) south of Colter Bay, you can take an unpaved, 1-mile (1.5km) road heading east from the highway to the **Grand View Overlook.** A large, flat area at the end of the road offers a commanding view of the Grand Tetons, and an excellent picnic spot. This road is great for autos, hikers, and bicycles, but not for large RVs.

You'll also get excellent views of the Cathedral Group on the trails and roads that ring **Jenny Lake** (see "Seeing the Highlights," below).

Signal Mountain, southeast of Jackson Lake, may not rank up there with the other Tetons, but you can drive right up it to an excellent lookout spot. Navigating the twisting, narrow road pays off at the summit, where you can gaze out over the valley, Cascade Canyon, Jackson Lake, and the Tetons.

Slightly north of Jenny Lake is the underrated, yet astoundingly humbling, **Mount Moran** (elevation 12,605 ft.), the fourth-largest peak in the range; its curiously flattened, sheared-off summit is the result of erosion back in geologically volatile times.

SEEING THE HIGHLIGHTS
JACKSON LAKE & THE NORTH END OF THE PARK

A great many people enter Grand Teton National Park from the north end, emerging from Yellowstone's south entrance with a 7-day park pass that gets them into Grand Teton as well. Yellowstone is connected to Grand Teton by a wilderness corridor through which the **John D. Rockefeller Jr. Memorial Parkway** runs for 8 miles (13km). Along it, you'll see an interesting area of meadows sometimes dotted with elk; the Snake River as it runs into Jackson Lake; and forests that in some places still show the impact of the 1988 fires. Some people complain about the sight of blackened tree trunks, but others are heartened to see the mosaic shapes of natural burn and the soft green of new trees sprouting.

Along the parkway, not far from Yellowstone, you'll pass your first lodging option, the recently modernized **Flagg Ranch** (see "Where to Stay in the Park," later in this chapter), with gas, restaurants, and other services. In the winter, this is a busy staging area for the snowcoach and snowmobile crowds.

JACKSON LAKE The north end of the park is dominated by giant **Jackson Lake,** a huge expanse of water that fills a deep gorge left 10,000 years ago by retreating glaciers. Though it empties east into the Snake River, curving around in the languid **Oxbow Bend**—a favorite wildlife-viewing float for canoeists, the water from Jackson Lake eventually turns south, then west through Snake River Canyon and into Idaho. In 1911, potato farmers downstream were instrumental in getting Congress to fund Jackson Lake Dam, which raised the lake about 40 feet and waterlogged the forest around the shoreline. Stream flow is now regulated at the dam for both farmers and rafters in the canyon, and, for better or worse, we have an irrigation dam in a national park. The dead trees have long since been cleared out and the dam was rebuilt with an eye for aesthetics in 1989. In general, the lake looks quite natural, except when water level plummets in the fall.

LEEKS MARINA As the road follows the east shore of the lake from the north, the first development travelers encounter is **Leeks Marina,** where boats can launch, gas up, and moor from mid-May to mid-September. There is a casual restaurant serving light fare and pizza during the summer. But drivers also have the option of stopping at numerous picnic pullouts along the lake.

COLTER BAY Just south of Leeks is **Colter Bay,** a busy outpost of park services where you can get groceries, postcards and stamps, T-shirts, and advice. If this is your first stop in the park, get maps and information at the **Colter Bay Visitor Center.** Here you can view park and wildlife videotapes and attend a park-orientation slide program throughout the day. Ranger-led activities include museum tours, park-orientation talks, natural history hikes, and evening amphitheater programs. Colter Bay has lots of overnight options, from its cabins to its old-fashioned tent camps to its trailer park and campground. There are also a general store and do-it-yourself laundry, two restaurants, a boat launch and boat rentals, and tours. You can take pleasant short hikes in this area, including a walk around the bay or out to **Hermitage Point** (see "Hiking," below).

The **Indian Arts Museum** ✦ (✆ **307/739-3594**) at the Colter Bay Visitor Center is worth a visit, though it is not strictly about the Native American cultures of this area. The artifacts are mostly from Plains Indian tribes, but there are also some Navajo items from the Southwest. The collection was assembled by David T. Vernon, and includes pipes, shields, dolls, and war clubs sometimes called "skull crackers." Visiting Indian artists work in the museum all summer long and sell their wares onsite. Admission is free.

JACKSON BAY JUNCTION From Colter Bay, the road veers east and then south again past **Jackson Lake Lodge** (see "Where to Stay in the Park," below), a slick, 1950s-style resort with a magnificent view of the Tetons and brushy flats in the foreground where moose often roam. Numerous trails originate here (see "Hiking," below), heading both to **Jackson Lake** and east to **Emma Matilda Lake**. The road then becomes **Jackson Lake Junction,** where you can either continue west along the lakeshore or go east to the park's **Moran Entrance Station.** Here the park's odd entrance configuration comes into play: If you go out through the Moran entrance you are still in the park, and may turn south on U.S. 26/89/191 and drive along the Snake River to Jackson, making most of your journey within the park's borders, though you might not know it.

SIGNAL MOUNTAIN But if you're here to enjoy the park, you'd probably turn west on **Teton Park Road** at Jackson Lake Junction, and arrive after only 5 miles (8km) at **Signal Mountain.** Like its counterpart at Colter Bay, this developed recreation area, on Jackson Lake's southeast shore, offers camping sites, accommodations in cabins and multiplex units, two restaurants, and a lounge with one of the few live televisions in the park. This is also the place to fill up on gasoline and provisions from the small convenience store. Boat rentals and scenic cruises of the lake also originate here.

If you turn east instead of west off Teton Park Road at Signal Mountain, you can drive up a narrow, twisting road to the top of the mountain, 700 feet above the valley, where you'll have a fine view of the ring of mountains—Absarokas, Gros Ventres, Tetons, and Yellowstone Plateau—that create Jackson "Hole." Note also the potholes created in the valley's hilly moraines left by retreating glaciers. Below the summit, about 3 miles (5km) from the base of the hill, is **Jackson Point Overlook,** a paved path 100 yards long leading to the spot where the Hayden Expedition's photographer, William Henry Jackson, shot his famous wet-plate photographs of Jackson Lake and the Tetons more than a century ago—proof to the world that such spectacular places really existed in the Rockies.

JENNY LAKE & THE SOUTH END OF THE PARK

JENNY LAKE   Continuing south along Teton Park Road, you move into the park's southern half, where the tallest peaks rise abruptly above a string of smaller lakes strung together in the foothills—**Leigh Lake, String Lake,** and **Jenny Lake,** which is the favorite of many park visitors. At North Jenny Lake Junction you can take a turnoff west to **Jenny Lake Lodge** (see "Where to Stay in the Park," later in this chapter)—the road then continues as a one-way scenic loop along the lakeshore before rejoining Teton Park Road about 4 miles (6km) later.

Beautiful **Jenny Lake** gets a lot of traffic throughout the summer, both from hikers who circumnavigate the lake on a 6-mile (10km) trail and from more sedentary folks who pay for a boat ride across the lake to Hidden Falls and the short, steep climb to **Inspiration Point** (see "Hiking," below). The parking lot at **South Jenny Lake** is often jammed, and there can be a long wait for the boat ride, so you might want to get there early in the day. There is also a tents-only campground, a visitor center, and a general store stocked with a modest supply of prepackaged foods, and even less fresh produce and vegetables. You can take a fairly level and easy hike around the south end of the lake to Hidden Falls or grab a ride with the **Teton Boating Company** (© 307/733-2703); round trips cost $6 for adults and $4 for children.

SOUTH OF JENNY LAKE   South of the lake, Teton Park Road crosses open sagebrush plains with never-ending views of the mountains. You'll pass the **Climbers' Ranch** (see "Climbing," below)—an inexpensive dorm-lodging alternative for climbers—and some trail heads for enjoyable hikes to **Taggart Lake** and elsewhere. Look closely in the sagebrush for the shy pronghorn, an antelope-like creature. This handsome animal, with tan cheeks and black accent stripes, can spring up to 60 miles (97km) an hour. If you wander in the sagebrush here, you may encounter a badger, a shy but mean-spirited creature that sometimes comes out of its hole at morning or twilight.

The **Teton Glacier Turnout** presents a view of a glacier that grew for several hundred years until, within the past century, it reversed direction, pressured by hotter summer temperatures, and began retreating.

MOOSE VISITOR CENTER   The road arrives at the park's south entrance again, actually well within the park's boundaries—and the sprawling **Moose Visitor Center,** which is also park headquarters. If you are approaching the park from the south rather than the north, this is where you can find maps, advice, and some interpretive displays.

⌒
Tips **Insider Tips**

Some of the best spots aren't highlighted on the map. On the west side of the road from Signal Mountain to the Jenny Lake cutoff, a little over a mile (2km) north of the Spring Lake–Jenny Lake scenic drive cutoff, is an unmarked, unpaved road that leads to **Spalding Bay.** You'll travel through bumpy moose habitat before curling down a steep hill to a back bay of the lake, where you'll find a small campsite, boat launch with parking for trucks and boat trailers, and primitive restroom. Use of the campsite requires a park permit, but we think this site provides an excellent opportunity to find seclusion with excellent views of the lake and mountains. The road is easily negotiable by an automobile or sport-utility vehicle; we would not recommend a motor home or towed trailer.

Just behind the visitor center is **Menors Ferry.** Bill Menor had a country store and operated a ferry across the Snake River at Moose back in the late 1800s. The ferry and store have been reconstructed, and you can buy items similar to the ones Menor used to sell here. Nearby is a historic cabin where a group of locals met in 1923 and planted the seed for the protection of the natural and scenic quality of the area, an idea that eventually led to the creation of the national park.

Also in this area is the **Chapel of the Transfiguration.** In 1925, this chapel was built in Moose so that settlers wouldn't have to make a long buckboard ride into Jackson. It's still in use for Episcopal services spring through fall and is a popular spot for weddings, with a view of the Tetons through a window behind the altar.

DORNAN'S   This is a small village area just south of the visitor center on an inholding of private land owned by one of the area's earliest homesteading families. There are a few shops and a semi-gourmet grocery store, a post office, a bar where there is sometimes live music, and, surprisingly, a first-rate wine shop.

OTHER PARK HIGHLIGHTS

The highway route through the park on the east side of the Snake has several turnouts for shutterbugs (better have a wide-angle lens!). Among the stops you can make are the **Glacier View Turnout** (where you can view an area that was filled with a 4,000-foot-thick glacier 150,000 years ago) and the **Blacktail Ponds Overlook** (a beaver-dam subdivision). Gazing out across **Snake River Overlook** at the plateaus that roll from riverbed to valley floor lends vivid insight into the power of the glaciers and ice floes that sculpted this landscape. If you want to go a ways off-road and down to the river, you can try the **Schwabacher Landing** dirt road or the newly repaved trip to **Deadman's Bar.**

Only 5 miles (8km) north of Jackson on U.S. 26/89/191, you can turn east on the **Gros Ventre River Road** and follow the river east into its steep canyon; a few miles past the little town of Kelly, you'll leave the park and enter the **Bridger-Teton National Forest.** In 1925, a huge slab of mountain broke off the north end of the Gros Ventre Range on the east side of Jackson Hole, a reminder that nature still has an unpredictable and violent side. The slide left a gaping open gash in the side of Sheep Mountain, sloughing off nearly 50 million cubic yards of rock and forming a natural dam across the Gros Ventre River half a mile wide. Two years later, the dam broke, and a cascade of water rushed down the canyon and through the little town of Kelly, taking several lives. The town of **Kelly** is a quaintly unconventional community with a large number of yurts.

Up in the canyon formed by the Gros Ventre River there are a roadside display with photographs of the slide area and a short nature walk from the road down to the residue of the slide and **Lower Slide Lake,** with signs identifying the trees and plants that survived or grew in the slide's aftermath.

RANGER-LED ACTIVITIES

It's got to be the best bargain in the world: National parks offer all sorts of free presentations and guided hikes throughout the summer days, and the rangers are generally personable and knowledgeable. At Grand Teton, you can sit on the back deck at Colter Bay and chat with a ranger while you look through a spotting scope at twilight, watch an evening slide show at an outdoor amphitheater, or walk among the wildflowers around Taggart Lake with a naturalist who knows their names.

At the north end of the park, based around the Colter Bay Visitor Center, you can take a **lakeshore stroll** with a ranger and learn about the geological and glacial forces that shaped the lake and mountains, or, if that hour-long walk seems too strenuous, sit out on the Jackson Lake Lodge deck and chat with the ranger while you look for moose through the spotting scope. There are summer **campfire programs** nightly June through September at the Colter Bay amphitheater and the Flagg Ranch campfire (check at the information center). From the Colter Bay Marina (fee charged for boat ride; © **307/543-2811**) you can join a daily cruise around the lake with a ranger telling you what's what.

At the south end of the park there are daily wildflower walks from the **Taggart Lake** trail head in June and July, **campfire programs** at Signal Mountain and Gros Ventre campground in the evenings, slide shows, and a twilight hike with a ranger around the south shore of Jenny Lake that takes about 3 hours—well worth it. You can also take a trip by boat across Jenny Lake ($6 round-trip for adults, $4 for children) and hike with a ranger to **Hidden Falls** and **Inspiration Point.** It's not a difficult hike (you can journey around the lake and save the boat fare), and you may be inspired to go on up Cascade Canyon on your own.

OTHER ORGANIZED TOURS & ACTIVITIES

The **Teton Science School** ⚓ (© **307/733-4765;** www.tetonscience.org) is a 30-year-old institution with a cabin campus in the park that offers summer programs for students and adults that discuss the ecology, geology, and wildlife of the park, with workshops in photography and tracking, too. The school's **Wildlife Expeditions** (© **307/773-2623**) offers trips on open-roofed vans, rafts, and sleighs, and by foot. These tours bring visitors closer to the wildlife than they're likely to get on their own, and guests sometimes participate in radio tracking and other research projects. The **Grand Teton Natural History Association** is a not-for-profit organization that provides myriad information about the park, including information for travelers through its bookstores at visitor centers in and around the park. These materials are available by writing the association at P.O. Drawer 170, Moose, WY 83012 (© **307/739-3403;** www.grandtetonpark.org).

HIKING
DAY HIKES

Many people cross Jenny Lake, either by boat or on foot around the south end, to hike up into **Cascade Canyon** ⚓⚓, a steep but popular journey that takes you first to **Hidden Falls** (less than 1 mile [1.5km] of hiking if you take the boat; 5 miles [8km] if you walk around) or another half mile to **Inspiration Point.** Skip the boat shuttle to avoid the crowds; the easy hike around the south end of the

Tips Picture Perfect

A meadow near the summit of Signal Mountain presents an excellent opportunity to look to the west for photos of both Mount Moran and the Grand Tetons. The best time to take those photos is before 11am, when the sun will be mostly at your back, or in the early evening, when the sun will backlight the crests to the west.

lake is refreshing, uncrowded, and a good prelude to heading up the canyon. Most people go no farther than Inspiration Point, but if you're physically up to it you really should go on. It's a steep climb to the entrance of the canyon, followed by a gentle ascent though a glacially sculpted canyon. At a fork in the trail around 4 miles (6km) from Inspiration Point you can follow either the north fork of Cascade Creek to Lake Solitude (3 miles; 5km) or the south fork to Hurricane Pass (5 miles; 8km). Try the north fork for a more relaxed day hike. Wildflowers carpet the area, ducks nest along Cascade Creek, and moose and bear may be spotted. The round-trip up into the canyon is about 4½ miles (7km).

A less-taxing alternative to the Cascade Canyon trip discussed above is a detour to **Moose Ponds,** which begins on the Inspiration Point trail. The ponds, located 2 miles (3km) from the trail head, are alive with birds. The area near the base of Teewinot Mountain is populated with elk, mule deer, black bears, and moose. The trail is flat (at lake level), short, and easy to negotiate in 1 to 1½ hours. The best times to venture forth are in early morning and evening.

Just down the road from South Jenny Lake is the trail head to **Taggart Lake,** a particularly interesting hike that winds through a recovering burn area to a glacial lake. The hike from the parking lot to the lake (a decent fishing spot) is only 1⅗ miles (2.5km) along the eastern route, and rarely crowded. After reaching the lake, you can return by the same trail or continue the loop on the **Taggart Lake Trail,** which leads around one end of the pond and loops back to the trail head through a more heavily forested area. This route adds ⅗ mile (1km) to the trip, and the elevation gain is 467 feet. At its highest point, the trail overlooks all of Taggart Lake and the stream that flows from it.

Upon reaching Taggart Lake, a second alternative is to continue north 1⅖ miles (2km) to **Bradley Lake,** the smaller of the two, and then return to the Taggart Lake trail head. Like others in Grand Teton, this hike is best made during the early morning or early evening hours when it is cooler and there is less traffic.

Yet another hike in this busy area begins at the **Leigh Lake trail head,** next to String Lake at the String Lake Picnic Area. This trail head is between Leigh Lake and Jenny Lake (String Lake is a smaller body of water between the two). The Leigh Lake trail is well marked and relatively flat, and goes through a forested area that is always within sight of the lake. Picnickers willing to hike roughly ⅖ mile (.5km) from the String Lake Picnic Area to the edge of the lake will find themselves eating in a less-congested area that provides spectacular views of the Tetons. The trail continues along the shore of Leigh Lake, but is rather uninteresting; a better option, if time allows, is to return to the picnic area, cross the String Lake inlet, and explore the western edge of Jenny Lake.

Just footsteps from the entrance to the Signal Mountain Lodge is a sign marking the trail head for the 3-mile (5km) **Signal Summit Mountain Trail** ★, one not generally described in commercial trail books. Though it's well marked, it's not well traveled, since most visitors drive their automobiles in this area. The trail begins steeply, and subsequently opens onto a broad plateau covered with lodgepole pines, grassy areas, and wildflowers. Cross the paved road and you'll arrive at a large, lily-covered pond at the opening of a meadow, home to frogs and waterfowl. The trail then winds along the south and east perimeter of the pond before turning east and heading toward the summit, which will take up to 2 hours. Shortly after passing the pond, you'll come to a fork in the road that converts the trip into a loop trail. Take the northern route and you'll travel the rim of the mountain, meandering to the summit through a forest of sagebrush and pine trees. On the return, a southern trail skirts large alpine ponds where you'll find waterfowl, moose—and, perhaps, black bears.

The day hikes at the north end of the park are less crowded. The easy but lengthy trip to **Two Ocean Lake** begins off the Pacific Creek Road north of Moran Junction and eventually circumnavigates the lake, with much of the mostly level walk through cool conifer forest. Or there is the **Hermitage Point trail head,** located near the marina, which branches out into trips ranging in distance from 1 to 9 miles (1.5–14km), mostly in lodgepole pine, with recurring views of the lake and the peaks on the other side. With careful planning, you can start the day with a hike from Colter Bay that leads past **Cygnet Pond** across **Willow Flats** to Jackson Lake Lodge (for lunch). Then, take the same path back to Colter Bay in time for the evening outdoor barbecue—all told, that's 9⁹⁄₁₀ miles (15km) round-trip.

Among the loops you can take from the Colter Bay trail head are trails to **Swan Lake** and **Heron Pond** (which share the same point of origin), the kind of country where wildflowers, Canada geese, moose, beaver, and bears all thrive. The two most prominent flowers here are heart-leaf arnicas and Indian paintbrush. Don't be put off by the fact that the first 200 yards of the Swan Lake/Heron Pond trails are steep; after reaching the top of a rise, the terrain levels out and has only moderate elevation gains from that point on. Within minutes, this trail opens to a broad meadow covered with sagebrush and, later in the summer, blooming wildflowers. Here you'll find one of the most spectacular views of Mount Moran, and the peaks reflect on the surfaces of the water.

Finding swans at Swan Lake requires a trip to the south end, where a small island affords isolation and shelter for nests. There are also osprey, kingfishers, and white pelicans in this neck of the woods. The distance from Swan Lake through a densely forested area to the Heron Pond intersection is ³⁄₁₀ mile (.5km); Hermitage Point is 3 miles (5km) from this junction, along a gentle path that winds through a wooded area popular with bears. Circumnavigation from the Colter area is doable in 2 hours.

A shorter hike in the Colter area, the **Lakeshore Trail** is a wide, shady thoroughfare that skirts the bay, leading to gravelly beaches that present views across Jackson Lake of the entire Teton range. The views leap out at you when you arrive at the end of the trail; water gently laps at the shore and, thankfully, you're out of the dense roadside traffic. This 2-mile (3km) loop can be completed in about 1 hour of brisk walking.

LONGER HIKES

If you decide a day hike isn't enough, you must get an overnight permit and camp in one of the various camping zones reserved through the visitor centers. Much longer trips can be strung together into the mountainous backcountry, crossing the mountains' spine to **Teton Canyon** on the Idaho side, or, at the north end of the park, exploring deep into the **Jedediah Smith Wilderness.**

Within the park, you can go far behind the day hikes described above—extending a Cascade Canyon hike, for instance, by going north to Lake Solitude, then coming down into **Paintbrush Canyon** (where you can camp, with a permit) and out at String Lake. You can also take the tram to the top of the ski area in Teton Village and follow the **Teton Crest Trail** north into the park, eventually dropping down through **Death Canyon** (another camping area) to **Phelps Lake.** A trip like this is more than 20 miles (32km) and will take several days.

The Park Service has a helpful brochure that delineates the 20 or so backcountry camping zones and lakeshore sites. You'll need to reserve sites, and rangers can brief you on the quality of different routes, the areas where you're likely to encounter bears, and "leave no trace" camping techniques.

OTHER SPORTS & OUTDOOR ACTIVITIES

For lovers of outdoor recreation, Grand Teton National Park offers one of the most accessible playlands of rock and water in the Lower 48. In addition to hiking, mountaineers and technical climbers can attack the highest hills; paddlers glide across the smooth waters of the lakes or splash along the livelier flow of the Snake River; and there are also waters open to motorized vessels and sailboats.

BIKING   The roads in Grand Teton were not built with bicyclists in mind, though the flats of the valley seem perfect for pedaling. The problem is safety—there are huge RVs careening about, and some roads have only narrow shoulders. Teton Park Road has been widened somewhat, but traffic is heavy here; road bikers should try **Antelope Flats,** beginning at a trail head 1 mile (1.5km) north of Moose Junction and going east. Sometimes called **Mormon Row,** this paved route crosses the flats below the Gros Ventre Mountains, past old ranch homesteads and the small town of Kelly. It connects to the unpaved **Shadow Mountain Road,** which actually goes outside the park into national forest, climbing through the trees to the summit. Total distance is 7 miles (11km) and the elevation gain is 1,370 feet, and you'll be looking at Mount Moran and the Tetons across the valley.

Mountain bikers have a few more options, but keep in mind that bikes are prohibited on backcountry trails and boardwalks. Try **Two-Ocean Lake Road** (reached from the Pacific Creek Road just north of Moran Junction) or the **River Road,** a 15-mile (24km) dirt path that parallels the Snake River's western bank. Ambitious mountain bikers may want to load their overnight gear and take the **Grassy Lake Road,** once used by Indians, west from Flagg Ranch on a 50-mile (80km) journey to Ashton, Idaho. A map that shows bicycle routes is available from the Park Service at visitor centers or at **Adventure Sports** (© 307/ 733-3307) in Moose, where you can also rent mountain bikes for $25 a day.

BOATING   Boaters have quite a few opportunities here. Motorboats are permitted on Jenny, Jackson, and Phelps Lakes. Rafts, canoes, dories, and kayaks are allowed on the Snake River within the park. No boats are allowed on Pacific Creek or the Gros Ventre River. Bigger boats find room on Jackson Lake, where powerboats pull skiers, sailboats move noiselessly in summer breezes, and fishermen ply the waters in search of wily trout. Those who venture on the big lake need to be aware that the weather can change suddenly, and late-afternoon lightning is not uncommon; sailors should be particularly wary of the swirling winds that accompany thunderstorms. **Scenic cruises** of Jackson Lake, as well as twice-a-week floating steak-fry cruises, are available daily at the **Colter Bay** marina May through September, water level permitting. See "Fees & Backcountry Permits" earlier in this chapter for information on boat permits. Boat and canoe rentals, tackle, and fishing licenses are available at **Colter** and **Signal Mountain.** Shuttles to the west side of Jenny Lake, as well as cruises, are conducted by **Teton Boating Company** (© 307/733-2703).

CLIMBING Every year there are rescues of climbers who get trapped on Teton rock faces, and many years there are fatalities. Yet the peaks have a strong allure for climbers, even inexperienced ones, perhaps because you can reach the top of even the biggest ones in a single day. But it isn't easy. The terrain is mixed, with snow and ice year-round—knowing how to self-arrest with an ice axe is a must—and the weather can change suddenly. The key is to get good advice, know your limitations, and if you're not already skilled, take some lessons at the local climbing schools (see "Getting Outside," in section 1).

Climbers who go out for a day do not have to register or report to park officials, so they should be sure to tell friends where they're going and when they'll be back. Overnight climbers must pick up a free permit. Climbing rangers who can lead rescue efforts are on duty at the **Jenny Lake Ranger Station** at South Jenny Lake from June until the middle of September. The American Alpine Club provides inexpensive dormitory beds for climbers at the **Grand Teton Climbers' Ranch** (Climbers' Ranch, Moose, WY 83012). Guided climbs of Grand Teton are offered by **Jackson Hole Mountain Guides** (© 800/239-7642; www.jhmg.com) and by **Exum Mountain Guides** in Moose (© 307/733-2297; www.exumguides.com).

CROSS-COUNTRY SKIING You can ski flat or you can ski steep in Grand Teton. The two things to watch out for are hypothermia and avalanches. As with climbing, know your limitations and make sure you're properly equipped. Check with local rangers and guides for trails that match your ability. Your options include the relatively easy Jenny Lake Trail, starting at the Taggart Lake Parking Area, about 8 miles (13km) of flat and scenic trail that follows Cottonwood Creek. A more difficult ski is the Taggart Lake–Beaver Creek Loop, a 3-mile (5km) route that has some steep and icy pitches coming back. About 4 miles (6km) of the Moose-Wilson Road—the back way to Teton Village from Moose—is unplowed in the winter, and is an easy trip through the woods. You can climb the winding, unplowed road to the top of Signal Mountain—you may encounter snowmobiles—and have some fun skiing down. There is an easy ski trail from the Colter Bay Ranger Station area to Heron Pond—about 2⅜ miles (4km), with a great view of the Tetons and Jackson Lake. Get a ski-trail map from one of the visitor centers.

FISHING The lakes and streams of Grand Teton are popular fishing destinations, loaded with lively cutthroat trout, whitefish, and Mackinaw (lake) trout in Jackson, Jenny, and Phelps Lakes. You'll most likely catch fish under 20 inches, fishing deep with trolling gear from a boat during hot summer months. The Snake River runs for about 27 miles (43km) in the park, and has cutthroat and whitefish up to about 18 inches. It's a popular drift-boat river for fly-fishing. If you'd like a guide who knows the holes, try **Jack Dennis Fishing Trips** (© 307/733-3270; www.jackdennis.com), **Triangle X-Osprey Float Trips** (© 307/733-5500), or **Fort Jackson River Trips** (© 800/735-8430). As an alternative, stake out a position on the banks below the dam at **Jackson Lake,** where you'll have plenty of company and just may snag something. You'll need a Wyoming state fishing license (see "The Active Vacation Planner," in chapter 2, "Planning Your Trip to Montana & Wyoming").

RAFTING & FLOAT TRIPS The upper end of the Snake River in the park can be deceptive—its smooth surface runs fast during the spring, and there are deadly snags of fallen trees and other debris. Check with rangers before putting your boat in—they'll discourage you if they think your skills may not match the river—and proceed with caution. It's a wonderful river for wildlife, too, with moose, eagles, and other animals coming, like you, to the water's edge. There are many commercial float operators in the park who will allow you to relax more and look around. They mostly run from mid-May to mid-September (depending on weather and river-flow conditions). These companies offer 5- to 10-mile (8–16km) scenic floats, some with early-morning and evening wildlife trips. Try **Fort Jackson River Trips** (© 800/735-8430), **Barker-Ewing Float Trips** (© 800/365-1800), **Grand Teton Lodge Company** (© 307/543-2811), and **Flagg Ranch Float Trips** (© 307/543-2861).

CAMPING

Since Grand Teton is so much smaller than its counterpart to the north, the mileage between campgrounds is much shorter. As a consequence, selecting a site in one of the five National Park Service campgrounds within the park becomes a matter of preference (rather than geography) and availability. Fees in all campgrounds are $12 per night, and all have modern comfort stations. Campgrounds operate on a first-come, first-served basis, but reservations are available to groups of 10 or more by writing **Campground Reservations,** Grand Teton National Park, Moose, WY 83012. You can get recorded information on site availability by calling © **307/739-3603.** Reservations for **trailer sites** at Colter Bay campground may be made by contacting the **Grand Teton Lodge Co.,** P.O. Box 240, Moran, WY 83013 (© **800/628-9988** or 307/543-3100). Additionally, **Grand Teton Campground** is a concessionaire-operated campground located in the **Flagg Ranch** complex on the John D. Rockefeller Jr. Memorial Parkway. The area has 93 sites with utility hookups, 74 tent sites, showers, and a laundromat. For reservations, contact Flagg Ranch, P.O. Box 187, Moran, WY 83013 (© **800/443-2311**).

All the campgrounds but Jenny Lake can accommodate tents, RVs, and trailers, but there are no utility hookups at any of them. **Jenny Lake Campground,** a tents-only area with 49 sites, is situated in a quiet, wooded area near the lake. You have to be here first thing in the morning to get a site.

The largest campground, **Gros Ventre,** is the last to fill, if it fills at all—probably because it's located on the east side of the park, a few miles from Kelly on the Gros Ventre River Road. It has 360 sites, a trailer dump station, a tents-only section, and no showers. If you arrive late in the day and you have no place to stay, go here first.

Signal Mountain Campground, with views of the lake and access to the beach, is another popular spot that fills first thing in the morning. It has 86 sites overlooking Jackson Lake and Mount Moran, as well as a pleasant picnic area and boat launch. No showers or laundry, but there's a store and service station nearby.

Colter Bay Campground and Trailer Village has 350 sites, some with RV hookups, a general store, showers, and a laundromat. The area has access to the lake but is far enough from the hubbub of the village to offer a modicum of solitude; spaces are usually gone by noon.

Lizard Creek Campground, at the north end of Grand Teton National Park near Jackson Lake, offers an aesthetically pleasing wooded area near the lake with views of the Tetons, bird-watching, and fishing (not to mention the mosquitoes: bring your repellent). It's only 8 miles (13km) from facilities at Colter Bay and has 60 sites that fill by 2pm.

Amenities for Each Campground, Grand Teton National Park

Campground	# sites	Fee	Showers	Laundry	Flush Toilets	Disposal
Colter Bay	310	$12	yes	yes	yes	yes
Gros Ventre	360	$12	no	no	yes	yes
Jenny Lake*	49	$12	no	no	yes	no
Lizard Creek*	60	$12	no	no	yes	no
Signal Mountain	86	$12	no	no	yes	yes

* tents only

WHERE TO STAY IN THE PARK

If you plan to visit Grand Teton during a "fringe" season—usually the best, least-crowded time to go, in the fall or spring—you better check first to see if the inn is open. Three different companies run the lodgings in the park, and they all run on different schedules. In early May, you'll find padlocks on the doors everywhere but at Flagg Ranch, which technically isn't in Grand Teton anyway, but in the limbo of the John D. Rockefeller Jr. Memorial Parkway. Likewise in late fall: By mid-October, there are hardly any beds available in the park, and you'll be bunking in Jackson.

You can get information about or make reservations for Jackson Lake Lodge, Jenny Lake Lodge, and Colter Bay Village through the **Grand Teton Lodge Company,** Box 240, Moran, WY 83013 (© **800/628-9988** or 307/543-2811; www.gtlc.com); for **Signal Mountain Lodge,** contact Signal Mountain Lodge Co., Box 50, Moran, WY 83013 (© **307/543-2831;** www.signalmtnlodge.com); and reservations at **Flagg Ranch** are made though Flagg Ranch, Box 187, Moran, WY 83013 (© **800/443-2311**).

EXPENSIVE

Jackson Lake Lodge   Much the way Old Faithful Inn or the Lake Hotel captures historic eras of Yellowstone tourism, Jackson Lake Lodge epitomizes the architectural milieu of the period when Grand Teton became a park. Unfortunately, that era was the 1950s, an era of right angles, flat roofs, and big windows. Still, the lodge is popular, particularly for its wonderful setting overlooking Willow Flats, the lake in the distance, and towering over it, without so much as a stick in the way, the Tetons and Mount Moran. You don't even have to go outside to see this impressive view—the lobby has 60-foot-tall windows. Guest rooms are in the three-story main lodge and in cottages scattered about the property, some of which have large balconies and mountain views. Lodge rooms are spacious and cheery, and most offer double beds, electric heat, and newly tiled baths. Both the lodge and cottage rooms are comparable to an upper-tier chain hotel, with an American Indian motif. For a premium, the view rooms provide guests with a private picture window facing the Tetons.

P.O. Box 240, Moran, WY 83013. © **800/628-9988** or 307/543-3100. www.gtlc.com. 385 units. $120–$210 double; $146–$210 cottage; $385–$550 suite. AE, DC, MC, V. Closed mid-Oct to mid-May. **Amenities:** 2 restaurants, lounge; heated outdoor pool; activities desk.

Jenny Lake Lodge ★★   This lodge justifiably prides itself on seclusion, award-winning food, and the individual attentions that come with a cabin resort kept intentionally small. The property is a hybrid of mountain lake resort and dude ranch, with various activities included in its prices, such as horseback riding, meals, and bicycles. The cabins are rustic on the outside, luxurious within. Inside are bright braided rugs, dark-wood floors, beamed ceilings, log furniture with cowhide upholstery, and tiled combination baths. Rooms have one queen, one king, or two double beds. No televisions, of course.

Catering to an older, affluent clientele, the style here is an odd mixture of peaceful rusticity and occasional reminders of class and formality (dinner jackets are "appreciated"). Generally, though, if you aren't sweating the prices, Jenny Lake Lodge offers a wonderful chance to unwind in a fairly isolated, feet-up-on-the-rail atmosphere with scenery that can't be matched.

Box 240, Moran, WY 83013. (*C*) **800/628-9988** or 307/543-3100. www.gtlc.com. 37 units. $418 double; $565–$590 suite. Rates include MAP (modified American plan). AE, DC, MC, V. Closed mid-Oct to May. **Amenities:** Restaurant, lounge; activities desk. *In room:* No phone.

MODERATE

Colter Bay Village ☆ *Kids* *Value*   You might call this the people's resort of Grand Teton, with simpler lodgings, lower prices, and a lively, friendlier atmosphere that seems particularly suited to families. Situated on the eastern shore of Jackson Lake, Colter Bay Village is a full-fledged recreation center. Guest accommodations are in rough log cabins perched on a wooded hillside; they are clean and simply furnished with area rugs on tile floors and reproductions of pioneer furnishings— chests, oval mirrors, and extra-long bedsteads with painted headboards.

If you want to take a trip back to the early days of American auto travel, when car-camping involved unwieldy canvas tents on slabs by the roadside, you can spend an inexpensive night in "tent cabins." (Bring your own sleeping bags.) The shower and bathroom are communal. The village provides an excellent base of operations for visitors, since it has the most facilities of any area in the park.

P.O. Box 240, Moran, WY 83013. (*C*) **800/628-9988** or 307/543-3100. www.gtlc.com. 166 units. $33–$125 log cabin; $33 tent cabin. AE, DC, MC, V. Closed late Sept to late May. **Amenities:** 2 restaurants; activities desk; shopping arcade; self-serve laundry. *In room:* No phone.

Flagg Ranch Resort   A few years back this place by the Snake River just outside Yellowstone National Park was showing its age—the sort of place where a hunter would rent a drafty room to collapse in after a few days in the woods. Not anymore: It's all fixed up, transformed into an all-seasons resort with log-and-luxury ambience.

A century ago there was a military post near here, and travelers in those wagon-road days would stop for a meal when they saw the flag waving—hence, the subsequent name Flagg Ranch, dubbed by original owner Ed Sheffield, who made a swimming hole out of a nearby hot spring and started serving tourists without much initial concern that he was doing so on public land (he eventually got a lease).

The newest accommodations are duplex and four-plex log cabins constructed in 1994, featuring king-size beds, spacious sitting areas with writing desks and chests of drawers, wall-to-wall carpeting, and baths with tub-shower combinations and separate vanities. There are also 171 RV sites (call for current rates and other information).

P.O. Box 187, Moran, WY 83013. (*C*) **800/443-2311** or 307/543-2861. www.flaggranch.com. 92 units. Spring and fall $100 cabin double; winter $110 cabin double; summer $135 cabin double. AE, DISC, MC, V. **Amenities:** Restaurant, lounge; activities desk.

Signal Mountain Lodge   Signal Mountain has a different feel, and different owners, from the other lodgings in Grand Teton, adding to the sense that any place you choose to stay in this park is going to give you a fairly unique atmosphere. What they all have in common is the Teton view, and this lodge, located right on the banks of Jackson Lake, may have the best. To top it off, it's got lakefront retreats, which you can really inhabit, with stoves and refrigerators

and foldout sofa beds for the kids. Other accommodations, mostly rustic log cabins, come in a variety of flavors, from motel-style rooms in four-unit buildings set amidst the trees to family bungalows with decks, some enjoying beach frontage. The carpeted cabins feature handmade pine furniture, electric heat, covered porches, and tiled baths; some have fireplaces.

P.O. Box 50, Moran, WY 83013. ✆ 307/543-2831. www.signalmtnlodge.com. 80 units. $95–$225 double. AE, DISC, MC, V. Closed Nov–Apr. **Amenities:** 2 restaurants; activities desk. *In room:* kitchenette.

WHERE TO DINE

Flagg Ranch AMERICAN   The food at this oasis is better than what's typically found in what most refer to as a "family restaurant," and servings are generous. The dinner menu includes fish, chicken, and beef dishes, as well as home-style entrees like ranch beef stew and chicken pot pie. The ambience is also pleasant, during both winter and summer months; wooden chairs and tables with colorful upholstery liven up this newly constructed log building.

John D. Rockefeller Jr. Pkwy., Moran. ✆ 800/443-2311. Breakfast $2–$6; lunch $4–$9; dinner $10–$25. AE, DISC, MC, V. Summer 7am–1:30pm and 5–9:30pm.

Jenny Lake Lodge Dining Room ★★ CONTINENTAL   The finest meals in the area are served here, where a cordon bleu chef creates culinary delights for guests and, occasionally, a president of the U.S. Three meals are served daily, but the five-course dinner is the bell-ringer; guests choose from appetizers that may include chilled lobster salad or smoked sturgeon ravioli, buffalo mozzarella and plum tomato salads, and entrees that may include grilled salmon, rack of lamb, or prime rib of buffalo. Desserts are equally decadent. Price is no object, at least for guests, since meals are included in the room charge; nonguests should expect a hefty bill, and if you're wearing shorts and hiking boots, your first and only course may be a plateful of chilly snobbery.

At Jenny Lake Lodge. ✆ 307/733-4647. Prix-fixe breakfast $14; prix-fixe dinner $45.50, not including alcoholic beverages. AE, MC, V. Summer daily 7:30–9am, noon–1:30pm, and 6–9pm.

John Colter Cafe Court DELI/FAST FOOD   These are the two sit-down restaurants in the village (though there's also a snack shop in the grocery store). Three meals are served daily during the summer months. The **Deli** serves sandwiches, chicken, pizzas, salads, and soup, with prices that range from $4.50 for an individual pizza to $12.99 for a chicken dinner. The **Chuckwagon Steak and Pasta House's** breakfast menu dishes up everything from plain eggs to a Chuckwagon omelet, with a huge and quite wonderful all-you-can-eat buffet available. Lunch is soup, salad, and hot sandwiches; dinner is a buffet with a nightly special each evening. Among the dinner entrees are trout, lasagna, pork chops, beef stew, and New York strip steaks. The ambience is very casual and straightforward, since these restaurants cater mostly to families.

Across from the visitor center and marina in Colter Bay Village. ✆ 307/543-2811. Breakfast $3–$6; lunch $5–$8; dinner $6–$14. DISC, MC, V. Daily 6am–10pm. Closed Oct–Apr.

The Mural Room ★ BEEF/WILD GAME   Jackson Lake's main dining room is quiet and fairly formal, catering to a more sedate crowd as well as corporate groups; it's also more expensive than other park restaurants. The floor-to-ceiling windows provide stellar views across a meadow that is moose habitat, to the lake and the Cathedral Group. Walls are adorned with hand-painted Western murals (what else?). Three meals are served daily in summer. Breakfast items include a continental breakfast, Belgian waffles, and vegetarian eggs Benedict. Dinner may be a grand, five-course event that includes a shrimp cocktail, French-onion soup, and Caesar salad, followed by an entree of Idaho trout, buffalo strip loin, vegetable lasagna, or rack of lamb. On the other side of the wall on which the murals are painted is the **Pioneer Grill,** which serves casual food in a 1950s-atmosphere, soda-fountain-style restaurant. Entrees are lighter and less expensive, and a takeout menu is available. A children's menu is available here.

At Jackson Lake Lodge. © 800/628-9988 or 307/543-2811, ext. 1911. Breakfast buffet $10.25; lunch $6–$9; dinner $16–$22. AE, MC, V. Summer daily 7–9:30am, noon–1:30pm, and 6–9:30pm.

Signal Mountain Resort _Value_ SANDWICHES/MEXICAN/ECLECTIC There are actually two restaurants here, serving delicious food in the friendliest style in the park. The fine dining room and lounge are called **The Peaks** and **Deadman's Bar,** respectively, and the **Trapper Grill** supplements that top-notch fare with Mexican entrees and plump sandwiches. You eat up the scenery, too, with a view of Jackson Lake.

Here's an insider's word of advice: When the bargain-hunting ladies and gentlemen who work for the park's concessionaires head out for dinner, chances are good they land here and order Nachos Supreme from the bar menu. A nutritionist's nightmare (and an appetizer, actually), the slew of melted cheese and spicy beef or chicken, served on a bed of corn chips and topped with sour cream, will generally satisfy the appetite of two adults. Since the bar has one of three televisions in the park, and is equipped with cable for sports nuts, the crowd tends to be young and noisy.

As an alternative, full meals are served in the proper dining room. Entrees include chicken pot pie, Mediterranean pasta, and veal saltimbocca, the most expensive entree.

At Signal Mountain Resort. © 307/543-2831. Breakfast $4–$8; lunch $6–$8; dinner $8–$30. AE, DISC, MC, V. Summer daily 7–10am and 11:30am–10pm.

3 A Side Trip to Dubois & the Wind River Range

86 miles (138km) NE of Jackson

For years, Dubois was a kind of doppelganger to Jackson, a blue-collar logging town with some quietly wealthy folks living on nice ranches up the nearby draws. Now the sawmill is closed, and wealthy folks who want to stay ahead of the latest real estate fashion are wandering over Togwotee Pass and buying up the beautiful Upper Wind River Valley. That means Dubois is poised for some serious development, but it hasn't quite happened yet, which dismays some residents and pleases others. Lying as it does along one of the Yellowstone access roads, Dubois is just far enough from the park entrances to be spared the West Yellowstone gateway syndrome, and if locals keep their heads, they'll protect the great trout streams, uncluttered wilderness, and small-town ambience from uncontrolled growth. So far, so good. It's a fun town, often with several bands playing in the bars on weekends. **To get there** from Jackson, go north on U.S. 26/89/191 to Moran Junction, then east over Togwotee Pass on U.S. 26/287.

Tips Travel Tip

Before arriving in Dubois, practice pronouncing the name without sounding like a city slicker. There are many ways to pronounce it, but only "DOO-boys" is correct. Sure, there is the inclination to say "doo-BWAH," but quell that urge—this isn't France.

Dubois wasn't quite ready for fine Italian dining—its finest restaurant closed its doors and moved to Jackson—but the **Rustic Tavern Steakhouse** (123 E. Ramshorn; © **307/455-2772**) does a good job with beef, seafood, and pasta; or you can get a great salad and sandwich on home-baked bread (and great barbecue ribs) at **Cafe Wyoming** (106 E. Ramshorn; © **307/455-3828**), hidden off the parking lot of Dubois Hardware with a pleasant porch overhanging Horse Creek.

In the lake-dotted Whiskey Basin, just south of town, hundreds of bighorn sheep migrate down in the winter to get away from the deep snows, and so there is a **National Bighorn Sheep Interpretive Center** (907 W. Ramshorn; © **307/ 455-3429**) located just off the highway in the center of town. Just across the street, at the **Dubois Museum** (909 W. Ramshorn; © **307/455-2284**), is a look at the past of the town, the Sheepeater Indians, and other interesting artifacts with local flavor. The museum is open from 9am to 5pm daily May through September. Contact the **Dubois Chamber of Commerce,** P.O. Box 632, Dubois, WY 85213 (© **307/455-2556;** www.duboiswyoming.com), for additional information on the community.

WHERE TO STAY

Absaroka Ranch *Kids*   High in the Absaroka Mountains northeast of Dubois is a rustic, comfortable ranch that can host up to 20 people (often families with children in tow). The main lodge, all wood, has the usual and hospitable large stone fireplace for evening gatherings, as well as a dining area where guests gather around three tables for family-style meals. The mainstay of visits here are half- and full-day horseback trips over miles of trails winding through high mountain meadows and cool forests 8,000 feet above sea level. Guides escort guests to nearby streams, and help them learn the tricks for catching wily cutthroat and brook trout.

The ranch's four cabins surround a large, grassy area and a fire pit where evenings are often spent listening to local entertainers. Each cabin has two bedrooms, electric heat, and full carpeting. Menus are eclectic and varied, with a healthful bent. Frittatas, omelets, Greek pizza, and Western fare make appearances, but the chef will cater to the dietary requirements of vegetarians and nondairy eaters. Lunch can be taken outdoors at picnic tables. This is a great spot for children, who especially enjoy sleeping in the nearby tepees.

P.O. Box 929, Dubois, WY 82513 (10 miles [16km] west of Dubois on U.S. 26; turn north on Dunoir Rd. and follow signs to the ranch). © **307/455-2275.** 4 2-bedroom units. $1,050 per person per week. Rate includes all meals. No credit cards. Hunting trips in fall. Closed Oct–May. **Amenities:** Activities desk.

Brooks Lake Lodge ★   For many years, this remote and historic mountain lodge, once an overnight stop on the road to Yellowstone, languished; in 1989, it was painstakingly restored and reopened to a good deal of well-deserved hype. It sits above the shores of Brooks Lake, a prize fishing lake surrounded by soaring pinnacles. This is the entry point to some of the most remote and challenging wilderness in the Rockies, packed with elk, trout, and grizzly bears. Yet the handsome lodge, with its hand-stripped timbers and deep porch overlooking the lake, is as cozy and comforting as anyone could ask. You can lounge, or take advantage of the riding stock, guided up steep trails to incredible views.

Accommodations are seven guest rooms in the lodge (one room is a suite with a Jacuzzi and a fireplace) and six cabins along the tree line. The cabins, each decorated with a distinct frontier motif, are comfortable, spacious affairs that have large decks or porches with views of the lake, and Western pine furniture.

458 Brooks Lake Rd., Dubois, WY 82513. © **307/455-2121.** www.brookslake.com. 13 units, including 1 suite. Summer (minimum 3-day stay) $195–$250 per person per night; winter $180–$215 per person per night. Rates include all meals. AE, DISC, MC, V. Closed May, Oct–Dec. **Amenities:** Restaurant; activities desk.

12

Cody & North Central Wyoming

Deep, broad valleys, cupped by daunting mountain ranges, provide some of the most livable pockets of the Rocky Mountain West. Not only do the mountains provide some protection from howling storms, but their snowmelt keeps streams running through the summer and their beauty supplies a spectacular backdrop for the communities nestled below.

Such a valley runs down the center of Wyoming, cradled by the Bighorn Mountains in the east and the Absarokas and Yellowstone Plateau in the West. Though the area around the town of Cody gets only about 10 inches of moisture annually, founder William "Buffalo Bill" Cody recognized a century ago that with a few dams and ditches in the right places, the mountains' snowpack could supply water year-round. His legacy continues to shape the basin's economy today: A great summer scene of cowboy fun attracts hordes of visitors, and green fields of sugar beets and grains stretch for miles from the mouth of the Wapiti Valley.

While Cody was staking claims to water rights along the Shoshone River in the early 20th century, the U.S. Bureau of Reclamation was storing that water behind the Buffalo Bill Dam, the world's tallest when it was completed in 1910. The reservoir today irrigates some 93,000 acres in central Wyoming, and the swift winds that skim the lake's surface attract the bravest of windsurfers.

In the post–"Buffalo Bill" era, the charms of north central Wyoming have taken many a visitor by surprise on their journey to and from Wyoming's famous national parks. And quite a few travelers find reason to linger longer in the nearby valleys, exploring a wealth of American Indian and Wild West history, geology, mountain scenery, outdoor recreation, and small-town charm. Highlights include fun-loving Cody, the Bighorn Canyon National Recreation Area, the gushing hot springs of Thermopolis, and the forests and rivers of Shoshone National Forest and other public lands.

The combination of stunning scenery and historic cattle operations makes the Cody area a natural center for dude ranches, where visitors can saddle up and swing a lariat. Or you can mount a more stationary seat in the stands at one of the summer rodeos. Cody's rodeo grounds light up every night in the summer, and nearly every town in the basin has its special rodeo weekend. On the Wind River Indian Reservation, the evening outdoor entertainment is often a powwow, featuring drum groups, colorful garb, and traditional dancing, with visitors welcome, and food stands offering Indian tacos and other treats.

North Central Wyoming

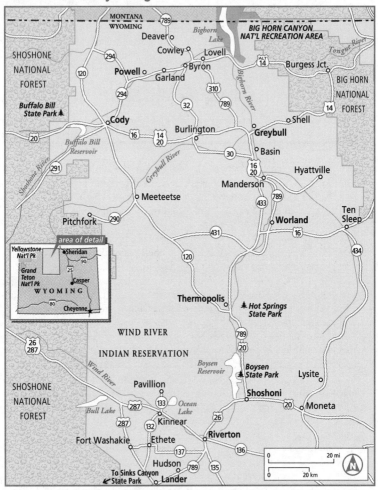

1 Scenic Drives

The two-lane roads of north central Wyoming follow the contours of a craggy landscape, tracking the twists and turns of the river and switchbacking over the mountain passes; the roads are narrow but generally not too crowded, except for the constant stream of traffic to Yellowstone's east entrance. **U.S. 14/16/20,** the east entrance road (also called the Yellowstone Highway), is the major east-west route through this region. The breathtaking views as it snakes through the Wapiti Valley and up over Sylvan Pass into Yellowstone make the traffic and seemingly interminable road repairs worthwhile. West of Cody, almost any road you take will reward you with a canyon or a climb, but many of them narrow into rough dirt byways as they delve deeper into the forest. **Wyo. 291** does that, as it follows the **South Fork of the Shoshone River** upstream toward the white-capped peaks of Yellowstone's Thorofare country. Along the way are prominent volcanic rock formations like Castle Rock, a succession of picturesque ranches, and sometimes a lucky glimpse of bighorn sheep, before the road finally dead-ends on the fringes of the Absaroka Range.

Cody is also an alternative starting point for the **Chief Joseph Scenic Highway,** which links up to the Beartooth Byway into Montana (see chapter 8).

Note: Most of the sights mentioned in the following driving tours are discussed in greater detail later in this chapter.

DRIVING TOUR #1: BIGHORN MOUNTAIN LOOP

This moderately easy day trip will open your eyes to an extraordinary mountain range, on a route that encompasses the towns of **Powell** and **Lovell,** as well as the scenic **Shell Canyon area.** Begin in Cody by taking U.S. 14A northeast to Lovell and the **Bighorn Canyon National Recreation Area.** A side trip north along Wyo. 37 provides views of the wild horses of the Pryor Mountain Wild Horse Range and Bighorn Lake from the Devil Canyon Overlook (see chapter 9 for more information on this recreation area).

After crossing the Bighorn River, U.S. 14A rises through the foothills and up the steep flanks of the Bighorns, not far from the footpaths of prehistoric travelers who built the **Medicine Wheel,** a 74-foot stone circle with 28 spokes. Like other mysterious wheel designs in the Rockies, it may have served ancient peoples as an astronomical key or a long-distance travel marker. To get here, turn off U.S. 14A at the Medicine Wheel sign and hike 1½ miles (2km) from the parking area to the site. American Indian spiritual leaders still conduct ceremonies here. Visitors are asked not to remove offerings or disturb American Indians using the site for prayer or fasting. For more information, contact the Medicine Wheel Ranger District of the Bighorn National Forest (© **307/548-6541**).

Once you have crested the divide of the Bighorn Mountains, take U.S. 14 southwest at Burgess Junction toward Shell Canyon and the towns of Shell and Greybull. The road drops sharply amidst steeply cut canyons, and you can stop at the **Shell Falls Interpretive Center** and follow a paved path to a close-up view of the creek, tumbling and twisting amidst tall granite slabs. As the road flattens out near the town of Shell, you're surrounded by the deep red sandstones of the **Chugwater Formation,** set off by the rich greens of cultivated fields. This area enfolds some well-packed dinosaur fossil beds. U.S. 14/16/20 takes you back to Cody, toward the embrace of the Absaroka Mountains and Yellowstone. This driving tour can be enjoyed year-round, though winter drivers should proceed cautiously on the steep grades around Burgess Junction.

DRIVING TOUR #2: BIGHORN BASIN LOOP

This all-day trip keeps to the Bighorn River Basin, navigating rolling sagebrush hills, cultivated farmlands, hot-spring terraces, and one-pump (formerly one-horse) Western towns.

Depart from Cody and travel south along Wyo. 120 to the tiny burg of **Meeteetse** on the banks of the Greybull River. From here, continue on Wyo. 120 to **Thermopolis,** self-proclaimed home of the world's largest free-flowing hot springs (New Zealand does not agree). After a relaxing soak and a brief drive east for a glimpse of the bison herd that roams Hot Springs State Park, travel northeast on U.S. 16/20 to **Worland,** an important agricultural center. Then, drive east along U.S. 16 to **Ten Sleep,** which lies at the base of another steep-sided canyon cutting down through the Bighorn Mountains. You may want to hike and cast a line in Ten Sleep Creek.

Here, take the Nowood Road north, which joins Wyo. 31 to Manderson and follows the base of the Bighorns. From Manderson, follow U.S. 16/20 north to

Basin, take Wyo. 30 west to the junction of Wyo. 120, and continue north to Cody. Along the way, you'll enjoy views of the Bighorn River and the Greybull River Valley. Winter isn't too harsh on this loop, which could include a detour south of Meeteetse on Wyo. 290 to the **Wood River Ski Touring Park.** If it's summer, rangers at Hot Springs State Park have a map and key to Legend Rock petroglyph sites north of Thermopolis, where you can hike around the cliffs.

2 Cody ⟨★⟩

52 miles (84km) E of the east entrance of Yellowstone; 177 miles (285km) NE of Jackson; 214 miles (345km) NW of Casper

The legendary scout and entertainer William F. "Buffalo Bill" Cody really knew how to put on a show, and he also knew where to put a town. Cody, founded by its namesake in 1887, is beautifully situated near the juncture of rivers that pour from the rugged Absaroka Range. Every summer, the town of Cody stages a cowtown circus that would do the founder proud, entertaining throngs of visitors on their way to and from Yellowstone 52 miles (84km) west. And the way to Yellowstone is nonpareil: Teddy Roosevelt called the Wapiti Valley "the most scenic 50 miles in the world."

Stop by Cody before the mid-May opening of Yellowstone National Park's east entrance and it's rather lifeless. For 3 months every summer, though, the town parades its Western charm for masses of travelers. When the sun goes down, the lights come on at the rodeo grounds, and nightly the broncs do a little busting of their own. A world-class museum, a reassembled Old West town, and retail shops all attract visitors. Though lacking the resort density and sophistication of Jackson, Cody's Western charm feels more authentic.

ESSENTIALS

GETTING THERE   Cody's **Yellowstone Regional Airport,** 3001 Duggleby Dr. (✆ **307/587-5096**), serves the Bighorn Basin as well as the east and northeast entrances of Yellowstone National Park with year-round commercial flights via **United Express** (✆ **800/241-6522**) and Delta feeder **Skywest** (✆ **800/ 453-9417**).

If you're driving from **Cheyenne,** travel north on I-25 to Casper, then west on U.S. 20/26 to Shoshoni, where U.S. 20 turns north to Thermopolis. From there, it's another 84 miles (135km) to Cody on Wyo. 120. From **Jackson,** take U.S. 191 to the West Thumb Junction in Yellowstone, drive east along the northern boundary of Yellowstone Lake, and continue on U.S. 14/16/20 to Cody. Coming from the west, drive north from Rock Springs on U.S. 191 to Farson, Wyo. 28 to Lander, Wyo. 789 to Thermopolis, and Wyo. 120 to Cody.

VISITOR INFORMATION   For printed information on this area of Wyoming, contact the **Park County Travel Council,** 836 Sheridan Ave., P.O. Box 2454, Cody, WY 82414 (✆ **307/587-2777;** www.pctc.org), or the **Wyoming Business Council Travel and Tourism Division,** I-25 at College Drive, Cheyenne, WY 82002 (✆ **800/225-5996** or 307/777-7777; www.wyomingtourism.org).

GETTING AROUND   If you haven't come by car, you'll probably need to rent one; there's little public transportation. **Budget** (✆ **800/527-0700** or 307/587-6066), **Thrifty** (✆ **888/794-1025** or 307/587-8855), and **Hertz** (✆ **800/654-3131** or 307/587-2914) maintain desks at Yellowstone Regional Airport.

The Mystery of Buffalo Bill's Grave

Buffalo Bill's legend looms large over Cody, but some locals believe that it's more than his spirit looking down from the surrounding peaks. Rumor has it that Buffalo Bill is buried not atop Lookout Mountain in Golden, Colorado, but on Cedar Mountain, just outside of Cody. After the legendary showman's 1917 demise, the mayor of Denver and the *Denver Post* arranged to buy his body as the centerpiece to a tourist attraction. As the story goes, a trio of Cody residents took it upon themselves to see to it that Cody be laid to rest outside the town that bears his name. They swapped his body with that of an anonymous old cowboy who died in Cody without any kin, and Buffalo Bill on Cedar Mountain. While there's more than one story floating around regarding the true whereabouts of Cody's grave, longtime Cody residents (and many of Buffalo Bill's descendants) swear that a nameless cowboy is buried on Lookout Mountain in Colorado and that William Cody's final resting place is where he wanted it—in Cody, Wyoming.

SPECIAL EVENTS   The Buffalo Bill Historical Center is a tremendous resource for unique events in Cody. The April festival of **Cowboy Songs and Range Ballads** features storytelling, poetry, and some fine yodeling and balladry. In mid-June, the **Plains Indian Powwow** brings alive the Robbie Powwow Garden on the south end of the Buffalo Bill Historical Center parking lot with whirling color. Traditional dance competitions are coupled with craft shows and American Indian food, and non-Indians are welcomed into round dances. Call the Buffalo Bill Historical Center (✆ **307/587-4771**) for exact dates of these and other events and exhibits.

Every July 1 to July 4, during the **Cody Stampede,** the streets are filled with parades, fireworks, street dances, barbecues, and entertainment, capped by a top-notch rodeo. Call ✆ **800/207-0744** or 307/587-5155 for tickets (see **www.codystampederodeo.org** for more information). For 2 days in July, the cool rhythms of jazz and the brassy sound of big-band and swing music take over the lawn of the Elks Club at 1202 Beck Ave. (next to the Cody Convention Center) during the **Yellowstone Jazz Festival.** Featured musicians come from afar, and all varieties of jazz are heard from 11am until dark. Call ✆ **307/587-3898** for additional information.

In mid-August, the Buffalo Bill Historical Center (✆ **307/587-4771**) stages the **Buffalo Bill Invitational Shootout,** where celebrities and local shooters test their skills in trap, skeet, sporting clays, and five-stand shooting. It's a more serious test of marksmanship than the melodramatic shootout staged every summer evening at 6pm in front of The Irma Hotel, when a group of local actors regress to their flop-dead gunfighter childhoods. In late September, Cody hosts the **Western Design Conference** (✆ **888/685-0574**) at the Cody Auditorium and the Buffalo Bill Historical Center, a gathering of artisans to show off their work in Western-style furniture, decorations, and clothing fashions.

GETTING OUTSIDE

If you'd rather not drive in the park's heavy summer traffic, guided Yellowstone tours are available locally through **Grub Steak Expeditions,** P.O. Box 1013,

Cody, WY 82414 (© **800/527-6316** or 307/527-6316; www.grubsteak.com), and **Powder River Tours** (© **800/442-3682,** ext. 114, or 307/527-3677). Bob Richard, Grub Steak's proprietor (and one of the most knowledgeable guides you'll find), can spin a tale with the best of them. His roots in the area run deep, as a third-generation Cody resident and former Yellowstone ranger.

Cody has fewer organized recreation options that Jackson does, but there is no shortage of places to go outdoors. **Buffalo Bill State Park,** located along the canyon and reservoir 6 miles (10km) west of Cody, is a hot spot for recreationists, with opportunities for hiking, fishing, and a variety of water sports, particularly windsurfing. The park also has facilities for camping and picnicking.

BIKING
Mountain-bike rentals (for $12–$20 a day) and local trail maps are available at **Olde Faithful Bicycles,** 1231 16th St. (© **307/527-5110;** bikecody@ wyoming.com). Though there isn't a marked network of bike paths in the Cody area, the Forest Service trails west of town off U.S. 14/16/20 in the Shoshone National Forest are available for biking. For specific trail information, call Olde Faithful Bicycles or the Forest Service at © **307/527-6921.**

CROSS-COUNTRY SKIING
If you favor a groomed course for cross-country skiing, try the **North Fork Nordic Trails** in Shoshone National Forest near the east entrance to the park off U.S. 14/16/20. You can circuit 25 kilometers (16 miles) of trails adjacent to the Sleeping Giant downhill area (see below) and the Pahaska Tepee resort.

DOWNHILL SKIING
Near the east entrance to Yellowstone National Park, 50 miles (81km) west of Cody, is an inexpensive, family-oriented ski area. **Sleeping Giant Ski Area,** 349 Yellowstone Hwy., Cody, WY 82414 (© **307/587-4044** or 307/527-SNOW for the snow report; www.skisleepinggiant.com), is rated 20% beginner, 60% intermediate, and 20% advanced, with two lifts and a 600-foot vertical rise from a base of 6,700 feet. There are 17 trails, up to ¾-mile (1km) long. The area is open Friday, Saturday, Sunday, and holidays from 9:30am to 4pm during the ski season, with rates of $18 adults and $8 for children 11 and younger. There's a ski school and equipment rentals are available. For a bigger resort, drive north to Red Lodge, Montana, and **Red Lodge Mountain** ski area (see chapter 8).

FISHING
Yellowstone's legendary fly-fishing waters are a short drive away, but the smaller streams west of Cody are also excellent angling destinations: **the Clark's Fork of the Yellowstone, the North and South Forks of the Shoshone,** and **Sunlight Creek.** They're located northwest of Cody along Chief Joseph Highway—go north on Wyo. 120, 17 miles (27km) to Wyo. 296 (which is Chief Joseph). To the east, the warmer and slower **Big Horn River** and **Big Horn Lake** nurture catfish, walleye, and ling for boat fishermen. For advice on the trout streams near Cody, ask at **North Fork Anglers,** 1107 Sheridan Ave. (© **307/527-7274;** www.northforkanglers.com), where they stock gear and clothing and also guide short day trips or longer, overnight excursions. If you like to troll or cast from a boat, **Buffalo Bill Reservoir,** 6 miles (10km) west of Cody on Yellowstone Highway (U.S. 14/16/20), has produced some big Mackinaw, as well as rainbow, brown, and cutthroat trout. You have a shot at landing a 10-pound rainbow at **Monster Lake** (© **800/840-5137;** www.monsterlake.com), a private 150-acre body of water on the Fraser Ranch 10 miles (16km) south of

Cody. It's strictly catch-and-release for these lunker rainbows (and brooks, browns, and salmon), and there's a hefty fee per rod ($175 for the first day, $150 thereafter).

GOLF
The **Olive Glenn Golf and Country Club,** 802 Meadow Lane, is an 18-hole PGA championship course that is open to the public daily from 6am to 9pm. Greens fees are a modest $20 for nine holes, $35 for 18. Call © **307/587-5551** for tee times.

RAFTING
There aren't a lot of Class IV, serious white-water rapids on the rivers around Cody, but the upper stretches of the North Fork of the Shoshone River rip pretty fast in the spring. The upper river is the province of **Wyoming River Trips,** 1701 Sheridan Ave. (© **800/586-6661** or 307/587-6661; www.wyomingrivertrips. com), which also runs rafts on the smoother, Class II waters below the dam, along with **River Runners,** 1491 Sheridan Ave. (© **307/527-RAFT;** www.west wyoming.com/rafting). Prices run from about $18 to $50, depending on the length and difficulty of the trip.

SNOWMOBILING
The most popular Cody snowmobiling trails originate from nearby Pahaska Tepee Resort, located 51 miles (82km) from Cody on U.S. 14/16/20 (see the listing in "Where to Stay," below). The **Pahaska Tepee Trail** connects to the Yellowstone National Park trails and the lengthy Continental Divide Snowmobile Trail, and offers breathtaking views including Avalanche Peak (10,566 ft.) and Cody Peak (10,267 ft.). Don't take it if you're afraid of heights. The **Sunlight trail system** is located 36 miles (58km) north of Cody and winds through the wilds to a stunning view of the Beartooth Mountains. You start from a parking area at the junction of Wyo. 296 and U.S. 212 and follow the Beartooth Scenic Byway east for 16 miles (26km) to a warming hut. To the east, there are 70 miles (113km) of snowmobile routes in the Bighorn Mountains. Snowmobiles can be rented at **Pahaska Tepee Resort** and in Cody at **Mountain Valley Engine Service,** 422 W. Yellowstone Ave. (© **307/587-6218**).

WINDSURFING
The **Buffalo Bill Reservoir** (see "Seeing the Sights," below) sucks wind from three mountain gorges, making one of the top 10 windsurfing destinations in the continental United States, according to *Outside* magazine. The temperature is tolerable June through September. There is a boat ramp near the campground on the north side of the reservoir just off U.S. 14/16/20.

SEEING THE SIGHTS
Buffalo Bill Historical Center ★★ This impressive museum casts a scholarly eye on the relics of the West's young history while offering some flash and entertainment for the easily distracted. From its beginnings in a rustic log building, the museum has evolved into a sprawling modern edifice that houses five different museums in nearly 300,000 square feet of space.

The **Buffalo Bill Museum** is a monument to one of the earliest manifestations of America's celebrity culture, displaying the wares that turned a frontier scout and buffalo hunter into a renowned showman. Posters trumpet his world-famous Wild West shows featuring "Custer's Last Rally" and "Cossack of the Caucasus," and there are some grainy film clips of the show itself.

The **Whitney Gallery** showcases work by the adventurous artists who carried their palettes to the frontier to record firsthand the wilderness beauty, the proud American Indian cultures, and the lives of trappers and cowboys in the 19th century. Bygone Western artists including Frederic Remington, Charlie Russell, Albert Bierstadt, and Gutzon Borglum share exhibition space with modern practitioners such as Jim Bama and Harry Jackson. Many of the works are an invaluable record of how disappearing American Indian tribes looked and dressed.

The **Plains Indian Museum** is devoted to the history of Plains tribes including the Blackfeet, Cheyenne, Crow, Gros Ventre, Shoshone, and Sioux. Exhibits explain the migrations and customs of the tribes, and display art and artifacts including cradle boards, ceremonial clothing, pipes, and beadwork.

Situated in an eye-catching rotunda surrounded by a herd of bison statues, **the Draper Museum of Natural History** is the center's newest addition, opening its doors for summer 2002. The $17 million museum re-creates the natural environment with a variety of fascinating multi-sensory exhibits focusing on man's investigation of nature over time, with specific attention on the Greater Yellowstone ecosystem.

The **Cody Firearms Museum** displays weaponry dating back to 16th-century Europe in its collection of more than 5,000 pieces. There are also exhibits of world-record game trophies and an arms-manufacturing facility.

The center also features rotating special exhibitions, and its research library is an unparalleled resource for all things Western. Additionally, numerous educational programs are held throughout the year. Late September's annual Plains Indian Seminar brings in scholars for an in-depth examination of American Indian issues.

720 Sheridan Ave. © 307/587-4771. www.bbhc.org. Admission $10 adults, $6 students (18 and over), $4 youth (6–17), free for children under 6. Admission is good for 2 consecutive days. Open daily year-round, peaking at 7am–8pm from June to mid-Sept; call for seasonal hours.

Buffalo Bill Reservoir

The **Buffalo Bill Dam** drops like a slim concrete knife 328 feet into the gorge carved by the Shoshone River west of Cody, and you can walk out atop the dam and look down the steep canyon or back across the deep blue water of the reservoir. Several workers died building it, and when it was completed in 1910, it was the tallest dam in the world. The lake behind it serves anglers, boaters, and windsurfers, while providing irrigation water to farmers downstream. An octagonal visitor center perched next to the dam contains exhibits on the reservoir, wildlife, and area recreation. There is a boat-launch ramp along the north lakeshore off U.S. 14/16/20 and a clean, spacious campground that lacks only adequate shade.

6 miles (10km) west of Cody on U.S. 14/16/20 at the top of Shoshone Canyon. © 307/527-6076 for visitor center. Free day admission; $6 per campsite. May–Sept daily 8am–8pm.

Cody Nite Rodeo ☆ (Kids)

If you want to see an authentic Wyoming rodeo, Cody offers a sure thing: a nightly tussle between bulls, broncs, and cowboys, as well as roping, cutting, and kids' events like the "calf scramble." Pay an extra two bucks and you get a seat just above the chutes in the Buzzard's Roost. The 6,000-seat stadium sits out on an open terrace above the Shoshone River west of town—not a bad place to be on a cool Wyoming evening beneath the stars. Once a year, some of the nation's top rodeo competitors show up for the Fourth of July Cody Stampede (see "Special Events," above).

Stampede Park (on U.S. 14/16/20 as you head west of town toward the Wapiti Valley). © 800/207-0744. Admission $11 adults, $5 children 7–12, free for children under 7. Memorial Day–Labor Day nightly at 8:30pm.

Old Trail Town   Walking the creaky boardwalks here, you'll pass by gray store-fronts and clapboard cabins gathered from ghost towns around the region and assembled on the original town site of Cody City, a short jog from the rodeo grounds. Archaeologist Bob Edgar hasn't wasted any paint on these relics, which include an 1883 cabin from Kaycee where Butch Cassidy and the Sundance Kid once conspired, a saloon decorated with bullet holes, and what must be the largest collection of worn-out buckboard carriages in the U.S. Many of the structures house artifacts, taxidermy, or archaeological finds. On the west end of the "town" are the relocated graves of a number of Western notables, including Jeremiah "Liver Eatin'" Johnston, the model for Robert Redford's *Jeremiah Johnson*.

1831 Demaris Dr. ✆ **307/587-5302.** www.oldtrailtown.com. Admission $5. May 15–Sept 15 daily 8am–8pm; call ahead for hours at other times of the year.

Tecumseh's Old West Miniature Village and Museum   You have to pass through a trading post of ordinary Western tourist plunder to get to this finely detailed miniature diorama of Wyoming and Montana history. Described by proprietor Jerry Fick as his "lifetime work," the room-sized landscape depicts everything from fur trappers floating the rivers to Custer's last moments at Little Big Horn. There is also a collection of American Indian and pioneer artifacts.

142 W. Yellowstone Ave. ✆ **307/587-5362.** Admission $3 adults, $1 students, under 6 free. June–Aug daily 8am–8pm; winter call for hours.

WHERE TO STAY

If you want to book lodging before you arrive, contact **Cody Area Central Reservations** (✆ **888/468-6996**), which can set you up at myriad different properties, from chain motels to frontier-style lodges. Another good accommodations resource is **Cody Guest Houses,** 927 14th St. (✆ **800/587-6560** or 307/587-6000; www.codyguesthouses.com), which manages a dozen properties, from Victorian B&Bs to three-bedroom houses.

Buffalo Bill Village Resort: Comfort Inn, Holiday Inn & Buffalo Bill Village Historic Cabins   This is not exactly a "resort," but an oddly matched cluster of lodgings with a convenient downtown location. The Holiday and Comfort Inns are similar to their chain brethren elsewhere, while the village of aged cabins offers a rustic exterior and a more Western feel, with modern conveniences inside. Family cabins provide two bedrooms. There is also a brief "Ol' West" boardwalk where you can shop for curios or sign up for tours and river trips; an outdoor heated pool; and several restaurants.

Two of the standout properties in town, the Comfort Inn and Holiday Inn are priced nearly identically and have similar amenities (the rooms at the Holiday Inn are slightly newer, but the Comfort Inn includes continental breakfast in the rate). The cabins at Buffalo Bill Village are simply equipped—not much beyond a bed, phone, and TV—and resultantly less expensive.

17th and Sheridan Ave., Cody, WY 82414. ✆ **800/527-5544.** Fax 307/587-2795. jblair@wavecom.net. Comfort Inn: 75 units. $75–$140 double. Holiday Inn: 189 units. $75–$150 double. Buffalo Bill Village Historic Cabins: 83 units. $50–$130 double. AE, DC, DISC, MC, V. Buffalo Bill Village closed Oct–Apr. **Amenities:** 2 restaurants; outdoor pool. *In room:* A/C, cable TV, coffeemaker, hair dryer.

The Irma Hotel   Buffalo Bill's entrepreneurial gusto ultimately left him penniless, but it also left us this century-old hotel (named for his daughter) in the heart of town. Cody hoped to corral visitors who got off the train on their way to Yellowstone, and one of his lures was an elaborate cherry-wood bar, a gift from straightlaced Queen Victoria. You can still hoist a jar on Her Royal

Majesty's slab in the Silver Saddle Saloon, or spend the night in a renovated room that may have once housed a president or prince.

Suites are named after local characters from the town's early days: The Irma Suite, on the corner of the building, has a queen-size bed, a writing table, a vanity in the bedroom area, a small sitting area, and an old-fashioned bathroom with a tub-shower combination. While The Irma's aura will surely please history buffs, those acclimated to modern convenience will probably want to look elsewhere.

Every summer night (except Mon), a gang of mustachioed gunfighters draws crowds as they fire blanks at each other in front of the hotel on 11th Street.

1192 Sheridan Ave., Cody, WY 82414. ✆ **800/745-4762** or 307/587-4221. www.irmahotel.com. 40 units, including 15 restored suites. $69–$92 double; $96–$119 suite. AE, DC, DISC, MC, V. **Amenities:** Restaurant. *In room:* A/C, TV.

The Mayor's Inn ✿   This two-story A-frame, built in 1905 for Mayor Frank Houx, found itself in the path of a wrecking ball in 1997. Before it was demolished, it was sold and moved to its current location, just a few blocks away. It's now one of Cody's best B&Bs, with rooms like the Yellowstone, featuring a lodgepole-pine bed frame and black-and-white photos of the park's early years, and the romantic Hart Mountain Suite, with floral decor in spades. There's also a well-equipped guest kitchen and a fully licensed bar on the enclosed back porch, the perfect spot to unwind after a long day. The breakfasts here are a hearty treat, featuring sourdough flapjacks and buffalo sausage.

1413 Rumsey Ave., Cody, WY 82414. ✆ **888/217-3001** or 307/587-0887. www.mayorsinn.com. 5 units, including 1 suite. $80–$155 double; $205 suite. MC, V. *In room:* A/C, no phone.

GUEST RANCHES & RESORTS

Double Diamond X Ranch ✿✿   Ranches along the South Fork of the Shoshone River don't see the kind of traffic that streams along the North Fork into Yellowstone, but they have their own incredible scenery, including green horse pastures, volcanic rock spires, a tumbling river, and snowcapped peaks. Guests visit the Double Diamond X to ride, fish, see wildlife, and just kick back. Guests are coddled with bounteous meals, amenities, and activities. There are five free-standing log cabins, quaint but quite charming, each sleeping between four and seven, and seven units in the Trail House, similarly rustic in their creature comforts. Cozy bedding, modern bathrooms, and omnipresent front-porch rockers are just a few of the perks. As with most dude ranches, guests sign up by the week, not the day, and the price includes all ranch activities.

3453 Southfork Rd., Cody, WY 82414. ✆ **800/833-RANCH.** Fax 307/587-2708. www.ddxranch.com. 12 units. $1,460 per adult per week, $1,020 per child per week. Lower rates in shoulder season. Rates include all meals. MC, V. Drive 34 miles (55km) SW of Cody on Southfork Rd. (aka Wyo. 291) and look for the sign on the west side. **Amenities:** Indoor pool; Jacuzzi; on-site fishing; horseback riding; children's program. *In room:* No phone.

Pahaska Tepee Resort ✿   Buffalo Bill's hunting lodge, only a mile from the east entrance to Yellowstone, was dubbed with his Lakota name, "Pahaska" (longhair), when he opened the lodge to park visitors in 1905. Near the top of the beautiful Wapiti Valley along U.S. 14/16/20, Pahaska is a popular stop. Far from town and close to the park, it's not unusual to find moose and elk on your doorstep, and it's also nice to have the modern conveniences of a grocery store, gas station, and gift shop. The old river-rock fireplace still burns in the main building, overseen by trophy elk on the walls.

The cabins scattered on the hill behind the lodge close in the winter, while the A-frames by the lodge are open year-round. (There's also a lodge with 11 queen beds and a condo with 4 available for nightly and weekly rentals.) Accommodations have no TVs, phones, or air-conditioning, and might best be described as "mini-motels" with two to five rooms, each with a private entrance. Some bathrooms have only showers, some tubs—it's best to ask in advance.

Pahaska has not kept up with every advance in resort amenities, but its location and reasonable prices more than make up for its shortcomings. For a fee, the resort offers trail rides and pack trips, and in the winter you can rent snowmobiles and cross-country ski gear.

183 Yellowstone Hwy., Cody, WY 82414. ℂ **800/628-7791** or 307/527-7701. Fax 307/527-4019. 48 units. Mid-June to Aug $100–$130 double, lodge $895, condo $450; off-season $65–$99 double, lodge $650, condo $295. DISC, MC, V. Closed Nov and Apr. **Amenities:** Restaurant; self-serve laundry. *In room:* No phone.

Rimrock Ranch   Tucked along Canyon Creek at 6,300 feet above sea level, the Rimrock Ranch has an intimate feel not found on larger dude ranches. The cabins, nestled alongside Canyon Creek, are fairly modern and definitely a cut above some of the more "rustic" cabins in the area. The weekly package includes backcountry rides and a roping arena, rodeo trips, fishing, cookouts, and river floats. A small outdoor pool perches next to the lodge with a view down the canyon. In the winter, snowmobile packages are available.

2728 North Fork Rte., Cody, WY 82414. ℂ **307/587-3970.** Fax 307/527-5014. www.rimrockranch.com. 8 cabins. Mid-May to mid-Sept $1,250 per person per week; children $975 per child per week. 3-day snowmobiling $975. MC, V. Drive 25 miles (40km) west of Cody on U.S. Hwy. 16/20/14 (aka Yellowstone Hwy.); ranch is on the south side of highway. *In room:* No phone.

7D Ranch ⭐   Beautiful Sunlight Creek runs through this venerable ranch, which has a homey, lived-in quality missing in slicker operations. The Dominick family has run the spread for three generations, and they know the nooks and crannies of the Sunlight Basin and the Beartooth Mountains, which guests explore on daylong rides, hikes, and fishing expeditions. Riding and casting lessons, naturalist-led wildflower walks, weekly square dances, and bonfires are all part of the package. And the cabins, cheerfully decorated with heaps of frontier charm, have more personality than the bulk of the 7D's peers.

Sunlight Basin, Box 100, Cody, WY 82414. ℂ **307/587-9885.** www.7dranch.com. 11 cabins. May–Sept $1,390–$1,560 per person per week. Discount for children under 13. Rates include all meals. MC, V. Drive north from Cody on Wyo. 120 to Wyo. 296, then west. Ranch is 50 miles (81km) from Cody via Sunlight Rd. **Amenities:** Game room. *In room:* No phone.

WHERE TO DINE

Before the east entrance to Yellowstone opens (usually in mid-May), Cody is a pretty quiet place, and sometimes it's a bit difficult to find an open restaurant. Therefore, we suggest that especially from fall to late spring you call the restaurant of your choice to check on its current hours and state of operation.

If you need something less than a formal sit-down meal, Cody has a good supply of familiar fast-food joints and a few informal, inexpensive places. **Peter's Cafe Bakery,** at 1191 Sheridan Ave. (ℂ **307/527-5040**), across the street from The Irma, serves a full breakfast starting at 6:45am, with fresh-baked bagels, pastries, and espresso, plus subs and burgers for lunch and dinner. **Maxwell's Bakery,** 937 Sheridan Ave. (ℂ **307/527-7749;** see the listing for Maxwell's Restaurant, below), offers croissants and other fragrant bakery items, along with coffee, in the early hours before the adjacent restaurant opens. There is also the **Cody Coffee Co. & Eatery,** 1702 Sheridan Ave. (ℂ **307/527-7879**), for coffee, fresh-made pastries, soups, and sandwiches. One of the best places day or night to get a beer 'n burger (or Rocky Mountain oysters!) is the thoroughly Western **Proud Cut Saloon,** 1227 Sheridan Ave. (ℂ **307/527-6905**).

Cassie's Supper Club WESTERN Cassie's is the sort of place you might expect and look for in the West: big platters of beef, four bars serving drinks, and roadhouse decor, including taxidermy and assorted cowboy ephemera. They've been in business since 1922. Located along the highway west of town in what was once a "House of Ill Fame," Cassie's is now very respectable and very busy. Besides the requisite steaks, there's seafood (including a great rainbow trout dinner), pasta, and chicken, plus a full menu of specialty drinks. You can get free Western swing lessons several evenings a week and there's live country music every night in summer.

214 Yellowstone Ave. ⓒ 307/527-5500. Main courses $16–$30. AE, DISC, MC, V. Mon–Sat 11am–2pm and 5–10pm; Sun 5–10pm.

The Gardens ⭐⭐ MEDITERRANEAN Chef-owner John McCormack's splashy new entry into the Cody culinary scene is worlds apart from the region's typical meat-and-potatoes establishments. Trained in Paris and at some of the finest restaurants in New York and Las Vegas, McCormack now stamps the Gardens' menu with his unique style: wild game and seafood prepared with French and Italian flair. This combination results in pheasant ravioli, boar and elk sausage, and incredible seafood pasta dishes. The restaurant also looks a lot different from the norm: It's a melding of Old West and funky cosmopolitan, with a sinfully red wine bar, an adjacent Internet bar, Victorian furnishings, and three stages for live music, including one on the big, breezy patio. To complete your visit, order up a dessert—bananas Foster is our choice.

1313½ Sheridan Ave. ⓒ 307/587-1101. Reservations recommended on weekends. Main courses $8–$25. AE, MC, V. Daily 11am–10pm (bar open later).

Mack Bros. Brew Co. BURGERS/BARBECUE Formerly the Silver Dollar Bar & Grill, this down-and-dirty eating and drinking establishment is a Cody institution. A stuffed cougar stands guard over the eclectically decorated room, where the walls are plastered with the likes of Woodstock posters and longhorn skulls. The menu is equal parts gourmet burgers and Southern-style barbecue, and the beers—brewed nearby in Red Lodge, Montana—are first-rate. Try the Sundance Wheat with a lemon wedge after a day in the great outdoors.

1313 Sheridan Ave. ⓒ 307/587-3554. Reservations not accepted. Most dishes $7–$14. AE, MC, V. Daily 11am–10pm (bar open later).

Maxwell's Restaurant 𝘒𝘪𝘥𝘴 ECLECTIC AMERICAN A family restaurant in which "family" does not translate to "bland," Maxwell's has some spicy chicken and pasta dishes to go with its salads, seafood, and beef. The gourmet pizzas (especially the garlicky Margherita) aren't a bad choice, nor is the pork tenderloin Marsala, sautéed in a light wine sauce with shitake mushrooms. You can even order a Philly cheese steak for lunch, uncommon in Wyoming. The low-backed booths and varnished wood tables are sometimes packed with boisterous families, raising the noise level and waitress stress, but it's a friendly crowd.

937 Sheridan Ave. ⓒ 307/527-7749. Lunch $7–$10; dinner $10–$20. AE, DISC, MC, V. Mon–Sat 11am–9pm.

Stefan's Restaurant ⭐ CONTEMPORARY Stefan Bennett is a restless chef, so the menu of his restaurant changes often—but everything is made from scratch with an eye for invention. A sign reads, "We don't do giddy-up here," and it's right: The gourmet fare bears little resemblance to typical Wyoming cuisine. Among the entrees are a filet mignon stuffed with Gorgonzola cheese, sun-dried tomatoes, and portobello mushrooms; an "Untraditional Meatloaf" with spicy buffalo; a crustless chicken pot pie; and Stefan's delectable honey-soy salad dressing. There are separate lunch and Sunday brunch menus—for the latter, Stefan smokes his own salmon and makes hollandaise sauce from scratch—and a "little bites" menu with $4 to $5 children's meals.

1367 Sheridan Ave. (℗ 307/587-8511. Reservations recommended. Lunch $5–$9; dinner $10–$23. AE, DISC, MC, V. Summer daily 11am–10pm; off-season Mon–Sat 11am–8pm.

3 A Side Trip Around the Bighorn Basin

Greybull: 40 miles (64km) E of Cody; 60 miles (97km) W of Sheridan

The prehistoric past of this region is written in the rock, and nowhere in Wyoming is that more true than in **Greybull,** named for a legendary albino bison sacred to American Indians. The town lies amidst red-rock formations rich in fossils and archaeological treasures. **The Greybull Museum** (325 Greybull Ave.; (℗ 307/765-2444) houses one of the largest fossil ammonites in the world, as well as petrified wood, agates, and American Indian artifacts. This fine museum is open Monday through Saturday, from 10am to 8pm from June to Labor Day, and more restricted hours in the winter, with free admission. Just north of town you'll find a spectacular 15-mile-long (24km), 2,000-foot-high natural fortress named **Sheep Mountain,** a textbook example of a "doubly plunging anticline," geo-lingo for a natural arch folded into layered rock.

Greybull is a gateway town to the Bighorn Mountains on scenic U.S. 14 up Shell Canyon. Just 7 miles (11km) outside of town heading east is the **Stone Schoolhouse,** listed on the National Register of Historic Places. The one-room schoolhouse was built in 1903 of locally quarried sandstone, and in recent years was converted to a bookstore/gallery, though its hours are unpredictable. Less than a mile farther along the highway, turn south on Red Gulch Road and drive 5 miles (8km) to a signed parking area where you can view dinosaur tracks.

U.S. 14 climbs through steep and beautiful **Shell Canyon** (see Driving Tour #1, above) to the Antelope Butte Ski Area, just 38 miles (61km) east of Greybull. It's a small ski area with nice views and short lift lines.

Fifty miles (81km) south of Greybull and east through little Hyattville brings you to the **Medicine Lodge State Archaeological Site** ((℗ 307/469-2234), where prehistoric peoples decorated the sandstone cliffs along Medicine Lodge Creek with carved petroglyphs and painted pictographs of hunting scenes. You can fish the small stream for brown trout. There is a shady, inexpensive, 26-site campground here, open May through October, with no RV hookups. To reach the site and campground, take Wyo. 789/U.S. 16/20 for 20 miles (32km) from Greybull to Manderson, then drive 22 miles (35km) along Wyo. 31 to Hyattville. In Hyattville, drive north and turn right onto Cold Springs Road. Follow the signs 5 miles (8km) to the site.

4 Thermopolis

84 miles (135km) S of Cody; 130 miles (210km) NW of Casper; 218 miles (351km) E of Jackson

Steaming water cascades over pastel-colored terraces and down to the Bighorn River at Hot Springs State Park, one of the undiscovered treasures of Wyoming. Trumpeted as the largest hot springs in the world (it's not quite: New Zealand's Whakarewarewa rightfully claims that honor), the 134° F water from the Big Spring supplies two indoor/outdoor pool facilities, two hotels, and a state-run soaking spa. The town of Thermopolis grew up around the hot springs after it was sold to the U.S. government by the tribes of the Wind River Indian

Reservation in 1896. Developers dreamt of a health spa to rival Saratoga, but it never quite happened. What did happen is a small, peaceful town with a great place to soak or slide, a nearby canyon of exciting white water, and surrounding hills holding a trove of dinosaur bones and prehistoric petroglyphs.

ESSENTIALS

GETTING THERE   The closest airports are the **Riverton Regional Airport** (55 miles [89km] south of Thermopolis, off U.S. 26 W. at 4700 Airport Rd., Riverton, WY 82501) and Cody's **Yellowstone Regional Airport** (84 miles [135km] northeast on Wyo. 120 to U.S. 14/16/20, north on Duggleby Dr. to 3001 Duggleby Dr., Cody, WY 82414; ✆ 307/587-5096). There is a small airport in Thermopolis used by private fliers.

United Airlines affiliate **Great Lakes Aviation** (✆ 800/241-6522) is the sole provider of air service into Riverton, with several daily connecting flights to Denver and north to Worland. Cody service is provided by both **United Express** (✆ 800/241-6522) and Delta feeder **Skywest** (✆ 800/453-9417).

To reach Thermopolis from Cody, drive 84 miles (135km) southeast on Wyo. 120. From Cheyenne, drive north on I-25 to Casper (178 miles; 287km), west on U.S. 20/26 to Shoshoni (98 miles; 158km), and north on U.S. 20 to Thermopolis. From Rock Springs, take U.S. 191 to Farson, Wyo. 28 to Lander, and Wyo. 789 through Riverton and Shoshoni to Thermopolis.

VISITOR INFORMATION   The **Thermopolis–Hot Springs Chamber of Commerce** (✆ 800/SUN-N-SPA or 307/864-3192; www.thermopolis.com) sends out packets of information about local attractions.

GETTING AROUND   If you've arrived by plane at one of the area airports, you'll need to rent a car to get around. **Hertz** (✆ 800/654-3131) maintains counters at both the Riverton and Cody Airports, and **Rent-a-Wreck** (✆ 307/864-2488) has a location at the Hot Springs County Airport in Thermopolis.

GETTING OUTSIDE

Hot Springs State Park (see the detailed listing below) offers a variety of outdoor activities, from splashing in mineral water to picnicking on the lawn. South and upstream on the Bighorn River is twisting **Wind River Canyon,** a tricky but bountiful fishing and floating section (you'll need permits from the Wind River Indian Reservation), topped by 19,000-acre **Boysen Reservoir,** about 20 minutes from Thermopolis on U.S. 20. The 11 campgrounds ($4–$8 a site, plus the requisite $2 day-use fee) on the largely treeless shore of this state park can be a bit buggy and hot in August, but the water attracts boaters to sail, fish, and waterski. There are three small public beach areas, on the reservoir's northeastern and western shores. For more information on the park, contact **Boysen State Park,** Boysen Route, Shoshoni, WY 82649 (✆ 307/876-2796), or call Wyoming State Parks and Historic Sites headquarters in Cheyenne at ✆ 307/777-6323.

FISHING

Whether you like fishing lakes or streams, this area has trophy-size opportunities—Boysen grows record-setting walleye, as well as trout and perch, while the Bighorn River grows some fat brown and cutthroat trout. Check locally to be sure you've got the right fishing license: The canyon requires a tribal permit; the reservoir and other stretches of river require a state license—both available at local sporting-goods stores. If you have your own boat, or hire an outfitter, you can float and fish from the bottom of the canyon at the Wedding of the Waters (where there's a wheelchair-accessible boat ramp) to Thermopolis. During the warmest part of summer, algae can darken the river and hamper fishing, but spring and fall are anglers' dreams. One reputable local guide service is **Wyoming Adventures** (℃ **307/864-2407**; www.anglingadventures-wy.com).

GOLF

The Legion Golf Course is a nine-hole course that overlooks the city from Airport Hill. Call ℃ **307/864-5294** to book a tee time at affordable prices—nine holes for $11 on weekdays and $13 on weekends; 18 holes for $16 and $18, respectively. The pro shop offers cart rentals, a driving range, and lessons. An adjacent restaurant, the Legion Supper Club (see "Where to Dine," below), is open daily for lunch and dinner.

HIKING

A boardwalk allows you to explore the bulbous travertine terraces without scalding your soles in the hot spring water that flows over them. The paths extend to a suspended footbridge across the Bighorn River and a riverside walkway below. For more earnest hikers, there is the approximately 6-mile (10km) **Volksmarch Trail,** one of several around the state that are marked with a trademark brown-and-yellow insignia. This one loops through the park and downtown Thermopolis. Just north of town off U.S. 20 you can hike **T Hill** for a bird's-eye view of Thermopolis, the Wind River Canyon, and the Owl Creek Mountains. The 2-mile (3km) round trip up **Roundtop Mountain** is another rewarding hike, culminating in spectacular views of the Hot Springs and Thermopolis, with the trail head beginning near the Monument Hill Cemetery on Airport Road.

WHITE-WATER RAFTING ★★

The tribes of the **Wind River Indian Reservation** virtually gave away the hot springs, but not the canyon upstream, through which the Wind River tumbles and twists (for reasons no one can explain, the Wind River becomes the Bighorn River as it leaves the canyon). A Shoshone-owned company now takes rafters through rapids named after historic tribal figures like Chief Washakie and Sharp Nose. "Sphincter Rapid" is not an Indian name, but it tells you there are some Class III–IV white-water thrills ahead. You can run half the canyon or the whole thing, take a more leisurely fishing trip, or camp overnight with **Wind River Canyon Whitewater,** 210 Hwy. 20 S., Thermopolis (℃ **307/864-9343** in season or 307/486-2253 during off-season; www.windrivercanyonraft.com). White-water trips run $35 to $38 for a half-day or $75 for a full day.

HOT SPRINGS STATE PARK ★★

Few state parks in Wyoming are as nice as **Hot Springs** (℃ **307/864-2176**), with its shady trees, striking flower gardens, and a stretch of the Big Horn River running through it, as well as a roaming buffalo herd and the main event: the magnificent hot springs, with some of its water funneled into swimming pools and slides. It's located at the north side of town off U.S. 20 and admission is free. The park's only shortcoming is that you can't camp overnight, which must please nearby private campgrounds and lodgings. As a Wyoming tourist attraction, the hot springs places a distant third to Yellowstone and Grand Teton National Parks, but the sparse crowds allow Thermopolis to retain its small-town style.

   At the north end of the park, you can climb a few stairs to look down into the bottomless blue-green depths of the Big Spring—the placid surface belies the fact that it pumps around 15 million gallons of aqua vitae a day.

SOAKING IN THE BATHS

You can't just plop yourself down in this 135° F water, but there are three bathing facilities in the park. To get to them, take the loop road—at the north end are the bathing areas. First, and simplest, is the **State Bath House** (© **307/864-3765**), a small spa open to the public free of charge thanks to famed Shoshone Chief Washakie. When the tribes sold the federal government the hot springs in 1896—it would later become state property—Washakie noted that the springs had always been a place of peace and neutrality among tribes, and should therefore always be free to all people. The small, clean indoor and outdoor pools aren't for frolicking or swimming laps—just soaking, wading, and perhaps conversing with some of the old-timers who come here. Soaks are limited to 20 minutes per session. You can rent a towel, locker, and bathing suit for under a dollar each, and it's open Monday through Saturday from 8am to 5:30pm, Sunday and holidays from noon to 5:30pm. On either side of this peaceful place are the more raucous commercial pools.

STAR PLUNGE The big lure at the Plunge are its three big slides—the kids' favorite "Little Dipper," the outdoor "Super Star," and the enclosed "Blue Thunder," the latter a 300-foot spin around a 60-foot tower that will thrill you to your claustrophobic, free-falling toes. Indoor and outdoor pools, hot tubs, Jacuzzis, a snack bar, and an arcade make this the favorite of the young set. On a crowded summer afternoon, there are lines at the slides, splashing all around, and a teenage volume level, but you can still find stillness in the "vapor cave." For more information call © **307/864-3771.** Admission is $8 for children over 4 and adults; $3 for children 4 and under; $5 for seniors. It's open daily from 9am to 9pm. Closed first 3 weeks of December.

HELLIE'S TEPEE SPA The Spa (© **307/864-9250**), sometimes called Hot Springs Water Park, is a little more peaceful under its big dome than its neighbor to the east, but it has its share of lively teens and a contingent of young families. The slides are not as big here, but you can hear yelps of delight as bodies zip down the twisting indoor open tube. There is a fast-moving open slide outdoors, too, and often a wet basketball game in the roomy outdoor pool. Soaking pools, a steam room, a sauna, and a game room complete the scene. Admission is $8 for ages 6 to 62, $4 for ages 4 to 5, $5 for 63 and over, and free for children under 3. Open daily from 9am to 9pm.

SEEING THE SIGHTS

Hot Springs County Historical Museum and Cultural Center   The original cherrywood bar from the Hole-in-the-Wall Saloon—Butch Cassidy's hangout—is the biggest draw at this local museum, which has some gems amidst the musty clutter that you learn to expect of rural repositories of historic artifacts. Various modes of transportation are represented, including a turn-of-the-century stagecoach, a caboose, and a wagon used to tour Yellowstone. Exhibits trace the local economic threads, primarily coal mining, petroleum extraction, and agriculture. On the lower level are a fully outfitted print shop, general store, and dentist's office. The museum's cultural center features local artwork and crafts on a rotating basis. Call for information on current exhibits.

700 Broadway. © **307/864-5183.** $10 families, $4 adults, $2 seniors and children 6–12. Mon–Sat 8am–5pm.

Legend Rock Petroglyph Site ♠ *(Finds)*   Petroglyphs—prehistoric drawings inscribed in rock—are scattered throughout the foothills of Wyoming's mountains. Legend Rock is one of the richest petroglyph sites in the Rockies, and

Gift of the Waters Historical Indian Pageant

An annual production, the pageant reenacts the sale of the hot springs and surrounding lands by the Shoshone and Arapaho peoples to the federal government in 1896. The pageant makes the sale out as an act of peace and neighborly brotherhood. In fact, the tribes were starving and desperate. Indians from Wind River play some of the roles in the pageant. The pageant is performed annually during the first weekend in August, along with a powwow. Contact the **Thermopolis Chamber of Commerce** (✆ **800/SUN-N-SPA** or 307/864-3192) for information.

---

it is managed—rather informally—by state agents at Hot Springs State Park (see above). Visitors can pick up a gate key at the park and then drive up Wyo. 120 to the Hamilton Dome turnoff, then continue 8 miles (13km) west, partly on a dirt road, to the site. There you can hike up and down Cottonwood Creek to find pecked representations of turtle-like creatures, bird glyphs, hunters, and musicians. To get a good view of some of the panels you need to scramble up on ledges. Weather has taken its toll on this soft sandstone, and so have souvenir hunters—hands off, please! Be sure to ask for a map to the site when you pick up the key between 9am and 5pm at the park office; the route is not well marked. You can drive down by the creek, but you're better off, particularly when it's wet and muddy, parking up by the gate and taking the short hike down.

Near Hamilton Dome, about 25 miles (40km) northwest of Thermopolis. For information contact Hot Springs State Park (see above) or the Thermopolis Chamber of Commerce (✆ 800/SUN-N-SPA or 307/864-3192).

Outlaw Trail Ride   Butch Cassidy was a well-known character around Thermopolis, although not by any means the only outlaw who favored this rugged country. Visitors who want to relive a Wild West getaway can join the annual Outlaw Trail Ride in August, and journey 100 miles (161km) up through the dry, hidden canyons of Hole-in-the-Wall country. Only about 100 people can participate in the weeklong event, and it's popular, so book well in advance. You must BYO horse and sleep on the ground.

Outlaw Trail, Inc., Box 1046, Thermopolis, WY 82443. ✆ 888/362-RIDE or 307/864-2287. www.trib.com/~outlaw. The ride occurs annually in mid-Aug.

Wyoming Dinosaur Center ✦ (Kids   This dinosaur museum is located right at the site where modern-day paleontologists have dug up dinosaur bones from the Jurassic period. There are 12 full skeletons on display at the center, as well as eggs, shells, and other remnants from around the world. Except in winter, visitors can take guided tours of dig sites, and then watch workers clean and prepare bones in the laboratory at the center.

110 Carter Ranch Rd., Thermopolis, WY 82443. ✆ 800/455-3466. www.wyodino.org. $6 adults 19–59, $3.50 children 5–18 and seniors; group rates available. Summer daily 8am–8pm; winter daily 10am–5pm. Closed major holidays.

WHERE TO STAY

Thermopolis has a number of motels and campgrounds with a little age on them, so if you're arriving in the busy summer season you should have a reservation, or risk landing in a room with the amenities of a closet. Recently, chain affiliates have taken a new interest in lodgings here, so the choices are growing.

Holiday Inn of the Waters (Kids   This is no cookie-cutter Holiday Inn—it's a hot-springs resort along the Bighorn River within Hot Springs State Park. The huge volume of superheated water that surges from the upturned sandstones is piped into the outdoor Jacuzzi next to the big pool. If lolling under the stars doesn't soften you up, take a turn in the health club and submit to the ministrations of a licensed masseuse. Unique to this Holiday Inn are its location in the park, several antiques-furnished rooms, and frequent promotions (2 weekend nights, dinner, and champagne for two for $160 from Sept–May). Certainly no other Holiday Inn has a restaurant like the Safari Room, arrayed with enough big-game trophies from around the world to make Ernest Hemingway blush and vegetarians gag.

Hot Springs State Park, Thermopolis, WY 82443. (**C**) **800/HOLIDAY** or 307/864-3131. www.holidayinn thermopolis.com. 80 units. $63–$120 double. AE, DC, DISC, MC, V. **Amenities:** Restaurant; outdoor pool; health club; Jacuzzi; massage. *In room:* A/C, TV.

Quality Inn & Suites Plaza Hotel *⚜* If you'd rather not have a wildebeest staring at you on your way to breakfast, but still want to be in the park, try this alternative, a funky old brick place that once operated as a hostel but now has been nicely fixed up by Quality Inns. The 1918 structure is on the National Register of Historic Places and the aura is more urban inn than chain motel. Several of the rooms and suites still have working fireplaces, and new owners have completely renovated the inner courtyard. It's an easy walk to pools, but you may enjoy the old-fashioned ambience here enough to linger over your coffee.

116 E. Park St. (P.O. Box 866), Thermopolis, WY 82443. (**C**) **888/919-9009** or 307/864-2939. www bestofwyoming.com. 36 units. $85–$125 double; reduced rates in winter. Rates include continental breakfast. AE, DC, DISC, MC, V. **Amenities:** Outdoor pool; Jacuzzi. *In room:* A/C, TV.

Roundtop Mountain Motel The Roundtop is one of several clean and comfortable budget alternatives in Thermopolis, offering lodging in either a motel room or a log cabin. A redwood deck and patio complement some of the newly renovated units, and kitchenettes are available, which puts the Roundtop ahead of its competition. Though not directly adjacent to the hot springs, the motel is located downtown and within a short drive or walk of the mineral baths.

412 N. 6th, Thermopolis, WY 82443. (**C**) **800/584-9126** or 307/864-3126. Fax 307/864-3905. www.round-topmotel.com. 12 units. $35–$69 double. DISC, MC, V. *In room:* A/C, cable TV, kitchenette.

Super 8 Hot Springs *Kids* The tile-roofed Southwest style of architecture distinguishes this new motel from other Super 8's, and from the many older, somewhat drab lodgings in Thermopolis. Inside, the decor is not particularly distinguished, but there is a big indoor pool, a pleasant lobby and eating area for the continental breakfast, and a honeymoon suite with a marble Jacuzzi. And it's a good bet for kids, offering eight family rooms, each with two bunk beds, two queen-size beds, a VCR, and a Nintendo for only $10 extra.

Lane 5 S., Hwy. 20, Thermopolis, WY 82443. (**C**) **800/800-8000** or 307/864-5515. Fax 307/864-5447. 54 units, including 2 junior suites. Summer $79–$95 double, $175 honeymoon suite; winter $65–$75 double, $145 honeymoon suite. Rates include continental breakfast. AE, DC, DISC, MC, V. *In room:* A/C, cable TV, fridge.

CAMPING

The **Fountain of Youth RV Park** (**C** **307/864-3265**) has tent and RV sites available almost year-round (they're closed in Dec and Jan) and is located 1½ miles (2km) north of town by the river on U.S. 20. The campground features a large mineral pool, barbecue grills, showers, laundry room, dump station, and camp store. RV sites cost about $20 (tent sites are lower), and MasterCard and Visa are accepted. Facilities are wheelchair accessible and an EMT is on-site. When things are busy in the summer, you may find yourself overhearing the unmuffled conversation of the Harley riders parked in the next slot. The **Eagle RV Park** (✆ 888/864-5262 or 307/864-5262) is a similar facility with similar rates and almost identical amenities, although there is a bit more space—and peace and quiet. It's located on U.S. 20 south of Thermopolis, and accepts American Express, Discover, MasterCard, and Visa.

WHERE TO DINE

Legion Supper Club AMERICAN   Up in the hills above Thermopolis, the Legion's pasta, steak, and prime rib menu is the fanciest fare offered in these parts. Lunch is a festive affair, with a Mexican menu that includes smothered burritos and a taco salad as well as standard sandwich fare; the crab-and-cheese melt and shrimp salad are local favorites. The cheerful ambience during lunch becomes decidedly more polished and romantic at dinner, when linen table-cloths, flowers, and candles grace the tables and entrees of prime cuts of beef and seafood are served. The restaurant also has a quiet, full-service bar.

142 Airport Rd., at the Legion Golf Club. ✆ 307/864-3918. Lunch $5–$10; dinner $8–$19. AE, DISC, MC, V. Tues–Sun 11am–2pm and 5–10pm; Sun brunch 10am–2pm. Turn west off U.S. Hwy. 20 on Broadway, then north on 7th St., which becomes Park St. and climbs Airport Hill to the golf course and supper club.

Pumpernick's *Finds* AMERICAN   The three rooms where meals are served at Pumpernick's clearly weren't designed as a restaurant, but the semi-cramped, bric-a-brac–bedecked quarters add a friendly intimacy to good food. In the sum-mer, you can escape the elbows by eating outside in the roomy adjacent arbor. Around town it's sometimes called the Local Yokel Club, and they come for breakfast, lunch, and dinner every day but Sunday. Pumpernick's serves three-egg omelets to breakfast noshers, then crepes and plump specialty sandwiches for lunch. Dinner features generous portions of T-bone steaks and seafood, including sautéed scallops, rainbow trout, and steamed shrimp. They bake their own breads, which they use for hoagies, soup bowls, and dinner loaves. Try the Hertle Turtle for a melt-in-your-mouth chocolate treat.

512 Broadway. ✆ 307/864-5151. Breakfast $2–$8; lunch $3–$7; dinner $9–$17. AE, DISC, MC, V. Mon–Thurs 7am–9pm; Fri–Sat 7am–10pm.

5 Wind River Valley

Lander: 160 miles (258km) SE of Jackson; 117 miles (188km) N of Rock Springs; 163 miles (262km) S of Cody

The deep curve of the Wind River Valley is shaped by the snowcapped Wind River Mountain range to the West and the Absaroka and Owl Creek Ranges on the east, forming a cottonwood-lined bottom that many consider one of the most beautiful areas in Wyoming. A sizable portion of the valley belongs to the Eastern Shoshone and Northern Arapaho tribes of the **Wind River Indian Reservation,** where there is considerable poverty, but also productive ranches and spectacular wilderness reaching up to the Continental Divide. The largest towns are Riverton and Lander, but there are smaller communities like Dubois, Shoshoni, Fort Washakie, and the historical gold-mining town of Atlantic City.

RIVERTON

Notched in a big bend of the Wind River is **Riverton,** a settlement that was carved out when the federal government opened the northern portion of the reservation to non-Indian people a century ago. Riverton has established itself as a retail commercial center for west central Wyoming. Contact the **Riverton Area Chamber of Commerce,** First and Main, Riverton, WY 82501 (✆ **800/235-2732** or 307/856-4801; www.rivertonchamber.org), for information, including useful suggestions for day trips in the area and a list of events. That calendar includes a summer **Riverton Rendezvous and Balloon Rally,** held during the third week in July, when colorful balloons from all over the Rockies rise against the majestic backdrop of the Wind River Range, and the town puts on arts and crafts fairs, a demolition derby, a family dinner with live entertainment, and even a treasure hunt. Also in the summer, there is the nostalgic **1838 Rendezvous** staged at the junction of the Wind River and the Little Wind River, with black-powder shooting, Indian dancing, tomahawk throws, and bead-trading. Wyoming's largest **cowboy poetry gathering** is held here in the early fall, and there is the **Wild West Winter Carnival** with drag races, ice sculpting, and fishing derbies on the frozen surface of Boysen Reservoir.

GETTING THERE   From Thermopolis, take U.S. 20 south through scenic Wind River Canyon to Shoshoni, then U.S. 26 south to Riverton.

WHERE TO STAY   If you plan to stay overnight in Riverton, your best bet is the **Holiday Inn** (© **800/HOLIDAY** or 307/856-8100). Located at 900 E. Sunset, it has 121 rooms that typically rent for $75 to $99 double. Or you could head 24 miles (39km) farther west on Wyoming 789 to **Lander** (see below).

SHOSHONI

Shoshoni, which translates as "Little Snow," is located 22 miles (35km) east of Riverton on U.S. 26. Peek behind the shabby exterior of the little town and you'll find what are reputedly the state's best milkshakes at the endearing **Yellowstone Drug Store,** 127 Main St. (© **307/876-2539**); some interesting sites for rockhounds amidst abandoned copper mines in the Owl Creeks to the north; and, on Memorial Day weekend, the state's premier **Old Time Fiddlers' Contest.** Contact the **Shoshoni Chamber of Commerce,** Box 324, Shoshoni, WY 82649 (© **307/876-2273**), for more information.

LANDER

If you head 24 miles (39km) farther west of Riverton on Wyo. 789, you hit **Lander,** tucked snugly into the foothills of the Wind River Mountains where the three fingers of the Popo Agie River draw together. When railroads were the nation's primary mode of travel, Lander was "where the rails end and the trails begin": the takeoff point for backcountry trips to hunt, fish, or explore the lake-dotted wilderness that climbs to the Continental Divide. The trains are gone, but this is still where you put on your hiking or riding boots. For more information, contact the **Lander Area Chamber of Commerce,** 160 N. 1st St., Lander, WY 82520 (© **800/433-0662** or 307/332-3892; www.landerchamber.org).

Just west of town on Wyo. 131 is **Sinks Canyon State Park** (© **307/ 332-6333**), where the Middle Fork of the Popo Agie disappears into a limestone cave and reappears farther down the canyon at a pool with an overlook where you can feed kibble to giant trout (no hooks allowed!). Day use is free. The park has a nature trail, a visitor center with naturalist displays, a campground ($4 a night), and tumbling waterfalls for those willing to hike some switchbacks. For a different kind of experience, drive south 37 miles (60km) on U.S. 287 to the **South Pass City Historical Site** (© **307/332-3684**), which re-creates a gold-mining town from the 1860s, and where Esther Hobart Morris became the nation's first female justice of the peace.

Lander has a justly famous **Fourth of July parade and Pioneer Days Rodeo** (© **800/433-0662**), and later in July it hosts the **International Climber's Festival** (© **307/332-6697**; www.climbersfestival.org). Slide shows by climbing greats, clinics, an equipment show, and climbers testing their mettle on the walls of Sinks Canyon and Wild Iris draw hundreds of serious climbers to the event. Some of the climbers are resident here, partly thanks to the **National Outdoor Leadership School** ⚘, which has been teaching outdoor types responsible ways of enjoying the wilds for more than 35 years, and now has branches all over the world. For course offerings from India to the Rocky Mountains, write the school's Lander headquarters at 288 Main St., Lander, WY 82520 (✆ **307/ 332-5300;** www.nols.edu).

If you want an exotic element to your trail adventure, try the **Lander Llama Company,** 2024 Mortimore Lane, Lander, WY 82520 (✆ **800/582-5262** or 307/332-5624; www.landerllama.com). Their naturalist-led Red Desert trip is as enlightening as it is enjoyable, incorporating ancient American Indian history and fossil viewing with stunning Wyoming scenery. If you'd prefer to horse around, check out **Allen's Diamond Four Ranch,** P.O. Box 243, Lander, WY 82520 (✆ **307/332-2995**), for guided horseback tours in the Popo Agie Wilderness and Wind River Mountains. The ranch's overnight accommodations are bare-bones—woodstoves, propane lights, bring your own bedding—but the emphasis is on riding, fishing, and seeing the high country. There are special programs for kids.

Winter transforms this country into a snowmobiler's playground, with 250 miles (402km) of the **Continental Divide Trail** reaching from Lander all the way to Yellowstone. Call the **Wind River Visitors Council** (✆ **800/645-6233**) or the Lander Area Chamber of Commerce (see above) for information on this and other snowmobile trails in the area.

WHERE TO STAY & EAT

As far as lodging and grub go, there are quite a few options in Lander, from pizzerias and roadside motels to supper clubs and historic B&Bs. The **Budget Host Pronghorn Inn,** 150 E. Main St. (✆ **307/332-3940**), is a reliable choice, with frontier-style trappings and a riverfront setting. Doubles run $60 to $75 in the high season. The Lander Llama Company (see above) rents **The Bunk House,** a stylishly rustic cabin (with a kitchenette) on the Popo Agie River, for $75 a night, with a five-guest limit. For dining, try the **Gannett Grill,** 126 Main St. (✆ **307/332-8228**), with a more-interesting-than-it-sounds menu of thick burgers, sandwiches, pizza, and salads.

WIND RIVER INDIAN RESERVATION

Note: The starting point for a tour of the Wind River Indian Reservation is Fort Washakie, located 14 miles (23km) north of Lander on U.S. 287, or 146 miles (235km) from Jackson (U.S. 26/89/191 to Moran Junction, then U.S. 287 over Togwotee Pass to Dubois and then on to the reservation).

More than two million acres of the **Wind River Indian Reservation** surround the town of Riverton, encompassing an area that stretches 70 miles (113km) east to west and 55 miles (89km) north to south. Wyoming's sole reservation is home to more than 2,800 Eastern Shoshone and 3,700 Northern Arapaho tribal members, governed by a council made up of representatives from both tribes.

The Shoshone were given a huge reservation to buffer westward travelers from more hostile tribes to the north like the Sioux and Blackfeet. A reservation that once included parts of Wyoming, Utah, and Colorado was reduced greatly when non-Indians discovered gold, grazing land, and water on tribal lands. Today, the Wind River Indian Reservation is a still-sizable 2.3 million acres, including oil and gas fields, several small communities, and some of the most pristine wilderness—and best fishing—in the United States.

The Northern Arapaho came to Wind River in the late 1870s for what they thought was a temporary placement before moving to their own reservation farther east. However, government promises were forgotten or ignored, and the Arapaho settled in to stay. The two tribes have unrelated languages and a history of warfare, but their relationship has gradually improved.

There are poverty and high unemployment on the reservation, but there is pride, too, quite evident at the powwows. Outsiders are welcome at these dances, which are held May through September at various sites (the Wind River Visitors Council can provide a schedule; © **800/645-6233**) where you'll see a more open, friendly side of Arapaho and Shoshone, as long as you are respectful. Sun dances are more spiritual affairs, and while visitors are not banned, these moving ceremonies are not for tourists, and no photographs or videos are allowed.

Services for visitors are not well developed on the reservation, but you can learn more about the Shoshone tribe at the **Shoshone Tribal Cultural Center** (© **307/332-9106**) in Fort Washakie, and about the Arapaho tribe at the **St. Stephen's Mission** (© **307/856-7806**). At St. Michael's Mission, in Ethete (5 miles [8km] east of Fort Washakie), there is a museum of Arapaho cultural artifacts. There is also a newly refurbished hot-spring spa on the reservation, **Chief Washakie Plunge** (© **307/332-9106;** between Fort Washakie and Ethete) with a pool, Jacuzzi, and private baths. Call for fees and hours.

Sacajawea, the famed Shoshone scout for the Lewis and Clark expedition, is supposedly buried on a reservation that bears her name, west of Fort Washakie. There is some debate about whether she is buried there, but it's a beautiful cemetery on a hill, and worth a visit (ask for directions in Fort Washakie). You might also stop by nearby **Roberts Mission**—John Roberts was an Episcopal minister who lived most of his life on the reservation and had a tremendous influence on the tribes, founding a school and recording useful historical and anthropological information about the tribes. Chief Washakie, the venerated Shoshone chief, is buried in a cemetery along the Little Wind River on the north side of Fort Washakie. He lived to be over 100 and was buried with full honors by the U.S. Army—the only Indian chief to be so honored.

In late June, American Indians from around the country converge at Fort Washakie for **Shoshone Treaty Days,** a celebration of American Indian tradition and culture. The **Eastern Shoshone Powwow and Indian Days** follow a week later, with one of the West's largest powwows and all-American Indian rodeos, including thrilling bareback relay horse races.

There are hundreds of lakes in the reservation's high country, and in the summer they come alive with trout—browns, cutthroats, brook, and golden. You can purchase a reservation fishing permit at local sporting-goods stores and find your way with maps to Bull Lake and Moccasin Lake by car, or pick up U.S.G.S. topographical maps and head for the high country on foot. Check with the fly-tying experts at **Rocky Mountain Dubbing Company,** 115 Poppy St. (© **307/ 332-2989**) on U.S. 287 just south of Lander, for permits, maps, equipment, and advice. If you want a guided horseback trip, contact **Paradise Outfitters,** Star Route, Box 2815, Kinnear, WY 82516 (© **307/856-2950**).

13

Sheridan & Eastern Wyoming

As you enter Wyoming from the east, the plains begin to roll like ocean swells, rising and falling until they break against the Rockies. As the elevation rises, the grass grows shorter. Rains taper from dependable downpours to sporadic cloudbursts. The wind races across the surface, combing down the grass and sculpting the snow.

Bison once roamed these prairies in enormous herds, and people were few. But the modern era brought rapid change. In the 18th century, Indian bands mounted horses that had escaped from Spanish conquistadors and enjoyed a brief era of prosperity on the plains, hunting buffalo with great skill. Then the white men arrived: trappers searching for beaver pelts, and pioneers who either wanted to settle here or just pass through on their way to Utah, California, or Oregon. But it was the Texas trail drives, moving north, not west, that most shaped the history and culture of eastern Wyoming.

The landscape hasn't changed much since then. There are still widely scattered settlements; a few small, irrigated fields; and lots of grass and cattle. The billboards announce "Welcome to the Cowboy State," but these days it's the coal and oil and gas beneath the prairies that subsidize life

in the wide-open spaces. But the cowboy life is still vibrant, and friendly to visitors: You can see rodeos or join a cattle drive, or just buy a hat and pair of boots and pretend. You can explore the mostly unchanged landscapes where cattle barons and their hired guns battled homesteaders in the Johnson County War, where outlaw Butch Cassidy and the Hole-in-the-Wall gang did their "work," and Indian chiefs Crazy Horse and Red Cloud clashed with the cavalry.

Adventurers come to climb **Devils Tower,** a natural skyscraper of volcanic rock that suddenly rises over 1,000 feet from the flatlands of Eastern Wyoming. Visitors also come to hike and fish in the Bighorn Mountains, a handsome range somewhat overshadowed by the peaks of the Continental Divide farther west.

You can explore this region by interstates—I-25 runs north-south, while I-90 dips down from Montana and then east to Devils Tower—or take small highways like U.S. 18 and Wyo. 59 to reach smaller towns and more remote country. But since Sheridan is often the target of travelers to the area, this chapter begins there, exploring south to Buffalo and then east to Gillette and Devils Tower. Then we backtrack to Casper for a look at Wyoming's second-largest city.

1 Sheridan

144 miles (232km) N of Casper; 130 miles (209km) S of Billings; 156 miles (251km) E of Cody

Sheridan looks right at home on the windblown plains, its deep roots evident in its well-preserved historic downtown. The Bighorn Mountains cast afternoon shadows in this direction, across the ranches in the foothills where "dude" ranching was defined and perfected. One of the largest Wyoming small towns, with 13,900 residents, Sheridan, named after Civil War general Phil Sheridan, retains its small-town charm with century-old buildings along Main Street and the mansions of cattle barons.

The source of prosperity in more recent times lies in the massive coal deposits to the north and east. After decades of production, the big strip mines are in a slow decline, and tourism is on the rise, with an influx of adventurous mountain bikers, rock climbers, paragliders, snowmobilers, and cross-country skiers who are lured by the Bighorns. Ranching these days is less about beef and more about providing saddle time for vacation dudes and retreats for wealthy corporate kings. Or queens—Queen Elizabeth of England, who has distant relations here, stopped by in the 1980s, and like any sensible horsewoman would, she dropped by **Kings Saddlery,** known worldwide for hand-tooled tack and ropes.

ESSENTIALS

GETTING THERE   The **Sheridan County Airport,** just southwest of town on **Airport Road** (take exit 25 off I-90), has daily service from Denver on **United Express** (© **800/241-6522**).

If you drive from Billings, take I-90 south 125 miles (201km) to Sheridan. From Sheridan you can continue south on I-25, sliding along the eastern side of the Bighorn Mountains, 147 miles (237km) to Casper, or drive the full 325 miles (523km) to Cheyenne. From Yellowstone and Cody, follow U.S. 14 across the basin and over the Bighorns, and drop into Ranchester, where you'll take I-25 15 miles (24km) south to Sheridan.

VISITOR INFORMATION   The **Sheridan Convention and Visitors Bureau** (© **800/453-3650** or 307/672-2485; www.sheridanwyoming.org) is located at the State Information Center, off I-90 at exit 23. Across the street is the **Wyoming Game and Fish Visitors Center** (© **307/672-7418**), with interactive displays and information on wildlife habitats, fishing, hunting regulations, and the best places to spot wildlife.

GETTING AROUND   You can rent a car from **Avis** (© **800/831-2847**) or **Enterprise** (© **800/736-8222**) at Sheridan's airport. Or call **Sheridan Taxi** (© **307/674-6814**).

GETTING OUTSIDE

The **Bighorn National Forest** offers some of the best outdoor recreation in the country, with hundreds of miles of marked trails for hiking, mountain biking, cross-country skiing, snowshoeing, and snowmobiling; plus fishing streams and fantastic wildlife-viewing opportunities. For maps and advice, contact the forest headquarters and Tongue Ranger District office, 2013 Eastside 2nd St. (© **307/ 674-2600;** www.fs.fed.us/r2/bighorn).

For advice on local hot spots for hiking, mountain biking, fishing, and camping, plus topographical maps, check with **Big Horn Mountain Sports** ⭐, 334 N. Main St. (© **307/672-6866;** www.bighornmountainsports.com). This extremely well-stocked sporting-goods store sells equipment and supplies, and also rents practically anything you might need for fly-fishing, backpacking, camping, snowshoeing, downhill and cross-country skiing, and snowboarding. Affiliated with the shop is a full-service mountain-bike facility (© **307/ 672-2453**), with sales, repairs, and rentals. Big Horn Mountain Sports also coordinates classes and guided trips through the **Sheridan Recreation Department** (© **307/674-6421**) and **Sheridan College** (© **307/674-6446**).

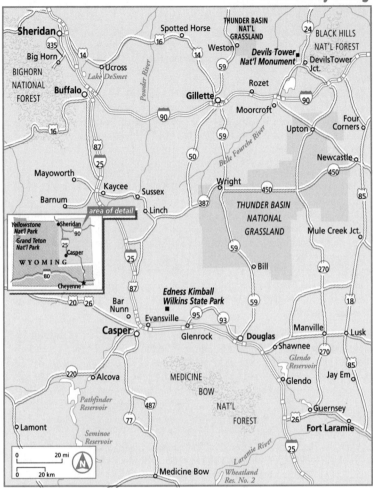

Although visitors are encouraged to participate in these classes, reservations—usually 1 month in advance—are necessary. Call for specific course offerings and dates. Past classes have included instruction in fly-tying, kayaking, cross-country skiing, and rock climbing at nearby Tongue River Canyon.

EQUESTRIAN EVENTS

Polo? In Wyoming? Well, they ride horses, don't they? Introduced by early English cattle barons, the tradition continues with matches every summer weekend (and practice most Wed and Fri evenings) at **Big Horn's Equestrian Center,** south of Sheridan toward the town of Big Horn at 351 Bird Farm Rd. (© **307/ 674-4812;** www.bighornpoloclub.com). Admission to both practices and matches is free (unless a benefit match is scheduled).

FLY-FISHING

The Tongue River is the Bighorns' blue-ribbon stream. There are browns, rainbows, and brook trout up to 20 inches. Inquire at the **Game and Fish Division,**

700 Valley View Dr. (© **307/672-7418**), for local catch limits and licenses. For equipment needs and advice, stop at Big Horn Mountain Sports (see above), and for guided fishing trips, contact the **Fly Shop of the Big Horns,** 227 N. Main St. (© **800/253-5866;** www.troutangler.com).

GOLF
Sheridan offers several 18-hole golf courses with views of the Bighorn Mountains, including the **Sheridan Country Club** (west of Sheridan on W. 5th St.; © **307/674-8135**), with greens fees of $16 and the mandatory cart fee of $8; and the **Kendrick Golf Club** (on Big Goose Rd.; © **307/674-8148**), charging $16 on weekdays and $20 on weekends.

SEEING THE SIGHTS
King's Saddlery and Museum ★   Don King's Main Street emporium is a cowboy's candy store, with an extensive collection of Western tack, and any size, length, and lay of ropes. Wander the shop to see the tools of the modern cowboy, and watch the King brothers hand-tool leather. Then step back in time to their museum, housing one of the largest collections of Indian artifacts and cowboy trappings—including high-back saddles, chaps, Spanish bits, silver spurs, and quirts. Don is often around to chat. Next door is the Kings' **Bozeman Trail Gallery,** 190 N. Main St., which displays Western-subject paintings and sculpture.

184 N. Main St., Sheridan, WY 82801. © **307/672-2702** or 307/672-2755. Fax 307/672-5235. Free admission. Mon–Sat 8am–5pm.

Bradford Brinton Memorial Ranch ★   From a distance, surrounded by cottonwoods and dwarfed by the hills and horizon, the Brinton ranch house doesn't look much different from most other two-story, white wood-frame homes. But the house, as interesting and historic as it is (it dates back to the late 1800s), is not the real reason to visit. Yes, this 20-room residence offers a fine example of how a "gentleman rancher" lived in the early 1900s—the tables are set with china and the shelves filled with gold- and leather-bound volumes—but on the walls hangs a first-class art collection. Here you'll see *Fight on the Little Bighorn* by Frederic Remington, and *When Ropes Go Wrong* by Charles M. Russell. Will James, John Audubon, and a host of other notable Western artists show up in one of the best but least-known Western art collections in the Rockies.

239 Brinton Rd., Big Horn, WY (10 miles [16km] south of Sheridan on U.S. 87). © **307/672-3173.** Fax 307/672-3258. www.bradfordbrintonmemorial.com. $3 adults, $2 seniors and children. May 15–Sept 6 daily 9:30am–5pm.

Trail End State Historic Site   The Kendrick Mansion, the only example of Flemish Revival architecture in Wyoming, sits on 3.8 acres of manicured grounds. John Kendrick, orphaned in Texas, arrived in Wyoming at age 22 on a cattle drive. By 1912 he'd built a 200,000-acre cattle ranch and amassed a net worth of one million dollars. The next year, he completed construction on a home so large it took a ton of coal a day to warm its 20 rooms. He later became Wyoming's governor, then U.S. senator. Visitors today can marvel at materials not common in pioneer Wyoming: silk, mahogany, Italian marble, Georgia pine beams, and a maple floor in the ballroom. Also on the grounds is a carriage house, which serves as a community theater.

400 Clarendon Ave., Sheridan, WY 82801. © **307/674-4589** or 307/672-1729. Fax 307/672-1720. www.trailend.org. $2 adults over 18. June–Aug daily 9am–6pm; off-season call for hr.

The Sheridan Inn   The majestic Sheridan Inn was hailed as the finest hotel between Chicago and San Francisco when it opened in 1893, and visitors today can step back to that time as they explore the restored first floor and get a glimpse of its grandeur on guided tours through the yet-to-be-restored second and third floors. Modeled after Scottish hunting lodges, the hotel had dormer windows for each of the 62 rooms, and three impressive river-rock fireplaces. The back bar was imported from England, and the building boasted the town's first electric lights, running water, and telephone. Buffalo Bill Cody led the grand march for the first dance on opening night, and Cody returned annually to stand on the long veranda auditioning riders for his *Wild West Show.* The Sheridan Inn has hosted a variety of other visiting celebrities and dignitaries, including Calamity Jane, Pres. Theodore Roosevelt, Will Rogers, and Ernest Hemingway. Although it hasn't operated as a hotel since 1965, the Sheridan houses a restaurant—and the handsome and historic bar still serves drinks. Fund-raising is underway for a complete restoration of the hotel that will allow overnight stays.

Broadway and 5th St., Sheridan, WY 82801. ℭ **307/674-5440.** www.sheridaninn.com. $2 self-guided tour of the first floor; $5 guided tour of all 3 floors. May–Sept daily 9am–9pm; rest of year call for hr.

The Ucross Foundation   Retreats for writers, artists, and musicians are not all that common in the West, but Ucross has gained an international reputation by providing a quiet, beautiful setting for seclusion and creativity. This ranchland, 30 miles (48km) east of Sheridan, was once the headquarters of the Pratt and Ferris Cattle Company, established in 1879. Now over half of the 22,000-acre ranch is protected with a conservation easement with The Nature Conservancy. You don't need an artist's residency to stop in and visit **Big Red,** a magnificently restored structure that once served as the main ranch house but today is a showcase of antique furniture; and the **Big Red Gallery,** which every year mounts four exhibits. If you're in the area on the Fourth of July, this is the place to be; more than 4,000 people show up for the fireworks.

30 Big Red Lane, Clearmont, WY 82835. ℭ **307/737-2291.** Fax 307/737-2322. www.ucrossfoundation.org. Free admission. Mon–Fri 8:30am–4pm.

WHERE TO STAY

Piney Creek Inn   Why pay $90 a night for a generic motel room when for $125 you can stay in the "Hideaway" cabin nestled in the trees and warmed by a fireplace and Jacuzzi? Why pay for two motel rooms when a family can easily fit in the "Pine Lodge" cabin with its gnarled-pine spiral staircase leading to the loft bedroom? Both cabins have kitchenettes and gas grills. Owners Vicky and Mel Hoff try to keep their rates low and their service high. They'll connect you with local horse or wagon rides, or point you toward trails to hike. Piney Creek was once one of Wyoming's best-kept secrets, but good news travels fast; be sure to book at least 3 months in advance.

11 Skylark Lane, P.O. Box 456, Story, WY 82842. ℭ **307/683-2911.** www.pineycreekinn.com. 4 units. $85–$150 double. Rates include full breakfast. MC, V. 7 miles (11km) west of I-90 from exit 33 or 44. **Amenities:** Whirlpool.

Spahn's Big Horn Mountain Bed and Breakfast ★★   Spahn's Bighorn Mountain B&B prides itself on being the oldest B&B in Wyoming, and it's certainly one of the best. Picture this: a four-story log cabin surrounded by pines; a common room with a crackling fire, shelves of books, and a piano; and outside, a deck with a 100-mile (161km) view of prairie stretching to the east. The rooms glow with varnished peeled logs, and have such country comforts as patchwork quilts and claw-foot tubs. Nightly wildlife safaris visit Teepee Creek in search of moose, elk, and deer, and kids explore the trail underneath nearby Little Goose Falls. The secluded "Eagle's Nest" guest cabin is perfect for honeymooners. The property is smoke-free.

P.O. Box 579, Big Horn, WY 82833. ℂ 307/674-8150. www.bighorn-wyoming.com. 4 units. $100–$165 double. Rates include full breakfast. MC, V for reservation deposit only; payment by cash or check. 15 miles (24km) southwest of Sheridan via U.S. 87 and Wyo. 335. *In room:* Some fridges, no phone.

Spear Ranch B&B   Pam and Lonnie Wright have restored this beautiful former dude ranch along Little Goose Creek and decorated it with art and antique furniture that gives it the comfortable feel of a well-heeled country estate. Most of the rooms have their own gas fireplaces. The dining- and living-room areas have a formal air, and there is a very informal recreation room in the basement with a huge collection of movies. You can also relax with a cup of tea or coffee in the sun room, or sit on the deck overlooking the creek and listen to the water. The separate cottage is perfect for a large family: It sleeps six and has a complete kitchen and its own TV and VCR. A couple of sweet old dogs will greet you outside if you wander along the creek or the country road that leads to the historic Bradford Brinton Memorial Ranch, discussed above under "Seeing the Sights."

170 Brinton Rd. (P.O. Box 607), Big Horn, WY 82833. ℂ 307/673-0079. www.spearranch.com. 5 units, 2 share bathroom; 1 cottage. $70–$90 double; $150 cottage. No credit cards. **Amenities:** Rec room with exercise equipment. *In room:* No phone.

GUEST RANCHES

HF Bar Ranch ⭐ *Kids*   With reasonable rates and plenty of activities for children, the HF Bar Ranch really caters to families—nannies are encouraged to come along at no extra charge (but are allowed only limited activities). This hospitable ranch is a real hoedown of old-fashioned fun, with weekly hayrides and square dances. Ice is delivered daily to a wooden box on each of the cabin's front porches, and hearty family-style meals are served in the main lodge. Guests can take daily trail rides or arrange a pack trip to the remote and rustic "mountain camp" 15 miles (24km) into the Bighorns. You can also ride your own horse if you have one. The sportsman (or woman) of the group can fish the miles of stream banks, shoot on one of the five sporting-clay courses, or hunt pheasant and chukar on a private bird reserve. In fall, the ranch outfits hunts for elk and deer.

Shell Creek Rd., Saddlestring, WY 82840. ℂ 307/684-2487. www.hfbar.com.com. Reservations required at least 6–12 months in advance. 29 cabins. $175 per person per day. Mid-June to mid-Sept, 1-week min. stay required. Rates include all meals and ranch activities. Round-trip transfers from Sheridan airport can be arranged for an additional $10 per person. No credit cards. Take I-90 35 miles (56km) south of Sheridan to exit 47. Turn west on Shell Creek Rd. for 7 miles (11km) to ranch. **Amenities:** Dining room; activities desk; babysitting. *In room:* No phone.

Paradise Guest Ranch   Aptly named, this dude ranch 45 miles (72km) south of Sheridan adds modern conveniences to the ambience and activities you expect on a ranch. The log cabins not only have decks with views of the surrounding valley, mountains, or streams, but also come equipped with their own washers and dryers. As with most resort ranches in the West, several trail rides depart daily for guests of all levels of ability. And if you're riding all day, you can get a chuck-wagon dinner. There are ample after-dark activities for the entire family, with evening entertainment in the ranch's French Creek Saloon and recreation center.

Box 790, Buffalo, WY 82834. ℂ 307/684-7876. www.paradiseranch.com. 18 cabins. $1,830–$2,750 double per week, depending on season. Rates include all meals and ranch activities and round-trip transportation to the Sheridan airport. No credit cards. Closed Nov to mid-May. **Amenities:** Dining room; lounge. *In room:* Kitchenette, fireplace, washer and dryer.

CAMPING

The **Sheridan/Bighorn Mountain KOA Campground,** 63 Decker Rd., Box 35A, Sheridan, WY 82801 (℃ **800/562-7621** for reservations, or 307/674-8766), one-half mile (1km) north of Sheridan at the Port of Entry exit, offers quiet and shady tent and RV sites, plus all the usual commercial campground amenities, including an outdoor swimming pool and miniature golf. The campground is open from May to early October, with rates from $18 to $27. For those who prefer roughing it, the **Bureau of Land Management** has several primitive campgrounds in the area, with sites costing $5 per night. Contact the Sheridan office (see "Getting Outside," above) for information.

WHERE TO DINE

Golden Steer STEAKS/SEAFOOD/MEXICAN   Ask around, and the locals point to the north end of town, to the Golden Steer steakhouse. And we agree. If you crave a big T-bone or sirloin (grilled, charbroiled, or however you want it), or a plateful of fried shrimp, this place will satiate your needs. At lunchtime the Golden Steer specializes in homemade Mexican food—try the burrito smothered in green chile sauce. The large dining room has Western decor and a family-friendly feel. On Saturday nights there's usually live music.

2071 N. Main St. ℃ 307/674-9334. Lunch $4–$8; dinner $10–$20. AE, DISC, MC, V. Lunch Mon–Thurs 11am–2pm and 4–9pm; Fri 11am–2pm and 4–10pm; Sat 4–10pm; Sun 4–8:30pm.

Sanford's Grub & Pub CAJUN   The maze of rooms at Sanford's, located in a 1907 historic building, is decorated like the dorm room of a junkman's son: Televisions, beer signs, and license plates are crammed to the rafters. You might even say the same about the dinner menu, which leans toward Cajun dishes, with really good jambalaya and Cajun-flavored burgers and steaks—try the New York strip Cajun-style. But the restaurant also has a whole lot of other things, including some items, like fried okra, that you wouldn't expect to see above the Mason-Dixon line. Sanford's is a good spot for beer drinkers, with a seemingly unlimited selection of bottled beers, plus the restaurant's own Cloud's Peak Raspberry Wheat, a stout, and two amber ales.

1 E. Alger St. (at N. Main St.). ℃ 307/674-1722. Reservations not accepted. Lunch $5–$9; dinner $10–$19. AE, DC, DISC, MC, V. Daily 11am–10pm.

SHERIDAN AFTER DARK

WYO Theater   The WYO is a model for other old theaters in the West. It was a broken-down movie palace facing the wrecking ball when locals stepped in and saved it, restoring the proscenium and reviving live entertainment in Sheridan. Classical music, local choral groups, touring dance companies, and popular performers like Michael Martin Murphey and Baxter Black fill the house. 42 N. Main St. (P.O. Box 528), Sheridan, WY 82801. ℃ 307/672-9084. www.wyotheater.com. Tickets $5–$20. MC, V. Performances at various times.

2 Buffalo

35 miles (56km) S of Sheridan; 182 miles (293km) E of Cody

Though Sheridan remains the busy hub of this Wyoming region, it is surrounded by interesting little towns like Dayton, Story, and Ranchester, plus one big enough to deserve its own slot: Buffalo. A short drive south of Sheridan on I-90, this old ranching town is near the site of the infamous Johnson County War (between cattle- and sheepmen), and not far from the Hole-in-the-Wall country favored by Butch, Sundance, and other outlaws.

Though this was a favorite area of Indian bison hunters, it was not named for a shaggy beast: The original settlers drew names from a hat, and the winner had written his New York hometown.

The historic downtown area is compact enough to explore on foot. Follow the **Clear Creek Centennial Trail** on a wheelchair-accessible path from downtown to a pleasant grassy area where it joins a 3-mile (5km) unsurfaced road to the base of the Bighorn Mountains. Maps are available from the **Buffalo Chamber of Commerce,** 55 N. Main St., Buffalo, WY 82834 (© 800/227-5122 or 307/684-5544). You'll see the old **Occidental Hotel** at 10 N. Main, possibly a model for a hotel in Owen Wister's *The Virginian,* and now the site of concerts and other community activities. At the excellent **Jim Gatchell Museum,** 100 Fort St., you'll find American Indian artifacts like arrowheads and medicine rattles, as well as cavalry items and the bridle Tom Horn braided while awaiting execution. Open from 8am to 8pm from mid-May to mid-October; $4 adults, free for kids.

Buffalo lies on the route of the Bozeman Trail, a 19th-century shortcut to the gold country of Montana that cut right through the hunting grounds of several resentful tribes. The U.S. Army built forts to protect travelers, and engaged in skirmishes with the resident Sioux, Cheyenne, and Arapaho. The largest fort was **Fort Phil Kearny** (exit 44 off I-90; © 307/684-7629), where soldiers endured repeated raids by hostile Indians. Though the original fort is gone, the site today is a national historic site with a visitor center and tours of two major battle sites nearby: the 1866 Fetterman Massacre, in which Crazy Horse and his band overwhelmed a small army contingent; and the Wagon Box Fight, which went the other way. The visitor center is open from 6am to 8pm Monday through Saturday from June to Labor Day; shorter hours the rest of the year; with a $1 admission.

Robert LeRoy Parker (Butch Cassidy) and his partner, Harry Longabaugh (Sundance Kid), assembled their infamous group of bandits known as the Wild Bunch to rob trains and banks, and steal herds of horses and cattle. One of their favorite places to hide was the **Hole-in-the-Wall,** a red-rock canyon area above the Middle Fork of the Powder River. The Hole-in-the-Wall is located about 45 miles (72km) south of Buffalo near the town of Kaycee. Take I-25 south from Kaycee to the Triple T Road exit, continue south 14 miles (23km) to County Road 111, then go west 18 miles (29km) to County Road 105, then north 8 miles (13km) to the U.S. Bureau of Land Management directional sign for Hole-in-the-Wall. It's a 3-mile (5km) hike into the actual site. The Hole itself is no more than a notch in a butte, disappointing to folks used to Disney-like re-creations of outlaw hideouts. But for the intrepid on horse or in four-wheel-drive vehicles, you can explore the spacious **Outlaw Cave.** There are tepee rings in the surrounding area and large pictographs and stenciled handprints under a rock overhang.

Note: Most of this area is private land. Be sure to check with the U.S. Bureau of Land Management office in Buffalo (© 307/684-1100) before exploring on your own.

Range Wars

The Johnson County War was a struggle between immigrant homesteaders and the cattle barons over the open range. One of the skirmishes in that struggle took place at the **TA Ranch**—ask to see the bullet holes—which now hosts guests (Box 313, Buffalo, WY 82834; © 307/684-5833; www.taranch.com; 13 rooms, $150 per person). The ranch is located 13 miles (21km) south of Buffalo on U.S. 87.

Just a few miles northwest of Buffalo along I-90 is **Lake De Smet,** an excellent fishing and boating destination, with opportunities for picnicking and camping.

3 Gillette

103 miles (166km) E of Sheridan; 243 miles (391km) E of Billings

Gillette is "Energy Capital of the World," boasts the local Convention and Visitors Bureau, "where just a century ago it was a frontier land with open ranges." Out on what used to be open range, you can now see several massive surface coal mines, like the RAG Coal West–Eagle Butte Mine. The mine, which opened in 1978, shipped its 250th million ton of coal on April 15, 1998. The huge coal mines, along with recently discovered coalbed methane gas, have made Gillette a prosperous community, which means that this is a very pleasant place to live (or visit), with a variety of modern facilities, including a first-class swimming pool and water park. There is still plenty of undeveloped plains habitat, too, particularly in the 1.8-million-acre **Thunder Basin National Grassland.** Anyone who likes geological wonders, and anyone who enjoyed *Close Encounters of the Third Kind,* will want to visit the nearby **Devils Tower** (see section 4, "Devils Tower National Monument," below).

ESSENTIALS

GETTING THERE   United Express (© 800/241-6522) offers daily commuter flights to the Gillette Airport, off U.S. 14/16.

By road, Gillette is 103 miles (166km) east of Sheridan via I-90 and 61 miles (98km) from Devils Tower National Monument.

VISITOR INFORMATION   Contact the **Gillette Convention and Visitors Bureau,** 1810 S. Douglas Hwy., Gillette, WY 82718 (© **800/544-6136** or 307/686-0040; www.visitgillette.net or www.gillettewyoming.net). Ask for the brochure *Campbell County Natural History Loop Tours,* which presents a brief history of the area and outlines two loop tours through areas populated by deer, pronghorn, turkeys, and other wildlife.

GETTING AROUND   You can rent cars from **Avis** (© **307/672-2226**), **Hertz** (© **307/686-0550**), or **Enterprise** (© **307/686-5655**); or get a taxi from **City Cab** (© **307/685-1000**).

GETTING OUTSIDE

Golf addicts can get their fix at either the **Gillette Country Club,** 1800 Country Club Rd. (© **307/682-4774**), or the **Bell Nob Golf Course,** 1316 Overdale (© **307/686-7069**). The country club has a nine-hole course; Bell Nob has 18.

Bird-watchers will enjoy the waterfowl of **McManamen Park,** near the corner of Gurley Street and Warlow Drive. **Hunters** are drawn here to bag elk, mule deer, pronghorn, and upland birds. Numerous hunting guides operate in the Gillette area; contact the Convention and Visitors Bureau (see "Visitor Information," above) for assistance in finding one.

SEEING THE SIGHTS

If you are impressed by big holes and big machinery, you've come to the right place. The RAG Coal West–Eagle Butte Mine has an impressive overlook near mile marker 100 on U.S. 14/16, about 1 mile (1.5km) north of Gillette's airport. The mine company and the Gillette Convention and Visitors Bureau jointly sponsor **free summer tours** to the mine site, where you can see the massive equipment used to extract the coal. Tours take place June through August, Monday through Friday, at 9 and 11am. Reservations should be made by calling ✆ **800/544-6136** or 307/686-0040.

The **Campbell County Rockpile Museum** 🐾, 900 W. 2nd St. (✆ **307/ 682-5723**), is the place to go to learn something about the history of this area. Displays include artifacts of the area's past such as saddles, rifles, arrowheads, and the like, but we prefer the big stuff—antique vehicles, including several Ford Model Ts, and a wagon collection that includes a horse-drawn hearse and an old sheep wagon. Kids like the vintage tractors they can climb on, as well as the other hands-on displays, including one that helps children identify the area's animals. There's also a "Grandma's Attic" section, where kids can dress up in historic (and funny-looking) fashions from days gone by. Adjacent to the museum building is a historic schoolhouse, completely furnished, that dates to the early 1900s; and a furnished homesteader's cabin from the same era. Both of these buildings were relocated to the museum grounds from other parts of the county. Finally, for those who like firecrackers—we mean really, really big firecrackers— don't miss the 10-minute big-screen video on coal mining that shows what dynamite can really do! Admission to the museum is free. May through September it's open Monday through Saturday from 9am to 8pm and Sunday from 12:30 to 6:30pm; the rest of the year it's open Monday through Saturday from 9am to 5pm.

The **CAM-PLEX,** a massive event pavilion, has been the host in recent years of the National High School Rodeo Finals, as well as an array of other exciting events. Call ✆ **800/358-1897** or 307/682-8802 to find out what's scheduled.

WHERE TO STAY & DINE

Lodging rates in Gillette are highest in summer, and sometimes as much as a third less at other times. The largest lodging property in town is the **Best Western Tower West Lodge,** 109 N. U.S. 14/16, Gillette, WY 82716 (✆ **800/ 762-7375** or 307/686-2210), which charges $60 to $110 double. The **Clarion Western Plaza,** 2009 S. Douglas Hwy., Gillette, WY 82718 (✆ **307/ 686-3000**), charges $59 to $85 double; and **Days Inn,** 910 E. Boxelder Rd., Gillette, WY 82718 (✆ **800/329-7666** or 307/682-39990, has rates for two of $60 to $120. Campers will want to head to the **Green Tree's Crazy Woman Campground**—how can you pass up a place with a name like that?—located on U.S. 14/16 off I-90 exit 124 (✆ **307/682-3665**), which rents shady sites for tents and RVs for $15 to $30, and is open from mid-April to late October.

Among restaurants we like in Gillette are **The Prime Rib Restaurant & Steakhouse,** 1205 S. Douglas Hwy. (✆ **307/682-2944**), an upscale steak and seafood place where you can get tender, slow-roasted prime rib, charbroiled filets, sautéed halibut, and shrimp scampi, among other items. Lunch prices are in the $5 to $10 range, and most dinner entrees cost $8 to $21. The restaurant is open Monday through Friday from 11am to 10pm, Saturday and Sunday from 4 to 10pm. We also recommend **Bailey's Bar & Grill,** 301 S. Gillette Ave. (✆ **307/686-7678**). It's located in the restored 1935 Gillette Post Office building and resembles an old Irish pub. Bailey's offers good burgers, steaks, seafood, and pasta (and especially good homemade pies) in a casual atmosphere, with lunches from $4 to $9 and dinners from $7 to $16. It's open Monday through Saturday from 10am to 9pm (usually closed Sat in winter).

4 Devils Tower National Monument ✸

62 miles (100km) NE of Gillette; 230 miles (370km) SE of Billings; 110 miles (177km) W of Rapid City, South Dakota

Once upon a time, so the Kiowa legend goes, seven sisters were playing with their brother when he suddenly turned into a bear. Fleeing, the girls scrambled onto a small rock and prayed. The rock started to grow, pushing them into the sky. While the bear clawed at the rock's sides, trying to get at the girls, the rock thrust them so high that they became the points of the Big Dipper. The 1,267-foot-tall rock became named (in various spellings) Mato Tipila, or "Bear Lodge." The site is sacred to the Sioux and other tribes of the northern plains.

Col. Richard I. Dodge, who commanded a military escort to a U.S. Geological Survey party that visited the Black Hills in 1875, is credited with giving the formation its current name. In his book *The Black Hills,* written the year after his journey, Dodge described Devils Tower as "one of the most remarkable peaks in this or any other country." In 1906, Congress declared it the nation's first national monument. The tower was further popularized in the 1977 movie *Close Encounters of the Third Kind.*

While the 60-million-year-old tower itself is composed of hard igneous rock, much of the remaining exposed rock within the 1,347-acre monument is composed of soft sediments from the warm, shallow seas of the Mesozoic era. These colorful bands of rock encircling the igneous core include layers of sandstone, shale, mudstone, siltstone, gypsum, and limestone.

Any visitor will understand immediately the allure of this striated column of volcanic rock. It's especially evocative in the evening—as darkness shrouds the surrounding hills, Devils Tower stands above the horizon, glowing amber.

ESSENTIALS

GETTING THERE   From Gillette, take I-90 east to Moorcroft (exit 154) and follow signs to Devils Tower; from Jackson, take U.S. 26/287 to Riverton, then U.S. 26 to Casper, then I-90 through Gillette to Moorcroft (see above); from Sheridan, take I-90 to Gillette, then see above.

VISITOR INFORMATION   Contact **Devils Tower National Monument,** P.O. Box 10, Devils Tower, WY 82714-0010 (© **307/467-5283;** www.nps. gov/deto). The **Devils Tower Natural History Association,** P.O. Box 37, Devils Tower, WY 87214-0037 (© **307/467-5283**), operates a bookstore at the monument's Visitor Center and offers a variety of publications.

VISITOR CENTER   Open from early April to late November only, the Visitor Center is located 3 miles (5km) from the monument's entrance, with exhibits about the tower's history and geology.

FEES & REGULATIONS   There is an entrance fee of $8 per vehicle or $3 per person on foot, motorcycle, or bike. Disturbing any wildlife or gathering items such as rocks or flowers is prohibited. Especially do not feed, chase, or disturb prairie dogs; they bite and may carry diseases. Abandoned prairie-dog holes are often homes to black widow spiders and rattlesnakes. Also see "Climbing the Tower," below.

SEEING THE MONUMENT

It's easy to experience much of what Devils Tower has to offer in less than a day. Rangers recommend that you allow 2 to 4 hours to walk a trail, stop at the visitor center, and view the prairie dogs.

Impressions

"A dark mist lay over the Black Hills, and the land was like iron. At the top of the ridge I caught sight of Devils Tower upthrust against the gray sky as if in the birth of time the core of the earth had broken through its crust and the motion of the world was begun. There are things in nature that engender an awful quiet in the heart of man; Devils Tower is one of them."

—N. Scott Momaday, author of *House Made of Dawn*

Surrounded by ponderosa pines and bathed in blue sky, the towering rock obelisk is visible for miles, and it's easy to imagine the reaction of the first lonely American Indian scouts and French fur trappers who stumbled upon this stunning geologic anomaly a few centuries ago. The paved 1⅗-mile round-trip (2km) **Tower Trail,** rated easy, goes all the way around the formation, offering close-up views of the tower on fairly level ground. Wayside exhibits tell the Devils Tower story.

Home to the feisty black-tailed **prairie dog,** the grounds of Devils Tower National Monument are perfect for picnicking and viewing wildlife. You can watch the sociable prairie dogs in their colony, or "town," just inside the park's east entrance station. The critters excavate elaborate networks of underground passageways, then guard their burrows with warning "barks" when predators such as hawks, eagles, bullsnakes, coyote, red fox, and mink come too close. Walk the leisurely ⅗-mile round-trip (1km) **Valley View Trail** to see a prairie-dog town, or savor a picnic lunch among the wildflowers at the monument's picnic area on the banks of the sleepy Belle Fourche River.

CLIMBING THE TOWER

Climbers have been wedging their fingers in the tower's cracks for more than a century, at a rate in recent years of about 5,000 climbers annually. Climbers must register with a ranger before starting their climb and on their return, but otherwise there are no permits or requirements for climbing the tower. Be prepared for sudden storms; carry rain gear and a flashlight. Rockfall is common, so climbing helmets are advised. Ask a ranger for additional safety and climbing information. A voluntary climbing ban is observed each June out of respect for American Indian religious ceremonies that are planned on Devils Tower at that time.

CAMPING   Located a mile from the monument's headquarters, **Belle Fourche Campground** is open April through October. Its 30 sites accommodate RVs (up to 35 ft. long) and tents on a first-come, first-served basis. Each campsite has a cooking grill, table, and nearby drinking water. There are no showers, RV hookups, or dump stations. Sites costs $12 per night, and there are three group sites, which cost $2 per person per night, with a six-person minimum. The adjacent Valley View Trail skirts a giant prairie-dog town, and the campground's amphitheater offers excellent interpretive ranger programs.

Those looking for a commercial campground with RV hookups, hot showers, and all the usual amenities will find the **Devils Tower KOA,** P.O. Box 100, Devils Tower, WY 82714 (© **800/KOA-5785** or 307/467-5395; www.devils towerkoa.com), just outside the monument entrance. Open May through September, it offers 56 campsites and 11 camping cabins (which share the bathhouse and other campground facilities). Rates for two adults are $24 to $28 in hookup sites, $19 for tents, and $50 for cabins. Amenities include a heated swimming pool, self-service laundry, game room, cafe, two interesting gift shops, horseback rides, hayrides, and a nightly showing of *Close Encounters of the Third Kind,* filmed at Devils Tower.

5 Casper

153 miles (246km) S of Sheridan; 178 miles (287km) NW of Cheyenne; 300 miles (483km) S of Billings; 240 miles (386km) NW of Denver

Casper is a pleasant little city between the Great Plains and Rocky Mountains that owes much of its success to the oil and gas industry. Its first oil refinery was built in 1895, and though, like most boom towns Casper has had its share of ups and downs, the petroleum industry continues to help the economy keep rolling along. But what keeps many residents here, and what makes the community of interest to many visitors, is not what's under the ground but what is on the ground.

Casper has a small but fun ski area, and there is a lot of wildlife in the vicinity, including more than 75% of the world's pronghorn. Also look for mule and white-tailed deer, fox, and a variety of birds. The North Platte River, which meanders through the city, is a premier year-round trout fishery.

This is also an ideal spot to see the real history of the West. Casper stands at the crossroads of westward expansion, and you stand in the ruts of the Oregon, Mormon, and Pony Express Trails. Fur traders stopped here in 1812 on their way back East, building a hovel from rocks and buffalo hides, perhaps the first building constructed by non-Indians in Wyoming. Later, pioneers and Mormons crossed the North Platte River here. Then came the oil miners, and Casper boomed.

Today, Casper is the second-largest city in the state, with almost 50,000 residents. It was also the hometown of United States Vice President Dick Cheney and his wife, Lynn.

ESSENTIALS

GETTING THERE   Casper's **Natrona County International Airport,** 8500 Airport Pkwy. (© **307/472-6688**), 12 miles (19km) northwest of Casper on U.S. 20/26, provides daily service on **Skywest** (© **800/453-9417**) from Salt Lake City, and **United Express** (© **800/241-6522**) from Denver.

To reach Casper from **Sheridan,** drive 153 miles (246km) south on I-25. From **Cheyenne,** take I-25 north for 180 miles (290km). From **Jackson,** take U.S. 191 to the Moran Junction, then drive 255 miles (410km) east on U.S. 26/287.

VISITOR INFORMATION   The visitor center, 500 N. Center St., is open from Memorial Day to Labor Day, weekdays from 8am to 6pm, weekends from 9am to 5pm; the rest of the year it's open weekdays from 8am to 5pm. For printed information on this area, contact the **Casper Area Convention and Visitors Bureau,** P.O. Box 399, Casper, WY 82602 (© **800/852-1889** or 307/ 234-5362; www.casperwyoming.org/visitors).

GETTING AROUND   Rent a car with **Avis** (© 800/331-1212), **Budget** (© 800/527-0700), **Enterprise** (© 800/736-8222), or **Hertz** (© 800/ 654-3131) at the airport. Need a cab? Call **RC Cab** (© 307/235-5203) or **Tom's Taxi** (© 307/237-8178).

SPECIAL EVENTS   Casper draws its largest crowds during the 5-day **Central Wyoming Fair and Rodeo,** which takes place each summer in mid-July. Call © **307/235-5775** for details. On the third weekend of July each year, the

Beartrap Summer Festival (© 307/235-9311; www.beartrapfestival.com) takes place on top of Casper Mountain, with blues and bluegrass musicians plus the Wyoming Symphony Orchestra.

GETTING OUTSIDE

To escape the heat of the summer or ski a few runs in the winter, head up **Casper Mountain,** being sure to stop at the pullouts to take in the view of the plains stretching north toward the Bighorn Mountains. The mountain rises 8,000 feet above sea level, and there are campgrounds, hiking trails (try Garden Creek Falls), ski tracks, groomed snowmobile tracks, and mountain-biking trails. Another popular destination for outdoor recreation is **Muddy Mountain.** Much of the public land here is under the jurisdiction of the **Bureau of Land Management,** 2987 Prospector Dr., Casper, WY 82604 (© 307/261-7600). The office has maps and other information available, and is open Monday through Friday from 7:30am to 4:30pm. Another good source for information, as well as equipment sales and rentals of cross-country skis and snowshoes, is **Backcountry Mountain Works,** 4120 S. Poplar St., at Sunrise Center (© 307/234-5330). At **Mountain Sports,** 543 S. Center St. (© 800/ 426-1136 or 307/266-1136), you'll find winter and summer outdoor equipment (including camping supplies), plus rentals of skis in the winter and mountain bikes in the summer.

There are some great hiking opportunities on Casper Mountain, including the **Braille Trail,** which enables visually impaired visitors to enjoy the beauty of Beartrap Meadow, with interpretive Braille markers describing the area's ecology. The **Casper Area Convention and Visitors Bureau** (see "Visitor Information," above) can help you with maps detailing this and other hiking trails.

Edness Kimball Wilkins State Park (© 307/577-5150) is a pleasant day-use park just 6 miles (10km) east of Casper off I-25, where you'll find huge old cottonwoods over the North Platte River. The park has hard-surfaced walking paths, a canoe- and raft-launch ramp, a swimming area, picnic tables, a playground, a handicapped-accessible fishing pier, and excellent bird-watching opportunities for species including cormorants, yellow-billed cuckoos, golden and bald eagles, and numerous ducks. The park is open daily from 7am to 10pm; admission costs $3 per vehicle.

SKIING

A cheerful little ski area is a big plus in an area of sometimes howling winters, and Casper has a fine one in the **Hogadon Ski Area** ★ (© 307/235-8499), situated atop Casper Mountain (drive south on Wyo. 258 from I-25 to Casper Mountain Rd.). It has a 600-foot vertical rise to a top elevation of 8,000 feet. Two double chairs and a Poma lift cover its 60 acres of groomed trails, and there are also onsite equipment rentals, a snack bar, and a ski and snowboarding school. A series of cross-country ski trails (tickets $5 per person) is groomed for skating and track skiing. The ski area generally opens around the first of December and closes sometime in April. Lift tickets are $23 for adults, $19 for students, and $15 for children. During ski season, Hogadon is open Thursday through Sunday, plus holidays (except Christmas Day), from 9am to 4pm.

SEEING THE SIGHTS

A new historic attraction, the **National Historic Trails Interpretive Center,** is scheduled to open in Casper in 2002, using state-of-the-art exhibits to give us modern travelers an idea of what life on the "road" was like to the emigrants who passed through here in the mid-1800s on the Oregon, Mormon, California, and Pony Express Trails. Get current information on the center from the Casper Area Convention and Visitors Bureau (see "Visitor Information," above). Those interested in the history of Casper should check with **Painted Past Enterprises** (© **307/265-6890**), which presents living-history walking tours of Casper 4 nights each week during the summer. Call for current rates and reservations.

Fort Caspar Museum and Historic Site   Come to Fort Caspar for a look at what the "good old days" in these parts were really like. The first occupation of this site was in 1847 when Brigham Young and the Mormon Pioneer party constructed a ferry to cross the North Platte River. In 1859 Louis Guinard built a toll bridge and trading post at the site. The post also served as a relay station for the Pony Express, and the transcontinental telegraph crossed the river on the Guinard Bridge. The U.S. army occupied the site in 1862, naming the post Platte Bridge Station. While attempting to reach an army supply train on July 26, 1865, Lt. Caspar W. Collins and troops from the fort were attacked by members of the Sioux and Cheyenne tribes. Collins and four other soldiers were killed during the Battle of Platte Bridge, and the fort was renamed Fort Caspar to honor the lieutenant. Later that same day at the Battle of Red Buttes, the army supply train was attacked and 22 of the 25 soldiers were killed. There are no records available to indicate Sioux and Cheyenne losses during the two battles.

Today the site includes the reconstructed fort buildings furnished as they would have appeared in 1865—the mess hall, telegraph hall, officers' quarters, store, blacksmith shop, stables, commissary, and the like. There's also a modern museum featuring exhibits on the social and natural history of central Wyoming, including displays on westward migration, a Plains Indian diorama, and weapons and other artifacts excavated from the fort. On the grounds there's a native plant exhibit, and during the summer there are living-history programs and lectures.

4001 Fort Caspar Rd. © **307/235-8462.** www.fortcasparwyoming.com. Free admission. Summer Mon–Sat 8am–7pm, Sun noon–7pm; winter Mon–Fri 8am–5pm, Sun 1–4pm. The museum is open year-round, but the fort buildings are open May–Sept only.

Nicolaysen Art Museum and Discovery Center   This attractive facility presents changing exhibitions of works by national and regional artists, with an emphasis on art by Western artists or with a Rocky Mountain West theme. There's one large and six small galleries, and three exhibitions take place simultaneously, for a total of a dozen different shows each year. Works range from traditional Western to contemporary. The Discovery Center is a hands-on self-guided studio with about a dozen stations, some often related to the current exhibits, where participants of all ages can create their own art. The Nicolaysen also hosts lecture programs and other activities (call for the current schedule), and has a gift shop.

400 E. Collins Dr. (Collins and Kimball). © **307/235-5247.** $2 adults, $1 children under 12. Free admission Thurs 5–8pm. Tues–Wed 10am–5pm; Thurs 10am–8pm; Fri–Sat 10am–5pm; Sun noon–4pm.

(Fun Fact   **Historical Footnote**

Both the city of Casper and Fort Caspar Museum and Historic Site were named for Lt. Caspar W. Collins, who was killed in an Indian attack here in 1865. However, it's the city and not the fort that is misspelled. Most of the army post communications were misspelled and the city picked up the incorrect spelling when it incorporated in 1889.

(*Moments* Time Travel

Historic Trails West, P.O. Box 428, Mills, WY 82644 (© 307/266-4868; fax 307/266-2746; www.historictrailswest.com), organizes trips that take you back in time as you rattle in a wagon, or sway in the saddle, along the Oregon, California, Pony Express, and Mormon Trails. Trips range in length from 3 hours ($35 adults, $25 children 10 and under) to all day ($85 adults, $65 children 10 and under), which includes lunch. Prices are slightly higher for those who opt to ride horses instead of sitting in the wagons. There are also overnight and multiday wagon-train trips, plus a 6-day working cattle drive, at $1,495, which includes horse, saddle, and all meals. Trips are scheduled May through October.

Tate Mineralogical Museum   You like rocks? If so, this is the place to come. You can see a vast collection of Wyoming jade, a variety of minerals, and meteorites here. The Tate also has a section on dinosaur excavations from the Natrona County area, including a T. Rex skull, and the leg and skull of a brontosaurus. There's also an interactive computerized weather station, plus "please touch" exhibits of fossils and minerals.

Tate Earth Science Center, Casper College, 124 College Dr. © 307/268-2447. Free admission. Mon–Fri 9am–5pm; Sat 10am–4pm.

Casper Planetarium   This planetarium offers a multimedia jaunt into space, with changing programs ranging from a basic exploration of the night sky to trips through the solar system. There are also other astronomy-related programs, such as one on the possibility of life beyond earth; plus special kids' programs. The planetarium also offers telescope-user workshops, instruction on how to build your own rocket, and lectures. There are hands-on science displays and exhibits of meteorites and tektites, plus a gift shop.

904 N. Poplar. © 307/577-0310. $2.50 per person per program. Summer showings daily at 4, 7, and 8pm; and Thurs 2pm. Winter each Thurs and the first 3 Sat of each month, 7pm. Call for additional holiday programs.

WHERE TO STAY

In addition to the lodging properties discussed below, reliable chains in Casper include the **Best Western Casper,** 2325 E. Yellowstone Hwy., Casper, WY 82609 (© 800/675-4242 or 397/234-3541), which charges $49 to $89 double; the **Days Inn,** 301 E. "E" St., Casper, WY 82601 (© 800/329-7666 or 307/234-1159), with rates for two of $60 to $75; the attractive **Holiday Inn,** 300 W. "F" St., Casper, WY 82601 (© 800/465-4329 or 307/235-2531), with rates for two of $85 to $129; and the **Super 8,** 3838 Cy Ave., Casper, WY 82604 (© 800/800-8000 or 307/266-3480), with rates for two of $55 to $75. Those on a strict budget might check out the independent **Royal Inn,** 440 E. "A" St., Casper, WY 82602 (© 877/234-3501 or 307/234-3501), which offers basic lodging at rock-bottom prices: $30 to $35 double for standard rooms and $35 to $45 double with kitchenette.

Hotel Higgins ⟨★⟩   Built by area oil tycoon John Higgins in 1916, the Hotel Higgins is a small historic hotel—listed on the National Register of Historic Places—that is plain on the outside but beautiful within, and a wonderful place to soak up the post-Victorian ambience of the early-20th-century American West. It has mahogany and oak woodwork with distinctive decorative touches that include alabaster chandeliers, beveled glass doors, and terrazzo tile floors. Standard rooms are somewhat small by today's standards (as is the case in most historic hotels), decorated with antiques, including some original pieces from the hotel. The brass, iron, or massive wooden beds have attractive chenille bedspreads, and dressers are oak or walnut. The excellent Paisley Shawl restaurant is one of the best places to eat in the Casper area (see "Where to Dine," below).

416 W. Birch St. (P.O. Box 741), Glenrock, WY 82637. © 800/458-0144 or 307/436-9212. www.hotel higgins.com. 9 units, 2 suites. $70 double; $80 suite. Rates include full breakfast. DC, DISC, MC, V. From Casper, take I-25 east for 20 miles (32km) to the first Glenrock exit. **Amenities:** Restaurant, lounge. *In room:* TV, no phone.

Parkway Plaza Hotel and Convention Centre This sprawling hotel is a friendly and busy place, with all the amenities you'd expect of a major convention center and 25,000 square feet of meeting space. There are a variety of units here, ranging from luxurious suites and mini-suites to spacious standard rooms and some smaller units. All have attractive modern American hotel decor—pleasant but somewhat nondescript—and some of the older, smaller rooms are set way back from the lobby, and therefore a healthy walk. Some units have kitchenettes. Pets are accepted with a deposit.

123 W. "E" St. (P.O. Box 823), Casper, WY 82602. © 307/235-1777. Fax 307/235-8068. 279 units. $55 single, $5 for each additional person. AE, DC, DISC, MC, V. **Amenities:** 2 restaurants, lounge; outdoor heated pool; weight room; spa; Jacuzzi; airport shuttle; salon. *In room:* A/C, TV, dataport, kitchenette (some).

WHERE TO DINE

In addition to the restaurants discussed below, you can get a good burger or traditional American breakfast at a reasonable price at **Granny's,** 1705 E. 2nd St. (© 307/234-4204), a '50's-style diner open daily from 6:30am to 9pm (10pm Fri and Sat). Another restaurant we like is the **Elk Horn Canyon Café and General Store,** 8455 Casper Mountain Rd. (© 307/473-8707), which offers a limited menu but excellent food, and has a great location adjacent to the national forest. Summer hours are Wednesday through Saturday from 11am to 9pm and Sunday from 8am to 5pm; call for hours at other times.

Bosco's Italian Restaurant ITALIAN   Other than cowboy cooking—translate that as beef, beef, and more beef—the only cuisine that seems to shine throughout Wyoming is Italian. This friendly little restaurant is no exception. It serves excellent food, and stays open as long as the customers keep coming (usually about 10pm). The scampi is excellent, or you can create your own fettuccini dish from ingredients such as fresh vegetables, lamb, smoked salmon, and shrimp.

847 E. "A" St. © 307/265-9658. Lunch items $5–$9; dinner entrees $8–$21. AE, DC, DISC, MC, V. Tues–Fri 11am–2pm and 5pm–close; Sat 5pm–close.

The Paisley Shawl ★★ CONTINENTAL   This is the area's best fine-dining establishment. Located inside the historic Hotel Higgins, 20 miles (32km) east of Casper, the Paisley Shawl is the dining complement to an unbeatable guest inn/restaurant combination. Specialties include shrimp scampi, veal Florentine, and the ever-popular Paisley Shawl chicken breast, lauded by locals and *Bon Appétit.* Set inside the hotel's former ballroom, the restaurant is expansive, with seating for 60. There aren't many restaurants in Wyoming that make you feel as if you're indulging yourself by dining there. This is one of them.

In the Hotel Higgins, Glenrock (from Casper, take I-25 east for 20 miles [32km] to the first Glenrock exit). © 800/458-0144 or 307/436-9212. www.hotelhiggins.com. Reservations recommended on weekends. Lunch $3–$9; dinner $12–$28. DC, DISC, MC, V. June–Aug daily 11:30am–1:30pm and 6–9:30pm; Sept–May Tues–Sat 11:30am–1:30pm and 6–9:30pm.

6 Fort Laramie National Historic Site

125 miles (201km) SE of Casper

On a hot day in 1834, mountain man William Sublette stopped his pack train laden with goods for the Green River rendezvous. Looking at the confluence of the Laramie and Platte Rivers, then to the east, across the dusty plains, and then to the west, toward the mountains, he decided that this was a good place for a trading post. Over the next 15 years, the fort served as a hub of the buffalo trade, then as a way station for weary travelers who needed a break on their way to the Pacific.

In 1849—the year of the California gold rush—the U.S. Army bought the fort to "defend" the rising tide of immigrants from the "savages." The Indian Wars hadn't really started yet, not until 1854, when a lame Mormon-owned cow wandered off and was eaten by a starving Miniconjou. A young lieutenant marched into the Sioux camp and demanded that the cow-eater be turned over for swift justice; soon his troops opened fire on the village, and the wars had begun. Many battles later, the Indian tribes gathered here to negotiate the Treaty of 1868, which gave the Sioux and their allies the Powder River country and the Black Hills for "as long as the grass shall grow and the buffalo shall roam." That turned out not to be very long, after gold was discovered in the Black Hills.

Within a few years, the Army had corralled the Indians onto reservations, the railroad had replaced the wagon trails, the beaver and the buffalo had been exterminated, and the fort was abandoned. It wasn't until 1938 that Franklin Roosevelt designated Fort Laramie a national historic site. In its time, travelers from Jim Bridger to Mark Twain had stopped at the fort; today almost 100,000 tourists ramble through many of the site's 22 original structures.

For an in-depth look at life at the fort, stop by the **visitor center** and watch the 18-minute video about the fort and its role in the settlement of the West. You'll see historic photos there, and a gift shop sells a wide selection of Western-themed books and gift items. Pick up a paper copy of the self-guided tour of the fort's historic buildings, or for $3 rent the audio tour, which not only tells the history of the fort but brings it alive with the voices and sounds of the past.

Some of the more notable (and restored) buildings you'll see are the **cavalry barracks,** where dozens of soldiers slept, crowded into a single room; **Old Bedlam,** the post's headquarters, which later served as housing for officers, bachelors, and married couples; the **guardhouse,** a stone structure that housed the fort's prisoners; and the **bakery.**

Living-history programs are conducted every summer, from June to mid-August, when rangers dress in period costumes, give talks, and answer visitors' questions.

Before leaving the fort, consider driving to the **Old Bedlam Ruts** (ask for a map from the visitor center), 2 miles (3km) northwest of the fort. The bumpy gravel road allows you to view the rutted trail marks left by the wagon trains of early Western settlers. Look for Laramie Peak and the grave of Mary Homsley, one of the many who died along the trail.

The grounds and buildings are open daily from sunrise to sunset. From mid-May to mid-September, the visitor center is open daily from 8am to 7pm, and daily from 8am to 4:30pm the rest of the year. Admission costs $3 for adults, free for those 16 and under. To get to the fort from Casper, take I-25 east past Douglas to U.S. 26 (exit 92), head east to Wyo. 160, which you take southwest to Fort Laramie. For more information, contact **Fort Laramie National Historic Site,** National Park Service, HC 72, Box 389, Fort Laramie, WY 82212 (© **307/837-2221;** www.nps.gov/fola).

14

Southern Wyoming

Southern Wyoming has long been less a destination than a land passed through. All the famous trails—the Bozeman, the Californian, the Emigrant, the Mormon, the Overland, and the Pony Express—lead somewhere else. Even today, if you stand on a hill just outside the state capitol of Cheyenne, where two major interstates intersect, you'll see a cluster of mega-gas stations crowded with RVs, autos, and semis, fueling up before speeding east or west.

In the middle of the 19th century, nearly a half-million people passed through Wyoming on the Oregon Trail. They paused at Independence Rock only long enough to rest and to carve their names in the stone (it's still there—west of Casper on Wyo. 220). This cross-state journey, which can now be done in less than a day, took a month in the 1840s. Along this route travelers left wagon tracks, cast-iron stoves, worn-out boots, crippled livestock, and their dead. It was no easy passage: On average, they dug 10 graves for every mile of trail.

By 1868, the railroad had forged across the plains, following the more southerly route of the Overland Stages. The arrival of the railroad brought shantytowns of gambling tents, saloons, and brothels, known as "Hell on Wheels." Left behind as the rails moved on, the makeshift towns collapsed, and a cycle of booms and busts began. New discoveries of coal, oil, gold, or uranium would spur a revival, followed by another bust.

That legacy colors the character of towns along I-80 today. A new generation of miners dig coal and trona (a gray-white or yellowish mineral used in cleaning agents) and keep the oil and natural gas flowing. Mineral money builds sparkling new schools and government buildings, but there is still a rough-and-ready quality to the downtown districts.

But unlike the old days, the communities now have a better grip on the landscape. **Cheyenne** is the state capital, home to thousands of government workers. The remnants of the ranching families that once dominated the area come out in force every year for **Frontier Days,** a rodeo extravaganza known the world over. West over the pass in **Laramie,** the University of Wyoming is a cultural and intellectual nexus. From Laramie west, I-80 climbs around Elk Mountain and races across the high desert—an expansive (some might say bleak) view from behind the windshield, and a sometimes harrowing drive during winter blizzards.

Cross-country travelers often miss the unexpected beauty in this land because they steadfastly stick to the interstate instead of the two-lane roads that lead to chalk buttes and rust-colored mesas. Take an off-ramp and head north among the stirring buttes of the Red Desert, read the ancient archaeological record at Fossil Butte, hike the mountain cirque of the Snowy Range, or dip in the clear waters of Flaming Gorge. On summer afternoons, the dry air turns humid, the sky black, and lightning dances on the red rims. When the sun breaks again, the cliffs burn copper.

1 Scenic Drives

I-80 runs the length of southern Wyoming along the same path followed by the first transcontinental railroad: straight, fast, convenient, but not often scenic. To the curious eye, though, there are interesting sights along the way.

Geology buffs will be interested in the road cuts made by the interstate—eons of geologic history are revealed. Historians will appreciate the remnants left more than a century ago: take exit 272, 41 miles (66km) west of Laramie, and visit **Little Arlington,** where you'll find what's left of an old stage station and a log cabin, back in the trees. Here along the interstate you'll also see Wyoming's latest contribution to the nation's energy pool: a wind farm of spinning propellers lining the ridges like an infantry on stilts.

But to break the monotony of the long drive across southern Wyoming, you need to take a loop off the interstate. There's plenty of great scenery out there, including the landscapes you'll see on the following trips. Many of the sights mentioned here are discussed in further detail later in this chapter.

DRIVING TOUR #1: THE SNOWY RANGE SCENIC BYWAY: LARAMIE TO SARATOGA

The **Snowy Range Road** (Wyo. 130), designated the nation's second scenic byway, twists up and over the Medicine Bow Mountains south of I-80 and west of Laramie, through corridors of pines and between snow banks (even in midsummer), and tops Snowy Range Pass at 10,847 feet. During the winter, heavy snows block the pass, but you can reach a ski area (both Alpine and Nordic) on the Laramie side, 6 miles (10km) past Centennial.

To reach the Snowy Range Scenic Byway from Laramie, take exit 311 off I-80 and head west along Snowy Range Road. Once past the little town of Centennial, the road switchbacks uphill at a steep grade. As you top the pass, you'll see sharp granite peaks to the north, often skirted by snow, that border on a group of snowmelt-fed lakes. This is the top of the range, with elevations more than 12,000 feet above sea level. On a summer day you'll have plenty of company at the turnouts—people stopping to look, to fish, to hike a nature trail, to picnic. Half a day of vigorous hiking (if you're adjusted to the altitude) will get you atop Medicine Bow Peak, the highest summit in the range. The road then descends the east side of the range, following French Creek to the **Upper North Platte River** (known as the Miracle Mile), which is popular with anglers. When you come to a *T* in the road, turn right on 130 and drive 8 miles (13km) north to **Saratoga,** a friendly little town where many boats are launched to fish the excellent waters of the Platte. Continue north from here to rejoin I-80 at Walcott Junction.

FINISH THE LOOP: A DIFFERENT WAY BACK TO LARAMIE You can return on I-80 to Laramie, or take a more adventurous route by going north from Walcott on U.S. 30/287 toward Medicine Bow. This road follows the rail line and, as such, bypasses the mountains—in the winter, it's often a better route than the interstate. The landscape is sagebrush plains and hills, where antelope roam. Every 20 miles (32km) or so, you'll hit a crumbling town. One community with a little life still left in it is **Medicine Bow,** location of the Virginian Hotel (another model for Owen Wister's *The Virginian*) and of a watering hole with character, the Diplodocus Bar. Take a look at the bar itself—a solid slab of Wyoming jade, 40 feet long. Some of the great historic dinosaur discoveries were made in this area, at nearby Como Bluff. Continue east to finish the loop in Laramie.

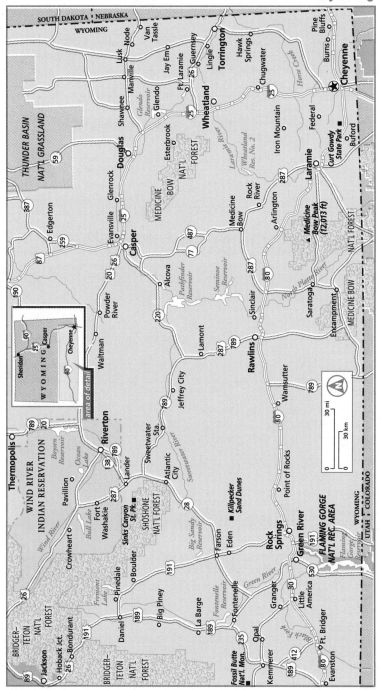

⎛Tips⎞ Travel Tip

Because of the altitude of this journey, be alert to weather, especially on the edges of winter. Contact **Wyoming Road and Travel Information** services for regularly updated road conditions at 📞 **888/996-7623** within Wyoming or 📞 307/772-0824 from outside of the state.

DRIVING TOUR #2: THE RIVERS ROAD & HIGHWAY 70: LARAMIE TO BAGGS

This scenic drive goes from Laramie to the town of Baggs along Wyo. 230 and a recently completed stretch of Wyo. 70. **Wyo. 230** (also known as "The Rivers Road") winds its way southwest from Laramie along the Laramie River to the town of **Mountain Home,** where the road dips south into Colorado. Here it makes a loop along Colo. 127/125 for 18 miles (29km) and reenters the state of Wyoming on the other side of the Medicine Bow Range. The route then continues northwest along Wyo. 230 to the old logging town of Encampment. This last portion offers beautiful river scenery with aspen and lodgepole pines, and opportunities for trout fishing. From Encampment, take Wyo. 70 west to Baggs across 58 miles (93km) of Carbon County land in the Sierra Madre Mountain Range. Because of the altitude, views can stretch for miles around this virtually uninhabited belt of southern Wyoming. But the altitude also causes road closures in the winter. Wyo. 70 climbs to 9,955 feet to Battle Pass, named for a nearby conflict that took place in 1841. Here it crosses the Continental Divide before descending to the small towns of **Savery, Dixon,** and **Baggs,** a trio of hamlets with a combined population of less than 500. Early settlers came to the area in search of gold and silver. The history of Baggs also includes a different kind of business: Outlaw Butch Cassidy pulled off several robberies here, and quick-triggered livestock detective Tom Horn frequented the area during the late 1800s.

Turn north off Wyo. 70 onto Wyo. 789 at Baggs, then drive north for 51 miles (82km) through high-plains ranching country. At Creston Junction, you'll rejoin I-80. From here, you can either drive west to Rock Springs and the Utah border or return east to Laramie. You won't have traveled as far as you think, but you'll have seen a lot more along this route than you would have staring at the back of an 18-wheeler along the interstate.

2 Cheyenne

93 miles (150km) N of Denver; 180 miles (290km) S of Casper

Cheyenne is located in the southeast corner of the state. Legend has it that when Gen. Grenville M. Dodge's surveying crew trudged across the prairie, picking a route for the transcontinental railroad, night came, they were tired, they stopped and said, "Good as any," and thus was born the present site of Cheyenne.

By horse or by highway, you can't miss Cheyenne, not only the largest city in Wyoming (population 55,000) but also its capital. Visitors enjoy the many historic and political sights, from the **Capitol Building** to the **Historic Governors' Mansion.** But Cheyenne's biggest event, hands down, is that wild and woolly weeklong cowboy extravaganza, **Cheyenne Frontier Days.**

ESSENTIALS

GETTING THERE   United Express (📞 **800/241-6522** or 307/635-6623) flies daily into the **Cheyenne Municipal Airport** on East 8th Avenue, off

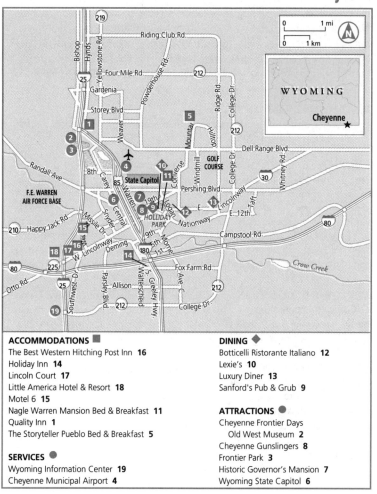

ACCOMMODATIONS ■
The Best Western Hitching Post Inn **16**
Holiday Inn **14**
Lincoln Court **17**
Little America Hotel & Resort **18**
Motel 6 **15**
Nagle Warren Mansion Bed & Breakfast **11**
Quality Inn **1**
The Storyteller Pueblo Bed & Breakfast **5**

SERVICES ●
Wyoming Information Center **19**
Cheyenne Municipal Airport **4**

DINING ◆
Botticelli Ristorante Italiano **12**
Lexie's **10**
Luxury Diner **13**
Sanford's Pub & Grub **9**

ATTRACTIONS ●
Cheyenne Frontier Days
  Old West Museum **2**
Cheyenne Gunslingers **8**
Frontier Park **3**
Historic Governor's Mansion **7**
Wyoming State Capitol **6**

Central Avenue, but most people choose to fly directly in and out of **Denver International Airport** (✆ **800/247-2336**), 101 miles (163km) south of Cheyenne in Colorado on I-25, and rent a car to drive into Wyoming from there.

By bus, you can get here with **Greyhound** (✆ **307/634-7744**). **Powder River Transportation** (✆ **307/635-1327**) buses leave for intrastate destinations from the bus terminal at 222 Deming St., under the I-80 overpass at U.S. 85.

To get to Cheyenne from **Casper,** take I-25 south for 180 miles (290km). From **Rock Springs** in the southwest part of the state, take I-80 east for 258 miles (415km).

VISITOR INFORMATION The **Cheyenne Area Convention and Visitors Bureau** at 309 W. Lincolnway, Cheyenne, WY 82001 (✆ **800/426-5009** outside Wyoming, or 307/778-3133; www.cheyenne.org), has a variety of brochures and local maps, including the *Cheyenne Historic Downtown Walking Tour,* and the *Downtown Cheyenne Map.* Once you're in town, you can also get information at the **Wyoming Information Center,** operated by the Wyoming Division of Tourism, located just off I-25 at College Drive.

GETTING AROUND   Avis (© 888/897-8446 or 307/632-9371) and **Hertz** (© 800/654-3131 or 307/634-2131) both have counters at the Cheyenne airport. Should you need a taxi, **Yellow Cab** can be reached at © **307/635-5555.** There is no taxi stand at the airport.

CHEYENNE FRONTIER DAYS ★★

In the world of rodeo, there are three must-see classics: The Pendleton Round-up, the Calgary Stampede, and the "Daddy of 'em All," Cheyenne Frontier Days. Since the inaugural event in 1897, it has grown into one of the largest rodeos in the world. The Frontier Days committee and thousands of volunteers organize this 10-day-long Western spectacle of parades, rodeo, dances, and concerts each summer, the last full week of July. It's safe to say that this is the most vivid demonstration of Western hospitality you'll encounter in the modern world.

Though the rodeo lasts for a full 10 days, picking and choosing activities carefully can save you a lot of time and money. Rodeo ticket prices range anywhere from $8 to $18 per person, and nightly shows featuring popular country music acts cost $15 to $20.

VISITOR INFORMATION   Contact the **Cheyenne Frontier Days Ticket Office** for brochures, ticket forms, and information on all shows and activities during upcoming Frontier Days celebrations at Cheyenne Frontier Days, P.O. Box 2477, Cheyenne, WY 82003-2477 (© **800/227-6336** or 307/778-7222; www.cfdrodeo.com).

GETTING AROUND DURING THE FESTIVAL   Parking is provided at Frontier Park for $5 per vehicle, but shuttle parking is also available and makes much more sense. The shuttle picks up visitors at several locations and delivers them to the rodeo grounds; round-trip fare is $4 per carload. The city also runs a special bus service to Frontier Park from downtown Cheyenne that stops at nearby campgrounds. Contact the **Cheyenne Area Convention and Visitors Bureau** (© 307/778-3133) for bus stop locations and scheduled pickups.

The Parade   With the exception of Buffalo Bill's walk through the streets of Cheyenne in 1898 and a docile march led by Teddy Roosevelt in 1910, Cheyenne's Frontier Days Parade in its early days was similar to a stagecoach holdup. Guns blazed as cowboys rode through the streets with little regard to form or style. In 1925, things took a turn toward civility when the "Evolution of Transportation" theme was introduced. Today, many horse-drawn vehicles make their way through the streets of Cheyenne as part of the Old-Time Carriage section of the parade. In addition to the carriages and antique cars, marching bands, local clubs, and various Plains Indians groups march. Viewing sites

---

⌐ _Tips_ Money-Saving Tip

To get the most for your money at Frontier Days, order a 1-day package for $28 that includes a ticket to the afternoon's rodeo and the evening concert; these tickets are good between Monday and Wednesday. For more information call © 800/227-6336 or 307/778-7222, or check out www.cfdrodeo.com.

are as near as the closest curb, but you'll want to claim a position 45 minutes before the start.

The parade starts at Capitol Ave. and 24th St., runs down Capitol Ave. to 17th Ave., and continues up Carey Ave. to the finish at Carey Ave. and 24th St. Free admission. During Frontier Days, Sat, Tues, and Thurs, commencing at 9:30am.

The Pancake Breakfast   Since their inception in 1952, these free breakfasts have become increasingly popular. On Monday, Wednesday, and Friday from 7 to 9am, a cement mixer moves in to mix enough pancake batter to cook more than 100,000 flapjacks for 30,000 people. The breakfasts are held downtown at the Cheyenne City Center parking lot on the corner of Lincolnway and Carey and served by the local Kiwanis Club, including, sometimes, an unassuming governor.

Cheyenne City Center parking lot, corner of Lincolnway and Carey. Free admission. During Frontier Days, Mon, Wed, Fri 7–9am.

The Rodeo   An anthropologist might see rodeo as a fading ritual to a passing way of life, but don't tell that to the fans who pack the stands at Frontier Days. It's actually one of the most popular spectator sports in the nation, as American as apple pie and baseball. Cheyenne's annual rodeo draws people from across the nation, and the best of the best cowboys.

Spectators from around the world pack into the stands to watch events like steer wrestling, barrel racing, team roping, and the classic event—and Wyoming's state symbol—saddle bronc riding. It's enormous fun, but part of the attraction is that these men and women put themselves in harm's way, working enormous animals with a wild streak. In a world where risk is often an illusion created by entertainers, this is the real thing. Champion bull-rider Lane Frost died in the ring at Frontier Days in 1989.

Daily ticket prices start at $10 for bleachers at the far end of the arena; $12 for seats closer to the roping gates; and $22 for the center of the action—the bucking chutes. Each night after the rodeo, top country stars take the stage. Concert tickets range from $16 to $30.

Frontier Park, exit 12 off I-80. (℗ 800/227-6336 or 307/778-7222. Tickets $10–$22. During Frontier Days, daily at 1pm.

SEEING THE SIGHTS

Stop in at the **Nelson Museum of the West** at 1714 Carey Ave. ((℗ **307/ 635-7670**) to see a collection of cowboy trappings, American Indian artifacts, taxidermy trophies, and Western memorabilia. Train buffs will enjoy the **Wyoming Transportation Museum,** located in the historic Cheyenne Union Pacific Depot, 121 W. 15th St. ((℗ **307/637-3376**). For a different perspective on the area, the **Warren ICBM and Heritage Museum,** accessible by getting a permit at Gate #1 of Warren Air Force Base ((℗ **307/773-2980**), offers a behind-the-scenes look at thermonuclear weaponry. A more serene option is a stroll through **Cheyenne Botanic Gardens,** 710 S. Lions Park Dr. ((℗ **307/ 637-6458**), a showcase of lush flowerbeds. These attractions have free admission, save the Nelson Museum of the West ($3 adult, $2 senior, under 12 free).

Cheyenne Frontier Days Old West Museum   Frontier Days has been around long enough that folks have become interested in its history, so sponsors established this museum to warehouse memorabilia from the rodeo and other historic artifacts. The Old West Museum, located next door to the rodeo arena, is a convenient place to take a break from the action. There are carriages, temporary exhibits (a display on the history of Wyoming tourism is slated to run through 2002), photos, a video-screening room, and a treasure trove of rodeo gear.

4610 N. Carey Ave., Frontier Park, Cheyenne, WY 82001. ℂ 307/778-7290. www.oldwestmuseum.org. $5 adults, free for children under 12. AE, DISC, MC, V. Mon–Fri 9am–5pm; Sat–Sun 10am–5pm; longer hr. in summer and during Frontier Days.

Cheyenne Gunslingers *Kids*   June through July, this nonprofit Cheyenne group puts on an Old West shootout downtown in "Gunslinger Square." You'll recognize it by the stage set of an Old West saloon, jail, and gallows. The volunteer actors love to ham it up. Their show dramatizes a jailbreak, a near-hanging, and a fast-draw—starring a corrupt judge, wily villains, and the white-hatted good guys. It's not necessarily the most accurate portrayal of the Old West (and it's not intended to be), but it is great entertainment for the family.

Gunslinger Sq., Lincolnway and Carey. ℂ 307/635-1028 or 307/631-0968. www.cheyennegunslingers.org. Free admission. June–July, shows held nightly at 6pm, Sat at noon; during Frontier Days, the show runs twice daily at noon and 6pm at the Soda Saloon in the Old Town Square.

Cheyenne Street Railway Trolley   No longer used as a mode of mass transit, the local trolley offers visitors a ride around Cheyenne's main tourist sites, including the Governors' Mansion, the Wyoming State Capitol, and the historic homes of the area's turn-of-the-century cattle barons. For something different, take the 90-minute "ghost" tour, departing Thursdays and Fridays at 7:30pm ($6 adults, $3 children). As you visit the Air Force base and the hotel district, you'll hear eerie tales of Cheyenne's haunted past.

Purchase tickets at the Cheyenne Area Convention and Visitors Bureau, 309 W. Lincolnway. ℂ 800/ 426-5009 or 307/778-3133. Tour $8 adults, $4 children. MC, V. Mid-May to mid-Sept 2-hr. tours Mon–Sat 10am and 1:30pm, Sun 1:30pm.

Historic Governors' Mansion   If you're interested in the political history of the state, you should continue 6 blocks from the capitol to the Historic Governors' Mansion. Built in 1904, it housed Wyoming's first families until 1976; today, many of the rooms have been restored to their 1905 appearances. Over the years, the decorative styles mixed, and you'll find everything from Chippendale to Colonial Revival to Art Nouveau. There's even a steer-horn chair in the entrance hall. The building itself, with its four Corinthian columns, looks more like an old fraternity house than a governor's mansion. A videotape and tour provide a worthwhile look into the political past of Wyoming's governors.

300 E. 21st St. ℂ 307/777-7878. www.wyo-park.com. Free admission. Tues–Sat 9am–5pm.

Wyoming State Capitol   In the summer, when the streets of Cheyenne are shaded by large old oaks, it's easy to come upon the capitol building a bit by surprise. It's not a large capitol, as such things go, but it's a traditional one, with a gold-leaf dome and carved stone. The main structure was built in 1888; the wings were added in 1917, but otherwise, the stately building has undergone little change over the years. Inside you can admire the beautiful woodwork, stained glass, and sparkling marble floors, and view historic photos and exhibits on the state's wildlife. Outside, you can stop by three statues: the first female justice of the peace, Esther Hobart Morris; a bronze bison; and the Spirit of Wyoming—the wild bucking horse emblazoned on every license plate in the state.

Capitol Ave. at 24th St. ℂ 307/777-7220. Free guided group tours by reservation or self-guided tours, Mon–Fri 8:30am–4:30pm, except holidays.

WHERE TO STAY

Thanks to its crossroads location, there's a plethora of accommodations in Cheyenne, from basic mom-and-pop and chain motels to ornate B&Bs and friendly guest ranches. The chain properties include: **Holiday Inn,** adjacent to the junction of U.S. 85 and I-80 at 204 W. Fox Farm Rd. (*C* **307/638-4466**), offering double rooms for $79 to $99 ($189 during Frontier Days); **Motel 6,** 1735 Westland Rd. (*C* **800/466-8356** or 307/632-8901), with rates of $46 to $54 for two ($72 during Frontier Days); and **Quality Inn,** 5401 Walker Rd. (*C* **800/228-5151** or 307/632-8901), with doubles for about $79 ($145 during Frontier Days). The 1950s-style **Lincoln Court,** 1720 W. Lincolnway (*C* **307/638-3302**), is a reliable bet among the nonchain options, with double rates of $50 to $60 ($130 during Frontier Days).

A reservation caution: Hotels fill up quickly during Frontier Days, and rack rates are much higher. Unlucky visitors who haven't made reservations up to a year in advance spill into Laramie and Fort Collins motels.

Best Western Hitching Post Inn   Located along the motel strip on Lincolnway near the junction of I-25 and I-80, the Hitching Post is where most of the legislators stay during their annual sessions at the capitol, so it has an air of importance and deal-making. With that comes some of the best service in town. It's also got spacious, well-appointed rooms. On occasion, there is live entertainment in the lounge.

1700 W. Lincolnway, Cheyenne, WY 82001. *C* **800/221-0125** or 307/638-3301. Fax 307/778-7194. 168 units. May–Sept $99 double; Oct–Apr $79 double; during Frontier Days, $200 double. AE, DC, DISC, MC, V. **Amenities:** 3 restaurants; indoor pool. *In room:* A/C, TV, dataport.

Little America Hotel and Resort ⭐   This is one of the largest hotels in Wyoming and a noteworthy oasis. The main building and low-rise brick lodges are surrounded by an executive golf course, duck pond, and mature evergreens. The main building harbors a tasteful lounge warmed by a fireplace and Navajo rugs; three shops offer boutique clothing, jewelry, and Western souvenirs. Accommodations, in four low-rise brick lodges, all refurbished since 2000, provide 31-inch TVs, balconies, and bathrooms with shower/tub combos and marble counters. Rooms come in three categories: standards, mini-suites with king-size beds, and executive suites. Meals are available in the Western Gold Dining Room (the house specialty is prime rib) and the lounge, and the coffee shop is open from 5am to 1am with very modest prices. The Olympic-size pool is open summer only, but a fitness center and jogging path can be used year-round.

2800 W. Lincolnway (I-80 at I-25), Cheyenne, WY 82009. *C* **800/445-6945** or 307/775-8400. Fax 307/775-8425. www.cheyenne.littleamerica.com. 188 units. $68–$160 double; during Frontier Days, $129–$169 double. AE, DC, DISC, MC, V. **Amenities:** 3 restaurants; outdoor pool; small health club. *In room:* A/C, TV, dataport.

Nagle Warren Mansion Bed & Breakfast ⭐⭐   This gem of an inn is the centerpiece of an increasingly hip stretch on 17th Avenue. Originally built in 1888 by famed architect Erasmus Nagle (it was the first house in the state with indoor plumbing), the mansion was converted into an elegant bed-and-breakfast in 1997. Grand and spacious, the three-story structure oozes luxury, from the furnishings (almost exclusively regional antiques) to the stately spire that anchors the building's southeast corner. The rooms, named after the mansion's former residents, feature lavish, turn-of-the-century style, tempered by a few modern perks—CD players, televisions, and modem-ready phones. Half of the rooms are located in the main building, and half are in the adjoining carriage house (the latter have fireplaces), but they all have their own unique allure.

222 E. 17th St., Cheyenne, WY 82001. ℂ **800/811-2610** or 307/637-3333. www.naglewarrenmansion.com. 12 units. $98–$158 double; during Frontier Days, $245 double. Rates include full breakfast. AE, MC, V. **Amenities:** Jacuzzi; small health club; courtesy car; massage. *In room:* A/C, TV, dataport.

The Storyteller Pueblo Bed & Breakfast Located on the northern tip of Buffalo Ridge on the northeast fringes of Cheyenne, this modern suburban home's exterior starkly contrasts with the decor within. Innkeepers Peggy and Howard Hutchings' private collection of American Indian artifacts is on display in both the private rooms and the public areas, representing 50 tribes from Alaska to Florida. The downstairs parlor features a sitting room stocked with games and a fireplace, alongside a pair of rooms bedecked with peace pipes, beadwork, and moccasins. Plains Indians and Victorian motifs commingle in the third room, located upstairs, and the backyard is serene and immaculately maintained. The American Indian theme continues into the breakfast menu with *ojibwa,* a dish made with hand-harvested wild rice, eggs, mushrooms, and green peppers.

5201 Ogden Rd., Cheyenne, WY 82009. ℂ **307/634-7036.** 3 units, including 1 suite. $60–$80 double; during Frontier Days, $100 double. Rates include full breakfast. No credit cards. Located 3 miles (5km) NE of downtown via Converse Ave. **Amenities:** Self-serve laundry. *In room:* A/C, cable TV.

CAMPING

The **Greenway Trailer Park,** 3728 Greenway St. (ℂ **307/634-6696**), offers paved RV pads and cable TV hookups for $15; $25 during Frontier Days. The biggest campground is the **Restway Travel Park** off Whitney Road, 2 miles (3km) east of Cheyenne (ℂ **800/443-2751** or 307/634-3811). Catering to RV and tent campers alike, Restway boasts a heated swimming pool, miniature golf, and a store stocked with basic supplies; nightly rates run from $15 for a basic tent site to $28 for a site with full hookups during Frontier Days. For something a bit different, head to **Terry Bison Ranch** ⚐, located 6 miles (10km) south of Cheyenne via I-25, exit 2 (ℂ **307/634-4171**), a working buffalo ranch with tent ($12–$15 per night) and RV sites ($14–$24 per night), as well as a bunkhouse, guest cabins, gift shop, and restaurant. The ranch also offers a variety of tours.

WHERE TO DINE

Botticelli Ristorante Italiano ⚐⚐ ITALIAN Located in a majestic Victorian mansion, Botticelli is Cheyenne's most romantic and intimate restaurant. Praised by locals and tourists alike, the food here is classic, savory, and rich. There's an ample selection of pastas, pizzas, chicken, and veal on the menu here, and a formidable wine list to boot. Our favorites: for lunch, the Botticelli panini on toasted focaccia with prosciutto and sun-dried tomatoes; for dinner, the marinated rack of lamb (unless it's Wed, when the seafood specials hold court). Top it all off with fresh cannoli or tiramisu, both Cheyenne's best.

300 E. 17th St. ℂ **307/634-9700.** Lunch $5–$9; dinner $8–$17. AE, MC, V. Mon–Thurs 11am–2pm and 5–9pm; Fri 11am–2pm and 5–9:30pm; Sat 11:30am–9:30pm; Sun 5–9pm.

Lexies AMERICAN Locals like to take out-of-town guests to this converted two-story wooden home for lunch. It's conveniently located only a few blocks from the town center, and in nice weather you can sit on the deck and enjoy a glass of iced tea or a microbrew. Sandwiches include the tenderloin steak, the sourdough club, and the pepper-jack chicken. Come dinnertime, Lexies is known for its ribs and steaks. If you're in town on a Wednesday, head over for the restaurant's soul-food special, complete with catfish and collard greens.

216 E. 17th St. © 307/638-8712. Lunch $7–$10; dinner $9–$20. AE, DISC, MC, V. Mon–Thurs 7:30am–9pm; Fri–Sat 7am–10pm.

Luxury Diner ★ Finds AMERICAN   A favorite blue-collar breakfast counter, the Luxury Diner is a real down-home greasy spoon. We say that affectionately, of course; the food is good, the coffee always hot, and the waitresses sassy. Breakfast is served all day. The pie: apple. The special: meatloaf. It's the real thing—no Buddy Holly posters, no 45s dangling from the ceiling for that "retro" look. In fact, the small dining area ran as a trolley from 1896 to 1912, before becoming a diner in 1926. Pictures of trains cover the walls, Christmas lights blink around the trim, and the menu says, "Friendliest place in town." They're right.

1401-A W. Lincolnway. © 307/638-8971. Breakfast $2–$8; lunch $4–$8. AE, MC, V. Daily 6am–4pm.

Sanford's Pub & Grub PUB FARE/CAJUN   This family-friendly place is overflowing with nostalgic junk of all stripes, from the truck bed that doubles as a canopy above the door to the antique advertisements and pop culture icons in the dining room to the kegs in the rafters. The menu is similar: There's a lot to look at and it's all over the place, from the 1-pound Elvis burgers and other sandwiches to gyros, grilled tuna, and steaks. If you dare, try the Atom Bomb burger, a Cajun-spiced patty piled high with ham, jalapeños, and blue cheese. The restaurant is also known for its Cajun offerings, from jambalaya to crawfish étouffée.

115 E. 17th St. © 307/634-3381. Lunch $5–$10; dinner $8–$15. AE, DISC, MC, V. Daily 11am–10pm.

3 Laramie ★

49 miles (79km) NW of Cheyenne; 360 miles (580km) SE of Yellowstone/Grand Teton; 207 miles (333km) E of Rock Springs; 124 miles (200km) N of Denver

Though the political capital is 49 miles (79km) to the east, Laramie is the cultural capital of Wyoming. It's home to the state's only university, public or private. Unlike Jackson, which has a prefabricated feel designed to appeal to visitors, Laramie has an earnest charm that seems to have developed by accident, and it has been this way for nearly a century. Located just east of the beautiful Medicine Bow Mountains, at an altitude of more than 7,000 feet, Laramie is sometimes buffeted by chill winds. But it has university-town amenities like bookstores and coffee shops, and a few Western features to boot, including outlying ranchlands and some rowdy downtown bars.

ESSENTIALS
GETTING THERE   The **Laramie Regional Airport,** 555 General Brees Rd. (© **307/742-4164**), west of town along Wyo. 130, services daily flights on **United Express** (© **800/241-6522**) from Denver.

Or go **Greyhound** (© **307/742-5188**) at **Tumbleweed Express,** a bus depot/convenience store at 4700 Bluebird Lane (© **800/231-2222** or 307/721-7405). The bus stops at several Wyoming cities along I-80, including Rock Springs and Cheyenne.

Laramie is an easy 49-mile (79km) drive from Cheyenne on I-80; driving from Salt Lake, it's just more than 300 miles (483km) once you hit Evanston. The fastest route from the Yellowstone–Grand Teton area is via U.S. 287 south for 259 miles (417km) to Rawlins and I-80 east for 101 miles (163km) to Laramie.

Laramie

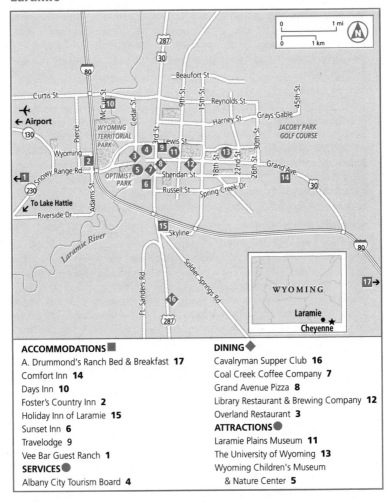

ACCOMMODATIONS ■
A. Drummond's Ranch Bed & Breakfast **17**
Comfort Inn **14**
Days Inn **10**
Foster's Country Inn **2**
Holiday Inn of Laramie **15**
Sunset Inn **6**
Travelodge **9**
Vee Bar Guest Ranch **1**
SERVICES ●
Albany City Tourism Board **4**

DINING ◆
Cavalryman Supper Club **16**
Coal Creek Coffee Company **7**
Grand Avenue Pizza **8**
Library Restaurant & Brewing Company **12**
Overland Restaurant **3**
ATTRACTIONS ●
Laramie Plains Museum **11**
The University of Wyoming **13**
Wyoming Children's Museum
  & Nature Center **5**

VISITOR INFORMATION The **Albany County Tourism Board,** 210 Custer St. (© **800/445-5303** or 307/745-7339; www.laramie-tourism.org), provides brochures, city maps, and area maps that cover outdoor activities, shopping, dining, and tours for Laramie and the surrounding area.

GETTING AROUND Avis (© **800/831-1212** or 307/745-7156) and **Enterprise**(© **800/736-8222** or 307/721-9876) maintain outlets in Laramie. Taxi service is available through **Classic Taxi** (© **307/761-8294**).

GETTING OUTSIDE

Curt Gowdy State Park, named for the television sportscaster who hails from Wyoming, is quite pleasant, if not spectacularly beautiful. Just outside Laramie, and 1,645 acres in size, it's a great spot for a picnic. Or stay the night in one of the five campsites for $5 per night. There are two lakes here, but no swimming is allowed (they provide part of Cheyenne's water supply). Both power and non-power boating is permitted, but no rentals are available at the park. Call

© **307/632-7946** for further information. To get to the park, take I-80 east until you see the exit for Wyo. 210, the scenic back road to Cheyenne.

Southeast of Laramie, on the edge of the Medicine Bow National Forest, are **Pole Mountain** and the **Vedauwoo Recreation Area** (© **307/745-2300**). Vedauwoo and the Happy Jack trail head near the Summit exit of I-80 have some excellent summer and winter recreational opportunities. The name Vedauwoo (pronounced "VEE-duh-voo") is Arapaho for "earth-born." The rock formations—soft-edged blocks shaped like stools, turtles, and mushrooms—were considered the sacred creations of animal and human spirits, and young Indian men sought visions there. Today rock climbers pursue their quests for challenging climbs here, and find tough technical pitches. Other folks see a great place to mountain bike, hike, and scan the vistas. To get there, take I-80 east toward Cheyenne, past the second biggest Abe Lincoln head in these parts (10 miles [16km] outside town) to exit 329, the Vedauwoo turnoff.

SEEING THE SIGHTS

The **Laramie Plains Museum,** 603 Ivinson Ave. (© **307/742-4448**), is a three-story Queen Anne Victorian home built by Laramie settler Edward Ivinson, with furnishings from the 1890s (some furniture was handcarved at the local penitentiary). Admission is $4. **The Wyoming Children's Museum and Nature Center,** 968 N. 9th St. (© **307/745-6332**), has enough things to keep kids busy, including a frontier general store where children can handle things and do face painting. Admission is $3 children and $2 adults.

Jubilee Days (© **866/876-1012** or 307/745-7339) is another Western party that runs the second full week in July with rodeos, parades, and fireworks. The Jubilee Days cattle drive, which runs through the streets of downtown, is a must-see, and participation is open to the public.

The Wyoming Territorial Park *Kids*   Formerly a penitentiary where Butch Cassidy served time, the Territorial Prison transmogrified into an experimental livestock station before becoming the tourist park it is today. Almost everything having to do with frontier life before the turn of the 20th century can be found here, from a funky frontier town, to stage-coach rides, to tepees (which rent for $15–$60 per night). Also housed here is the **National U.S. Marshall's Museum,** with exhibits covering 2 centuries of the federal law enforcement agency. The **Horse Barn Theater** features melodrama performances and music revues, and dinner is served in the theater's restored loft.

975 Snowy Range Rd. (just east of I-80, exit 311). © 800/845-2287 or 307/745-6161. www.wyoprison-park.com. Park admission $12, free for children under 13; dinner-theater tickets for both park admission and the Horse Barn Dinner Theater show $30 adults, $19 children. Park open daily 9am–6pm. Shows Wed–Sat 6–9pm.

The University of Wyoming   The university's history began in 1887 with the funding of Old Main, its first building. At that time, there were five professors, two tutors, and 42 students on the 20-acre campus, which included Prexy's Pasture, where the school's first president kept his cows. Today, the University of Wyoming has more than 2,000 faculty and staff members and an enrollment of nearly 11,000 drawn from across the United States and 65 countries, though a majority of the undergraduates hail from Wyoming. The university has boomed along with oil and gas prices and the coal-bed methane market, with the legislature loosening the purse strings in recent sessions. However, some departments have been closed or cut back in order to concentrate on other fields—like geology, anthropology, and molecular biology—where UW is nationally recognized.

The campus consists of charming elderly sandstone buildings and the requisite extensive athletic facilities of a Division I school. For visitors, there is also a good dinosaur-fossil collection and an interesting piece of new architecture in the Centennial Complex, which houses an excellent research facility, the American Heritage Center.

To catch a glimpse of student life in Laramie, swing by Prexy's Pasture, where students hang, especially in fall. It's located in the heart of the campus, accessed off Ivinson Street or Grand Avenue by turning north on 13th Street (stop at the **Visitors Services Center,** 1408 Ivinson Ave., for a map). Those visiting during the school year may also want to contact **UW news line** (© 307/766-5000) to find out what's on the schedule, from classical music to modern dance to international speakers. An auto tour of the campus is worth the effort, if for no other reason than to check out the campus architecture, which ranges from the solid sandstone castles of a century ago to the spaceship designs of today.

With no professional sports teams in Wyoming, the college's football and basketball programs take on special importance. In the fall and winter, fans drive from around the state to root for the **Cowboys** in the university's excellent outdoor stadium and indoor arena. The UW Cowboys have been giant-killers in recent years, knocking off some national top-ranked teams and competing for Western Athletic Conference crowns. For event information and tickets, contact the ticket office at © 307/766-4850; www.wyomingathletics.com.

In a state where many towns have only small, local museum collections to display and inform visitors, the university plays an important role with its museum spaces, and most of the exhibits are free. Worth visiting are the **Geological Museum** (© 307/766-4218; located in the Geology Building, northwest corner of Prexy's Pasture), with plenty of dinosaur fossils, open Monday through Friday from 8am to 5pm, Saturday and Sunday from 10am to 3pm; and the **Rocky Mountain Herbarium** (© 307/766-2236), open Monday through Friday from 8am to 5pm (7:30am–4:30pm when school is out of session). The **Insect Museum** (© 307/766-2298; in room 1408 of the Ag Building, just north of Prexy's Pasture) is primarily a research facility and a bit esoteric to the average visitor; it is open to the public Monday through Friday from 8am to 5pm year-round. The **Centennial Complex** (on the east side of campus, east of 15th St.) houses the **UW Art Museum,** with works by Audubon, Charlie Russell, Thomas Moran, and even Gauguin. It's open Monday through Saturday from 10am to 5pm. Also in this building—which looks like a volcanic cone tipping sideways—is the **American Heritage Center** (© 307/766-4114), a top-notch research facility with extensive collections of Western-history materials and some unexpected archives, like some of Jack Benny's papers.

SHOPPING

Since Laramie is a university town, it has its fair share of bookstores. There is of course a giant and useful chain store, **Hastings Books, Music, and Video,** at 654 N. 3rd St. (© 307/745-0312), but there are also some fine and idiosyncratic locals, including the peaceful **2nd Story Books** and **Personally Recommended Books,** both located at 105 Ivinson Ave. (© 307/745-4423), where you can tap into the latest literary currents without the distraction of noise or bustle. To see what's hot on campus, visit the extensive **University Bookstore** 1 block north of Ivinson Avenue and 13th Street (© 800/423-5809, ext. 2). **The Grand Newstand** at 214 E. Grand Ave. (© 307/742-5127) has a more limited and mainstream selection, but an enormous array of periodicals and newspapers.

If you're looking for the gear you need for an adventure in the Medicine Bow, try **Cross-Country Connection** at 222 S. 2nd St. (© 307/721-2851) for skiing and climbing equipment (you can rent, too). For Western clothing and souvenirs, hit **Martindale's,** downtown at 211 E. Grand Ave. (© **307/721-4100**).

Downtown Laramie is also home to all kinds of artists and craftspeople. **Artisans' Gallery** at 215 S. 2nd St. (© **888/616-6409**) specializes in crafts and artwork by Wyoming artists. **Earth, Wind, and Fire** (© **307/745-0226**), just across the road at 216 S. 2nd St., is a pottery lover's dream come true. **Green Gold,** at 215 S. 1st St. (© **307/742-0003**), has lots of silver and Wyoming jade.

WHERE TO STAY

There's a number of chain motels and roadside mom-and-pops, but don't expect much in the way of B&Bs or hotels. The most reliable chain properties in town are **Travelodge,** 165 N. 3rd St. (© **800/742-6671** or 307/742-6671), with rooms for $50 to $75 double; **Days Inn,** 1368 McCue St. (© **307/745-5678**), with doubles for $76; and **Comfort Inn,** 3420 E. Grand Ave. (© **307/ 721-8856**), with double rates from $69 to $99. Outside of the chains, the **Sunset Inn,** 1104 S. 3rd St. (© **800/308-3744** or 307/742-3741), is a small motel that doesn't have many perks, other than an outdoor pool and indoor hot tub. Doubles cost $40 to $70.

A. Drummond's Ranch Bed-and-Breakfast ⭐ *(Finds)* A short drive from either Laramie or Cheyenne, the Drummonds' house sits above peaceful hills of pine and sage. Here you can ride mountain bikes in summer, cross-country ski in winter, or even take a llama to lunch. That's right. For $65 per person, the Drummonds will pack your lunch by llama. Or guests can bring their own horses, and owner and horse-lover Taydie Drummond can set your steed up with its own bed-and-breakfast.

Inside, guests relax in the living room or sit on the porch and gaze. The inn isn't particularly historic, large, or quaint, but it feels exactly like what it is: a home. It's a grand place to kick back, take walks, and pet the animals. Second-story rooms have two beds and share a bath. The aptly named Hummingbird Room looks out over Colorado's Rocky Mountain National Park, 75 miles (121km) away. Those in love will want to stay in the Carriage House Loft, with its private deck, hot tub, gas fireplace, and steam shower.

399 Happy Jack Rd., Laramie/Cheyenne, WY 82007 (25 miles [40km] east of Laramie off I-80). © 307/ 634-6042. www.adrummond.com. 4 units. $65–$80 2nd-story room; $120 garden room; $160–$200 carriage-house room. Rates include breakfast. MC, V. *In room:* No phone.

Foster's Country Inn A stone's throw from I-80 (depending on how well you throw), this locally owned motel is doing its best to come up to speed in the hospitality game. Built around a central parking area, it lacks variety or elbow room, but it does offer well-kept, reliable lodging as well as an airport shuttle.

1561 Snowy Range Rd., Laramie, WY 82070. © 307/742-8371. 112 units. $55–$102 double. Rates include continental breakfast. AE, DC, DISC, MC, V. **Amenities:** Restaurant; indoor pool. *In room:* A/C, TV, dataports.

Holiday Inn of Laramie In a city that lacks a truly fine hotel, this is the best of the bunch. The layout has no particular logic, extending around an inner courtyard that goes mostly unused, but the rooms are above average, the property is well maintained, and the service is very good. The sports bar here fills to the rafters and goes absolutely nuts when the UW Cowboys play an away game.

2313 Soldier Springs Rd. (exit 311 of I-80 and U.S. 287), Laramie, WY 82070 © 307/742-6611. 100 units. $99–$109 double. AE, DC, DISC, MC, V. **Amenities:** Restaurant; indoor pool; Jacuzzi. *In room:* A/C, TV, dataports.

Vee Bar Guest Ranch ★★ A jewel of a guest ranch, the Vee Bar is definitely pricey, but perfect for those looking to delve into the ranching lifestyle as they get away from it all. The property itself, 800 acres in all, features lush fields, cottonwood and willow groves, and a stretch of the crystalline Little Laramie River. Alongside the historic main lodge, the accommodations here are comfortable cabins and a trio of "Riverside Suite" duplexes that manage to balance the rustic with the convenient. Two of the freestanding cabins are more than a century old, restored and furnished with antiques of local origin; the third is modern (1990), but blends into the old-fashioned atmosphere with ease. Activities such as horseback riding, fishing, river tubing, and overnight camp-outs are included, as are all meals. For breakfast, expect flapjacks, eggs, and bacon; for dinner, steaks and seafood. Guests can unwind in the historic John Wayne Saloon.

2091 Wyo. 130, Laramie, WY 82070. ℃ **800/745-7036** or 307/742-8371. Fax 307/745-7433. www.vee-bar.com. 9 cabins. $2,895 per week for 2 people; $700 per week each additional person. Rates include all meals and activities. In the fall, winter, and spring (and summertime Sat), single-night stays are available for $100–$150 for a double room. AE, DISC, MC, V. Located 21 miles west of Laramie via Snowy Range Rd. (Wyo. 130). **Amenities:** Restaurant; Jacuzzi; small health club; children's programs; self-serve laundry. *In room:* No phones.

CAMPING
The **Laramie KOA,** off I-80 at 1271 Baker St. (℃ **307/742-6553**), is open April through October, depending on the snows. There are 100 pull-through sites here, as well as a rec room, small store, and unobstructed mountain views. Full hookups cost $23. There is also a campground at Curt Gowdy State Park (see "Getting Outside," earlier in this chapter).

WHERE TO DINE
Laramie should do better than it does in the restaurant department, but it has a few good ones. You'll find more character in the old downtown area, where thinkers and talkers fuel up on good java at the **Coal Creek Coffee Company,** 110 E. Grand (℃ **307/745-7737**); there is sometimes live music in the evenings. You can get a small portion of excellent pasta or pizza at **Grand Avenue Pizza,** 301 Grand Ave. (℃ **307/721-2909**), which hides in an old corner space downtown.

The Cavalryman Supper Club STEAKS/SEAFOOD This restaurant with an unusual atmosphere and decor, located south of town, is perfect for big appetites—it's also perfect for big spenders with its admittedly high prices. It pays tribute to the 7th Cavalry, a regiment that once used this site as a post on its march north to the Battle of the Little Bighorn. Previously a schoolhouse— and at one time, a brothel—it has a colorful past. There are always at least eight entrees from which to choose on the ever-changing menu; selections often include lobster, prime rib, and prawns. All meals include an appetizer of deep-fried mushrooms, tea or coffee, an after-dinner drink, and dessert.

4425 S. 3rd St. (U.S. 287). ℃ **307/745-5551.** Main courses $15–$28. AE, DC, DISC, MC, V. Daily 4:30–10pm. Located 3 miles south of downtown.

The Library Restaurant & Brewing Company AMERICAN This small microbrewery, located adjacent to the University of Wyoming campus, has an air of scholarliness amidst its obvious passions for good food and good beer. The domed ceiling covers a spacious, sunny room with shelf after shelf of books. The literary theme extends to the menu, with lunch dishes like the Catcher in the Rye (a variation on the Reuben); dinner entrees such as East of Eden (a grilled chicken breast with sautéed artichokes in a lemon-herb sauce); and desserts including the Great Gatsby (cheesecake with a rich chocolate or strawberry topping). The beers are also tasty, especially the Bantam Pale Ale.

1622 Grand Ave. ℂ 307/742-0500. Main courses lunch $5–$8; dinner $6–$15. AE, DISC, MC, V. Sun–Wed 11am–9pm; Thurs–Sat 11am–10pm.

Overland Restaurant ⭐ ECLECTIC   A great place to savor a meal while watching the trains come and go, the refreshingly unpretentious Overland shines the most in the evening, when wine lovers choose from the 2,000-bottle cellar filled with California and Italian wines. Those fine wines will go well with the wild game specials, including venison, ostrich, and Rocky Mountain trout. The pork medallions, chicken artichoke fettuccine, and Cajun dishes are also noteworthy. Beyond dinner, the Overland's Reubens are legendary, and chocoholics can't go wrong with the decadent Triple Chocolate Cake.

100 Ivinson Ave. ℂ 307/721-2800. Main courses $8–$17. AE, DISC, MC, V. Mon–Fri 11am–8pm; Sat–Sun 8:30am–8pm.

4 A Side Trip for the Outdoor Enthusiast: The Snowy Range & Carbon County

Snowy Range: 32 miles (52km) W of Laramie

You can very quickly leave behind the dry plains around Laramie and find yourself up among lakes, forest, and substantial peaks in the north end of the Medicine Bow Mountains, known as the **Snowy Range.** Just take Wyo. 130 west, through the foothill town of Centennial, past the **Snowy Range Ski Area** (ℂ **800/462-7669;** www.snowyrange.com), and up into the mountains, where peaks rise well over 10,000 feet. Though **Medicine Bow Peak** is 12,013 feet tall, it's a relatively easy day climb, starting at the parking lot by Lake Marie and covering about 5 miles (8km). You can loop around the west side of the hollow in which the peak stands and return on the east side among the lakes. Trails are well marked and you'll meet people as you hike. Just keep an eye on the thunderheads, as you'll be above timberline, exposed to lightning. For **detailed trail maps** of the Medicine Bow National Forest, contact the **Medicine Bow National Forest Service** in Laramie at ℂ **307/745-2300.**

If you drive on over the Snowies—it takes only about an hour—you'll drop down into the valley of the **North Platte River,** with its old mining and timber towns such as Encampment and Saratoga. **Saratoga** is the roost of several fishing outfits that guide on the North Platte, one of the finest trout fisheries in the state. If you spend the night, you'll probably enjoy the creaky, old-fashioned style of the historic **Hotel Wolf** at 101 E. Bridge St. (ℂ **307/326-5525**), or the peaceful (and expensive) spa **Saratoga Inn** (ℂ **307/326-5261**), with its own hot spring–fed pool and golf course. Another area attraction of note is **Woods Landing** (ℂ **307/745-9368**), a historic Western dancehall built on 24 boxcar springs.

CAMPING
Medicine Bow National Forest (ℂ **307/745-2300**) maintains more than 30 public sites June through September, scattered throughout the range west of Laramie. All are semiprimitive, which means no showers, no RV hookups, and no flush toilets. Fees range from $7 to $10 per night.

FISHING
The Upper North Platte River cuts right through Saratoga, and those in the know consider it one of the state's top trout-fishing spots. The Orvis-endorsed **Great Rocky Mountain Outfitters,** at 216 E. Walnut, Saratoga

(© **307/326-8750;** www.grmo.com), has been guiding anglers along the Upper North Platte since 1981. They charge $375 for a full-day, two-person float-fishing expedition (including lunch), and $300 for a half-day excursion with no meal. **Platte Valley Anglers,** located 1 mile (1.5km) west of Saratoga on Route 83 (© **307/326-5750**), offers drift fishing, white-water fishing, and white-water float trips. Or contact **Medicine Bow Drifters** (© **307/326-8002;** www. medbow.com).

5 Rock Springs

258 miles (415km) W of Cheyenne; 178 miles (287km) S of Jackson

Rock Springs began as a stage station on the Overland Trail, named after a natural spring that dried up after extensive mining in the area. In 1894, Jack London wrote of Rock Springs: "It seems to be a mining town . . . It seems to be the Wild and Woolly West with a vengeance." It's still true: Rock Springs shows the rougher side of Wyoming, powered by a coal-burning power plant, freight trains roaring through, and all-night truckers stopping for coffee, adding to a pervasive blue-collar sensibility. But it's not without pockets of culture and intellect, particularly at Western Wyoming College.

This is also a pocket of unionism in a conservative state. In 1875, the Union Pacific Railroad demanded more coal to fuel its transcontinental trains, but simultaneously cut wages. When the local miners went on strike, the railroad imported about 500 Chinese laborers. More and more Chinese came to the area, and within a decade, the white miners felt displaced. Animosity festered, then burst in 1885 when a mob of laid-off miners murdered 28 Chinese and burned Chinatown to the ground. Now on the site, ironically, stands a church.

Boom followed bust followed boom, and in the late 1970s, oil, gas, and coal caused the area population to double. Wages skyrocketed. So did the crime rate, and corruption raised its ugly head. Motels and bars and quickly assembled pre-fab homes multiplied. The streets in historic downtown can get a bit ornery, but it's interesting to walk among the weathered brick and wooden buildings. You might even stumble upon a hidden treasure in one of the many pawnshops.

And you're not far from some fine outdoor attractions: **Fossil Butte National Monument** (see section 7)—an astonishing natural storehouse of ancient plants, insects, and miniature horses—and **Flaming Gorge National Recreation Area** (see section 6 for more information), where a dam has backed up the Green River and made excellent fishing waters above and fine raft-floating waters below.

ESSENTIALS

GETTING THERE United Express (© 800/241-6522) flies into the Rock Springs Airport, 15 miles (24km) east of town on I-80, and the **Greyhound** bus rumbles in four times a day at 1665 Sunset Dr. (© **307/362-2931**).

Northeast of Flaming Gorge National Recreation Area, Rock Springs squats at the intersection of U.S. 191 and I-80. From Cheyenne, drive I-80 west for 258 miles (415km). From Jackson, take U.S. 191 south for 178 miles (287km).

VISITOR INFORMATION The **Rock Springs Chamber of Commerce,** 1897 Dewar Dr. (© **800/463-8637** or 307/362-3771), puts a positive spin on Rock Springs and its immediate area. The *Welcome to Sweetwater County* travel guide, available from the chamber, is a good resource, as is a website, **www.tourwildwyoming.com.** For maps and information about **Flaming**

Gorge National Recreation Area, contact the Green River Forest Service office (© **307/875-2871**).

GETTING AROUND   Avis (© **800/331-1212** or 307/362-5007) and **Hertz** (© **800/654-3131** or 307/382-3262) both maintain counters at the airport in Rock Springs. For a **Taxi,** contact **Don's Taxi Service** (© **307/382-5207**) or **City Cab** (© **307/382-1100**).

SEEING THE SIGHTS

While strolling around town, pop into the **Community Fine Arts Center,** at the Sweetwater County Library, 400 "C" St. (© **307/362-6212**), which contains a few original paintings by Grandma Moses and Norman Rockwell. Though not their most famous pieces by any stretch, these are early works that admirers may find notable. The **Rock Springs Historical Museum,** at 201 "B" St. (© **307/362-3138**), is a great piece of Romanesque architecture. Formerly City Hall, the building now houses exhibits covering the city's mining history. The **Western Wyoming Community College Natural History Museum,** 2500 College Dr. (© **307/382-1600**), has several dinosaur displays and a few fish and plant fossils. All three museums are free.

For a rundown on upcoming local events, call the county **Events Complex** at © **307/352-6789.**

WHERE TO STAY

The three hotels listed below may not be the fanciest in the state, but they have swimming pools and well-maintained modern rooms. The **Inn at Rock Springs,** 2518 Foothill Blvd. (© **307/362-9600**), offers rooms for $50 to $80 double. The **Comfort Inn,** 1670 Sunset Dr. (© **307/382-9490**), offers free continental breakfast every morning and a free cocktail each evening, as well as a heated outdoor pool, hot tub, and exercise room—all for $60 to $70 a night for two. You'll find the same amenities at the **EconoLodge,** at I-80 exit 104 (© **800/548-6621** or 307/382-4217), for $55 to $75 a night.

WHERE TO DINE

Bitter Creek Brewing ⚡ AMERICAN/ITALIAN   "Life is too short to drink cheap beer," reads the sign behind the oak bar. If you agree, then Bitter Creek is the place for you. In four fermenting vats adjacent to the bar, they concoct their own special microbrews, including the popular Mustang Pale Ale, and the cleverly named Coal Porter, a darker beer with a slight chocolate aftertaste. The menu includes blackened-salmon salad, garlic-chicken and pesto pizza, and portobello-mushroom linguine. Maybe because the prices are a touch high, and the bar doesn't serve hard alcohol, not a lot of locals eat here. But tourists accustomed to the stylish brewpubs found in Missoula and Jackson will surely appreciate Bitter Creek's addition to Rock Springs.

604 Broadway. © **307/362-4782.** Lunch $5–$8; dinner $10–$17. AE, MC, V. Mon–Thurs 11:30am–10pm; Fri–Sat 11:30am–11pm; Sun 11:30am–8pm.

Sands Cafe CHINESE/AMERICAN   If you're hankering for Chinese food while in Rock Springs, then head for the Buddha statue across from the Sands Inn. More like a coffee shop than a Chinese restaurant (one side looks like Anywhere, U.S.A., the other like a Beijing storefront), the food is actually quite good, running the gamut from kung pao plates and steaks to burgers and breakfast (anytime). A bonus for the road-weary: free delivery to local motels.

1549 9th St. © **307/362-5633.** Breakfast $4–$7; lunch and dinner $6–$15. AE, DISC, MC, V. Daily 10:30am–10pm.

White Mountain Mining Company STEAKS/SEAFOOD   Overhauled in 1995, this eatery is now one of the nicer supper clubs in southern Wyoming. The dining-room tables are covered with mauve linens, and the barn-style walls give the place the feel of, well, a barn. Like most other supper clubs, this one serves a mean prime rib, but the deep-fried shrimp is a close second.

10 Clearview. ⊘ **307/382-5265.** Main courses $11–$22. AE, DISC, MC, V. Mon–Sat 5–10pm. Bar stays open later, depending on crowd.

6 Flaming Gorge National Recreation Area (★

24 miles (39km) W of Rock Springs

By May of 1869, the Union Pacific had laid its tracks across Wyoming and pinned them to the eastbound rails with a golden spike. The town of Green River, 15 miles (24km) west of Rock Springs, was only a year old. And that May, 10 frontiersmen and ex-soldiers climbed off the train, lead by a veteran who'd lost his arm in the Civil War. They jumped into stout wooden boats and set off down the Green River. As they slid through red canyons with the cliffs peaking high above, almost singed yellow along the rims, they named the place "Flaming Gorge."

The expedition continued down the Green, which merged into the Colorado River, and then continued on into the Grand Canyon, weaving through boulders, portaging sandbars, and being sucked through rapids. Three men decided to hike out rather than risk the rapids. They were later found bristling with arrows. The remaining seven survived. And the leader would go on to map and record the *Great American Desert* and later to help organize and then direct the U.S. Geological Survey. The one-armed Civil War veteran, the famous river runner was, of course, John Wesley Powell.

Today a 455-foot dam, 15 miles (24km) into Utah, backs the river onto itself for 91 miles (147km), nearly to the town of Green River. Each summer, jet-boaters, water skiers, and anglers skim the surface of the reservoir, while paddlers drop in below the dam for scenic and adventurous floats in the wake of Powell's boats.

ESSENTIALS

GETTING THERE   Take I-80 west from Rock Springs for 15 miles (24km) to the town of **Green River** at the junction of Wyo. 530. (See "A Driving Tour," below, for information on driving through the area.)

VISITOR INFORMATION   For information before you arrive, contact the **District Ranger,** Flaming Gorge National Recreation Area, USDA Forest Service, Box 279, Manila, UT 84046 (⊘ **435/784-3445;** fax 435/781-5295; www.fs.fed.us/r4/ashley). The **Dinosaur Nature Association,** Flaming Gorge Division, 1291 E. U.S. 40, Vernal, UT 84078-2830 (⊘ **800/845-3466** or 435/789-8807; fax 435/781-1304; www.dinosaurnature.com), sells maps, books, and other publications. Once you're in the area, stop at the U.S. Forest Service's **visitor center** in **Green River** at 1450 Uinta Dr., Green River, WY

Impressions

The river enters the range by a flaring, brilliant red gorge, that may be seen from the north a score of miles away . . . We name it Flaming Gorge.
—Explorer Major John Wesley Powell, May 26, 1869

82935 (© **307/875-2871**) to pick up maps and brochures, including detailed information about hiking and mountain-biking trails.

ADMISSION & REGULATIONS   Admission to the 200,000-acre Flaming Gorge National Recreation Area is $2 per vehicle per day, $5 for 16 days, or $20 for an annual pass. The Forest Service's regulations here are mostly common sense, aimed at preserving water quality and protecting the forest and historic sites. In addition, Wyoming and Utah fishing and boating regulations apply in those states' sections of the recreation area. Dogs are permitted on trails, but not indoors, and should be leashed at all times. For more information, call the Green River Game and Fish Department office (© **307/875-2332**) or the Green River office of the U.S. Forest Service (© **307/875-2871**).

A DRIVING TOUR

As you drive south on Wyo. 530, the cactus and sagebrush–filled **Devils Playground** badlands and the rock formations of **Haystack Buttes** will be to your right. Wyo. 530 runs the length of the recreation area's west side and provides access to the Flaming Gorge Reservoir at the **Buckboard Crossing Area,** 20 miles (32km) south, where a full-service marina is in operation during the summer.

From Wyo. 530, pick up Utah 44 just across the state line in Manila, Utah. Utah 44 runs south then east for 27 miles (43km) to pick up U.S. 191. Along this route you'll catch glimpses of Utah's Uinta Mountains to the west and may see bighorn sheep in nearby **Sheep Creek Canyon,** which has been designated a special geological area by the Forest Service because of its dramatically twisted and upturned rocks. A mostly paved 11-mile (18km) loop road cuts off from Utah 44, offering a half-hour tour of this beautiful, narrow canyon, with its lavish display of rocks that have eroded into intricate patterns, a process that began with the uplifting of the Uinta Mountains millions of years ago. This loop may be closed in winter.

Eventually, you'll come to the **Red Canyon Overlook** on the southern edge of the gorge, where a rainbow of colors adorns 1,000-foot-tall cliffs. The **Red Canyon Visitor Center** (open 9:30am–5pm in summer) is nearby, as is **Flaming Gorge Dam.**

To head back to Wyoming, take U.S. 191 away from the eastern edge of the gorge. From the junction of Utah 44 and U.S. 191, it's 16 miles (26km) to the border. Once you're at the state line, it's 30 miles (48km) to the turnoff for **Firehole Canyon,** an access to the gorge that offers views of the magnificent spires known as **Chimney Rocks.** Keep going north on 191 and you'll hit I-80 again.

GETTING OUTSIDE

For more information about the Utah portion of Flaming Gorge National Recreation Area, including additional outdoor recreational activities and outfitters, lodging options, and other nearby sites of interest, see *Frommer's Utah.*

BOATING   Boaters get to enjoy a unique perspective of some memorable scenery, with the wide-open badlands of Wyoming in the north and the magnificent fiery red canyons surrounding the lake in the Utah section. During the summer, the **Buckboard Marina** (© **307/875-6927**) rents 14-foot boats for $8 an hour and $60 a day. Or if big-engine water-skiing boats are more your speed, they rent those for $30 an hour and $250 a day.

From Buckboard, it's another 25 miles (40km) to **Lucerne Valley** and the **Lucerne Marina** across the border in Utah (© **435/784-3483**). During the

summer season, you can rent a houseboat, minimum of 3 nights, for $598 (36')
or $950 (50'). For the whole week, they're $1,060 and $1,650, respectively.

CAMPING   The U.S. Forest Service maintains about 20 RV and tent sites in
the area ($6–$26), and there are also many primitive riverside sites. Visit their
office in Green River (listed above) for maps and other information.

FISHING   You might want to bring along a muscular friend if you plan to fish
Lake Flaming Gorge, which is famous as the place to catch record-breaking
trout, such as the 51-pound, 8-ounce lake (Mackinaw) trout caught in 1988, the
26-pound, 2-ounce rainbow caught in 1979, or the 33-pound, 10-ounce German brown caught in 1977. You'll also see other cold-water species such as
smallmouth bass and kokanee salmon. Fishing is popular year-round, although
ice-fishermen are warned to make sure the ice is strong enough to hold them.
For fishing information and excursions, call **Creative Fishing Adventures**
(② **435/784-3301**) or **Van Beacham's Solitary Angler** (② **307/877-9459**).
Van will take two people out for a day for $300.

WHERE TO DINE
Penny's Diner AMERICAN   Step back in time at the retro Penny's Diner.
Although more replica than real McCoy, this growing chain presents a reasonable facsimile of a classic greasy spoon with lots of chrome, a juke box, open
short-order grill, milkshakes, cherry pie a la mode, hot (albeit weak) coffee,
and—of course—breakfast served all day.

1170 W. Flaming Gorge Way (in the Oak Tree Inn), Green River. ② **307/875-3500**, ext. 550. Breakfast $3–$6;
dinner $4–$9. Daily 24 hr. AE, DISC, MC, V.

7 Killpecker Sand Dunes & Fossil Butte National Monument

Killpecker Sand Dunes: 40 miles (64km) N of Rock Springs; 140 miles (225km) SE of Jackson

KILLPECKER SAND DUNES
North of Rock Springs and east of Eden (we're not kidding . . . it's a small town)
swell the **Killpecker Sand Dunes**—the largest active dunes in North America.
Here hikers can scale and descend the heaving hills of white sand, where the
noon heat shimmers and the midnight cold cuts. Rock climbers trek to **Boar's
Tusk,** a standing volcanic plug, while ethnography buffs seek the **White Mountain Petroglyphs,** and photographers with high-powered telephoto lenses
should be on the lookout for wild horses.

Bird-watchers will especially enjoy the **Seedskadee Wildlife Refuge,** where
they may see geese, sandhill cranes, and great blue herons along the miles of
marshes along the Green River.

GETTING THERE   To get to the dunes, drive Wyo. 191 north from Rock
Springs 36 miles (58km) to Eden. Turning east, you'll bump along at least 20
miles (32km) of gravel road. Bring a compass, plenty of emergency water, and a
map. It's best to contact the Bureau of Land Management (② **307/352-0256**)
before blazing the trail on your own. *Note:* When it rains, the bentonite on these
rough roads turns to glue, and smart drivers stop trying.

FOSSIL BUTTE NATIONAL MONUMENT
Standing at the base of Fossil Butte, gazing up 1,000 feet at the rust and
ochre–stained cliffs, with the crackling desert wind rattling sage and tumble-
weeds, you'd never guess that eons ago you'd have been looking up from the bottom of a subtropical ocean. Some 50 million years ago, during the Eocene

Epoch, millions of fish wriggled across what's now the sky. With the ebb and flow of millennia, they sifted into the mud and fossilized.

Today, visitors join paleontologists during the summer to dig for the ancient remains of fish, insects, turtles, birds, and even bats. You can also hike (be watchful for rattlesnakes) on two short trails—the 1½-mile (2.5km) Fossil Lake Trail and the 2½-mile (4km) Quarry Trail. This is also a prime wildlife-viewing area, where you're likely to see pronghorn, mule deer, white-tailed prairie dogs, and ground squirrels, and you might be lucky enough to spot moose, elk, and beaver as well. A variety of birds is also seen here, including Canada geese, great blue herons, Clark's nutcrackers, yellow-headed blackbirds, great horned owls, and red-tailed hawks.

The excellent **Fossil Butte Visitor Center** (© 307/877-4455) exhibits more than 75 fossils, including a 13-foot-long crocodile and the oldest known bat, plus it offers video programs. It's open daily from 8am to 7pm June through August, but only until 4:30pm the rest of the year, and closed during winter holidays and bad snow.

GETTING THERE   From Green River, head west on I-80 to U.S. 30 (exit 66), which you follow north about 40 miles (64km). Past Kemmerer, follow the signs to the visitor center (about 3½ miles; 6km). Admission to both the monument and visitor center is free. Advance information is available from Superintendent, Fossil Butte National Monument, P.O. Box 592, Kemmerer, WY 83101-0592 (© **307/877-4455;** www.nps.gov/fobu).

ALSO WORTH A LOOK   No need to rush through Kemmerer, an old mining town with a pleasant central square and some fine old buildings, set along the Hams Fork River. Why not visit the very first **JCPenney store** (© 307/877-3164) and the original home of its founder, James Cash Penney? The store, despite being small, historic, and selling nostalgic souvenirs, is a regular JCPenney, open year-round from 9am to 5:30pm. (The house is open 11am–6pm in summer, with free admission.) The "mother" store is located on the town's central square, at 722 JCPenney Dr.; the home is 1 block north on the same street.

There's a handful of motels in town, the best of the bunch being the **Fairview Motel,** 61 U.S. 30 (© **800/247-3938** or 307/877-3938), featuring standard motel units with in-room fridges and microwaves, and rates for two of $40 to $50.

Appendix:
Montana & Wyoming in Depth

Spectacular scenery combines with a genuine frontier history to create what we consider the real American West. The land is mostly uncluttered—even the so-called cities are little more than overgrown cow towns—and the setting is one of rugged beauty: the remote wilderness of Yellowstone's Thorofare country, the Gallatin valleys where Sacajawea led Lewis and Clark, and the sandstone arroyos of famed outlaw Butch Cassidy's Hole in the Wall country.

There's a little more pavement here than there was 75 years ago, but the open horizon and hospitality—along with a pronounced independent spirit among the locals—still exist in Montana and Wyoming. Your first visit will likely be centered on the scenery, the outdoor recreation, and the region's Wild West history, but these two states have even more to offer.

1 The Natural Environment

In Montana and Wyoming, the earth seems to have turned itself inside out, its hot insides leaking into hot springs and geysers, its bony spine thrust right through the skin of the continent to form the Continental Divide, making it a geologist's dream. And to a biologist it's heaven, one of the last regions in the United States with enough open space for animals like elk and pronghorn and grizzly bears to roam free.

Plains, basin, and range alternate in this high-altitude environment that is in large part defined by its extremes of weather and climate. These changing landscapes make Montana and Wyoming two of the best vacation spots in the country for travelers who like their scenery dynamic and dramatic.

The western side of both states is mountainous, dragging moisture from the clouds moving west to east and storing it in snowpack and alpine lakes. Because the ridge of the Rockies wrings moisture from the atmosphere, you find deeper, denser forest extending far to the west, while on the east side, the lodgepole pine, spruce, and fir forests give way to the Great Plains, a vast, flat land characterized by sagebrush, native grasses, and cottonwood-lined river bottoms.

But a lot of the landscape dates back over 100 million years to when the collision of tectonic plates buckled the earth's crust and thrust these mountains upward. Later, glaciers (of which some vestiges remain) carved the canyons. The tallest peaks in Wyoming are located within the Wind River Range, which rises from the high plains of South Pass and runs northwest to the Yellowstone Plateau. Nine of the peaks in the Winds have elevations over 13,000 feet; **Gannett Peak,** at 13,785 feet, is the highest in the state. Several other mountain ranges are found to the south of Yellowstone—including the Absarokas and the stunning Tetons— and from Yellowstone north into Montana run more dramatic ranges, including the Gallatin, Madison, Missions, Bitterroots, Cabinets, and Beartooths, where you'll find Montana's highest point, **Granite Peak,** at 12,799 feet.

The **Continental Divide** enters Montana from Canada and traces a snaking path through the two states. Both Montana and Wyoming have rivers flowing west to the Pacific and east to the Atlantic.

Here you'll also find the headwaters of major river systems—the Flathead and Clark Fork heading west into the Columbia from Montana, along with the Snake from Wyoming; the Yellowstone, North Platte, and Madison joining the Missouri bound east; and the Green from Wyoming emptying into the Colorado heading south. These rivers are the lifeblood of the region, supplying irrigation, fisheries, and power from dams. Montana also boasts the country's largest freshwater body of water west of the Mississippi River: **Flathead Lake. Yellowstone** and **Jackson Lakes** are Wyoming's two largest natural bodies of water.

Montana is the greener of these two states, with more abundant alpine wilderness and bigger rivers. Wyoming, however, has been dealt a more interesting hand of natural wonders: Waterfalls, geysers, and other geothermal oddities at Yellowstone; **Devils Tower,** near the state's Black Hills region of the northeast, is a natural landmark of clustered rock columns that rise more than 1,280 feet above the surrounding plains. At Wyoming's Red Desert, south of Lander, the Continental Divide splits to form an enclosed basin where no water can escape, and nearby you find **Fossil Butte National Monument,** an archaeological treasure chest of fossilized fish and ancient miniature horses.

The states are characterized by long, cold winters and short summers of hot days and chilly nights. Temperature ranges are dramatic, and are largely dependent on elevation. Except along the far western edge of Montana, precipitation here is less than 30 inches a year. It's considerably less as you journey east and south. But the snowpacks in the high mountains—over 300 inches accumulate in some areas—melt through the summer and keep the rivers running.

2 Environmental Issues

The environmental issues that get attention in the Northern Rockies usually have to do with the national parks: Should we try to stop the building of expensive second homes around the edges? How do we reduce the impact of cars and snowmobiles? How do we keep the free-roaming herds of elk and bison from spreading brucellosis—a disease that causes cattle to abort—outside the park?

But many important issues are occurring away from the parks, in areas less popular and less noticed by the outside world. Oil and gas development continues in "elephant" fields around the region, particularly south of Jackson, Wyoming. Big mining operations have been proposed in delicate areas like the Stillwater Complex in southern Montana.

Ranchers and farmers have always been powerful forces in this region, and they often want wildlife protection to take a back seat to livestock and irrigation and farming. But the livestock industry's power seems to be waning—certainly the reintroduction of wolves in Yellowstone showed new muscle in the region's conservation forces. Exotic species present a new problem, particularly in the fisheries, where lake trout crowd out native cutthroat, and whirling disease has infected some of the region's trout streams.

Logging in the northern Rockies has cost the region not just scenery but critical wildlife habitat. But the timber industry, too, has seen better days—over the last 20 years, money-losing sales on public lands have been challenged and sometimes stopped. Forest managers are modifying plans to reduce the amount of logging in slow-growth forests.

As these longtime stalwart industries of the region decline, tourism is advancing. However, tourism brings its own problems, not the least of which are traffic congestion and building construction, and some say that this economic "cure" may be worse than the disease.

3 The Northern Rockies Today

The northern Rockies have been discovered by a new group of immigrants, many seeking a quieter, less stressful life away from the crowds, pollution, and crime of city life. But these newcomers are quite different from the settlers who discovered this region a hundred or more years ago. Those people were homesteaders, putting down roots, raising families, and building communities. The much greater wealth and mobility of today's Americans have brought a different crowd. Many come only for a particular season. A growing number make their livings long-distance, often via a computer modem. Cities with scenery and recreation are thriving—Missoula, Jackson, Bozeman—and new residents are bringing some cosmopolitan tastes. Once they're here, these newcomers often resist growth—trying to shut the gate behind them.

Whether Wyoming and Montana can build year-round economies with tourism as the engine remains to be seen. The natives know the value of patience and withholding judgment, and in many cases that's what they're doing in regard to the newcomers and the new economy—they know that if you wait 5 minutes the weather will likely change, and so may a lot of other things.

4 History 101

MONTANA

IN THE BEGINNING The first people believed to have wondered at the land we now call Montana was Folsom Man, who arrived sometime after the end of the last Ice Age about 12,000 years ago, and lived here until superseded by the Yuma culture about 6,800 years ago.

Then, about 3,000 years ago, a more modern American Indian culture began to emerge, eventually evolving into the Kootenai, Kalispell, Flathead, Shoshone, Crow, Blackfeet, Chippewa, Cree, Cheyenne, Gros Ventres, and Assiniboine that lived across the state when Europeans first encountered them.

Buffalo provided food, clothing, shelter, and ornamentation for the tribes. There have been more than 400 pishkun, or buffalo jump sites, uncovered in Montana, and you can see a few of them preserved on your travels through the state.

EUROPEAN EXPLORERS The first European known to enter Montana was Pierre Gauliter, Sieur de Varennes de la Verendrye.

Verendrye had heard of a river that flowed to the western sea and was

Dateline

- 11,000 B.C. Earliest evidence of humans in Montana.
- 1620s Arrival of the Plains Indians.
- 1803 The eastern part of Montana becomes a territory through the Louisiana Purchase.
- 1805–06 Explorers Lewis and Clark journey through the northern Rockies to and from the Pacific coast.
- 1864 Montana becomes an official territory. Gold is discovered at Last Chance Gulch in Helena.
- 1876 Defeat of George A. Custer at the Battle of the Little Bighorn.
- 1877 Chief Joseph of the Nez Perce tribe surrenders to U.S. soldiers in the Bear Paw Mountains.
- 1880 The Utah and Northern Railroad enters Montana.
- 1883 The Northern Pacific Railroad crosses Montana.
- 1889 Montana, on November 8, becomes the 41st state in the Union.
- 1893 The University of Montana in Missoula and Montana State University in Bozeman are founded.
- 1910 Glacier National Park is established.
- 1914 Women's suffrage amendment passes.
- 1917–19 Missoula native Jeannette Rankin, a Republican, becomes the first woman elected to U.S. Congress

looking for the Northwest Passage. He came in 1738, but retreated. His sons, Pierre and François, returned in 1743 and described the "shining mountains," generally believed to be the Bighorns of southern Montana and northern Wyoming. But threats of a looming Indian war discouraged the brothers and they returned to Montreal. No other white men are known to have come here for another 60 years.

When they finally did arrive, they were with the expedition of Lewis and Clark. The explorers reached the mouth of the Yellowstone River on April 26, 1805, and pushed upriver to the Shoshone, where they were warmly greeted, the result of having coincidentally brought Shoshone chief Cameahwait's long-lost sister Sacajawea with them as one of their guides.

SETTLEMENT The first industry in Montana, at least for non-Indians, was trapping. John Jacob Astor, Alexander Ross, and William Ashley brought in their hearty voyageurs to clear the country of beaver for the European hat market.

The first steamboat landed at Fort Benton—the westernmost navigable section of the Missouri River—in 1859. Until 1862, four cargo boats a year landed there, increasing to 39 a year after gold was discovered at Bannack.

and votes against U.S. participation in World War I.

- 1940 Fort Peck Dam is completed. Jeannette Rankin is again elected to the U.S. House of Representatives; she is the only member of Congress to vote against U.S. involvement in World War II.
- 1965 Construction of Yellowtail Dam is completed.
- 1973 Montana's third state constitution goes into effect; it includes the right to a clean and healthful environment and the goal of preserving the cultural integrity of the state's American Indians.
- 1983 Anaconda Copper Mining Company shuts down.
- 1986 Montana spends $56 million on environmental protection programs.
- 1995 Wolves are reintroduced into Yellowstone National Park. Daytime speed limits are abolished (but later reestablished).
- 1996 Recluse Theodore Kaczynski, dubbed the Unabomber, is arrested at his cabin near Lincoln, and is later sentenced to life in prison for sending a series of mail bombs that killed three people.
- 1998 The $6 million Lewis & Clark National Historic Trail Interpretive Center opens in Great Falls.
- 2000–2001 A series of forest fires— most wildfires but some caused by careless humans—drive thousands of people from their homes and do millions of dollars in damage.

The discovery of gold opened Montana's Wild West era for real, a period you can see preserved in the Bannack/Virginia City/Nevada City area. The lure of easy money plus the fact that these towns were some 400 miles from official justice attracted outlaws, con artists, and ladies of the night from all over the West.

In 1864, just as gold was discovered in Last Chance Gulch in present-day Helena, the Montana Territory was formed and Sidney Edgerton became the first territorial governor. The capital was moved to Virginia City and a constitutional convention was called as the first step toward statehood. A constitution was drafted and sent to St. Louis for printing, but was lost somewhere along the way.

In 1884, another constitution was drafted. This one didn't work either, for one reason or another, and in 1889, the now well-practiced delegates came up with a third one. Taking no chances, they prefaced it with the Magna Carta, the Declaration of Independence, the Articles of Confederation, and the U.S. Constitution. Montana finally became a state in November 1889.

TROUBLE BETWEEN THE INDIANS & THE SETTLERS Montana's Indian tribes were not at first invariably hostile to the whites, and signed a number of treaties signaling their peaceful intentions. But the influx of settlers and the confinement of tribes to the reservation resulted in dissatisfaction among the original inhabitants, and escalating hostilities against the whites. In 1876, the War Department launched a campaign against the Sioux and Cheyenne. At the end of June that year, this culminated in the **Battle of the Little Bighorn** and the death of all of the command under Gen. George Armstrong Custer.

The Indian victory was only a temporary setback for the whites, however, and by 1880 all the Indians had been forced onto reservations. The last action of the Indian War period occurred in Montana with the heroic flight of Chief Joseph's Nez Perce from their northern Idaho reservation toward Canada in 1877.

INDUSTRIALIZATION   When copper was first discovered in the silver mines in Butte, no one could have foretold its effects on Montana's future. When copper wiring became an integral part of several new electrical technologies, Butte copper became an important resource for America. One of the first men to profit was Marcus Daly, an Irish immigrant, who arrived in Butte in his mid-30s and purchased his first mine, which yielded incredibly large amounts of the purest copper in the world. Soon a smelter was built near the source at Warm Springs in Anaconda, the town that took its name from the company Daly founded.

William Clark, another copper-mine baron, was a Horatio Alger type. An average youth from Pennsylvania, he rooted around in mines until his efforts took him to Montana. He had a keen business acumen that prompted him to purchase mining operations, electric companies, water companies, and banks. He quickly amassed a great deal of wealth; then his inflated ego drove him to the political arena. His was the major voice in the territorial constitution proceedings in 1884, and when Montana held its last territorial election, Clark was determined to get into public office as Montana's representative.

A war commenced between Daly and Clark, rooted in Clark's determination to hold political office and Daly's unwillingness to see him do it. Montana finally became a state in 1889, after 5 tough years of appeals to the U.S. Congress. The bellicose millionaires were so set on controlling the young state's political interests that they purchased or created newspapers to give themselves a printed voice. They stuffed money into the pockets of voters and agreed on nothing. In Montana's first congressional election, Clark fell three votes shy of his bid, and the legislature adjourned without selecting a second senator, leaving Montana with only half of its due representation in Washington.

The fight for capital status came along in 1894. Helena had been the capital, but the constitution held that the site must be determined by the voters. Daly wanted his newly created Anaconda to be the capital; Clark was happy with the status quo. The fact that Anaconda was ruled by the strong arm of the Anaconda Mining Company caused voters to turn to the diversified ways of Helena. For once in his life, William Clark was not only rich, but appreciated by the masses. Or so it seemed.

With his thirst for public office revitalized, Clark did his best to buy his way into the U.S. Senate, and actually pulled it off. Daly, infuriated by the way his bitter enemy achieved his seat, demanded an investigation by the Senate. The investigation uncovered a wealth of improprieties on Clark's part, so he resigned. Down, but not out, Clark took a deep breath and plunged immediately back into the thick of things. Once when Robert Burns Smith, governor of Montana and hardly an ardent admirer of Clark's, was out of town, Clark arranged for his friend, A.E. Spriggs, the lieutenant governor, to appoint Clark to the Senate.

This lunatic act embarrassed the state of Montana, causing Smith to nullify the appointment upon his return. Meanwhile, Daly had sold his Anaconda Copper Company to Standard Oil to form the Amalgamated Copper Company, and Clark was now up against a nameless, faceless opponent.

He chose to link his fate with another, younger copper king, Augustus Heinze, hoping to form an alliance that Amalgamated couldn't match. At this time, Heinze was more influential than the older, less active Clark, and the team of Heinze and Clark soon had complete control of the mining world in Montana. It seemed as if Clark's last wish—to garner the Senate post he had been denied for so long—would be realized with Heinze's help. And so it was—Clark served his state as a senator from 1901 to 1907.

Though the discovery of copper in Montana was important economically, today it is also considered by many as just another chapter in the history of the state's misuse of natural resources. Montana's copper-mining industry also brought its share of unmitigated disaster to future generations. Marcus Daly died in 1900 without control of his beloved Anaconda Copper Company. Augustus Heinze sold his interest in mining in 1906 and lost his fortune on Wall Street. William Clark died in 1925 at the age of 86 in New York with a net worth estimated at $150 million. Their legacy: a reputation as the ultimate robber barons and polluters.

THE 20TH CENTURY   At the beginning of the 20th century, Montana experienced a boom of a different type. The Indian Wars had ended, and white settlers declared the land a safe and fertile haven for farming. The U.S. government helped things along in 1909 when it passed the Enlarged Homestead Act, giving 320 acres to anyone willing to stay on it for at least 5 months out of the year for a minimum of 3 years. Homesteaders arrived from all over the country to stake a piece of land.

Sentiment for the homesteaders was never good, and the generalization that homesteaders were stupid, dirty people became increasingly popular. Even the renowned cowboy artist Charlie Russell, who had no stake in the matter, expressed anti-farming sentiments. The truth is, Montana's agricultural backbone was created by these extraordinary people who came west to establish farms. Wheat became—and still is—the major crop in such areas as the Judith Basin in the center of the state and Choteau County north of Great Falls.

As more and more homesteaders came to settle in Montana and farming became a mainstay of the state's economy, women began to emerge from their submissive roles in the home and take part in a suffrage movement on a large scale. In the middle of it all was young Jeannette Rankin from Missoula. In 1914, voters narrowly passed the amendment for women's suffrage; 2 years later, Rankin, a Republican, became the first woman elected to the U.S. Congress. Though her stay was brief, she was there long enough to vote against United States involvement in World War I. In 1940, she was elected to the U.S. House of Representatives, and, as an avowed pacifist, became the only member of Congress to vote against American involvement in World War II.

When the Great Depression hit Montana, farming was enduring some rather dry difficulties, and jobs were nowhere to be found. Roosevelt's New Deal was a lifesaver. Without the jobs created by the Civilian Conservation Corps and the Works Progress Administration, the state might have never recovered its economic balance. Of particular help was construction of the Fort Peck Dam in the mid-1930s, which employed more than 50,000 workers. The earth-filled dam, the largest of its kind in the world, took almost 5 years to complete.

Since the 1950s, the story of Montana has been an evolving one, with tourism and agriculture playing key roles. While farming and cattle-ranching methods have become much more sophisticated, many of the younger generation, expected to carry on the farming tradition, have opted to settle in the larger cities. Though agriculture still drives the economic engine of the state, tourism makes a huge financial contribution. The face of ranch life has changed, with many ranches now filled with guests paying to participate in ranch activities.

WYOMING

IN THE BEGINNING   The earliest indications of man in what is now Wyoming date back some 20,000 years. No one knows the identity of these early inhabitants, nor can anyone say with certainty who created the Medicine Wheel in the Bighorn Mountains or the petroglyphs found in various parts of the state. The earliest identified settlers were the Crow, Sioux, Cheyenne, and Arapahoe—tribes that came from the east—as well as the Shoshone and Bannock, who came from the Great Basin, more closely related to the peoples of Central America. The lifestyles of these tribes were greatly changed by the arrival of two European innovations—the horse and the gun. The first white men in Wyoming were fur trappers, and the first of them was John Colter, who left the Lewis and Clark expedition in 1806 to wander south through Yellowstone and possibly Jackson Hole.

SETTLEMENT   The Oregon Trail and other major pioneer routes west cut right through Wyoming and the territories of the Sioux, Shoshone, Arapaho, and other tribes. Without much regard for the people they were displacing, the non-Indians killed a great deal of the game the Indians depended on; Indian bands, in turn, harassed and sometimes attacked

Dateline

- **1807** John Colter explores the Yellowstone area, coming as far south as Jackson Hole.
- **1812** Fur trader Robert Stuart discovers South Pass, the gentlest route across the northern Rockies.
- **1843** Pioneers begin traveling west on the Oregon Trail through Wyoming.
- **1848** U.S. Army moves into Fort Laramie to protect Oregon Trail travelers from Indians.
- **1852** The first school in the state is founded at Fort Laramie.
- **1860** The Pony Express begins its run from Missouri to California, through Wyoming.
- **1867** The Union Pacific Railroad enters Wyoming.
- **1868** The Treaty of Fort Bridger creates the Shoshone Reservation in northwest Wyoming.
- **1868** The Territory of Wyoming is created by Congress.
- **1869** Wyoming Territorial Legislature grants women the right to vote and hold elective office.
- **1870** Esther H. Morris becomes the nation's first female justice of the peace.
- **1872** Yellowstone National Park is established as the nation's first national park.
- **1884** First oil well drilled in Wyoming.
- **1886–87** Great blizzard decimates ranches of eastern Wyoming, sending many "cattle barons" into bankruptcy.
- **1889** The state constitution is adopted.
- **1890** Wyoming becomes the nation's 44th state.
- **1892** The Johnson County War breaks out over a dispute about cattle rustling.
- **1897** The first Cheyenne Frontier Days rodeo is staged.
- **1906** Devils Tower is established by President Roosevelt as the country's first national monument.
- **1910** Buffalo Bill Dam is completed.
- **1925** Nellie Taylor Ross becomes the nation's first female governor.
- **1927** Man claiming to be Butch Cassidy visits Wyoming from Washington, suggesting that the outlaw was not killed in Bolivia as was generally believed.
- **1929** Grand Teton National Park is established, consisting of only the peaks.

the travelers. Indian tribes were increasingly pushed west into tighter spaces, and there was warfare among tribes.

In a series of treaties, beginning with the Fort Laramie Treaty of 1851, the tribes gave up rights to some of their homelands in return for reservations and other considerations. The discovery of gold in areas like the Black Hills and South Pass, and the routes of settlers, led to numerous treaty violations and continued conflict. Tribes in the east were being evicted and shipped west. Treaties that might have protected Indian rights were modified and broken, and U.S. Army troops were sent in to keep the peace. Some tribal leaders, recognizing the inexorable advance of the whites, decided the only alternative was to fight the invaders.

- 1929 Oil thefts discovered on federal land at Teapot Dome, a scandal that rocks the Harding Administration.
- 1950 National forest and private lands are added to form Grand Teton National Park as it is today.
- 1965 Minuteman missile sites are completed near Cheyenne.
- 1973 The Arab oil embargo sends oil prices skyrocketing, instigating a huge oil-drilling boom in Wyoming.
- 1988 Five fires break out around Yellowstone National Park, burning through the summer and blackening approximately one-third of the park.
- 1995 Wolves are reintroduced into Yellowstone.
- 1996 The National Park Service institutes a voluntary ban on climbing Devils Tower during June to respect American Indian religious ceremonies.
- 1998 Gay University of Wyoming student Matthew Shepard murdered.

TROUBLE BETWEEN THE INDIANS & THE SETTLERS   Sitting Bull and Crazy Horse of the Hunkpapa Sioux joined forces with members of the Cheyenne and Arapaho tribes along the Little Bighorn River. It was here in June 1876, that a huge gathering of Indians defeated George Custer and his men. Inevitably this led to a backlash, a series of attacks on Indian communities, culminating in the death of Sitting Bull and the massacre of Big Foot and his Sioux followers in 1890 at Wounded Knee, South Dakota. Chief Washakie of the Shoshone was one of the few great Indian leaders still alive, though his star was diminished by his decision to ally his tribe with the whites. That alliance got his people one of the finest reservations in the West, and the only one in Wyoming—Wind River. Then the U.S. Army moved the now threadbare Arapaho, traditional enemies of the Shoshone, to Wind River "temporarily," and the two tribes began an uncomfortable coexistence that continues to this day.

INDUSTRIALIZATION & THE 20TH CENTURY   Big cattle operators moved into Wyoming in the 19th century, controlling the territory's economy and political scene through organizations like the Cheyenne Social Club. A couple of severe winters in the 1880s and the influx of new settlers building fences raised tensions. When the cattle "barons" brought in hired guns to clear out the newcomers, the Johnson County War of 1892 erupted. The wealthy cattlemen claimed the newcomers were rustlers. But that show of muscle was futile in halting the longtime decline of the big livestock owners.

Though the ranch community would long dominate Wyoming politics, the true economic hammer in the state would soon be the energy industry. The state's fate has been closely tied to oil, gas, and coal, with the economy rising and falling in synch with world prices. The boom and bust of the energy industry has prompted repeated calls for a more diversified economy, and in recent years Wyoming's tourism industry has begun to have an impact. But for the most part, Wyoming remains a predominantly rural state where you have a job in the energy industry or, like your parents and grandparents, work the ranch.

Index